THEMATICALLY RECONSTRUCTED
&
DILIGENTLY REVISED

THE KNOWLEDGE

OF

GOOD & EVIL

DEFINITIVE EDITION

A STUDY OF THE FALL OF MAN

JOSHUA COLLINS

Post Gutenberg™

AN IMPRINT OF
GLOBALEDADVANCEPRESS

The Knowledge of Good and Evil

Definitive Edition

A Study of the Fall of Man

Copyright © 2008, 2014, 2015 by Joshua Collins

Library of Congress Control Number: 2013955777

Collins, Joshua 1980 -

ISBN 978-1-935434-29-0

Subject Codes and Description: 1: REL006210; Religion - Biblical Studies 2: SOC046000; Social Science - Abortion 3: REL006410; Religion: Biblical Reference - Language Study

Cover artwork by Barton Green
Printed in Australia, Brazil, France, Germany, Italy, Spain, UK, and USA.

Published by
Post-Gutenberg Books™
an imprint of
GlobalEdAdvance Press

www.GlobalEdAdvance.org

"There still remains indeed a most important operation of nature... the true nature of each plant can only be fully understood by studying its medicinal effect, the vast and recondite work of divine power, and the greatest subject that can possibly be found."

(*Natural History: Book 19*, Pliny the Elder)

"...I will give no deadly medicine to anyone if asked, nor suggest any such counsel; and in like manner I will not give to a woman a pessary to produce abortion. With purity and with holiness I will pass my life and practice my Art...."

("The Oath," Hippocrates)

"The whole system of the Hebrew rites is one great and complicated allegory, to the study and observance of which all possible diligence and attention were incessantly dedicated by those who were employed in the sacred offices."

(*Lectures on the Sacred Poetry of the Hebrews*, Lowth)

TABLE OF CONTENTS

Note: Quotations within this book are often highlighted by small capital type such as, "IN THE BEGINNING God created the heavens and the earth" (Genesis 1:1). The highlighting with small capital type is used by the author for the purpose of calling attention to specific parts of quotations in an attempt to prove a point. Similarly, the translations offered by the author where original language is used are displayed by showing the original language and immediately following it with English in italicized type. For example, the Hebrew word בראשית is commonly translated as "In the beginning"; this book displays the original language and its translation as בראשית *in the beginning.*

Note: The Hebrew roots are in the third-person, singular, masculine, perfect in the active voice; but, in order to facilitate English reading, they are expressed herein as infinitive phrases in the active voice. For example, the word "ברך *knee*" is literally from the root "he kneeled," but it is communicated in this book as "to kneel." So long as the reader is aware of this manner of translation, the points asserted relative to Hebrew roots will prove clearer in this book.

Note: Often in this book, quotations are offset by margins smaller than the surrounding text contrary to standard practice. The reason for this format is to avoid having key points lost on account of quotations and the surrounding text running together so often that they appear difficult to distinguish readily. By isolating certain quotations through the adjustment of the margins, it is the hope of the author to strike the nerve of various points in a manner that causes them to be received by the reader with as much facility as possible.

Thanks are due my Editorial Assistants:

S. Collins, and Rev. D. Kasik

A special acknowledgement is due S. Collins for correcting the digital difficulties of printing sinistrograde language, for her labor in this matter saved me more time than I would like to think about.

FOREWORD

The Holy Bible was written over millennia and translated many times into numerous languages. Joshua Collins examines and clarifies God's messages that are emphasized again and again from Genesis to Revelation through the writings of Moses, the Prophets, and the Apostles written in Hebrew and Greek. As a lay Christian who loves the Scriptures and Jesus Christ, I recommend this scholarly work to you. It has provided me a deeper understanding concerning God's plan by returning to the writings in Hebrew and Greek through his insights. This commentary brings cohesiveness, consistency, and an incredible depth to the Holy Bible as a unified whole, revealing God's purpose and His desire for you.

In his definitive edition of *The Knowledge of Good and Evil*, Collins returns to the original languages of the Holy Bible as the foundation of his commentary. The goal is to encourage us to rediscover the remarkable messages revealed in the Scripture. Our opportunity is better discernment when studying the Holy Bible as a whole instead of relying on selected texts and verses sometimes taken out of context. You will gain deeper understanding of God's Word often written mysteriously in riddles, puzzles, and parables in the stories, teachings and prophecies. The work compares western Christian thinking to God's thinking about major themes that may have not been readily apparent to us.

This scholarly work also draws on the agriculture, architecture, astronomy and culture of ancient times in order to provide a richer insight into the mysteries of God's Word. We become more aware of the richness of God's plan. English translations from the original languages force the choices of the meaning of key words, use of language, and the types of logic. Our knowledge has been shaped further with the use of study programs, books and commentaries. Many have been beneficial to us, strengthening our faith, but the sole use of these sources without anchoring and testing them in the Scriptures makes us vulnerable in forming our own personal theologies. Returning, however, to the times and the original languages provides deeper insights in our knowledge and strengthens our wisdom about God, the Father, Jesus Christ, our Savior and Advocate, and the workings of the Holy Spirit.

This commentary delves into the rich meanings of concepts and words that we might have taken for granted, or at times, might have appeared confusing, conflicting, or beyond our capability. The author tackles important messages about communion, faith, thresholds, libation, the law, sacrifice, the womb, the vine, salvation, good vs. evil, love, relationships, and most importantly, our covenant with God. These are God's recurring messages from the beginning to the end times. The author has provided an excellent scholarly work requiring serious study, and you will be emboldened when taking this journey. Your discernment and love of His glory will grow as you continue to read the Scriptures. I applaud his thought-provoking effort.

— **Leonard Heller, Ed.D.**

Professor & Vice President of The University of Kentucky (Retired)

"It is not that we have a short space of time, but that we waste much of it. Life is long enough, and it has been given in sufficiently generous measure to allow the accomplishment of the very greatest things if the whole of it is well invested. But when it is squandered in luxury and carelessness, when it is devoted to no good end, forced at last by the ultimate necessity we perceive that it has passed away before we were aware that it was passing. So it is—the life we receive is not short, but we make it so, nor do we have any lack of it, but are wasteful of it. Just as great and princely wealth is scattered in a moment when it comes into the hands of a bad owner, while wealth however limited, if it is entrusted to a good guardian, increases by use, so our life is amply long for him who orders it properly."

("On The Shortness of Life," Seneca)

PREFACE

IT often bothers people to consider the possibility that a long-held, heartfelt tradition bolstered by many could be inaccurate in spite of its sincerity. Dr. Sayce, Professor of Assyriology, said in his *Lectures on the Origin and Growth of Religion as Illustrated by the Religion of the Ancient Babylonians* (1898),

> I have undertaken to treat of Babylonian religion only, not of Semitic religion in general. For such a task there are others far more competent than myself; great Arabic or Syriac or Hebrew scholars, who have devoted their lives to the study of one or more of these better-known Semitic tongues. My own studies have of late years lain more and more in the ever-widening circle of Assyrian research; here there is enough, and more than enough, to fill the whole time and absorb the whole energies of the worker; and he must be content to confine himself to his own subject, and by honest labor therein to accumulate the facts which others more fortunate than he may hereafter combine and utilize. This is the day of the specialists; the increased application of the scientific method and the rapid progress of discovery have made it difficult to do more than note and put together the facts that are constantly crowding one upon the other in a special branch of research. The time may come again — nay, will come again — when once more the ever-flowing stream of discovery will be checked, and famous scholars and thinkers will arise to reap the harvest that we have sown. Meanwhile I claim only to be one of the humble labourers of our own busy age, who have done my best to set before you the facts and theories we may glean from the broken sherds of Nineveh, so far as they bear upon the religion of the ancient Babylonians. It is for others, whose studies have taken a wider range, to make use of the materials I have endeavoured to collect, and to discover in them, if they can, guides and beacons towards a purer form of faith than that which can be found in the official creed of our modern world.

The duration of a thought-system's existence and the number of its adherants are very often viewed as an indication of correctness, but let us consider time and populace in a different light. The majority of books written about the Bible begin with an accepted theology. Accordingly, these books are theologically dependent on someone outside the Bible who developed the theological foundation accepted as a premise. The situation, then, is that a man penned his own thoughts about Scripture, and his followers patterned their thoughts after his; this then points to the fact that, at its most concentrated level, there are few original theologians relative to their adherents. If we consider roughly 2,000 years of original theologians, and if we allot 50 years to each of them, then time and strength-in-numbers take on a different aspect. Again, giving the first original theologian in our scenario a 50-year reign that is followed by another original theologian who began immediately after the end of the previous 50 years, etc., then the total number of original theologians would only equate to 40 over 2,000 years. I do not find it difficult to believe that only 40 people — over the span of two millennia — were mistaken about a single point; furthermore, I do not find it difficult to accept that all of the followers of the 40 originals were also mistaken regarding that single point since they began from a premise that did not anticipate or allow for that single point. Being mistaken at a single point does not necessitate that everything the originals said was wrong, but it does allow for nothing of what the originals said to have addressed the correctness of a single point of which none of them were aware. This scenario is not something that I find shameful; it is something that I merely find probable; it is something to which we are all subject to one degree or another. Imagine, however, if the answers to the greatest questions regarding Scripture all ramified from a single point that was not seen by any of the theologians. For instance, it is not commonly known that the Hebrew word for "knowledge" used to describe the forbidden tree in Eden can mean "union," as its Hebrew root explains in Genesis 4:1. A standpoint ignorant of the understanding that the forbidden tree was the "union" of good and evil would seem to indicate that God desired a limit to human understanding, and this stance — though tremendously common — is in flagrant contradiction to James 1:5 that states, "If any of you lacks wisdom, let him ask of God, who gives to all liberally and without reproach, and it will be given to him."

It is often the case that collective agreement is viewed as correct because it is collective, but such a situation is never true and strength in numbers is merely strength in numbers. Fiduciary matters tend to influence collective agreement, especially when the institution is sustained through donation. A fair amount of vagueness and plasticity within an institution allows for fascile adaptation designed to suit the desires of the donators. Generalities are often used to pretend uniformity by the deliberate avoidance of specificity.

When truth is revealed in specificity as opposed to abstraction, and when specific truth resonates with an established philosophical or theological abstraction, it is common to hear someone respond by declaring that many traditions and many individuals certainly understood the specific truth of the given topic at hand based on the fact that various traditions and individuals were pointed in the same general direction. Such a manner of reasoning inadvertently inhibits the recognition of discovery based on the fact that specific truths precede their receivers, and it assumes that the same specific truths were perceived in the same exact way for identical purposes with congruent results. Surely, such a situation cannot be true.

When the same exact words forwarding the same specific truths are given to one man for the purposes of privately educating his daughter to recognize God as sovereign with the aim of maintaining her integrity until marriage, and when those same exact words forwarding the same specific truths are given to another man for the purposes of corporately educating a church he founded that it may recognize God as sovereign with the purpose of maintaining its integrity in bearing Christ's name, general and parallel truths are obviously shared in both situations *by analogy*; however, the situations differ with respect to the number of people involved and the manner of "fruit" produced. That one couple speaks verity and produces fruit based on the truth of God does not necessarily mean it does so because it understands the corporate functions of the Church; rather, the couple does so because the same truth is as applicable to its marriage as it is to the functionality of the Church. When truth in one situation resonates in another, the parallel observed does not evince that one situation recognized the other or saw any immediate connection; but, the parallel observed does elucidate that both situations function in parallel as bound and guided by uniform truth. Correlation does not prove causation.

It is because of the mistakenly and retroactively viewed parallel noted above that when one identifies something that harmoniously reinforces connections already seen, others may be quick to believe that all of the people who saw similar connections also saw what an individual pointed out to reinforce those connections — and this is not necessarily correct. Such a retroactively viewed parallel would be like claiming an ancient priest who witnessed lightning 4,000 years before the light bulb understood bulbs every bit as well as the inventor of the light bulb, or that the inventor understood lightning in an identical sense as an ancient priest 4,000 years ago who viewed lightning atop a mountain. The constant, the truth of both situations is electricity. That an ancient priest saw electricity contained in the sky and that the inventor enclosed it in glass means that they both experienced the truth of electricity, not that they both experienced the reality of the mountain experience or the light bulb. It is therefore evident that it would be errant to tell the light-bulb's inventor that he had not necessarily accomplished anything because innumerable individuals before him already witnessed what was contained in his invention. It would be like telling Edison that his ability to sustain incandescence was of little importance or originality because people before him had produced incandenscence (although unsustainably). Unfortunately, it is often the practice of many thinkers to grasp truth forwarded by one and then claim that all the men who preceded the one understood the same truth in precisely the same way for exactly the same purposes based on the fact that the truth bound common threads of the same pattern. That is, people who ponder specific points over long spans of time can often accidentally superimpose the specific points onto their readings of people who moved towards the same goal but who did not accomplish the same end. Consider how foolish it would be to think that the invention of the light bulb necessarily anticipated video games by the fact that both the light bulb's inventor and video-game makers share the common thread of electricity. In short, such error stunts the appreciation of and impetus for discovery. Discovery recognizes something that existed before the discoverer's ability to notice it, so of course the discoverer is secondary. Truth exists prior to its discovery in much the same way a diamond exists before it is mined. The discovery does shed light on previous thought, but it does not necessarily admit that previous applications of that thought were worse, better, or identical to the current applications of the discovery, for that would be like claiming that a diamond was necessarily meant for gold rings by the fact that ring-makers mean to set diamonds in their works of gold. Let us, for example, consider the infamous Golden Calf of Exodus.

    The Golden Calf has rarely been regarded in the light of child-sacrifice. When Amos discussed the Golden Calf at Sinai, he said,

> "Did you offer Me sacrifices and offerings In the wilderness forty years, O house of Israel? You also carried Sikkuth YOUR KING, and Chiun, your idols, the star of your gods, which you made for yourselves. Therefore I will send you into captivity

beyond Damascus," says the LORD, whose name is the God of hosts (Amos 5:26-27).

In Hebrew, "your king" is one word (מלככם), and it can also be read in Hebrew as "your Molech" (מלככם). Molech was a child-sacrificial false deity. In other words, Amos understood that children were ritually slaughtered at the base of Mount Sinai. This knowledge then explains that when the Golden Calf (Molech) was ground up by Moses, the gold-dust was, of course, tainted with the ash of the children who were burned on it. Children, often being called the "fruit of the womb" in Scripture, were, in this sense, eaten. Thus, the Israelites ate golden fruit (so to speak) at the base of Mount Sinai in direct punishment for the children they slew upon the pagan image they fashioned. We can begin to see in this scenario why Moses was so angry and why he smashed the tablets after he desceneded Sinai. The Molech-worshipping Israelites took innocent life. Accordingly, when the innocent Stephen was about to be killed, he quoted Amos in Acts 7:

> This is he who was in the congregation in the wilderness with the Angel who spoke to him on Mount Sinai, and with our fathers, the one who received the living oracles to give to us, whom our fathers would not obey, but rejected. And in their hearts they turned back to Egypt, saying to Aaron, "Make us gods to go before us; as for this Moses who brought us out of the land of Egypt, we do not know what has become of him." And they made a calf in those days, offered sacrifices to the idol, and rejoiced in the works of their own hands. Then God turned and gave them up to worship the host of heaven, as it is written in the book of the Prophets:

> "Did you offer Me slaughtered animals and sacrifices during forty years in the wilderness, O house of Israel? You also took up the tabernacle of Moloch, and the star of your god Remphan, images which you made to worship; and I will carry you away beyond Babylon."

Stephen quoted Amos who commented on Moses. Moses was understood by Amos and Stephen to have communicated that the Israelites killed the innocent in pagan worship at the base of Sinai. Stephen, who was innocent, was likewise killed after having pointed to the truth. That many have commented on the Golden Calf incident in Scripture does not mean that they understood it as Stephen did, as Amos did, or as Moses did; this fact does not mean that commenters who were unaware of the child sacrifice in the wilderness were *altogether* wrong in what they said, but it does mean that, without the knowledge of the refrences to child sacrifice, their comments were incomplete with respect to the severity of the matter. The same story can be experienced with different hues of varying vividness whereby the variations are correct within their scope, even if they are not definitive in their application.

The manner in which something is experienced by the brain has much to do with one's language usage. For instance, according to Professor Lidwell's research (on the affects of color) produced by The Great Courses, the Himba Tribe of Northern Namibia cannot distinguish easily between the colors green and blue *because* of their language; their language tunes their brains to experience color differently than people with another language system, and this was proven when the Himba Tribe was able to distinguish shades of green much easier than its Western counterparts. In other words, the distinctions and associations of language have an effect on perception to the extent that even the physical world is experienced relative to one's linguistic relationship to it. Two people can experience an *absolute* and not experience uniformity if they do not share the same language (and ability with it). I stress the word "absolute" because perception of an entity does not affect that entity even though it does affect one's experience of that entity. Whatever one believes about a tree does not affect the fruit, leaves, bark, or roots, but it does affect one's experience of that tree to some degree that may or may not be accurate if one cannot perceive an inherent detriment based on one's inability to describe it according to its own standards.

The invention of categories in order to compartmentalize constituent parts produces a type of cartography designed to view components for specialized purposes. If those constituent parts are, with time, not perceived as members of the whole from which they were taken, it is quite easy to discuss them with categories that are incongruent with their source to the extent that the experience of those parts differs from the absolute function they have within a whole no longer seen easily (if at all). For instance, people can sit around academic facilities, coffee houses, or churches and debate the theology of, say, Zwingli. The same people, through course of reason, argumentation, Scripture reference, and so forth, can come to a collective agreement concerning Reformational arguments about the "real presence" and think they have accomplished, to some degree, the potential to affect masses as Zwingli did based on their views of the Eucharist; yet, it is often the case that these same people only understand the writings produced from Zwingli's views as writings concerning theology without realizing that Prince Philip of Hesse attempted to resolve Zwingli's differences with Luther at his castle in Marburg in terms of the imminence of warfare. When Zwingli could not form an alliance on account of his views, he returned to Switzerland to face the Catholics to the extent of warfare in 1531 wherein Zwingli personally led his forces into fighting that ultimately took his life. The Peace of Kappel ended the war and Switzerland was left politically and religiously divided. The point stressed here is that Zwingli's theological arguments preserved on paper were political and had an enormous effect on national policy — not merely on the private beliefs of worshippers sitting in church somewhere. It can be seen, however, that the attendees of academic facilities, coffee houses, and churches often revere those educated in such theology as elites when such people are merely educated theologically to the extent that they are restricted to no-risk argumentation that affects but a small populace that only exists through theological agreement and not to the extent of national policy and the mortality of physical conflict. Mere philosophical or theo-logical stances expressed in books or through other media have a limited effect when the option to ignore is present and active. It is another matter altogether when an entire army, poised to kill and plunder, is standing in your backyard. Arguing opinions with theology and stabbing throats with swords are two very different things; in the case above, these very different things are reflected similarly in pages, but the pages must be understood in their context and milieu; otherwise, they remain merely pages to uniniti-ated eyes.

Again, the invention of categories in order to compartmentalize constituent parts produces a type of cartography designed to view compo-nents for specialized purposes. If those constituent parts are, with time, not perceived as members of the whole from which they were taken, it is quite easy to discuss them with categories that are incongruent with their source to the extent that the experience of those parts differs from the absolute function they have within a whole no longer seen easily (if at all). The various usages of the artificial "chapter" and "verse" divisions of Scrip-ture have proven this point efficiently and disastrously to the extent that it is fashionable to believe the Bible to be a conglomeration of disjuncture slapped sloppily together by unevolved simpletons who conceived of the world through a vocabulary-poor language system that disallowed specific-ity and sufficient categories to describe what we know easily today. Such a belief mocks its believer. The categories of "theology" and "tradition," like linguistic categories of color, can disallow one from seeing the apparently obvious distinctions based on the vocabulary of the theology or tradition. Collective agreement concerning vocabulary is a way of beholding a sub-ject askance.

Looking straight ahead, one should also acknowledge the fact that being a linguist does not provide absolute authority over a subject that requires the powers of linguistics. The language of a subject, at the level of diction and grammar, does not function in a vacuum since it is tethered to associations that may be physical, mental, concrete, abstract, blatant, subtle, cultural, personal, or any category not shared or comprehended by the linguist who observes the subject. Associating the word "green" with verdure allows one to experience verdure differently than one who associates it otherwise; thus, if the one who associates "green" with verdure desired to understand one who does not experience verdure as such, it would be essential to understand what associations the one who does not understand verdure as such makes concerning verdure. For instance, the Hebrew letters עצה mean *counsel* (if derived from the root יעץ) or *tree* (if derived from the root עצה); the word אכל can mean *to eat* and it is used sometimes to indicate the act of *comprehension*; thus, *to eat from a tree* can mean, by the exact same words, *to understand from counsel*. Linguistically, a translator is forced, by the very categories of translation, to make a choice in how information is represented, and this choice often results in a predetermined philosophical, theological, or traditional bent siphoning the original into a compartment only able to contain a portion of it. In Eden, the "serpent" enticed humanity *to eat from a tree*. Physically, a translator may be unaware that the geography of a narrative assumes the words "the tree" to indicate a fruit tree that is used as a trellis for a grapevine whereby two trees exist geographically as one, for Genesis 2:9 discusses two trees in the midst while Genesis 3:6 discusses them as "the tree"; furthermore, Ezekiel 15:1 categorizes vines as "trees"; without knowing these geographical associations, it has been propounded by many that we are viewing the literary patchwork of the unsophisticated when such a claim is itself unsophisticated. Mentally, a translator is compelled to attempt to distinguish one from another. If the whole is not kept in mind for any one part, the translated part may be mistranslated, and this danger relies on one's ability to keep in mind the whole while attempting to discern meaning. Concretely, one should realize that a translation can be likened to a classification of color that, by default, bars one from seeing what is obvious to another, even though the same subject is being examined by both. Imagine if the subject "eaten fruit" were viewed by one person as masticated plantlife and by another person as the charred corpse of a child... and what if both people were correct, but one person only saw one while the other person saw both simultaneously? — it would be nearly impossible for the one person who saw the two apparently disconnected subjects simultaneously to explain the morbidity of "eaten fruit" to one who could but see a grape and the verdent serpent upon which it grew. The level of philosophical or theological simplicity to which categories could be designed in order to explain something apparently basic (like "blue" or "green") is of little or no value if one's experience is received by a brain whose language and reference-point are not of the same mind as the information's provider. A vine's physical properties are not changed by the words we use to describe it, but our perception of a vine's physical properties are affected by those words and the associations they encapsulate. Conveying an idea to another who exists in a realm of different categories is nearly impossible if both the conveyor and the receiver are convinced that they are in disagreement and that the other is wrong. The difficulty is increased if one bolsters his stance with the view that collective agreement is proof for his understanding, for, at this point, "reality" is perceived to be synonymous with "popularity." Associating popularity with reality functions by the anachronistic tendency to confuse causes with results whereby collective agreement denominates a subject that compels any usage of that new name to fit within an unoriginal category determined by consensus, i.e. it is so because we say it is so.

Biblical scholarship often begins with what some call a "theology" and what others call a "tradition." For scholarship to eventuate into a theology is one matter, but for theology to begin scholarship is another. What happens when there is no apparently extant tradition concerning a certain aspect of Scripture? The position of originating Biblical exploration from a documented theological standpoint necessarily compels the researcher to read with a certain lens that may or may not be accurate; furthermore, this approach would then inadvertently dismiss the notion of an undocumented understanding that preexisted the tradition utilized for the Biblical research. In essence, beginning with a predetermined theological view will result in that particular theology's end, and assuming that all there is to know about Scripture exists in widely accessible auxiliary documents nullifies the possibility of discovery or rediscovery that preexists documented, or apparently documented, traditions. A tradition is a delivery of preserved knowledge; such a delivery has a tendency not to anticipate, require, or even desire discovery, for tradition is often thought to contain all that needs to be contained — and this is a self-limiting proposition.

It is often Tradition's aim to mandate adherence to itself in order to contextualize Scripture with a specific bent. In other words, an adherence to Tradition compels a student to read into Scripture what Tradition supplies as an explanation to Scripture, and, when the Scriptures appear silent concerning the specificities of Tradition, it is purported that those very silences reveal the primary necessity of the Tradition; this form of reasoning demands that the Tradition is both the beginning and the end of the religion. By mandating that the Tradition be the origin and conclusion of the Text it claims to explain, the theology — and not the Scriptures — becomes the religion, and such a situation gives birth to the establishment of a drastically minute body of Scripture-readers and a multitude of adherents who receive primarily oral theological reflections upon Tradition that is supposed to mirror the Scriptures that so few read. In short, holding theology as a substitute as opposed to a supplement supplants the apparent need for the Bible, and this reasoning also is established upon the principle that all that is known (or needed to be known) has already been documented in supplemental fashion — thus ruling out the possibility of discovery and rediscovery.

That documentation of supplementary thought does not exist (or appear to exist) materially does not mean that such thought never occurred; rather, an absence of material access only indicates that such thought either was not written down or that the written record of it no longer exists (or appears to exist). Lack of recognition does not prove lack of existence. Germs existed before germs were discovered, and what is called "science" is often the verifiable success of what was formerly called "magic," for chemistry is essentially the alchemy that worked. The fact that mighty institutions with lengthy histories and verifiable successes did not grasp the entirety of a matter does not mean that those institutions deserve blame; however, such institutions may not have all of the necessary aspects of a matter to succeed any further than they already have, for such success may be insufficient when they encounter another entity capable of greater proficiency aimed in the same direction. It proves contradictory for those who believe in the totality of Traditional understanding on the one hand and the evolution of thought on the other, because such duplicity would demand that all there is to be known about a matter exists among a populace who will necessarily excel beyond the limits of what is currently established and maintained... and we may notice that this manner of thinking leads to the assumption that people can transcend the restrictions of Scripture on the basis of being more evolved than the scribes utilized to pen the Scriptures and the Mind that inspired them. Such inherently fallacious reasoning could conclude that the "Old" Testament was good in its time, the "New" Testament was good in its time as well, but now we can go on to something better than what both have offered collectively since the restrictions within the Scriptures would only be necessarily beneficial to a populace less advanced than ourselves because we are more recent. If the state of being recent is evidence of excellence, then every infant should be inherently more advanced than his parents. Such a stance is immature.

According to Scripture, the moral taintlessness of man preceded man's fall from ethical perfection. If the precedent is not known, then a false point of origin is assumed and accidentally superimposed retroactively as original; this has happened in the case of man's diet. It seems that few schools of thought have recognized that the original diet of all of earth's creatures was vegetarian (Genesis 1:29-30), and that the consumption of one another only occurred following the consumption of the forbidden tree. It would seem consistent to connect consumption unto death with death unto consumption as a reflection of the disinheriting fall that God wages against with the offer of adoption. If the precedent is not known, then the "point of origin" is a misnomer relative to the entirety of the matter and can only be applicable to a fragment that proceeds from the origin and that may not reach fully back to the origin. Cicero said, "Time in the sense in which we now use it — for to define it absolutely and in general terms is difficult — time is a part of eternity definitely indicated as being of a certain length, a year, a month, a day, or night" (*De Inventione*). If one does not know the origin, then one cannot possibly say that what proceeded from an unknown point is known to excel the unknown. If another comes along and, in beholding the same assumed point of origin, sees another aspect of something (perhaps not according with the existing body of information in a given time-period), the aspect seen may, in fact, be more correct than what appears to define a collectively agreed upon point of origin. Collective agreement proves nothing beyond collective agreement. If collective agreement purports to be orthodox by the fact that it believes itself to extend directly from the point of origin and not from at least a secondary snippet, then it will be collectively agreed that anything found not in total congruence (let alone in opposition!) to the "orthodox" must necessarily be unorthodox and therefore untrue.

Assuming that the primary state of the world was less advanced than the current state (based on available records and the various theories derived therefrom) compels one, even if moral degradation is allowed in the argument, to assume superiority over an unknown precedent. What if what is thought to be archetypical is at least secondary? If something that is not original is thought to be primary, then mistakenness will grow into something that is not itself in total accordance with what preceded it. The Scripture says of Christ that "He was in the beginning with God" and "yet the world did not know Him" (John 1). If the world did know Him Who preceded the ignorance under discussion, then ignorance cannot be the point of origin. If ignorance cannot be the point of origin, then man has not progressed in quality from his origin. Ignorance must be at least second-ary. Ignorance must have resulted from something that occurred following primacy. Scripturally, we can understand why the failure darkly commu-nicated in the account of our first human parents concerned wisdom pri-marily and the נפל *Fall* secondarily. Humanity did not fall in ascension, for such an inversion is a flat contradiction that has resulted in fruitless moral perversion and not abundant ethical progress. Scripturally, we can see that God said, "Let there be light" in Genesis 1 and comprehend why Paul discussed "wisdom" relative to this statement in the Book of 2 Corinthians 4:6:

> For it is the God who commanded φως *light* to shine out of darkness, Who has shone in our hearts to give the light of the knowledge of the glory of God in the face of Jesus Christ.

Paul used the Greek φως *light* in the Hebrew sense of *wisdom*, for the Hebrew word אור means both *light* and *wisdom,* which are synthesized in our English word *Enlightenment.* Imagine the confusion that would en-sue if a populace considered *Enlightenment* to be one thing when it was another... and consider how such confusion can occur by the simple giving of names. At the same time, consider how the Garden of Eden story dis-cusses the first man naming entities relative to wisdom along with the fact that the Hebrew word שכל can mean both *name* and *wisdom.* Consider also that the Book of Job is arguably the oldest Book of Scripture, and one of its speaker's asks,

> Do you not know this of old, since Adam was placed on earth, that the triumphing of the wicked is short, and the joy of the hypocrite is but for a moment? Though his haughtiness mounts up to the heavens, and his head reaches to the clouds, yet he will perish forever like his own refuse; those who have seen him will say, "Where is he?" He will fly away like a dream, and not be found; yes, he will be chased away like a vision of the night. The eye that saw him will see him no more, nor will his place behold him anymore. His children will seek the favor of the poor, and his hands will restore his wealth. His bones are full of his youth-ful vigor, but it will lie down with him in the dust. THOUGH EVIL IS SWEET IN HIS MOUTH, AND HE HIDES IT UNDER HIS TONGUE, THOUGH HE SPARES IT AND DOES NOT FORSAKE IT, BUT STILL KEEPS IT IN HIS MOUTH, YET HIS FOOD IN HIS STOMACH TURNS

SOUR; IT BECOMES COBRA VENOM WITHIN HIM. He swallows down riches and vomits them up again; God casts them out of his belly. He will suck the poison of cobras; the viper's tongue will slay him (Job 20: 4-16).

That a given connection has not been widely observed within a given section of eternity that we qualify as a point in time does not mean that such a connection does not exist, nor does it mean that such a fact was not seen in a different time. Furthermore, that facts are written down overtly in one time-period does not mean that they were written overtly in other time periods. If facts were written in deliberate obscuration for a select group of initiates, then any search for the obvious would not yield blatant finds even if a search yielded a multitude of subtle findings that, viewed as a sum, made a grand picture obvious in the end. It can therefore be concluded that an obvious picture may be the end of subtle, hidden fragments reconsidered in an original light that has the appearance of being innovative. For instance, let us reexamine the so-called 40-day duration of Noah's flood. Genesis 7:17-8:14 states,

IN THE SIX HUNDREDTH YEAR OF NOAH'S LIFE, IN THE SECOND MONTH, THE SEVENTEENTH DAY OF THE MONTH, on that day ALL THE FOUNTAINS OF THE GREAT DEEP WERE BROKEN UP, AND THE WINDOWS OF HEAVEN WERE OPENED. And the RAIN WAS ON THE EARTH FORTY DAYS AND FORTY NIGHTS. On the very same day Noah and Noah's sons, Shem, Ham, and Japheth, and Noah's wife and the three wives of his sons with them, entered the ark— they and every beast after its kind, all cattle after their kind, every creeping thing that creeps on the earth after its kind, and every bird after its kind, every bird of every sort. And they went into the ark to Noah, two by two, of all flesh in which is the breath of life. So those that entered, male and female of all flesh, went in as God had commanded him; and the Lord shut him in. Now THE FLOOD WAS ON THE EARTH FORTY DAYS. The waters increased and lifted up the ark, and it rose high above the earth. The waters prevailed and greatly increased on the earth, and the ark moved about on the surface of the waters. And the waters prevailed exceedingly on the earth, and all the high hills under the whole heaven were covered. The waters prevailed fifteen cubits upward, and the mountains were covered. And all flesh died that moved on the earth: birds and cattle and beasts and every creeping thing that creeps on the earth, and every man. All in whose nostrils was the breath of the spirit of life, all that was on the dry land, died. So He destroyed all living things which were on the face of the ground: both man and cattle, creeping thing and bird of the air. They were destroyed from the earth. Only Noah and those who were with him in the ark remained alive. And THE WATERS PREVAILED ON THE EARTH ONE HUNDRED AND FIFTY DAYS. Then God remembered Noah, and every living thing, and all the animals that were with him in the ark. And God made a wind to pass over the earth, and the waters subsided. The FOUNTAINS OF THE DEEP AND THE WINDOWS OF HEAVEN were also stopped, and the rain from heaven was restrained. And the waters receded continually from the earth. At the end of THE HUNDRED AND FIFTY DAYS the waters decreased. Then the ark rested in the SEVENTH MONTH, THE SEVENTEENTH DAY OF THE MONTH, on the mountains of Ararat. And the waters decreased continually until the tenth month. In the tenth month, on the first day of the month, the tops of the mountains were seen. So it came to pass, AT THE END OF FORTY DAYS, that Noah opened the window of the ark which he had made. Then he sent out a raven, which kept going to and fro until the waters had dried up from the earth. He also sent out from himself a dove, to see if the waters had receded from the face of the ground. But the dove found no resting place for the sole of her foot, and she returned into the ark to him, for the waters were on the face of the whole earth. So he put out his hand and took her, and drew her into the ark to himself. And he waited yet another seven days, and again he sent the dove out from the ark. Then the dove came to him in the evening, and behold, a freshly plucked olive leaf was in her mouth; and Noah knew that the waters had receded from the earth. So he waited yet another seven days and sent out the dove, which did not return again to him anymore. And it came to pass iN THE SIX HUNDRED AND FIRST YEAR, IN THE FIRST MONTH, THE FIRST DAY OF THE MONTH, that the waters were dried up from the earth; and Noah removed the covering of the ark and looked, and indeed the surface of the ground was dry. And IN THE SECOND MONTH, ON THE TWENTY-SEVENTH DAY OF THE MONTH, the earth was dried.

The flood consisted of two water-sources: the "FOUNTAINS OF THE GREAT DEEP" and the "WINDOWS OF HEAVEN." That it rained 40 days and 40 nights says nothing to the duration of the fountains surging forth. The Text then states that "THE FLOOD WAS ON THE EARTH FORTY DAYS," but it does not say that the flood ended after 40 days only; instead, it is written, "THE WATERS PREVAILED ON THE EARTH ONE HUNDRED AND FIFTY DAYS."

Immediately, one cannot state that Scripture discusses a flood that lasted 40 days when the very Scripture in question states that the waters prevailed for 150 days. The flood began in the 600th year of Noah's life, but it ended in the 601st year of his life; so, if Noah was 600 years old before the 150 days under discussion, and he was 601 years old on the other end of the 150 days, then the years of Noah's life also indicate a flood that lasted longer than 40 days. The flood began "IN THE SECOND MONTH, THE SEVENTEENTH DAY OF THE MONTH," but the earth was dried "IN THE SECOND MONTH, ON THE TWENTY-SEVENTH DAY OF THE MONTH"; therefore, the flood would have lasted longer than 150 days based on the dates of its beginning and ending . It would seem fitting that 12 moons comprising 354 days are accounted for here, thus a surplus of 11 days (in order to account for the seasonal harmonization of lunar and solar time) would mark neatly that Noah's flood lasted the duration of a solar year: 365 days. The reader can observe that the dates of Noah's life in conjunction with the dates of the flood are carefully included in the Narrative. Again, by mandating that the Tradition be the origin and conclusion of the Text it claims to explain, the theology becomes the religion. That no tradition existed, or appeared to exist, to explain Noah's flood does not mean that a tradition was necessary to explain it, nor does it mean that apparently accessible theologies are the only way of discovering the Text.

The Astronomer G. Shiaparelli noted the facts above in his book *Astronomy in the Old Testament* in the year 1905, and he rediscovered something understood prior to his time on the earth — but something that did not exist in the exact same form in which he penned the previously comprehended substance of his observations. He commented that "...it cannot be doubted that the habit of reckoning times by weeks of years, or by weeks of weeks of years, had its root, not in astronomical phenomena, but simply in the superstitious veneration with which the Jews (and not they only) have always regarded the number seven." On the contrary, this assertion can be doubted because the "superstitious veneration" of "the Jews" played no part in the Book of Genesis since no "Jew" yet walked the earth. Furthermore, the superstition suspected is actually a literary device connoting a *covenant*, for the root שׁבע *to swear an oath (as in a covenant)* produces the word שׁבע *seven*. The point here is not in any way to criticize the work of Shiaparelli. The point here is in every way to demonstrate that the assumption of "superstitious veneration" criticized by Shiaparelli is the result of Collective Agreement's name "Jew" retroactively superimposed upon a people-group who preceded the Jews historically. On top of this, what was not seen was the literary association of the number *seven* with a *covena*nt, like that which was signified by Noah's rainbow, for rainbows comprise seven colors. "I set My RAINBOW [of *seven* colors] in the cloud, and it shall be for the sign of the COVENANT [etymologically related to the word *seven*] between Me and the earth" (Genesis 9:13). The mind of Shiaparelli was superior, but the categories of "Jew" and "seven" received through an unoriginal language system and by an anachronistic tradition of naming did not allow a sharp man to see the scientific colors that signify a nonmaterial covenant by the number of its linguistic association.

I write to you concerning a topic unseen, or apparently unseen, for nearly 2,000 years, but I am convinced this topic was last known by the men who penned the so-called "New Testament" Scriptures. When material evidence is lacking, truths can be preserved in traditions. The limit of tradition is that it relies on some preexistent knowledge to be understood in order to grasp the tradition's reflection of its origin. Unfortunately, it is often the case that devotees are bereft of direct access or evidence and are unavoidably compelled to rely (at least for a time) on what they can glean from tradition and what they can observe from the reflection. It is my conviction that we live in an era (that has existed slightly less than 2,000 years) that has had the privilege of beholding the reflection but not the very substance being reflected, and this situation explains why there is no, or apparently no, documentary evidence pointed in the exact same direction of thesis asserted within this publication. Today, such a situation can be observed in that a dire multiplicity of religious fervors and tax-exempt businesses all claim origin from the same Book and yet function in internal and external discord. The fractions would seem to admit a common source, and the present reality appears as shards of a mirror that often cut those who attempt to reconstruct a surface capable of sharper reflection.

My thesis is this: The Garden of Eden rendering, understood to involve a talking snake, mythical fruit, and an uncultivated form of humanity that was too ignorant to realize it stood without clothing, is but a childish *version* of the Truth that is beheld askance. I forward this thesis because of the following: (1) Many adherents to what is now called "Christianity" received the Text from adherents to what is now called "Orthodox Judaism," and there was a time in history (as recorded in the Talmud) when expounding Scripture's Creation account was unlawful for what later became called "Orthodox Judaism." (2) The inability to expound the historical origin of life thus obscured the ramifications that ensued. (3) Observations were made concerning the ramifications as opposed to the original source. Traditions were devised to preserve those observations, but they were not able make defectless sense of those observations. (4) Since Tradition is more quickly available than personal study, Tradition superseded personal study of the source. (5) After Tradition superseded personal study, it became the religion itself. (6) At this point, the tradition painted any contradictory knowledge of what preceded the tradition as contrary to the basic tenets of the religion the tradition was supposed to elucidate; thus, Brandolini proves incisively correct: *"For when causes change, effects must necessarily change too"* (*Republics & Kingdoms Compared*). It is the claim of this book that what is thought to be "original" to the Faith actually exists in oblique reflection of the Faith's origin, and it is for this reason that the claims of this book can seem innovative and not foundational if they are read within a vacuum. Knowing, however, that nothing is written in a vacuum, the claims of this book will, I hope, prove to be true if the Scriptures are searched with relentless scrutiny. It is also my fervent hope that anything that might be accidentally incorrect in my work may be exposed, dismissed, and forgotten by the grace of God... which brings me to the reason for this second edition.

When I first observed the discovery that led to the composition of the first edition, my plan was strained by unavoidable time limitations and resource constraints. The plan of the first edition was frustrated even more by the traditions I was taught since my youth through a very wide variety of organizations who shared a single title in inadvertent incoherence. In short, I had to unlearn almost as much as I had to learn in order to bring about this second edtion.

I still hold to my original thesis. The thesis of the first edition did not need revision. The form of my first edition did need revision because, with further study, I disagree considerably with what is considered "Orthodox." I formerly thought — based on what I was taught by institutions — that a multitude has always known the depths of Scripture, based on its "faith" in Christ, and that the particular aspects concerning my book have only been recently forgotten but were known widely in the time of Christ; this point I find to be false because I Corinthians 2:6-8 states, "...we speak wisdom among those who are mature, yet not the wisdom of this age, nor of the rulers of this age, who are coming to nothing. But we speak the wisdom of God in a MYSTERY, the HIDDEN WISDOM which God ordained BEFORE THE AGES for our glory, which <u>NONE</u> OF THE RULERS OF THIS AGE KNEW; for had they known, they would not have crucified the Lord of glory." The stance that "Orthodox Judaism" knows the majority of the Hebrew Bible's intricacies based on its tradition is ignorant of the fact that this tradition confounds the terms "Hebrew," "Israelite," and "Jew" by falsely assuming them to be synonymous when they are not. Furthermore, a Benjamite Jew distinguished such categories by discussing the "Seed of Abraham" (II Corinthians 11:22, etc.). I believe that there is a Great Secret that binds the entirety of Scripture into a provably seamless whole. It is this secret, this mystery, that is the subject of the book you are reading.

In closing, I ask God for mercy if anything found within this work is lacking or errant, and I ask the reader to check against the assertions of this text by turning to the Bible itself. My hope is that whatever errors found within this book are forgiven and are not permitted to mislead others, for my hope is to help point towards a source far superior to my best work. The reader should understand that I do not view Scripture as simple, nor do I think it can be apprehended with ease. The attention-span formed by mass-media has no place within this study. I adamantly assert that the technical skills required for critical reading are experiencing diminution as today's mind willfully suffers degradation by trading the mass media's Screen for wisdom and by exchanging digitized "clicks" for substantial answers to the extent that the greatest way today to hide information is by writing it in a physical, tangible codex. How sardonic an irony!

Sincerely,

Joshua Collins

INTRODUCTION

K<small>EEP</small> in mind the ancient term "womb-serpent" throughout your reading of this book. This "serpent" is to be understood emblematically. Consider the cuneiform writing of the ancient East. Ancient Mesopotamian writing, impressed into clay, is three-dimensional writing. The play of light and shadow causes this writing to be revealed or concealed since this writing can only be read properly if the light comes from a certain direction. Translations of cuneiform writing as such are often accompanied by transcriptions since a large problem with interpretation stems from the difficulty of transforming three dimensions into the two with which we, in English, employ to read and to write. As a result of only thinking about writing in two dimensions, we English speakers must adapt our understanding of language by considering a third dimension in terms of the physical construction of ancient Eastern writing, and we must also take into account a fourth dimension: time. The world of the time of clay writing, the geography in which it is found, and the cultures it reflects are all different from our world of two-dimensional ideas of words, our physical landscapes, and our culture. We must conceive of the world through their eyes in order to understand what they meant by impressing their words into the very soil from which they sprang. Information and knowledge was, for a long while, primarily oral. Writing was very much concerned with the future, but in terms of memory; for ancient commemorative inscriptions, when read, perpetuate the name of their commissioner; thus, writing was, in a sense, a seed that germinated within the future's readers so that the name of the original commissioner would be perpetuated through yet another human vessel; consider Christ, "The Word," in this sense:

> "My LITTLE CHILDREN, for whom I LABOR IN BIRTH again until Christ is formed In you..." (Galatians 4:19).

Ancient inscriptions, like the Stela of Vultures (about 2,400 BC), paired iconography with text in order to account for illiteracy: the literate understood the words; the illiterate understood the pictures. Iconography, however, was often emblematic. In the case of the Stela of Vultures, the defeated enemies of Ningirsu are depicted as vultures trapped in a net. The vultures are emblems of people. Consider now the union of writing and iconography, not side-by-side on a carving, but in two-dimensional words themselves:

> For man also does not know his time: like fish taken in a cruel net, like birds caught in a snare, so the sons of men are snared in an evil time, when it falls suddenly upon them (Ecclesiastes 9:12).

Ezekiel 13:20 discusses hunting "souls like birds." Genesis 49 calls Judah a "lion's whelp," Issachar a "strong donkey," Dan a "serpent," Naphtali a "deer," Joseph a "fruitful bough," and Benjamin a "ravenous wolf." Jacob's children, like himself, were human even though their descriptions, like the vultures discussed above, are not. In a manner of speaking, the iconography intended for the illiterate is absorbed into the writing of the literate, so that initiated eyes might perceive the truest meaning of the Text while uninitiated eyes might see but not understand.

> And He [Christ] said, "To you it has been given to know the mysteries of the kingdom of God, but to the rest it is given in parables, that 'Seeing they may not see, and hearing they may not understand.'"

A mystery can be simultaneously proclaimed openly and discerned clandestinely. Familiarity with a certain writing does not necessarily admit familiarity with that writing's meaning. The emblems, the symbols, of a "lion's whelp" or a "serpent" are, in the cases above, ways of discussing people. Knowing what a "lion's whelp" or a "serpent" is helps one begin to understand the people these symbols describe. When we consider the conversion from three-dimensional writing into two-dimensional writing, statements like these are perceived more vividly:

> You are our EPISTLE written in our hearts, known and read by all men; clearly you are an epistle of Christ, ministered by us, written not with INK but by the Spirit of the living God, not on TABLETS OF STONE but on tablets of flesh, that is, of the heart (2 Corinthians 3:2-3).

> For we are His ποιημα poem, book, workmanship created in Christ Jesus for good works, which God prepared beforehand that we should walk in them (Ephesians 2:10).

Cuneiform was impressed upon clay. Ziggurats were constructed of clay. The first man was made of clay. Likewise, 2 Corinthians 3:2-3 and Ephesians 2:10 describe man as work of writing; 1 Corinthians 3:16

describes man as a temple; Genesis 2:7 describes man as clay. That man is described in these three ways that are all united by the constant of clay is here made obvious, but to what effect? Writing, in ancient Mesopotamia (which is where Adam was created), was understood to bestow life upon the material on which it was written. At the same time, motion was thought by the ancient Easterners to indicate life. The ideas of animating clay or writing upon clay are, in this sense, essentially one and the same. Mesopotamian clay, three-dimensional writing was considered to be alive. Ancient tablets state how people "listened to the tablet" and discuss the "mouth of the tablet." When a tablet was made void, it was said to be "killed," but when a tablet was renewed it was said to be "brought back to life" (*Reading and Writing in Babylon*, Charpin). Without understanding the way the ancient Mesopotamians described the world, we today can easily superimpose artificiality on top of their writings just as easily as we can, through habit, take on a new nature that is not original and that cannot understand the original:

> In Him was life, and the life was the light of men. And the light shines in the darkness, and the darkness DID NOT COMPRE-HEND it (John 1:4-5).

Christ, The Light, was incomprehensible to the "darkness," and Christ is thus called "The Wisdom of God" (1 Corinthians 1:24). The Wisdom of God is the Creator (Colossians 1:16). We may say, in a manner of speaking, that the Creator took clay and animated it concerning the creation of Adam, thus, "...we are His ποιημα *poem, book, workmanship* created in Christ Jesus for good works, which God prepared beforehand that we should walk in them" (Ephesians 2:10). Christ, The Wisdom of God, the Creator, was "killed" by those who made void His word, for He accused them of "...making the word of God of no effect through your tradition which you have handed down" (Mark 7:13). Since what is "handed down" (i.e. tradition) perpetuates the name of its commissioner, then the tradition that rendered God's Word "of no effect," so to speak, can be considered abortive in that it sought to obstruct what God Himself handed down. Abortive birth was said to be accomplished by a "womb-serpent" in Sumerian cuneiform. In Genesis 3, it was the "Serpent" who challenged what God "said" orally. After the Fall of Man, Psalm 19 says, "The HEAVENS declare the glory of God; and the firmament shows His HANDIWORK"; Ephesians 2 says that "...we are His ποιημα *poem, book,* WORKMAN-SHIP..."; Job 20 says, "The HEAVENS will reveal his iniquity." Considering that the "Serpent" challenged the bride's recollection of God's Word orally, it should be understood that the ancient tablets were personified in a manner that permitted no difference between written evidence and personal testimony. What a person (whose first human father was made of clay) spoke of the law, his testimony could not be distinct from what was written (on clay). God said X, the "Serpent" asked the bride what God said, the bride repeated something that was not X, something that God did not say; thus, her word differed from clay from which she was made since she chose to walk in evil works: "For we are His ποιημα *poem, book, workmanship* created in Christ Jesus for good works, which God prepared beforehand that we should walk in them" (Ephesians 2:10). Likewise, it is written that "He created them male and female, and blessed them and CALLED THEM ADAM in the day they were created" (Genesis 5:2). Adam was condemned to return to the dust, not the clay, from where he originated (Genesis 3:19). The dust, or soil, is mingled with water in order to produce clay; the "Spirit" or "Breath" of God is described often in Scripture as being "poured out"; Genesis 2:7 states that God "breathed" into man in order to animate him; the clay of which man was made was the mixture of dust with the "Breath" or "Spirit" of God; the dust to which man's body returned was, logically, devoid of the "Breath" or "Spirit" of God.

> Then the dust will return to the earth as it was, and the spirit will return to God who gave it (Ecclesiastes 12:7).

The demise of man resulted from departure from The Word of God, for man's testimony was found errantly distinct from God's Word. The tablet of man was "killed." When The Word of God came in clay to the earth in order to save, He was "brought back to life" through the renewal of a covenant that was once made void by man, that was once aborted by man; He came as an infant, and His Father brought Him back to life in accordance with the original design: "And the LORD God formed man of the dust from the ground, and breathed into his nostrils the breath of life; and man became a living being" (Geneis 2:7). We must remember that "there is a spirit in man, and the breath of the Almighty gives him understanding" (Job 32:8) and "The Spirit of God has made me, and the BREATH OF THE ALMIGHTY gives me life" (Job 33:4); thus, 1 Corinthians 15 tells us that

> [t]here is a natural body, and there is a spiritual body. And so it is written, "The first man Adam became a living being." The last Adam became a life-giving spirit. However, the spiritual is not first, but the natural, and afterward the spiritual. The first man was of the earth, made of dust; the second Man is the Lord from heaven. As was the man of dust, so also are those who are made of dust; and as is the heavenly Man, so also are

those who are heavenly. And as we have borne the image of the
man of dust, we shall also bear the image of the heavenly Man.

Again, when a tablet was made void, it was said to be "killed," but
when a tablet was renewed it was said to be "brought back to life." Christ
was killed and brought back to life. Christ is The Word. There could be
no discrepancy between the personal testimony of a man and the written
record of the law, and it was "The Law" that was contended over by Christ
and His adversaries that He called a "brood of vipers," i.e. serpents.

The Law of God was a covenant, an oath. In the ancient East, oaths
were said to be "sworn" or "eaten." The eating of an oath was understood
as the consumption of a substance that linked the lives of the swearers or
eaters. The violation of an oath was thought of symbolically in terms of the
destructivity of what was swallowed originally in the constructive covenant
as symbolized by the constructive "eating." In this way covenantal "sacrifice" was meant to be constructive, but the violation of the "eating" forced
a destructive "sacrifice," i.e. death in the belly of the perpetrating "eater."
Covenants required mutual fidelity in order to keep from "being killed" like
a tablet rendered void. Oral testimony was considered, in the ancient east,
as valid as written testimony. Concerning covenants in the ancient East,
oral testimony was often concluded by symbolic gestures. The act of "driv-
ing a stake" into land was a sign that a land owner's boundaries were verified by oath and symbolized by the driven stake.

Do not remove the ancient landmark which your fathers have
set (Proverbs 22:28).

The officials in charge of the various territories of a kingdom were themselves called "stakes." A person was as the stake he drove into the soil
in the symbolic gesture that accompanied covenantal declarations. The
words translated as "cross" in Scripture are actually ξυλον *a stick, club,* or
tree and σταυρος *a stake, a post, a support.* It was after Christ was crucified, descended, and rose that He said, "All authority has been given to Me
in heaven and on earth" (Matthew 28:18), as it was in the beginning. A
tree's roots descend underground, its trunk is terrestrial, and its branches
stretch celestially. Christ reclaimed His creation. He was and is The Stake,
so to speak. Like a renewed covenant, like a revitalized clay tablet, Christ
rose from the dead:

There shall come forth a Rod from the stem of Jesse, and a
Branch shall grow out of his roots (Isaiah 11:1).

Christ, The Stake, The Living Tree, rose again. Christ, The Light, The Menorah, shined again. Christ renewed the covenant with life originally intended before the fall. The three-dimensionality of clay writing was revitalized in animate form and is, today, witnessed by the two-dimensionality of ink writing. The Hebrew Scriptures unifiy three-dimensional reality with a two-dimensional record in a manner that is both historical and timeless.

The Hebrew Scriptures were written originally without breaks between words, vowels, or punctuation. The Massorite Scribes solidified a Traditional Text by inserting word-breaks, vowels, and punctuation that locked over the top of the Hebrew Scriptures an oral tradition concerning how the Scripture is to be read (at least initially). It has been stated often, both in speech and in writing, that the original Hebrew Scriptures were delivered though an unevolved form of writing and that, with the advancements inserted into this writing that account for word-breaks, vowels, and punctuation, we can now have a fuller understanding of the Text. Such a standpoint is errant, for the insertions placed into the Text anticipate translation and thus a singular reading. The insertions of which I speak, like translations, cannot allow for every interpretive possibility. A translation of Biblical Hebrew is not a facsimile but a representation of a portion of the Message.

The intentionally incomplete representation of speech sounds in Ancient Hebrew would seem to admit that the orality involved in expounding the Text utilizes more words than the written Text itself. That is, the deliberately imperfect record of speech sounds typifies action and thoughts into an initially nebulous scheme stylized by formulaic repetitions so that focus sharpens by repetitive exercise with the Text. Simply put, the ancient Eastern method employed here demands consistent reading to the point of memorization, and the memorization allows for a patterned map to be created in the mind of the reader wherein the initial varieties become recognized as consistent representations of an original whole. Accordingly, this manner of writing conceals itself in the open to those who, without practice, exempt themselves from discerning the pattern and subsequently supply a foreign context to writing that cannot unify with it without expressing apparent contradictions.

Though I am beyond grateful for translations, I wish here to assert resoundingly that translations have their place. Translation necessarily reduces the Message of the Text. Such things like the insertion of vowels are essential for translation, but not for comprehending the original Text. The absolute qualification of Scripture through such linguistic facets as vowels does not elucidate the Message but rather a version of the Message because such qualification cannot permit permutations in reading the original Text. For example, the Hebrew letters עבד can mean substantively a *work, deed, servant, slave,* and *a son* depending on the pronunciation (vowels) and context; the pronunciation is not written, the context is infrequently obvious, and translation can only select one definition. These letters (עבד *work, deed, servant, slave,* and *a son*) descend from the root עבד which is commonly considered to mean *to work, to labor, to till, to cultivate, to serve,* i.e. *to perform some deed of service.* Yet, since the substantive עבד can also mean *a son,* it should not be forgotten that it is reflective of its root and thus allows for the understanding of the cultivation of woman for the purposes of lineage as it discusses the cultivation of land for the purposes of fruit; this fact can be observed in that the Hebrew word פרי *fruit* means a product of agriculture and a product of conception. As such, the root עבד *to cultivate* can be understood also to mean *to sire a son.* When it is written, "The Lord God took the man and placed him in the garden of Eden לעבדה *to cultivate her* and to protect her" (Genesis 2:15), it can be reasonably induced that the passage could also be read as "The Lord God took the man and placed him in the garden of Eden לעבדה *to sire a son in her* and to protect her" — which makes clear the first command: "Be fruitful and multiply...." (Genesis 1:28). There is no translation of Genesis 2:15, of which I am aware, that discusses the siring of a son within the precinct of Eden, and this is probably attributable to the various traditions that preceded (and are reflected by) the various translations. In fact, the first procreation is consistently considered to have occurred outside of Eden to the result of Cain — and this is incorrect. Consider: "wisdom is justified by her εργων *works*" (Matthew 11:19) and "wisdom is justified by her τεκνων *children*" (Luke 7:35); in this, we can see that *a work is a child, a work is a fruit.*

I was taught since youth that writing is devised to disclose; therefore, Scripture is written to be understood; thus, Scripture should be easy to understand if it is read. The conclusion, "thus, Scripture should be easy to understand if it is read," is incorrect because it does not take into account the method by which ancient Hebrew sought to protect, as though in a garden, a message for posterity whereby a lineage would be perpetuated abstrusely as though hidden in our midst. Ancient Hebrew's lack of vowel representation in writing mandates guesswork and so functions by subtlety that requires repetition and memorization. With this system of writing, the reader must determine the vowels, and this determination qualifies a meaning that the reader must test in order to discover the validity thereof.

At first glance, it might seem as though interpretation is meant to be individually distinct and therefore functionally malleable; yet, such a glance lacks precision because it does not consider that this form of writing can be multitiered and homogeneous simultaneously in a manner that points to an original whole that is communicated with intentional vagueness. For instance, Genesis 3:8 is commonly understood to mean, "... and the man hid himself and his wife from the face of the יהוה אלהים בתוך עץ הגן *Lord God in the midst of the trees of the garden*" on account of their "nakedness" (Genesis 3:10). Why would the humans hide themselves from One Who sees all unless they could no longer see Him? Genesis 3:8 could very easily be translated "... and the man hid himself and his wife from the face of the יהוה אלהים בתוך עץ הגן*Lord God Who was in the midst of the trees of the garden,*" i.e. God was in the midst of the garden observing their sin right in front of them, but they could not see Him, and it seems that this translation is the very sense through which Hebrews 4:12-13 states,

> For the word of God is living and powerful, and sharper than any two-edged sword, piercing even to the division of soul and spirit, and of joints and marrow, and is a discerner of the thoughts and intents of the heart. And there is no creature HIDDEN FROM HIS SIGHT, BUT ALL THINGS ARE NAKED and open to the eyes of Him to whom we must give account.

Furthermore, the word עץ can mean *trees* or *tree*. If Adam hid in a tree, it would seem fitting that he climbed it. Consider the similar rebellion and fall of Satan who told humanity, in Genesis 3:5, "you will be like God":

> How you are fallen from heaven, O Lucifer, son of the morning! How you are CUT DOWN to the ground [like a tree], you who weakened the nations! For you have said in your heart: "I will ascend into heaven [as though climbing a tree], I will exalt my throne above the stars of God; I will also sit on the mount of the congregation on the farthest sides of the north; I will ascend above the heights of the clouds, I will be like the Most High" (Isaiah 14:12-14).

Similarly, Job 20:4-6 states,

> Do you not know this of old, Since אדם *Adam/man* was placed on earth, that the triumphing of the wicked is short, and the joy of the hypocrite is but for a moment? Though his haughtiness mounts up to the heavens, and HIS HEAD REACHES TO THE CLOUDS, [as though Adam climbed a tree, like the ziggurat of Babel with " וראשו בשמים*his head in the heavens]* (Genesis 11:4).

In both instances (humanity in Eden and humanity at Babel), language was confused in the midst of pride. The first Adam and God, it would seem, were in a tree where humanity could only see Adam; this situation was rectified by the Last Adam Who is God and Who was in a tree where humanity could only see a man.

The Hebrew Scriptures are riddles. The Biblical stories are often reflections of things unstated. The Text conveys a message to a select group who seeks to learn the meaning. Terms that seem common (like "serpent," "garden," "prayer," "amen," etc.) but are not conceived of in a Hebrew and Eastern historical setting accidentally cause tremendous confusion that leads to the assumption of textual error instead of interpretive error, and this situation places the critic in the accusatory role of Adam's fallen state when he blamed God by saying, "The woman whom *You* gave to me, she gave to me from the tree...." God's Word, and not man's mind, is often first accused by man. For instance, I have heard it stated and restated that "Christianity" declares that people are wicked since they are sinful and that the problem of sin was solved by The Father rejecting His Son and sacrificing Him for humanity's sake. "Christianity" has been preached to this extent consistently without realizing it is describing its opposite: the ceremonial slaughter of children. I assert that what was once understood as child-sacrifice (like Molech-worship) is now erroneously called "Christianity" and that the opposite of the truth has parasitically adopted the guise of the Standard. It is Molech worship that obscures the Son from our eyes whereas it is what Scripture calls "The Way" (Genesis 3:24; Malachi 2:8; John 14:6; Acts 24:13-14) that allows us to see Him revealed in our midst. Scripture is a recondite record of the evidence of things unseen, and it is our privilege to seek the catalyst for the words we read upon the pages of Scripture. Hebrews 2:2 states that "every transgression and disobedience received a just punishment" which should point to the fact that the punishment fits the crime perfectly and thereby the remedy fits the punishment congruently as though in a mirror. **The punishment fits the crime, and the grace fits the punishment**. The womb was punished as a result of the sin in Eden (Genesis 3:16). What crime did the womb commit? Hanging was the punishment for the ritual slaughter of children (Numbers 25:4). Why is Christ called the "Holy Child" (Acts 4:27)? The word "child" utilized here is the Greek παις which can mean *a child, a servant, and a slave*, for it is the translation of the Hebrew עבד *a slave, a servant,* and *a son* which allows us to recall that "The Lord God took the man and placed him in the garden of Eden לעבדה *to sire a son in her* and to protect her" -- which makes the connection clear between the commands, "Be fruitful and multiply...." (Genesis 1:28) and, "Go therefore and make disciples of all the nations, baptizing them in the name of the Father and of the Son and of the Holy Spirit, teaching them to observe all things that I have commanded you..." (Matthew 28:19-20). That is, the word עשה *to do, to make* can also mean *to convert* (Genesis 12:5) and *to reproduce* (Genesis 2:3). This Hebrew connection is seen lucidly in Greek when Phillip converted the Eunuch (Acts 8) who was reading Isaiah 53, for Isaiah continues in this place by calling God עשיך *Your Maker (or Converter or Reproducer),* גאלך *Your Redeemer (thus Converter),* and בעליך *Your Hus-band (thus Reproducer)* in 54:5 in order to lead into the declaration,

> Do not let the son of the foreigner who has joined himself to the Lord Speak, saying, "The Lord has utterly separated me from His people"; nor let the eunuch say, "Here I am, a DRY TREE." For thus says the Lord: "TO THE EUNUCHS who keep My Sabbaths, and choose what pleases Me, and hold fast My cov-enant, even to them I will give in My house and within My walls a place and a name better than that of sons and daughters; I will give them an everlasting name that shall not be cut off" (Isaiah 56:3-5).

The quotation of Isaiah 53 in Acts 8 triggers the promise to the faithful eunuch, and we read in Acts 8:35-39 the following:

> Then Philip opened his mouth, and BEGINNING at this Scripture [and ending probably in Isaiah 56], preached Jesus to him. Now as they went down the road, they came to some water. And the eunuch said, "See, here is water [nor let the eunuch say, 'Here I am, a DRY TREE.']. What hinders me from being baptized [wa-tered]?" Then Philip said, "If you believe with all your heart, you may." And he answered and said, "I believe that Jesus Christ is the Son of God." So he commanded the chariot to stand still. And both Philip and the eunuch went down into the water, and he baptized him. Now when they came up out of the water, the Spirit of the Lord caught Philip away, so that the eunuch saw him no more; AND HE WENT ON HIS WAY REJOICING,

as predicted in the section of Isaiah where the eunuch was reading.

The Hebrew Scriptures are the prerequisite memorization key for the so-called Greek "New Testament." By understanding that the root עשה *to do, to make* can also mean *to convert* and *to reproduce,* we can begin to understand the "image" man was created to accord with in Creation. Likewise, the root דמה *to resemble* produces the word דמות *similitude, par-able, likeness, pattern, model.* The declaration, "נעשה אדם בצלמנו כדמותנו Let

Us make man in Our image according to Our likeness" could just as well be translated, " נעשה אדם בצלמנו כדמותנו *Let Us convert man in Our image according to Our parable,"* which is exactly what Christ did: "For whom He foreknew, He also predestined to be CONFORMED TO THE IMAGE OF HIS SON, that He might be the firstborn among many brethren" (Romans 8:29). The Greek παραβολη *parable (a placing beside, a juxtaposition, a parallel, a similitude)* is a translation of the Hebrew חידה *riddle, hard saying,* and the Book of Hebrews employs the word *parable* to discuss physical reality and not just orality (9:9, 11:19). The conformation to the image of God repeats the original creation of man by the Image of God, and this seems to indicate that sin's effects labor to efface God's image. The image is understood here as both mental and physical whereby a pattern, that is, a similitude is the reflection of a substance that, at first, exists in an unseen manner. Exodus 3 tells us that the "angel of the Lord appeared to him in flames of fire from within a thorny bush," but it proceeds to say that Moses was awe-struck that the thorny bush was not consumed by the fire. The Text does not say that Moses was awe-struck that the "angel of the Lord" was "in flames of fire" and that this angel was "within a thorny bush." The Text only says that Moses was awe-struck by the flames' lack of destruction of the thorny bush and not the lack of destruction of the angel within them and within the thorny bush. The angel was in the midst of the plant, so to speak. It seems quite plain that Moses saw the thorny bush and the fire but not the Divine Being, even though the angel was immediately before him (as it seems was the case with Adam in the garden). Later, Moses understood "...him who dwelt in the burning bush" (Deuteronomy 33:16) whereas, formerly, Moses only saw the fire; thus, Adam first saw God, rebelled, and then did not see Him in the midst of the plant at the point of his physical demise, whereas Moses first did not see God, obeyed, and then did see Him in the midst of the plant at the point of his physical demise.

The Biblical method of understated repetition demands consistent reading to the extent of memorization, and the memorization allows for a paradigm to be fashioned in the brain of the reader wherein types become recognized as constituents of an unfractured original. This manner of writing hides itself in the open to those who, unused to such exercise, are exempt from seeing the pattern and accidentally supply an unoriginal context to writing that cannot meld well with it without presenting apparent contradictions. The "contradictions" in Scripture do not exist in reality, but the contradictions in our minds do, and such contradictory reality appears to have been the scheme of the "serpent" who was allowed by man to induce a laborious question that ramified into the marred image recognized obliquely in fallen human progeny. In Sumerian cuneiform texts, birth defects are described as being the result of demonic activity wherein evil forces are "coiled up... like a serpent in the human womb"; the so called "womb-serpent" of these texts bears a connection to the goddess of childbirth, "the mother goddess" (*Cult of the Serpent*, Mundkur). The point is that defective birth was, in the ancient east, described as the result of a "womb-serpent." When we consider that it was the "serpent" who enticed our first human mother, it should be kept in mind that she received punishment in her womb (Genesis 3:16).

THE LEXICON

CONSIDER what are called "word-studies." Often, we may experience a statement like this:

> The book of Jonah never uses the word "whale." The word translated "whale" [דג] really means *a great fish*; it is from the root "דגה *to increase, to multiply*." Since we know that fish have gills and whales have lungs, Jonah could not have been swallowed by a whale because the Bible tells us — in the original language — that it was *a great fish*, and this means it was a *great, multiplying animal with gills*.

In the opinion of this author, such a statement is inadmissible for several reasons: (1) The translators were not ignorant men, and they rendered the Hebrew word "fish" in the English tongue as "whale" because a whale is large enough to swallow a human entirely, and they never asserted that it must necessarily have been a whale but only an animal comparable to a sea-dwelling creature of great proportions. (2) Asserting that a "fish" in English has identical taxonomy in Hebrew is presumptuous because our English usage for "fish" does not bring immediately to mind the concept of multiplication any more than the Hebrew usage of "fish" brings immediately to mind the characteristic of gills. That English-speaking taxonomists classified fish as animals that have gills says nothing to the possibility that ancient Hebrew taxonomists admitted any such characteristics beyond the commonality of any animal that lives in water. Leviticus 11:9 states literally "from all that are in the waters," not all water-dwelling animals that breathe through gills; therefore, current English classification cannot be retroactively superimposed on ancient Hebrew classification to distinguish a "whale" from a "fish" Biblically. (3) That a given Hebrew word "really means" anything other than an English word is obvious by the fact that Hebrew is being translated, not reproduced; if it were reproduced, it would not be a translation at all since no two language systems have entirely identical correspondences between their respective dictions in their entireties. For the foregoing reasons, a simple reference to a dictionary/concordance is a good (if not necessary) start to understanding the Language of Scripture, but it cannot necessarily be the end of understanding words because the design of the average lexicon does not often admit every single usage of a word in the context of the Narrative but only the lexicographer's conclusions based upon a given word's various usages.

Numbers 14:20-23 states "Then the Lord said: 'I have pardoned, according to your word; but truly, as I live, all the earth shall be filled with the glory of the Lord — because all these men who have seen My glory and the signs which I did in Egypt and the wilderness, and have put Me to the test now these ten times, and have not heeded My voice, they certainly shall not see the land of which נשבעתי *I swore* to their fathers, nor shall any of those who rejected Me see it.'" Psalm 95:11 recounts this swearing, this oath, in this manner: "So נשבעתי *I swore* in my wrath, 'They shall not enter מנוחתי *My rest*.'" Hebrews 3:11 quotes Psalm 95:11: "So I swore in my wrath, 'They shall not enter καταπαυσιν μου *My rest*.'" The reader will notice that, among Numbers 14, Psalm 95, and Hebrews 3, the act of entering into the Promised Land is equivalent to מנוח *rest*. The reader will then note that this *rest* is connected with an *oath*, a *swearing*, and this *swearing* is from the root שבע *to swear* and produces the cardinal number שבע *seven*. Etymologically, the number *seven* is linked to the concept of *a covenant, an oath, a solemn swearing intended to be vindicated practically*. Accordingly, the people who rejected God rejected also His covenant (*covenant* being synonymous with *rest*), so God did not allow them to enter His rest (*rest* being synonymous with the *covenant* the people rejected). In the manner of usage displayed here, we may observe that *rest* can be employed as a programmatic substitution for *covenant* and that by merely referencing the word *rest* in the dictionary, there is hardly a necessary link to the word *covenant* that is immediately apparent... which says nothing to the fact that the words *rest* and *covenant* are Scripturally employed as synonyms under the topic at hand.

The very fact that there was a border to be crossed to enter the Promised Land admits the presence of a threshold, and a threshold was historically held synonymously with an altar (where covenants are often made). A threshold and a basin were held synonymously, even to the extent that the Hebrew word סף means a *bowl*, a *basin*, and a *threshold*; therefore, a threshold, a bowl, and a basin can be linked to an altar upon which an oath is uttered and where a covenant is cut; the covenant indicates a rest acquired by the passing over into the oath. Marriage was once understood as a threshold covenant (See *The Threshold of Paradise*, by Collins.), and the word לקח can mean both *to marry* and *to take*. In the sense of a ברית *covenant*, לקח *to marry* indicates an *oath to the death, a solemn swearing*, and Genesis 2:15 says that "The Lord God לקח *took* (covenanted with) the man, ויניחהו *and He put him to rest* in the Garden of Eden...." i.e. God covenanted with man by having him pass over the garden's threshold into covenant with his garden (ultimately, his wife, for Song of Songs 4:12 calls a woman a "garden"). A threshold covenant is a type of marriage, and marriage is a type of threshold covenant; so, when the bride "fell into transgression" (1 Timothy 2:14), the bride rejected God's rest, God's covenant, God's wedding supper in preference for the Seducer's wedding supper, the Seducer's communion, the Seducer's new covenant and new testament. As a result, "The Lord God שלח divorced..." (Genesis 3:23) His bride, since she asked for the divorce by rejecting His rest (rest being a circumlocution or substitution for covenant), and man was "גרש divorced" (Genesis 3:24) — divorce being understood as a breach of covenant, oath, rest, marriage, etc. Roundly (not precisely) the divorce necessitated work, for the rest of the covenant was rejected by man. In other words, "וינחהו and He put him to rest in the Garden of Edenלעבדה to work/cultivate/serve her and to guard her" (Genesis 2:15), and we see an apparent difficulty in that God both put the man to rest and to work in the Eden simultaneously when the very punishment of man for breaking the covenant was "work" (Genesis 3:17-19). Was man to rest or to work in his perfection prior to the Fall? — The answer is perceived when one recognizes that a covenant, an oath, a solemn swearing, is used Scripturally in conjunction with rest and as its synonym, and this rest is not incongruous with work even though rest and work appear to be antonyms; for, נוח to rest is a synonym of שבע to swear and the rest is employed to indicate protection, not lack of labor. That is, "work" was not the punishment outside of Eden any more than "rest" was the avoidance of work inside of Eden. The "work" inside of Eden was covenantally connected to God whereas the "work" outside of Eden was covenentally connected to the Enemy to which man defected. We may recall that the letters עבד can mean work, deed, servant, slave, and a son, and this descends from the root עבדto work, to labor, to till, to cultivate, to serve. It would seem that there was an intended "rest" (covenant) that anticipated a son (work); when this intention was thwarted, it would seem that there was a resulting "work" (son) who reflected an unholy covenant (lack of holy "rest") and that this son was Cain who condemned himself to be a restles "fugitive and vagabond" (Genesis 4:14). We may read this same principle in Joshua 21:44:

> The Lord gave them REST all around, according to all that He had SWORN to their fathers. And not a man of all their enemies stood against them; the Lord delivered all their enemies into their hand.

The pattern is clear: part of the blessing of the swearing of the oath (the covenant) is protection that Scripture calls "rest," and this protection is necessitated in an oath because both covenanting parties stake their lives for each other's; this explains why "...the Lord God took the man וינחהו and He put him to rest in the Garden of Eden לעבדה to work/cultivate/serve her ולשמרה and to guard her" (Genesis 2:15). God covenanted with Adam concerning Eden, and this covenant, this rest, necessitated the protection expected of Adam, for the word גן *garden* is from the root גנן *to defend*. God made a defended place wherein He set his worker to rest and to labor, that is, to labor without the intrusion of an enemy. God's worker, who was in covenant with Him, was, in turn, to perform his duty to defend the garden God planted during both his rest and his labor. We may see that the first sin was not eating of the forbidden tree, but allowing the enemy in the covenantal garden in the first place; this explains why a negative command (2:8) was given to Adam immediately after covenanting with him (2:7) positively, for the initial positive injunction followed immediately by a negative is what is called in a covenant the "blessing" and the "curse" or "binding" of a covenant, i.e. the anticipated and required fruit or blessing of the covenant and the policed insurance of retribution for stunting or eliminating the fruit of the union. The Torah shows negative commands to be the result of error. That a negative command was given to Adam means that he was in error prior to eating of the forbidden tree. We know this error to be that he allowed the Enemy's intrusion in the very place Adam had covenanted with God, the very place that both parties in this *covenant* swore an oath to defend in both *labor and rest* (*rest* being synonymous with *oath* and *oath* being synonymous with *protection*).

Similarly, נח *Noah* means *Rest*, and God *protected* Noah during his *labors* to build the ark and during the deluge that left the remaining world unprotected. Genesis 8:9 states, "But the dove found no RESTING PLACE for the sole of her foot, and she returned into the ark to him, for the waters were on the face of the whole earth." The "מנוח *resting place*" of the dove was not found amidst the destructive waters, for the *covenant* (rest) had not yet been made regarding the earth's future destruction that God promised not to exact by water (Genesis 9:11). When the flood ended, God gave a seven-colored sign of His covenant, and the root שבע *to swear* produces the cardinal number שבע *seven*. The sabbatical covenant mandates undaunted defense at all times, not just six days per week. We may see a perfect example of this defensive/covenantal/rest/labor principle in Matthew 12 where Christ protected His disciples concerning the grain they plucked on the Sabbath and where He protected a man with a withered hand that He healed on the Sabbath. Both stories in Matthew 12 concerning food and a hand are juxtaposed to His teaching concerning "good" and "evil" trees; Adam's covenant with God was broken, and, after he ate, God said, "...lest he stretch forth his hand..." (Genesis 3:22); God restored, reaffirmed, and renewed the covenant when He said, "Stretch forth your hand" (Matthew 12:13) just after His defense concerning food and just before His discussion of good and evil trees. In short, *rest* is synonymous with *covenant* that is related to *protection*, which, it would seem, is why it is written, "...the Lord God took the man וינחהו *and He put him to* REST in the Garden of Eden לעבדה *to* WORK/*cultivate/serve* her ולשמרה *and to* GUARD *her*" (Genesis 2:15).

Internally, Scripture employs definite meanings programmatically in order to make connections through various employments of words. Such employments of diction utilize definite meanings expansively without defying their original and definite meanings in order to evince symmetry of thought beyond the capability of a single word. Simply referring to a masterful dictionary is a wonderful way to begin understanding the language of Scripture, but it is not a masterful end of such study. The logic of the connections presented above is not English in spite of the fact that the record of this logic is in English. Translations of Scripture may be blessedly erudite, but they are not nor cannot be perfectly definitive. Furthermore, mastery of language alone cannot give mastery of understanding, for individual words can be misunderstood contextually on account of not knowing the reference to which they refer. For instance, one can understand that the Hebrew word we render as "firmament" is רקיע *a beaten out sheet of metal*, but to what effect? The natural question would be, "Why is the sky compared to a sheet of metal?" and the answer can be seen to lie outside of the limits of linguistic mastery. Definite meanings also have definite references, and syntax allows diction to transcend individual meaning for the purposes of a descriptive whole.

TRANSLATION
&
INTERPRETATION

TRANSLATION is not reproduction. So called "word-for-word" translation is not a facsimile of the original. A translation is an interpretation. A translation is one way of viewing part of the original whole. A translation is the conveyance from an original through a medium whereby the essence, not the specificity, is hopefully retained, but the retention exists in an altered state much in the same way perfume is the translation of a flower's scent into a foreign but reminiscent form. Though both perfume and flower petals smell similar, a bottle of perfume is not a flower. A good translation cannot possibly capture the entirety of a message, for a translation is only capable of conveying a version of a message or a piece of a story. In my opinion, the main limitation of translating Biblical Hebrew into English is that the logic of Hebrew's etymology cannot be reproduced with English diction.

In Genesis 42:23, Joseph spoke through a מליץ *translator, interpreter,* which is, in ancient Egyptian, a *repeater* or *narrator* who serves as a type of linguistic mirror. The word מליץ *translator, interpreter* is from the root לוץ *to turn, to twist, to speak obscurely, to interpret,* but the same root can also mean *to mock, to deride;* hence, it produces the word מליצה *obscure saying, enigma* and also *satire.* The word מליץ *translator, interpreter* resembles the root מלץ *to be smooth, agreeable, slippery* from which the word מלצר *master of wine* is derived. Scripturally, it seems as if there is a thematic connection between clever words and wine and that the link between the roots לוץ *to turn, to twist, to speak obscurely, to interpret* and מלץ *to be smooth, agreeable* can be observed in the synonymous employment of the root חלק *to be smooth, flattering* and also in the root ישר *to be straight, even, smooth.* For instance, Proverbs 5:1-4 states:

> My son, pay attention to my WISDOM; Lend your ear to my UN-DERSTANDING, that you may preserve DISCRETION, and your lips may keep KNOWLEDGE. For the lips of an immoral woman drip HONEY, and her mouth is *smoother [חלק]* than OIL; but in the end she is bitter as wormwood, sharp as a two-edged sword.

Likewise, Proverbs 23:31-32 says,

> Do not look on the wine when it is red, when it sparkles in the cup, when it swirls around *smoothly [מישרים]*; at the last it bites like a serpent, and stings like a viper.

In both of the passages from Proverbs listed above, something seemingly smooth (adultery and drunkenness) results in bitter incisiveness (sharpness and venomousness). Consider the words of the serpent and the woman in Genesis 3. The "serpent" first acted as an מליץ *interpreter* or *translator* (from the root לוץ *to turn, to twist*) by speaking an מליצה *obscure saying, enigma,* and the woman proceeded to imbibe his folly and to act likewise. In other words, the "serpent" asked, "Did God say...?" hence the root לוץ *to turn, to twist, to speak obscurely, to interpret;* the woman responded with her own interpretation as to what God said. The poison, like the wine of the forbidden tree, slid down smoothly and became bitter to the point of vomiting (Job 20:15). In like, Genesis 44 depicts a wrangling over a cup through an interpreter. Since Scripture classifies a vine as a "tree" (Ezekiel 15), we can smoothly and agreeably perceive how a vine would be a twisted and turning tree. Since the letters עצה spell both *tree* and *counsel,* we can interpret how obscure speech can be understood along with wine and the serpentine tree that produces it.

Consider the word *dragoman,* which stems back to the Akadian *targumanu* or *interpreter*. The similarly sounding *dragon* is from the Latin *draco,* which can mean *a snake* (particularly a sacred temple serpent and guardian of treasure) as well as *the main stem of a vine that has hardened with age.* Dragomen were often employed by Eastern Monarchs to procure exotic wines, and such wine was indeed a special treasure for these ancient kings; for the dragoman was the only other person, besides the cupbearer, who knew what the monarch's personal wine tasted like. In Acts, the Spirit-filled followers of Christ were falsely assumed to be like drunken dragomen, i.e. inebriated translators. An מליץ *interpreter* or *translator* (from the root לוץ *to turn, to twist, to speak obscurely, to interpret*) also means *a mediator* (Job 33:23), and Job 33 describes an angel as being such a mediator, for an מלאך *angel* is a *messenger.* Knowing that Satan was the "Anointed Cherub" (Ezekiel 28:14) who acted as a false interpreter to the Bride, we can understand more as to why a "serpent" is an ideal image for the root לוץ *to turn, to twist, to speak obscurely, to interpret,* particularly with respect to a forbidden fruit (like a grape). The title כרוב Cherub is from an unused root that seems to mean כרב *to cover, to guard.* Again, Ezekiel 28:14 explains that Satan was ordained כרוב ממשח הסוכך *the anointed guardian cherub;* a literal translation elucidates the synonymous wordplay: *the covering one who covers with outstretched wings,* or *the guardian who guards with outstretched wings.* Such a figure can be observed through representation in Solomon's temple described in I Kings 6:23-28:

> Inside the inner sanctuary he made two cherubim of olive
> wood, each ten cubits high. One wing of the cherub was five
> cubits, and the other wing of the cherub five cubits: ten cubits
> from the tip of one wing to the tip of the other. And the other
> cherub was ten cubits; both cherubim were of the same size

and shape. The height of one cherub was ten cubits, and so was the other cherub. Then he set the cherubim inside the inner room; AND THEY STRETCHED OUT THE WINGS OF THE CHERUBIM SO THAT THE WING OF THE ONE TOUCHED ONE WALL, AND THE WING OF THE OTHER CHERUB TOUCHED THE OTHER WALL. And their wings touched each other in the middle of the room. Also he overlaid the cherubim with gold.

Job 33 describes an angel as being a "mediator," that is, an מליץ *interpreter* or *translator* (from the root לוץ *to turn, to twist, to speak obscurely, to interpret*) for an מלאך *angel* is a *messenger*. Satan was an angel (a cherub). The word הסכוך *the guardian* also means *the interweaver* from the root סכך *to cover, to conceal oneself, to guard, to interweave*. Translation compels a translator to select one definition, and there is no apparent link in English to connect *covering* with *concealment, guardianship,* and *interweavement,* though conceptually connecting these definitions makes sense. For example, an מלאך *angel* is a *messenger,* and a כהן *priest* is supposed to "guard knowledge... because he is the מלאך *angel* of the Lord of Hosts" (Malachi 2:7) who interweaves or interprets Scripture for the congregation, and it is probably for this interpretive quality that Daniel marks the Antichrist with " שכל*wisdom,*" the same as that which described the tree in Eden (Genesis 3:6). Succinctly put, the connections displayed plainly here are obscured on account of translation — not bad translation — but translation itself, for translation is not reproduction, but it is a reweaving of words that often speaks obscurely about an internal logic it does not itself possess. Such a fact has produced thousands of years of striving over, "Did God say...?" A *translator* is, in Hebrew, a *twister* and a *turner.*

Misunderstandings and accidental cultural superimpositions affect reading dramatically, especially through translation. Consider the fact that Rabbinic Judaism believes what Christians call the "Old Testament" to count time from sundown based on the "and there was evening and there was morning" refrain in the Creation Narrative when, in reality, the Babylonian reckoning of time was overlayed atop the Jewish rendering of the Hebrew Scriptures so that it became believed that the two systems were somehow always in agreement even though they were and are not. The most glaring proof of this mistake can be seen in that "Rosh Hashannah" is nowhere to be found in the Torah, but Leviticus 23:23-25 is taken as "Rosh Hashannah" in spite of the fact that this title is not in the Hebrew Text and the New Year is counted in the Spring as described by Exodus 12:2. In other words, the Hebrew Bible's New Year is obvious, but the Jewish New Year is something different. The Hebrew Bible's New Year is in the

First Month, on the first day of the month whereas the Jewish New Year is in the Seventh Month, on the first day of that month; these two celebrations are half-a-year apart. The sacred occasion the Torah describes in Leviticus 23:23-25 became called the New Year by those who were captured by Babylon probably because the Babylonian New Year was at the time of the occasion Leviticus celebrates in the Seventh Month. Thus, the Babylonian reckoning of time became superimposed atop the Hebrew reckoning of time to the extent that the year was, essentially, flipped as though in a mirror. This fact is the first clue that Hebrews and Jews are not necessarily the same people group, for the term "Jew" is but an anachronism thrown back upon Moses who was not a "Jew," properly speaking. Genesis 18:14 counts the equinotical rising of the seasonal sun as the עת חיה *time of life* or *spring* (as opposed to the autumnal and contrabiblical, or at least, extrabiblical "Rosh Hashanah"), and Exodus 12:2 plainly states that the ראש *beginning* or *head* (pronounced "*rosh*") of the year is in the Spring. The vernal equinox could be viewed macrocosmically as the annual sunrise just as the dawn is as the daily sunrise. If the vernal equinox begins the year, the dawn begins the day, just as Matthew 28:1 states, "After the σαβ–βατων *week, sabbath*, in the επιφωσκουση *dawning* towards the FIRST of the σαββατων *week, sabbath*, Mary Magdalene and the other Mary went to the tomb." The dawn was toward the "first," and time could not possibly be enumerated beginning from sundown if dawn is the first. The Torah and the Book of Matthew count time beginning with the rising of light (a fact that should be obvious in that the Creation, or recreation, begins with "Let there be light." Notice that the end transferring to the dawn marked the beginning of the next apparent circuit of the sun, for it was in this microcosmic עת חיה *time of life* that Christ was born again from what, conceptually, Psalm 110:3 calls the רחם משחר *womb of the dawn*. As Christ was born in a cave, so He was born again from a cave; that is, as Christ was laid in a manger (and the Hebrew word ארון means *ark, manger,* and *coffin*), we can note that the bones of corpses were eventually transferred from the stone slabs of cave tombs to *ossuaries* or *grain boxes*, that is, to *mangers*. The gate of Eden flanked by cherubs is described as being in the קדם east or *in front* (Genesis 2:8). Psalm 110:3 refers to the קדם *front* or *east* as the משחר רחם *womb of the dawn,* for it is apparent that the *dawn* begins the reckoning of time as gestation begins the reckoning of a life. It was at the קדם *front* or *east* of עדן Eden, *Fertility*, that is, the רחם *womb of* Fertility, where God placed the cherubs, the threshold guardians who flanked the "flame of the sword" (Genesis 3:24), and it is probably to these angels that Christ referred when He said, "Take heed that you do not despise ONE OF THESE

LITTLE ONES, for I say to you that in heaven THEIR ANGELS always see the face of My Father who is in heaven" (Matthew 18:10).

A translation is an interpretation. The Hebrew word מליץ *translator* also means *interpreter*. Interpretation provides a way of viewing the source but not the source itself, and, in this instance, it can be seen how drastically the source can be misunderstood by superimposing one's own culture over a text that was written apart from such a culture. At the same time, mastery of language is not mastery of Scripture. Satan was once a Cherub, that is, a threshold guardian, a defender of the gate, womb, or opening from which the dwellers issued forth. Specifically, Satan was הסוכך כרוב ממשח *the guardian messiah who conceals himself* (through *interweaving* — like the *speech* of a dragoman, like the *embroidered* cherubs on the curtain of the tabernacle), for an *anointed one, a christ* (Greek) or *messiah* (Hebrew) was a priest or a king who could be either righteous or wicked, hence Jesus Christ and the antichrist. Satan was an מליץ *interpreter* or *translator, that is, a mediator* who twisted words falsely regarding the fruit dragomen were so experienced in procuring. If Satan is the parasitic opposite of Christ, for an "anti-" requires a standard (not the antithesis), how much more is Christ the "mediator of a better covenant" (Hebrews 12:24)? As a grape's essence is preserved through a transformation that results in wine, and as a flower's scent is guarded by the glass walls of a perfume bottle, so Scripture's essence is hedged with thistles in translation whereby a transformation occurs to maintain a semblance, though a bleary one, of a clear yet concealed image painted with the thorny embroidery of obscure words wrought in time by the Eternal Mind.

THE PROOF TEXT

CITING portions of the Text as "proof" regarding one doctrine or another is common. It is also common to witness portions of Scripture cited textually or quoted orally in a malleable manner that seems to suit a given argument that has little or nothing to do with the topic at hand. The flagrant misapplication of Scripture for the purpose of fortifying an argument metaphorically has given rise to the corrupt belief that the Holy Bible can substantiate nearly any moral position because it is an internally inconsistent collection of apparently disparate documents. It is often the case that witnesses to or participants in the misapplication of the Text reason thus: One party claims position A based on a given portion of Scripture while an opposing party asserts position Z according to the same portion; therefore, the Bible is internally inconsistent. Such reasoning (or lack thereof) functions on the propositions that (A) it is impossible for both parties to be incorrect, (B) it is possible that both parties are right according to apparently conflicting passages, which leads ultimately to the conviction that (C) given the choice between incorrectness being applied to people or the Bible, the Bible must be at fault. That people will misuse Scripture to substantiate a stance and its opposite means that people, not Scripture, are guilty of contradiction. A safer vantage-point from which to reason might be that everyone who has read Scripture has, at least once, accidentally misapplied the Text to the extent of detriment; therefore, the Text needs to be reexamined regularly in order to weed out the obviously inherent defects in human reasoning throughout the process of maturation with the Text. A prime example of one party apparently taking position A while another party apparently taking position Z according to the same passage can be seen in the so-called "faith vs. works" conundrum: Catholics quote Ephesians 2:10 in defense of the necessity for good works whereas Evangelicals quote the previous passage, Ephesians 2:8-9, in defense of the privilege — not the necessity — of doing good works. Let us view both passages:

> For by grace you have been saved through faith, and that not of yourselves; it is the gift of God, not of works, lest any one should boast. For we are His workmanship, created in Christ Jesus for good works, which God prepared beforehand that we should walk in them (Ephesians 2:8-10).

It appears as if the first portion states that we are not saved by our works and therefore have no right to boast in them. Reasoning thus, the second portion would seem to indicate that we are created for the very thing that does not save us. Surely, a misapprehension is present. The

Greek literally says, "For by grace you have been saved *through faith*," and the mistake is to assume that the *faith* spoken of here refers simply to *belief, trust,* and *confidence*. The Greek word πιστις *faith* also means *pledge* and is used in Romans 17 to translate the Hebrew word אמנה *covenant* in Habakkuk 2:4, which makes perfect sense in Greek regarding a *pledge*. In other words, the reformation debate cycloned around a distinction between faith and works even though the "belief" of the matter was not the issue. The issue was the fruit of a covenant, not merely a belief, and both "covenant" and "belief" are accounted for in the word "pledge" even though only "belief" has been considered in the essential argument. The main problem centered upon a knowledge (or lack thereof) of the covenantal thrust of the Greek word "faith" utilized here, for it was overlooked on account of the more common Greek understanding of "covenant" found in the word διαθηκη relative to the more common Hebrew understanding of "covenant" found in the word ברית. Simply put, we are beholding a confusion of synonymous terms:

1)   ברית *covenant, pledge*

2)   אמנה *covenant, pledge, faith*

3)   διαθηκη *covenant, pledge*

4)   πιστις *faith, pledge*

Habakkuk 2:4 uses the Hebrew word (2) for *covenant* when it states, "...the just shall live by אמנה *covenant, pledge, faith*," and Romans 1:17 uses the Greek word (4) for *covenant* in translation when it states, "the just shall live by πιστις *faith, pledge*," i.e. *by covenant, an oath which necessitates actions to vindicate it.* The stance that necessitates good works, and the stance that necessitates right belief are not opposites but are one and the same, for both sides are unified in the Greek word πιστις *faith* that is used by Scripture programmatically to translate the Hebrew word אמנה *covenant* that is from the same root as אמן*Amen, I covenant,* i.e. *I pledge my life in order to vindicate the oath to the death I have taken in my petition to God,* i.e. *I believe, I trust.* One of the most obvious examples of the Greek πιστις *faith* being used to translate the Hebrew אמנה *covenant* is the Septuagint's version of Genesis 15 where the actual covenant was made prior to its signification (which is a typical pattern in Scripture). We see that Abraham's πιστις *faith* is a translation of the Hebrew word אמנה *covenant* (Genesis 15:6) while the sign of Abraham's διαθηκη *covenant, pledge* is a translation his ברית *covenant, pledge* (Genesis 15:18). Abraham's bloody sacrifice at sundown was the physically antithetical and conceptually mirrored sign of the bloodless sacrifice at the sunrise of Isaac's birth — both of which nearly merge atop Mount *Moriah*.

Quoting one passage and stating that we are required to do good works, and quoting another passage as proof that what is really gotten after is right belief are not two different arguments from two different sentences; instead, these two "proof texts" are two separated stances taken mistakenly in the absence of the other. Furthermore, the word we often render simply as πιστις *faith* means *proof* (Acts 7:31), and this fact is made plain by Hebrews 11:1: "Now πιστις *faith, proof* is the SUBSTANCE of things hoped for, the EVIDENCE of things not seen." Of course "substance" and "evidence" are "proof," so the wretched stance that asserts faith to be apart from fact is fallacious; all such a stance seeks to accomplish is a preemptory prohibition against falsification for the purpose of thwarting verification.

Covenanters are unified through sacrifice. Like the difficulty with the word "faith," the difficulty with the English word "sacrifice" is that it is used to translate more than one Hebrew word that have, in a sense, the same starting-point but can sometimes travel in opposite directions. The English word "sacrifice" is a translation of several Hebrew words. For instance, קרבן *[constructive* or *living] sacrifice* is used to indicate, essentially, the *motivation* behind both a bloody offering (Leviticus 1:2) and an bloodless offering of salt (Leviticus 2:13), and this "sacrifice" is from the root קרב *to draw near*. A זבח *[destructive* or *dead] sacrifice* is also utilized to signify a bloodless offering in that the מזבח *altar* of incense, where there is no blood, and is from this root which means זבח *to slaughter*. Likewise, Genesis 4 and Exodus 29:41 illustrate how yet another word for "sacrifice" (מנחה), which is from an unused root thought to mean מנח *to give*, can mean both bloody and bloodless sacrifice. Sacrifice is worship and worship is sacrifice, i.e. they were both an *offeratory approach*.

In Ephesians 2:1-10, it can be easily seen that we are not saved by our own blood but by Christ's, and we are to live as living sacrifices (constructively until our deaths) since we formerly chose to live as dead sacrifices (destructively throughout our lives):

> And YOU HE MADE ALIVE, WHO WERE DEAD in trespasses and
> sins, in which you once walked according to the course of this
> world, according to the prince of the power of the air, the spirit
> who now works in the sons of disobedience, among whom
> also we all once conducted ourselves in the lusts of our flesh,
> fulfilling the desires of the flesh and of the mind, and were by

nature children of wrath, just as the others. But God, who is rich in mercy, because of His great love with which He loved US, EVEN WHEN WE WERE DEAD IN TRESPASSES, MADE US ALIVE TOGETHER WITH CHRIST (by grace you have been saved), and raised us up together, and made us sit together in the heavenly places in Christ Jesus, that in the ages to come He might show the exceeding riches of His grace in His kindness toward us in Christ Jesus. For by grace you have been saved through πιστις *faith (pledge, covenant)*, and that not of yourselves; it is the gift of God, not of works, lest anyone should boast. For we are His workmanship, CREATED IN CHRIST JESUS FOR GOOD WORKS, which God prepared beforehand that we should walk in them.

It can be seen plainly that a covenant is necessary in order for us to have life after death since we broke covenant with God by choosing death to end our lives. The just shall live by Christ's covenant with us, and the just must therefore work in order to vindicate the covenant into which they pledged themselves by an oath to the death. There is no such thing as a workless covenant. Both covenanting parties pledge or stake their lives for each other, thus both offer a defense of sorts; this defense is called "rest" in Scripture as we have already noted; in this way, work and rest are brought together as work and belief (pledge, covenant, faith) are brought together; this is made plain by James 2:26: "...πιστις *faith, pledge, covenant* without works is dead," and the word εργον *work* used here is the substantive form of the verb εργαζεσθαι *work, cultivate* used by the Septuagint to translate the Hebrew עבד *work, cultivate* in Genesis 2:15 — for the very next passage (Genesis 2:16) discusses death which will occur should the *faith*, that is, the *covenant* not be kept. A "covenant without *works* is dead," and "...sin, when it is full-grown, gives birth to death" (James 1:15). Specifically, James uses the "faith/covenant without works" metaphor relative to the body and the spirit. The main problem that has arisen is the assumption that works are to be paralleled to the body and that faith is to be paralleled to the spirit; this accident is literally monumental! Faith is not analogous to the spirit but to the body, and works are not analogous to the body but to the spirit.

James 2:26 says, "For as the (A) body without the (B) spirit is dead, so (A) faith without (B) works is dead also." The synonymous parallel is straight-forward even though the reference is subtle. Let us deal first with the synonymous parallel: **(A) body** is paralleled to **(A) faith, covenant, proof; (B) spirit** is paralleled by **(B) works**. When discussing a "living sacrifice," we may grasp that a body cannot be animated without a spirit any more than a covenant can be vindicated without enactments. James said 2:15-16: "If a brother or sister is naked and destitute of daily food, and one of you says to them, 'Depart in peace, be warmed and filled,' but you do not give them the things which are needed for the body, what does it profit?" The covenant (faith) is as the body, and the work is as the spirit that animates the body, and so James establishes an analogy where a body is not cared for because no work has been exerted in order to provide the care. The parallel is plain, but the reference is arcane. The reference is ultimately to Adam who, prior to sin, was "naked" and unashamed/un-afraid (Genesis 2:24); however, humanity was both naked and ashamed/afraid after sin (Genesis 3:11). In order to clothe the nakedness, Luke 24:49 compares being filled with the Holy Spirit to being "CLOTHED with power from on high," and John 20:22 parallels this by stating, "So Jesus said to them again, 'PEACE to you! As the Father has sent Me, I also send you.' And when He had said this, He BREATHED ON THEM, and said to them, 'RECEIVE THE HOLY SPIRIT.'" The divine clothing was spiritual; receiving the Holy Spirit is being converted or "reborn"; Job 10:8-12 refers to cloth-ing of skin in terms of human gestation, whereby the flesh is formed in the womb; thus, "My LITTLE CHILDREN, for whom I LABOR IN BIRTH again until Christ is FORMED in you..." (Galatians 4:19). The protection, the oath, the rest, and the work are all as the Spirit and the Clothing from on high that covers (Hebrew: כפר atones, covers) the sins committed in the flesh, that is, the errors committed against the covenant.

Since it is the body (not the spirit) that is compared to "faith" or covenant, we can understand that a child is the expression of an unseen covenant in that each human is a mark of proof that two parents unified in order to produce the evidence of their union: "Now faith [covenant] is the substance of things hoped for, the evidence of things not seen" (Hebrews 11:1). A person is the substance and evidence of his parents' covenant. By seeing a person, you see, in a physical sense, his parents' unification. Even if a man's parents are dead and you have never met them, the man is the proof of at least two more people of whom he is 50% of both; a per-son is physically the two "sides" of his parents, and it is written that the Lord God "took אחת מצלעתיו one from his sides... ויבן and He built the side into a woman," like a carpenter builds a house or, in this case, the bride, the temple, the body. The covenant is as the body, and the works are as the spirit. A living body displays a substantial and evidential covenant with God "Who is our Life" (Colossians 3:4). The first "body without the spirit" of which we read (relative to the first humans) is Adam's body:

And the Lord God FORMED MAN OF THE DUST of the ground, and BREATHED INTO HIS NOSTRILS THE BREATH OF LIFE; and man became a living being. The Lord God planted a garden eastward in Eden, and there He put the man whom He had formed (Genesis 2:7-8).

First, God formed man; then, He breathed His Spirit into Him. Man sinned. In order to renew the covenant (the body requiring enactment), we see God breathing His Spirit again into man after displaying His body, His covenant, in John 20 and Luke 24; but, let us return to Adam. Literarily, God formed Adam's physical body and then He animated it. In this literary case, Adam's body without the Spirit was dead. Likewise, faith/covenant/proof (body) without works (spirit) is dead. A covenant involves and is itself a sacrifice. Death is recognized while life is anticipated initially and required ultimately. When James stated that "faith/covenant/proof without works is dead," it seems that he was referring to Adam's body prior to its animation that allowed it to cultivate, to work, and to guard the garden which leads ultimately to an understanding that perpetuates the covenant. Consider: "there is a spirit in man, and the BREATH OF THE ALMIGHTY gives him understanding" (Job 32:8) and "The Spirit of God has made me, and the BREATH OF THE ALMIGHTY gives me life" (Job 33:4); in this, we can see that the breath that animated Adam's corpse seems to have the dual signification of (1) the life-breath of the lungs as well as (2) the divine wisdom, the wisdom that was capable of maintaining the covenant and thus positive fertility. The reader will also notice that Adam's body was formed first, animated secondly, and placed in the garden thirdly which shows us that his life was in symbiosis with *Eden* (Hebrew " עדן *Fertility*"), which hints at how his death and expulsion were synonymous. In a manner of speaking, outside of Eden was the realm of the dead (and thus the unenlightened), and this is implied in his name ("Adam") given to him prior to entering Eden, for its feminine form is אדמה *red ground, sterile ground*, i.e. the opposite of "Eden" or "Fertility." Adam's body was animated in order to be fertile, that is, in order to perpetuate animation and wisdom; this is implicit regarding the "Tree of Life" since the Hebrew nominal "Life" is properly חיים *Lives* and can be read adjectivally as "Living" with special respect to the fact that *animation* was regarded in the ancient East as *life*, which is maintained in the expression מים חיים *moving water, living water*. Adam, without God's breath, was a corpse. Humanity without wisdom is dead, and this fact is apparent in that the forbidden tree gave death as opposed to wisdom since "Wisdom gives life" (Ecclesiastes 7:11-12). In Hebrew, the *viable womb* is understood as *wisdom*; Genesis 30:1 describes *child-*

lessness as *death*; childlessness would be the opposite of wisdom since wisdom is equated with a viable womb and life; therefore, a person without wisdom is a corpse, an incapable vessel. *Breath* is the same word as *wind* and *spirit* in both Hebrew and Greek. Adam, without God's Spirit, was a corpse as is the case with an unbeliever, the dead, the unenlightened, who has rejected "the breath of the Almighty," i.e. the life-giving wisdom that sires positive perpetuity. The double entendre is therefore apparent in the denomination translated "living soul" in Genesis 2:7 which is in Hebrew " נפש חיה *animate life*" (since חיה *living* was signified by animation and נפש also meant *life* in Genesis 9:4) or "*animate corpse*" (since חיה *living* was signified by animation and נפש also meant *corpse* in Numbers 6:6). Furthermore, the "living soul" could not have referred to Adam's physical exterior since נפש *soul, life, corpse* also means *breath* and since Genesis 3:30 says that this נפש *soul, life, corpse, breath* was within animate creation. It can be seen then that one could have either a breath of life or a breath of death within him, and this diametric possibility is accomplished either positively or negatively through man's choice that determines the nature of the spiritual clothing of his נפש *soul*:

> In Him you were also circumcised with the circumcision made without hands, by PUTTING OFF THE BODY OF THE SINS OF THE FLESH, by the circumcision of Christ, buried with Him in baptism, in which you also were raised with Him through *faith* [= covenant/body] in the working of God, who raised Him from the dead. And you, being DEAD IN YOUR TRESPASSES [while yet your fleshly body moves and breathes] and the uncircumcision of your flesh, He has made alive together with Him.... (Colossians 2:11-15).

The connections made above offer a multitude of proof-texts that are strung together to prove a point. At the same time, we must discern the validity of the string by seeking verification that therefore opens the claim to falsification as a test. If the claim cannot be verified with some other portion of Scripture, one wields a weak claim as to the "proof" of the texts provided to support the claim. A further difficulty arises if corresponding passages of Scripture have been accidentally misperceived or, at least, have not been proven to support the doctrines that have sprung forth In reaction to them. In reaction to the claim that, "The Bible can support nearly any position," I claim the following: Nearly any written document, if repunctuated, if reemphasized, if planted within a foreign context or within a vacuum, can support a wide variety of contradictory positions. For instance, I have heard it asserted more than once that Moses only

writes about the righteousness of the Law *as opposed to* the righteousness of faith (covenant/proof), and that Christians ought not to say who is,
or who is not, going to Hell, based on this passage:

> For Moses writes about the righteousness which is of the law,
> "The man who does those things shall live by them." But the
> righteousness of faith [covenant/proof] speaks in this way, "Do
> not say in your heart, 'Who will ascend into heaven?'" (that is,
> to bring Christ down from above) or, "Who will descend into the
> abyss?" (that is, to bring Christ up from the dead). But what
> does it say? "The word is near you, in your mouth and in your
> heart" (that is, the word of faith which we preach): that if you
> confess with your mouth the Lord Jesus and believe in your
> heart that God has raised Him from the dead, you will be saved.
> For with the heart one believes unto righteousness, and with
> the mouth confession is made unto salvation. For the Scripture
> says, "Whoever believes on Him will not be put to shame." For
> there is no distinction between Jew and Greek, for the same
> Lord over all is rich to all who call upon Him. For "whoever calls
> on the name of the LORD shall be saved" (Romans 10:5-13).

If man truly has no choice in the matter of his salvation, then the
crux of my argument which states, "...one could have either a breath of
life or a breath of death within him, and this diametric possibility is accomplished either positively or negatively through man's choice that determines the nature of the spiritual clothing of his נפש *soul*," is errant. So, let
us first examine the claim that Moses only writes about the righteousness
of the Law *as opposed to* the righteousness of faith. The quotations, "The
man who does those things shall live by them [Leviticus 18:5]," and "Do
not say in your heart, 'Who will ascend into heaven?'... or, 'Who will descend into the abyss?'... [Deuteronomy 30:12]" are both quotations from
the Law scribed by Moses; so, it cannot be that the Law here contradicts
the Faith/Covenant/Proof if the very Faith/Covenant/Proof in question
is found written in the Law itself, unless one wishes to assert an internal contradiction in the Law based on the passage from Romans above.
One should consider the subtlety of the fact that Romans is using a proof-
text from the covenant of Moses in order to discuss "faith," and the word
"faith" means both "proof" and "covenant." Taking the Romans passage
above, removing it from its original context in the Torah, and viewing it in
a vacuum might yield a supposed teaching of not discussing the personal
application of salvation and damnation.

Congruent reasoning could also state that the Bible communicates
that "There is no God" in Psalm 14:1. Such error comes about by fractur-

ing the Text into divisions that did not originally exist to the extent that isolated words are referred to as the basis for entire doctrines. Psalm 14:1 begins, "The fool has said in his heart, 'There is no God'...." Indeed, Scripture does state that "There is no God," and it does so in the context of a "fool's" heart. Since such is true at the sentence-level, the entirety of Scripture should be accounted for when viewing individualities within the Text. As such, the Law states what the Faith should be, and this faith is "Do not say in your heart, 'Who will ascend into heaven?'... or, 'Who will descend into the abyss?'...." The notion that the Law negates the Faith of righteousness cannot be if the Law itself states the Faith of righteousness.

As to the Faith of righteousness, it is again written, "Do not say in your heart, 'Who will ascend into heaven?'... or, 'Who will descend into the abyss?'...." (Deuteronomy 30:12) — but the entire passage states,

> For this commandment which I command you today is NOT TOO MYSTERIOUS FOR YOU, nor is it far off. It is not in heaven, that you should say, 'Who will ascend into heaven for us and bring it to us, that we may hear it and do it?' Nor is it beyond the sea, that you should say, 'Who will go over the sea for us and bring it to us, that we may hear it and do it?' BUT THE WORD IS VERY NEAR YOU, IN YOUR MOUTH AND IN YOUR HEART, THAT YOU MAY DO IT. See, I have set before you today life and good, death and evil, in that I command you today to love the LORD your God, to walk in His ways, and to keep His commandments, His statutes, and His judgments, that you may live and multiply; and the LORD your God will bless you in the land which you go to possess. But if your heart turns away so that you do not hear, and are drawn away, and worship other gods and serve them, I announce to you today that you shall surely perish; you shall not prolong your days in the land which you cross over the Jordan to go in and possess. I call heaven and earth as witnesses today against you, that I have set before you life and death, blessing and cursing; therefore choose life, that both you and your descendants may live; THAT YOU MAY LOVE THE LORD YOUR GOD, THAT YOU MAY OBEY HIS VOICE, AND THAT YOU MAY CLING TO HIM, FOR HE IS YOUR LIFE AND THE LENGTH OF YOUR DAYS; and that you may dwell in the land which the LORD swore to your fathers, to Abraham, Isaac, and Jacob, to give them. (Deuteronomy 30:11-20).

The teaching would seem not to concern itself with who will or will not go to Hell; rather, the teaching would seem to command that we not give the sluggardly excuse that we cannot know the will of God, for He has given us a Text that is "not TOO mysterious" to be grasped. The Text is certainly mysterious; yet, it is not "too mysterious" to be grasped. We are, therefore, commanded not to give false reasons for Scriptural ignorance, which, when referring back to Paul's quotation, becomes clearer within its original context inside the Law: "But the word is very near you, in your mouth and in your heart, that you may do it." Again,

> For Moses writes about the righteousness which is of the law, "The man who does those things shall live by them." But the righteousness of faith [covenant/proof] speaks in this way, "Do not say in your heart, 'Who will ascend into heaven?'" (that is, to bring Christ down from above) or, "Who will descend into the abyss?" (that is, to bring Christ up from the dead). But what does it say? "The word is near you, in your mouth and in your heart" (that is, the word of faith which we preach): that if you confess with your mouth the Lord Jesus and believe in your heart that God has raised Him from the dead, you will be saved. For with the heart one believes unto righteousness, and with the mouth confession is made unto salvation. For the Scripture says, "Whoever believes on Him will not be put to shame" (Romans 10:5-13).

Since Christ, "The Word" (Revelation 19:13) both descended into the Abyss (1 Peter 3:19) and ascended into Heaven (Acts 1:9), we can understand why Paul wrote,

> But the righteousness of faith speaks in this way, "Do not say in your heart, 'Who will ascend into heaven?' (THAT IS, TO BRING CHRIST DOWN FROM ABOVE) or, 'Who will descend into the abyss?' (THAT IS, TO BRING CHRIST UP FROM THE DEAD)."

Paul immediately proceeds by saying, "'The word is near you, in your mouth and in your heart' (that is, the word of faith which we preach): that if you confess with your mouth the Lord Jesus and believe in your heart that God has raised Him from the dead, you will be saved." The Word in our mouth might otherwise be called "Communion," for the Word in our heart would require discernment: "For he who eats and drinks in an unworthy manner eats and drinks judgment to himself, not DISCERNING the Lord's body" (1 Corinthians 11:29). It would seem as though the "judgement" here comes from a lack of "discerning" the covenant, i.e. the faith, i.e. the body since the body without the spirit is dead. Essentially, we are not to make excuses for avoiding the diligent study of the Word, that is, the diligent consumption of God's Teaching or the diligent meal of God's Daily Bread lest we die.

As an example of daily study of God's word, Matthew 6 records the Lord's Prayer which says, "Give us this day our daily bread." Surely, the "daily bread" is a reference to the Holy Word, the unleavened bread of Passover, and the manna provided in the wilderness: "Then the Lord said to Moses, "Behold, I will rain BREAD from heaven for you. And the people shall go out and gather a certain quota DAILY, that I may test them, whether they will WALK IN MY TEACHING OR NOT" (Exodus 16:4). Furthermore, Exodus 13:7-9 describes the unleavened bread of the Passover in terms of "The Lords TEACHING" in the "mouth" of His followers. The Lord's Prayer was given in response to the request, "Lord, TEACH us to pray, as John also TAUGHT his disciples" (Luke 11:1). The "daily bread" is, it would seem, the teaching of God as signified by food or "bread"; but what of the wine?

Usually, wine that was suitable for drinking was mingled with water and was called "fruit of the vine" as opposed to unmixed wine that was called "fruit of the tree." Wine is called "blood" in Genesis 49:11. Psalm 105:41 recounts that the Rock's waters זוב bled forth; the description of "bleeding" waters from the Rock is a foreshadowing of the water and wine that flowed from Christ's circumcised heart on the cross:

> Moreover, brethren, I do not want you to be unaware that all our fathers were under the cloud, all passed through the sea, all were baptized into Moses in the cloud and in the sea, all ate the same SPIRITUAL FOOD, and all drank the same spiritual drink. For they drank of that spiritual Rock that followed them, AND THAT ROCK WAS CHRIST. But with most of them God was not well pleased, for their bodies were scattered in the wilderness (I Corinthians 10:1-5).

Just after Christ *walked on the sea*, He said, "I am the BREAD OF LIFE. Your fathers ate the MANNA in the wilderness, and are dead. This is the BREAD WHICH COMES DOWN FROM HEAVEN, that one may eat of it and not die. I am the LIVING BREAD WHICH CAME DOWN FROM HEAVEN. If anyone eats of this bread, he will live forever; and the bread that I shall give is My flesh, which I shall give for the life of the world" (John 6:48-51).

Grapes can ferment upon the vine under the right conditions. Jeremiah 11:19 uses the word usually translated as לחם *bread* to mean *fruit*; thus, the daily bread from Heaven could at once be considered figuratively to be as the Eucharist in that, according to diction, the manna could be at once considered a type of intinction. The Israelites who travelled in the wilderness (parabolically) took communion daily in that they ate and drank a signification of bread and of wine mingled with water. The word לחם can mean *fruit*, *bread* and *flesh* (לחום), and the word דם is used to indicate *wine* and *blood*. According to Rawlinson, manna is gathered from trees (particularly the dwarf oak) by placing cloths beneath the limbs and shaking them. It can also be found on shrubs, rocks, and stones, and the ground. Manna is abundant after fogs. Manna can also be used as a purgative if prepared so but can otherwise be eaten in large quantities (*Seven Great Monarchies: Assyria*, Rawlinson). It would seem to be the case that the lack of discernment regarding manna could cause the opposite of a full stomach. Likewise, it would seem to be the case that the lack of discernment regarding Christ's body produces a judgement illustrated by purgation. The antithesis of Holy Communion or Christ's body would be an unholy communion or Satan's body. With respect to Adam, we may note the following that accords with an unholy purgation:

> Though evil is sweet in his mouth, and he hides it under his tongue, though he spares it and does not forsake it, but still keeps it in his mouth, yet his food in his stomach turns sour; it becomes cobra venom within him. He swallows down riches and VOMITS THEM UP AGAIN; God casts them out of his belly. He will suck the poison of cobras; the viper's tongue will slay him (Job 20: 4-16).

Vines were called "trees" in Hebrew and they were trained onto fruit trees, and, under the right conditions, grapes fermented and became wine within skins; thus, two trees in the midst, conformed as one, could produce bread that falls from on high and wine that grows directly from the branches. Fruit trees were often planted by digging a hole, placing a foundational rock in the hole, and planting the tree atop the rock, causing the roots to spread out beneath the soil as opposed to straight down into the ground. The labyrinthine route in the wilderness was headed by a pillar (tree) of smoke and fire, a Tree of Light (Menorah) or a Tree of Life; this maze was followed by the Rock Who bled water. A tree's fruit is called "לחם *bread*" (Jeremiah 11:19), and the Israelites' desert wandering was compared to a marriage (Jeremiah 2) wherein the collective Israelite bride aborted God's Child by treating His "heritage as an abomination" by worshipping Baal (v.8) through child-sacrifice, for this is the "abomination" discussed concerning Molech-worship in Deuteronomy 12:31 in which "they burn even their sons and daughters in the fire." We see that Holy Communion is accomplished in "The True Vine" (John 15:1) since a vine was considered to be a "tree" in Hebrew, since a vine produced the "the blood of grapes," and since the rock served as the foundation of its trellis (its cross, its supportive tree). The opposite would be, therefore, a false vine that produced abortive wine. The Israelites ate and drank unto the Lord in an oath to the death, a covenant, as they tread the maze with Him. What appeared to be an aimless death-march was a spiritual trek through the labyrinth (like that of Eden) designed to teach them God's ways. The Fall was an unholy communion unto death that was issued by a tree and that caused Adam to wander outside of the paradise (the royal orchard and pleasure-ground stocked with animals) of God. Our redemption, signified by the marriage supper (communion) is discussed in this way: "...'To him who overcomes I will give to eat from the tree of life, which is in the midst of the Paradise of God'" (Revelation 2:7). Our "daily bread" is our continual reception of God's Word that nourishes unto life.

The proof-text may prove either the accuracy or inaccuracy of a particular doctrine based on Biblical passages, but the misapplication of a proof-text cannot prove inaccuracy within the Bible. If the abuse of Scripture casts a negative shadow on the value of Scripture, then the abuse becomes the standard and a gross inversion occurs. Such reasoning would then state that marriage resides within a negative shadow because infidelity exists, therefore infidelity is the standard... or the that Eucharist cannot be administered with wine because various people struggle with drunkenness, therefore drunkenness is the standard by which the administration of the Eucharist will be judged. Such perverse inversions mandate that abuse should be the standard that determines use rather than use being the standard from which abuse falls away. Citing misapplications as reasons for doubts in the standard is itself internally contradictory. It is therefore necessary that the entirety of Scripture be kept in mind when one provides proof-texts to assert points or even when Scripture employs proof-texts within itself.

One is not to make the poor excuse that Scripture is too high to be understood because he may not presently comprehend it—for he is not the standard; Scripture is the standard. That one may not understand something does not mean that something cannot be understood. That one group does not comprehend something does not mean that another group cannot understand that same thing. The very fact that Scripture is viewed in translation coupled with the mistaken belief that translation is a facsimile has contributed even more to the Heaven/Hell question. Consider Romans 9.

Romans 9 is often viewed as though it directly stated that God selects some but not others for salvation because "...the Scripture says to the Pharaoh, 'For this very purpose I have raised you up, that I may show My power in you, and that My name may be declared in all the earth.' Therefore He has mercy on whom He wills, and whom He wills σκλερυνει

He hardens. You will say to me then, 'Why does He still find fault? For who has resisted His will?'" (Romans 9:17-18). The first problem with believing that God "hardened" Pharaoh's heart to proceed against God's will is that 1 Samuel 6:6 says, "Why do YOU HARDEN your hearts AS THE EGYPTIANS AND PHARAOH DID? When <u>Israel's God dealt harshly with them,</u> did they not send the Israelites out so they could go on their way?" This passage blatantly sates that the Egyptians and Pharaoh — not God — hardened their own hearts against God and not according to God's will. This proof-text refers to Exodus 10:2: "that you may tell your children and grandchildren how <u>I dealt harshly with the Egyptians</u> and how I performed my signs among them, and that you may know that I am the Lord." At first glance, it would seem plain to think that the Scripture says openly that God dealt harshly with the Egyptians by hardening their hearts as is stated in Exodus 10:2; however, since I Samuel 6:6 states that the hardening was performed by the Egyptians and not by God, another understanding must be possible on account of 1 Samuel. The main problem here is that we are dealing in the realm of translation, for translation is not exact reproduction. Leading up to Exodus 10:2, there are three different words that are all translated as "hardened": (1) כבד, (2) חזק, and (3) קשה. The first word in our list comes from the root *to be heavy,* but it can be used positively as *to be honored.* The second word in our list is derived from the root *to be strong* and is used positively as *to be empowered.* The third word in our list is from the root *to be harsh* and is usually used negatively with the exception of passages like Exodus 7:3 where it is used as a synonym for our second word. The point is that all of the words for "harden" used in the account of Pharaoh have positive meanings as well, despite the fact that Tradition remembers them in negative unison. According to Romans 9, Scripture states that God "hardened" Pharaoh's heart in Greek, but it is translating the Hebrew original of Exodus; however, the word חזק *to harden, to encourage* is how Hebrew communicates "to strengthen, to become strong" as in, "I am going the way of all the earth וחזקת *be strong* and become a man" (I Kings 2:2) as opposed to being obstinate and remaining immature as did Pharaoh. In other words, the "hardening" under discussion and relative to Pharaoh is not negative, for the exhortation stated above is exceedingly positive; being "hardened" here means being fortified positively, i.e. being *encouraged.* To *harden the heart negatively* is discussed with a different and fourth word in 2 Chronicles 36:13 where it written " ויאמץ את לבו *and he hardened his heart"* in rebellion, and this word for "harden" is from the root אמץ *to be strong, to encourage,* which is a synonym for חזק *to harden, strengthen,* and which can also be taken positively (as in Deuteronomy

31:6) as can that which was applied to Pharaoh. When David's family was kidnapped in I Samuel 30:6, it is written that "ויתחזק דוד ביהוה אלהיו" which can be read as, "*and he* STRENGTHENED [ENCOURAGED] *himself in the Lord his God*" or "*and he* HARDENED *himself against the Lord his God*" — and it is obvious that, according to the Divinely ordained reclamation of David's family, the first rendering is the correct one and relates the Divine strength David received from God. Again, in 2 Chronicles 16:9, we read, "For the eyes of the Lord range throughout the earth להתחזק *to harden/strengthen* those whose hearts are fully committed to Him," for it is more than obvious that God does not cause those who are committed to Him to stray from Him through *hardening*, but He does draw His faithful to Himself in order to increase their faith through *strengthening*. Furthermore, the particle ו can be both conjunctive and disjunctive. Consider, "And the Lord said to Moses,

"When you go back to Egypt, see that you do all those wonders before Pharaoh which I have put in your hand. ואני אחזק את לבו ולא ישלח את העם *But I will harden his heart, and he will not let the people go*" (Exodus 4:21); this classically controversial passage only contains controversy in its translation because of an errant disjunctive-conjunctive sense has been placed upon it instead of a conjunctive-disjunctive sense. The very same words can read, " ואני אחזק את לבו ולא ישלח את העם *And I will strengthen his heart, but he will not let the people go*."

In other words, God will help Pharaoh to believe, but Pharaoh himself will choose not to believe. God elected to make one of the most powerful men on the earth an example of victorious repentance, but this man chose not to repent and was thus made an example of unrepentant destruction; the exact opposite of this negative story of Israel's captor occurs positively with Cyrus in Ezra 1. Cyrus freed the Israelites at God's behest unlike Pharaoh who did not; in both situations, the Israelites left free and funded "...that their hearts may be ENCOURAGED, being knit together in love, and attaining to all RICHES of the full assurance of understanding, to the knowledge of the mystery of God, both of the Father and of Christ, in whom are hidden all the TREASURES of wisdom and knowledge" (Colossians 2:2-3). It is, now, plain to see the sense of Romans 9:16-24:

So then it is not of him who wills, nor of him who runs, but of God who shows mercy [as God showed on Pharaoh 10 times before giving Pharaoh his own way]. For the Scripture says to the Pharaoh, "For this very purpose I have raised you up, that I may show My power in you, and that My name may be declared in all the earth [for, imagine what the earth would have thought

had Pharaoh denounced himself and proclaimed Jehovah]."
Therefore He has mercy on whom He wills [as He did on Pha-
raoh], and whom He wills He *hardens* [i.e. he *strengthens*, for
God "strengthening" someone is an act of mercy: "Then an
angel appeared to Him from heaven, STRENGTHENING Him"
(Luke 22:43)]. You will say to me then, 'Why does He still find
fault? For who has resisted His will ? [for Salvation, not for
destruction; God "...desires all men to be saved and to come
to the knowledge of the truth" (1 Timothy 2:4)].' But indeed, O
man, who are you to reply against God [As Pharaoh did again
and again, despite the *strength* God gave him]? Will the thing
formed say to him who formed it, 'Why have you made me like
this? [Why have you made me a king since my Egyptian authority falsely says that I myself am a son of god as opposed to
Israel, whom You consider your "firstborn son" (Exodus 4:22)?']
Does not the potter have power over the clay, from the same
lump to make one vessel for honor [in repentance] and another
for dishonor? [— if one chooses not to acknowledge God by
resisting Him]. What if God, wanting to show His wrath and to
make His power known, ENDURED WITH MUCH LONGSUFFERING
THE VESSELS OF WRATH prepared [by themselves] for destruction
[who elected to reject God], and that He might make known
the riches of His glory on the vessels of mercy [who chose to
repent], which He had prepared beforehand for glory, even us
whom He called, not of the Jews only, but also of the Gentiles?

If one assumes that God created certain people for the strict purpose of
damnation, then why would God "endure with much longsuffering" His
own choice to do so? Scripture is very clear on this matter:

I urge, then, first of all, that petitions, prayers, intercession
and thanksgiving be made for all people — FOR KINGS AND ALL
THOSE IN AUTHORITY, that we may live peaceful and quiet lives
in all godliness and holiness. This is good, and pleases God our
Savior, WHO WANTS ALL PEOPLE TO BE SAVED AND TO COME TO A
KNOWLEDGE OF THE TRUTH. For there is one God and one *mediator* [*translator, arbiter*] between God and mankind, the man
Christ Jesus, who gave Himself as a ransom for ALL. This has
now been witnessed to at the proper time (1 Timothy 2:1-6).

Romans 9:22 says that He "endured" that He "might make known the
riches of His glory on the vessels of mercy" who accepted His predestined
plan for all humanity to be saved, despite the fact that much of humanity
has chosen not to accept God's original, predestined design and would

rather follow Pharaoh's path. Furthermore, the "riches," relative to the "vessels," is a plain reference to clay containers, that were filled with money and sealed with an air-tight lid and were buried for the purposes of long-term savings. The only way to utilize the money long-saved was to unearth and shatter the vessel. In the ancient east, "a dust storm" or "cloud of dust" was terminology applied to the dead. In the ancient east, corpses were also buried in earthen jars and fired within them, whereby the skeletons remained intact until unearthed; once the jars were exhumed and broken, the skeletons, upon being touched, instantly became dust. The comparison between the spirit placed into the body of dust regarding Adam is negatively paralleled by the corpse placed into the clay tomb, and this is explained neatly by the fact that the word נפש means both *soul* and *corpse*; both of these images are paralleled by money placed within a clay jar and buried for future reclamation: "Now this I say, brethren, that flesh and blood cannot inherit the kingdom of God; nor does corruption inherit incorruption" (1 Corinthians 15:50); this passage, in turn, is the explanatory antitype of Leviticus 11:33: "Any earthen vessel into which any [unclean thing] falls you shall break; and whatever is in it shall be unclean"; for, once sin is committed in the flesh, only the riches implanted within the flesh may be exhumed and reclaimed by God Who first breathed them in; and, in coming full-circle, the argument of Romans 9 is restated in Ephesians 2:4-8:

> But God, who is RICH in mercy, because of His great love with which He loved us, even when we were DEAD IN TRESPASSES, MADE US ALIVE together with Christ (by grace you have been saved), and RAISED US UP together, and made us sit together in the heavenly places in Christ Jesus, that in the ages to come He might show the exceeding RICHES of His grace in His kindness toward us in Christ Jesus. For by grace you have been saved through faith....

The hardening of the earthen vessel is for the strict purpose of making it capable of holding the gift intended for it. Should the vessel reject being hardened by the fires of Divine Grace, the vessel is but a lump of clay incapable of bearing fruit by receiving riches. Should the hardened vessel refuse to hold the contents intended by the Potter, all that is left for the vessel is brokenness in order for another vessel to receive the wealth — and the Israelites left Egypt full of riches given to them by their former, obstinate captors who were in the process of committing their own riches (their firstborn) to dust. A similar situation can be observed in that Judas held the money-pouch (near his loins), and, after committing Christ to the dust, the former location of his money-pouch burst open with blood upon the clay (the "field of blood") as a result of serpentine asphyxiation whereby his payment was signified literally as "blood-money"— for he refused to contain both the riches God gave him initially (in his acceptance of Christ) and the riches Satan gave him terminally (in his rejection of Christ). Ironically, both Christ and Judas were hanged, The One as the "True Vine" like the serpent on the pole, and the other like the false vine whose contents spilled out like a burst wineskin. The One was born again through His shed blood; the other bore blood from his penniless, fleshy belly (womb) upon the poverty-stricken, earthy womb that received his corpse.

As it was in Eden, so it was with the Israelites under Egyptian and Roman rule successively: God elected all people, but not all people elected God. People's rejection of God in spite of His election of us should be apparent by the fact that the first sin involved man's choice as opposed to God's choice, a point that is reflected by man's election of Barabbas after God already elected all people; for His covenantal election was vindicated by dying and rising for the sins of the whole world and not just part of it. Likewise, Pharaoh, in spite of God actively STRENGTHENING HIS HEART, chose to fall into the abysmal sea of unrepentance:

> For Moses writes about the righteousness which is of the law, "The man who does those things shall live by them." But the righteousness of faith speaks in this way, "Do not say in your HEART, 'Who will ascend into heaven?'" (that is, to bring Christ down from above) or, 'WHO WILL DESCEND INTO THE ABYSS?' (that is, to bring Christ up from the dead). But what does it say? "The word is near you, in your mouth and in your HEART" (THAT IS, THE WORD OF FAITH WHICH WE PREACH): that if you CONFESS WITH YOUR MOUTH the Lord Jesus and BELIEVE IN YOUR HEART that God has raised Him from the dead, you will be saved. For with the HEART one believes unto righteousness, and with the mouth confession is made unto salvation. For the Scripture says, 'Whoever believes on Him will not be put to shame" (Romans 10:5-13).

Thus,

> Do not think that I [Jesus] shall accuse you to the Father; there is one who accuses you — Moses, in whom you trust. For if you believed Moses, you would believe Me; for he wrote about Me. But if you DO NOT BELIEVE HIS WRITINGS, how will you BELIEVE MY WORDS? (John 5:45-47),

for

> By faith Moses, when he became of age, refused to be called
> the son of Pharaoh's daughter, choosing rather to suffer afflic-
> tion with the people of God than to enjoy the passing pleasures
> of sin, esteeming the reproach of CHRIST greater riches than
> the treasures in Egypt; for he looked to the reward (Hebrews
> 11:24-26).

To say that God *hardened* Pharaoh's heart, to say that the so-called
"Old Testament" God was a God of wrath, and to say that the so-called "Old
Testament" is opposed to the so-called "New Testament" is to commit error. "Α εντολεν καινεν *new commandment* I give to you, that you love one
another; as I have loved you, that you also love one another" (John 13:34).
Surely this word "new" is referring to the Hebrew word חדשׁ*renew*. Moses
said, "Yet now, if You will forgive their sin — but if not, I pray, blot me out
of Your book which You have written" (Exodus 32:32), the Lamb's Book of
Life (as though written upon the vellum of His Body): "He who overcomes
shall be clothed in white garments, and I will not blot out his name from
the Book of Life; but I will confess his name before My Father and before
His angels" (Revelation 3:5). Reconsider the expression "clothed in white
garments" relative to Luke 24:49 which compares being filled with the Holy
Spirit to being "CLOTHED with power from on high." John 20:22 parallels
this by stating, "So Jesus said to them again, 'Peace to you! As the Father
has sent Me, I also send you.' And when He had said this, He BREATHED
ON THEM, and said to them, 'RECEIVE THE HOLY SPIRIT.'" The divine clothing was spiritual and analogous to libation; receiving the Holy Spirit is being converted or "reborn"; Job 10:8-12 refers to clothing of skin in terms
of human gestation whereby the flesh is formed in the womb; thus, "My
LITTLE CHILDREN, for whom I LABOR IN BIRTH again until Christ is FORMED
in you..." (Galatians 4:19). Moses esteemed "the reproach of Christ" as
superior to earthly riches, for he loved his neighbor similar to how Christ
loved him which is why Moses was willing to suffer Hell innocently on account of his guilty brethren (Exodus 32:32). It would seem that Christ said,
according to Hebrew (חדשׁ), "A *renewed commandment* I give to you, that
you love one another as I have loved you, that you also love one another"
(John 13:34). Moses was a human paragon of this love, and Paul adopted
his example when he penned,

> I tell the truth in Christ, I am not lying, my conscience also bear-
> ing me witness in the Holy Spirit, that I have great sorrow and
> continual grief in my HEART. FOR I COULD WISH THAT I MYSELF
> WERE ACCURSED FROM CHRIST FOR MY BRETHREN, my country-

men according to the flesh, who are Israelites, to whom pertain the adoption, the glory, the covenants, the giving of the law, the service of God, and the promises; of whom are the fathers and from whom, according to the flesh, Christ came, who is over all, the eternally blessed God. Amen (Romans 9-1-5).

Paul then proceeds to the so-called "Predestination" argument which, we may see, is the discussion of God's plan for salvation that many have rejected regardless of how much God strengthened them, for it is they who elect not to follow God and not God Who elects for them not to follow Him.

The proof-text requires previous contextual knowledge that is not always stated within the proof-text itself, but rather exists in understated propositions contained in the standard from which the proof-text is drawn. The proof-text demands a skill-set that existed prior to the proof being presented. The proof-text is but a stated portion of a whole that is presently unstated, and the comprehension of this portion necessitates a familiarity of that which preceded the argument containing the proof-text. Accordingly, the proof-text merely triggers the memory of something that is supposed to be familiar as it points towards a whole; the proof-text is not the whole itself. A proof-text is a supplement, not a substitute. An individual "verse" is not the whole itself, for it is a portion of a whole that exists in symbiosis with what preceded it and with what follows it as is the case with the Romans 9 example above. It is apparent that the so-called "Greek New Testament" is but in Greek garb; it assumes a familiarity with the Hebrew terms it explains. If one is unaware that the "Greek New Testament" is constructed according to Hebrew, then one might assume that God makes certain people for the sole purpose of having them tortured forever in Hell while, in contradiction, the same Text explains how Christ died for all... one might assume that the "Old Testament" God is of wrath while, in contradiction, the "New Testament" God is of mercy... one might assume incorrectly.

It should be further noticed that the fiery descriptions of Hell are not arbitrary, for Gehenna is certainly described in the manner of a *Tophet*, a child-sacrificial pyre of "shame." In Hebrew, "בוש to be ashamed" is as "יבש to be dried up, to be ashamed," and it is such a חרף *shame* that Daniel discusses: Daniel 12:2: "And many of those who sleep in the dust of the earth shall awake, some to everlasting life, some to shame and everlasting contempt." The root חרף to *shame, to scorn, to* PLUCK FRUIT under discussion produces the word חרף AUTUMN, the time when the leaves fall and fruit is taken away (and also one of the seasons when manna falls redemptively along with the ripening of grapes). "To fall" is the Hebrew נפל which begets the word נפל *abortion*. When we consider how Hannaiah, Mishael, and Azariah were delivered from the furnace in Daniel, we may notice how I Kings 8:51 describes the Exodus, that occurred immediately following the death of the firstborn, as God's people being brought "out of the iron furnace"; this explains these descriptions of damnation and salvation:

> But concerning the times and the seasons, brethren, you have no need that I should write to you. For you yourselves know perfectly that THE DAY OF THE LORD so comes as a thief in the night. For when they say, 'Peace and safety!' then sudden de-struction comes upon them, AS LABOR PAINS UPON A PREGNANT WOMAN. And they shall not escape" (1 Thessalonians 5:1-3); "Now if anyone builds on this foundation with gold, silver, pre-cious stones, wood, hay, straw, each one's work will become clear; for THE DAY WILL DECLARE IT, because it will be REVEALED BY FIRE; AND THE FIRE WILL TEST each one's work, of what sort it is. If anyone's work which he has built on it endures, he will receive a reward. If anyone's work is burned, he will suffer loss; but he himself will be saved, YET SO AS THROUGH FIRE (I Corin-thians 3:12-15).

"Baptism", religiously applied, was a lustration understood in the time of Christ to indicate *conversion* and *rebirth* and thus salvation (the opposite of נפל *falling, abortion* as by a Tophet, a child-sacrificial pyre of "shame"). It is clear why damnation and abortion are linked to the autumn, for autumn is the opposite of spring, and spring is called the "time of life" in Genesis 18:14. Contrary to Jewish reckoning, the Hebrew Torah states that the year begins in spring (Exodus 12:2), and the first full moon after the institu-tion of the Hebrews' first month was the Passover, the time of life when the Egyptian firstborn died and the Israelite people, God's "firstborn" (Exodus 4:22), were יצא *birthed out of* Egypt (Exodus 12:31), the "iron furnace" (I Kings 8:51), and עלה *went up, ascended, like a burnt offering* (Exodus 12:38) untouched by the fire of Pharaoh, the Serpent whose line sanc-tioned the killing of Hebrew babies. "Pharaoh" means "Great House", and the word בית *house* also means *womb*; thus, the Great House was obligat-ed to יצא *birth out of* Egypt God's "Firstborn" in opposition to the Hebrew innocents who were consumed in Egypt formerly. In other words, having made the Hebrews fruitless, the Great House, the Abortive Womb, the Ser-pent, the Pharaoh was compelled to be fruitful despite the former miscon-duct in Egypt; consider "the great city which spiritually is called Sodom and

Egypt, where also our Lord was crucified" (Revelation 11:8) along with, "I will greatly multiply your sorrow and your conception" (Genesis 3:16) in light of God's first command: "Be fruitful and multiply" (Genesis 1:28).

In order to employ an individual proof-text, one must keep the whole of Scripture in mind. A proof-text is like a point on a sphere: it is always in the midst of the whole, but the entirety makes the equation of the point and the center possible. The matrix makes collective sense that can be observed by its individual output, and the only sensible output is vitality.

CIRCUMLOCUTION

&

PERIPHRASIS

A circumlocution is a roundabout or indirect method of explanation and can be viewed as a periphrasis, the employment of multiple words where one or a few would suffice. Sometimes, Scripture appears to use one word in conjunction with the definition of a synonym. Other times, it seems to give a definition of a word without actually using the word under indirect discussion; this situation is quite common within the art of riddle-telling, the skill of parabolic discourse, and the craft of dark speaking. For example, Exodus 32:4 discusses the sin of the golden עגל calf, and it seems as if "calf" is a circumlocution for the word פר bull. The English reader may be quick to say that, "Though they are technically the same animal, one is younger and one is older"; this statement is true and can be seen in the juxtaposition of the "lamb" and "ram" concerning the binding of Isaac. However, the Hebrew (as opposed to the English) would still seem to admit that a tacit circumlocution is being employed in the usage of "calf" in Exodus 32:4 because of the description of what Moses did in Exodus 32:20: "Then he took the calf which they had made, burned it in the fire, and ground it to powder; and he scattered it on the water and made the children of Israel drink it." The word עגל calf is from an unused root that carries with it the concept of *rolling*, and it is related to the word for עגיל *earring*. Immediately, the circumlocutions begin to become clear, for Aaron avoided the word עגיל *earring* by speaking its definition, by circumlocution: "Take off THE GOLD THAT IS IN THE EARS of your wives, your sons, and your daughter...." when he could have just said, "Take off your gold earrings." Aaron employed multiple words by way of definition instead of using the word of which he spoke; therefore, "calf" connects the reader to the "earrings," but the synonym "bull" (instead of "calf") seems to be implied in conjunction because Moses "...took העגל*the calf* which they had made, burned it in the fire, and ground it to powder; and he scattered it...." The word פר *bull* comes from the root *to break in pieces* (which is what Moses did to the *calf*); thus, the reader may observe that "calf" aligns with what Aaron did according to the "earrings" he used to construct the infant-sacrificial idol, and "bull" aligns with what Moses did according to his destruction of it. Both a "calf" and a "bull" are common nouns that can be used as circumlocutions for the idol Molech (and those like him), the metal bull upon which children were sacrificed as whole burnt offerings. The wretched irony here is that the whole burnt offering for unintentional sin in Numbers 15:24 is a פר *bull* sacrificed by man, and, in Exodus, we have an account of a whole burnt offering by intentional sin of man sacrificed on a bull. Darkly, the words פרי העץ *fruit of the tree* can also mean פרי העץ *bulls of the cross*:

> Many BULLS have surrounded Me; strong BULLS of Bashan have encircled Me. They gape at Me with their MOUTHS, like a raging and roaring lion. I am POURED OUT LIKE WATER, and all My BONES are out of joint (Psalm 22:12-14).

> Then he took the CALF which they had made, BURNED it in the fire, and ground it to powder; and he scattered it ON THE WATER and made the children of Israel DRINK it (Exodus 32:20).

The reader will notice that these examples juxtapose "calf" and "bull" while discussing open mouths and "water," that is, both passages discuss the destruction of the innocent. That "fruit of the tree" and "bulls of the cross" are the same Hebrew words would appear to highlight the fact that the sin of the Golden Calf and crucifixion are connected in Psalm 22. Adam declared, "I heard your voice in the garden, and I WAS AFRAID because I was naked; so I hid," after he hid in the midst of the trees (or tree) in Genesis 3:8-10. Adam was "afraid" of his nakedness before God in Genesis 3:10 ("afraid" being a circumlocution for not "ashamed" of his nakedness in Genesis 2:25); after the second commandment tablets were constructed following the sin of the Golden Calf, the people were "afraid to come near him" (Exodus 34:30). Adam was "afraid" before God after his sin with the "fruit of the tree," and the people were "afraid" before Moses after their sin with the Golden Calf. Since it is obvious that "afraid" is utilized as a circumlocution for "shame" in the case of Adam, it is worthwhile to note that the word בוש *to be ashamed* is cognate to יבש *to dry up, to be ashamed*. The people were "AFRAID" (i.e. *ashamed*, DRIED UP) before Moses immediately after Moses "was there with the Lord 40 days and 40 nights without eating bread OR DRINKING WATER" (Exodus 34:28); FAMISHED land was understood as "cursed" ground (Genesis 3:17) and "naked" land (Genesis 42:9), and Adam was afraid (ashamed, DRIED UP) because of his nakedness. "Nakedness" can also mean "childlessness" in Hebrew as can be observed when Abram distresses about his lack of a male heir in Genesis 15:1-2:

> After this, the word of the Lord came to Abram in a vision: 'Do not be AFRAID, Abram....' But Abram said, O Sovereign Lord, what can you give me since I remain עֲרִירִי NAKED, CHILD-LESS...?"

Having considered the avoidances of circumlocutions, let us consider the avoidances of euphemisms.

Sometimes translators resort to euphemistic renderings in order to accord with certain predetermined convictions, to avoid what might be considered indelicate expression by a certain people, etc. Such euphemistic renderings can obscure the Text and point passages down paths that are insufficient or even originally unintended. At the same time, euphemistic translations can often result from being unfamiliar with information that is unavailable by the time of the translation. For instance, an altar is a table, and both were anciently held as feminine illustrations at which a male priest was to officiate by offering forth his life in covenantal congruence with the Deity. As a function, life was to be offered up by way of the altar: the priest's (sacrificer's) life was dedicated to the service, he poured out life upon his altar (his bride), and she was the vessel that yielded the life upon her up in the worship of the Deity. In Hebrew, a "threshold" and a "basin" are the same word (סף), for a "house" and a "womb" were held synonymously. The "womb," the "belly," and a "basin" are also the same Hebrew word (בטן). An altar and a table were essentially the same entity, so we may observe the connection of a feminine table/altar being a place of "eating" and a threshold/basin/womb also being a place for "eating" by the fact that the Hebrew אכל *to eat* can mean to CONSUME food as on a table (Genesis 31:38)/to consume or BURN by flame (Nahum 3:13)/and to pass over the concave threshold of the womb to COPULATE and therefore render up life (Proverbs 30:20); thus, "eating" was understood ceremonially as a covenant of life, for life, with the purpose of perpetuating life by way of marriage via pouring out life upon an altar, i.e. libation, i.e. copulation, i.e. the marital covenant. We may observe the connection between the "woman" and the "altar" by the fact that the word אשה means *woman*, *fire offering*, and GIFT; thus, Adam said, "The woman You GAVE to stand with me, she GAVE me...." with a darkly clever wordplay. With respect to both the altar and the wife (which were understood as one and the same), the priest (sacrificer) was understood to be in covenant with the Deity *through* his altar/his wife.

I repeat, the sacrificer was not merely in covenant with his wife but, more importantly, *through* his wife to God... the priest was said to be "bound" to God in this covenant, and this covenant was called "The Right of the Firstborn," a title that blatantly connects officiating at the altar and marriage. For example, "Levi" means "The Bound One," for "Levi is from the root לוה *to bind*. The tribe of Levi is also taken as God's "Firstborn" in Numbers 3:12 as a result of Levi "eating" ("devouring with the sword," in Hebrew thought) his brethren in Exodus 32 as a punishment since they sacrificed the life of the altar, the children of the womb, the firstborn. Succinctly put, not knowing the connections between the altar and the wife has caused very learned men to euphemize Genesis 2:24: "For this reason a man will leave his father and mother and cling *to his wife*...." Individually, a priest is a husband to his altar as a man is a husband to his wife. Collectively, the congregation led by the priest is the bride who willfully unifies with her lord, her husband, the Deity. The concept described here is clearly seen in the term "bride of Christ."

Genesis 2:24 does not say cling לאשתו *to his wife* in the dative case; it says באשתו *in his wife* in the locative case and *through* his wife in the ablative case. The idea of clinging "in his wife" is anatomically explicit and is thus softened by saying "to his wife" by deflecting the physicality of the matter. At the same time, the rendering of "to his wife" is not outrageous because באשתו *in his wife* is determined by the prefix ב which can mean "in, within, among, at, near, on, before, by, with, and through." If the translators viewed the Hebrew as "cling near his wife" or "cling by his wife," then rendering the dative case is not necessarily errant. Consider William Tyndale when he wrote about the Hebrew expression found all throughout the Greek New Testament that he translated into English:

> If ought seem changed, or not altogether agreeing with the Greek, let the finder of the fault consider the Hebrew phrase or manner of speech left in the Greek words. Whose preterperfect tense and present tense is oft both one, and the future tense is the optative mode also, and the future tense is oft the imperative mode in the active voice, and the in the passive ever. Likewise person for person, number for number, and an interrogation for a conditional, and such like is with the Hebrews a common usage" ("Unto the Reader" of Tyndale's English New Testament).

The great translators were not ignorant men, and they sought to capture the overall sense of Scripture in a manner they thought best relatable to their audience relative to the available information of the times. Again, a translation is not a reproduction or a facsimilie. Accordingly, it would appear that a man will "cling in his wife" physically as an official of the altar God "gave" him because he understands his priestly duty is one of joy and life to be started and finished in pleasurable adoration through the worship of God; then, ultimately, a man will cling "though his wife" to God in covenant... man will cling "though his wife" to God in life, for life, with the perpetuity of life constantly before him. The reader may observe the precisely negative inversion of this principle of a man officiating at an altar through which he is bound to the deity in Numbers 25.

In Numbers 25, the Israelites become seduced by the people of Moab. The Moabites descended from the polluted altar of incest, from

Lot's libation upon his older daughter's altar in Genesis 19. We must keep in mind that Lot's daughters were products of the cities condemned for inverting the officiation at the altar/threshold/house/temple = womb, hence the weighted emphasis made concerning the filthy Sodomites and the "door of the house" (Genesis 19:9-10) they attempted to "break down." Following the destruction of the perverts, Lot became drunkenly induced by his older daughter which, literarily, appears to be a mockery of worship by holy libation in that her method was to give wine to acquire her father's water... for מים *water* is sometimes a Scriptural euphemism for *semen*. The older daughter gave wine in hopes that her father would give water. The older daughter succeeded in acquiring her father's water, and she gave birth to Moab (which means "Water of the Father"). It does not appear that the woman under discussion attempted to sacrifice herself in covenant to God by having her altar officiated unto His glory. In the same way, the descendants of Moab seduced the Israelites. The Moabite women "...invited them to the sacrifices of their gods. The people ate and bowed down before these gods. So Israel joined in worshipping Baal of Peor. And the Lord's anger burned against them" (Numbers 25:1-3). Again, an altar and a table were essentially the same entity, and so we may observe the connection of a feminine table/altar being a place of "eating" and a threshold/basin/ womb also being a place for "eating" by the fact that the Hebrew אכל *to eat* can mean to CONSUME food as on a table (Genesis 31:38), to consume or BURN by flame (Nahum 3:13), and to pass over the concave threshold of the womb to COPULATE (Proverbs 30:20); thus, "eating" was understood ceremonially as a covenant of life, for life, with the purpose of perpetuating life by way of sacrifice and marriage via pouring out life upon an altar, i.e. libation, i.e. copulation, i.e. the marital covenant. We may observe the Numbers 25:1-3 accordingly: The Moabite women

> ...invited them to the SACRIFICES [eating/fire] of their gods. The people ATE AND BOWED DOWN   [clung to these women in physical union]   before these gods. So Israel joined Baal of Peor [clung to the child-sacrificial and false deity through these women]. And the Lord's anger BURNED [eating/fire] against them (Numbers 25:1-3).

Of course, "bowing down" is employed in terms of intercourse (Job 31:10 and 39:3) and worship (Numbers 25:1-3), for intercourse is a form of worship, which is partly why the desire for it is strong enough to be let out of control easily. "Baal" means "husband, lord, and master," and it is derived from the root בעל *to have dominion, to marry*; thus: "'Return, faithless people,' declares the Lord, 'For I am your Baal [Husband]...'" (Jeremiah 3:14).

"Baal" can mean a "husband" generically, it can indicate God in union with his people to the extent of perpetuating life and perpetual life, and it can name the consistent inhibiter of life, Satan. Again, The Moabite women

> ...invited them to the SACRIFICES of their gods. The people ATE AND BOWED DOWN before these gods. So Israel joined the Husband of the Opening [= "Baal Peor"]. And the Lord's anger BURNED against them (Numbers 25:1-3).

Now the euphemism is clear: The sensual misconduct of the Israelite men with the Moabite women was analogous to Satan lending out his bride in order to ensnare the people of God... and this is the negative, the perversion of the standard that gives birth to death. The standard is thus: The copulative union is a sign of the covenantal joining of man and wife that is analogous to God offering libation for the purpose of multiplying His Life through His people. Consider that an ancient eastern prophet (like one of those of the Babylonians) was called "the pourer out," a man who poured out water and wine. Since Genesis 9 equates "blood" with "life" and since Genesis 19 equates "water" with "semen," we may notice that the unifying theme of "Life" is illustrated with blood and water. Numbers 25 states that the perverse death that ensued by the joining or clinging of the Israelites through the Moabites to Satan was thwarted by Phineas thrusting a spear through an Israelite man as he coupled with a Moabite woman; the English reads, "He drove the spear through both of them — through the Israelite and into the woman's body" (Numbers 25:8). The word "body" here is an English euphemism because the Hebrew says קבתה *her womb* (from the root קב *to bore through, to pierce*). Removing the translated euphemisms, the woman of her Father's Semen enticed the man of Israel to the extent that he was willing to participate in the profanation of the altar unto death; therefore, his punishment was to be pierced negatively unto death as a bride (who is intended to be pierced positively unto life by her husband), and the Moabite woman received both a fleshly masculinity and a spear where life and death mingled unto destruction as her punishment.

Genesis 2:24 states, "For this reason a man will leave his father and mother ודבק *and cling* THROUGH his wife...." to God, for it is written, "Fear the Lord our God and serve Him. תדבק *Cling* to Him and take your oaths in His Name" (Deuteronomy 10:20). Both passages employ the same Hebrew word for "cling." It appears that man was made to be the priest of his house, i.e. man was made to officiate at the altar of his God, i.e. God instituted the marriage of man and woman as an illustration of man's intended unity with God that is described as a "marriage supper" or "wedding feast," ideas we more commonly refer to as "Holy Communion." Adam was to worship God through the altar, the wife God provided for him in order to take part in eternity, i.e. in order to participate in perpetuity through seed (as befits a gardener). Baal Peor (The Husband of the Opening, Satan) wished to be worshipped through the altar he desecrated (his wife whom he seduced away from God) in order for man to take part in death, i.e. in order to participate in the thwarting of perpetuity through seed (as befits a hunter).

Wine is called "the blood of grapes" (Genesis 49:11), and Christ called Himself "The True Vine" (John 15:1). The "fruit of the vine" was wine mingled with water, as opposed to what the Talmud remembers as "fruit of the tree," or wine that was not mingled with water. Again, blood and water indicate life, and "water" can sometimes mean seed, that is "semen." The issue is not merely intercourse, but worship unto life or worship unto death... an altar unto life or an altar unto death, the worship of God or the worship of Satan, the Tree of Life or the Tree of the Knowledge of Good and Evil. The reader will notice that the punishment of the Israelites for having become the bride of Satan through the Moabite women (and, thus, for having sacrificed children) was this: " והוקעעDISLOCATE, ALIENATE, HANG them before the Lord BEFORE THE SUN...." The punishment for killing the children was hanging (Numbers 25) or stoning (Leviticus 20). Psalm 22:1... 14:

> My God, My God, why have You forsaken Me [ALIENATE]? *Why are You so* far from helping Me, *and from* the words of My groaning [ALIENATE]? O My God, I cry in the daytime [BEFORE THE SUN], but You do not hear [ALIENATE].... I am poured out like water and all My bones are out of joint [DISLOCATE]; My heart is like wax; it has melted within Me. My strength is dried up like a potsherd, and My tongue clings to My jaws; You have brought Me to the dust of death.

The "death" discussed immediately above is, of course, crucifixion, which is why Christ uttered this Psalm on the cross... as The True Vine hung on the Tree of Death; the opposite of this would be The False Vine hanging on The Tree of Life. God is perfectly just and perfectly merciful. **The punishment fits the crime and the grace fits the punishment**. It is obvious that crucifixion is the punishment for killing children as a result of an unholy union as we have just read in Numbers 25. If crucifixion is the punishment, then killing a child is the crime. If the Last Adam was hung on a tree, then the reader should ask, "What child was sacrificed in order to bring the crucifixion of Christ about? Furthermore, why would child-sacrifice have any necessary connection to a tree in the first place?" At this point, I leave the reader with this observation: God made Adam a helper "כנגדו *before him*" (Genesis 2:18), and God told Moses to "והוקע *hang* them before the Lord נגד השמש *before the sun*...." (Numbers 25:4); the word "before" in both passages is the same Hebrew word implicit of marriage, i.e. the man's worship of God through his wife, a priest officiating at the altar God gave him, a sacrificer yielding forth life at the threshold basin God carved out for him, as opposed to the perverse Sodomites and Moabites. Blood and euphemistic "water" mingled unto death by a spear in the womb of the Moabite woman as her Israelite lover "clung" to her and "joined" himself to Satan. Christ slept, and then both blood and water poured forth from his circumcised heart when He clung to God that His bride might live. Adam slept and had his heart circumcised by God so that his bride might live. Let it be understood clearly that there are many euphemisms within the Scripture's original languages, and even more so in translations of Scripture. The greatest euphemism, the grandest periphrasis, the most magnitudinous circumlocution can be found within the Eden Narrative of Genesis symbolized at the gate of expulsion as a result of unsuccessful birth.

PROPOSITIONS

&

UNDERSTATEMENT

STATEMENTS and questions forward propositions that can be of a greater magnitude than the statements and questions themselves. Propositions are often forwarded subtly and not stated overtly. Careful syntactic constructions can state the obvious and simultaneously establish veiled implications. The willingness to dialogue based on an initial statement, or the willingness to answer a question, is a willingness to accept the proposition(s) behind the statement or question. For example, if someone were to ask, "Which do you like better: X or Y?" the proposition that is forwarded by this question assumes that the receiver likes both X and Y and has a preference for one over the other. If the receiver likes neither X or Y, but persists in answering the question asked, the receiver has already admitted something that is not true and, therefore, he cannot continue in an accurate dialogue.

When we view Christ and Satan dueling in the midst of Satan's attempt to tempt Christ, it might seem as if Scripture can bolster any opinion if one views individual passages as independent entities without total uniformity with each other. In other words, it can be assumed falsely that Satan employed Scripture to fortify his points and Christ wielded Scripture to mandate His points also to the extent that Satan relented; however, this supposition disregards the fact that Scripture was not necessarily being questioned. The intentions of the heart were being questioned via the propositions behind the employment of the given Scriptural references. Consider Luke 4:9-12:

> Then he brought Him to Jerusalem, set Him on the pinnacle of the temple, and said to Him, "If You are the Son of God, throw Yourself down from here. For it is written: 'He shall give His angels charge over you, to keep you, 'and, 'In their hands they shall bear you up, lest you dash your foot against a stone.'" And Jesus answered and said to him, "It has been said, 'You shall not tempt the Lord your God.'"

The reader will notice that Satan employed Scripture in his arguments; however, Satan did not seem to be challenging Scripture itself. Satan, it appears, knew that the Scripture is true, but he seemed to challenge first Christ's knowledge of Scripture and then, ultimately, Christ's faith in it — both of which were intended to exist in symbiosis. The proposition of Satan's Scripturally based question appears to challenge the skill of Scriptural knowledge entwined with the faith, the covenantal trust of Scripture's truth, for Satan himself seemed not to doubt the veracity of the Text. In other words, Satan appeared not to question whether or not "...In their hands they shall bear you up..." is true, but the unspoken proposition with which Satan challenged Christ was whether or not Christ was willing to jump in order to prove the Scripture to be true, i.e. whether or not Christ was willing to test God to prove God's Word to be true — which is fallacious reasoning because God's Word says not to test God. One cannot violate God's Word in order to keep God's Word. Man is to be tested in order for man to know that God's Word is true, hence Exodus 16:4:

> Then the Lord said to Moses, "Behold, I will rain bread from heaven for you. And the people shall go out and gather a certain quota every day, THAT I MAY TEST THEM, whether they will walk in My law or not"

The provision of manna put man, not God, to the test. The proposition that Satan forwarded against Christ did not involve whether or not Christ would be protected solely. Satan's proposition involved whether or not Christ would test God in order to see if He would be protected, and testing God is an inversion of the logic of Scripture: *Man is to be tested* in order for man to know God's Word to be true, but *God is not to be tested* in order for man to know God's Word to be true; it is for this reason that it is written that God "may test them, whether they will walk in My law or not" (Exodus 16:4) as opposed to something like "that man may test God, whether man will walk in God's law or not." Since Satan's proposition was aimed at whether or not Christ would test God; Christ then responded, "It has been said, 'You shall not tempt the Lord your God,'" for Christ responded to Satan's proposition, not Satan's Scripture citing. Had Christ responded to Satan's Scripture citing, He would have answered in a manner that would attempt to prove that He could jump and therefore obligate God to make good on promises that were never questionable by Christ or Satan in the first place.

The lack of recognizing the propositions of questions and statements forces the receiver to answer challenges that are beside the point and that ultimately defeat by way of superior wit; it is for this reason that it seems impossible to exercise significant faith in God without significant knowledge of God. The very notion that one can have faith in God without knowledge of Him would place one in the position of taking the Enemy's words as truth (since Satan is able to quote Scripture) and therefore obeying the Enemy's demands in order to prove, somehow, that God is true by meeting the request of God's Enemy — which is a logical fallacy at least! After having observed propositions behind individual questions and statements, let us view individual words.

It can be argued that God allows Himself to be tested with respect to finances based on Malachi 3:10: "'Bring all the tithes into the storehouse, that there may be food in My house, and try Me now in this,' Says the Lord of hosts, 'If I will not open for you the windows of heaven and pour out for you such blessing that there will not be room enough to receive it.'" We may notice the imperative "try Me now in this" and state that the message is plain: we may test God with our contributions. It is, however, observable that this statement rests upon the proposition that people first part with money, and the very act of parting with finances is a test for humanity. It can therefore be seen that man's faith can be tested by parting, and that such a test opens ample opportunity for the King to pour out blessing in whatever way He sees fit. Adam had first to sleep in order for his bride to live as a result of his circumcised heart. Ultimately, the first Adam failed, but, eventually, the Last Adam succeeded. Christ's heart was circumcised, and He poured out a baptism of blood and water ("fruit of the vine," i.e. wine) and thus blessed us with His ability to renew us; yet, this particular event was not viewed initially as joyous, and it was only in due time that Paul could write of the propositions forwarded:

> In Him you were also circumcised with the circumcision made without hands, by putting off the body of the sins of the flesh, by the circumcision of Christ, buried with Him in baptism, in which you also were raised with Him through faith in the working of God, who raised Him from the dead. And you, being dead in your trespasses and the uncircumcision of your flesh, He has made alive together with Him, having forgiven you all trespasses, having wiped out the handwriting of requirements that was against us, which was contrary to us. And He has taken it out of the way, having nailed it to the cross. Having disarmed principalities and powers, HE MADE A PUBLIC SPECTACLE OF THEM, TRIUMPHING OVER THEM IN IT (Colossians 2:11-15).

Notice that Paul considered what appeared at first glance to be a rebel freedom-fighter's execution as a triumphant military conquest. Surely such an image was not conceived of at the foot of the tree by the majority of onlookers... for, surely, the Last Adam was hiding victoriously in the midst of the trees of Golgotha when He seemed to be most defeatedly exposed to counter Adam hiding unvictoriously in the midst of the trees of Eden after he was most disastrously naked; but, before pursuing the matter further, let us review Exodus 17 in order to prove the point.

In Exodus 17, we read of how God gave drink to the Israelites and then how He made provision for a victorious war over Amalek. Cornwall & Smith's *Exhaustive Dictionary of Bible* Names defines "Amalek" as "a people that lick up" and "a strangler of the people," both of which seem to point to negative serpentine, pythonic imagery: "They shall lick the dust like a serpent..." (Micah 7:17). "Amalek" is from the root עמל *to labor, travail,* and Job 15:35 uses the related masculine noun עמל *toil, mischief* with reference to *abortive birth...* so, it would seem that we have in this title, Amalek, a subtle link among "toil," "labor," and "abortive birth" with respect to serpentine allusions. Amalek attacked Israel in Exodus 17:8 immediately after, "And he called the place 'Testing' and 'Qarreling' because the Israelites quarreled and because THEY TESTED THE LORD saying, 'Is the Lord among us or not?'" (Exodus 17:7); thus, people tested God, and then a serpent, Amalek, came to fight with them. Again, with respect to the temptations of Christ, the serpent's proposition involved whether or not Christ would test His Father — which is a reversal of the logic of Scripture, for God is not to be tested in order for man to know God's Word to be true. Once the war with the serpent, Amalek, was underway, *Aaron* (אהרון *Shining One*; consider נחש *serpent, shining one*) and *Hur* (חור *aperture, hole*) held Moses's hands aloft in order for the Israelites to be victorious in battle. If we observe the names involved here, then we can notice that the concepts of "shining," "serpent," and "aperture" are all found in the word מאורה *something lighted, an aperture, a hole of a serpent.* It can be reasonably deduced that we are observing, in the war with Amalek, a wicked serpent battling a righteous Serpent, the false vine contending with "The True Vine" (John 15:1), Satan warring with Christ. As an example, consider how serpents were used to chastise the Israelites in Numbers 21 and how the remedy for their bites was the Serpent on the pole, which was a direct reference to Christ on the tree (John 3:14-16); immediately after this episode, the Text states, "The Israelites moved on and camped בבאבות *at Wineskins*" (Numbers 21:10). Now that it is established that the Israelite war with Amalek was a spiritual battle between "serpents," we may return specifically to the temptations of Christ.

Psalm 91: 11-13 states:

For He shall give His angels charge over you, to keep you in all your ways. In their hands ישאונך *yi they shall bear you up,* lest you dash your foot against a stone. You shall tread upon the lion and the cobra, the young lion and the serpent you shall trample underfoot.

Satan quoted a portion of Psalm 91 in an effort to persuade Christ to test God; however, since Titus 2:13 calls Jesus "our great God and Savior," it appears likely that Christ was convicting Satan of testing God when He said, "You shall not tempt the Lord your God." Nevertheless, the Psalm states that ישאונך *they shall bear you up* which is from the root נשא *to lift up.* After Aaron (Shining One) died, and before the Israelites traveled to the land of Wineskins (Oboth, Serpents), the Israelites were bitten by serpents and were saved by gazing upon a serpent (Numbers 21). Christ recounted the episode in this way: "And as Moses lifted up the serpent in the wilderness, even so must the Son of Man be LIFTED UP, that whoever believes in Him should not perish but have eternal life. For God so loved the world that He gave His only begotten Son, that whoever believes in Him should not perish but have everlasting life" (John 3:14-16). The point is that Satan employed the 91st Psalm's description of "lifting up" to indicate the preservation from a fall, whereas Christ enacted this Psalm by enacting a fall: death. The root נפל *to fall* (as in battle) is what God did not permit the Israelites to do before the serpent, Amalek, and Christ properly quoting the Word of God did not allow Himself to fall in battle either. At the same time, Satan attempted to get Christ to consider ישאונך *they shall bear you up* as a means of preventing a fall, whereas Christ utilized the image of Moses "lifting up" the serpent as a prefiguration for Salvation's gift upon a tree. The root נפל *to fall* produces the נפל *an untimely birth, an abortion (i.e. a dead innocent).* Ironically, Satan told Christ to make Himself fall, and Christ negated Satan's words by making Himself fall... that is, Satan told Christ to plunge in order that He might be "lifted up," but Christ took on the form of a dead innocent (literally "a fallen one") by being "lifted up" on the tree. Ironically, Numbers 25 illustrates how the punishment for killing an innocent on a sacrificial pyre (i.e. wood and fire) is being hung on a tree before the sun (i.e. wood and fire), and this Narrative follows Moses lifting up the serpent for Salvation in Numbers 21. "Jesus" means "Salvation, He saves." So, when Satan challenged Christ to become guilty of testing God by falling in order that He be lifted up, Christ negated Satan's temptation by falling (dying as an innocent) in order that He be lifted up (on the tree, destructively, and in the Resurrection, constructively), just as Moses "lifted up" the shiny, fiery, blood-colored serpent in the wilderness; therefore, He received the punishment of killing an innocent, but He died as an innocent.

It can be seen that Satan took the Word of God and applied a different and deceitful sense to the strict letter of the passage, and Christ responded by reestablishing the original sense to the strict letter of the passage in truthful opposition to the false sense that Satan superimposed. Satan's words seemed original in that he quoted Scripture, but his words were deceitfully innovative (the chief deceit being in that his words seemed original). Christ's words were original when He quoted Scripture. Knowing that a "vine" is a circumlocution for a "serpent," we can observe a war between the "True Vine" (John 15:1) and the false vine. It can therefore be deduced that Christ was not speaking innovation but origin, and thus He told the "brood of vipers," "And no one, having drunk old wine, immediately desires new; for he says, 'The old is better'" (Luke 5:39), referring to Himself (and not his enemies) as the "old wine." In Luke's example, we can comprehend the link between a serpent and a vine by way of "wineskins," which is the same Hebrew word as Oboth, the land to which the Israelites travelled after they were saved through the Serpent on the pole as a result of having been bitten by snakes. In Luke 5, the Serpent (soon to be on the pole) battled a "brood of vipers." In short, Christ did indeed fall and was certainly lifted up, but not in the sense that Satan forwarded; this teaches that not only was Satan's application of Scripture incorrectly innovative, but that the original prediction of the so-called "Old Testament" was that the Savior would die on a tree to undo the ravages of sin birthed in Eden. Furthermore, the term "old wineskins" uses the same Greek word for "old" in Luke 5:36 as the term "old testament" does in 2 Corinthians 3:14; the Hebrew would allude to *hidden, eternal* wine... not merely "old" wine, thus, "...this is My blood of the new [חדש *renewed*] covenant, which is shed for many for the remission of sins" (Matthew 26:28) on the tree where Christ was "lifted up." Christ poured forth the hidden wine of the original as opposed to Satan's errantly liberal treatment of Scripture. Satan proposed testing God, not following God.

The word ישאונך *they shall bear you up* is derived from the root נשא *to lift up (as the hand in solemn prayer, or as the head i.e. resurrection), to carry away, to aid, to lift (as the voice), to utter (as a parable or prayer), to present (as a gift), to take (i.e. to get married, take a wife), to bear (as in bearing away sin, thus) to forgive, to pardon.* Observe how Christ must have held His head up during the crucifixion since John tells us that, "When Jesus had received the wine, He said, 'כי עשה *It is finished* [Psalm 22:31].' Then he bowed His head and gave up His Spirit" John 19:30). Notice how Christ was "led away" to be crucified in Matthew 27:31, how Mark 15:37 says, "And Jesus cried out with a loud voice, and breathed His last," how Christ prayed Psalm 22 parabolically, how He gave us grace as a "free gift" (Romans 5:15) that we may be pardoned, and that He views us as a "bride," having born our sins away. All of these ideas are encapsulated in the root נשא *to lift up*; Satan challenged our Salvation by misappropriating the Scripture, "ישאונך *they shall bear you up*," for he conveniently did not mention, "You shall tread upon the lion and the cobra, the young lion and the serpent you shall trample underfoot." After Adam hid "in the midst of the trees of Eden" (Genesis 3:9), it was prophesied that the "serpent" would be tread underfoot (Genesis 3:15); hence, it would seem that, if Christ was "borne up" or "lifted up," He could then crush the head of the serpent: "Jesus answered and said, 'This voice did not come because of Me, but for your sake. Now is the judgment of this world; now the ruler of this world [the "serpent"] will be cast out. And I, if I AM LIFTED UP from the earth, will draw all peoples to Myself.' This He said, signifying by what death He would die" (John 12:30-33), i.e. death on a tree. Ancient eastern warfare was initiated by sacrifice. If Christ was lifted up in order to tread on the head of the serpent as an ancient eastern monarch treads upon the head of his vanquished foe, then it would seem that the crucifixion was the acceptable sacrifice in order to initiate the war on Satan, the hidden war that revealed Christ victorious three days later. In other words, it seems as if Christ, the Righteous Serpent, initiated the war on Satan, the unrighteous serpent, in the arrow of time on the tree at Golgatha in order to win the war in eternity as evidenced by rebirth from the dead otherwise called "resurrection." The real war, it would seem, took place in the realm of eternity, in the realm where the arrow of time is not as we perceive it on earth.

Satan tried to tempt Christ into being lifted up from a fall Satan wanted Christ to take, but Christ resisted the temptation by being willing to be lifted up from a fall He was willing to take. Certainly, the *sense* of the words is what is being argued. Satan, the opener (i.e. gouger, blinder) of spiritual eyes used his powers to deceive the world into beholding a condemned criminal. It appears as if the crucifixion is described in terms similar to that of Moses having his hands held aloft by his compatriots (like a crucified man) as he stabilized himself upon a rock to the effect that the Israelites triumphed in the war of Exodus 17 immediately after they received water from a rock: "Moreover, brethren, I do not want you to be unaware that all our fathers were under the cloud, all passed through the sea, all were BAPTIZED INTO MOSES in the cloud and in the sea, all ate the same spiritual food, and all drank the same spiritual drink. For they DRANK OF THAT SPIRITUAL ROCK that followed them, and that Rock was Christ" (I Corinthians 10:1-4). When Psalm 105 recounts the flowing of water from the rock, it states specifically that the waters ויזובו *flowed out (as is often applied to the flowing of blood),* thus connecting it to the water and the blood that flowed out of Christ when His heart was circumcised physically on the Cross in part by a Roman's blade. God told Moses, "I will stand before you by the rock בחרב, *with a blade, at Horeb.* Strike the Rock, and water ויצאו *will birth out* of it for the people to drink" (Exodus 17:6). "This is He who came by water and blood — Jesus Christ; not only by water, but by water and blood. And it is the Spirit who bears witness, because the Spirit is truth" (I John 5:6), and we can see why it is written that "By faith Moses, when he became of age, refused to be called the son of Pharaoh's daughter, choosing rather to suffer affliction with the people of God than to enjoy the passing pleasures of sin, esteeming the reproach of CHRIST greater riches than the treasures in Egypt; for he looked to the reward" (Hebrews 11:24-26).

Genesis 17:11 states that the cutting of the foreskin is the "sign" of the covenant of circumcision and not the circumcision itself, and this explains why Deuteronomy 10:16; 30:6, Jeremiah 4:4 and Romans 2:29 state that circumcision is truly of the לב *mind, heart.* In the same way, I Peter 3:21 explains that the washing of water is the sign of baptism, not the baptism itself, and this explains why Peter connects Noah's flood to baptism, for Noah was not himself washed in that water. The reader will also observe that circumcision was to take place on the 8th day (Leviticus 12:3), and that 8 people were saved during Noah's flood (I Peter 3:20). Both circumcision and baptism were understood in terms of fertility, thus שמנה means both *fertile* and *eight.* To be converted was to be baptized, i.e. to have one's mind and heart circumcised — both of which mean *to be born again.* In the same way, we can see why Adam's heart was circumcised in order for his bride to be born; the creation of Adam's wife was the fertility of circumcision and baptism, which indicates more of why Scripture tells us, "HUSBANDS, LOVE YOUR WIVES, just as Christ also loved the church and gave Himself for her, that He might sanctify and cleanse her with the WASHING OF WATER BY THE WORD (Ephesians 5:25-27). The creation of Adam's wife was a type of pruning and lustration. Such a situation explains why unpruned vines are called ערל *uncircumcised vines, forbidden vines* which is etymologically related to the word ערלה *foreskin.* The foreskin of Adam's heart was pruned, so to speak.

> I am the true vine, and My Father is the vinedresser. Every branch in Me that does not bear fruit He takes away; and every branch that bears fruit He prunes, that it may bear more fruit. You are already clean because of the word which I have spoken to you. Abide in Me, and I in you. As the branch cannot bear fruit of itself, unless it abides in the vine, neither can you, unless you abide in Me. I am the vine, you are the branches. He who abides in Me, and I in him, bears much fruit; for without Me you can do nothing (John 15:1-5).

Moses' hands were lifted up by others in order to triumph over the Amalekites, the serpents. Let us behold the glory of the tacit confluence elucidated by Colossians 2:11-15:

> In Him you were also circumcised with the CIRCUMCISION MADE WITHOUT HANDS, by putting off the body of the sins of the flesh, by the CIRCUMCISION OF CHRIST, buried with Him in baptism, in which you also were raised with Him through faith in the working of God, who raised Him from the dead. And you, being dead in your trespasses and the UNCIRCUMCISION OF YOUR FLESH, He has made alive together with Him, having forgiven you all trespasses, having wiped out the handwriting of requirements that was against us, which was contrary to us. And He has taken it out of the way, having nailed it to the cross. Having disarmed principalities and powers, HE MADE A PUBLIC SPECTACLE OF THEM, TRIUMPHING OVER THEM IN IT.

The very fact that Christ, The True Vine, was "chastised" in Luke 23 demonstrates subtly to us the agricultural terminology of the time, for Theophrastus' *De Causis Plantarum* states that vines can be "chastened" to bear fruit by piercing holes into them. In short, everything that Satan attempted to do negatively to Christ was used positively for Christ's bride by Christ. Again,

> But Moses' hands became heavy; so they took a STONE and put it under him, and he sat on it. And Aaron and Hur SUPPORTED HIS HANDS, one on one side, and the other on the other side; and his hands were steady until the going down of the sun. So Joshua [= Jesus] defeated Amalek [Serpent] and his people with the edge of the sword [like the blade that pruned Christ's heart and allowed the baptism to flow forth] (Exodus 17:12-13).

Since Moses was "as God to Pharaoh" (Exodus 7:1), since both Pharaoh and Amalek were as serpents, and since Moses sat enthroned upon a mountain while his hands were raised as the limbs of a tree in victory while Joshua [Jesus] fought beneath him victoriously, it would seem as if The Father, flanked by His angels, did with His own hands what His Son did below as He battled the brood of vipers on one level and the Serpent on another as the heavenly lights indicated the victory by the lunar eclipse that occurred, like the first Passover in Egypt, on the 14th Day of Nissan over Jerusalem in 33 AD.

> Reconsider,

> For He shall give HIS ANGELS charge over you, to keep you in all your ways. In their hands ישאונך THEY *shall bear you up*,

lest you dash your foot against a stone. You shall tread upon the lion and the cobra, the young lion and the serpent you shall trample underfoot."

Christ triumphed over the assaulter of His bride, and He slept in order for His heart to be pruned so that His bride could live and be cleansed; he gave "Himself for her, that He might sanctify and cleanse her with the WASHING OF WATER BY THE WORD [as in cleansing an altar prior to offering gifts upon it], that He might present her to Himself a GLORIOUS CHURCH…" (Ephesians 5:25-27) of people as opposed to the corrupt temple of stone from which Satan tried to coax Christ into jumping. "In Him you were also circumcised with the circumcision made without hands, by putting off the body of the sins of the flesh, by the circumcision of Christ, buried with Him in baptism, in which you also were RAISED WITH HIM THROUGH FAITH IN THE WORKING OF GOD, WHO RAISED HIM FROM THE DEAD" (Colossians 2:11-15). It is my personal conviction that, when Christ prayed the 22nd Psalm on the Tree, the criminal who recognized Christ saw how "…He shall give His angels charge over you, to keep you in all your ways. In their hands ישׂאונך THEY *shall bear you up*, lest you dash your foot against a stone." When this penitent criminal realized that The successful King of Heaven was mistaken by a spiritually blinded world of opened (gouged) eyes who thought Him to be a failed king of earth, he then said, "'Do you not even fear GOD? … LORD, remember me when YOU come into YOUR kingdom.' And JESUS said to him, 'Assuredly, I say to you this day, you will be with ME in Paradise.'" This resurrection is the rebirth, for the last words of the Psalm are in Greek "It is finished" or "Paid in full"; and, in their Hebrew original, they can be conceived of as "כי עשׂה *for He reproduced*" because the word עשׂה *he did, he made* is the word used for *reproduction* in Genesis 2:3, the opposite of the word נפל *abortion,* which is from the root נפל *to fall*.

Propositions underlie questions and statements. To accept statements or questions is to accept the propositions that bear them, and if the premise of the proposition is errant, the statements and questions can only lead to error, whereby the acceptance of them connects to further error. The acceptance of a faulty proposition led to the נפל *Fall, Defection, Abortion*.

THE ORGANIC HOUSE
OF WISDOM

I N Hebrew thought, a *womb* and *wisdom* are connected with particular respect to the concept of *renewal*. The word קרב can mean *womb* (Genesis 25:22), *mind* (Jeremiah 31:33), and *midst* (Zephaniah 3:17). After referring to the ברית חרשה *renewed covenant* or *reaffirmed covenant* of Jeremiah 31:31 in Romans 11:27, Romans goes on to say in 12:1-2,

> I beseech you therefore, brethren, by the mercies of God, that you present your bodies a θυσιαν ζωσαν *living sacrifice*, holy, acceptable to God, which is your reasonable service. And do not be conformed to this world, but be transformed by the ανακαινωσει *renewing* of your νοος *mind*, that you may prove what *is* that good and acceptable and perfect will of God.

We can observe the referential juxtaposition of "renewed covenant" to the "renewing of your mind," for the "renewed covenant" is the "law בבקרבם *in their minds*" (Jeremiah 31:33) that is written "on לבם *their hearts*," for לב means both *heart* and *mind* with specific reference to the *midst* and the *womb* (*womb* being connected to *wisdom*). Again, the word translated קרב *mind* here can also mean *womb* (Genesis 25:22) and *midst* (Zephaniah 3:17) since, in Hebrew thought, a man's heart is analogous to a woman's womb (as we read of Adam birthing his wife from his circumcised heart). This word קרב *womb, midst* is from the root קרב *to draw near, to approach*, and it produces the word קרבן *offering, oblation, sacrifice*, and these facts demonstrate that Hebrew קרבן *sacrifice* was originally constructive and generative whereby life is produced, not destroyed, as is the case with the intended function of the womb. (The confused assumption that "sacrifice" is necessarily deprivational has occured, in part, because the "sacrifice" is utilized to translate the word קרבן *sacrifice (constructively)* — from where "קרב *womb*" is derived — and זבח *slaughter*; obviously, "slaughter" serves an unnatural function antithetical to that of the natural womb. *Womb and midst* are the Hebrew קרב that are birthed from the same root as קרבן *sacrifice (constructively)* as opposed to זבח *slaughter, sacrifice*. The womb and the mind can both be renewed, and it would seem that such a facet is why the "renewed covenant" of Jeremiah 31 (commonly, and mistakenly, called the "New Testament") deals with an extremely significant birth whose issue can renew our minds. In Hebrew thought, a *womb* and *wisdom* are connected with particular respect to the concept of *renewal*.

Again, after referring to הבברית חרשה *the renewed covenant* of Jeremiah 31:31 in Romans 11:27, Romans goes on to say in 12:1-2,

I beseech you therefore, brethren, by the mercies of God, that you present your bodies a θυσιαν ζωσαν *living sacrifice*, holy, acceptable to God, which is your reasonable service. And do not be conformed to this world, but be transformed by the ανακαινωσει *renewing* of your νοος *mind*, that you may prove what *is* that good and acceptable and perfect will of God.

We can observe the referential juxtaposition of "renewed covenant" to the "renewing of your mind," for the "renewed covenant" is the "law in their minds" that is written "on their hearts," for לב means both *heart* and *mind* and is analogous to the *womb*. The womb would seem to be made comparable to a written document, hence the Scripture, "For we are His ποιημα *poem, book, workmanship* created in Christ Jesus for good works, which God prepared beforehand that we should walk in them" (Ephesians 2:10); this might help explain the θυσιαν ζωσαν *living sacrifice* reference, for this expression seems to be a literal Greek translation of the Hebrew קרבן *generative offering, i.e. sacrifice* which is etymologically related to קרב *womb* which is from the root קרב *to draw near, to approach*; hence, "present your bodies a θυσιαν ζωσαν *living sacrifice*" would then indicate that believers are to present themselves generatively, like a fertile bride, "created in Christ Jesus for good works," i.e. to produce good fruit or the "Fruit of the Spirit" (Galatians 5:22-23), for the Hebrew word עבד *work* also spells *son*. The bride is to *draw near* to Christ as capable of producing His fruit, that is, as a *"living sacrifice"* that leads to viable fruit (and not a slaughtering womb that leads to nonviable fruit), for Jeremiah's "Renewed Covenant" is stated in the same place where God says "I was a HUSBAND to them" (Jeremiah 31:32). Hebrews 8 translates Jeremiah 31 accordingly.

Jeremiah 31:31-33 says,

> Behold, the days are coming, says the LORD, when I will make a ברית חדשה *renewed covenant* with the house of Israel and with the house of Judah—not according to the covenant that I made with their fathers in the day that I took them by the hand to lead them out of the land of Egypt, My covenant which they broke, though I was a Husband to them, says the LORD. But this is the covenant that I will make with the house of Israel after those days, says the LORD: I will put My law בקרבם *in their wombs, minds, midsts* and write it on לבם *their hearts, minds, midsts*; and I will be their God, and they shall be My people.

Hebrews 8:8-10 says in Greek quotation,

> Behold, the days are coming, says the LORD, when I will make a

διαθηκην καινην *new covenant* with the house of Israel and with the house of Judah — not according to the covenant that I made with their fathers in the day that I took them by the hand to lead them out of the land of Egypt, My covenant which they broke, though I was a husband to them, says the LORD. But this is the covenant that I will make with the house of Israel after those days, says the LORD: I will put My law in their διανοιαν *minds*, and write it on their καρδιας *hearts*; and I will be their God, and they shall be My people.

It can be seen that the logic of the Greek quotation makes little sense without knowledge of the Hebrew original. First, the Greek διαθη–κην καινην *new covenant* might suggest something different and not orig-inal. That is, indeed the covenant discussed is "new" relative to the Mosaic covenant given on Sinai; but, knowing the Hebrew original ברית חדשה *renewed covenant,* the reader can realize that Sinai is in the midst of an original and then renewed covenant since Sinai is not the first covenant. The so-called "New Testament" is here communicated to have preceded Sinai, to have been broken, and to have been revitalized following Sinai — a fact that makes perfect sense for One Who calls Himself "The First and the Last" and the "Last Adam" relative to the "First Adam." Second, the Greek term διανοιαν *minds* is but the translation of the Hebrew term קרבם *their wombs, minds, midsts.* That is, the "mind" discussed is also the "womb" and the "midst"; it is something generative and focal, not merely something mental — a fact that makes perfect sense in the case of Eden where the focal point is in the "midst" of the Garden relative to the first command to "be fruitful and multiply." Third, the Greek word καρδιας *hearts* is a rendering of the Hebrew לבם *their hearts, minds, midsts.* That is, the "heart" considered is also something mental and central — a fact that makes perfect sense in the case of the consumption of the venomous false vine on the Tree of Life being corrected by the True Vine on the tree of death consuming fatal poison in John 19:30.

The Greek "New Testament" is a commentary and exposition on the Hebrew "Old Testament" that is analogous and infinitely superior to the "Oral Law" of the Rabbis. The Greek translation does not fix the Hebrew original so much as it explains it. The Greek does not have an indepen-dent meaning, as we have seen in the above comparisons. In a sense, the Greek "New Testament" renews nuances otherwise lost in the remaining belief-systems that claim Biblical authority. There is, however, a trace of this logic in what is now called "Orthodox Judaism," i.e. the oral religion of the Rabbis or Pharisees.

Jews of the Pharisaic school begin to learn the Hebrew Alphabet (Aleph-Beth) in this way: "Teach wisdom." The imperative "Teach wisdom" is based on the first two letters of the Hebrew alphabet: א and ב respectively. To consider this in English, the letters A and B can be spelled out phonetically as Ay and Bee. The Hebrew letters א and ב can be spelled out as אלף and בית. As an illustration, spelling out the full name of the letters yields A = א = אלף = *to teach* and B = ב = בית = *temple, house*, both of which are understood as a *womb* and *wisdom* (Exodus 1:10-21). As such, we have the expression A-B = ב-א = Aleph-Beth = Teach wisdom. Solomon (the wise) built God's physical temple (house/womb) and One built God's spiritual temple (womb/rebirth). 1 Chronicles 17:10-11 says "...I tell you that the Lord will *build you a house*. And it shall be when your days are fulfilled, when you must go to be with your fathers, that I will *set up your seed after you, who will be of your sons*...." which is a statement that ultimately referred to Christ who rebuilt the Temple in three days as He was reborn out of a cave. Seneca, in Epistle XLI entitled "On the God Within Us," calls a cave a "place NOT BUILT WITH HANDS" in that it was made by God Himself; Hebrews 9 discusses how Christ entered the "more perfect Tabernacle NOT MADE WITH HANDS," before the discussion of His death, and subsequently discusses how Christ did not officiate in the earthly temple that was a mere copy "MADE WITH HANDS" and not by God Himself. Consider:

> In Him you were also circumcised with the circumcision MADE WITHOUT HANDS, by putting off the body of the sins of the flesh, by the circumcision of Christ, BURIED WITH HIM in baptism, in which you also were raised with Him through faith in the working of God, who RAISED HIM FROM THE DEAD. And you, being dead in your trespasses and the uncircumcision of your flesh, He has made alive together with Him.... (Colossians 2:11-15).

The womb is wisdom i.e. an organic house, a temple that grows into a holy habitation:

> Now, therefore, you are no longer strangers and foreigners, but fellow citizens with the saints and members of the HOUSEHOLD of God, having been BUILT on the *foundation* [Hebrew סוד *secret, mystery, foundation*] of the apostles and prophets, Jesus Christ Himself being the *chief cornerstone*, in whom the whole BUILDING, BEING FITTED TOGETHER, GROWS into a holy TEMPLE in the Lord, in whom you also are being BUILT TOGETHER for a DWELLING PLACE of God in the Spirit (Ephesians 2:18-22).

We may observe the organic "house-temple-womb" in Psalm 139:13-16 from where it seems the Ephesians quote was derived:

> For You formed my inward parts; You covered me in my mother's WOMB... My frame was not hidden from You, when I was MADE in *secret*, and SKILLFULLY WROUGHT in the lowest parts of the earth [earth/mother]. Your eyes saw גלמי *my fetus*, being yet unformed. And in Your BOOK they all were written, the days FASHIONED for me....

The reader can see that ב = בית = *house* = *temple* = רחם*womb*, "womb" being held synonymously with "wisdom"; therefore, א Teach ב wisdom, for אב spells the Hebrew words *father* and *verdure* along with a Chaldee word *fruit* (like that of a Tree). "Be FRUITFUL and multiply" (Genesis 1:28); "...I tell you that the Lord will BUILD YOU A HOUSE...." (1 Chronicles 17:10-11). The reader can see that a Hebrew "house" can be a "womb" with a specific connection to "wisdom": "Through wisdom a house is built, and by understanding it is established" (Proverbs 24:3); "The wise woman builds her house, but the foolish pulls it down with her hands" (Proverbs 14:1) abortively, i.e. a *house* (*wisdom/fertility*) is torn down by foolish (unfruitful) hands. Surely the forbidden tree did not grant both wisdom and death, since the wise woman builds her house. Let us now turn our attention to Eden.

The Hebrew root עדן, from where the name *Eden* is derived, does not occur in Scripture, but an Arabic cognate means *to be soft, pliant, and lax* and carries with it the idea of *delight*. From here, it appears this root and its derivatives are consistently interpreted relative to the Arabic definition; however, the employments of this root's derivatives shed light on the original concept of the Hebrew root. When viewing these derivatives, it would seem that Eden is more clearly understood under the context of fructification, perpetuity, life, i.e. *the inheritance given through fertility* as in fruitful land, and, ultimately, the *Fruitful Womb*. It is the conviction of this author that *Eden* indicates *Fertility*, for it was the Garden of Fertility from which Adam was expelled, contrary to the difficult and accursed soil over which he was to toil, since he was made from the אדמה *ground* which is the Egyptian *red ground* or *accursed soil* that is difficult to cultivate: "In the sweat of your face you shall eat bread until you return to the אדמה *ground*, for out of it you were taken; for dust you are, and to dust you shall return" (Genesis 3:19). Adam was made from the sterile ground outside of the land of Fertility and, choosing infertility, he chose to dwell outside of Eden. "And the Lord God formed man of the dust of the אדמה *sterile ground*, and breathed into his nostrils the breath of life; and man became a living being" (Genesis 2:7); "THEN the Lord God took the man and put him in the garden of *Eden* [*Fertile ground*] to cultivate and guard it" (Genesis 2:15). Adam was taken from infertility in order to be made fruitful, for his body was from "red ground," that is, ground that had been burned (like pottery) and the currency put into his vessel animated him towards fruitfulness, for it is written that the Lord God יצר *formed like pottery* the man from the red ground so that his body was initially dead and then received inspiration to sustain and reproduce life... a situation that indicates a אמנה *covenant,* which, in Greek, is πιστις *faith* (Habakkuk 2:4; Galatians 3:11): "For as the BODY WITHOUT THE SPIRIT IS DEAD, so faith without works is dead also" (James 2:26). Sarah was astounded at the concept of bearing a child, not at the idea of having mere "pleasure" when she said, "After I am worn out and my master is old, will I now have this עדנה *pleasure*?" The word rendered "pleasure" here is derived from the same root as "Eden." Thus, Sarah was contemplating a rejuvenated, fruitful womb, not simple "pleasure," and the word she used to describe this fertility is of the same family as "Eden." Consider Isaiah 47:1-9:

> Come down and sit in the dust, o virgin daughter of Babylon; sit on the ground without a throne, o daughter of the Chaldeans! For you shall no more be called TENDER and DELICATE. Take the millstones and grind meal. Remove your veil, take off the skirt, uncover the thigh, pass through the rivers. Your NAKEDNESS shall be uncovered, yes, your shame will be seen; I will take vengeance, and I will not arbitrate with a man. As for our Redeemer, the LORD of hosts is His name, The Holy One of Israel. Sit in silence, and go into darkness, o daughter of the Chaldeans; for you shall no longer be called The Lady of Kingdoms. I was angry with My people; I have profaned My inheritance, and given them into your hand. You showed them no mercy; on the elderly you laid your yoke very heavily. And you said, 'I shall be a lady forever,' so that you did not take these things to heart, nor remember the latter end of them. Therefore hear this now, עדינו *you who are given to pleasures*, who dwell securely, who say in your heart, 'I am, and there is no one else besides me; I shall not sit as a widow, nor shall I know the loss of children'; but these two things shall come to you in a moment, in one day: the LOSS OF CHILDREN, and widowhood. They shall come upon you in their fullness because of the multitude of your sorceries, for the great abundance of your enchantments.

Notice that the "eden-like-one = עדינו *you who are given to pleasures*" is juxtaposed to a "loss of children." Since the loss of children is opposed to the one "given to pleasures," it would seem as if this "pleasure" is a similitude of a womb's fructification that forwards inheritance. Consider Nehimiah 9:22-25:

> Moreover You gave them kingdoms and nations, and divided
> them into districts. So they took possession of the land of
> Sihon, the land of the king of Heshbon, and the land of Og
> king of Bashan. You also multiplied their children as the stars
> of heaven, and brought them into the land which You had told
> their fathers to go in and possess. So the people went in and
> possessed the land; you subdued before them the inhabitants
> of the land, the Canaanites, and gave them into their hands,
> with their kings and the people of the land, that they might do
> with them as they wished. And they took strong cities and a rich
> land, and possessed houses full of all goods, cisterns already
> dug, vineyards, olive groves, and fruit trees in abundance.
> So they ate and were filled and grew fat, ויתעדנו *and delighted
> themselves* in Your great goodness.

Notice that they "delighted, Edened" themselves in vineyards, olive groves, and fruit trees... they delighted themselves in the INHERITANCE of a fruitful land, they delighted in Fertility. Consider 2 Samuel 1:24:

> O daughters of Israel, weep over Saul, who clothed you in
> scarlet, with   עדנים *luxuries*; who put ornaments of gold on your
> apparel.

This passage connects the "daughters" of Israel to "עדנים *eden-like things, luxuries*." Consider Psalm 36:7-8:

> How precious is Your lovingkindness, O God! Therefore the
> children of men put their trust under the shadow of Your wings.
> They are abundantly satisfied with the fullness of Your house,
> and You give them drink from the נחל *river, inheritance* of עדניך
> *Your Edens, pleasures.*

Notice that Psalm 36:7-8 above discusses "inheritance" relative of God's "Edens", a word-picture tantamount to a fruitful inheritance. "Eden" is also related to "time" in Chaldee, for in Daniel 2: 8, 9, 21; 3: 5, 15; 4:16, 23, 25, 32; and 7:12, 25, a form of the letters that spell "Eden" is rendered "time." It may prove beneficial here to consider "gestation" as a parallel to "time" regarding the fulfillment of God's Word through fertility. Accordingly, we may also compare "time" to gestation in Genesis 18:11-13:

Abraham and Sarah were already old and well advanced in years, and Sarah was past the age of childbearing. So Sarah laughed to herself as she thought, "After I am worn out and my master is old, will I now have this עדנה *pleasure, Eden*?" Then the Lord said to Abraham, "Why did Sarah laugh and say, 'Will אלד *I really bear* a child, now that I am old?... I will return to you כעת חיה *at the time of life, Spring*, and Sarah will have a SON."

Sarah said "have this עדנה *pleasure, fertility, Edenlike existence*" and God recounted her thoughts as "bear"... a "son"; therefore, we can see that *Eden* indicates fertility and is analogous to the Spring season, the "Time of Life." The name "חוה **Eve**" means "Life," and Song of Songs 4:12 calls a woman a "**garden**." Furthermore, Genesis 13:10 compares the physical beauty of Sodom and Gomorrah to that of **Eden**, and the Narrative concerning Sarah's fertility, Sarah's Eden (Genesis 18) is juxtaposed to the Narrative concerning the destruction of Sodom and Gomorrah (also Genesis 18), the annihilation of gross infertility from sickeningly unfruitful and unnatural unions. It is interesting to note that Sodom (Flaming) and Gomorrah (Rebellious People) were destroyed along with Admah (Red [**Adam**]) and Zeboiim (Shiny), as Deuteronomy 29:23 recounts, for a נחש *serpent* literally means a *shining one*, as does the word נהר *river*, the serpentine fertilizer of dry land.

Genesis 2:10 is commonly rendered, "Now a river went out of Eden to water the garden, and from there it parted and became four riverheads" The word ארבע *four* comes from the root רבע which can mean "*to lie with, carnally*," i.e. *copulation* as it is employed in Leviticus 19:19. Reexamining the rivers of Eden, the reader may now conclude that "Eden" is analogous to a "Fruitful Womb":

> Now a river went out of *Eden* [*Fertility*] to water the garden, and from there it parted and became four riverheads. The name of the first is פישון *Diffusion of Waters*; it is the one which skirts the whole land of חוילה *The Bringing Forth of Pregnancy*, where there is gold. And the gold of that land is good; bdellium and the onyx stone are there. The name of the second river is גיחון *Belly, as the Source of the Fetus*; it is the one which goes around the whole land of שוכ *The Cup, The Womb**. The name of the third river is חדקל *Light, Swift*; it is the one which goes toward the east of אשור *Lifted Up, Exalted* [like a גגביע *cup, a womb, the bell of a flower as the tops of the menorah are described*]. The fourth river is the פרת *Fruitful*, (Genesis 2:10-14). (*See *Did God Plant the Forbidden Tree?* Collins p. 167-170).

Here we have a description of the privileged ease of birth that was the orthodox design of gestation which, because of sin, became belabored and even dangerous. The point is that what is considered to be "orthodox" may not, indeed, be original because the historical demarcation was not drawn far enough back in time. *Eden* seems to mean *Fertility*, which, had sin not entered it, would have rendered a more "pleasurable" birth process along with its "delightful" fruit.

In Hebrew, *heart* and *mind* are the same word; *wisdom* and *womb* are the same idea; *womb* and *house* are the same word; thus, *heart* and *womb* are related. For instance, we read of Adam's circumcised heart being utilized for the creation of his wife; this situation makes his heart analogous to the intended fertility of the womb. Again, *heart* and *mind* are the same Hebrew word (לב), which Hirsch considers to be from the root *to conjoin in the central core*. Davidson's Lexicon states that לב *heart and mind* are understood as *middle and core*. To be "בתוך *in the midst*" is to be in the "heart" and "mind," in the place of *life, vitality*, and (positively) *wisdom*, according to Hebrew diction. Proverbs 17:16 employs לב *mind, heart* to indicate *understanding*; so, the Tree of Life stood in the *place of understanding, the midst*. To be *in the midst, middle* is to be in the *heart, mind*; therefore, the quotidian tradition that states, "You can have God in your head but not in your heart," is at fundamental odds with the diction of Scripture, and it admits an impossible proposition that dissuades the diligent from delving into the Written Word by a preference for emotional and ephemeral responses. The name *Eden* means *Fertility,* and the *womb* is held in complementary parallel to the mind, the heart, the place of *understanding* in Scripture. The Hebrew B is ב = בית = *temple, house*, both of which are understood as a *womb* and *wisdom* (Exodus 1:10-21). The Male *heart and mind* are synonymous to the female *womb and mind* also via the word הרה *to become pregnant, to conceive in the mind* (conception), which was probably originally spelled consonantally identically to the word הר *mountain* (like a pregnant womb from which gemstones may be mined), and which is similar to the Chaldee concept of *thinking* (yet another parallel between *womb* and *wisdom*). We may observe the bride being birthed by way of Adam's exposed heart (Genesis 2:22), and the provision made for her was that she would be granted greater "conception" (Genesis 3:16) since she was "deceived" and "fell into transgression" (1 Timothy 2:14) — which should indicate to the reader that, as wisdom is parallel to a fruitful womb, folly is parallel to an abortive womb, thus the provision of greater "conception." The Hebrew letter ב, which begins the Creation Days in Genesis, signifies both a "womb" and "wisdom," therefore, life and light.

Psalm 110 says, "...in the DAY of Your power; in the beauties of holiness, from the WOMB OF THE MORNING...." The garden was planted in Fertility (where wisdom resides), and, in the midst, the mind. Since the focal-point before us is the midst of the garden, as opposed to elsewhere, we are, it would seem, viewing a literary reference to a maze-garden — a garden that has the physical pattern of the brain. The brain is in the head, and the "head" of a ziggurat is its top tier whereupon was the altar (womb); herein we see a connection between *womb* and *wisdom*. The "Tower of Babel" or Ziggurat of Babel is described by Genesis 9:4 as having " ראשו בשמים *his head in the heavens*"; the "head" or top of such a tower functioned as a celestial observatory, an altar, and was crowned with verdure. A garden (like that of Eden) could easily be compared to a fertile brain in that it was in the head of a ziggurat, and the fact that the focus is upon Eden's midst would seem to suggest that Eden was a labyrinth (at least in literary typification in that the punishments administered mirrored the crimes that necessitated them). Thus, a maze in the head of a ziggurat that slithers around an altar is quite neatly accomplished if we consider the location of the story's focus with respect to it being atop "My holy mountain" (Isaiah 11:9). A tower with a "head" in which there is a maze-garden makes it easy to conceive of the structure below the head to be the remaining body or temple or house so that one may consider this man-made mountain as resembling a person. A temple or house typifying a person could be under-stood paternally in that, from the top down, the decisions of the high priest and his successive priesthood filter down throughout the ziggurat-temple-house to the lay humanity below so that the choices of one man affect the situations of all over whom he has authority: "...the Head, from whom all the body, nourished and knit together by joints and ligaments, grows with the increase *that is* from God" (Colossians 2:19). A temple populated by people and run by its head is as a father with his children within him who descend from his wisdom (which is a type of womb). It was also a custom regarding ancient eastern monarchs that their funerals were the sights of mass, institutionalized suicide so that the fate of a man was intimately and ultimately connected to the life and death of his king... this fact says much as to the state of fallen humanity following Adam's choice. Consider: "For if we have been united together in the likeness of His death, certainly we also shall be in the likeness of His resurrection" (Romans 6:5). The "curse" (or "binding") against the soil resulted in thorns, and so we ob-serve the binding of thorns around our Head, for "...Christ is the head of the church, His body, and is himself its Savior" (Ephesians 5:23). We may also observe thorns encircling the Garden of Fertility... bound thorns encompassing wisdom... twined thorns defending positive conception... for the Hebrew word גַן *garden* is derived from the root גנן *to defend*, and gardens, like sheepfolds, were once defended by hedges of thorns. Even the idea of encircling thorns being viewed negatively is smoothly comparable to a corrupt priesthood atop a ziggurat and around its altar, for Ezekiel 2:6 calls wicked people "thorns."

The labyrinthine, serpentine path of Eden is an exquisite parallel of the Hebrew concept of parables, riddles. The Word חידה *riddle* is a παραβολη *parable (a placing beside, a juxtaposition, a parallel), i.e. a type of mirror.* Riddles or parables were more often statements than questions. Why would one think that the mysteries, the secrets, the enigmas, the mazes of God, would be initially easy to discern? — for it would seem the answer to this question is: errant tradition. In opposition, Scripture states, "It is the glory of God to conceal a thing: but the honor of kings is to search out a matter" (Proverbs 25:2). Ancient Eastern kings and their satraps ("defenders of the kingdom") possessed walled landscapes that combined the patterns of vivariums (or, antithetically, hunting grounds), orchards, and military campgrounds, called פרדסים *paradises*; inside these paradises were gardens, and, in their midst, were central trees. Since ancient eastern warfare could not be waged without first offering sacrifice, we might grasp the following:

> Now a great sign appeared in heaven: a woman clothed with the sun, with the moon under her feet, and on her head a garland of twelve stars. Then being with child, she cried out in labor and in pain to give birth. And another sign appeared in heaven: behold, a great, fiery red dragon having seven heads and ten horns, and seven diadems on his heads. His tail drew a third of the stars of heaven and threw them to the earth. And the dragon stood before the woman who was ready to give birth, to devour her Child as soon as it was born. She bore a male Child who was to rule all nations with a rod of iron. And her CHILD WAS CAUGHT UP TO GOD and His throne (Revelation 12:1-5).

A child being "caught up" is an expression used by Ovid (*The Heroides*, XI, 73-74) just prior to the child's violent death caused, in Ovid's case, by "mountain wolves" instead of a "dragon." The letters עלה spell *burnt offering*, and *elevation.* 1 Samuel 15:32-33 states,

> "Then Samuel said, 'Bring Agag king of the Amalekites.' Agag came to him מעדנת *edenically*, thinking, 'Surely the bitterness of death is past.' But Samuel said, 'As your SWORD has נשים שכלה

made women childless, so your mother תשכל *will be childless among women*. And Samuel put Agag to death before the Lord at the PLACE OF TURNING."

We must keep in mind that the Lord God יצר formed like pottery, and this formation necessitates turning. Similarly, a threshing-floor was also a place of turning, and a threshing-floor served as the foundation of the first temple. Furthermore, perverted foundation-covenants involved slaying children and burying them beneath the threshold of a house and thus beneath its ceremonial foundation whereupon the fire was kindled, for the idea of this burial was that the fiery spirit of the sacrificed child would guard the entrance to the home as a threshold guardian. Likewise, we read that "...He drove out the man; and He placed cherubim at the east of the garden of Eden, and a לחט החרב *flame of the blade* which TURNED every way, TO GUARD the way to the tree of life" (Genesis 3:24). The word להשכיל *to make childless* used above is the same consonantal spelling as *to make wise* in the Eden Narrative (Genesis 3:6) with a play on the diaphanous sibilant (or the serpentine sound) in the way that mirrors the antithetical usages of the word חטאת *sin* (negatively) which also means *sin offering* (the positive remedy for sin). The diaphanous sibilant ש is used wisely to play upon a diametrically opposed meaning that revolves around the concept of the *womb*, that is, of *wisdom*: the wise are fertile and the unwise are infertile. We understand that humanity acted foolishly in Eden. Of course, playing upon the sibilant is reminiscent of a "serpent," so to speak, for Agag was an Amalekite, and "Amalek" means "a people that lick up" and "a strangler of the people," which references negative serpentine imagery: "They shall lick the dust like a serpent..." (Micah 7:17). Again, we can perceive the imagery of Fertility and child sacrifice, a man and a "serpent" (Genesis 3:1) or "dragon" (Revelation 12:3) or "cherub" (Ezekiel 28:14). Consider the relations of a turning blade and circumcision that leads to fertility like the pruning of Adam's heart for the purpose of bearing fruit, i.e. for the cause of wisdom.

The Scriptures are not straight-forward, they are not simple narratives, and they are not easily understood. The Scriptures are filled with repeated and varied images that link to form a composite whole that, over time, reveals itself as though birthed from the mystery of an unseen womb. Within the boundaries of Scripture, there is a growth that is only perceived if the whole is accounted for all at once. It should be noted that the Tower of Bable, a ziggurat, was a place of child-sacrifice; גבר means *a strong man, warrior*, and *male child* (Job 3:3). The "strong man's house" (Matthew 12:29) is the womb, the temple. Consider:

> And He Himself [The Deity] gave some [who descend from Him]
> to be apostles, some prophets, some evangelists, and some
> pastors and teachers, for the equipping of the saints for the
> work of ministry, for the edifying of the body of Christ, till we
> all come to the unity of the faith and of the knowledge of the
> Son of God, to a perfect man, to the measure of the stature of
> the fullness of Christ; that we should no longer be CHILDREN,
> tossed to and fro and carried about with every wind of doctrine,
> by the trickery of men, in the cunning craftiness of deceit-
> ful plotting, but, speaking the truth in love, may grow up in all
> things into HIM WHO IS THE HEAD — Christ — from whom the
> WHOLE BODY, JOINED AND KNIT TOGETHER by what every joint
> supplies, according to the effective working by which every part
> does its share, causes GROWTH OF THE BODY for the edifying of
> itself in love (Ephesians 4:11-16).

Job 10:8-12 describes human gestation in this way:

> Your hands have made me and fashioned me, an intricate uni-
> ty... Remember, I pray, that You have made me like clay. And will
> You turn me into dust again? Did You not pour me out like milk,
> and curdle me like cheese, clothe me with skin and flesh, and
> KNIT ME TOGETHER WITH BONES AND SINEWS? You have granted
> me life and favor, and Your care has preserved my spirit.

Consider the ziggurat, tower, temple, house again:

> Now, therefore, you are no longer strangers and foreigners, but
> fellow citizens with the saints and members of the household
> of God, having been built on the *foundation* of the apostles and
> prophets, Jesus Christ Himself being the *chief cornerstone*, in
> whom the whole BUILDING, BEING FITTED TOGETHER, GROWS
> into a holy TEMPLE in the Lord, in whom you also are being built
> together for a dwelling place of God in the Spirit (Ephesians
> 2:18-22).

It would seem as if the construction of a ziggurat for worship whereby humanity unites with God in the air (i.e. at the apex, the mind in the head of
the body) is designed to beget children (worshippers) who will disseminate
the religion of the Deity as directed by the high priest and king. So, to think
that Babel possessed a tower whereby male children were hunted (i.e.
that practiced child sacrifice) would be a temple that proclaimed Satan as
God and is evidence of a war made directly on the gates of Heaven in the
heavenly places (i.e. atop the thorny crown of the corrupted temple). The
opposite of this putridity is the righteous renewal exhibited where Christ,

reborn from death, sent His spirit to enflame the minds of His priests who descended to disseminate the religion of God as it was intended from the beginning (and not merely 2,000 years ago). The followers of Christ were as His temples in miniature whose fiery descent was not destructive (like child-sacrifice) but constructive, generative, and accordant with the dictum, "Be fruitful and multiply." At the time of the fiery tongues of Pentecost, the vernal equinox, through the celestial movement called The Precession of the Equinoxes, had taken up residence in the constellation of Pisces. The summit of a temple, a mountain, a ziggurat was where the priesthood (like the Magi) would observe celestial matters for agricultural purposes. The recognition that the end of an astronomical age had occurred and the beginning of a new age was now manifested by The Precession of the Equinoxes as signified in the Fish was, it would seem, evidenced in the Ichthus or Fish symbol traced by the early followers of The Way that later became called "Christianity." This symbol, this fish is, in Hebrew דג, which is from the root דגה to *increase, to multiply*. The command to "Be fruitful and multiply" was carried out in a fertively ignescent manner in contrast to the infertively ignescent Babel that God Himself overthrew. The Temple is supposed to be generative, not abortive. When one considers the first command given to humanity in light of humanity's expulsion that is connected with the womb's punishment, one may reflect on how,

> ...since Adam was placed on earth, that the triumphing of the wicked is short, and the joy of the hypocrite is but for a moment? Though his haughtiness mounts up to the heavens, and his head reaches to the clouds, yet he will perish forever like his own refuse; those who have seen him will say, "Where is he?" He will fly away like a dream, and not be found; yes, he will be chased away like a vision of the night. The eye that saw him will see him no more, nor will his place behold him anymore. His children will seek the favor of the poor, and his hands will restore his wealth. His bones are full of his youthful vigor, but it will lie down with him in the dust. Though evil is sweet in his mouth, and he hides it under his tongue, though he spares it and does not forsake it, but still keeps it in his mouth, yet his food in his stomach turns sour; it becomes cobra venom within him. He swallows down riches and vomits them up again; God casts them out of his belly. He will suck the poison of cobras; the viper's tongue will slay him (Job 20: 4-16).

The idea of a child-sacrificing temple/ziggurat would say much to the "spiritual hosts of wickedness in the heavenly places" (Ephesians 6:12). With respect to a body, the womb, the wisdom, the head, the heart, and the midst are all related; anatomically, if one were to connect them with a line, one would behold a body split into two sides, and such was the pretended threat of King Solomon in order to exhibit his wisdom when he determined who the living half of the disputed child mirrored. A "house" is not to be divided against itself; rather, it is to exhibit the cell-division that is a component of its growth.

COVENANT

THE verb שבע to swear, to enter into an oath, to covenant is spelled consonantally identically to the cardinal number seven. To enter into an oath is to be connected with the number seven, and this can be observed by the consistent employment of the number seven in Scripture to indicate covenantal union and the fruit thereof. Correspondingly, the verb שבע to become satisfied, to become filled is spelled similarly to the number seven and the verb to swear (accounting for the diaphonous sibbilant שׁ). Satisfaction, seven, and an oath are all represented in the Creation account once God finished His work and "rested" (covenanted) on the "seventh Day." An oath or covenant is a binding, and such a binding is expressed in the word שבעה (from the root שבע) in passages like Numbers 5:21, where a soul is so bound. The circuit of Creation was completed on the seventh "Day," the Day of the Oath or the Covenantal Day. It must be remembered that "Day" is the title given to אור light, and this light also means life, fire, and wisdom as 2 Corinthians 4:6 translates. Creation was completed on the seventh light, that is, the covenantal wisdom of life, for life was created to perpetuate life according to God's dictum for Creation. Connectedly, the letter ב 2, house, temple, womb, wisdom is the first letter in the word בראשית in the beginning or with the Firstborn. The second word of the Creation account ברא is from the root ברא to create, and this word is related to the verb to cut and the noun ברות food. The beginning and end of the Creation deals with covenant as is indicated by initiating the process with cutting and by completing it with satiation, i.e. descriptions of a meal. It follows that Creation was breached by a meal. The fact that seven stages of development are described indicates numerically that a covenant is being discussed, and the fact that the greatest number of zodiacal constellations that can be seen at once is seven as indicated by the menorah or "Tree of Life," the shining plant that is aflame and yet unconsumed, discussed following the kindling of the seven Lights or "Days" which is reflected in Jeremiah 33:20-21:

> "Thus says the Lord: 'If you can break My covenant with the day and My covenant with the night, so that there will not be day and night in their season, then My covenant may also be broken with David My servant, so that he shall not have a son to reign on his throne, and with the Levites, the priests, My ministers.'"

The horizon, the marker of the seven visible zodiacal constellations, illustrates the covenant with the day and with the night, for the stars mark the seasons upon the edge that cuts or delineates the circular horizon where heaven meets earth, conceptually speaking. Heaven and earth meet also at the summit of a mountain or tower (temple, ziggurat). So, from a per-spective that places a summit east of an observer in the morning, the sunrise would appear to be birthed out of the horizon and the summit simultaneously, as is recalled obliquely in the ancient hymn to the fire god discussed by Dr. Sayce in Lecture V of his discussion of Babylonian reli-gion. A good case could be made that the Divine title "El *Shaddi*" can be connected to the Assyrian *sadu* or *mountain,* so that the title El Shaddi could also be considered "God of the Mountain," for this is the name that Genesis 17 uses to discuss the eventual birth of Isaac who, on a moun-tain, was raised to perpetuate God's Name, Linneage, and Temple through Abraham who concluded "...that God was able to raise [Isaac] up, even from the dead, from which he also received [Isaac] in a figurative sense" (Hebrews 11:19).

    That the Creation itself is evident of a covenant, and that the cov-enant involves creativity, compels, in Hebrew, the notion of eating, and it is this set of stipulations that necessitates that the only way this covenant of life could be broken is by eating. A ברית *covenant* is *a binding oath (often to the death)*; it is from the root ברה *to cut,* TO EAT, *to choose,* and is related to the root ברא *to create* which anticipates a product, a fruit. With respect to fruit production (offspring), it would seem that the act of creation in-tends for perpetuity that is itself covenantal. The words ברותת *food* and ברית *covenant* are derivatives of the same source, which reflects the concept that the act of eating itself was viewed as religiously sacrificial. Since the act of eating involved cutting (at least with one's teeth), and since the root ברה *to cut, to eat, to choose* is related to the root ברא *to create, to form, to make, to carve out, to cut, to fashion,* and TO BE BORN, we can observe why the Hebrew word בריאה A NEW, WONDERFUL THING along with the Chaldee word בר A SON are linked to the word ברית *covenant,* for a covenant anticipates and requires a product, a fruit, that is, viability and perpetuity. Perpetuity is a type of salvation since it preserves. As such, we can observe the link between דם *blood* and אור *light* since both can mean or indicate *life* with particular reference to birth. For instance, Ezekiel 16 describes God's beloved as a child left for dead in an open field. This child was still attached to the placenta through the umbilical cord and was "struggling in [her] blood." God commanded, "Live," which means that the cord must be cut so that life is not attached to or mingled with death, for such a union of opposites leads to death. The cut cord resulted in the life of God's beloved thereby exemplifying how the root ברה *to cut, to eat, to choose* is related to the root ברא *to create, to form, to make, to carve out, to cut, to fashion,* TO BE BORN. That the root ברה *to cut, to eat, to choose* is related to the root ברא *to create, to be born* can be seen in Proverbs 30:20 where "eating" is utilized euphemistically for copulation. A covenant made one individual part of another as eating makes the edible part of the consumer. Both consumed the same meal that united them, and this union was evidenced by the fruit thereof.

A covenant was "cut," meaning that a deliniation of sorts was made and consumption was involved, both of which were by choice. The very act of cutting a covenant involved a choice between two things and the adherence to one. If one chose to be in covenant with another, the covenantal union, i.e. the choice to be unified until death, was deemed more binding than inherent familial relation since siblings have no choice regarding physically familial bonds. A covenant was of life, for life, and it sought to perpetuate life; thus, we understand the blessing of a covenant as illustrated by the thanksgiving, and we understand, as well, the curse of a covenant or the נקם ברית *vengeance of the covenant*, as a result of violating perpetuity. The vengeance or curse of the covenant was often executed by a חרב *cutting instrument,* or *sword,* so to speak (Leviticus 26:25); this explains more of the expression "cut a covenant," which indicates both the blessing and the curse involved in such a trust, that is, two edges of the same cutting instrument based upon actions relative to words: "... Now out of His mouth goes a sharp, TWO EDGED sword..." (Revelation 19:15). Violating God's covenant caused a soul to be "cut off" (Genesis 17:14). Two people in covenant were thought of as one life in two bodies, not merely two lives in serious agreement; one can see this principle in the word ערבה *pledge*, which is from the root ערב *to intermix, to pledge*. If one member of the covenant gave his life for the other member, and that other member's life was saved, then the one who died did not technically lose his life; rather, the dead member saved his life by perpetuity through the life of the covenantal counterpart.

Generally, covenants were sealed by a meal and the sharing of blood: the meal indicated a truce, and the blood and/or wine sealed the sharing of two natures that combined to form a new being, a new creation. Specifically, the natures mingled when the blood was shared between them. A covenant is something substantial and is symbolized by physical reality that is sacrificial. Another word for ברית *covenant* is אמנה *covenant* (these are two different Hebrew words). This word אמנה *covenant* — which is translated by the Greek word πιστις *faith* in Galatians 3:10 and Hebrews 10:38 — is from the root אמן *to support, to stay,* TO NURSE, *to bring up, to be firm, faithful, and true*, and it produces the words אמוןCHILD *(even adopted child)*, אומונה *steadiness, truth, faithfulness,* אאמנה *beam, lintel,*

אמנה *education, nursing,* אמת *truth, as opposed to deceit,* and אמן *Amen.* It is apparent that a mother's and father's obligation to their child is as much a product of their covenant as the child itself; therefore, a couple cannot participate in reproduction rightfully without an oath to the death (a covenant) that is carried out in both signification and in practicality through the care and cultivation of their fruit. Covenants aim towards fruit production by first binding and then begetting: the physical binding is the sign, the true binding is the initiator of the physical binding that carries through to the product. In a sense, a covenant constructively divides two parties in half and unites half of one to half of the other so that there is a bond between two formerly distinct wholes; this bond is expressed wholly in a child who is the link between two families; this bonding process continued results in community as signified by the oath to the death, the covenant, the marriage we call Holy Communion. In other words, the spiritual binding of two is illustrated by their physical binding and is proven by their fruit (in Holy Communion's case, the "Fruit of the Spirit"). Fruit production as a result of physical binding, but devoid of righteous spiritual binding, is a covenant of death... that is, a covenant cut for a purpose antithetical to the very nature of a covenant's design to be of life, for life, and maintained by producing more life. Cutting a covenant with no intended viable product is a grim inversion and mockery of the standard: Life. There is a division that is the standard that produces life through the bond of a covenant, and there is a division that is a parasitic mocker that reduces life through the bond of a covenant; the first is of life, the second is of death. Life itself is mocked by the production of fruit that is the output of insubstantiality since the substance is supposed to be followed by the sign and epitomized by the fruit. According to the brilliant work of H. C. Trumbul, a covenant was initiated by a truce (a meal) and then sealed by blood (a drink of blood, wine, or a mixture of the two). The consumption of blood (wine) was understood to be the unification of the covenanting parties, for the ענב *cluster* of grapes is derived from the root ענב *to join together, to bind together,* and wine is called the "blood" of the grape in Genesis 49:11. Since vines were called "trees" in Hebrew (Ezekiel 15), a grapevine is, in effect, a tree of blood that is supposed to unite its partakers constructively, not destructively as in the case of Noah. Christ called Himself the "True Vine" in John 15:1.

Covenants came with a blessing and a curse (or vengeance). The blessing looked towards the fruit, the creative nature of the covenant. The curse or vengeance of a covenant was its referee, its patrolman. In other words, if either party defected, or if both of the covenanting parties were to fracture mutually from the oath by which they bound themselves, the curse would take effect as a penalty for deceit by the fact that the boundary of the covenant was transgressed. Confusion regarding "curses" has ensued because of an ignorance of covenants, and the ignorance of covenants has caused many to believe that the Law of Moses was accursed as opposed to the fact that the Law of Moses was a Covenant that contained a curse to guard it.

> For as many as are of the works of the law are under the curse;
> for it is written, "Cursed is everyone who does not continue in
> all things which are written in the book of the law, to do them."
> But that no one is justified by the law in the sight of God is
> evident, for "the just shall live by faith." Yet the law is not of
> faith, but "the man who does them shall live by them." Christ
> has redeemed us from the curse of the law, having become a
> curse for us (for it is written, "Cursed is everyone who hangs
> on a tree"), that the blessing of Abraham might come upon the
> Gentiles in Christ Jesus, that we might receive the promise of
> the Spirit through faith. (Galatians 3:10-14).

In fact, the word אלה means both a *covenant* and a *curse* since covenants were oaths to the death and therefore under penalty of death if broken. That is, if the faith was broken, the offender necessitated the "curse" or the "vengeance" to be exacted upon himself. A covenant is a binding oath, and should one break this binding until death, then one is cursed. The Hebrew word ארר *to curse* also means *to bind*, and this is made apparent in that God "cursed" Satan in Genesis 3:14 and had Satan "bound" in Revelation 20:2. A covenant is binding by being maintained and this maintenance is blessed, whereas a curse is the exchange of a blessed binding for a nonviable binding that is maintained consistently and unfavorably. Again, a ברית is a *covenant, a binding oath*; it is from the root ברה *to cut, TO EAT*, and its synonym אמנה *covenant* or *faith* is derived from the root אמן *to support* from which the words אמון *child, atificer* (one who cuts, like a carpenter), אמת *truth*, and אמן *Amen* extend.

The word אמנה *covenant* is from the same root as אמת *truth*, so breaking a covenant was considered deceit. "...Adam was not deceived, but the woman being deceived, fell into transgression..." (1 Timothy 2:14), and we see that the woman "took of his [Satan's] fruit, and she ate" (Genesis 3:6), which indicates that the woman broke covenant with God by entering into covenant with Satan. Furthermore, "she gave also to her husband with her, and he ate" (Genesis 3:6) from her hand, which means that Adam became joined to Satan through his bride. In other words, the bride broke covenant with Adam to join Satan, and Adam broke covenant with

God to join his wife. Thus, Adam was joined to Death by proxy of his bride, even though he was not deceived mentally. That Adam was not deceived indicates that he openly rebelled against God on account of his heart, for the bride was made from the exposure of his heart, " אחת מצלעתיו *one from the sides of him*," which seems to indicate the "circumcised heart," in one respect. In another respect, the "sides" seem also to indicate literarily the "sides" of Abraham's sacrifice that are often translated as "the halves opposite each other" (Genesis 15:10) but are literally, " איש בתרי לקרא רעהו *half of a man to meet his neighbor*," i.e. the two halves are composed of a *man* and his *neighbor*, the neighbor being the אשה *wife* of the man. In this, we can note the following connections: "You shall love your NEIGHBOR as yourself" (Leviticus 19:18); "Let none of you think evil in your heart against your NEIGHBOR; and do not love a false oath. For all these are things that I hate" (Zechariah 8:17); "So husbands ought to love their own WIVES as their own bodies; he who loves his WIFE loves himself" (Ephesians 5:28); "...the Lord has been witness between you and the WIFE of your youth, with whom you have dealt treacherously; yet she is your companion and your wife by covenant. But did He not make them ONE, having a remnant of the Spirit? And why ONE? He seeks godly offspring" (Malachi 2:14-15). The "side" is as the "half," and these two halves are expressed genetically in the offspring as is the fruit that results from the circumcised heart or the pruned plant. Man can take a blade and cut a body in two, but such a splitting brings death. God can take a blade, "The Sword of The Spirit," "The Flaming Sword," and cut a body in two so that such a splitting brings life as expressed in the halves that constitute a child. A child is, genetically, half of his father and half of his mother. A child is the expression of the human uniting with God in that life, not death, results in the mingling that is procreation. Killing a child is severing the divine half (i.e. God) from the body of the child; therefore, killing a child is a way to brandish a destructive blade against God; thus, Uriah's death resulted in Solomon's nameless older brother's death as Nathan declared, "Now therefore, the sword shall never depart from your house, BECAUSE YOU HAVE DESPISED ME, and have taken the wife of Uriah the Hittite to be your wife" (2 Samuel 12:10). This "sword" was destructive, not constructive. The "Sword of the Spirit" (Ephesians 6:17) is "The Word of God" (Hebrews 4:12) that is "like fire" (Jeremiah 23:29), for it is constructive, not destructive, like the "Flaming Sword which turned every way, to guard the way to The Tree of LIFE" (Genesis 3:24). God's Sword begets offspring through the proclamation of Good News that unites DNA with the One Who gave it. God's sword does not slay His own children, thus the destructive fire and the knife were not, by The Word of God, applied to Isaac. The ancient east regarded lightning as a sword as it also regarded storms as illustrations of fertility as evidenced by the verdant growth that ensued on account of land's hydration.

The problem of the first sequence of sin is that the First Adam proceeded against the will of God by joining himself to death through and on account of his bride. The solution to sin came about by the Last Adam proceeding according to the will of God by joining himself to mortality through and on account of His bride and then annulling the covenant (or marriage) to death whereby "one from his sides" who "struggled in her blood" (Ezekiel 16) could be severed from her attachment to death (as a child is cut from its dead placenta) by being washed in the blood of the One who bore her as Adam once bore his bride by the hand of God from his exposed heart, so to speak. It would seem that such a situation brings more clarity to the expression "born again" which, at the time of Christ's earthly days, indicated "conversion" as the result of repentance signified by being washed in water. Another birth is necessary in order to complete a covenant with life if abortion occurs, for breaking a covenant is, essentially, to commit an abortion. Severing an oath to the death is equivalent to wishing death upon the other constituent who entered into and maintained the covenant faithfully, and this dismality is as taking innocent life that grew as a result of the mingled natures of the covenantal constituents. The "curse" or "vengeance" of a covenant takes effect upon the covenant's severance because it thwarts the attack against the innocent party by turning the deceit and the consequences thereof back upon the offender in due time; thus, the "curse" or "vengeance" is effectually a covenant's guardian:

> Christ has redeemed us from the curse of the law, HAVING BE-
> COME A CURSE FOR US (for it is written, "Cursed is everyone who
> hangs on a tree"), that the blessing of Abraham might come
> upon the Gentiles in Christ Jesus, that we might receive the
> promise of the Spirit through πιστεως = אמנה *covenant* (Gala-
> tians 3:10-14).

That is, Christ became a "curse" for us in the sense that He became our Defender. If we live until death in covenant with Christ, then our marriage is solidified by death so that its conclusion cannot be altered. Since Christ can no longer die, and we die as he died once, we can only die once and must therefore live eternally as He lives eternally. Not living in marriage to Christ until death solidifies the divorce, whereby one dies eternally being married eternally to Death as opposed to Christ, which means that one would exist forever with the Accuser and not the Defender. That the curse of the covenant would involve death is obvious when a covenant is an oath *to the death*: if the covenant was broken, *death* would pursue the guilty party. In essence, one's choice to break a covenant is a silent admission that one wished his covenanting counterpart to be dead because a covenant is an oath (often to the death, unless otherwise specified as in the case with Abraham's servant in Genesis 24:41). Since one deceitfully wished death upon his own counterpart, the curse of the covenant was in place to throw back onto him justly what destruction he wished for his counterpart unjustly. We can observe the "curse of the Law" in Deuteronomy 28. A covenant ultimately was to produce life by initially joining counterparts. For instance, Adam was to join to God *through* (ב) his bride (Genesis 2:24) in order to receive the blessing of the covenant: "Be fruitful and multiply...." The blessing sought fruit, and the curse punished the subversion of the fruit production by the fact that the curse took effect when the covenant was broken which therefore nullified any further possibility of producing the same fruit production that was thwarted.

To be "naked" (עֵרִירִי) means, in Biblical Hebrew, to be "childless" and also to be "dead" as we see illustrated plainly when Abraham laments his "nakedness" regarding not having a naturally born heir in Genesis 15:2 and this "nakedness" being recounted as walking in a "dead body" in Hebrews 11:12. Numbers 25:1-5 mandates that the punishment for consuming the fruit of the womb by fiery wood is crucifixion, thus, "If a man has committed a sin deserving of death, and he is put to death, AND YOU HANG HIM ON A TREE, his body shall not remain overnight on the tree, but you shall surely bury him that day, so that you do not defile the land which the Lord your God is giving you *as* an inheritance; FOR HE WHO IS HANGED IS ACCURSED OF GOD" (Deuteronomy 21:22-23). One cannot compel God to curse another by hanging the other on a tree. Rather, one puts himself under God's curse by violating the covenant of life spiritually in taking innocent life physically. The unholy fruit of this decision is the corpse suspended from a tree symbolizing the fruit of death and signifying the curse that the dead fruit called down by his own actions in opposition to the life his former covenant anticipated and required.

In short, there are several Hebrew words for "covenant." Summarily, a covenant is an oath to the death. Such an oath must, of necessity, be vindicated by the actions of the covenanting parties. Should those actions not be accomplished, or should those actions be worked against, the covenant is broken. The breaker of a covenant necessarily wishes the death of the other constituent of the covenant when a violation of an oath *to the death* has occurred, and this situation is analogous to both murder and abortion in that an innocent's life is taken despite the former stipulations whereby the unified path was to be tread (murder) and in that the innocent party cannot compel his counterpart's maintenance of the covenant (abortion). The blessing (fruit) of the covenant (binding blessing) is thwarted when the covenant is broken which causes the curse (binding vengeance) to reflect the wickedness of the offender back upon the offender in order to thwart a further breach. As such, death, which is the result of breaking an oath to the death, limits the amount of evil one can perform since the covenant with life has been broken. The fact that we move and breathe is evidence of a covenant made prior to our birth that resulted in our birth. The fact that we die is evidence of both a covenant made prior to our birth and a covenant we made after our birth. Death is the curse of the covenant, and this curse is two-fold: (1) For those who reject the original covenant with Life, death limits their decision against life and perpetuates their deaths; thus, we may comprehend eternal death; (2) For those who reject the secondary covenant with Death in order to embrace the original covenant with Life, death limits the amount that the secondary covenant with death affects those seeking to return to the pristine state of perfection; thus we may comprehend eternal life in that one can die in covenant with life in an oath to the death where death is no longer possible.

God is innocent. By breaking covenant with Him, we necessarily wish His death, and such a death would be analogous to murder and to abortion. The punishment for killing the innocent by wood and fire is hanging (Numbers 25) or stoning (Leviticus 20). It should be noted that the word עץ means *wood, gallows, cross* and *tree* while the word אור means *light, life, fire,* and *wisdom*. It should also be recalled דם *blood is* called life (Genesis 9:4). A "Tree of Life" could at once be tree of fire as well as a cross of blood, a menorah and a vine, for wine is the "blood of grapes" (Genesis 49:11). Christ is called "The True Vine," and He was hung on a tree even though He was and is "The Light of the World." In other words, Christ was punished as if He had killed an innocent by wood and fire (since Numbers 25 says that such murder is to be punished by crucifixion) when it was humanity that punished Christ for mankind's sin. Christ, therefore, "bore our transgressions" literally through covenant. According to the connected meanings of the synonymous words for "covenant," Christ is a murder victim and a type of abortion, for it is obvious that Christ was "murdered," as it is written, "The God of our fathers raised up Jesus whom you murdered by hanging on a tree" (Acts 5:30). Since Christ is raised (i.e. born again) and can no longer die, He is the "Holy Child" (Acts 4:27) who is the Initiator and Fruit of our covenant with the Father, despite the fact that our sin, our breach of the covenant, made us the terminators, the slayers, and the consumers of our God's Fruit, His Firstborn, our Redeemer.

HEBREW IN GREEK ATTIRE

SCRIPTURE is a library of riddles, which means that there is something to be discovered. The logic of the riddles is found chiefly in Hebrew, and it is essential to view the so-called Greek "New Testament" through a Hebrew lens. It proves beneficial to consider the "New Testament" as a Greek explanation of the Hebrew Scriptures that surpasses mere translation. If one tests the proposition forwarded here, a previously unseen and startling uniformity should become apparent in both the "Old Testament" and the "New Testament."

Hebrews 5:12-14; 6:1-6 states,

> For though by this time you ought to be teachers, you need someone to teach you again the first principles of the oracles of God; and you have come to need milk and not solid food. For everyone who partakes only of milk is unskilled in the word of righteousness, for he is a babe. But solid food belongs to those who are of full age, that is, those who by reason of use have their senses exercised to discern both good and evil. Therefore, leaving the discussion of the elementary principles of Christ, let us go on to perfection, not laying again the foundation of repentance from dead works and of faith toward God, of the doctrine of baptisms, of laying on of hands, of resurrection of the dead, and of eternal judgment. And this we will do if God permits. For it is impossible for those who were once enlightened, and have tasted the heavenly gift, and have become partakers of the Holy Spirit, and have tasted the good word of God and the powers of the age to come, if they fall away, to renew them again to repentance, since they crucify again for themselves the Son of God, and put Him to an open shame.

The discussion of renewal, recrucifixion, and shame are covenantal references that describe the breach of an oath. In a covenant, the act of breaking it is a silent admission of the wish of death for the innocent party that subsequently induces the "curse" or "vengeance" of the covenant to be ruled against the infractor; however, ignorance of covenants has led to a variety of misapplications that aim at the lowest, and not the highest, common denominator so that the common man remains common and the wisest of them exists in stunted growth. The passage above discusses what is useful for "babes" and is equivalent to "milk" as opposed to "solid food." In short, what seems to be a staple of much organized "Christianity" is here recounted as infant food; and, if maturation does not ensue with positive fruitfulness, Christ is said to be put to "an open shame." Similarly, Strabo, born some six decades before Christ, said in his *Geography*,

In the first place, I remark that the poets were not alone in sanctioning myths, for long before the poets the states and lawgivers had sanctioned them as a useful expedient, since they had an insight into the natural affections of the reasoning animal; for man is eager to learn, and his fondness for tales is a prelude to this quality. It is fondness for tales, then, that induces children to give their attention to narratives and more and more to take part in them. The reason for this is that myth is a new language to them — a language that tells them, not of things as they are, but of a different set of things. And what is new is pleasing, and so is what one did not know before; and it is just this that makes men eager to learn. But if you add thereto the marvelous and the portentous, you thereby increase the pleasure, and pleasure acts as a charm to incite to learning. At the beginning we must needs make use of such bait for children, but as the child advances in years we must guide him to the knowledge of facts, when once his intelligence has become strong and no longer needs to be coaxed. Now every illiterate and uneducated man is, in a sense, a child, and, like a child, he is fond of stories; and for that matter, so is the half-educated man, for his reasoning faculty has not been fully developed, and, besides, the mental habits of his childhood persist in him. Now since the portentous is not only pleasing, but fear-inspiring as well, we can employ both kinds of myth for children, and for grown-up people too. In the case of children we employ pleasing myths to spur them on, and the fear-inspiring myths to deter them. Most of those who live in the cities are incited to emulation by the myths that are pleasing, when they hear the poets narrate mythical deeds of heroism, such as the Labors of Heracles or of Theseus, or hear of honors bestowed by gods, or, indeed, when they see paintings or primitive images or works of sculpture which suggest any similar happy issue of fortune in mythology; but they are deterred from evil courses when, either through descriptions or through typical representations of objects unseen, they learn of divine punishments, terrors, and threats—or even when they merely believe that men have met with such experiences. For in dealing with a crowd of women, at least, or with any promiscuous mob, a philosopher cannot influence them by reason or exhort them to reverence, piety and faith; nay, there is need of religious fear also, and this cannot be aroused without myths and marvels. For thunderbolt, aegis, trident, torches, snakes, thyrsus-lances,—arms of the gods—are myths, and so is the entire ancient theology.

The "ancient theology" to which Strabo referred is pagan, and his cynicism regarding its literal interpretation could hardly be avoided by the fact that the "deities" involved were obvious inventions crafted for ulterior purposes. The point is that Strabo did not believe that a reasonable man could reason with unreasonable men. Instead, a reasonable man would appeal to reasonable men with reason, but a reasonable man would not appeal to unreasonable men with reason. Both the scribe of Hebrews and Strabo himself, though different in their respective religious beliefs, adhered to the same constant, the same truth that unskilled and unlearned men are "babes." The argument of Hebrews appears more hopeful by the fact that it appeals to babes with the hopes of cultivating them towards mature fruit, whereas Strabo relies on versions of the truth to affect masses of the uninitiated while sharper images of the same truth guide the elite who rule the masses. Consider that "Nahash" the Amonite in I Samuel 11 is the same word as the Hebrew "serpent" of Genesis 3. For the majority, a "serpent" deceived our first human mother — which is not necessarily a false statement; rather, it is a version of the truth that is forwarded by deflection and potential abstraction even though the word is precise and elusively explanatory. Though Scripture utilizes riddles at the highest level, the basic concept of intentional obscurant is not unique to the Bible. For instance, when the Babylonian or Assyrian priesthood wished to hide something with words, it did so through riddles. Whenever they wanted their words to be taken without misinterpretation, they wrote plainly and in an unmistakable manner. Yet, the religions of the Babylonians and Assyrians often robed themselves in linguistic arcana in order to preserve and protect its secrets. In the ancient east, religious texts were written to be read with intentional difficulty in order to mask hidden knowledge from the unitiated. In the astronomical work called "The Observations of Bel," we are informed that "on the high-places the son is burnt"; a prescribed prayer (recorded by Sayce in his *Lectures on Babylonian and Assyrian Religion*) that accompanied child-sacrifice discusses the "establisher of *law*," and this word "*law*" is, literally, "*secret wisdom*." One can see in this gruesome word-picture that the ritualistic *slaughter of children* was related to *secret wisdom*. Likewise, the Hebrew letters שכל spell both *wisdom* and *abortion* (depending on how the sibilant ש is pronounced). One should consider the punishment against the womb of our first mother (Genesis 3:16) relative to the ability "*to make one wise*" discussed in Genesis 3:6.

It is the conviction of this author that the constant of truth has been moving through time for various purposes since the Fall of Man and that it has been grasped by some abstractly through analogy and by others specifically by way of proof. "Now faith is the substance of things hoped for, the evidence of things not seen" (Hebrews 11:1). Let us consider a forest relative to a garden. Both a forest and a garden can comprise similar and identical entities. The one is uncultivated and the other is cultivated; accordingly, positively untouched nature is nature in its infancy, whereas positively cultivated nature is nature in its maturity. It seems that Scripture is the positively cultivated record of intended nature set in the midst of an unintended lack of cultivation, and it is therefore our obligation to recognize our Scriptural immaturity so that we may cultivate the seed implanted within us as opposed to being satiated by infantile formula suitable for controlling masses enough to grow wealthy in gold and impoverished in the riches of the knowledge of God simultaneously, i.e. two states of diametric opposition. People are Biblically commanded to grow from cognitive infancy and are not to remain in it "that their hearts may be encouraged, being knit together in love, and attaining to all riches of the full assurance of understanding, to the knowledge of the mystery of God, both of the Father and of Christ, in whom are hidden all the treasures of wisdom and knowledge" (Colossians 2:2-3). What then is this "mystery of God"? It is useful to notice that the Hebrew word סוד secret also means an assembly sitting together for consultation, deliberation, and intimacy; this word is from the root יסד to lay the foundation, and it produces the יסוד the base of an altar, like the altar at which the high priest officiated. By definition, officiating at the altar contains or is a "secret" — which is why the High Priest alone could but enter the Holy of Holies once per year in the marital ceremony called "Atonement" or literally "Covering."

"For every high priest taken from among men is appointed for men in things pertaining to God, that he may offer both gifts and sacrifices for sins. He can have compassion on those who are ignorant and going astray, since he himself is also subject to weakness. Because of this he is required as for the people, so also for himself, to offer sacrifices for sins. And no man takes this honor to himself, but he who is called by God, just as Aaron was. So also Christ did not glorify Himself to become High Priest, but it was He who said to Him: 'You are My Son, today I have begotten You.' As He also says in another place: 'You are a priest εις τον αιωνα FOREVER [Hebrew: עולם HIDDEN, of old, in indefinite time] according to the order of Melchizedek': who, in the days of His flesh, when He had offered up prayers and supplications, with vehement cries and tears to Him who was able to save Him from death, and was heard because of His godly fear, though He was a Son, yet He learned obedience by the things which He suffered. And having been perfected, He became the author of eternal salvation to all who obey Him, called by God as High Priest 'according to the order of Melchizedek,' of whom we have much to say, and hard to explain, since you have become *dull of hearing* [Hebrew ערל *uncircumcised* regarding hearing, comprehension]. For though by this time you ought to be teachers, you need someone to teach you again the first principles of the oracles of God; and you have come to need milk and not solid food. For everyone who partakes only of milk is unskilled in the word of righteousness, for he is a babe. But solid food belongs to those who are of full age, that is, those who by reason of use have their senses exercised to discern both good and evil" (Hebrews 5:1-13).

People are Biblically commanded to grow from cognitive infancy (uncircumcised comprehension) and not to remain in it "that their hearts may be encouraged, being knit together in love, and attaining to all riches of the full assurance of understanding, to the knowledge of the MYSTERY of God, both of the Father and of Christ, in whom are HIDDEN all the treasures of wisdom and knowledge" (Colossians 2:2-3).

When viewing the parallel of various traditions maintained by diverse populaces, and when observing the discoveries (or rediscoveries) of the minority within seemingly disparate traditions throughout time, an observer might notice the uniformity of truth manifesting itself in a variety of related, but not identical, ways. That more than one group or individual experienced the uniformity of truth does not necessarily admit that the group or individual experienced the truth in an identical fashion, even if the result was similar. It is therefore the aim of this book to be able to observe original truth continually manifesting itself in multiple ways in numerous times through a variety of circumstances eventually pointed towards a common goal that reveals the constituents to be related by uniform truth. To illustrate this goal, let us consider the fig-tree that Christ destroyed, but let us also keep in mind that the "right of the firstborn" meant the right to officiate at the altar, the privilege to lead the rites of familial priesthood.

In Mark 11, Christ told the fig tree, "Let no one eat fruit from you ever again." Peter recounted Christ's words by saying, "Rabbi, look! The fig tree which You cursed has withered away."

> Now the next day, when they had come out from Bethany, He was hungry. And from afar a fig tree having leaves, He went to see if perhaps He would find something on it. When He came to it, He found nothing but leaves, for it was not the season for figs. In response Jesus said to it, 'Let no one eat fruit from you ever again.'... Now in the morning, as they passed by, they saw

the fig tree dried up from the roots. And Peter, remembering, said to Him, 'Rabbi, look! The fig tree which You cursed has withered away'" (Mark 11:12-21).

Christ mandated the fruitless death of the tree, and this fruitlessness is referred to by Peter as a "curse." (A) When considering the fact that the fruit under discussion was a fig, we may notice that the letters בכורה can spell *the early fig, firstborn,* and *birthright*; these words are from an unused root בכר whose Arabic cognate means *to be early* and it forms the idea of *bearing early fruit*. A "fig" tree is intended to bear fruit, by raw definition, as opposed to being fruitless and accursed. (B) The individual words are being employed and acted out situationally to teach a lesson, for a "parable" can also be a physical reality and not merely a metaphor, as we see demonstrated outright in Hebrews 11:19. The Narrative says that fig tree "dried up from the roots," which is expressed in Hebrew by the root יבש *to dry up, to be ashamed*; so, a "dried up" tree is an "ashamed" tree; thus an ashamed tree is a fruitless tree, which also makes it accursed; an "ashamed" tree is a dead tree ("shame" being synonymous with death in Daniel 12:2). Genesis 2:5 discusses "shame" relative to "nakedness," and "shame" is referred to as "fear" in Genesis 3:8-10; that is, they were not "ashamed" of their nakedness positively in Genesis 2, but Adam was "afraid" because he was naked negatively in Genesis 3. To "dry up" is to be "ashamed," and to be "ashamed" is to be "afraid"; between Christ's pronouncement against the fig tree and Peter's recognition of the effects of the pronouncement, we read that the scribes and chief priests "feared" Christ (Mark 11:18). (C) Considering "nakedness" leading to "fear," "shame," and "drying up," the word ערירי *naked* also means *childless*. A "childless" person is a "naked" person, and a naked person can indicate a "dead" person (Hebrews 11:12). "Children" are referred to as the "fruit of the womb" (Luke 1:42) and Christ is identified as Luke 2:7 calls Christ Mary's "firstborn"; the letters בכורה can spell *firstborn* and *the early fig*. It would appear uniform that Christ did not see His image reflected well by His creation since, "He is the image of the invisible God, the FIRSTBORN over all creation. For by Him all things were created that are in heaven and that are on earth, visible and invisible, whether thrones or dominions or principalities or powers. All things were created through Him and for Him. And He is BEFORE ALL THINGS, and in Him all things consist. And He is the head of the body, the church, who is THE BEGINNING, the FIRSTBORN FROM THE DEAD, that in all things He may have the preeminence" (Colossians 1:15-18). That is, since Christ is Firstborn, and the early fig is, in a sense, a firstborn, it would appear that the early fig is indicative of or related to

Christ — especially with respect to the custom of ancient eastern kings naming principle trees after themselves along with Scripture's tendency to refer in simile and in metaphor to people as trees (Psalm 1, Isaiah 61, Matthew 15, and, most importantly for our purposes, Genesis 2-3). (D) Since "early fig" is the same word as "firstborn," it is curious why Christ would seek the firstborn before due time, "for it was not the season for figs," hence, an untimely firstborn. The root נפל *to fall* (literally *he fell*) produces the word נפל *an untimely birth, an abortion*, which is, in Greek, εκτρωμα *an abortion, a baby prematurely born*. (E) Fruitlessness is referred to as a "curse." Though the fig tree parable is adorned in Greek, we may note that the Hebrew makes the following connections:

(A) Fig	=	(A) Firstborn
(B) Dry Up	=	(B) Shame, Fear
(C) Fruitlessness; Fruit	=	(C) Childlessness, Nakedness, Death
(D) Untimely Fig	=	(D) Aborted Firstborn
(E) Fruitlessness, Curse	=	(E) Fruitlessness, Curse, Death

FIG = FIRSTBORN: "And SEEING from afar a FIG tree having LEAVES, He went to see if perhaps He would find something on it. When He came to it, He found NOTHING BUT LEAVES..." (Mark 11:13). "Then THE EYES OF BOTH OF THEM WERE OPENED, and they knew that they *were* naked; and they sewed FIG LEAVES together and made themselves coverings" (Genesis 3:7).

DRY UP = SHAME, FEAR: "Now in the morning, as they passed by, they saw the fig tree DRIED UP from the roots" (Mark 11:20). "So he said, "I heard Your voice in the garden, and I was AFRAID..." (Genesis 3:10).

FRUITLESSNESS = CHILDLESSNESS = NAKEDNESS; UNTIMELY FIG = ABORTED FIRSTBORN: "...When He came to it, He found NOTHING BUT LEAVES, for it was not the season for figs" (Mark 11:13). "...I was afraid BECAUSE I WAS NAKED..." (Genesis 3:10).

FRUITLESSNESS = CURSE: "And Peter, remembering, said to Him, "Rabbi, look! The fig tree which You CURSED has withered away" (Mark 11:21). "...You are CURSED more than all cattle, and more than every beast of the field..." (Genesis 3:14).

We may now observe that a story about untimely fruitlessness that resulted in the drying up of a fig tree is quite literally (according to Hebrew diction) explanatory of a story about the abortive birth of a firstborn child that resulted in nakedness... childlessness that brought shame and a curse on account of fruitlessness. The reader must keep in mind at all times that God is perfectly just and perfectly merciful. Scripturally speaking, **the punishment fits the crime, and the grace fits the punishment.** Without recognizing the absolute uniformity of the Scriptural judgments, the punishments can appear random and the grace can appear unfitting. I repeat, the **punishment fits the crime, and the grace fits the punishment**; it is by this knowledge that one can behold the mirror in an effort to distinguish the substance from its reflection; furthermore, I assert that what is chiefly commented on is not the substance but the reflection. Returning to the point, if grace is given through the death of The Firstborn, and if this grace perfectly fits the punishment, then what was the crime in Eden?

The letters אדם spell *Adam, mankind*, and I WILL BE SILENT. Notice how Egypt is compared to the "Garden of the Lord" in Genesis 13:10. Notice that Moses sealed his expulsion from Egypt after he "HID" a corpse in the sand, and he became "AFRAID" on account of his known actions (Exodus 2:12-14). Notice that Adam sealed his expulsion from Eden after he "HID"... and he became "AFRAID" on account of his known actions (Genesis 3:8-10). Now, consider Job 31:33-35:

> If I have COVERED my transgressions as Adam, by HIDING my iniquity in my bosom, because I FEARED the great multitude, and DREADED the contempt of families, ואדם SO THAT I KEPT SILENCE *and* did not go out of the door — Oh, that I had one to hear me!

The reader may ask, "If nakedness was covered, was nakedness the originally intended state of man or the eventually chosen state of man?" Tradition states that nakedness was original, and I object to this assertion staunchly. Childlessness could not have been originally intended based on the first command to "Be fruitful and multiply," and the obsession with deeming the physical unity of man and woman to be inferior and sullied is only induced by the obsession with misusing and abusing the physical unity intended only for husband and wife; it is this misuse and abuse which is itself inferior and sullied, and it is this misuse that is the negative reflection of a substance called "The Way" that is illustrated through Holy Communion, marriage, and The Wedding Feast of the Lamb. The first command given to humanity anticipated and required fruit, which communicates to us resoundingly that the first command was covenantal. The first command was an oath, which is why life, work, and guardianship were required for the purpose of repeating and enlarging the vital cycle whereby halves are joined and community increases. The womb is the orb of perpetuity, the wine-skin of life, the heart where the True Vine was intended to dwell, and the midst where unification unto vivification was designed to flourish and not to be aborted. Many ancients, like Seneca (Epistle CII), understood pregnancy as being 10 months long, and this method of counting is lunar, not inclusive. Thus, in opposition to the 10 plagues wherein the 10th exhibited the death of the firstborn, the 10 lunar months of gestation (the 280 days of pregnancy) typified in the reflection commonly called the 10 Commandments were discussed clandestinely by the teaching commonly called The Sermon on the Mount. In other words, the arrow of time was to be encompassed by the womb in a sinless, endless life of perfection as established in Eden. Compare Romans 8 to Ecclesiastes 1. The sin in Eden reversed or reflected the intended design whereby the arrow of time was birthed out instead to the extent that it became the dictator of the womb's viability upon a segment so that "The Way of women" (Genesis 31:35) became subject to difficulty and, in sorrowful cases, futility.

LIBATION

THE English word *libation* means *the pouring of a liquid offering as a ritual, the liquid poured,* and *an intoxicating beverage*; it is derived from the Latin *libatio,* from *libare, to taste, pour out as offering.* Generally, a drink was poured out in reverent service to deity. Specifically, a priest poured wine sacrificially upon a flaming altar (and sometimes the victim of unoriginal and destructive "sacrifice") and the heat thereof converted the liquid into an exalted aroma that ascended to the heavens. A libation is a drink offering, and it is frequently used as a translation for the Hebrew word נֶסֶךְ *drink offering, libation,* which is from the root נסך *to pour out.* Hebrew diction, unlike English, equates a *molten image* with a *libation* by using the same word for both (נסך) so that, technically, a pagan or an apostate could imbibe idolatry as though being inseminated by an idol; the positive opposite and original that apostacy mimics would be one filled with the Spirit of the Living God to the extent that "The Fruit of the Spirit" is generatively manifested. Such a fact as this shows the antithetical juxtaposition between Melchizedek and the King of Sodom in Genesis 14, for Melchizedek offered what became known as the Eucharist or Holy Communion, whereas Sodom was a place of idolotrous mingling and child-sacrifice. Drinking the wine of a covenant proclaimed a unity until death that formed a new nature (like a child), and from Eden we can begin to understand the conflicting natures contained within mortal bodies as a result of sin, illustrated through libation:

> I find then a law, that evil is present with me, the one who wills to do good. For I delight in the law of God according to the inward man. But I see ANOTHER LAW in my members, warring against the law of my mind, and bringing me into captivity to the law of sin which is in my members. O wretched man that I am! Who will deliver me from this body of death? I thank God — through Jesus Christ our Lord! (Romans 7:21-25).

Shortly after Hannah offered libation, we read of her pregnancy with Samuel. Right after Jacob offered libation upon the rock at Bethel, we read of his wife birthing Benjamin. It was immediately after Abraham's worship and covenant through the Eucharist administered by Melchizedeck that a prophecy of his future Son was given. The covenantal wine of God's table was received by Abraham through obedience as it was epitomized by Christ, Abraham's "Son" (Matthew 1:1), through flawless obedience. Negatively, since a *molten image* and a *libation* are the same word, it can be understood why Moses ground up the golden calf of child-sacrifice and made the sinners drink it and its burned, human remains. Consider: "Now they sin more and more, and have made for themselves molded images, idols of their silver, according to their skill; all of it is the work of craftsmen. They say of them, 'Let the men who offer זבחי אדם *human sacrifices* KISS the calves!'" (Hosea 13:2). Biblically, libation is linked to children and is typified by a kiss that can represent or be connected to wine. In ancient Egyptian, "to kiss" meant "to feed," thus feeding a calf with human sacrifices can be understood in the context of Molech worship (like drinking alcohol while pregnant).

Wine has been associated with a kiss for countless years. We see a reflection of this fact in Song of Songs 1:2: "Let him kiss me with the kisses of his mouth — for your love is better than wine." Generally, wine has been understood as analogous to life, vitality, and invigoration. Similarly, wine was viewed as medication (or, at least, the conduit through which medication was administered). Wine, furthermore, was conceived of as transformative on account of the fermentation required for its production. Let us focus here on the transformative properties and associations of wine: wine was seen as the end result of a seed, for the seed was planted, the vegetation that broke the soil was nourished and trained upon a steak or tree or cross, the vine stock was bifurcated, pruned, "chastised" by having its limbs pierced so that fruit was produced amply, and the liquid therefrom was fermented or transformed into a product of invigoration distinct from the plain juice of its former state. Along with its obvious physical resemblance, wine was considered in the same light as blood, for both blood and wine were comprehended illustratively as life. It is here that we can notice how a bloodline through children by covenant connects to the ceremony of libation. We may note that Genesis 49:11 calls wine "blood," and Genesis 9:4 calls blood "life"; wine, blood, and life are employed synonymously.

The grape and the kiss were understood as unifying entities. *To join* and *to kiss* are the same Hebrew root (נשק), and the word ענב *grape* comes from the root ענב *to bind together, to join*. It can be seen why wine was used in covenants, for it resembled blood; the unification of parties through wine unified two formerly separate beings as though through mutual blood in order to transform them into one new being living in two bodies. The expression of the two bodies fused into one new being would be seen in the fruit or child, the work or offspring of the covenant expressed in unified halves that join two formerly distinct people and two formerly distinct families. A child is, thus, the splitting and melding of two formerly distinct halves into the bond of life. Accordingly, if Chist is the "Vine" and we are the branches, then the fruit of this union would be expressed by the ענב *grape* (and this word comes from the root ענב *to bind together, to join).* The grape is the child of the vine that is born by the maternal brach as sired by the paternal Vine as seems to be indicated in John 15:5-8:

> I am the vine; you are the branches. If you remain in me and I in you, you will bear much fruit; apart from Me you can do nothing. If you do not remain in Me, you are like a branch that is thrown away and withers; such branches are picked up, thrown into the fire and burned. If you remain in Me and My words remain in you, ask whatever you wish, and it will be done for you. This is to my Father's glory, that you bear much fruit, showing yourselves to be My disciples.

The fruit or child is the work or offspring of the covenant, and such fruit is the substance of libation itself. As wine joined through liquid, a kiss joined through breath; wine was poured like a kiss that was breathed out, and wine was imbibed as an aroma was inhaled. Consider: "Yes, and if I am BEING POURED OUT AS A DRINK OFFERING on the SACRIFICE and service of your faith, I am glad and rejoice with you all" (Philippians 2:17) along with, "And walk in love, as Christ also has loved us and given Himself for us, an offering and a SACRIFICE to God for a SWEET-SMELLING AROMA" (Ephesians 5:2). Both the root נשק (= NSK) *to join, to kiss* and נסך (= NSK) *to pour out, to make libation, to cover* are spelled similarly. Libation is linked to garments in that the root נסך *to pour* out can also mean *to weave,* for when we recall Christ bedecked in the High Priest's wine-colored robe that Pilate had formerly confiscated, we can smoothly connect this scene to the Treader of the wine press in Isaiah 63; that is, He was covered with libation as though He was the Victim upon whom libation was poured destructively (His blood and the garment) and, being the "High Priest forever, according to the order of Melchizedek" (Psalm 110) was the One to offer libation for the world, a libation that poured generatively from His circumcised heart to vivify His bride, as was the case with the first Adam.

The root נסך *to pour out, to make libation* indicates the truce that precedes and is reflected by a covenant, for it produces the word מסכה *libation, truce, a fusing* which is also used for metals, particularly with respect to *molten* idols. Idols are falsities to which people bind themselves. The binding of idolatry that produces a sordid truce can be observed in that the worship of the molten calf — the child-sacrificial false deity — involved the covenantal pouring out of blood from the ear (Exodus 32:2) that mocked the servitude signified by the pierced ear described in Exodus 21:6, and the contradictory mingling of this truce involved the pouring out of gold along with "fellowship offerings" (Exodus 32:6) coupled by the slaying of an innocent child at the very foot of Mount Sinai (Amos 5:25-27, Acts 7:43).

In other words, the viable offering of a child to God was intended for vitality and life as evidence and assurance of communal peace, but the nonviable offering of a child to Satan was concocted in stillness and death as evidence and assurance of a lurid pact. Child-sacrifice was sometimes ritually accompanied by sensuous deviancy, that is, unsuitable *mingling,* whereby a spirit was poured out in vain and not to induce righteous perpetuity. The נסך *molten image (מסכה), libation* of the golden calf was the lifeblood of a child poured out upon that wretched golden altar, and the punishment was that the sinners were compelled to drink the ground, molten metal mingled with the charred remains of its victim, for the murderous group נשק *kissed,* and *joined* themselves to the innocent child by first consuming his life and then by imbibing his remains.

Scripture often describes the distribution of spirit in terms of being *poured out*, in terms of libation. Hannah said, "No, my lord, I am a woman of sorrowful spirit. I have drunk neither wine nor intoxicating drink, but have poured out my soul before the Lord" (I Samuel 1:15). Isaiah 29:10 says, "For the Lord has POURED out on you the SPIRIT of deep sleep, and has closed your eyes, namely, the prophets; and He has covered your heads, namely, the seers." Ezekiel 39:29 states, "And I will not hide My face from them anymore; for I shall have POURED out My SPIRIT on the house of Israel,' says the Lord God." Joel 2:28 says, "And it shall come to pass afterward that I will POUR out My SPIRIT on all flesh; your sons and your daughters shall prophesy, your old men shall dream dreams, your young men shall see visions." Consider Acts 2:33: "Therefore being exalted to the right hand of God, and having received from the Father the promise of the Holy SPIRIT, He POURED out this which you now see and hear." Ponder Acts 10:45: "And those of the circumcision who believed were astonished, as many as came with Peter, because the gift of the Holy SPIRIT had been POURED out on the Gentiles also." Review Romans 5:5: "Now hope does not disappoint, because the love of God has been POURED out in our hearts by the Holy SPIRIT who was given to us." The link between "spirit" and "pouring" is obvious, but the context has remained hidden for ages. The context is *libation*, the pouring out of wine upon a fiery altar that transforms the red liquid into an aromatic vapor that ascends Heavenward.

We can understand clearly that when Christ offered His "blood" at the so-called "Last Supper," He had not yet been pierced. The "blood" he offered was His life, not His death — for His death sealed the limits of his defectless life so that this taintlessness endured eternally without fault. The "blood" Christ offered was His wine, that is, His covenant whereby we might be joined with Him in life first, not in death first — for it is evident that both the saved and the lost all experience temporal life and temporal death in the physical body, but the saved receive eternal life in the spiritual body as vindicated by a league with Christ in the temporal body, whereas the damned elect eternal death inherited by a truce with Satan in the physical body. Judas did not receive Christ's communal wine, so he (invertedly) gave Christ *wine*, that is, *a kiss*. The death of the physical body seals the life of the physical body. The "living sacrifice" is the life, not the death, of a person; it is the life lived in servitude to God as opposed to the life lived in servitude to Satan. Christ offered His wine in life before His morally perfect life was finished and sealed by death. He "breathed on them" so that they would receive His "Spirit" in John 20:22. In other words, He offered His wine in the temporal life that was poured out and that ascended to Heaven vaporously like a libation, and He offered this transformed wine in His eternal life after rising from the dead when He breathed His Holy Spirit upon the disciples. Since the altar is understood as a symbol of the bride, it can be understood why the evidence of this Libation, this Spirit, would express itself in fire upon the heads of His bride, His altar, at Pentecost, for אור *light, wisdom, fire* was understood as *life* as were *blood* and *wine*. The ancient Babylonians described the glistening of a helment to be "light like fire" and, if I may draw a simple parallel between the Babylonians and the Hebrews, the tongues of fire on the heads in the upper room probably signified the "Helmet of Salvation" (Isaiah 59:17; Ephesians 6:17) since Salvation was preached immediately after the ignescence described like a libation of wine poured onto a heated altar.

Zechariah 12:10 says, "And I will POUR on the house of David and on the inhabitants of Jerusalem the SPIRIT of grace and supplication; then they will look on Me whom they pierced. Yes, they will mourn for Him as one mourns for his only son, and grieve for Him as one grieves for a FIRST-BORN." The libation is the pouring out of life in liquid that is heated by a fiery altar in order to ascend vaporously. A firstborn is connected beautifully with libation in Job 10:10: "Did You not pour me out like milk, and curdle me like cheese," for this passage describes the covenantal union of marriage by the act of physical worship wherein God Himself pours libation by equipping the husband with milk to pour out upon his altar (his bride) so that a spirit can be yielded up in the construction of the Officiant's image, that is, in the gestation of a child after the pattern of God reflected through the father.

God's image being formed reproductively can be observed outside of Eden where God formed the man. Genesis 2:6 describes the procreative union of "water" and maternal soil. Genesis 2:7 conveys the tender image of a Father kissing His newborn child, for "He breathed into his nostrils the breath of life." Consider Genesis 27:25-27 in light of the fact that Jacob served Isaac wine, and this serving was immediately followed by a kiss; this kiss was immediately followed by a Isaac's misperception based on the bloody smell that he thought falsely was of Esau. The Hebrew word רוח *spirit, wind, breath* is derived from the root רוח *to smell, to perceive* (and is used to indicate *touching fire* in Judges 16:9). The pattern of libation is that red liquid kisses fire and is converted to a "spirit"; in this, can see that Jacob offered unholy libation followed by his own unholy kiss that, when combined with his bloody smell, produced an unholy and incorrect stage upon which he deceitfully received what was already his even though he himself did not yet perceive it. Likewise, but as the positive standard and not as Jacob's heinous negative reflection, The True Vine kissed Adam who is called איש *man* (i.e. אש *fire*) in order to give him a life-giving spirit and Godly perception, for, "...*there is* a spirit in man, and the breath of the Almighty gives him understanding" (Job 32:8) and "The Spirit of God has made me, and the breath of the Almighty gives me life" (Job 33:4). A nostril-to-nostril exchange (so to speak) is as a face-to-face or mouth-to-mouth exchange, for the love required in this covenant was as wine shared in communal union, as the unifying breath expressed through a kiss of acceptance. Effectually, wine was poured out as a kiss was breathed out (so to speak), and wine was imbibed as an aroma was inhaled. Adam inhaled the "holy kiss" (to use the term provided in Romans 16:16, 1 Corinthians 16:20, 2 Corinthians 13:12, and 1 Thessalonians 5:26). That is, Adam received the holy libation that God Himself poured out. Libation is the illustration through which the "breath of life" and the "holy kiss" can be understood as linked, and such an illustration flows easily into the fact that the name "Adam" is derived from the root "*to be red, sparkling.*" Like the mockery induced through the destroyed innocent of the *molten* (= *poured out*) calf, we can understand more of the significance of Judas' betrayal of Christ concerning a deceitfully unholy kiss of death in a garden from which the Last Adam was removed as opposed to the holy kiss, or breath of life, outside of the garden that the First Adam was then placed within. It can be understood here that God first offered libation, that His libation was generative and not destructive, that He taught the first man to be a priest and to pour likewise the holy union that perpetuates God's timeless image. The image of God is transmitted ultimately in a spiritual sense, for we read of Moses learning the wisdom, or life, of the holy kiss in that Exodus 33:11 and Deuteronomy 34:10 describe Moses' relationship to God being " פנים אל פנים *face-to-face.*" Such invigoration, such a holy kiss, is made more explicit in Numbers 12:8 that further describes this union as " פה אל פה mouth-to-mouth" as was the case with Adam's inspiration and subsequent mobility and comprehension within the garden of wisdom and fertility. Surely, as womb and wisdom are essentially the same in Hebrew, the holy kiss is an illustration of divine wisdom as though it were received upon the altar like a libation; again: "...*there is* a spirit in man, and the breath of the Almighty gives him understanding" (Job 32:8) and "The Spirit of God has made me, and the breath of the Almighty gives me life" (Job 33:4). It was immediately after the spurning of wisdom, i.e. the slaying of the innocent child, that Exodus 33:11 describes the "face-to-face" parentally generative union of God and man, the union that saved Moses from Pharaoh's slaughter of the innocents. It is also immediately after the holy kiss, the breath of life, the libation poured into Adam, that we read of him being placed within the walls of עדן *Fertility, Eden*; it is this fact that helps explain why Deuteronomy 32:32 recalls the forbidden tree in venomously serpentine fashion and couples it with descriptions of unholy mixtures, since the מסכה *libation, truce, a fusing* can be understood darkly by unsuitable *mingling* whereby a spirit is poured out in vain and not to induce righteous continuence (which is obvious since all humanity died from that point forward). Even more, as the word נסך can mean both a *libation* and *an idol*, so the עצב *travail, toil* connected with childbirth that resulted from eating of the unholy fusion in Eden also spells *image, idol*. In other words, humanity drank the serpent's libation, his image, and we are all subsequently born as a contradictory and internally warring mixture of God's and Satan's image that requires rebirth in order to be one with God. In essence, Eve placed Satan's idol or image within her womb, and this image caused her death just as Rachel hid Laban's idol near her womb and died in childbirth.

It is important that one recognizes that it is God Who first poured the libation. אדם *Adam* means *Red Man*, for the אדמה *red ground* from which he was taken is an Egyptian term that means *sterile ground* as opposed to עדן *Fertility, Eden*. In other words, God took sterility and made it fertile, for this pattern is consistent in the genealogy from Adam to Christ and is epitomized through Mary. Ironically, the Red Man from the sterile, red ground was made fertile through the breath of life, which we know to be illustrated through libation that, in this case, would seem to be the pouring of red wine or the "the blood of grapes." The red theme here encompasses a dual meaning, for the life is illustrated with the same color that characterizes the absence of life. It would seem fitting that the maternal earth, the altar upon which life is to be yeilded up, will be set ablaze in the end (Zechariah 1 echoed by 2 Peter 3) in order to cause the blood spilled upon it to ascend in vaporous spirit as described in I Corinthians 15:

> But someone will say, "How are the dead raised up? And with
> what body do they come?" Foolish one, what you sow is not
> made alive unless it dies. And what you sow, you do not sow
> that body that shall be, but mere grain — perhaps wheat or
> some other grain. But God gives it a body as He pleases, and
> to each seed its own body. All flesh is not the same flesh, but
> there is one kind of flesh of men, another flesh of animals, an-
> other of fish, and another of birds. There are also celestial bod-
> ies and terrestrial bodies; but the glory of the celestial is one,
> and the glory of the terrestrial is another. There is one glory of
> the sun, another glory of the moon, and another glory of the
> stars; for one star differs from another star in glory. So also is
> the resurrection of the dead. The body is sown in corruption,
> it is raised in incorruption. It is sown in dishonor, it is raised in
> glory. It is sown in weakness, it is raised in power. It is sown
> a natural body, it is raised a spiritual body. There is a natural
> body, and there is a spiritual body. And so it is written, "The first
> man Adam became a living being." The last Adam became a
> life-giving spirit. However, the spiritual is not first, but the natu-
> ral, and afterward the spiritual. The first man was of the earth,
> made of dust; the second Man is the Lord from heaven. As was
> the man of dust, so also are those who are made of dust; and
> as is the heavenly Man, so also are those who are heavenly.
> And as we have borne the IMAGE of the man of dust, we shall
> also bear the IMAGE of the heavenly Man.

Even on Greek pottery, it is the pagan gods themselves who pour libation,
and it seems as if such depiction was devised to instruct people how to
worship. That is, the very idea of libation as a form of worship instituted by
Divinity is evidenced even in cultures who knew little to nothing of the true
God, and their ignorance often led to libation being destructive as opposed
to its originally constructive intentions. For instance, the January/Febru-
ary 1984 VOL.X NO.1 issue of *Biblical Archaeology Review,* along with the
Cult of Molech, by Heider, discuss how priests of the child-sacrificial idol
Molech often reddened their skin with ochre, for, in this, they and their victims appeared aflame with the tincture of wine. When substitutionary sacrifice was conducted for Molech, the words "Life for life, blood for blood, a
lamb as a substitute" were included in the ritual, and it is these very words
"life for life" that Scripture records concerning the defense of pregnancy
(Exodus 21:22-25) combined with the "eye for eye" (Leviticus 24:10-23
also) description that so many have ignorantly and profanely linked exclu-

sively to Hammurabi on account of missing the Molech reference in a vain effort to prove Scripture to be religiously unoriginal instead of historically referential; in this light, Matthew 5:38 will be seen to put the hearers in the place of the child.

Wine was thought to infuse one with divinity by illustration, and counterfeit inspiration was demonstrated through religious drunkenness, hence, "And do not be DRUNK WITH WINE, in which is dissipation; but be FILLED WITH THE SPIRIT" (Ephesians 5:18). As the grape was transformed into wine, so we are to be the "branches" of the "True Vine" (John 15:1-8) capable of making holy libation that perpetuates life: "I beseech you therefore, brethren, by the mercies of God, that you present your bodies a LIVING SACRIFICE, holy, acceptable to God, which is your REASONABLE service. And do not be conformed to this world, but be TRANSFORMED by the RENEWING OF YOUR MIND, that you may prove what is that good and acceptable and perfect will of God" (Romans 12:1-2); it is just prior to this directive that Romans says, "For if the first fruit is holy, the lump is also holy; and if the root is holy, so are the branches. And if some of the branches were broken off, and you, being a wild olive tree, were grafted in among them, and with them became a partaker of the root and fatness of the olive tree, do not boast against the branches. But if you do boast, remember that you do not support the root, but the root supports you" (11:16-18) in a fashion similar to the branches of the True Vine. Remember that the olive was for מאור light, fire, life according to Exodus 27:20 and that wine is understood symbolically as both blood and life. The Holy Spirit is the Person poured out, as though in a libation, into man by God as a generative act of worship that births fruit from the head, the heart, and the loins, i.e. the severing and reuniting expressed in the halves of a child's DNA. The Holy Spirit is described as Libation, as Fire, and as a Dove. We may notice that יונה Dove's, Jonah's connection to the kykeon vine described in Hebrew as a "son of the night" (Jonah 4:10) is mirrored Scripturally by 1 Thessalonians 5:5 and paganly by the kykeon drink provided the wounded soldier in connection to the gold cup designed with figures of doves in the Iliad (11.628-643). The word רוח spirit, wind, breath comes from the root רוחto smell, to perceive, to touch which is spelled similarly to the root רוה to become satiated with drink. If we consider the "renewing of your mind" physically, we may note that taste buds have sensory cells that respond to one of five different primary tastes that transform chemical information into electrical signals that pass through the brain's primary taste cortex located in the insula; our ability to smell and taste is united in the orbitofrontal cortex to effect the sensation of flavor; information from the senses of touch and vision combine with the aforementioned process and mingle to manufacture a sensation that is localized to the mouth. In short, we can, in a sense, taste spirit in liquid form and smell it in vapor form, and this process is accomplished through the union of the fire and the altar, the threshold where the same essence changes forms in order to ascend like a bird. The principle of understanding the vaporous to be birdlike can be observed even in the Egyptian idea of the soul as being something winged, for it requires little imagination to grasp the symbolism here. Biblically, the Spirit "poured out" upon a prophet was as a prophet receiving a Divine message from The Winged One (like the Dove Who appeared at Christ's baptism). The context here is the ancient system of messenger birds: the king attached a message to a bird, the bird flew to the king's spokesman, the spokesman gave the message from the heavens (i.e. from the bird that was in the sky) to whom the king intended to receive the message. A concept of heavenly warfare can be understood as in the birds of prey that might target the messenger bird along the way, or as in a deceiver who spoke falsely in the name of the king by the same kind of messenger bird. Thus, in a manner similar to a spokesman (prophet) receiving the Winged, Heavenly Message (Spirit) from the King (the Father), one can understand a bride (follower) receiving the spirit (impregnation) from her husband (the priest) as easily as one can understand how an altar received a libation that became vaporous as an act of worship conducted by a priest.

For the pagans, pouring out liquid as a form of worship was a unique form of giving because it prevented the recovery of the liquid. Meat offered to divinity was eaten after it was offered and cooked, but libation ascended to divinity without being drunk by the human officer. For those who exist in the knowledge of the true God, libation anticipated reciprocity initiated by God in the Creation and that perpetuated the worship of God through continuous life. God provided the liquid, the husband/priest poured out on to/into his bride/altar, the liquid was converted into a unique spirit, and this spirit was perceived in pregnancy through which the pattern could be continued anew. The word "ha-mah" spelled חמה means *heat*, but spelled חמא means *to curdle, to coagulate*. We can understand procreation illustrated by libation when Job asks God, "Did You not pour me out like milk, and curdle me like cheese" (Job 10:10). Again, we can see the fruit of such a union being cared for affectionately as illustrated by the "holy kiss" where the breath of life was transferred from mouth to mouth to our first human father which is analogous to a portion of a parent's life being invested in the physical fruit of marriage. In short, libation is constructive sacrifice, living sacrifice that renews and that ascends in vivacity. Likewise, we can imbibe the Spirit, if we are obediently willing to receive His outpouring, in order to be converted to a renewed form that allows us to ascend in continuous fellowship. Oppositely, we can ingest the Enemy, if we are defiantly willing to receive his libation, and thus be converted to a dying state that compels us to descend in abortive union.

Sacrifice

LET us reexamine the difficulties of translation. The English of Jeremiah 33:11 states, "Praise the Lord of hosts, for the Lord is good, for His mercy endures forever — and of those who will bring THE SACRIFICE OF PRAISE into the house of the Lord. 'For I will cause the captives of the land to return as at the first,' says the Lord." Likewise, the English of Hebrews 13:15 states, "Therefore by Him let us continually offer THE SACRIFICE OF PRAISE to God, that is, THE FRUIT OF OUR LIPS, giving thanks to His name." Since "the sacrifice of praise" is defined as "the fruit of our lips," it cannot be that we are killing and cooking with our mouths in praise of God consumptively but that we are offering worship resurgently. This "sacrifice" is not destructive but constructive, for it is the word תודה *thank offering,* and it is stated in the context of marriage or communion illustrated by a populated city with a restored Temple as opposed to a desolate woman, a desolate city with a corrupt Temple. Consider the confusion that has arisen in that the word *sacrifice* is used to translate תודה *thank offering, eucharist,* זבח *slaughter,* חג *feast,* מנחה *gift* or *bloodless offering,* and קרבן *approach.* The English usage of the word *sacrifice* indicates deprivation, destruction, and the like, and it is almost impossible to conceive of *sacrifice* in any other sense when using this word unless it is somehow qualified further. Nevertheless, the Hebrew קרבן *approach, sacrifice* for instance, is a type of sacrifice that can indicate construction and increase as opposed to destruction and decrease, which is why it is derived from the same root as קרב *womb, mind, midst*; thus, the expression *child sacrifice* could be interpreted as offering a child in divine service for life on the one hand or slaughtering a child in Satanic worship for death on the other. The main idea of קרבן *approach, sacrifice* concerns itself with a transfer from one to another, so the destruction of the object intended for transfer is the nullification of the intended transfer and no real קרבן *approach, sacrifice* at all. Birthing a child is literally a type of קרבן *approach, sacrifice* wherein one can observe the viable transfer from God to man, and this is etymologically observable in Hebrew by the fact that he word קרב *womb, mind, midst* is from the same root as קרבן *approach, sacrifice.* It can be seen that sacrifice viewed as destruction, as opposed to a viable transfer, is the opposite of the Hebrew קרבן *approach, sacrifice* and would indicate an abortive womb and a cognitive failure. Technically, one cannot give a gift by throwing it away unless the receiver is intended to be a container of refuse. God is not a container of refuse. Jeremiah 7 makes clear that God did not desire the blood of animals and that the various specificities concerning which animals die in what manner for certain sins is but the reminder of what should not have been committed and thus signified by further destruction.

The root אכל *to eat, to consume*, produces the words אכל *food* and מאכל *knife, blade,* and this relationship seems to suggest that a blade was thought of in the same sense as a tooth; hence, ברית *a binding oath, a covenant* is from the root ברה *to cut, to eat*. The synonymous root לחם *to eat, to consume, to war, to fight* produces the words לחום *flesh, body* and לחם *food, meat, fruit, feast, bread, and meal* as well as the word מלחמה *warfare*. In the sense of a covenant, the root ברה *to cut, to eat, to choose* seems to indicate a willful allegiance made over a meal as an oath (to the death) even to the extent of warfare; it is probably for this reason that battle was likened to a *devouring sword* since a blade was understood in the same sense as a sharp tooth: "I will make My arrows drunk with blood, and My *sword* shall devour flesh, with the blood of the slain and the captives, from the heads of the leaders of the enemy" (Deuteronomy 32:42).

"Eating" can indicate the consumption of food (Genesis 2:16), the "burning" of something (Ezekiel 15:4), a blade's destructive capability (II Samuel 18:8), and the overall destruction of something or someone (Numbers 16:45); Numbers 14:9 employs the word לחם *bread* to refer to *people* who are to be destroyed (eaten); in each of the preceding descriptions of "eating," the idea conveyed is one of breakdown. A חרב *cutting instrument, blade (as in a sword)* has an intimate connection with eating, and both eating and cutting have a close connection to a covenant. Marriage was also originally understood to be an oath to the death. That is, if one counterpart departed from the other, whether in physical separation or in promiscuity, the departing member was, in effect, invoking the curse of death upon himself or herself, since he or she had broken the binding to which he or she had been joined for life; thus, death was the only legitimate way to sever the marriage. In congruence, the punishment for adultery was death. Similarly, the word "eating" was used to indicate the sexual union (Proverbs 30:20), which was only considered legitimate within the context of the marital covenant of man and woman. Committing adultery was, of course, analogous to selecting food improperly, committing treason against a covenant, and invoking the binding curse of death.

Dr. Sayce, in his book *The Religions of Ancient Egypt and Babylonia*, stated, "When the Egyptian spoke of 'eating' his god, he mant no more than we do when we speak of 'absorbing' a subject.... Thus in the Pyramid texts... Unas is described as 'eating' the crowns of Upper and Lower Egypt." In Hebrew, "Eating" can also mean to "make part of oneself," i.e. *to bind, to join, to become one with*; hence, *to learn*: "Your words were found, and I ate them, and your words became to me a joy and the delight of my heart; for I am called by your Name, O Lord, God of Hosts" (Jeremiah

15:16)"; "... O Mortal, eat what is offered to you; eat this scroll... Then I ate it; and in my mouth it was as sweet as honey" (Ezekiel 3:1-3). Similarly, לקח means *to take, to marry* and can be employed to indicate continuous action (as in אש מתלקחת *continuous fire*), *captivating speech, and learning*. Food and understanding were held synonymously, as were marriage and learning. In fact, vines trained onto fruit trees (that served as trellises) were considered to be married to the fruit trees. The union of a vine and a fruit tree was understood as a marriage for the strict purpose of producing fruit by way of the blade. Concerning vines, Genesis 49:11 calls wine the "blood of grapes."

Blood was understood as life, not death (Leviticus 17:14), even though death often occurred in the procurement of blood. Blood is linked to cutting and therefore to covenants: "Whatever man of the children of Israel, or of the strangers who dwell among you, who hunts and catches any animal or bird that may be eaten, he shall pour out its blood and cover it with dust; for it is the life of all flesh. Its blood sustains its life. Therefore I said to the children of Israel, 'You shall not eat the blood of any flesh, for the life of all flesh is its blood. Whoever eats it shall be cut off'" (Leviticus 17:13-14). In a blood covenant, the act of sharing in the blood of another meant taking on the nature of the other so that, from the two, one new nature was produced in more than one body. As we can see, the root ברה *to cut, to eat, to choose* is related to the root ברא *to create, to be born,* which produces the Hebrew word בריאה *a new, wonderful thing related* to the Chaldee word בר *a son.* A covenant was understood to be a productive, not a sterile or a destructive, union that was accompanied by a similitude, a combination of two formerly distinct natures into one, new nature. Fittingly, the word דם *blood* is the same word as *similitude, likeness.* The word דם, read as *likeness, similitude,* is from the root דמם *to be silent,* but, when read as *blood,* is from the root אדם *to be red,* from where "*Adam*" and "*Edom (Esau)*" are derived.

In terms of a sacrifice where animate blood was concerned, blood could be acquired either destructively or constructively. Blood was acquired destructively in the shedding of blood as the result of a blade; it was acquired constructively in the she shedding of blood when the hymen was penetrated during the sign of the marital covenant. Such symbolism is retained well in Latin, for the Latin word for a "scabbard" for a blade is "vagina." When inanimate blood was acquired, it was called the "blood of grapes" (Genesis 49:11), i.e. wine. The acquisition of blood was a sign of the acquisition of life, and by partaking of the blood of another, one was using a physical sign to indicate an inward assent to take on the nature of another. The ancient Hebrews were not to partake of blood other than "the blood of grapes" for, had they consumed animate blood, they would have performed a sign of physical ingestion to proclaim an inward assent to take on the nature of an animal, and one whose fleshly body will die. Instead, a Hebrew could consume wine in order to perform a sign of physical ingestion that proclaimed the inward assent to accept the nature of a binding vine that perpetually returns from the dead, i.e. produces fruit repetitiously, which is similar to a snake shedding its skin cyclically. It is obvious why vines were likened to snakes, and why both were a symbol of rebirth: "And as Moses lifted up the serpent in the wilderness, even so must the Son of Man be lifted up, that whoever believes in Him should not perish but have eternal life. For God so loved the world that He gave His only begotten Son, that whoever believes in Him should not perish but have everlasting life" (John 3:14-16). Blood was binding, and the word ענב *grape cluster* is from the root ענב *to bind together*. Blood was utilized sacrificially to cover an altar, and the word "atone" is a derivative of the root כפר *to cover, to overlay, to forgive* and is related conceptually to the root נשא *to lift up, to bear, to forgive*; the idea of a basin, whether one as covered over or as one as lifted up, links these roots, and since blood was used to atone, we can see how wine was employed to bind one to another in the revivification of a covenant. As blood was poured upon an altar, so was wine used in libation. A priest, a sacrificer, was to pour out blood upon an altar in worship of the Deity as a sign of a perpetually revivitalized covenant that allowed the sacrificer to become like the Deity, to become one with the Deity, in humble submission to the Deity in a situation analogous to marriage, which was initiated at an altar. The fire united the libation with the altar in a manner similar to how the Pillar of Smoke and Pillar of Fire walked between Abraham's halves in reflection of the standard: "Many nations shall be joined to the Lord in that day, and they shall become My people. And I will dwell in your midst. Then you will know that the Lord of hosts has sent Me to you" (Zechariah 2:11). In other words, God desires to dwell in our MIDST constructively in order to develop fully the "Fruit of the Spirit" as expressed through the "fruit of the womb" that results from a covenant wherein "many nations shall be JOINED to the Lord." This juncture, it would seem, is the Holy Child we call "Jesus" Who unifies what are called commonly the "Old" and "New" Testaments, in a manner of speaking. It is often the case that, when the word "sacrifice" is used, the notion of some manner of deprivation is involved. Sacrifice in a Hebrew sense, however, does not revolve entirely around the notion of deprivation, but is separated into constructive and destructive categories; that is, sacrifices that generate immediately life and sacrifices that instantly take life. Hebrew קָרְבָּן *sacrifice, oblation, offering* comes from the root קרב *to draw near* which, causatively, means TO JOIN TOGETHER, and the adverb מִקָּרוֹב *for a short time* is derived from this root as well. In other words, a "sacrifice" is an act of worship that allows divine access of the offerer by being joined together with the Deity covenantally (and this does not necessarily involve killing) as we see that the first man was joined to his wife and through her to God. The rebellious Israelites of Numbers 25, on the other hand, joined to the Moabite women and through them to Baal Peor by the sacrificial destruction of their children that was punished by hanging.

It is evident that sacrifice implies religion because the English "religion" is the Greek θρησκεια *ceremonial worship*; the sense of repeated action and regular works displays itself openly by the fact that the Hebrew "festivals" are the מוֹעֲדִים *meetings together, the appointments*, thus, the *repetitious continuities of communal service, i.e. religion, a life of sacrifice*: "I beseech you therefore, brethren, by the mercies of God, that you present your bodies a LIVING SACRIFICE, holy, acceptable to God, which is your reasonable service," (Romans 12:1). A living sacrifice, applied to humanity, would indicate that humanity is to draw near to God in a state of perpetuity and constancy through continual revivification, thus making worship synonymous with life (not death) on a practical level. Furthermore, the festivals were also considered as מִקְרָאֵי קֹדֶשׁ *holy rehearsals* (Leviticus 23:1), ceremonial practices of divine service. Such a yielding up of oneself is more acquisition than deprivation, for the fact that the root קרב *to draw near* causatively applied means TO JOIN TOGETHER is blatant proof that the Biblical concept of marriage is itself a sacrifice: "Therefore a man shall leave his father and mother and BE JOINED בWITH / THROUGH HIS WIFE, and they shall become one flesh" (Genesis 2:24). Accordingly, communion through a table is directly analogous to sacrifice through an altar, for, in both instances, humanity is participating in the union with the Divine. Such a realization can be seen clearly in that the Law consecrated the Levites as the priestly (sacrificial) tribe, and "Levi" comes from the root ללוה *to be joined*, for, in the ancient east, priests (sacrificers) were understood to be "bound" to the Deity in a fashion similar to marriage.

The expression "wash the feet" (2 Samuel 11:8) indicated the proper covenantal coupling of marriage as opposed to the expression "to lie with" (11:4) which allows for fornication, adultery, or other forms of pollution. The directive for Uriah to "wash his feet" was applicable to what was rightfully his through covenant; ironically, this directive was coupled with a meal, and Proverbs 30:20 uses "eating" euphemistically for "copulation" with specific reference to adultery. Such a foot-washing was intended to be physically marital but was more so applied as spiritually communal since a sacrifice on an altar was comparable to food on a table and proper marriage is properly sacrificial. Among the most important and overlooked points concerning the covenanatally sacrificial act of foot-washing can be seen in Exodus 29:17 and Leviticus 1:9, for it was mandated that the sacrifice have its legs washed in preparation for the altar. John 13 depicts Christ washing His disciples' feet just prior to communion (at the table, the altar), and this illustration parabolically displays an ancient eastern sacrificially religious concept that long preceded Christ's fleshly course on earth, for, in so doing, Christ identified Himself as the Deity and His disciples as His "bride," that is, His religious devotees with whom He sought to share His table covenantally in order to produce life through the בשר *flesh, good tidings, Gospel, successful birth* (Jeremiah 20:15). It is plain that Christ first offered Himself as a sacrifice in expectation of us being living sacrifices in order to fulfill our end of the covenant which, it would seem, is why He washed the disciples' feet in the manner of how the sacrifice's legs were to be washed according to Moses. Such a covenantally religious union being comparable to a marriage (comparable to a union of natures) can be observed directly in that John 13:23 depicts the beloved disciple "in the bosom" of his Teacher over a meal as John 1:18 previously depicted Christ "in the bosom" of His Father, i.e. at a meal, at a union, in accord, in covenant sacrificially drawing near with a knit nature. It is in such a union that a man can, through the illustration of marriage, be unified to God through his wife: "Therefore a man shall leave his father and mother and be joined ב *with/through* his wife, and they shall become one בשר *proclamation of good news, Gospel, flesh, royal birthday, accession to the throne through succession by birth.*" (Genesis 2:24). Again, "a man shall... be joined with/through his wife..." to God, which is why we are commanded corporately as the collective bride to "cling" to God (Deuteronomy 30:20), and this is explained plainly in Ephesians 5:31-32: "'For this reason a man shall leave his father and mother and be joined to his wife, and the two shall become one flesh.' This is a great mystery, but I speak concerning CHRIST AND THE CHURCH." The Hebrew Text says "והיו *and they will be* one flesh," and the Greek translation in Ephesians says "οι δυο *the two* shall be one flesh" which displays that the "they" of Genesis 2:24 did not indicate the human man and his wife; rather, it indicated the Husband (Deity) and the bride (the followers of the Deity, in this case, Adam and his wife joined together) which is why the Apostle says, "but I speak concerning Christ and the Church," not merely Adam and his wife. As such, Christ is the "Last Adam"

(I Corinthians 15:45), as we are to be the last bride, the church, the house wherein the Deity resides: "Or do you not know that your body is the temple of the Holy Spirit who is in you, whom you have from God, and you are not your own?" (I Corinthians 6:19). In short, sacrifice is a religious service, a ceremonial worship, that intends to unite the bride and her Deity through a meal either by food and drink upon a table or by solid oblation and liquid libation upon an altar, both being one. The intended goal of sacrifice is drawing near unto unity and perpetual fructification, for the insemination of the bride is accomplished by libation, so to speak.

When sacrifice was brought to the temple, the service was accompanied by (often simultanously with) great feasting. The cooked meat did not endure long enough for the sacrifices to be consumed much later than shortly after the service, and, with the streaming influx of sacrifices, meals were made of them by one set of priests (sacrificers), while another set of priests cooked the sacrifices upon the Table of the Lord, the Altar. The priests, when reclining to eat the sacrificed meat, ate at the Lord's Table that typified the Altar. With the exception of the whole burnt offering, the religious sacrifice of flesh and blood was the priestly sustenance, and this situation unified the offering to God with the food of the sacrificer through the offering of the worshipper. Sacrifice indicated eating systematically, symbolically, and practically, and eating signified a bond between humanity and the divine, for eating positively perpetuates life. As sacrifices were being offered at the Temple, a great banquet occurred simultaneaously, for the Lord's Table is the Wedding Supper. More illustratively put, the worshipper was as the bride, the sacrificer was as the groom; however, the unified worshipper and priest functioned collectively as the bride relative to the Deity to Whom they both played their respective roles in offering sacrifice. The yielding of the sacrifice itself cost the worshipper, sustained the priest, and paid homage to God in a similar way to a bride bearing her child and sustaining the family line by producing a new sacrificer who would, in turn, renew the familial covenant; it would seem that it was partially for this reason that the privilege of priesthood was called the "Right of the Firstborn" because the sacrifice being consumed was paralleled by the priest (the firstborn) who offered it, for Hebrew "קרבן *sacrifice*" meant "drawing near" and not "deprivation."

Sacrifice was understood to be coupled with a meal, and such a communion was illustrative of marriage, thus Holy Communion is called the "Marriage Supper of the Lamb" (Revelation 19:19), and we may observe that the Lamb is both the Sacrificer and the Sacrifice. The only way a priest (a sacrificer) could also be the sacrifice is in the slaying of the firstborn or what is commonly called "child-sacrifice." If child-sacrifice was so sinful that it was punished by hanging (Numbers 25), then it proves enigmatic to ponder that the Son of God was crucified. In other words, it appears to be a riddle that the Victim of innocent death, called the "Last Adam," should be punished as if He were guilty of innocent death. A priest was a sacrificer. The only time the sacrificer and the sacrifice could be one and the same is in the sacrifice of the Firstborn, that is, the sacrifice of the Priest. If, therefore, there were two priests in such a situation, one would have to be, of necessity, wicked provided that the sacrificed priest be righteous since the sacrifice had to be perfect. The slaying of the first-born was punished by crucifixion (Numbers 25), and "Firstborn" is the title of the priest. If the sacrifice was morally pure, and the sacrifice was also the priest, then the priest also would have to be morally pure (which is humanly impossible and is but mirrored by ritual purity). It is confluent that the only priest who could offer a pure sacrifice that was identical to Himself would have to be the very God to Whom He sacrificed which means that God, the Sacrificer, and the Sacrifice would have to be One. The unity described here would mandate crucifixion since crucifixion is the punishment for taking the life of the firstborn sacrificially by wood and fire, according to Numbers 25. The opposite of God, the Priest, and the Sacrifice having their collective life taken selfishly and destructively would be that these three would give their lives selflessly and constructively which must, of necessity, involve some manner of renewed life. Should these three offer a constructive sacrifice in that their life was given to and for someone else, and this constructive sacrifice mandated the death of the Firstborn, then the Firstborn would have to be crucified for the life of the Firstborn He sacrificed, which would make plain the conclusion that the Deity assumed the punishment reserved for the murderer of a child while He Himself was that very Child whereby the bloodguilt of the wicked is covenantally atoned for by the washing of the Atoner. The One providing atonement would be, in some sense, the one needing atonement, and this conundrum is taken care of if both the sacrifice and the sacrificer are Adam ("The First and the Last"); in this way, we can observe the circuit of the "First Adam" (1 Corinthians 15:45) who needed atonement being provided with atonement by the "Last Adam" (I Corinthians 15:45) Who is the "Great God and Savior" (Titus 2:13), thus completing the cycle and renewing the Covenant of life, for life, with the purpose of perpetuating (not destroying) life through constructive (not destructive) sacrifice (drawing near) that is illustrated by the fruitful multiplication following a priest worshipping God *through* His altar. Since it was the "Last Adam" Who accomplished the absolute atonement in His own earthly day, the "Last days" do not necessarily refer to the end of time but rather the completion of the atonement that He articulated on the tree by stating, "τετελεσται *paid in full, it is finished*," which is a Greek translation of the Hebrew of Psalm 22 that is, " כי עשה *he produced, it is finished.*" It would seem as if the "Last days" is a reference to the time-period following completion of His sacrifice, which is why Hebrews 1:1 distinguishes between the "past" days and the "last" days in terms of what God "created" relative to what "He has spoken"; for He said during His sacrifice on the tree, "כי עשה *he produced, it is finished*"; the reader will notice this is the last line of Psalm 22 (John 19:30) and that the first line is spoken in Matthew 27:46, thus marking the death of Christ by the beginning and ending of the same Psalm, for the Crucifixion was at once the end of one life and the beginning of another. The point being asserted here is that Hebrews 1:1 separates time by Christ's sacrifice into two main categories, the past days and the last days; that is, the days before His sacrifice and the days following His sacrifice. It is inadmissable to think that the men who penned the so-called "New Testament" actually thought the world was going to end soon while they were putting to writing the Narrative that initiated the Last Days. Furthermore, the two main categories of time discussed here seem to be linked to the word "τετελεσται *paid in full, it is finished*," which is a Greek translation of the Hebrew, " עשה כי *he produced, it is finished,*" in light of the fact that Christ is "The True Vine" (John 15:1); for, Columella, in his work *On Agriculture*, describes the marriage custom of providing a dowry "in readiness for their vineyards," meaning that a bride-price was paid as the vine was "wedded" to the tree, i.e. a fruit tree was used as a trellis for the grapevine that was joined to it.

Numbers 25 indicates that the sacrifice of children necessitated the morbid unification with a tree, i.e. the death of the sacrificers and the assenting worshippers. We have already understood that Adam was to join himself to God "ב *through*" his wife. Negatively, Numbers 25:1-3 states, regarding the sacrifices to the gods of Moab, how the people "ate and bowed down before these gods" and "Israel joined to Baal Peor." Adam was to join to God through his bride in order to receive the blessing of the covenant: "Be fruitful and multiply..."; but, the Israelites of numbers 25 joined to Satan through his harlots and received the curse of death and hanging... for they killed the fruit of the womb and so they were killed and hung as fruit on trees themselves. The situation described here, of course, parallels adult people to trees and children to fruit which then puts the perpetrating adults in the very place of the children they victimized. Since the perpetrators consumed fruit, they had to become as the consumed fruit themselves; the blessing and the curse of a covenant, relative to the destruction of innocent fruit, can be seen in the first Psalm:

> BLESSED is the man who walks not בעצת *in the counsel of/with the tree of* the ungodly, nor stands in the path of sinners, nor sits in the seat of the scornful; but his delight is in the law of the Lord, and in His law he meditates day and night. He shall be LIKE A TREE planted by the rivers of water, that brings forth its FRUIT IN ITS SEASON, whose leaf also shall ולא יבול *not WITH-ER/not act foolishly/not shrivel like a wineskin*; and whatever he does shall prosper....

It can be seen, through the word "WITHER" employed here relative to "tree," that the Hebrew taxonomists listed vines amongst trees, hence Ezekiel's expression: "עץ הגפן *vine tree*" (15:2). The association of a vine to a snake is unmistakable, for "vine" was frequently used as a circumlocution for "serpent," as was "rope," "swollen feet," "chain," etc. A righteous man would, therefore, be as the opposite of the wicked "serpent" in Eden, for "Eden" means "Fertility," and the fruitful womb is indeed the house of the covenant. The right of priesthood is called the Right of the Firstborn or "בכרה *Birthright*" (Genesis 25:31-32) that is also spelled "בכורה" in the Traditional Text, which is the same consonantal spelling as "בכורה *the early fig*" (Hosea 9:10; Micah 7:1); thus, a poisonous vine on a fig tree could literally be described as a venomous snake constrictingly usurping the birthright, a serpent seeking the firstborn, a wicked priest practicing child-sacrifice. Killing the Firstborn (the one born to be the successive priest) forced the strange situation of a sacrificed sacrifcer. The opposite of a wicked priest orchestrating the sacrifice of a sacrificer would be a righteous priest who offered himself as the sacrifice willingly. If a priest (a sacrificer) offered himself as an acceptable sacrifice, he would not only have to be perfect, but he must therefore be connected to hanging according to Numbers 25. We may observe that Christ is the High Priest (Hebrews 5:6) and also the sin offering (2 Corinthians 5:21) which would mandate that He Himself make the offering, be whole according to the strictures of the sin offering, and be associated with a tree according to the sacrifice of the Firstborn Child. The Marriage Supper of the Lamb is offered by the Lamb, and this shows the Priest to be also the Sacrifice. Since Christ was indeed a Man, since He is certainly the High Priest, the only way He could be a "Lamb" beyond mere illustration is in the fact that the Aramaic word טליא (Hebrew: טלה *lamb*) means both *lamb* and *child* just as the word אמון means both *craftsman* and *little child*. The link is now clear: Christ is called the (1) "Holy Child" after His ascension in Acts 4:27, a (2) "craftsman" or "carpenter" in Mark 6:3, and the (3) "Lamb" in Revelation 19:19, for we can observe the "First Adam" (1 Corinthians 15"45) who needed atonement being provided with atonement by the "Last Adam" (I Corinthians 15:45), the (1) "Son of Man/Adam" (2) Who is the "Great God and Savior" (Titus 2:13) and the (3) "Lion of the Tribe of Judah" (Revelation 5:5).

It is worthwhile to reflect upon the fact that, during the earthly days of Christ, the sacrificial lambs were slaughtered and then placed upon cross-beamed racks (crosses) in the temple in preparation for the priests' meals. That Christ was hung between the morning and evening sacrifices explains much as to the symbolism of an innocent being ritually killed as was the case in child-sacrifice. In the Temple, lambs were, essentially, crucified and then eaten, and it should be recalled that, in Jeremiah, children had formerly been sacrificed in the Temple. A person sacrificing his own child parallels a woman deliberately participating in abortive birth. In other words, giving birth to a child is constructive sacrifice, whereas abortion is destructive sacrifice. Consider:

> While he was still speaking, another also came and said, 'YOUR SONS AND DAUGHTERS were EATING AND DRINKING WINE in their OLDEST BROTHER'S [FIRSTBORN SON'S] HOUSE, and suddenly a great wind came from across the wilderness and struck the four corners of the house, and it fell on the young people, and they are dead; and I alone have escaped to tell you!' Then Job arose, tore his robe, and shaved his head; and he fell to the ground and worshiped. And he said: "NAKED I CAME FROM MY MOTHER'S WOMB, AND NAKED SHALL I RETURN THERE..." (Job 1:18-21),

the "mother," of course, being the earth ready to consume the corpse in burial, in opposition to the fact that man was pulled from her womb by the hands of God. Such a return was not part of the original design and is an inversive response to the sin of Eden. Again, "Eden" means "Fertility." It should be noted that the Eden (Fertility) narrative concerns "eating" with the "mouth." Furthermore, in ancient Eastern warfare, kings sometimes banqueted with food and wine before their defeated foes who hung on trees, impaled and dismembered. The mingled situation of defeated foes' cadavers suspended from bloodied trees in the very location of lush feasts where wine flowed abundantly was a grim projection of raw and unflinching dominance in the midst of cultivated tenderness that was eerily analogous to the fact that the sacrificial animals mandated for slaughter in Leviticus were all herbivores and were slaughtered on account of man's sin, not God's bloodthirst, that is, man's uncultivated dominance that came about as a result of sin in opposition to the intended and refined diet of "every herb that yields seed which is on the face of all the earth, and every tree whose fruit yields seed" (Genesis 1:29):

> The wolf also shall dwell with the lamb, the leopard shall lie down with the young goat, the calf and the young lion and the fatling together; and A LITTLE CHILD shall lead them. The cow and the bear shall graze; their young ones shall lie down together; and the lion shall eat straw like the ox. The nursing child shall play by the cobra's hole, and the weaned child shall put his hand in the viper's den. They shall not hurt nor destroy in all My holy mountain, for the earth shall be full of the knowledge of the Lord as the waters cover the sea" (Isaiah 11:6-9).

Christ is called the "Holy Child" in Acts 4:30.

Originally "sacrifice" did not involve death at all. Sacrifice was קרבן *drawing near* to God habitually as a natural outflow of unsullied life. As such, the *whole burnt offering* is spelled עלה which is from the root עלה *to ascend*. Since it "never entered My [God's] mind" to sacrifice children (Jeremiah 32:35), and since God told Abraham to sacrifice Isaac, it could not be that God told Abraham to kill Isaac, which is exactly the reason He prevented Abraham from doing so. God told Abraham to "העלהו *cause him to ascend*," that is, *lift him up*, and Abraham did indeed cause Isaac to ascend the mountain with wood for the uplifting as an example of the Last Days to come. The word הר *mountain* or הרה *mountain* is, consonantally, spelled the same a הרה *pregnant with child,* which is from the root הרה *to conceive, to implant with seed,* and relates to the idea of teaching. Abraham, it would seem, was commanded to teach Isaac to be reborn, that is, to be converted to the Covenant of which he was intended to be Firstborn; this would also seem to indicate that the reception of the office of Firstborn is itself a ceremonial rebirth, and a mountain is a type of etymological and physically metaphorical womb. In other words, Isaac was to be reborn on the altar of the womb and not to be destroyed on the altar of the womb. Isaac was to be consecrated, not desecrated. Isaac was to be offered up as a living sacrifice, not condemned as a dead sacrifice. God did tell Abraham to cause his son עלה *to ascend*; He did not tell him to cause his son to die: "By faith Abraham, when he was tested, OFFERED UP Isaac, and he who had received the promises offered up his only begotten son, of whom it was said, 'In Isaac your seed shall be called,' concluding that God was able to RAISE HIM UP, even from the dead, from which he also received him in a parable" (Hebrews 11:8-19). Confusion regarding the binding of Isaac has come about because עלה *burnt offering* also means *ascension* which is why it is from the root עלה *to ascend*. It is our misconceptions that link *sacrifice* to death absolutely when, originally, "sacrifice" indicated a drawing near unto life, not a slaughter. Though the word מזבח *altar* is derived from the root זבח *to slaughter*, it should be noted that a שלחן *table* is also an altar and is from the root שלח *to send*. A gift sent ceremonially to the Deity was a sign of the inward conviction of servitude by which the sender attempted to draw near to the Lord with life, in life, and for life. God is not a child-sacrificer destructively, and neither should we be. God sacrificed Himself, as should we. Sacrifice was not destructive initially; therefore, God is a child-sacrificer in that He drew near to us; we, as His children, ought to draw near to Him; that is, we ought to sacrifice ourselves by the definition that preceded sin, the definition that begot life and did not extinguish it. James 4:8 translates Zechariah 1:3 by writing, "*Draw near* to God and He will *draw near* to you," i.e. *sacrifice* to God, and He will *sacrifice* to you (as He did destructively on the cross and constructively at the empty tomb) out of the love through which He saves you like the unabortive love a true parent has for his child. One cannot give a gift by throwing it away unless the receiver is intended to be a container of refuse. Birthing a child is literally a type of *transfer* or קרבן *sacrifice* wherein one can see the viable transfer from God to man, and this is etymologically discernable in Hebrew by the fact that he word קרב *womb, mind, midst* is from the same root as קרבן *sacrifice*.

PRIMOGENITURE

THE Right of "Firstborn" is the right to officiate at the altar, that is, the right to lead the worship of God. The office of Firstborn is the office of a כהן priest. Regarding the Temple and Tabernacle, the High Priest would be the Firstborn. Regarding the family house, the man, husband, and father of the private house is the Firstborn. The Firstborn is the leader of worship, and, as Malachi 2:7 states, a priest's lips were to guard דעת knowledge ותורה and instruction, for he was the מלאך messenger, angel of The Lord. Typically, but not always, the first male child born to the man of the house was the next firstborn who was, in a sense, one with his father since they worked in unity regarding the immediate worship of God and its sustenance after the death of the father, whereby the cycle would repeat once the son married and bore offspring; this would mean that a son would have to be born into office. The situation of one who was not physically born first but who attained the rank of Firstborn often played a part in a considerable deal of jealousy-induced strife from the older, rejected brother to his younger counterpart of higher ranking. Conferring the right of firstborn was as birthing a son into office, which is analogous to "begetting" a king, i.e. placing the next king upon the throne.

The title of Firstborn conferred upon its recipient the authority to redeem. For instance, Jacob discussed how he was redeemed in the pronouncement of his blessing upon Ephraim even though Manassah was physically firstborn (Genesis 48:13-19). God, as Firstborn, promised the redemption of Israel (Exodus 6:6). Sacrificially, the firstborn of a donkey was redeemed with a lamb (Exodus 13:13). Redemption is a mark of the Firstborn's authority. The root גאל to redeem is spelled identically to the root גאל to pollute, and מלאכי Malachl, My Messenger, My Angel, plays upon this dual meaning by accusing the Levites (the Firstborn) of offering "polluted bread" at the Lord's table (Malachi 1:7-12). That the Firstborn was to be the guardian of knowledge means that he was to be able to explain the wisdom of God's teaching, and a play upon sounds becomes immediately apparent relative to the priestly office of Firstborn. The root "pa-tar," spelled פטר means to burst open, to bud (as of flowers), to let out water, to dismiss, to slip away, as in "Consecrate to Me all the firstborn, whatever פטר opens the womb among the children of Israel, both of man and beast; it is Mine" (Exodus 13:2). Similarly, the root "pa-tar," spelled פתר means to interpret, to explain as in "Joseph [Israel's spiritual Firstborn] פתר interpreted" prophetic dreams (Genesis 40:22). Understanding is linked to birth, and we may see a further link amongst the concepts that surround the ב house, temple, womb, and wisdom. A Firstborn was the leading worshipper, sacrificer, and teacher whose birth was preeminent irrespective of its order through his mother physically. A Firstborn perpetuated the Name of God as well as his own name that was given to him at birth, through the familial name of his father, and in God's Name. Furthermore, since a priest was the protector of the altar, He was a liminal defender, a threshold guardian like the cherubs. It is interesting to note that the root כרב to cover (which produces the word כרוב cherub) is spelled similarly to the root קרב to draw near (which produces the word קרבן sacrifice). It was the priest who could make atonement. To atone is, in Hebrew, כפר to cover, to guard and cherub is from the root כרב to cover, to guard, a fact exemplified by the Ark of the Covenant's lid where atonement was made. Ezekiel 28 describes Satan as being adorned with the armor of High Priesthood (of the Firstborn Warrior), the same as those described regarding Aaron in Exodus 28; it says that Satan was the "Cherub with outstreatched wings who covers" who was anointed; it says that he also became "defiled," and it is this defilement that is conceptually linked negatively to the order of Firstborn in that the root גאל to redeem regarding the Firstborn is spelled identically to the root גאל to pollute. Ezekiel's description accords with Job 18 where what seems to be a reference to Molech/Satan worship (slaying and burning babies who were often firstborn males) is described as the "Firstborn of Death" eating human flesh, and this description appears congruent to the fact that Adam was made of dust (Genesis 3:19) and that Satan was to eat this dust (Genesis 3:14). Conversely, Christ is called "Firstborn from the Dead" in Colossians 1:18 and Revelation 1:5 Who cannot be consumed by Death because of the fact that He died the first death as a sinless and innocent Firstborn which disallows eternal destruction on account of fact that Christ fulfilled the entire Law of God as reflected in the Law of Moses, the Law that says, "Cursed is the one who does not confirm all the words of this law by observing them" (Deuteronomy 27:26). That cherubs, who are called "living creatures" in Ezekiel 1, 11, and Revelation 4, are to be connected conceptually with birth can be seen partially in that they are threshold guardians, and the womb is Biblically understood as a threshold, a gate, a door, etc. Consider Habakkuk 3:2: "Lord, I have heard of your fame; I stand in awe of your deeds, O Lord. בקרב in the midst שנים of two חייהו living creatures, בקרב in the midst, in the womb, in the mind שנים of two you make known; in wrath remember רחם mercy [the womb]," for this was the scene of Christ's birth in reaction to the closing scene of man's expulsion from Eden (Fertility), man's birth into death, in Genesis 3 with the cherubs standing guard; furthermore, it explains, "For where TWO or three are gathered together in My name, I am there IN THE MIDST of them." (Matthew 18:20). A Hebrew word for *manger* is ארון *ark, coffin.* That is, it would seem as though Joseph and Mary flanking the Christchild in the manger was a reflection of the Ark of the Covenant's lid, which was, in turn, a mirrored image of the entrance to Eden where Flame stood as the cencer's smoke upon the propitiation slab called the Mercy Seat, during Atonement or Redemption (Leviticus 16). We may thus consider the Child at Eden's gate relative to the Child at Molech's gate sealing the fact that the gates of Hell shall not prevail.

The right of the Firstborn was the right to officiate at the altar as the priest, the sacrificer. The Right of the Firstborn, along with its inheritance, was not simply a fiduciary inheritance but a religious inheritance. The ceremonial office of Firstborn required the firstborn to be knowledgeable about the religion, and it is therefore understandable why this right was not always conferred upon the eldest son if a younger son were more *devoutly* knowledgeable. The firstborn son was intended for the perpetuation of the altar's service; however, if he was unsuitable in his moral conduct by profaning his position at the altar, another would be found and given the right as the altar's officer. The tension that ensued from the loss of this right was immense, and we can see very clear examples of this between the "Christians" and the "Jews," John the Baptist and the Sadducees, Joseph and his brothers, Jacob and Esau (Edom), Isaac and Ishmael, Able and Cain, and Adam and Satan. The struggle between these pairs was/is the struggle over who would preside over worship and therefore the government, the rule of the family, the culture, the tradition, the reception of gifts for the altar, the maintainance of the house of worship, and the offerings for the service. The rites of this right involved sacrifice. The word קרבן *sacrifice* is derived from the same root as קרב *inward part, middle, midst, womb.* Ultimately, a sacrifice was something inward, which is why a way of life was considered a sacrifice far above any material gift. That a sacrifice involved the inward part, the heart, the middle, the midst, points us to the heart, the mind. The word לב *heart, mind* is understood as *the vital principle,* and it is applied to the will, judgement and understanding; it contains the concept of being in the center like the word קרבן *sacrifice.* A probing mind that seeks knowledge of the divine, a heart that yearns after the heart of the Deity, a mind that desires the will of God is literally a sacrifice, for it draws near the inward part, the midst of God's will. It can be readily understood how primogeniture could not overcome the desire and acquisition of divine knowledge, for the right of the firstborn was the right to officiate at the altar — an altar that he understood and to which he drew near in his knowledge and with his practice.

A כהן priest, sacrificer was understood as both a bride and a husband, i.e. as a covenanting official of God. The priest was a bride (so to speak) of God, the husband of the altar, the image of God to the congregation, and, as a member of the congregation, a constituent of the bride. More properly, a male considered as a "bride" or as part of the "bride" is better understood as a "bound one," as is pointed out by the fact that "Levi" (the priestly tribe) is derived from the root לוה to bind, i.e. in an oath, a covenant. The idea expressed here is similar to the sangu or one who was "bound" in the religion of ancient Nineveh. In this manner of thinking, the sexes are not confused; rather, the sexes are delineated for the purposes of designated worship that serves as a symbol of a marriage, a communion, a covenant of two parties in binding union to the death (or that is perpetual insofar as life is concerned). Libation was a strict part of the rites of the altar, for ענב a cluster of grapes comes from the root ענב to bind together, for a גפן vine comes from the root גפן to bend, which is synonymous to the root גחן to bend, which produces the word גחון Gihon (a river of Eden), the Belly, the Womb. Since the altar was understood as representative of the womb, then the pouring out of "binding" liquid that came from a "binding" plant by a "bound" sacrificer illustrates how covenants were supposed to be ever-fixed in communion, but organic and reproductive as a result of this communion as is the case with marriage and children. Quite often, ancient pottery samples depict the deity, not the human priest, pouring libation; this situation graphically displays the deity as a sacrificer himself which, therefore, designates him as the husband, lord, master, and possessor, for these three words are the same Hebrew word: either איש man, lord, husband, and בעל husband, lord, Baal (as a proper noun). The altar is collectively symbolic of devotees headed by a priest, a sacrificer.

The Firstborn was supposed to be male because this sacrificer was the head of the worshippers, the one who drew near to the deity immediately. It can therefore be clearly understood that the sex of the priest was a constant and was not brought into question, but his designation and position qualified him conceptually as leader of the congregation (head/man) and as a constituent of the congregation (body/bride) so that he understood the totality of functional worship in humble imitation of God as having accepted divine authority by God and under God. Without this specific mechanism in mind, designation has been confused with ability, and the subtle beauty of the gender designations and distinctions of pure religion are easily confused with sex-reversals that nullify the image that equates the worship of God to a marriage and a supper of both truce and covenant knit together in tender sacrificial love capable of reproduction through both birth and conversion. It was this very confusion that Satan played upon when he asked insidiously, "Did God say ' לא תאכלו *you [males] shall not eat...?'"* (Genesis 3:1) as opposed to what God said: "לא תאכלו" *you [male]/she shall not eat....*" (Genesis 2:17). The deliberate confusion of the sexes here was an intentional attempt by Satan to destroy marriage, to sever the covenant man had with God, to desecrate the altar of God by reversing the roles so that the altar sacrificed upon the priest instead of the priest sacrificing upon the altar... for the root גאל can mean *to redeem* as well as *to pollute*. Keep in mind that the First Temple was polluted when the priests sacrificed children upon Jehovah's altar (Jeremiah 7), which forced the situation of a Firstborn sacrificing a firstborn. When comparing the office of Melchizadek to that of Levi relative to Christ, it can be seen that Christ was both the Firstborn Sacrificer and the Firstborn Sacrifice, and this unique position allowed His Temple to be rebuilt on the Third Day, the day when Earth bore vegetation, the day when He resurrected or was "born again," literally, the Day of Firstfruits which is the Third Feast of the Torah. It can thus be perceived that the firstborn were thwarted through gruesome destruction in the First Temple, which is why it was destroyed in turn, and that Christ, the Firstborn, was killed gruesomely prior to the destruction of the Second Temple. It can further be perceived that the slaying of the firstborn relative to God's Temple was overcome by the re-birth that came through the rebuilding of God's Temple on the Feast of Firstfruits when He came up from the ground through the cave, which was reminiscent to the cave in which he was born.

The Firstborn priest must be male, for He is the husband to the congregation who, along with the bride, is responsible for bearing fruit. "Christ, the Firstfruits" (1 Corinthians 15:23) is both the head and the fruit, the husband and the child, the "Root and the Offspring" (Revelation 22:16) who is God and the Son of God, God and the Son of Man. By instituting a female priest to offer sacrifice, a type of homosexuality ensues; this very scenario can be observed in Genesis 14 when Melchizech brought out bread and wine to worship with Abraham as opposed to the King of So-dom who offered spoils. Obviously, Melchizedech represents Christ while the King of Sodom reflects the Knowledge of Good and Evil, i.e. the union of unsuitable mixture that is incapable of producing viable fruit, our first example of homosexuality, which is the rancidly grotesque ruination of all that is admirable, functionally consistent, life-giving, and natural. The con-fusion of gender breaks viable covenants and severs the line of worship from man to God.

Wine that was deemed acceptable for religious consumption was to be mingled with water and was called "fruit of the vine" in Hebrew, whereas unmingled wine was deemed unsuitable (especially for pregnant women) and was called "fruit of the tree." How sickeningly ironic it is that the forbidden tree that was the result of mingling against viability contained " עץ הפרי fruit of the tree" which was unmingled itself! — for this very title is the syntactic inversion of the Hebrew "עץ פרי fruit tree," which is a disgusting display of perverted logic that manifested itself upon the altar of life and which continues to display itself today in the destruction of viable fruit and the decadence of the family that is supposed to produce organic perpetuity with religious legitimacy. The wretched perversion described here pivots falsely around the unmingled wine of the forbidden tree that derived from a horridly mingled source: a Sodomite vine, so to speak, a serpentine homosexuality from which phallic filth and female antifecundity originated: "For their vine is of the vine of Sodom and of the fields of Gomorrah; their grapes are grapes of gall, their clusters are bitter. Their wine is the poison of serpents, and the cruel venom of cobras" (Deuteronomy 32:32-33).

The altar was understood as both a table and a threshold, for thresholds were indeed altars. The word מזבח altar is from the root זבח to slaughter, to sacrifice, and it produces the word זבח repast, banquet, and, by metonomy, flesh. Since a banquet was related to a slaughter, we can see a link in the positive and negative applications of covenants, for ברית a binding oath, a covenant is from the root ברה to cut, to eat, and the synonymous root לחם to eat, to consume, to war produces לחום flesh, body and לחם food, meat, fruit, feast, bread as well as the word מלחמה warfare (see Revelation 12:4-7), for warfare could not be rightfully initiated without a sacrifice. An altar was also a שלחן table, from the root שלח to send, to commission, to put forth, to extend, to divorce, and the words שלח spear and vegetation shoot are derived from here also, along with the word שלוחים gifts, dowry. The intricate imagery conveyed here is that an altar was understood maritally in the sense of binding, for the word אשה woman also means fire offering and gift, thus the שלוחים gifts, dowry regarding the bride, the table. The woman was taken from the exposed heart of the man, and לב heart, mind is understood as the vital principle that is in the center, the midst, as is the inward part, the womb, as is connected to the idea of drawing near, i.e. sacrifice. The Firstborn, the priest, was always male, for איש man (as masculine) was probably spelled originally in consonantal similitude to אש fire, shining brightness, splendor; thus, by placing the ה on the side of the אש man, fire, you can see the אשה, woman, the fire offering, *the gift.* Prior to sin (and therefore prior to death), sacrifice was performed on a שלחן *table, altar,* not on a מזבח *slaughtering place, altar.*

The אור *light, fire, wisdom, life* of the religious and marital union was viable and could perpetuate further life. The man was unified to the altar by his libation of wine (דם, חיים *blood, life*) that was converted into a gas (רוח *breath, spirit, aroma*) by fire, which is how we, while living, are the "aroma of life" (2 Corinthians 2:16) and at the same time a "living sacrifice" (Romans 12:1). The altar unified with the offering (libation, semen) by the fire, and, in this manner, we can understand how the child of this union was the sacrifice (product) raised from the altar who ascended to God by a אור *light, fire, wisdom, life*; that is, the altar was the woman, the priest was the man, and the expression of the life-giving unity was the child or the unifying light. The imagery expressed here must be understood constructively, for it is the גאל *redemption*: "Nevertheless she will be SAVED IN CHILDBEARING if they continue in faith [= covenant], love, and holiness, with self-control" (1 Timothy 2:15). Conversely, the גאל *pollution,* the profanation and defilement of the altar occurs when the altar was unified with the breathing child by fire, for in this manner we can understand how the child of this union was the bloody sacrifice raised from the altar by a אור *fire* so that the רוח *breath, spirit, aroma* was forcefully removed from its vessel in the horrid worship of Satan. Reversing the order of the same words, given the opposite sense by confusing imagery for physicality and physicality for imagery, inverts the entire order of the conduit of life so that it becomes a trash disposal of death like the Tophet of Hell as symbolized by Gehenna, that is, the Valley of Slaughter described in Jeremiah 7 and Isaiah 30.

If the gift and altar were rejected by the priest, it can be understood that he disregarded the שלחן *table, altar* for the root of "table" can mean שלח *to divorce,* and we can also see the lexicon's reflection of marriage alliances relative to warfare and the apparent physical similarity between combative wrangling and copulation. The altar, as a table, was analogous to (or often physically was) a threshold. A סף *threshold* is from the root *to expand, to extend* like the root שלח *to extend* that produces the word שלחן *table.* Ancient eastern thresholds were concave and served as basins for collecting the blood of slaughtered animals as will be noticed in the Passover and the subsequent legislation that mandated that sacrifices be brought to the "door of the Tent of מועד *Betrothal/Meeting/Drawing Near (i.e. Tent of Sacrifice or Marital Tent wherein the union was consumated),"* for the word בית *house* also meant a *temple* and a *womb.* The threshold was a physically concave delineation that was used sacrificially like an altar to draw near, to worship, with food dedicated to the Deity and partaken of in union with Him; if the service was not performed properly with a discerning heart, the penalty was death, as was the case on the first Passover and at Lot's house in Sodom (where the perverts attempted to open a door with unatural force and were thwarted by supernatural vengeance). A סף *threshold* was a basin, and a basin was a מבטן *womb, belly*; גחון *Gihon, Belly* is the name of the second river denominated in Eden, and the Hebrew number ב *two* is spelled בית *house, temple, womb, wisdom*, thus the watery threshold of the Gihon river. Both rivers and snakes were understood as *shining ones* and *thresholds*; the word נהר *river* is from the root *to flow, to shine* and the word נחש *serpent* is from the root *to shine*; the words מפתן *threshold* and פתן *snake* are from the same root: "... sin is crouching at the door..." (Genesis 4:7). In short, a threshold was a type of altar and an altar was a type of table, all of which had, in a religious sense, something to do with a "serpent," that is, a shining one, i.e. one who sought and acquired divine knowledge as the official firstborn who officiated at an altar to which he drew near in his knowledge and with his body. The first Levitical High Priest had the name of אהרון *Shining One, Aaron*.

A threshold was a demarcation of the center, for sacrifice was literally how to approach God since the word קרבן *sacrifice* is derived from the same root as קרב *inward part, middle, midst* that produces the word קרב *womb*. There were at least three partakers in the religious covenant of sacrifice: (1) The Deity to Whom the food was first offered on the threshold/altar, (2) The Firstborn who received the food from the altar and ate it on his table, and (3) the devotee who brought the food for the Deity Who, in turn, provided for the priest. It would seem as if the threshold/altar and the table/altar were the two ends of a communal table where humanity joined the deity; so, in a sense, each end of the table was occupied by the Groom and the bride while the Child was offered up constructively in the midst through libation; this seems to be the very image we see atop the ark where the libation of blood was offered, for דם means both *blood* and *likeness*; and, it was this very likeness that God created after He poured forth water atop the earth from beneath it to form the man. Since דעת *knowledge* and sacrificial love were essential components in this union, we may notice that ancient eastern eating often took place reclining. One person lay "in the bosom" of another, meaning the one person's head was close to the heart of the successive person around the table. As such, we may observe the confluence of the following passages: "But the poor man had nothing, except one little ewe lamb which he had bought and nourished; and it grew up together with him and with his children. IT ATE OF HIS OWN FOOD AND DRANK FROM HIS OWN CUP AND LAY IN HIS BOSOM; and it was like a daughter to him" (2 Samuel 12:3); "Now there was LEANING ON JESUS' BOSOM one of His disciples, whom Jesus loved" (John 13:23); and, "No one has seen God at any time. The only begotten Son, who is IN THE BOSOM OF THE FATHER, He has declared Him" (John 1:18) as though Christ is eating supper. Since "eating" and "learning" are sometimes the same in Hebrew, and since both man and woman are related to fire and fire offering, it would appear that seeking after the knowledge of God is as eating at His table, thus we read in Moses: "The sight of the glory of the Lord was כאש אכלת*like a consuming fire, like a Man [איש ~ אש] eating* on the top of the mountain in the eyes of the children of Israel" (Exodus 24:17). It was also quite often the case that both altars and thresholds were the tops of tombs, tombs of great men buried above ground and tombs of children buried below the foundations of houses; this seems to be the very image at the entrance of Eden (like the top of the Ark of the Covenant) following the parents' expulsion.

The common understanding of the word בית *house* is more properly rendered *dwelling*; it is the same word as "temple" and "womb," all of which were understood to have life dwelling within them; furthermore, such a dwelling could be an open-air precinct like a garden or, sickeningly, like a tophet, a child-sacrificial precinct. A בית *dwelling* could be organic and capable of locomotion, and we may observe this with the Tabernacle in the wilderness, the womb above the moving legs of the mother, and of the dwelling/body/temple of the Holy Spirit. "Dwellings" were said to be "built," and this is the literal expression employed in Genesis 2:21-22 where it says that The Lord God "took אחת מצלעתיו *one from his sides...* ויבן *and He built*" the side into a woman," like a carpenter builds a house. That is, a "אמון *craftsman, child*" is derived from the same root as אמנה *covenant*, which is synonymous to ברית is *a binding oath.* A child is the result of a holy libation poured out upon a house's altar, and this has a house built for him by God Who, through this craftsman, can continue the process. The idea of gestational creation is made here analogous to the construction of a dwelling, a place of worship; thus, a house, temple, and womb were all understood synonymously and were even the same word. Such structures had thresholds, as it is obvious that a child must proceed out of the door the father entered. Many eastern thresholds were concave and were the functional equivalents of basins. A basin is a type of cup, and such a basin can be viewed as either concave or convex depending on the perspective of the viewer. Accordingly, a גביע*cup* comes from the root גבע *to be high*, and this root produces the word גבעוןGibeon (where the Tabernacle was stationed when the Lord appeared to Solomon), the great altar that was also rebelliously used in child sacrifice -- for the synonymous term במה *high place* means an altar specifically designated for the religious slaughter of innocent children. A "high place" was a mortuary shrine. The convection of a cup held high explains the imagery of a mountain being held as analogous to a pregnant womb, for the word הרה can mean both *a mountain* and being *pregnant with child*. In connection, the word כוס (which seems to be spelled כוש in Genesis 2:13) also means *a cup*, but it descends from the root כסה *to conceal, to be covered* which produces the words כסות *garments* and *clothing* and is synonymous to the root כסא *to cover* which yields the words כסא *the renewal of the moon (new moon)* and כסאות *seat of a high-priest or judge, royal throne*. It is apparent, even from mere etymology, that a house, temple, womb, cup, and mountain all were understood gestationally, but with the distinct aim at preserving knowledge concerning life being ruled over and dwelling under the protection and exaltation of a covenant, an oath, by a lord and ultimately The Lord. Raising a cup was the sign of an oath, and overturning a cup indicated the pouring out of libation upon an altar in religious piety towards The Deity through which He was worshipped. Notice how Moses states that the Word of God is in our heart (Deuteronomy 30:14), that Moses placed this word in the side of the Ark of the Covenant that was a propitiation altar (Deuteronomy 31:26), and that the אשה *woman, fire offering, gift* was from the side of the man (Genesis 2:21). The dwelling place had a threshold. In perverted inversion, many often sacrificed their firstborn sons and buried them beneath the thresholds/cornerstones of their houses in a (false) attempt to procure divine favor and in the (false) expectation that the slain child would guard the entrance of the home. Such threshold/foundation covenants allowed for a child to be dedicated in the womb. The sickening ritual of child sacrifice was performed in order to gain success in a matter, but the (false) deity who was expected to procure favor through this slaughter would not be satisfied with a stillbirth. If a stillbirth occurred, the parents had to produce another male child as a representative advocate for his stillborn brother; this child was then sacrificed, and his bones were buried with the bones of his elder brother, both of which would be, in a sense, considered the Firstborn in Aramaic (Hebrew: טלה *lamb*), a טליא is both a lamb and a child, a slain child, an abortion, is called a נפל *fallen one*; the opposite would be a standing one: "And I looked, and behold, in the midst of the throne and of the four living creatures, and in the midst of the elders, STOOD a Lamb as though it had been slain," i.e. as though it had fallen. Melchizech brought out bread and wine to worship with Abraham as opposed to the King of Sodom who offered spoils; obviously, Melchizedech represents Christ as the King of Sodom reflects the Knowledge of Good and Evil, i.e. the union of unsuitable mixture that is incapable of producing viable fruit. Perversely, children were often sacrificed and buried beneath thresholds in order for the parents to gain success selfishly. It was thought that the slain child would bring good fortune and would protect the entrance to the domicile through flames for, from the outside, the light or fire of the house was seen at the doorway and it was conceived that such a child could stand guard and not be burned — unlike perpetrators. It is grossly apparent that the logic here is inverted since the parents were themselves the mistaken perpetrators and they actually put themselves outside the House of God by sacrificing to/unifying with the arch enemy of God through a sacrificial approach, through a religious binding that is analogous to marriage, to a covenant where the life poured out is not a holy libation that induces perpetuity through an innocent but an unholy libation of that induces the death of an innocent. Such a death is a breach of the covenant, which is comparable to both murder and abortion.

ONE FLESH

THE word אחד *one* is from the root *to unify*, which therefore means that *one* is a *unification* of sorts. The word בשר *flesh* also means *good news, gospel, proclamation of good tidings (with particular reference to successful birth)*. We may read " והיו לבשר אחד *and* THEY *will be as one flesh*" (Genesis 2:24) as *they will be one proclamation of good tidings*, for Job 3:3 discusses the day of his birth relative to the proclamation "a גבר *strong man, male baby* is conceived!" The most blatantly obvious example of "flesh" meaning the "gospel, proclamation of good tidings with particular reference to successful birth" is Jeremiah 20:15 that employs the Hebrew בבשר*flesh* to describe *the proclamation of Jeremiah's birth*, his incarnation and subsequent birth from the בית *house, the temple, the womb*: "...who brought בשר *good news, gospel* to my father, saying, 'A male child has been born to you!' Making him very glad...." We may therefore view the passage "and THEY will be as one flesh" as "and THEY will be as a unified proclamation of good news" and "and THEY will be as a unified gospel" and "and THEY will be as a unified gospel capable of successful birth in marriage" — not merely indicating copulation, but the covenant that preceded their physical union that eventuates in the perpetuity of life through a child, the fruit of the womb. Connecting the concepts above, we may notice that a male baby is called a "strong man" in Job 3:3 and that the expression "one flesh" can indicate the covenentally spiritual union to God that is illustrated by marital copulation that results in a proclamation of joy regarding successful birth as opposed to stillbirth. The proclamation of good news, the gospel, is not merely connected to birth, but to successful birth. The Gospel of Mark cleverly plays off of the word בשר *flesh, good news* = ευαγγελιον, *gospel* for the following reasons: (1) "Conversion" to the faith was understood as being "born again," and this rebirth, this renewal of the covenant with God, was symbolized by lustration (now formally called Baptism); (2) Being "born again," being converted to the Faith by the renewal of the covenant would, of course, make the convert analogous to an infant; (3) Mark does not mention the birth of Christ as a physical infant. Instead, Mark begins his book "The beginning of the GOOD NEWS of Jesus Christ, the SON of God," and then proceeds to discuss His BAPTISM, his REBIRTH. Galatians 3:26-27 states, "For you are all SONS of God through faith in Christ Jesus. For as many of you as were BAPTIZED into Christ have put on Christ," for the word נשא can indicate *lifting up, bearing, forgiveness* and the *putting on, the adornment, of a garment*: "...Then He said to them, "Thus it is written, and thus it was necessary for the Christ to suffer and to rise from the dead the third day, and that repentance and remission of sins should be preached in His name to all nations, beginning at Jerusalem. And you are witnesses of these things. Behold, I send the Promise of My Father upon you; but tarry in the city of Jerusalem until you are endued with power from on high." (Luke 24:46-49). Again, we read, "The beginning of the Gospel [בשׂרflesh, *good news, gospel, proclamation of good tidings, successful birth*] of Jesus Christ, the SON of God." Matthew began his account with Herod's threat to the successful birth of Christ, Luke recounted that the Voice from Heaven proclaimed "You are my SON" during Christ's rebirth (Baptism) followed immediately by the genealogy that connected Christ on one end to Adam on the other. Matthew penned that Satan attempted to abort Christ's mission by tempting Him immediately after His Baptism, His rebirth, i.e. The Father's proclamation of good news, "This is my SON, the Beloved, with whom I am well pleased" (Matthew 3:17). Thus, it follows that "והיו לבשר אחד *and they will be as one flesh*" has a direct reference to the marital covenant as signified by birth. "Flesh" indicates "Gospel," and "Gospel" indicates "successful birth."

When it is written, "והיו לבשר אחד *and they will be as one flesh*" (Genesis 2:24), this passage is recounted as, "...and the δυο TWO shall become one flesh" (Matthew 19:5). The original "they" is recounted as "two." Mark 10:8 states, "and the TWO shall become one flesh'; so then they are no longer two, but one flesh." I Corinthians 6:16 recalls the same principle for a warning against its perversion: "Or do you not know that he who is joined to a harlot is one body with her? For 'the TWO,' He says, 'shall become one flesh'" (I Corinthians 6:16). Surely "the two" (as a translation of "they") cannot begin and end with a man and his wife, for Ephesians 5:31-33 explains, 'For this reason a man shall leave his father and mother and be joined to his wife, and THE TWO shall become one flesh.' This is a great mystery, but I speak concerning [1] CHRIST [2] AND THE CHURCH. Nevertheless let each one of you in particular so love his own wife as himself...." So, the man and his wife are physical illustrations of the covenental relationship of Christ and His Bride, and this would show that the Genesis account is communicating that man was in covenant with God through his wife and that God, not man, joined Adam to his bride with the intent flowing through the two humans collectively to the extent that His image would perpetuate in this union. Accordingly, "and the two shall become one flesh"; so then they are no longer two, but one flesh. Therefore WHAT GOD HAS JOINED TOGETHER, let not man separate" (Mark 10:8-9), and "...Yet she is your companion And your wife by covenant. But did He not MAKE THEM ONE, Having a remnant of the Spirit? And WHY ONE? HE SEEKS GODLY OFFSPRING..." (Malachi 2:14-15). The reader can easily see that the oneness is of God with man, that this unification is illustrated in human marriage, and that the purpose thereof is for man to bear the fruit of God as human couples, as a בית *house, the temple, the womb*: "...so we, being many, are ONE BODY IN CHRIST, and individually members of one another..." (Romans 12:5). Conclusively, "they will be one flesh" is a reference to the union of God and man illustrated by the marital union where man is in covenant with God through his wife since "the two" are "Christ and the church," i.e. "one flesh, one Gospel, a unified proclamation that announces the fruit of Christ through humanity." The converse of this principle would be, of course, man uniting himself to Satan by sinning with an altar founded on destruction that does not seek "Godly offspring."

Many often claim that when Noah "lay uncovered inside his tent" and when "Ham, the father of Canaan, saw his father's nakedness" (Genesis 9:21-22) that Noah was embarrassed because his masculinity was seen by those it sired. Noah may have been ashamed of such nakedness, but the passages in question cannot be referring exclusively (if at all) to masculinity. Leviticus 20:11 states, "The man who lies with his father's wife has uncovered his father's nakedness; both of them shall surely be put to death. Their blood shall be upon them." It is clear that a "father's nakedness" is a description of a "father's wife." Immediately prior to the description of Noah's nakedness, Scripture states, "Whoever sheds the blood of man, by man shall his blood be shed; for in the image of God has God made man" (Genesis 9:8) followed by the "covenant" (like a marriage) signified by the rainbow. So, here we may observe the shedding of (1) BLOOD, the (2) COVENANT, and a (3) "FATHER'S NAKEDNESS" referring to a "father's wife"; thus, "The man who lies with his (2) FATHER'S WIFE has uncovered his (3) FATHER'S NAKEDNESS; both of them shall surely be put to death. (1) THEIR BLOOD shall be upon them." A man's "nakedness" refers to a man's wife. Next, Deuteronomy 27:20 says, "Cursed *is* the one who lies with his father's wife, because he has uncovered his father's *bed* [כנף *robe's corner, wing*]"; here, a "father's wife" is the one who lies beneath a "father's wing, a father's robe." One is "cursed" who uncovers his father's wing in order to see his nakedness, and, when Noah realized he was violated by Canaan, he said, "Cursed be Canaan" (Genesis 9:25). A man's "nakedness" refers to the marital covenant through which man is connected to God through his wife. Finally, Ezekiel 22:10 communicates, "In you men uncover their fathers' nakedness; in you they violate women who are set apart during their impurity" thus paralleling a "father's nakedness" to women; therefore, a man's nakedness is his covenantal and private altar, his wife's threshold, his altar, his bride. A man's body is his bride.

Expressions are vital to the meaning of the Text. When an individual Book of Scripture is read in isolation, or when a word is inadvertently severed from an expression, much is lost when attempting to focus on the picture Scripture paints before us. For instance, consider the idea of being *clothed with skin*. Genesis 3:21 states, "Also for Adam and his wife the Lord God made tunics of skin, and clothed them." An immediate assumption could be made that since the humans realized they were naked, God gave clothing to cover the shame of exposure. Such an assumption is, in a sense, true, though true through abstraction — accurate as a reflection of an unseen source. Consider the fact that the ancient Babylonians called the dead "fleshless ones," for to clothe with skin would be to bring a person to life, and such a life can be seen in that Job 10:8-12 describes human gestation in this way: "Your hands have made me and fashioned me, an intricate unity... Remember, I pray, that You have made me like clay. And will You turn me into dust again? Did You not pour me out like milk, and curdle me like cheese, CLOTHE ME WITH SKIN AND FLESH, and knit me together with bones and sinews? You have granted me life and favor, and Your care has preserved my spirit"; gestation would be, in this sense, a type of resurrection from the dead (i.e. parents whose bodies are moving towards death but, in the process, procreate bodies proceeding in opposition to death). We may observe several metaphors here. (1) The fashioning of humanity in the womb is first described here as being an intricate "יחד *unity*." The word "unity" here is from the same root as the word אחד *one*, as in "Therefore a man shall leave his father and mother and be joined to his wife, and they shall become אחד *one flesh*" (Genesis 2:24) which, anatomically, discusses the marital union as the conduit of the gestation under discussion. (2) Job said that God's hands "עצבוני *fashioned me*," and this is from the same root as "בעצב *In pain* you shall bring forth children" (Genesis 3:16); the Hebrew word "in pain" is derived from the "fashioning" Job mentions, i.e. the making of a statue or vessel, and can be used to indicate a *toiling* that parallels the man's punishment ("by the sweat of your brow"). The same idea is expressed where it is written, "And the Lord God יצר *formed* man of the dust of the ground..." (Genesis 3:7) because יצר *formed* was applied as a technical potter's term that is synonymous with עצב *fashioning, pain* since יצר *to form* also means *to distress* in Hebrew. God acted as a Potter, and he formed an image within the womb, thus making the womb analogous to a potter's wheel. Such an image follows the ancient Orient's way of conceiving of life; that is, movement indicated "life," and, since a womb does not move in a locomotive sense, it would appear to have been viewed as a centrifuge comparable to a potter's wheel and a whirlwind, thus the next passage: "You have made me like clay. And will You turn me into dust again?" i.e. You added water to dust and made the clay of humanity; would you now dry me up (make me ashamed, make me naked) so that I am but waterless dust? --- which would explain more of why Genesis 2:6 describes the water that fertilized the ground, and Genesis 2:7 describes the creation of the "man of dust." (3) The pouring of water onto earth is now made analogous to milk hardening into cheese: "Did You not pour me out like milk, and curdle me like cheese." This figure is a delicate description of a man's emission eventuating into the flesh of his offspring. (4) The next figure states "...clothe me with skin and flesh..." and we now arrive at the expression of our focus. To "clothe with skin" is a gestational term that describes the unborn maturation of a human being, for clothing covers nakedness, and to be עָרִירִי *naked* also means to be *childless*. Nakedness is covered by clothing; childlessness is overcome by gestation and successful birth. (5) The final portion of the quotation under discussion is "...and knit me together with bones and sinews...." and the gestational image is viewed as a knitting, like the veil to the Holy of Holies, for this veil is called Christ's "flesh" in Hebrews 10:19-22: "Therefore, brethren, having boldness to enter the Holiest by the blood of Jesus, by a new and living way which He consecrated for us, THROUGH THE VEIL, THAT IS, HIS FLESH [His Robe, His Bride, His Nakedness], and having a High Priest over the house of God, let us draw near with a true heart in full assurance of faith, having our hearts sprinkled from an evil conscience and our bodies washed with pure water." The same parallel of gestation and clothing can be observed in Psalm 139:13-16:

> For You formed my inward parts; You COVERED ME IN MY MOTHER'S WOMB. I will praise You,for I am fearfully and wonderfully made; Marvelous are Your works, and that my soul knows very well. My frame was not hidden from You, when I was made in secret, and SKILLFULLY WROUGHT in the lowest parts of the earth. Your eyes saw my substance, being yet unformed. And in Your book they all were written, the days fashioned for me, when as yet there were none of them.

Since it has been established that "to clothe with skin" is a reference to gestation, it is advantageous to keep in mind that people who are already born can also be clothed with skin; therefore, such an adornment would seem to be a symbol of rebirth. A human is clothed with skin in the womb as a baby, and an adult can be clothed with skin in renewal, in rebirth, in conversion symbolized by Baptism: "Therefore, brethren, having boldness to enter the Holiest by the blood of Jesus, by a new and living way which He consecrated for us, THROUGH THE VEIL, THAT IS, HIS FLESH, and having a High Priest over the house of God, let us draw near with a true heart in full assurance of faith, having our hearts sprinkled from an evil conscience and our bodies washed with pure water" (Hebrews 10:19-22). After the first two humans sinned, then "...for Adam and his wife the Lord God made tunics of skin, and clothed them" (Genesis 3:21). It would appear that God covered them in blood by clothing them with skin... that He atoned for them through the shedding of the blood of "The Lamb slain from the foundation of the world" (Revelation 13:8), the blood of Christ, "For you are all sons of God through faith in Christ Jesus. For as many of you as were baptized into Christ have PUT ON Christ," and the Aramaic word טליא (Hebrew: טלה *lamb*) means a *child*, a *lamb*, similar to how the letters אמון mean a *male youth*, an *artificer* (like *a carpenter*), and *truth*: "I am The Way, THE TRUTH, and The Life..." (John 14:6). God provided the opportunity for repentance through rebirth, "Behold, the days come, says the Lord, when I will make a διαθηκην καινην *new testament* = ברית חדשה *renewed covenant*, that is, through being clothed with skin, being renewed, putting on Christ, The Lamb Who was slain, the Truth, the Carpenter, the Male Youth. The English word "atone" is the Hebrew word כפר *to cover,* and "blood" is called "life" in Genesis 9:4: "But you shall not eat flesh with its life, that is, its blood." To cover with blood is, literally, to atone with life. "I put on righteousness, and it clothed me; my justice was like a robe and a turban" (Job 29:14). We may now appreciate more of the illustrations provided us in II Corinthians 5:1-4 relative to Job 10:8-12:

> Your hands have made me and fashioned me, an intricate unity. Will You now turn and תבלעני SWALLOW ME? Remember, I pray, that You have made me like clay. And will You turn me into dust again? Did You not pour me out like milk, and curdle me like cheese, CLOTHE ME WITH SKIN AND FLESH, and knit me together with bones and sinews? You have granted me life and favor, and Your care has preserved my spirit (Job 10:8-12).

> For we know that if our earthly house, this tent, is destroyed, we have a building from God, a house not made with hands, eternal in the heavens. For in this WE GROAN, EARNESTLY DESIRING TO BE CLOTHED with our habitation which is from heaven, if indeed, HAVING BEEN CLOTHED, WE SHALL NOT BE FOUND NAKED. For we who are in this tent groan, being burdened, not because we want to be unclothed, but FURTHER CLOTHED, that mortality may be SWALLOWED up by life. Now He who has prepared us for this very thing is God, who also has given us the Spirit as a

guarantee. So we are always confident, knowing that while we are at home in the body we are absent from the Lord. For we walk by faith, not by sight. We are confident, yes, well pleased rather to be absent from the body and to be present with the Lord (II Corinthians 5:1-4).

When comprehending the Heavenly garments offered to humanity, it is necessary to keep in mind that saved humanity is the bride, not the groom. Though males may find it difficult to conceive of such a metaphor, remember that it is the bride who is to bring forth fruit, it is this counterpart who is to be fruitfully receptive in receiving the Power from on High. Consider: "My little children, for whom I labor in birth again until Christ is formed in you" (Galatians 4:19). The imagery here would seem to suggest that Paul is speaking from the standpoint of the bride giving birth to Christ for the sake of others; in this respect, God is both the Sire and the Son. Christ said, "I and My Father are one" (John 10:30), for he is "The Root and the Offspring of David" (Revelation 22:16). When the bride was found to be עֵירֹם *naked, childless,* Her Husband clothed her with skins, gave her a means with which to renew the covenant... He gave her a Son. "And Adam was not deceived, but the woman being deceived, fell into transgression. Nevertheless SHE will be *saved in childbearing* if THEY continue in faith, love, and holiness, with self-control" (I Timothy 2:14-15). After the first humans swallowed the forbidden food, they were found naked, and God clothed them that death may be swallowed up in victory through repentance and renewal. Such a teaching is contained in the expression "to clothe with skin." Scripture is not informing us of the rude attire of cavemen and the uncouth clothing of childlike morons! The Text describes the heavenly attire of revivification and perpetuity birthed through a contrite spirit in the acceptance of a grace beyond capabilities of the English word "love." Hebrews 5:5-14 says,

> So also Christ did not glorify Himself to become High Priest, but it was He who said to Him: "You are My SON, today I have begotten You." As He also says in another place: "You are a priest forever according to the order of Melchizedek"; who, in the days of His FLESH, when He had offered up prayers and supplications, with vehement cries and tears to Him who was able to save Him from death, and was heard because of His godly fear, though He was a SON, yet He learned obedience by the things which He suffered. And having been perfected, He became the AUTHOR OF ETERNAL SALVATION to all who obey Him, called by God as High Priest "according to the order of Melchizedek," of whom we have much to say, and hard to explain, since you

have become dull of hearing. For though by this time you ought to be teachers, you need someone to teach you again the first principles of the oracles of God; and you have come to need milk and not solid food. For everyone who partakes only of milk is unskilled in the word of righteousness, for he is a BABE. But solid food belongs to those who are of full age, that is, those who by reason of use have their senses exercised to discern both **good and evil**.

Notice the opposition in Hosea 4:6: "My people are destroyed for lack of knowledge. Because you have rejected knowledge, I also will reject you from being priest for Me; because you have forgotten the law of your God, I also will forget your CHILDREN." Considering the fact that **The Tree of the Knowledge of Good and Evil** killed a bride who was "deceived and fell into transgression," it is perceptible that the bride was "unskilled in the words of righteousness" and therefore a "babe"; in other words, a lack of knowledge destroyed an infant... thus when the bride was found to be ערירי *naked, childless,* Her Husband, God, clothed her with skins in order to renew the covenant through the birth of The Son of Adam, The Son of Man. "Then she spoke out with a loud voice and said, "Blessed are you among women, and blessed is the fruit of your womb!" (Luke 1:42). "So when the woman saw that the tree was good for food, that it was pleasant to the eyes, and a tree desirable to make one wise, she took of its fruit and ate..." (Genesis 3:6). "Your hands have made me and fashioned me, an intricate unity. Will You now turn and בבלעני SWALLOW ME? Remember, I pray, that You have made me like clay. And will You turn me into dust again? Did You not pour me out like milk, and curdle me like cheese, CLOTHE ME WITH SKIN AND FLESH, and knit me together with bones and sinews...?" (Job 10:8-12).

A covenant was a binding oath that suggested creativity in the respect that two formerly distinct natures elected to mingle in order to form one new entity that shared a singular life in more than one body. With respect to any threat against the new life of a covenant, the new nature, having more than one body, was, at this point, capable of sustaining itself through sacrifice since the act of one counterpart giving its life for the other allowed for perpetuity. The two covenanting counterparts, in a state without immediately apparent threat, revivified their communal oath by symbollically performing a sacrifice that symbolized what each was in agreement to do for the other should the need arise; therefore, the symbol or sign of the covenant, though involving substance, was not itself the substance of the covenant; rather, the covenanting counterparts were the substance of the covenant. Mistakenly confusing the sign and the substance allowed for the covenant to be degraded into a mere performance of rites and not a way of life that reflected the mingled and new nature that was parabolically renewed through the clandestinely instructive rites that paralleled it. Confusing the symbolic gender roles of the covenant allowed for unnatural relations that defied the covenant itself. Covenants were "cut" through a deliberate choice that involved ingestion as a symbol of comprehension. Ingestion made the physical symbols part of the covenanting parties in the same way that mutual assent made the new, combined lifestyle able to be renewed continually through reminders instigated by the physical symbols. Keeping in mind that *eating* could indicate *copulation* (i.e. a physical symbol of covenantal truce), the bread or meal was the symbol of the truce between the two parties, and the blood was a symbol of the life-long binding to which both pledged themselves. Since a covenant was an oath, breaching the covenant was invoking Divine wrath unto death. Wine was indeed understood as blood, specifically the blood of grapes, for a grape cluster was understood conceptually and etymologically as a binding itself similar to how blood-relations bind families; yet, a covenant was an elective blood-relation which made it analogous to a marriage more so than a lineage because lineage is but the result of others' choices whereas a covenant was the choice that birthed the resulting lineage. As such, it is apparent why covenants involved creativity as mirrored by procreativity, for a covenant bound two separate natures into one new nature that was renewed through the creativity that was inherent in the nature of the covenant itself. The inheritance of the union is analogous to a firstborn, and the "Right of the Firstborn" was the title given to the priest who officiated at the altar of sacrifice that was used as a symbol of the union of the people who remembered their pledge before it ceremonially. If the priest, the sacrificer, the Firstborn was himself a covenanting party with another person, then he was the father or lord of the covenant and, at the same time, the Firstborn; in this respect, the Father and the Firstborn were one and the same person, and the Firstborn's covenant was inherently understood to create further life for the purpose of perpetuating the life, the blood, of the covenantal union. The type of the elected lineage through blood, through life, was signified through libation being lifted up in oath and overturned in libation so that the wine, the blood, the life covered the altar that was itself analogous to the bride. The Firstborn was as the husband, the altar was as the bride, and the offering was as the firstborn of the Firstborn's union who saw himself upon the altar reflected by the offering upon it; the Firstborn, the Priest, who was the Sacrificer was, in this sense, both the sacrificer and the sacrifice linked to his firstborn through the altar in a manner similar to how a father is linked to his child through his wife. It was critical that the altar and the sacrifice be understood in a strictly symbolic sense, for, if the symbol and the substance were mistakenly inverted, then the offering would actually be a human child, the altar would actually be a human mother... inhumanity would ensue. The priest was to guard the altar, for it was closed with the intimacy of a marriage. The altar itself was understood as a threshold to a dwelling, and the priest was understood to live within that dwelling; accordingly, the priest was positioned on one side of the altar while the offerer was positioned on the other; the guardian priest — not the offerer — possessed the license to pass the threshold of the altar and move to the side of the offerer in order to administer the shared, covenantal meal which, in turn, brought the offerer on the side of the priest. If the priest acted on behalf of the Deity alone, his officiation at the altar would place him in the role of a vicar of the Deity, and the Deity would be symbolized by the fire and the priest that received the gifts and caused them to ascend to the ethereal, divine dwelling — thus linking heaven and earth and showing earth to be only a copy and shadow of the hidden substance and source above. The priest had the right, and therefore the responsibility, to guard the altar so as not to let the boundary, the threshold, be transgressed by the bride (the congregation), for it was he who was to come to them first in the sign of the covenant, for it was the husband who was to propose to the bride. The priest officiated at the altar as a husband renews the life of the covenant by officiating at the threshold of his bride. The priest, along with the congregation, constituted the collective bride of the covenant which indicated that the Deity was willing to unify with His worshippers in order that His creativity might flow through them to the extent of gifts flowing from the congregation in a state that is analogous to a child passing through the bride — thus, the Deity was, in effect, the Sire and the Son of the covenant, and He symbolized himself in the Firstborn, the priest whom He chose to guard the altar and therefore the congregation of God.

Again, a covenant was a binding oath that suggested creativity in the respect that two formerly distinct natures elected to mingle in order to form one new entity that shared a singular life in more than one body. With respect to any threat against the new life of a covenant, the new nature, having more than one body, was, at this point, capable of sustaining itself through sacrifice since the act of one counterpart giving its life for the other allowed for perpetuity:

Then God blessed them, and God said to them, "Be fruitful and multiply; fill the earth and subdue it; HAVE DOMINION OVER THE FISH OF THE SEA, OVER THE BIRDS OF THE AIR, AND OVER EVERY LIVING THING THAT MOVES ON THE EARTH" (Genesis 1:28).

"[After the Lord's Supper...] ...Peter sat outside in the courtyard. And a servant girl came to him, saying, 'You also were with Jesus of Galilee.' But he denied it before them all, saying, 'I do not know what you are saying.' And when he had gone out to the gateway, another girl saw him and said to those who were there, 'This fellow also was with Jesus of Nazareth.' But again he denied WITH AN OATH, 'I do not know the Man!' And a little later those who stood by came up and said to Peter, 'Surely you also are one of them, for your speech betrays you.' Then he began to curse and swear, saying, 'I do not know the Man!' Immediately a rooster crowed. And Peter remembered the word of Jesus who had said to him, 'Before the rooster crows, you will deny Me three times.' So he went out and wept bitterly" (Matthew 26:69-74).

And you, who once were alienated and enemies in your mind by wicked works, yet now He has reconciled in the body of His flesh through death, to present you holy, and blameless, and above reproach in His sight — if indeed you continue in the faith, grounded and steadfast, and are not moved away from the hope of the gospel which you heard, WHICH WAS PREACHED TO EVERY CREATURE UNDER HEAVEN... (Colossians 1:21-23).

The two covenanting counterparts, in a state without an immediately apparent threat, revivified their communal oath by symbollically performing a sacrifice, a drawing near, that symbolized what each was in agreement to do for the other should the need arise; therefore, the symbol or sign of the covenant, though involving substance, was not itself the substance of the covenant; rather, the covenanting counterparts were the substance of the covenant. Knowing that "woman" is called a "garden" Scripturally, we may observe the following:

The Lord God planted a garden eastward in Eden [= Fertility], and there He put the man whom He had formed... Then THE LORD GOD TOOK THE MAN AND PUT HIM IN THE GARDEN [woman] OF EDEN [Fertility] to tend [serve] and keep [guard] it (Genesis 2:8).

To "wash the feet" was a euphemistic expression that connoted the MARITAL UNION and also a symbolic expression that indicated a COVENANT

THAT PRODUCED LIFE through mingled natures (Genesis 18:4; 2 Samuel 11:8). "Now before the FEAST OF THE PASSOVER, when Jesus knew that His hour had come that He should depart from this world to the Father, having loved His own who were in the world, He loved them to the end. And supper being ended, the devil having already put it into the heart of Judas Iscariot, Simon's son, to betray Him, Jesus, knowing that the Father had given all things into His hands, and that He had come from God and was going to God, rose from supper and LAID ASIDE HIS GARMENTS, TOOK A TOWEL AND GIRDED HIMSELF. AFTER THAT, HE POURED WATER INTO A BASIN AND BEGAN TO WASH THE DISCIPLES' FEET, AND TO WIPE THEM WITH THE TOWEL WITH WHICH HE WAS GIRDED" (John 13: 1-5).

> For He Himself is our peace, who has made both one, and has broken down the middle wall of separation, having abolished in His flesh the enmity, that is, the law of commandments contained in ordinances, SO AS TO CREATE IN HIMSELF ONE NEW MAN FROM THE TWO, thus making peace, and that He MIGHT RECONCILE THEM BOTH TO GOD IN ONE BODY through the cross, thereby putting to death the enmity (Ephesians 2:14-16).

Mistakenly *confusing the sign and the substance* allowed for the covenant to be degraded into a mere performance of rites and not a way of life that reflected the mingled and new nature that was parabolically renewed through the clandestinely instructive rites that paralleled it, and **confusing the symbolic gender roles** of the covenant allowed for unnatural relations that defied the covenant itself. Covenants were "cut" through a deliberate choice that involved ingestion as a symbol of comprehension. Ingestion made the physical symbols part of the covenanting parties in the same way that mutual assent made the new, combined lifestyle able to be renewed continually through reminders instigated by the physical symbols.

> **Because *you* have heeded the voice of your wife *[instead of the other way around]*, and have eaten from the tree** *[that unified unsuitable constituents against nature]* of which I commanded you, saying, 'You shall not eat of it': Cursed is the ground for your sake; in toil you shall eat of it all the days of your life. Both thorns and thistles it shall bring forth for you, and you shall eat the herb of the field. IN THE SWEAT OF YOUR FACE YOU SHALL EAT BREAD till you return to the ground, for out of it you were taken; for dust you are, and to dust you shall return. (Genesis 3:17-19).

> Now on the first day of the Feast of Unleavened Bread the disciples came to Jesus, saying to Him, "Where do You want us

to prepare for You to eat the Passover?" And He said, "Go into the city to a certain man, and say to him, 'The Teacher says, 'My time is at hand; I will keep the Passover at your house with My disciples.'" So the disciples did as Jesus had directed them; and they prepared the Passover. When evening had come, He sat down with the twelve. Now as they were eating, He said, "Assuredly, I say to you, one of you will betray Me." AND THEY WERE EXCEEDINGLY SORROWFUL, and each of them began to say to Him, "Lord, is it I?" He answered and said, *"He who dipped his hand with Me in the dish will betray Me [**for two men in one basin was unnatural as was the case with the forbidden tree**]. The Son of Man indeed goes just as it is written of Him,* BUT WOE TO THAT MAN BY WHOM THE SON OF MAN IS BETRAYED! *It would have been good for that man if he had not been* ***born***." Then Judas, who was betraying Him, answered and said, "Rabbi, is it I?" He said to him, "You have said it." And as they were eating, Jesus took bread, blessed and broke it, and gave it to the disciples and said, "Take, eat; this is My body" (Matthew 26:17-26).

Wives, submit to your own husbands, as to the Lord. For the husband is head of the wife, as also Christ is head of the church; and He is the Savior of the body. Therefore, just as the church is subject to Christ, so let the wives be to their own husbands in everything. Husbands, love your wives, just as Christ also loved the church and gave Himself for her, that He might sanctify and cleanse her with the washing of water by the word, that He might present her to Himself a glorious church, not having spot or wrinkle or any such thing, but that she should be holy and without blemish. So husbands ought to love their own wives as their own bodies; he who loves his wife loves himself. For no one ever hated his own flesh, but nourishes and cherishes it, just as the Lord does the church. For we are members of His body, of His flesh and of His bones. '*For this reason a man shall leave his father and mother and be joined to his wife, and* ***the two shall become one flesh***.' This is a great mystery, but I speak concerning Christ and the church. Nevertheless let each one of you in particular so love his own wife as himself, and let the wife see that she respects her husband" (Ephelsans 5:22-33).

Compare this passage to God's judgment of mercy towards the Bride: "Your desire shall be for your Husband, and He will rule over you" (Genesis 3:16) to counteract eating from the forbidden tree: "For their vine is of the vine of Sodom and of the fields of Gomorrah; their grapes are grapes of gall, their clusters are bitter. Their wine is the poison of serpents, and the cruel venom of cobras" (Deuteronomy 32:32-33).

Keep in mind that "eating" could indicate copulation (a physical symbol of covenantal blood was a symbol of the life-long binding to which both pledged themselves). Since a covenant was a solemn oath, breaching the covenant was invoking wrath. Wine was indeed understood as blood, specifically the blood of grapes, for a grape cluster was understood conceptually and etymologically as a binding itself, which is similar to how blood-relations bind families; yet, a covenant was an elective blood-relation which made it analogous to a marriage more so than a lineage because lineage is but the result of others' choices, whereas a covenant was the choice that birthed the resulting lineage.

> And the LORD God commanded the man, saying, "Of every tree of the garden you may freely eat; but of THE TREE OF THE KNOWLEDGE OF GOOD AND EVIL you shall not eat, for in the day that you eat of it you shall surely die" (Genesis 2: 16-17).

In opposition to the false vine on the Tree of Life, we can observe the True Vine on the tree of death: "I AM THE TRUE VINE, and My Father is the vinedresser. Every branch in Me that does not bear fruit He takes away; and every branch that bears fruit He prunes, that it may bear more fruit. You are already clean because of the word which I have spoken to you. Abide in Me, and I in you. As the branch cannot bear fruit of itself, unless it abides in the vine, neither can you, unless you abide in Me. I AM THE VINE, you are the branches. He who abides in Me, and I in him, bears much fruit; for without Me you can do nothing. If anyone does not abide in Me, he is cast out as a branch and is withered; and they gather them and throw them into the fire, and they are burned. If you abide in Me, and My words abide in you, you will ask what you desire, and it shall be done for you. By this My Father is glorified, that you bear much fruit; so you will be My disciples. As the Father loved Me, I also have loved you; abide in My love. If you keep My commandments, you will abide in My love, just as I have kept My Father's commandments and abide in His love. These things I have spoken to you, that My joy may remain in you, and that your joy may be full. This is My commandment, that you love one another as I have loved you. GREATER LOVE HAS NO ONE THAN THIS, THAN TO LAY DOWN ONE'S LIFE FOR HIS FRIENDS [the sacrificial covenant that sustains life instead of ending it]. You are My friends if you do whatever I command you. No longer do I call you servants, for a servant does not know what his master is doing; but I have called you friends, for all things that I heard from My Father I have made known to you. You did not choose Me, but I chose you and appointed you that you should go and bear fruit, and that your fruit should remain, that whatever you ask the Father in My name He may give you" (John 15:1-16).

> Therefore DO NOT BE UNWISE [as was the case with the forbidden tree], BUT UNDERSTAND WHAT THE WILL OF THE LORD is. And DO NOT BE DRUNK WITH WINE, in which is dissipation; but be filled with the Spirit, speaking to one another in psalms and hymns and spiritual songs, singing and making melody in your heart to the Lord, giving thanks always for all things to God the Father in the name of our Lord Jesus Christ, submitting to one another in the fear of God. Wives, submit to your own husbands, as to the Lord. For the husband is head of the wife, as also CHRIST IS HEAD OF THE CHURCH; AND HE IS THE SAVIOR OF THE BODY (Ephesians 5:17-23).

As such, it is apparent why covenants involved creativity as paralleled by procreativity, for a covenant bound two separate natures into one new nature that was renewed through the creativity that was inherent in the nature of the covenant itself. The inheritance of the union is analogous to a firstborn, and the "Right of the Firstborn" was the title given to the priest who officiated at the altar of sacrifice that was used as a symbol of the union of the people who remembered their pledge before it ceremonially. Again, if the priest, the sacrificer, the Firstborn was himself a covenanting party with another person, then he was the father or Lord of the Covenant and, at the same time, the Firstborn; in this respect, the Father and the Firstborn were one and the same person, and the Firstborn's covenant was inherently understood to create further life for the purpose of perpetuating the life, the blood, of the covenantal union.

> Do you not believe that I am in the Father, and the Father in Me? The words that I speak to you I do not speak on My own authority; but the Father who dwells in Me does the works (John 14:10).
>
> I and My Father are one (John 10:30).

The type of the elected lineage through blood, through life, was signified through libation being lifted up in oath and overturned in libation so that the wine, the blood, the life covered the altar that was itself analogous to the bride. The Firstborn was as the husband, the altar was as the bride, and the offering was as the firstborn of the Firstborn's union who saw himself upon the altar reflected by the offering upon it.

The Lord has sworn and will not relent, 'You are a priest forever according to the order of Melchizedek (Psalm 110:4).

For every high priest taken from among men is appointed for men in things pertaining to God, that he may offer both gifts and sacrifices for sins. He can have compassion on those who are ignorant and going astray, since he himself is also subject to weakness. Because of this he is required as for the people, so also for himself, to offer sacrifices for sins. And no man takes this honor to himself, but he who is called by God, just as Aaron was. So also Christ did not glorify Himself to become High Priest, but it was He who said to Him: 'You are My Son, Today I have begotten You.' As He also says in another place: 'You are a priest forever according to the order of Melchizedek'; who, in the days of His flesh, when He had offered up prayers and supplications, with vehement cries and tears to Him who was able to save Him from death, and was heard because of His godly fear, though He was a Son, yet He learned obedience by the things which He suffered. And having been perfected, He became the author of eternal salvation to all who obey Him, called by God as High Priest 'according to the order of Melchize-dek,' of whom we have much to say, and hard to explain, since you have become dull of hearing (Hebrews 5:1-11).

For He made Him who knew no sin to be $\alpha\mu\alpha\rho\tau\iota\alpha\nu$ = חטא *a sin offering* for us, that we might become the righteousness of God in Him (2 Corinthians 5:21).

The Firstborn, the Priest, who was the Sacrificer was, in this sense, both the sacrificer and the sacrifice linked to his firstborn through the altar in a manner similar to how a father is linked to his child through his wife.

To the woman He said: "I will greatly multiply your sorrow and your conception; IN PAIN YOU SHALL BRING FORTH CHILDREN; your desire shall be for your husband, and he shall rule over you" (Genesis 3:16).

Then Simeon blessed them, and said to Mary His mother, "Behold, this Child is destined for the fall and rising of many in Israel, and for a sign which will be spoken against (yes, A SWORD WILL PIERCE THROUGH YOUR OWN SOUL ALSO), that the thoughts of many hearts may be revealed" (Luke 2:34-36).

And He is the head of the body, the church, who is the beginning, THE FIRSTBORN FROM THE DEAD, that in all things He may have the preeminence (Colossians 1:18).

> Grace to you and peace from Him who is and who was and
> who is to come, and from the seven Spirits who are before His
> throne, and from Jesus Christ, the faithful witness, the FIRST-
> BORN FROM THE DEAD, and the ruler over the kings of the earth
> (Revelation 1:4-5).

It was necessary that the altar and the sacrifice be understood in an illustrative manner, for, if the symbol and the substance were mistakenly inverted, then the slaughtered offering would actually be a human child, the altar of slaughter would actually be a human mother... inhumanity would desecrate the beauty of what the constructive sacrificial union was supposed to be. It must be remembered that altars were often the tops of tombs, and the ignescent life atop the tomb served as a decisive contrast to the corpse beneath it. Such a parallel struck a demarcation between death and life that served as a poigniant reminder that the covenanting parties had life's binding under penalty of death's severence. The priest was to guard the altar, for it was closed with the intimacy of a marriage. The altar itself was understood as a threshold of a dwelling, a temple, and the priest was understood to reside inside that dwelling. The priest possessed the authority to pass over the threshold, to approach the altar in order to administer the shared, covenantal meal, which, in turn, brought the offerer near the priest regarding the oath to the death by blood. If the priest acted on behalf of the Deity alone, his service at the altar would place him in the role of a vicar of the Deity, and the Deity would be symbolized by both the fire and the priest that received the gifts and caused them to ascend to the ethereal, divine dwelling; this may be the link between the Hebrew words אש *fire* and איש *man*:

> Now the Lord spoke to Moses after the death of the two sons of
> Aaron, when they offered profane fire before the Lord, and died;
> and the Lord said to Moses: "Tell Aaron your brother not to
> come at just any time into the Holy Place inside the veil, before
> the mercy seat which is on the ark, lest he die; for I will appear
> in the cloud above the mercy seat (Leviticus 16:1-2).

Again, the offerers were not allowed to approach the altar, the table, the threshold, the tomb (in this case, the Ark of the Covenant) at any time, for the union of the Divine and human was under the direction of the Divine, not the human. Such a union would serve to join Heaven and Earth with the remembrance of death beneath, for such is the case with the ancient symbolism of a tree when considering its subterranean roots that ramify into the realm of the dead and its trunk that serves as an axis to the heavens where the tree's branches extend into the loftiness of the firmament. The priest, who guarded this (ה)עץ *wood, tree, counsel,* of wisdom, this sacrificial illustration of wisdom, had the right, and therefore the responsibility, to guard the altar of the feminine ארץ *Earth* upon which the עץ *wood, tree* was set for the fire of the קרבן *sacrifice, the drawing near to the divine.* The עץ *wood* of the אש *fire* bound the sacrifice to the איש *man* and the עץ *tree* as all three were unified in ascension, for the word עלה *burnt offering* is from the root עלה *to ascend (literally, he ascended).* Concerning the Passover and Communion, the שה *lamb* which is as a טליא *Lamb, Little Boy,* was the flesh and blood of the sacrifice; it was slaughtered at the threshold of the house and united with wood and fire by the man, the priest of the house, the sacrificer who officiated at the altar as a husband renews and reaffirms the life of the covenant by officiating at the threshold of his bride. We can see that such an offering distinguished between a live firstborn and a dead one:

> Thus says the Lord: "Israel is My son, My firstborn. So I say to you, let My son go that he may serve Me. But if you refuse to let him go, indeed I will kill your son, your firstborn" (Exodus 4:22-23).

> They departed from Rameses in the first month, on the fifteenth day of the first month; on the day after the Passover the children of Israel went out with boldness in the sight of all the Egyptians. For the Egyptians were burying all their firstborn, whom the Lord had killed among them. Also on their gods the Lord had executed judgments (Numbers 33:3-4).

The Firstborn (the Priest) of Israel slaughtered a lamb, and Egypt's obstinence came at the penalty of the death of its firstborn. Consider:

> Then he said, 'Look, the fire and the wood, but where is the lamb for a burnt offering?' And Abraham said, 'My son, God will provide for Himself the lamb for a burnt offering.' So the two of them went together (Genesis 22:7-8).

Another way to render this passage is, "Then he said, 'Look, האש *the fire* והעצים *and the wood,* but where is השה*the one of the flock* for a burnt offering?' And Abraham said, 'My son, God will provide for Himself the השה *the one of the flock* לעלה *for a burnt offering, ascension.'* So the two of them went יחדו *as one.*" The word שה *is one of the flock (whether sheep or goat);* consider, more specifically, the Aramaic word טליא *lamb* (Hebrew: טלה *lamb),* child. Both the father (who had possessed The Right of the Firstborn) and the son (The Firstborn) were "as one." The "Firstborn" was also called the "Only Begotten Son" even if he had brothers, as was the case with Isaac and Ishmael (Genesis 22:2): "For God so loved the world that He gave HIS ONLY BEGOTTEN SON, that whoever believes in Him should not perish but have everlasting life" (John 3:16), i.e. God gave his Firstborn, the One Who would inherit the eternal priesthood according to the order of Melchizedek. Furthermore, the word "gave" in John 3:16 is but a Greek translation of the נתן *child sacrifice (particularly of the firstborn)*: "For God so loved the world that He נתן *sacrificed (i.e. He sired successfully into the world) His Firstborn*, HIS ONLY BEGOTTEN SON, that whoever believes in Him should not perish but have everlasting life." Isaac asked concerning the שה *one of the flock, particularly a lamb*, but God provided a איל *ram* which is also *a certain ornament over doors* (like the passover blood of Communion), and this ram was caught in an סבך *interweavement* by his horns, like the Firstborn and His crown of thorns. Another way to render Genesis 22:7-8 quite literally (keeping in mind the fire/man relation) would be, "Then he said, 'Look, האש *the Man* והעצים *and the trees*, but where is the lamb [טליא *lamb, little boy*] for a burnt offering?' And Abraham said, 'My son, God will provide for Himself the lamb טליא [*lamb, little boy*] לעלה *for ascension*.' So the two of them went יחדו *as one*," for, after He ascended, Peter called Christ the "Holy Child" (Acts 4:30), and Proverbs 8:30 says that Wisdom was the אמון *craftsman, child* at the "side" of the Lord, for "No one has seen God at any time. The ONLY BEGOTTEN SON, who is IN THE BOSOM OF THE FATHER, He has declared Him" (John 1:18), i.e. at the side of the Father like a Holy Child and Carpenter. This word "אמון *craftsman, child*" is derived from the same root as אמנה *covenant*, which is synonymous to ברית is *a binding oath* from the root ברה *to cut, to eat, to choose*, and is related to the root ברא *to create*. The words ברותה *food* and ברית *a binding oath, covenant* are derivatives of the same source, which reflects the concept that the act of eating itself was religiously sacrificial and was therefore accompanied by a prayer of thanksgiving. Reconsidering thanksgiving, the root ידה *to throw, to cast, to confess, to give thanks*, produces the words ידות *hymns*, תודה *confession, praise, and thanksgiving, a company of persons singing songs of praise, a choir of singers*, and יהודה *Judah*. Christ came through Judah in the בשר *flesh, royal proclamation of good news*, Gospel:

> And behold, an angel of the Lord stood before them, and the glory of the Lord shone around them, and they were greatly afraid. Then the angel said to them, 'Do not be afraid, for behold, I bring you GOOD TIDINGS of great joy which will be to all people [בשר *flesh, successful birth, proclamation of good news*, Gospel]. For there is born to you this day in the city of David [from Judah] a Savior, who is Christ the Lord. And this

will be the sign to you: You will find a Babe wrapped in swaddling cloths, lying in a manger [Hebrew: ארון *ark, coffin,* as in the Ark of the Covenant].' And suddenly there was with the angel a multitude of the heavenly host [תודה *confession, praise, and thanksgiving, a company of persons singing songs of praise, a choir of singers*] praising God and saying: 'Glory to God in the highest, And on earth peace, goodwill toward men! [בשר *flesh, royal proclamation of good news,* Gospel]' So it was, when the angels had gone away from them into heaven, that the shepherds said to one another, 'Let us now go to בית לחם*House of Bread/Womb of Fruit [~Eden = Fruitful Womb] Bethlehem* and see this thing that has come to pass, which the Lord has made known to us.' (Luke 2:9-15).

Since לחם can mean both *bread* and *fruit,* we can see how in one tree, the grape vine, Holy Communion can take place. Adam was to "guard" the garden (Genesis 2:15), like a priest is to guard the altar, like a husband is to guard his wife. The Fall of man was accomplished by a mockery of Holy Communion through the false vine that *united* incompatability: "For their vine is of the vine of Sodom and of the fields of Gomorrah; their grapes are grapes of gall, their clusters are bitter. Their wine is the poison of serpents, and the cruel venom of cobras" (Deuteronomy 32:32-33). The threshold was a concave delineation that was utilized sacrificially as an altar to draw near, to worship, with food dedicated to God and eaten in *union* with Him; if the service was not performed properly with a discerning heart, the penalty was death, as was the case on the first Passover and at Lot's house in Sodom. Melchizek brought out bread and wine to worship with Abraham as opposed to the King of Sodom who offered spoils; obviously, Melchizedek represents Christ as the King of Sodom reflects the Knowledge of Good and Evil, i.e. the union of unsuitable mixture that is incapable of producing viable fruit. Let us now, however, consider the literary genius Scripture provides in the description of viable fruit production.

The entrance of Eden would have been understood as its foundation, its cornerstone, the place of judgment, the threshold upon which the sacrificial fire burned, and a portal that contained a secret, for the word בשר *flesh* also means *Gospel* and connotes a *successful birth.* Adam, as a priest and husband, did not guard the altar. Christ, The Last Adam, The High Priest Forever according to the order of Melchizedek, offered us His flesh and blood (His Gospel and Covenant) through His sacrifice that qualified Him as "Firstborn of the Dead" in whom "...we are members of His body, of His flesh and of His bones" (Ephesians 5:30), the "one flesh" of

Genesis 2:24. That the word בשר *flesh* also means *proclamation of good news* (i.e. gospel) with a specific reference to *successful birth* can be seen in Malachi's quotation and definition of Genesis 2:24. Genesis 2:24 states, "Therefore a man shall leave his father and mother and be joined to his wife, and they shall become one בשר *flesh*." Malachi 2:15 says, "But did He not make them one, Having a remnant of the Spirit? And why one? He seeks godly offspring. Therefore take heed to your spirit, and let none deal treacherously with the wife of his youth." Malachi quotes the "one" and defines the "flesh," for when he asks "And why 'one'?" concerning Genesis 2:24, he explains the word בשר *flesh* in terms of successful birth by defining it as "godly offspring." Immediately following the proclamation of God's Image through man, "The Serpent" enters the scene overtly. On account of his inducement, and man's participation in it, history had to wait for God's Image to come through flesh, through a successful birth, that is, through the Gospel that was abortively set in abeyance in Eden.

Genesis 5:2 states that God called both His male and female human creations "אדם *Adam* in the day He created them." Genesis 2:23 informs us that the male Adam named the female Adam אשה *woman* after proclaiming himself איש *man*. We may see, therefore, that God gave a single name to His first human (who was male) and the same name to His second human (who was female), but Adam called himself and his wife a name other than what we read of God providing. The name of איש *man* resembles the word for אש *fire*, and we might consider that God "... makes His מלאכיו *His angels/messengers* spirits and His ministers a flame of אש *fire*" (Psalm 104:4) and that a priest is called an *angel/messenger* in Malachi 2:7.. Adam, it would seem, referred to himself with a priestly title. A further clue to this assertion can be seen in the name he gave his wife before the title (Eve) he gave her after the fall. Before Adam named his bride Eve (i.e. Life, Living), before the Fall, our first human mother was named "Adam" by God and אשה *woman* by the male Adam. This word אשה *woman* is spelled consonantally identically to the word אשהfire offering. This word אשה *fire offering* also means *gift* as discerned by a Ugaritic cognate. That the name *woman* is connected to a *gift* can be observed when Adam blamed God by stating, " האשהthe woman, the gift whom נתתה *You* GAVE to be with me, she GAVE me of the tree" (Genesis 3:12). The name אשה *woman*, however, is connected to *fire*, and this realization helps us to view her as the constructive product of God's altar that He constructed from Adam's circumcised heart, for it is written that, " ויבןHe built her" into a אשה *woman,* and the word "built" is the same as when Sarah hoped to be "built up" through Hagar in Genesis 16:2, when Abraham "built" an altar for Isaac in Genesis 22:9, and when God "built" David a house, i.e. provided an altar of child-birth (not child-sacrifice) regarding his eventual son, Solomon, and Son, Jesus, in 1 Chronicles 17:10-11. We may notice in the concept of "building" that altars, child-birth, and child-sacrifice are connected so that the unifying theme is *gestation,* whereby a constructive altar generates life and a destructive altar takes life. The word אש *fire* is a synonym for אור *light, fire, life, wisdom* as in "Let there be אור *light, fire, life, wisdom*" (Genesis 1:3); thus, the fire of an altar can either signify life rising from the table or life being destroyed upon the table. The name אשה *woman* is provided in the Narration of Genesis 2:22 as a product of "building" from Adam's circumcised heart and, in this, the reader can see the constructivity and subsequent life generated from Adam's open heart.

The man's heart is analogous to the female's womb in Hebrew thematically and linguistically. Linguistically, the word לב *heart, mind* is derived from the root לבב *to be in the central core, in the middle;* the בית *womb, dwelling, house* is understood in connection to *wisdom* (Proverbs 24:3) and is, accordingly, connected to the mind. If one were to consider the physical body of humanity, then the mind, heart, and womb, if connected by a line, would mark the middle of the body. Genesis 2:21 states literally that God "took one מצלעתיו *from his sides*" which is usually translated as "one of his ribs." Nevertheless, the Text says *one from his sides.* In this expression, one may understand a circumcised heart and therefore a blade of some sort (literary or otherwise). One may also consider literarily a bisected man. As outrageous as this figure may sound at first, consider that this literary figure is reflected physically by Abraham's sacrifice wherein God prophesied the Savior through the birth of Isaac. In the case of both Adam and Abraham, their future offspring were generated following the same "תרדמה *deep sleep*" or incubation (Genesis 2:21; 15:12). Adam was caused to fall into his deep sleep and then had "one from his sides" taken from him while Abraham, as though in a mirror, split the animal carcasses in halves and then fell into his deep sleep. Adam's deep sleep preceded his constructive sacrifice, while Abraham's deep sleep followed his destructive sacrifice that was also followed by the prophetic promise of his Seed. The "halves opposite each other" that Abraham's blade carved out are described literally in Hebrew as "איש בתרו לקרא רעהו *a man split opposite his neighbor*" (Genesis 15:10). The "man" and his "neighbor" are the halves of one body, thus, "You shall love your neighbor as yourself" (Leviticus 19:18). The word "man" here is the same name that Adam called himself when he named his wife אשה *woman.* It would seem as if Adam was designating himself figuratively as one of the halves of his own body and his wife as his "neighbor." Consider, "You shall love your neighbor as yourself" (Leviticus 19:18) along with Ephesians 5:28-33:

> So husbands ought to love their own wives AS THEIR OWN BOD-IES; he who loves his wife loves himself. For no one ever hated HIS OWN FLESH, but nourishes and cherishes it, just as the Lord does the church. For we are members of His body, of His flesh and of His bones. "For this reason a man shall leave his father and mother and be joined to his wife, and the two shall be-come one flesh." This is a great mystery, but I speak concern-ing Christ and the church. Nevertheless let each one of you in particular so love his own wife AS HIMSELF, and let the wife see that she respects her husband.

Adam's title of איש *man* linguistically resembles fire and themati-cally signifies a *half*. The title Adam gave to his wife was אשה *woman* and is connected to a *fire offering* and a *gift* but is understood as a "neighbor" with respect to the other half. The two halves would then be bisected by fire, and in Genesis 15:17 we read of the pillar of smoke and of fire pass-ing between the halved carcasses of Abraham's sacrifice like that which halved the sea during the Exodus. The creation of woman is described as a halving that involved fire in a manner similar to the procreation of Abra-ham that was described in connection with a halving that involved fire. The names איש *man* and אשה *woman* appear to be priestly titles. The priest or firstborn was understood, in the ancient east, to be at once the ceremonial bride to the Deity and the ceremonial husband of the congregation (as though a mediating image of the Deity the congregation served). Individu-ally, the priest was as the bride; collectively with the body of the congrega-tion, the priest was a constituent of the bride. The priest was physically male, and he symbolized the Deity to the congregation. The congregation was physically male and female, and it was symbolized by the altar that was a symbol of femininity and fecundity. The priest symbolized God, and the altar symbolized the congregation; therefore, both the priest and the congregation could (in their respective senses) be viewed as simultane-ously male and female. It was imperative that the priest be physically male in that he worshipped upon the altar of God that was a female typification, for the worship service was supposed to signify a marriage between God and man that eventuated in God perpetuating Himself through man who was subsequently perpetuated in unison. The word לקח *to take* also means *to marry*, so it is written that God "*took*" or "*married* one מצלעתיו *from the sides of him.*" God, in this case, was the Priest Who made a threshold or altar in His pruning of Adam's heart or bisecting of the man into literary "sides" in order to signify a demarcation, threshold, or altar. In so doing, God is depicted as teaching man how to generate life through constructive sacrifice by giving him an altar, a bride, from his own heart and from His own heart that is expressed as the other "side" of the man and also as his "neighbor" who is as a אשה woman, fire offering, and gift. The word אור light, fire, life, wisdom, as a synonym, can be understood to point to the life-giving qualities of both woman and man as halves of an original whole that are capable by the "blessing" of God of being "fruitful" and multiplying through fruit that expresses the halves of physical parentage and the half that constitutes the parents unifying with the half God constitutes. In the case of both Adam and Abraham, the "one flesh" is the unified halves that had fire or life pass between them whereby the fusion of the halves can be understood blatantly in the face of the child produced. Again,

> So husbands ought to love their own wives as their own bodies; he who loves his wife loves himself. For no one ever hated his own flesh, but nourishes and cherishes it, just as the Lord does the church. For we are members of His body, of His flesh and of His bones. "For this reason a man shall leave his father and mother and be joined to his wife, and the two shall become ONE FLESH." This is a great mystery, but I speak concerning Christ and the church. Nevertheless let each one of you in particular so love his own wife as himself, and let the wife see that she respects her husband.

Since the other "half" of man is his "neighbor," we can understand how, ceremonially, the bride of the priest is the neighbor of the man. The ritual impurity incurred by contacting a corpse in the case of the priest and Levite (Leviticus 21:11) can be seen now as a ceremonial preparation for laying his life down for his friend by loving his neighbor as himself. It was this very preparation that was the sign of self-sacrifice in a constructive manner that became inverted so that the sign took the place of the substance to the extent that death rather than life emerged. Such is the substance of the parable of the Good Samaritan. In Luke 10:30, Christ describes the wounded man as "half dead." The essential question is, "Who will be the other half of this man that will restore him to full life?" Christ specifically points out that a "priest" and a "Levite" encounter the man and avoid him (10: 31-32). The specific mention of a priest and a Levite would have called to mind immediately those who were to avoid corpses; but, the problem is that the avoidance of death or potential death was a preparatory sign that refused to be the dead "half"; thus, the priest and the Levite were to be the living "half" of a congregation that was "half dead" in order to restore the congregation, the body, to life. Christ deliberate selected a hated Samaritan to be the life "half" for the dying man, and He even describes the Samaritan as a priest pouring libation on an altar by stating that he was "pouring on oil and wine" (10:34) on the wounded altar at which he was to officiate in a manner like the drink offerings of Leviticus -- for the very words "drink offerings, an אשה **offering made by fire**" (Leviticus 23:18) are the same spelling as אשה **woman, fire offering, gift** that the man Adam named called his bride who was his other half or "side" or "NEIGHBOR." Christ then asked, "So which of these three do you think was NEIGHBOR to him who fell among the thieves?" (10:36). The despised Samaritan acted in a superior priestly manner than the priest and Levite. The reader will notice, though, that the "neighbor" is supposed to be the wounded man, the half or side of the priest or "Firstborn"; but Christ calls the Samaritan the "neighbor"; this mirrored reversal displays the begetting through halves in that God passed between the two pieces or sides and was successfully birthed out into the heart of the next priest, the wounded man who would go "and do likewise" (10:37), the one who heard and understood the parable to whom Christ said, "Go and do likewise." It can be seen that Christ was the Priest Who worshipped His Father by instructing and repairing His broken altar (i.e. humanity) with a parable about an unseen priest who worshipped his father by repairing a broken altar by loving his neighbor as himself so that, in both cases, a subsequent priest was born from the heart of God and into the heart of man and from the heart of man by the heart of God. The two sides fused together are one flesh, one בשר *proclamation of successful birth* (Jeremiah 20:15), *a unified Gospel* that God initiates, passes through, and is birthed out of. Intentionally fruitless unions can be seen as a bifurcation that welcomes God in its midst and refuses to have Him "pass between the pieces" (Genesis 15:17). Abortion would be, therefore, a morbid attempt to banish God from one's midst, and this explains the reason for man's banishment by God from the Garden of Fertility. Consider the lid of the Ark of the Covenant: one may reflect on the fiery blade between the cherubs at Eden's eastern gate in light of the pillar of fire that walked between Abraham's pieces with respect to the intended output of the fusion of God and man that was thwarted and resulted in exile and death.

"NAME"

IN the ancient east, a name was considered identical (or nearly identical) with the entity it signified. As an example, the Sumerian word *Zi* signified *Life* and was denoted by a picture of a *flowering reed*. At the same time, *Life* was synonymous with *motion* in the ancient east. A living tree was a moving tree or a tree of life (like the fiery menorah), and if one considers the pillar of cloud and of fire that led the Israelites through a labyrinthine education, one will see an allusion to motion indicating life that was denoted by a picture of a plant. The Egyptians conceived of creeping plants, like vines, to grow "on the belly" (*Language of the Pentateuch*, Yahuda). When Leviticus 11 discusses animals that proceed on the belly, one can see how Satan, the "Serpent," is compared to a poisonous vine as hinted at in Deuteronomy 32:32. In Genesis 3:14, Satan is told, "On your belly you shall go...," which compares him to the forbidden animals of Leviticus 11 and the poisonous vine of Deuteronomy 32:32, i.e. the forbidden tree or "vine-tree" (Ezekiel 15:1). It can be understood that Satan destroyed man by offering his libation as a vine hanging on a fruit tree (so to speak), and it can be seen that Christ saved man by offering His libation from His circumcised heart by hanging on a barren tree. It is often true that symbolism is necessary in order to grasp the abstract, but with symbolism comes the threat that a symbol can become confused with the substance for which it stands so that the abstract becomes mistaken as the concrete. Dr. Sayce, in his 1902 book on the *Religions of Ancient Egypt and Babylonia*, said, "...the more literal is our translation of an old religious text, the more likely we are to misunderstand it." The bird was used to represent the soul by the ancient Egyptians (among others), and Ezekiel 13:20 discusses hunting "souls like birds." Consider how many of the devout believe in talking snakes. An Egyptian example of the importance of names standing parallel with the substances they signify can be seen in the doctrine of the *Ka* or *Double* from which Plato developed his *ideas*. This *Ka*, this *Double*, was as the shadow in the visible world. As the shadow cannot be separated from the object it reflects, so the Double is the reflection of the object as it is mentally conceived. In this way, a name was a Double for the person it stood. Egypt specifically is but one example of the ancient eastern concept of names and reflections, but the concept generally can be observed profusely in Scripture. A tree could be the Double of an animate being, and we may consider the fact that the two central trees of Eden's garden had specific names. The choice between two trees could easily be the choice between two people. The Pharaoh was described by the ancient Egyptians as a bull that tread down his enemies while the symbol of royalty adopted by the earliest Pharaohs was the cobra, a conquering and feared animal; thus, a Pharaoh was at once a bull and a cobra, so to speak, and we may consider that Genesis 3:1 (written by Moses who was educated as Egyptian royalty) states that the "*serpent was more subtle than any beast of the field....*" If one keeps in mind the infanticide that the infant Moses survived in light of the death of the firstborn at Passover, one can see how the Pharaoh was linked to infant death through symbols of snakes and beasts. In Hebrew, the *name* is connected sometimes to *offspring* and, in this sense, the father and his lineage can be one.

Some Hebrew words for "name" are שם and שכל as in, "Then the prophet Haggai and Zechariah the son of Iddo, prophets, prophesied to the Jews who *were* in Judah and Jerusalem, בשם *in the name of* the God of Israel, who was over them" (Ezra 5:1) and "Let not mercy and truth forsake you; bind them around your neck, write them on the tablet of your heart, and so find favor ושכל טוב *and a good name* in the sight of God and man" (Proverbs 3:3-4). The word שםname can mean *fame, renown,* and *reputation*; this word שםname also means *lineage* and *offspring* positively as we see in Genesis 25:13: "And these were the names of the sons of Ishmael, by their names, according to their generations..." for it is obvious that "names" is not stated here redundantly but to indicate lineage; consider: "And you shall not let any of your descendants להעביר *pass over* to Molech [a child-sacrificing deity], nor shall you profane the שם *name* of your God: I am the Lord" (Leviticus 18:21). The passover of Molech is the sacrifice of children, particularly the ritual slaughter of the firstborn — and it is this passover that profanes the Name, the lineage, of the Lord, for "God made האדם*the man* in His image" (Genesis 1:27). As is the case with child sacrifice overtly, the generational aspect of the word שם *name* is also darkly apparent relative to its connection with "cursing" one's "name," which can mean to destroy one's lineage by killing one's child. Regarding another word for *name*, the root נקבmeans *to bore through, to pierce, to mark out,* TO NAME, *to execrate, to curse, to blaspheme, to be specified by name,* and it produces the word נקבה *female* and קבה *womb*. When the act of naming is being discussed relative to "blasphemy," it is plain that abortive birth or child-sacrifice is being discussed as is the case with the "eye for eye" scenarios in Scripture in opposition to the root רחם *to love tenderly, to have compassion and mercy, to pity* that produces the word רחם *womb*. For instance, Exodus 21:22-25 states,

> If men fight, AND HURT A WOMAN WITH CHILD, so that she
> gives birth prematurely, yet no harm follows, he shall surely
> be punished accordingly as the woman's husband imposes on

him; and he shall pay as the judges determine. But IF any harm follows, THEN you shall give LIFE FOR LIFE, eye for eye, tooth for tooth, hand for hand, foot for foot, burn for burn, wound for wound, stripe for stripe.

It is probable that the "eye for eye" passage was an already well understood principle of reciprocity articulated as such and connected to the older "life for life" that was applied specifically to a baby. Stating "life for life" was a portion of the formula for Molech-worship or child-sacrifice: "Life for life, blood for blood, a lamb as a substitute." Similarly, the human sacrifices of the Accadians stated that the father must give the life of his child for his own sin, "the child's head for his head, the child's neck for his neck, the child's breast for his breast" in an absurd vicarious punishment (Sayce, *Lectures on the Religions of Babylonia and Assyria*). Consider Micah 6:7 in the response against child-sacrifice: "Will the Lord be pleased with thousands of rams, ten thousand rivers of oil? Shall I give my firstborn for my transgression, the fruit of my body for the sin of my soul?" Molech-worship also contained the formula "because he heard his voice." If we understand that "eye for eye" is actually referent to the "life for life" and "because he heard his voice" formulas for child-sacrifice, we can connect blasphemy to death as restitution for harming a child; in connection, we read,

Now the son of an Israelite woman, whose father was an Egyptian, went out among the children of Israel; and this Israelite woman's son and a man of Israel fought each other in the camp. And the Israelite woman's son BLASPHEMED [ויקב] THE NAME [השם] OF THE LORD ויקלל and *cursed*; and so they brought him to Moses. (His mother's name was Retribution the daughter of My Word, of the tribe of Dan [the "Serpent": Genesis 49:17].) Then they put him in custody, that the mind of the Lord might be shown to them. And the Lord spoke to Moses, saying, "Take outside the camp him who has *cursed*; then let all who heard him lay their hands on his head, and let all the congregation stone him. "Then you shall speak to the children of Israel, saying: 'Whoever *curses his God* shall bear his sin. And whoever BLASPHEMES THE NAME OF THE LORD SHALL SURELY BE PUT TO DEATH. All the congregation shall certainly stone him, the stranger as well as him who is BORN in the land. When he BLASPHEMES THE NAME of the Lord, he shall be PUT TO DEATH. 'WHOEVER KILLS ANY MAN shall surely be PUT TO DEATH. Whoever kills an animal shall make it good, animal for animal.' IF A MAN CAUSES DISFIGUREMENT OF HIS NEIGHBOR, AS HE HAS DONE,

SO SHALL IT BE DONE TO HIM— FRACTURE FOR FRACTURE, EYE FOR EYE, TOOTH FOR TOOTH; AS HE HAS CAUSED DISFIGUREMENT OF A MAN, SO SHALL IT BE DONE TO HIM. And whoever kills an animal shall restore it; but WHOEVER KILLS A MAN SHALL BE PUT TO DEATH. You shall have the same law for the stranger and for one from your own country; for I am the Lord your God.'" Then Moses spoke to the children of Israel; and they took outside the camp HIM WHO HAD CURSED, and stoned him with stones. So the children of Israel did as the Lord commanded Moses (Leviticus 24:10-23).

We read that men fought, but it is not stated that one man killed his combatant. It is stated explicitly that a man "blasphemed" and that he also "cursed" the "name," that is, the progeny. The blasphemy under discussion is from the same root as the word "female" as specifically marked out by her womb, and this word is juxtaposed to "name" with reference to killing. As Exodus 21 before it, this passage mandates the "eye for eye" principle as a remedy for opposing the "womb," "womb" being from the root "to love tenderly, to have compassion and pity." The blasphemer was KILLED because he KILLED his combatant's unborn child, as it is written, "If men fight, and hurt a woman with child, so that she gives birth prematurely, yet no harm follows, he shall surely be punished accordingly as the woman's husband imposes on him; and he shall pay as the judges determine. But if any harm follows, then you shall give LIFE FOR LIFE, eye for eye, tooth for tooth, hand for hand, foot for foot, burn for burn, wound for wound, stripe for stripe." It is therefore clear that the "eye for eye" ruling is to prevent further injury to the רחם womb, mercy, which is from the root רחם to love tenderly. The second "eye-for-eye" injunction, which we can see regards the unborn, immediately follows the feasts that were performed in the Tabernacle and, later, the Temple. The word "feast" is the Hebrew מועד, from the root יעד to appoint, to betroth, the point being that betrothal was intended to lead to a fruitful womb, and a womb is called a בית house, temple which was protected by the "eye for eye" mandate, for the Temple of God is for His "Name" (I Chronicles 28:3). The בית house, temple, place wherein the Deity resides is the full spelling of the letter ב which means wisdom and womb. Similarly, the word שכל name comes from the root שכל to act wisely, prudently, and wittingly.

It is apparent that the uniting factor in the words for "name" here is "high estimation through wisdom," for such would make for a "good name" as opposed to an infamous one. Regarding the womb-wisdom-temple-name link, we may note that the womb is the place where the wisdom of God enters in order to perpetuate His image and thus His name; the opposite of this would be that the womb is the place where the folly of Satan enters in order to erase God's image and establish his own name, his own seed: "And I will put enmity between you and the woman, and between your seed and her seed..." (Genesis 3:15).

To speak "in the name" of someone is literally to speak by the authority and thus with the power of the one in whose name something is being uttered. A police officer can enter one's home "in the name" of the authority that governs both the suspect and the police officer. To pray "in the name" of God is a bold admission that one speaks by the authority of God Almighty Himself and with His power. Unfortunately, many often apply the expression "in the name of Jesus" merely to indicate that their prayer is directed towards Him personally as opposed to being directed towards another. As such, multitudes pray "in the name" of God for antithetical purposes and thus "take His name in vain" by ignorantly claiming that God authorized the prayer and also that it is being uttered as if it is already in the process of fruition. "You shall not take the name of the Lord your God in vain, FOR THE LORD WILL NOT HOLD HIM GUILTLESS WHO TAKES HIS NAME IN VAIN" (Exodus 20:7). If we consider "name" as "progeny," the Name of God would then be Christ. Taking Christ for naught would then mean disregarding His requirements, thus, "Whoever believes in Him is not condemned, but whoever does not believe stands condemned already because they have not believed in the NAME of God's one and only Son" (John 3:18).

Consider the tradition of equating the terms "Hebrew," "Israelite," and "Jew." Certainly, the tradition under discussion is false since making these three terms synonymous is committing a gross anachronism. Not one place in the Torah of Moses will you find the term "Jew" because such a nation did not walk the earth during the days of Moses. The first mention of the term "Hebrew" is found in Genesis 14:13 as a designation for Abraham. The Jewish Publication Society's Torah Commentary called *Etz Hayim* states, "Israelites identify themselves as "Hebrew" (*ivri*) when addressing foreigners. It is a term used by the later when referring to Israelites. Many scholars relate the term to the nomadic mixed ethnic group called Hapiru in ancient Near Eastern documents. The origin and meaning of the term *"ivri"* ["Hebrew"] is unknown." If the meaning of the term is unknown, the fact that people employ it regularly indicates that they are assigning a foreign definition to it in ignorance fortified by a tradition that lacks apparent evidence. Let us work our way backwards. The term "Jew" is short for "Judean," which signified the Roman territory of Judea that was formerly the Judean district of Babylon. Prior to the Babylonian exile, its borders were larger when it was the self-contained Kingdom of Judah following the civil split of the Northern Kingdom of Israel and the Southern Kingdom of Judah. Prior to the fracture, both the Northern and Southern Kingdoms comprised the one Kingdom of Israel, which was named after the patriarch of the tribes whose name was formerly Jacob. This Jacob was the grandson of Abraham who is the first person that Scripture names as a "Hebrew" outright (though there were certainly "Hebrews" before Abraham). Thus, the term Jew is but a shortened national term reinforced by its subsquent captors but that came to be associated with the Judean religion, i.e. the religion of the people of the province of Judea which existed as such long after the acquisition of Canaan that was renamed after the patriarch who sired the tribes who occupied it. There was no "Judea" in the days of Abraham; there was no "Jew" in the days of Abraham the Hebrew. At the same time, there were Hebrews in the days of the Jews. The problem is cleared when one recognizes that the term Hebrew cannot be a hereditary one any more than it can be a nationalistic one, for this would be like saying that Christopher Columbus' grandfather was an American before Columbus was even born! The term "Hebrew" is one of religious belief and covenant that existed prior to so-called "Judaism," Judaism itself being the product of Judean and Babylonian amalgatation whose chief book is the Talmud, not the Hebrew Scriptures.

The word "Hebrew" is spelled עברי which is derived from the root עבר to pass over. A "Hebrew" is one who "passes over." The natural question is, "What is it that Abraham passed over so that he was denominated as a 'Hebrew'?" The reader will notice that the word "Hebrew" is applied to Abraham just after God pledged that Abraham's lineage his name, would be made like the dust of the earth and right after one of Abraham's relatives (Lot) was taken prisoner. Lot sired the Moabites from whom Ruth descended in order to procreate David of whom Christ is both "the root and the descendant" (Revelation 22:16). Had Lot been killed, the genealogy would not have flowed as it did down from and to our Savior. The reader will notice that Abraham was a Chaldean by nationality in a time when no "Jews" or people of "Judah" were yet born. Abraham (Abram at that time) obeyed God by relocating from Chaldea to Canaan in order to participate in God's covenant that Abram would be made into "a great nation" (Genesis 12:2). In other words, Abraham had to cross the Euphrates River in order to become fruitful, and "Euphrates" means "Fruitful." Abraham had to pass over the threshold of fruitfulness in order to become fruitful, and we may now realize that Abraham, the Hebrew, passed over a threshold into covenant with God; this physical and spiritual situation, this union of deeds and belief, constituted what can be called a "threshold covenant" whereby covenanting parties signify their union at a threshold. God intended to make Abraham fruitful, Abraham acted upon God's intent, God created the Fruitful river, Abraham crossed this watery fertility, Abraham was made fruitful according to God's intent, and Abraham's title was that of "One who passes over," that is, a "Hebrew." In fact, the root of the word "Hebrew" can also mean *to drop as a liquid* and *to conceive*, and *to become pregnant*; this root produces the word מעבר *place of passing*, and we may consider a child passing into the outer world from the womb, for the womb is called a בית *house* in Hebrew, thus the concept of the threshold at the "doors of the womb" (Job 3:10). A threshold covenant signified fidelity. For instance, in Xenophon's Anabsis (1.4), Cyrus' soliders proved their allegiance by crossing the Euphrates River in a *covenant, an oath to the death*, for they crossed this river in order to follow Cyrus into battle (hence the oath to the death).

Playing with words has abortive consequences as was the case in Eden, for "Eden" means "Fertility." When the first Adam had to pass over Eden's threshold negatively into exile, he was being born again to die based on his own will in opposition to the covenant of life thereby invoking what is called the "curse of the covenant." The Last Adam passed over the threshold of Paradise to be born into the world in order to die based on His own will, in opposition to the covenant with death the first Adam made, thereby receiving the blessing of life in order to overturn the curse. A "Hebrew" is one who passes over a spiritual threshold in accordance with God and as a new (or renewed) creation, and this process is often signified at a physical threshold. To transgress such a threshold, as a new creation, would be tantamount to a willfully abortive birth of oneself.

A threshold covenant is not something popularly known, but its history has been treated at beautiful length by one Henry Clay Trumbull in his book, *The Threshold Covenant*. (Enough cannot be said about Trumblull's contributions.) A few points will suffice for the purposes of our discussion of diction. The family altar in remote antiquity seems to have been the threshold, the entranceway to the house. In the same way that the family house was governed by the father, so was the temple governed by the priest, the sacrificer. This priest was said to have the "Right of the Firstborn" and was called "Firstborn," for this right and title marked him as the one whose responsibilty and privilege it was to officiate at the altar, the threshold. Sacrifices for the family were conducted in a manner that painted the doorway with blood in a fashion similar to how a priest spilled sacrificial blood upon the altar in the temple for the family of the deity to be connected to the deity himself through a covenant of blood, a covenant of life. Blood was understood as life, not death, which explains why Scripture calls blood "life" in Genesis 9:4. The blood of an animate being was forbidden regarding human consumption, but the "blood of grapes" or wine (Genesis 49:11-12) was commanded to be consumed in a threshold covenant, i.e. at Passover (Matthew 26). The word סף means both *a basin* and *a threshold* because the thresholds under discussion were concave, not convex. The ritual of pouring lifeblood upon an altar for sacrifice, the regular occurence of slaughtering the family meal religiously at the doorway of the house, the command to kill sacrifices at the door of the Tabernacle (Exodus 29), and the pouring of wine in libation are basically all illustrations of signifying a doorway to a house as a parallel to a womb; that is, they are all ways of discussing vital perpetuity through regular revivification, sustained life through continual renewal, maintained invigoration through an eternal state resignified through ceremonial worship, through religion that therefore necessitates action in a pure and undefiled manner. Of course, conception, gestation, and live birth connect all of these symbols neatly; accordingly, we read, regarding the Passover, that "...the Lord kept vigil that night להוציאם *to birth them out* from the land of Egypt, on this night all the Israelites are to keep vigil to honor the Lord for the generations to come" (Exodus 12:42). The Pharaoh, like Herod, slaughtered innocents as though he were an abortive womb; בית house also means*womb* in Hebrew; "Pharaoh" literally means "Great House"; a "Pharaoh" who murders children is a governmentally abortive womb. In counterbalance, since Pharaoh, with the compliance of Egypt, acted as an abortive womb, then Pharaoh, with the compliance of Egypt, had the Hebrews birthed out of the land. Abortive birth was overturned by live birth with a stark reminder to both Hebrews and Egyptians: "They departed from Rameses in the first month, on the fifteenth day of the first month; on the day after the Passover the children of Israel went out with boldness in the sight of all the Egyptians. For the Egyptians were burying all their firstborn, whom the Lord had killed among them. Also on their gods the Lord had executed judgments" (Numbers 33:3-4). Genesis 15 depicts Abraham crafting a delineation marked by animal parts cut in half, for Abraham was entering ito a threshold covenant whereby the halved carcasses provided the bloody threshold. Similarly, when the Egyptian firstborn were struck down, the killing took place *at midnight,* which is the Hebrew בחצי הלילה*in the halves of the night.*

Recall how people have consistently blamed God for killing the Egyptian babies at the first Passover, when He did not. We have a clue provided in Revelation 11:8: "And their dead bodies will lie in the street of the great city which SPIRITUALLY IS CALLED SODOM AND EGYPT, where also our Lord was crucified." We know that Christ was not crucified in the geographical Sodom or the geographical Egypt. The Passover in Egypt was the antitype of Lot's exodus from Sodom. Lot baked unleavened bread on the night before his escape from Sodom (Genesis 19:3); during the night, intruders attempted to enter Lot's house (Genesis 19:4); Lot was guarded — at the door of his house — by Divine protection (Genesis 19:10). In the same way, the Hebrews baked unleavened bread on the night and before their escape from Egypt; during the night a destroyer attempted to enter the Hebrew's houses; the Hebrews were guarded — at the door of their houses — by Divine protection. Both Sodom and Egypt experienced a rain of fire (Genesis 19:23; Exodus 9:24). "Hebrew" comes from the root that means "to pass over," i.e. into covenant with God. The Divine protection first passed over Lot's threshold in order to protect Lot, as was the case with the Israelites in Egypt. Exodus 12:23 specifically says that God would "pass over the entrance" of the Hebrews' houses so as not to permit "the destroyer to enter your homes"; the destroyer, Satan, was permitted to enter the homes of which God had not passed over the thresholds, as was true with Lot in Sodom regarding his angelic company. So, when it is written that God "smote every firstborn" (Exodus 12:29) because God had specifically said, "I will pass over in the land of Egypt on this night, and I SHALL STRIKE every firstborn" (Exodus 12:12), those who received such a warning would have understood the more-than-common imagery (at that time) of a King (the "Living God") coming with His executioner, "the one who has the power of death, that is, the devil," (Hebrews 2:14). God did indeed "pass over" Egypt (generally) and He did "pass over" the entrances to the Hebrews' houses (specifically). As God stood at the door to defend the "Hebrews" (those who "passed over" into covenant with God), so Divinity stood at the door to defend Lot from the wickedness of the Sodomites; we may grasp the historical reference: "...their dead bodies will lie in the street of the great city which SPIRITUALLY IS CALLED SODOM AND EGYPT, where also our Lord was crucified," for as the Passover lamb was slain, so Christ is the Lamb Who was slain (Revelation 5:6). Satan must have been already known by Moses to be the slayer of the firstborn since Moses composed the Torah and since Hebrews 11:28 indeed identifies Satan, not God, as this destroyer of the firstborn: "By faith he [Moses] kept the Passover and the sprinkling of blood, lest HE WHO DESTROYED THE FIRSTBORN should touch them." How could it be believed that Moses kept God's command in order to prevent God from doing something according to God's command? — for this produces a contradiction. Therefore, we can understand why it is written that, "For the Lord will pass through to smite the Egyptians; and when He sees the blood upon the lintel, and on the two side posts, the Lord will PASS OVER THE DOOR, and will not suffer THE DESTROYER to come into your houses to smite you," (Exodus 12:23). Of course, God was not the "Destroyer" (Satan); God was the Defender. Satan is but the executioner, for God is King. Satan's destruction of the firstborn is his blasphemy of God's "name." Such a blasphemy of the Name was punished by hanging the perpetrators (Numbers 25). It can therefore be seen that, when Deuteronomy 21:23 states that those who are hung on trees are cursed, the curse is the reason that they are hung. The hanging did not generate the curse. In other words, hanging someone cannot impel God to curse someone, but being hung is a symbol of being under God's curse for having killed an innocent, specifically a "name." The Sadducees, the Temple Levites of Christ's earthly days, deliberately persuaded Rome to hang Christ so that He could not be considered the Messiah based on their misunderstanding of Deuteronomy 21:23, which caused them absurdly to assume that they could compel the Father to curse Christ because they had the authority to mandate the Father doing so... when, in fact, they did not grasp that their murder of Christ necessitated *them* being hung on trees, which is an ironic proof that He took their punishment upon Himself without them knowing it and specifically according to their sins. Consider: "No, we declare God's wisdom, a mystery that has been hidden and that God destined for our glory before time began. None of the rulers of this age understood it, for if they had, they would not have crucified the Lord of glory" (I Corinthians 2:7-8); "Then Jesus said, 'Father, forgive them, for they do not know what they do'" (Luke 23:34). The fourth chapter of the Book of Acts discusses the error of the Temple Levites relative the murder of the "Holy Child" (verse 30) and the forbiddence of His "Name," and the connection to abortion can be seen in Ecclesiastes 6:4: "...I say that הנפל *the abortion, the stillborn child* is better than he — for it comes in VANITY and departs in darkness, and its NAME is covered with darkness"; "You shall not take the NAME of the Lord your God in VAIN, FOR THE LORD WILL NOT HOLD HIM GUILTLESS WHO TAKES HIS NAME IN VAIN" (Exodus 20:7). The punishment for taking His "Name" in vain, for causing His "Holy Child" to die, is hanging (Numbers 25) or stoning (Leviticus 20), which means that the fact God's Name was crucified means that "Surely He has borne OUR griefs and carried OUR sorrows; yet WE esteemed Him stricken, smitten by

God [as was the case with the Sadducean Levites], and afflicted. But He was wounded for OUR transgressions, He was bruised for OUR iniquities; the chastisement for OUR peace was upon Him, and by His stripes WE are healed. All WE like sheep have gone astray; WE have turned, every one, to HIS OWN WAY; and the Lord has laid on Him the iniquity of US ALL" (Isaiah 53:4-6). Essentially, The Holy Child sacrificed Himself for us when we should have received the vengeance, that is, the curse of the Covenant. The pattern described here can be observed in the tenth chapter of the Book of Hebrews, for the discussion of sacrifice is followed by a warning against transgressing the Covenant with Christ and being the recipient of God's vengeance accordingly. The vengeance, that is, the curse of the covenant is its justice, and the just punishment for killing an innocent (particularly a child) is hanging (Numbers 25) or stoning (Leviticus 20). The curse signified by being hung on a tree is a perpetrator becoming as dead fruit since he killed the fruit of the womb. It then makes perfect sense as to why humanity's sin in Eden (which means "Fertility") regarding a tree and concerning wisdom was atoned for by the Holy Child's death on a tree in Golgotha (the place of the Skull) where wisdom is supposed to reside. The Name was blasphemed through a tree, and a war was declared upon this Name, the Sire. The Name posted Himself upon the tree of blasphemy whereby He poured a libation from His circumcised heart that perpetuated His Name through renewal in Holy Communion wherein the symbol of new birth proclaims the eternal Name.

The term "Hebrew" comes from the root רבע to pass over, i.e. into covenant with God. If one enters into God's covenant, then one is forgiven. The "one who passes over," that is, the "Hebrew," is literally "The Forgiven One," as is proven in Job 7:21. Job 7:21 uses a derivative of the root of "Hebrew" to mean "to forgive" or "to pass over sin." The name "Hebrew" means "Forgiven," and it is the Book of Hebrews that explains specifically how Christ offered forgiveness to His Forgiven Ones, His "Hebrews," i.e. His Bride.

THE CONFUSION

OF

THE SEXES

KNOWLEDGE of diction is essential to understanding arguments, and reassigning innovative meanings to diction previously understood in another way induces confusion (at least) when, unbeknownced to the receiver, definition Y is superimposed upon definition X. The correct application of diction is also largely dictated by one's familiarity with references. For instance, when the word "Messiah" is used today, it is often simply assumed to refer to Jesus. In a sense, this word Messiah has begun to take on another definition that is to be distinguished from its Scriptural employment. A *messiah* is a *christ*, for our word *Christ* comes through Greek as a translation of the Hebrew word we pronounce as *Messiah*. An opponent to Christ would be an antichrist, but the simple term *christ* does not necessarily refer to Jesus exclusively. Scripture discusses more than one messiah, that is, more than one christ. A *messiah*, or *christ*, means literally *an anointed one*. Both kings and priests were anointed upon receiving their respective offices, and this fact displays openly that there were many *messiahs* or *christs* who had positive and negative traits, who were moral and immoral, etc. Saul was God's *Anointed*, that is, God's *Messiah* or *Christ*, but Saul did not have the same status by any means as the One Who is called The Christ Who is Jesus. In short, the reader must be careful to distinguish between distinct entities that go by the same title.

Consider a priest. In the ancient East, a *priest* was understood as a *bound one*, that is, bound to the Deity in a similar way a bride is bound to her husband. Congruently, *Levi* means *Bound One*, and Levi was the tribe who, in time, received the priesthood. In Hebrew, a כהן *priest* is from the root *to stand, to make ready, to prepare, to adorn, to minister, to officiate,* and this root appears to be synonymous with the root כון *to stand, to exist, to establish, to prepare, to fashion, to form*. Relative to the Deity, the priest was as a bride in the sense that the priest was ministered upon by the Deity in that he received holy libation, spirit, or inspiration. Relative to the worshippers the priest led, the priest was a representative of the Groom in that he ministered to the people who were, collectively, the bride and who were signified by the altar upon which the priest poured libation. In this sense, the priest had both masculine and feminine designations that were illustrated by his office ceremonially and not physically.

The divine order of the priesthood began with masculinity in that the Deity was understood as male. That God first created humanity male makes it plain that a succession of official worship was intended, and that God created the man from the feminine אדמה *red ground* illustrates the union of Heaven and Earth, whereby Earth is understood maternally as the altar upon which God, as Priest, "formed the man of dust" (Genesis 2:7). The union of Heaven and Earth is understood as generatively illustrated by the eastern horizon at morning, for Psalm 110:3 calls the sunrise the "womb of the morning." The creation of the first man is described as being the result of worshipping God even though it was done by God, and a similar message made its way to ancient Greece as evidenced by the Grecian artwork that consistently depicts the gods, not the people, pouring libation in worship. Children come through woman by way of man's libation upon her, and it can be understood illustratively why God would be depicted as a Father, first, Who poured libation upon the feminine altar of the ground to sire a son, first, who would continue the process that would of necessity require the production of both *male* and *female* successors, that is, future *priests* and *altars*. Distinguishing between the sexes becomes extremely important here. The Deity was understood as a Priest and therefore a Man, for a female priest would be an absolute contradiction in terms under this system. At the same time, this Man would have to be generative in some way, and it becomes clearer as to how the union of man and woman in the binding of marriage spiritually, ceremonially, and physically would be expressions of the Unity Who created both them and the institution by which they are joined as evidenced from a circumcised heart, so to speak.

Again, the Deity was understood as a Priest and therefore a Man without a divided nature; in this way, God could at once be the Father, the Groom, and the Son, and such is illustratively true for any human, married father. Accordingly, God sired the first man from the feminine earth, for a priest poured libation upon an altar in divine worship, and such divine worship was generative as is seen in the word כהן *priest* which is from the root that can be understood to mean *to form* (as stated above). In this sense, the Husband is God, the ground is the bride, and the man is the child; the man is an expression of the union of Heaven and Earth, whereby he bears the image of both and is so bound under the authority of the Divinity Who initiated the union and its fruit. The man, the son, fashioned in the image of his father, is then reared to continue the worship through imitation of the Father upon the earth, whereby all subsequent humans trace their heritage back towards a Heavenly Father and an Earthly mother formed by this Father so that, in a pure and ceremonial sense, the earth is as the bride and daughter of the Father just as Eve's relationship was to Adam, for Eve was not generated copulatively, which negates the otherwise lurid state of being both bride and daughter. The pattern cannot repeat without another son. The human daughter, who was not generated sexually, became the bride of the first human son, and the former unity of one man became signified sexually in that the familial nature of the relationship became generative through internally marital relations as opposed to externally familial relations; illustratively, the Deity Who first poured libation in His Divine union with earth that generated His son then instructed His fruit, his son, in how to perpetuate life physically by pouring his own libation of seed in honor of his father and mother upon the altar his father fashioned for him so that further fruit containing seed could continue the process. In this manner, the man was intended to be the mediator between his bride and God; so, to God, he was a specific constituent of the bride, and to the bride, he was a specific representation, or image, of God. In this sense, the man specifically was as humanity generally, as the usage of the name Adam implies (Genesis 5:2).

Several aspects of the ancient worship can be seen in this arrangement. (1) Life begins with the masculine. Life is generated through the union of the masculine and feminine with the aim of producing both masculinity and femininity in order to continue the process. (2) The process is initiated, at least illustratively, by the solely masculine because subsequent life is a continual expression of an initial, constructive unity that was not sexual (which explains the prohibitions against incestuous relationships). (3) The sexual distinctions being essential at this point have restrictions that avoid incest (among other taboos), and the lawfully willful union of suitable constituents in worship is a reflection of the willful creation of the One who began the process. (4) The process was begun by a Priest, and therefore a Man, Who poured libation upon an altar in order to raise up fruit. (5) The fruit was a man, and therefore intended to be a priest, who would in turn raise up fruit upon the altar his Father provided. (6) The arrangement here places the man as the priest, his wife as the altar, and his child as the offering. (7) The fact that the child is the offering mandates that the offering is not one of death but one of life so that the "sacrifice" is the life and not the death of the union initiated by Father Whose Name is passed on.

The masculine role of the priest makes him singly as the son of his Father, the Deity, for he is bound to his Father as fruit is bound to a Tree. This point seems to be hinted at when Christ said, "I am the vine, you are the branches" (John 15:5), for the word ענב *grape cluster* comes from the root ענב *to bind together*, for the grape is the child of this serpentine plant. The masculine role of the priest makes him as the representative of his father to others, a type or image of his Father and therefore his Father's son. The masculine role as the son of his Father makes this sonship ceremonial just as the feminine role of the altar is ceremonial and expects to receive generative libation. The feminine aspects of the priest are now obvious because, as a constituent of those he leads in worship, he is to receive his Father's Libation or Spirit or Inspriation as poured out generatively for the good purpose of bearing his Father's fruit, which takes the worship full circle in constructive binding as fruit is bound to The Tree. It is such an inspiration we read of when "He breathed into his nostrils the breath of life" (Genesis 2:7).

The delicate balance described here has the aim of perpetual life. A worship service was originally analogous to a marriage, for the libation poured upon the altar by the priest typified the initial creation and subsequent procreation of the marital covenant that was intended to be the union of Heaven with Earth as evidenced by the sustentation and perpetuity of life through fruit production—none of which is naturally possible if the sexes are confused or rearranged. Any union other than man and wife cannot reproduce viable fruit. Thus, if one were to confuse one tree for another, the result would be sterile, dry, and temporal. If one were to confuse the sexes, the entire process would be inverted to the extent that the fruit of a sordid union would be nonviable, for such was the situation of Abraham's choice between the King of Salem and the King of Sodom, that is, Abrahman's choice between the King of Peace and the king of homosexual child-sacrificers. In criticism of a priesthood divorced from God, Malachi 2:7 states, "For the lips of a priest should keep KNOWLEDGE, and people should seek the law from his mouth; for he is the messenger of the LORD of hosts." If one confuses the Hebrew usage of דעת knowledge with his own native language's approximate equivalent, the confusion of the sexes becomes a disturbingly easy blunder to commit.

The word דעת knowledge is conceived of often in simply cognitive terms, but the syntactic employments of this diction can be figurative in order to convey a message beyond the limits of isolated diction. For instance, Genesis 4:1 says, "Now Adam knew Eve his wife, and she conceived and bore Cain..." It is obvious that Adam did not sit down and think about his wife and that his cognition produced a child and induced labor. Adam's "knowledge" was his unification with his wife, and so "knowledge" is syntactically employed (perhaps by circumloctuion) to indicate the copulative process of begetting. The very same syntactic idea is expressed at the mere diction level with the word תחבולה wise counsel, for it comes from the root חבל to twist, to bind, and this root produces the word חבל birth pangs as well. Thematically, we can observe that Adam's "knowledge" of his wife is stated just after this statement: "I will greatly multiply your sorrow and your CONCEPTION; IN PAIN YOU SHALL BRING FORTH CHILDREN..." (Genesis

3:16). "Conception" and the bringing forth of children are obviously paralleled here, and the English word "conception" indicates both thought and begetting as does the Hebrew word הריון *conception* which is from the root הרה *to conceive, to become pregnant.* The point is that the word דעת*knowledge* has little or nothing to do with pregnancy at the raw level of diction, but its syntactic employment alludes to ideas contained within the raw diction of other words that are not written in that same sentence. Few or none of these observations could be grasped if we did not know synonyms or if we altered the definition of "knowledge." Again, the word דעת *knowledge* can be used to indicate *unification* even though its lexicon definition states that it means *intelligence* and *understanding.* Not knowing that a parable is a riddle, not realizing that a riddle can be declarative, and not referring to the entirety of the Bible when reading only one part of it might lead to a misunderstanding of דעת *knowledge.* When considering that Ecclesiastes 7:11-12 says that "...the excellence of KNOWLEDGE is that WISDOM GIVES LIFE to those who have it," and when reflecting on the fact that the Tree of the Knowledge of Good and Evil gave death, the forbidden tree could not possibly have given wisdom since it gave death. It is apparent that, especially regarding the consistent emphasis that the Creation Narrative places on things being according to their kind, the forbidden tree was not a tree that increased understanding but it *unified* opposites, a Tree of the *Unification* of Good and Evil, i.e. a lethal mingling of opposites, a deadly mixture of kinds that did not accord — and this fact was elucidated through the Apostle Paul when he penned in II Corinthians 6:14-18:

> Do not be unequally *yoked* TOGETHER with UNBELIEVERS. For what
> *fellowship* has RIGHTEOUSNESS with LAWLESSNESS? And what
> *communion* has LIGHT with DARKNESS? And what
> *accord* has CHRIST with SATAN? Or what
> *part* has a BELIEVER with an UNBELIEVER? And what
> *agreement* has THE TEMPLE OF GOD with IDOLS?

It is obvious that lawlessness opposes righteousness, that darkness opposes light, that Satan opposes Christ, that the unbeliever opposes the believer, and that idols oppose God's temple. Paul said not to be unified with unbelievers, i.e. not to know them in the sense of mingling, hence, קדש means *to be holy, to be set apart* and not to commingle opposites; ironically, the very same letters spell *male prostitute.* The forbidden tree mixed opposites, for it did not give positive understanding of anything. How in the world could sinning against God bring anything positive at all? — but, because the nature of the forbidden tree has largely been unknown, major belief systems actually hold that the eating of the forbidden tree was a good thing because it brought about the need for salvation which is evidence of the effected idiocy of the nonviable forbidden tree! Such an outrageous proposal only functions on the premise that salvation from sin is superior to sinlessness, that mended injuries are superior to health, and that learning from mistakes is superior to not making mistakes. Such an errant philosophy is a putrid sanctioning of sin that attempts to use wickedness to accomplish good in spite of the fact that Scripture says, "For if the truth of God has increased through my lie to His glory, why am I also still judged as a sinner? And why not say, 'Let us do evil that good may come'?—as we are SLANDEROUSLY REPORTED and as some affirm that we say. Their CONDEMNATION is just" (Romans 3:7-8).

Comprehension is largely dictated by one's ability with language. Grammar is a normative or prescriptive system of rules that set forth standard usage in language. It is common today to discredit the importance of grammar's strictures in favor of some overall concept that supposedly transcends the laws of language. To ignore the fact that grammar provides the structure necessary to grasp the fullness of a message is certainly an error. General comprehension of the written word degrades dramatically if basic linguistic rules are disregarded. Grammar is important. Rules are important. Without grammar, there are no rules in language, and, without rules, there is no mechanism with which to express or comprehend meaning. Lack of respect for grammar allows unhealthy plasticity with language that confuses reception and prepares fertile ground for deception. For instance, the current second person singular and second person plural "you" can be applied to one or to more than one with grammatical soundness, and, since English has no gender in "you," it can be applied to either sex. In the imperative, "Go," the subject is an implied pronoun that, without context, could be applied to either sex of one or more, or to both sexes simultaneously in the plural. A crafty speaker could easily mean the singular but deceive a receiver into mistakenly assuming the plural and therefore into agreeing to terms strictly and correctly stated but deceitfully exacted. The intricacies (or oddities) of English imperatives require explanation of some sort; similarly, the intricacies of oracular utterances can also require explanation (or contemplation) of some sort initially, especially since oracles were usually intended only to make full sense in due time.

The nature of oracles is not common knowledge in what is called the "Church" today. As a result, "parables" are misunderstood to be simple stories that illustrate simple truths. The mandate that asserts Scripture to be simple, straight-forward discourse uncovers an ignorance of oracles, and the simplicity in question (and in superimposition) does lower the bar to the extent that a devotee can crawl over it. Oracles are often parabloic. Parables are riddles that are told in parallel to the truths they ensconce. Riddles require the untangling of meanings held in juxtaposition; they are not simple; they are deflective; they exist on multiple plains of depth, and they can be instructive on multiple levels; they allow one to use few words in order to communicate many, thus it requires many words to explain parables, riddles, and, in this case, divine oracles. Oracles are usually constructed to be realized fully in the course of due time and not at the moment they are spoken. "Knowing" occurs and its comprehension is fully realized in the course of due time when the child is birthed.

It has been often argued against our first human father that "God's command to Adam regarding his abstinence from the forbidden tree was simple... that God said, 'If you eat of that tree, then you will die.'" I contend this blunt point of view sharply. Genesis 2:16-17 says, "And the Lord God commanded the man, saying, 'Of every tree of the garden you may freely eat; but of the tree of the knowledge of good and evil you shall not eat, for in the day that you eat of it you shall surely die'." Since the word כי could mean "if," one could possibly read the sentence this way: "Of every tree of the garden you may freely eat; but of the tree of the knowledge of good and evil you shall not eat, כי *if* in the day that you eat of it you shall surely die..." but, in my opinion, the construction does not seem altogether fitting, and, if a conditional is implied, I believe the condition to be in man's choice and not in God's commands. At the same time, suspecting some condition is not altogether outrageous. For instance, 1 Kings 2:37 and Ezekiel 33:8 and I Kings contain the same mandate as Genesis 2:16:

> For it shall be, on the day you go out and cross the Brook Kidron, know for certain מות תמות *you shall surely die*; your blood shall be on your own head (I Kings 2:37).

> When I say to the wicked, 'O wicked, מות תמות *you shall surely die*!' and you do not speak to warn the wicked from his way, that wicked shall die in his iniquity.... (Ezekiel 33:8).

> ... but of the tree of the knowledge of good and evil you shall not eat, for in the day that you eat of it מות תמות *you shall surely die*.... (Genesis 2:16).

The identical statements in all three passages above pronounce declaratives, but declaratives regarding the offense only if it is enacted. Furthermore, the statements are made to the wicked; the reason for this claim is that the Torah employs negative commands, not positive commands, in reaction to misdeeds. In other words, the Torah says, "Do not," in reaction to error as opposed to, "Do"; thus, we may observe that Adam had already begun his descent into sin prior to the eating of the tree as can be observed in these passages: "But each one is tempted when he is drawn away by his own desires and enticed. Then, when desire has conceived, it gives birth to sin; and sin, when it is full-grown, brings forth death" (James 1:14-15) and "(For until the law sin was in the world, but sin is not imputed when there is no law" (Romans 5:13). In James 1:14-15, the desire precedes the sin and sin precedes death, so it would seem that Adam's desire was wicked, and this wicked desire was prophesied to become sin and ultimately death provided Adam's choice of death. The wicked desire could not be counted sin without a law even though "sin was in the world," so a law was given in order that sin could be rightfully imputed, thus "Whoever commits sin also commits lawlessness, and sin is lawlessness" (1 John 3:4), for rules are indeed important. It can be deduced henceforth that Adam was already entertaining temptation through wicked desire, and a law was given in reaction to this wickedness. At the same time, it also appears that Adam had an option to escape the prophetic doom in that he was provided with a choice, for the identical Ezekiel passage states, "When I say to the wicked, 'O wicked, you shall surely die!' and you do not speak to warn the wicked from his way, that wicked shall die in his iniquity," which illustrates that God's prophetic declaration was a warning of doom, not certain doom. In other words, if Adam chose to continue in his errant way, then error would be his end, and it might be that this observation gave rise to the conditional interpretation of God's negative command regarding the forbidden tree. It would seem to be that man's reaction to God's declaration is conditional based on man's comprehension and adherence to God's declaration. The conditional option is apparent in the declarative command; the command is not conditional, but the adherence to the command is conditional, which would explain why the Ezekiel passage describes such condition as a "warning" for the wicked as opposed to fatalistic doom, i.e. the hope for salvation as opposed to the certainty of damnation. The principle forwarded here, relative to the Tree of Life and the deadly tree can be observed in Deuteronomy 30: 15-18:

> See, I have set before you today life and good, death and evil,
> in that I command you today to love the Lord your God, to walk
> in His ways, and to keep His commandments, His statutes, and
> His judgments, that you may live and multiply; and the Lord
> your God will bless you in the land which you go to possess. But
> if your heart turns away so that you do not hear, and are drawn

away, and worship other gods and serve them, I announce to you today that YOU SHALL SURELY DIE...

We may observe here that man's obedience, not God's declarations, are conditional. The conditional obedience to God is that, if man chooses death, then man shall surely die; but, if man chooses life, then man shall surely live. The divine declaration that becomes a negative command is in reaction to sin where there is no law; therefore, if man chooses lawlessness after a law has been provided, then sinfulness is imputed fairly, and this sin gives birth to death: "... but of the tree of the knowledge of good and evil you shall not eat, for in the day that you eat of it you shall surely die...." (Genesis 2:16). The birth of sin is preceded by its conception, and, if conception is prevented by abstinence, the birth will not eventuate because the conception never occurred: "But each one is tempted when he is drawn away by his own desires and enticed. Then, when desire has conceived, it gives birth to sin; and sin, when it is full-grown, brings forth death" (James 1:14-15). Abstinence, in order to prevent conception, would seem to be the principle behind this passage: "For the weapons of our warfare are not carnal but mighty in God for pulling down strongholds, [1] casting down arguments and every high thing that exalts itself against [2] the knowledge of God, [3] bringing every thought into captivity to the obedience of Christ, and being ready to punish all disobedience when your obedience is fulfilled" (2 Corinthians 10:4-6). [1] Consider Satan's argument to the woman that exalted itself against the knowledge of God in Genesis 3:1; [2] consider the false assessment of knowledge regarding the forbidden tree; [3] consider that humanity was commanded positively to rule over every locomoting thing in Genesis 1:28. God's negative command appears to be a declaration, not a condition, concerning man's conditional choice. Man sets the conditions of his own destruction through disobedience to the declarations of God, and this would seem obvious by the fact that Hell was made for Satan and his angels (not man), and that man can choose to reside with God or with Satan, i.e. man chooses to accept Salvation or damnation: "Then He will also say to those on the left hand, 'Depart from Me, you cursed, into the everlasting fire PREPARED FOR THE DEVIL AND HIS ANGELS'" (Matthew 25:41). It does not say that the everlasting fire was prepared for man. Furthermore, the everlasting fire is described explicitly as a "tophet" (a territory of child-sacrifice) wherein a "HIGH-PLACE" (a child-sacrificial altar) is set in Isaiah 30:33 (see Jeremiah 7:31). "For the weapons of our warfare are not carnal but mighty in God for pulling down strongholds, casting down arguments and EVERY HIGH THING that exalts itself against THE KNOWLEDGE OF GOD, bringing every thought into captivity to the obedience of Christ, and being ready to punish all disobedience when your obedience is fulfilled" (2 Corinthians 10:4-6). Keep in mind that God commanded Adam to "be fruitful" (Genesis 1:28) a process described as "knowing" (Genesis 4:1). All that God made was "good," so God commanded the "knowledge" of good and good, not the "knowledge of good and evil," which can be seen in the blatant fact that He declared, "... but of THE TREE OF THE KNOWLEDGE [UNION] OF GOOD AND EVIL you shall not eat, for in the day that you eat of it you shall surely die...." (Genesis 2:16).

Now, considering the negative application of God's negative command, we may note that there was a "day" in which Adam did eat from the forbidden tree, but so many often rail against Scripture by noting that Adam did not die that "day," within that 24-hour timeframe. One problem with Biblical translations is accounting for time in the Bible. Hebrew technically has no "tenses" and therefore has no time, for tense indicates time. The time of Hebrew is indicated contextually, not grammatically. Hebrew verb conjugation indicates state, not time, and this conjugation affords the condition of being either complete or incomplete, that is, finished or in the process of being finished. Imperatives are modal imperfects, and imperfects express incomplete action. The English "you shall surely die" is more precisely the Hebrew "dying, you shall begin to die," and we can see why most translators do not translate it the second way because, though it is sound Hebrew syntax, it is awkward English syntax. Reapplying the Hebrew syntax relative to the masculine Adam, we see this:

> Of every tree of the garden, EATING YOU MAY BEGIN TO EAT; but of The Tree of the Knowledge of Good and Evil you shall not begin to eat, for in the day YOU EAT OF IT, DYING, YOU SHALL BEGIN TO DIE (Genesis 2:16).

On an earthly level, Adam did begin to eat from the forbidden tree, and this initiation also started his aging towards death. Adam but tasted death, and such a tasting began his degeneration: "Though evil is sweet in his mouth, and he hides it under his tongue, though he spares it and does not forsake it, but still keeps it in his mouth, yet his food in his stomach turns sour; it becomes cobra venom within him" (Job 20:12-14). On the conditions that Adam set, Adam could determine whether or not his aging was constructive or destructive, which is similar to the constructive aging of youth as opposed to the destructive aging of the elderly. English, always grammatically demanding verbs to be in one of three major categories of time, cannot express the Hebrew original well when attempting word-for-word translation, and the very fact that time has been inadvertently superimposed of English necessity upon the Text has led to the readers' confusion of God's command similar to the bride's blunders with the serpent in Eden. Since time is not a grammatical function of Hebrew, it could be deduced that incomplete verb-states explain something about eternity. Eternity does not end and is, therefore, incomplete. Grammatical incompleteness is called "imperfection," and without some knowledge of grammar, "imperfection" could be misconstrued as the state of being flawed as opposed to the state of being unifinished and, for our purposes, perpetual. It could be reasonably deduced that the completion of eating from the forbidden tree is the completion found in death towards damnation, damnation being incomplete, eternal:

> But whoever causes ONE OF THESE LITTLE ONES WHO BELIEVE IN ME to stumble, it would be better for him if a millstone were hung around his neck, and he were thrown into the sea. If your hand causes you to sin, cut it off. It is better for you to enter into life maimed, rather than having two hands, to go to hell, into the fire that shall never be quench — where 'THEIR WORM DOES NOT DIE AND THE FIRE IS NOT QUENCHED.' And if your foot causes you to sin, cut it off. It is better for you to enter life lame, rather than having two feet, to be cast into hell, into the fire that shall never be quenched — where 'THEIR WORM DOES NOT DIE, AND THE FIRE IS NOT QUENCHED.' And if your eye causes you to sin, pluck it out. It is better for you to enter the kingdom of God with one eye, rather than having two eyes, to be cast into hell fire — where "THEIR WORM DOES NOT DIE AND THE FIRE IS NOT QUENCHED" (Mark 9:42-48).

Noticing the wretched timelessness of Hell, it is interesting to observe that this teaching immediately follows the causation of stumbling for "one of these little ones who believe in Me," for the everlasting fire is described explicitly as a territory of child-sacrifice wherein a child-sacrificial altar is set; thus, one who sacrifices a child (even by causing the little one to stumble) sacrifices himself upon Satan's altar, self-magnification, high place, child-sacrificial table — for the story concerns eating. When the whole world was subjugated to futility, the death that resulted from sin is comparable to an abortion, comparable to wicked desire leading to sinful conception eventuating in abortive and futile birth: "For the creation was subjected to futility, not willingly, but because of Him who subjected it in hope; because the creation itself also will be delivered from the bondage of corruption into the glorious liberty of the children of God. For we know that the whole creation groans and labors with birth pangs together until now" (Romans 8:20-22). Again, it does not say, "You shall surely die," literally in Hebrew, but "מות תמות *dying you shall begin to die*." Death is stated twice, the second "death" is imperfect, and this two-fold death seems to be the key to these passages:

> He who has an ear, let him hear what the Spirit says to the churches. He who overcomes shall not be hurt by the SECOND DEATH (Revelation 2:11).

> Blessed and holy is he who has part in the first resurrection. Over such the SECOND DEATH has no power, but they shall be priests of God and of Christ, and shall reign with Him a thousand years (Revelation 20:6).

> Then Death and Hades were cast into the lake of fire. This is the SECOND DEATH" (Revelation 20:14).

If Death is removed, and death is the price of sin, then life is eternal, chronologically incomplete, grammatically imperfect, and morally flawless.

> But the cowardly, unbelieving, abominable, murderers, sexually immoral, sorcerers, idolaters, and all liars shall have their part in the lake which burns with fire and brimstone, which is the SECOND DEATH (Revelation 21:8).

Again, the destruction includes fire, and Hell is described as a human-sacrificial altar. Two deaths are stated, and we can observe two distinct deaths in Daniel 12:2: "And many of those who SLEEP IN THE DUST OF THE EARTH [death one] shall awake, some to everlasting life, some to SHAME AND EVERLASTING CONTEMPT [death two, the same "shame" as the fig tree Christ cursed]."

Genesis 2:16 states, "Of every tree of the garden you may freely eat; but of the tree of the knowledge of good and evil you shall not eat, for in the day that you eat of it you shall surely die." Again, "Of every tree of the garden *you may freely eat [literally,* אכל תאכל *eating you may begin to eat]*; but of the tree of the knowledge of good and evil *you shall not eat [* לא תאכל *you shall not begin to eat]*, for in the day that you eat of it, *you shall surely die [literally,* מות תמות *dying you shall begin to die]*." The reader will notice more than one "eating" and more than one "dying."

We have already viewed examples of the "second death," and it would seem to follow logically that there is a second life — which would explain why the title "Tree of Life" is, in Hebrew " עץ חיים *Tree of Lives*." The Hebrew חיים can be understood as "life" substantively and as "living" adjectivally. If The Hebrew word "life" employed here is taken as a substantive as opposed to an adjective, then "Tree of Life" is, more properly, "Tree of חיים Lives," thus, one tree that contains more than one life. The word "עץ tree here is odd because the plural would otherwise be spelled "עצים trees," but the singular spelling can be conceived as plural as in "עץ פרי" fruit trees; so, "Tree of Life" could be "Tree of Lives" or "Living Trees." A similar peculiarity is noticed in that the word "face" is literally "פנים faces." Whether or not "faces" is a mere grammatical oddity and only means the singular "face" is another's burden. At the same time, it would seem that, when conceived of substantively, "Tree of Lives" would seem to agree in positive opposition to the two deaths. In other words, more than one death exists, one being temporal and one being perpetual. Since death is the end of life, then the standard would seem to be more than one life, one being finite, the other being infinite. Indeed, Revelation 22:2 translates "חיים עץ Tree of Life" by using the word for life (ζωη) eternal as opposed to life (βιος) temporal, and this seems to indicate that the original Hebrew "Tree of Life" is actually "Tree of Lives" in that it refers to something perpetual and not limited to time.

Next, the traditional rendering "you may freely eat" is literally " תאכל אאכלeating you may begin to eat," and so more than one manner of "eating" seems to be suggested. Indeed, to "eat" (אכל) can mean to consume as food, to burn, to destroy, to comprehend, to copulate, and to make something part of oneself (as in a covenant). Keeping in mind that we are contemplating the Eden Narrative, "comprehension" shall remain a focus relative to the word "eat." If we have more than one "eat," it might follow that we are to comprehend something beyond physical eating. Since לחם bread can also mean food (in general) and tree fruit (Jeremiah 11:19), and since there also seems to be more than one eating involved in " תאכל אאכלeating you may begin to eat," then it would also seem to follow that one eating is temporal and the other is eternal, for Christ said, "I am the bread of life" (John 6:35) and He employed the word for life (ζωη) eternal as opposed to life (βιος) temporal; consider: "I am the bread of life [ζωες eternal]. Your fathers ate the manna [God's physical bread from Heaven] in the wilderness, and are dead. This is the bread which comes down from heaven [another bread from Heaven], that one may eat of it AND NOT DIE. I am the living [ζων eternally] bread which came down from heaven. IF ANY-ONE EATS OF THIS BREAD, HE WILL LIVE FOREVER; and the bread that I shall give is My flesh, which I shall give for the life [ζωες eternal] of the world" (John 6:48-51). Conceived of in a Hebrew sense, the בשר means both "flesh" and "royal proclamation = gospel," and it would appear that Christ discusses two breads and two lives relative to His royal proclamation, His gospel... eternal bread and eternal life through the eternal gospel given on the earth in time and for eternity. Notice also that both a substantive and an adjectival form of the Greek word "eternal life" is used, and they match the fact that, in the Hebrew "Tree of Lives," חיים means "lives" substantively and "living" adjectivally.

The rendering ממות תמות *dying you shall die* also views the command as the second person, singular, masculine, i.e. you (male) shall die. It is imperative to notice that the feminine forms of the imperfects in Hebrew contain peculiarities that can cause confusion out of context. The second person, femenine, plural, imperfect "you (females) begin" is identical to the third person, femenine, plural, imperfect "they (females) begin." Also, the second person, masculine, singular, imperfect "you (male) begin" is identical to the third person, feminine, singular, imperfect "she begins." With such grammatical congruences, the only way to tell which of these is being used is through context; however, it could be that more than one is being used simultaneously. For instance, it is written, "...male and female He created them" (Genesis 1:27). Notice that Genesis 3:1 displays Satan's question directed towards the female and not the male. The reasoning here is terribly crafty, especially in light of Genesis 5:2: "...He blessed them and called their name 'Adam'." So, God called both man and woman "Adam" without the definite article (i.e. not "the man" but "Man"), and God's command of abstinence was to "the man" in Genesis 2:16. We can observe how confusion ensued. In other words, a grammatical proposition of Satan's question was that masculinity, not femininity, might be the only one restricted, and this seemingly ridiculous claim is not so ridiculous after all in light of Hebrew (not English) grammar. When God commanded the prohibition, the woman was not yet created. Since the woman was yet to be (not complete), Tradition took the prohibition strictly as masculine because Adam was alone. Unfortunately, Tradition did not view the prohibition as oracular, that is, to be fully realized in due time (incomplete, gestational) as opposed to the moment in which it was spoken. Had tradition accounted for the oracular relative to Hebrew grammar, the woman would have been a consideration when reading the prohibition given prior to her creation.

> Of every tree of the garden, eating you (male) [/she] may begin to eat; but of The Tree of the Knowledge of Good and Evil you (male) [/she] shall not begin to eat, for in the day you eat from it, dying, you (male) [/she] shall begin to die (Genesis 2:17).

At this point, one might question whether God told Adam (in the Second Person) not to eat, or whether God told Adam about His future creation and his future wife (in the Third Person) not to eat. If the second option is selected, then the passage would read,

> Of every tree of the garden, eating she may begin to eat; but of The Tree of the Knowledge of Good and Evil she shall not begin to eat, for in the day you eat from it, dying, she shall begin to die (Genesis 2:16).

One might argue that surely God did not tell Adam anything about the woman because He had not yet made her; but, surely God's command was oracular in that it discussed something that actually happened in the fullness of time. Again, we could conceive of the passage in this way: "Of every tree of the garden, eating she may begin to eat; but of The Tree of the Knowledge of Good and Evil she shall not begin to eat, for in the day you eat from it, dying, she shall begin to die" (Genesis 2:17), for the very next passage in Scripture is "And the Lord God said, 'It is not good that man should be alone; I will make him a helper comparable to him'" (Genesis 2:18). The very fact that God discussed woman immediately following the prohibition given to Adam that, grammatically, could very well apply to the bride appears to indicate that the command was intended for both Adam and his wife and that Adam was to guard his wife from Satan. The act of guarding is important here because it is written that "...the Lord God took the man and put him in the garden of Eden to tend ולשמרה *and to guard her*" (Genesis 2:15), for Song of Songs 4:12 calls a woman a "garden," and the word גן *garden* is derived from the root גנן *to guard*. That guarding is even mentioned indicates some threat, and the "serpent" challenger is called the "guardian cherub" in Ezekiel 28:14, a guardian angel. Ancient Egypt considered serpents to be guardians, and, if there is a reflected link between the Egyptians and the Hebrews here, then it would seem as if Adam was to be a righteous serpent who guarded Eden from the unrighteous guardian. Whichever way, Adam was to be a human guardian and that Satan was an angelic guardian. Furthermore, when we consider a story about "eating," it is useful to keep in mind that an angel is a "διακονος *table-waiter who serves food and drink, a deacon, a servant under authority*." Since we know that a focus of the Fall Narrative is food, the table-waiter (priest at an altar) theme is apparent, but the question of authority (deacon) and servitude is subtle when reflecting again upon the situation that "...the Lord God took the man and put him in the garden of Eden לעבדה *to serve her, to cultivate her* ולשמרה *and to guard her*." Subjugation is an issue here, for Adam was placed in The Garden of Eden, i.e. The Land of Fertility to serve her and to guard her, and this situation is initiated by the fact that, before any of God's commands to humanity, "זכר *male (as to remember)* and נקבה *female (as with an indentation)* He created them" (Genesis 1:27). The word for *male* also indicates *memory* in Hebrew, and this word is the synonym of the word guard used of Adam also (compare-Exodus 20:8 to Deuteronomy 5:12). Adam was given a gap to defend like a threshold is given a guardian. Satan is called the "guardian Cherub," and, when we consider the cherubic threshold guardians at the conclusion of the Fall Narrative, we can understand the consistent figure of the "whoredom" of sin in that Adam was to guard the Garden (woman) of Eden (fruitful womb) in response to God's command, "Be fruitful and multiply; fill the earth and subdue her. Rule over the fish of the sea and over the birds of the air and over every living creature that moves upon the earth" (Genesis 1:28). Subduction occurs through servitude positively; seduction occurs through servitude negatively: "...whoever desires TO BECOME GREAT among you shall be your SERVANT" (Mark 10:43); "And if you do not do well, SIN LIES AT THE DOOR. And its desire is for you, but YOU SHOULD RULE OVER IT" (Genesis 4:7).

Since Adam was commanded to "rule over every living creature that moves on the face(s) of the earth" (Genesis 1:28), it would appear that Satan was to be ruled over by Adam. Here we may begin to see part of Satan's envy. Ironically, Satan is described as a נחש *serpent or shining one*, and the word מפטן *threshold* is derived from the same root as פתן *asp, serpent*; this root is probably equivalent to פתל **to twist**, *to wrestle, to struggle, to be deceitful*, and the root the root חבל **to twist**, *to bind* produces the word חבל *birth pangs*. Consider how Jacob wrestled with the wicked angel whom he subdued (Hosea 12:4) immediately after he protected his wife, Rachel, at the threshold of where he originally attempted to escape from his sin in Genesis 31. Notice also how many traditions, without referring to Hosea 12, thought that Jacob actually fought God and won instead of having overcome Satan! Satan's goal is to appear "like God," as it is written of Satan:

> How you are fallen from heaven, O Lucifer, son of the morning! How you are cut down to the ground, you who weakened the nations! For you have said in your heart: "I will ascend into heaven, I will exalt my throne above the stars of God; I will also sit on the mount of the congregation on the farthest sides of the north; I will ascend above the heights of the clouds, אדמה *I will be like* the Most High" (Isaiah 14:12-14).

Both male and female are called "Adam" in Genesis 5:2; אדם *Adam* is the masculine of אדמה *red ground, (Egyptian) sterile soil*; אדם= *Adam, humanity, I will be silent* (Job 31:33-35) and אדמה = *red ground, sterile soil, I will be like*; thus, we notice Adam's silence in the presence of deceit since he did not guard against the Enemy during Satan's entire exchange with the bride, we notice the sterility of defiled ground since such is the case with violent bloodshed (Numbers 35:34) and sexual immorality (Leviticus 18:27), and we notice all of these things are connected within a single word, a word that can be translated as "I will be like...." When Satan said, "והיתם *and you will be* כאלהים*like God*" to the humans in Genesis 3:5, the gematria (numeric equivalencey) *"like God"* is כאלהים = כ 20 + א 1 + ל 30 + ה 5 + י 10 + ם 600 = **666**. "Here is wisdom. Let him who has understanding calculate the number of the beast, for it is THE NUMBER OF A MAN: His number is **666**" (Revelation 13:18); Satan is called "the man" in Isaiah 14:16 and Pilate, in John 19:5, calls Christ "the man." It is obvious that dire confusion has occurred by mistaking God and Satan for each other, for Satan is the false imitation of God: Jesus described Himself as a serpent in John 3:14, and Satan is referred to as a "serpent" in Genesis 3:1; Jesus described Himself as, "the bright Morning Star" in Revelation 22:1, and Satan is referred to as "morning star" in Isaiah 14:12; Jesus said, "Behold, I come like a thief..." in Revelation 16:15, and Jesus said of Satan, "The thief comes only to steal and kill and destroy" in John 10:10; Jesus is described as a "lion" in Revelation 5:5, and Satan is described as a "lion" in I Peter 5:8. Many mistakenly believe that Jacob conquered God in a wrestling match immediately after serving by protecting his wives and children, but Ephesians 6:10-12 states, immediately after discussing wives, children, and servants, "be strong in the Lord and in the power of His might. Put on the whole armor of God, that you may be able to stand against the wiles of the devil. For we do not wrestle against flesh and blood, but against principalities, against powers, against the RULERS OF THE DARKNESS of this age, against spiritual hosts of wickedness in the HEAVENLY PLACES," for the wicked spirit said to Jacob, "Let Me go, for the day breaks" (Genesis 32:26) referring to the dissipating darkness and the rising of the sun into its heavenly place. Such confusion has caused some Jewish traditions to think that there is no Satan at all and that God is both good and evil, and English translations say that Jacob prevailed over God.... Many traditions actually consider Satan to be a talking reptile, but what of this? -- "You brood of vipers! Who warned you to flee from the wrath to come?" (Luke 3:7), and the fact that Satan is described flatly as a "guardian cherub" in Ezekiel 28:14. I have yet to hear anyone say that he actually thinks God placed literal snakes at the entrance of Eden where it is written, "So He drove out the man; and He placed cherubim at the east of the garden of Eden..." (Genesis 3:24). Observing a bit of just how deceitful Satan is, let us reflect again upon the importance of grammar.

Satan employed the second person, masculine, plural, imperfect when he specifically asked, "Did God say אל תאכלו you [males] shall not begin to eat...?" (Genesis 3:1); this question is a riddle, for the emphasis should not be placed upon the general meaning of God's command but on the specific grammar of His command. Satan asked if God restricted more than one male, for the grammatical construction Satan used is plural and masculine only. The argument could be made that " בנים *sons*" describes both males and females generally, so Satan's question was directed at the human couple in general; however, this argument functions on the proposition that Satan merely asked if the humans could eat and not if God said, "אל תאכלו *you [males] shall not begin to eat*." In other words, Satan's question appears to ask whether or not God restricted eating, but his question does not revolve around the generality of eating. Satan's question revolves around the deceitful proposition that one, but not the other, could indeed eat legally based upon the oddity found within Hebrew grammar: the third person, feminine, singular, imperfect is identical to the second person, masculine, singular, imperfect, i.e. "she shall not begin to eat" is, in Hebrew, identical to "you (man) shall not begin to eat." The nature of this question challenges a knowledge of Hebrew grammar regarding the sense in which the command was given, and this is why I believe that the foundation of Scripture can only be understood fully in Hebrew because the Hebrew grammar is not identical to the English grammar. That is, this story only makes full sense in Hebrew. Hebrew does not distinguish grammatically between "you (male) shall not begin to eat" and "she shall not begin to eat"; these two are one: "תאכל." Satan used one conjugation to ask a question concerning what the bride thought God meant when He gave the prohibition that was given with another conjugation. If one first conceives of what God means and then refers back to what God said, then one can easily superimpose a meaning upon the Text that is not original. On the other hand, if one consults the original first and then attempts to understand what God said, one has a greater chance of success. When Satan asked "Did God say אל תאכלו *you [males] shall not begin to eat...?*" the answer should have been simply, "No," as in Joshua 5:13-14: "And it came to pass, when Joshua was by Jericho, that he lifted his eyes and looked, and behold, a Man stood opposite him with His sword drawn in His hand. And Joshua went to Him and said to Him, 'Are You for us or for our adversaries?' So He said, 'No...'." The bride did not say, "No," and the battle was in the process of being lost when she responded, "God has said "תאכלו *you [men or males] shall not eat...*," for she said explicitly that Satan's conjugation was indeed God's conjugation when, in fact, Satan's conjugation was different from God's. The bride accepted the proposition of Satan's question and therefore responded identically to the falsehood with which he propounded his riddle. God said specifically A, and Satan said specifically B:

A: "לא תאכל" =   2nd P. Sing. Masc. or 3rd P. Sing. Fem.

B: "לא תאכלו" =   2nd P. Plur. Masc.

The letter ו is the number 6 and means "a nail." Regarding the forbidden tree, Satan added a ו *nail* to what God said and thus implied that God restricted more than one male from eating of the forbidden tree. God used a form of the root אכל *he ate* that can be understood as the second person singular masculine, i.e. *you (male) may eat* or third person singular feminine, i.e. *she may eat*. So, one could question whether God said "you (male)" or "she"; but, a proposition of this question is "either or" which does not admit the possibility of "and." Oracles are usually declarative (as opposed to interrogative), and they usually are designed to make sense significantly after they are given so that one has to begin with the word itself before attempting to discern what it means. Since riddles or parables use few words to say many, it could be that God said any permutation of,

> Of every tree of the garden, אאכל תאכל *eating* **you (male)/she** *may begin to eat*; but of The Tree of the Knowledge of Good and Evil לא תאכל **you (male)/she** *shall not eat*, for in the day אכלך *of your eating*, מות תמות *dying* **you (male)/she** *shall begin to die.*

Since God prohibited the forbidden tree prior to the bride's creation, Tradition has assumed that the command was given in the masculine understanding of the verb... but what if the feminine is meant? If one asks whether or not God restricted the man *or* the woman from the forbidden tree, then one would have to concede that God permitted either the man *or* the woman to eat from the forbidden tree. If one, however, recognizes that an oracle is a riddle that makes sense in the fullness of time, and that God spoke an oracle recorded in a language that does not grammatically account for time in its verbs, then God could very well have spoken in eternity prior to the situation of time being detrimental; God could have spoken of the male and female simultaneously by speaking to the male. The reader should note the words immediately before the overt mention of Satan in Genesis 3:1: "Therefore a man shall leave his father and mother and be joined to his wife, *and they shall become* ONE FLESH. And they were both naked, the man and his wife, and were not ashamed" (Genesis

2:24-25). The discussion of unity immediately precedes the first words of Satan. It appears as if Satan precisely attacked that unity through his question that disallowed the grammatical construction of the command given imperatively in the second person, masculine point of view (in a grammatically imperfect state) — to the man (living before his wife in a chronologically imperfect and timeless state) — in reference to the third person, feminine point of view (in a grammatically imperfect state) — about a woman who was yet to be (in a chronologically imperfect state). Since the roots of Hebrew words are third person, singular, perfects (finished), it should be assumed that the issue begins from masculinity which is probably why Adam is the fleshly father, in a manner of speaking, of his bride. I assert that both the man and the woman were meant in God's prohibition because the two are one regardless of gender in the conjugation " לא תאכל *you (male)/she* shall not eat." Furthermore, it was Adam's responsibility to remember the rules and to teach his wife: "Husbands, love your wives, just as Christ also loved the church and gave Himself for her, that He might sanctify and cleanse her with the WASHING OF WATER BY THE WORD" (Ephesians 5:25-27). Since Adam was to serve firstly and guard secondly, but did not, we see the inversion in that he did not guard firstly and his wife served him food secondly. Remember that angels are described as "table-waiters, servants" in Hebrews 1:14, for Revelation 10:9 says, "So I went to the angel and said to him, 'Give me the little book.' And he said to me, 'Take and eat it; and it will make your stomach bitter, but it will be as sweet as honey in your mouth,'" for "to eat" can mean "to acquire knowledge," hence the deceitful tree and its corresponding name. Similarly, Ezekiel 3:1 says, "Moreover He said to me, "Son of man, eat what you find; eat this scroll, and go, speak to the house of Israel." It seems probable that, at least, this is a possible solution: Adam was responsible for his wife who "became the mother of all the living" (Genesis 3:20) and would be guilty of sin if he allowed her to eat, on top of the fact that he would be guilty also if he ate. The reason for this conclusion is because Ezekiel 33:7-8 illustrates the same principle:

> So you, son of man: I have made you a צפה *watchman* for the house of Israel; therefore you shall hear a word from My mouth and warn them for Me. When I say to the wicked, 'O wicked, מות תמות DYING YOU SHALL BEGIN TO DIE!' and you do not speak to warn the wicked from his way, that wicked shall die in his iniquity; BUT HIS BLOOD I WILL REQUIRE AT YOUR HAND.

A צפה *watchman* is a שמר *watchman* (two different Hebrew words that translate to the same English word *watchman*). Song of Songs 4:12 calls a woman a "garden." "Then the Lord God took the man and put him in the Garden of Eden עבדה *to serve her, to cultivate her* [i.e. make her fruitful] ולשמרה *and to guard her* [i.e. to be her watchman]" (Genesis 3:15). "Now let me sing to my well-beloved a song of my Beloved regarding His vineyard: My Well-beloved has a vineyard on a very fruitful hill. He dug it up and cleared out its stones, and planted it with the choicest vine. HE BUILT A TOWER IN ITS MIDST, and also made a winepress in it..." (Isaiah 5:1-2). It would seem that the bride should have been guarded by Adam from the forbidden tree that came to be in the midst of Eden, particularly since God נחהו *covenanted (as in a vow)* with the man in the garden (woman) of Eden " עבדה *to serve her* [i.e. make her fruitful] ולשמרה *and to guard her.* "And the Lord God COMMANDED THE MAN, 'Of every tree of the garden, eating she may begin to eat; but of The Tree of the Knowledge of Good and Evil she shall not begin to eat, for in the day of your eating, DYING YOU SHALL BEGIN TO DIE"; since Satan is called "the man (איש)" as Adam called himself, and since Satan said, אדמה *I will be like* which is the same Hebrew word (אדמה *sterile ground*) as the mother from which Adam was taken (Job 1:21), it could very well be that both Adam and Satan were condemned to die as a consequence of the bride's death. It could also be that humanity/Adam has a hope that, through humility, Satan covets. Whichever way, the discussion of בשר אחד *one flesh, one proclamation, one Gospel, one successful birth* — since they are all the same two words — seemed to be Satan's target, and he sought to fracture the unity of the command " ולא תאכל **you (male)** AND **she** shall not begin to eat" by suggesting "ולא תאכל **you (male)** OR **she** shall not begin to eat" with the rendition "לא תאכלו *not you males shall begin to eat.*" The bride's acceptance of Satan's proposition would then create a situation where Adam/humanity would have to die along with Satan because Adam did not annul his wife's vow before she sealed it in covenant by "eating." Recall: When I say to the wicked, 'O wicked, DYING YOU SHALL BEGIN TO DIE!' and you do not speak to warn the wicked from his way, that wicked shall die in his iniquity; but his blood I will require at your hand" (Ezekiel 33:7-8). Since man and wife were designed to be "one flesh," and since man was made to "guard" his bride, then it seems that when specifically the woman ate, her blood would be required at her husband's hands. Thus, it would follow that Adam could have prevented his wife from following through with her error based on the provision that ensued through the Torah:

If she vowed in her husband's house, or bound herself by an agreement with an oath, and her husband heard it, and made no response to her and did not overrule her, then all her vows shall stand, and every agreement by which she bound herself shall stand. But if her husband truly made them void on the day he heard them, then whatever proceeded from her lips concerning her vows or concerning the agreement binding her, it shall not stand; her husband has made them void, and the Lord will release her. Every vow and every binding oath to afflict her soul, her husband may confirm it, or her husband may make it void. Now if her husband makes no response whatever to her from day to day, then he confirms all her vows or all the agreements that bind her; he confirms them, because he made no response to her on the day that he heard them. But if he does make them void after he has heard them, THEN HE SHALL BEAR HER GUILT (Numbers 30:10-15).

Grammatically, the main problem here is the confusion of the sexes. The bride inverted the recitation of God's command by accepting the inverted proposition of Satan's supposed liberality. The confusion of the sexes should be glaringly obvious now that it is known that the forbidden tree was the Tree of the Union of Good and Evil, a perverse admixture. Furthermore, what should also now be obvious is that, since Melchizedech is a type of Christ then the King of Sodom is a type of Satan prefigured by the Tree of the Union of an Unsuitable Mixture. How perverted Satan's craft is! — for the Creation account explicitly discusses all that God made to be productive "according to its kind" and homosexuality is not productive "according to its kind." In other words, homosexuality is a union of unlike things by the very fact that they are alike anatomically. The very notion of such a union, let alone the permission and acceptance of it, are a grim mockery of the order of creation and the covenant of life to which creation was designed to adhere. The feminine word עצה *tree* also means *counsel*, and, when thought of in the masculine, we may notice that the bride today has elected עץ הדעת טוב ורע *The Counsel of the Union of a Ruinous Mixture* (*literally, The Tree of the Knowledge of Good and Evil*) to define marriage governmentally in flagrant opposition to The Great King's institution. The bride chose in Eden, the land of the Fruitful Womb, a sterile union to infect the earth, and this bride continues to choose the same today. Satan's grammatical deceit also serves to identify to the reader that Satan was not a mere "serpent" any more than the crowd who came to be baptized by John in Luke 3 was a collection of scaly vipers. Talking snakes are the substance of children's stories, the stuff of myth. We are to be mature readers who seek after wisdom. The gross error of social evolution runs counter to the Fall of Man because it assumes that man can fall upwards. "Assuredly, I say to you, among those born of women there has not risen one greater than John the Baptist..." (Matthew 11:11), but Adam was not born of woman and was therefore greater, for he was God's archetype. Adam was no child-like idiot! Adam was so wise that, when facing Satan, "...Adam was not deceived, but the woman being deceived, fell into transgression" (I Timothy 2:14). Since we have all been deceived before Satan, none of us has yet attained to the wisdom of Adam. Satan did not trip Adam by way of wisdom; yet, mere grammar causes us, the bride of Christ, to stumble. The reader must keep in mind that the word נחש serpent is also the name of a human being (I Samuel 11) and it is from the root נחש he shined; it is to be connected with wisdom, not an absence of appendages: "And many of those who sleep in the dust of the earth shall awake, Some to [1] EVERLASTING LIFE [the second life], some to shame and [2] EVERLASTING CONTEMPT [the second death]. Those who are WISE SHALL SHINE like the brightness of the firmament, and those who turn many to righteousness LIKE THE STARS FOREVER AND EVER."

When considering The Tree of the Knowledge of GOOD AND EVIL, we may reconsider these words: "For though by this time you ought to be teachers, you need someone to teach you again the first principles of the oracles of God; and you have come to need milk and not solid food. For everyone who partakes only of milk is unskilled in the word of righteousness, for he is a babe. But solid food belongs to those who are of full age, that is, those who by reason of use have their senses exercised to discern both GOOD AND EVIL...." (Hebrews 5:12-6:1-2).

Based on the law of a woman's vow quoted above, it is likely that this is a veiled teaching about the Judgment Day. Christ is the Bridegroom, and He has authority to annul to foolish vows of His bride. If this conclusion is correct, then we may be able to view the salvific subtlety contained within God's prohibition if we view the word. In the ancient East, the dead were understood to eat dust for food (Religions of Ancient Egypt and Baylonia, Sayce) and we can see Satan himself referred to in this way in Genesis 3:14. Based on the law of a woman's vow quoted above, it is likely that this is a veiled teaching about the Judgment Day. Christ is the Bridegroom, and He has authority to annul the foolish vows of His bride. If this conclusion is correct, then we may be able to view the salvific subtlety contained within God's prohibition if we view the word מות as a proper noun (מות Death) instead of only as an infinitive absolute (מות dying): "Of every tree of the garden, אכל תאכל eating you (male)/she may begin to eat; but of The Tree of the Knowledge of Good and Evil לא תאכל **you (male)/she** shall not eat, for in the day of your eating, מות תמות Death **you** shall begin to die." If I am correct, it would shed much light on these passages in relation to each other:

> The last enemy that will be destroyed is DEATH
> (I Corinthians 15:26).

> Depart from Me, you cursed, into the everlasting fire PREPARED FOR THE DEVIL AND HIS ANGELS (Matthew 25:41).

> Then I saw a great white throne and Him who sat on it, from whose face the earth and the heaven fled away. And there was found no place for them. And I saw the dead, small and great, standing before God, and books were opened. And another book was opened, which is the Book of Life. And the dead were judged according to their works, by the things which were written in the books. The sea gave up the dead who were in it, and Death and Hades delivered up the dead who were in them. And they were judged, each one according to his works. Then DEATH AND HADES WERE CAST INTO THE LAKE OF FIRE. This is the second death. And anyone not found written in the Book of Life was cast into the lake of fire (Revelation 20:11-15).

Again,

> Of every tree of the garden, אכל תאכל eating **you (male)/she** may begin to eat; but of The Tree of the Knowledge of Good and Evil אל תלכאת **you (male)/she** shall not eat, for in the day of your eating, מות תמות **Death, You** shall die eternally.

The eternity, or chronological imperfection, displayed here connects the masculine to the feminine in a single conjugation, and this conjugal union is a grammatical expression of perpetuity. Covenants entail both a blessing and a curse. The blessing of a covenant anticipates fruit production since a covenant is of life, for life, and innately seeks to perpetuate life. The productivity expected is the result of proper officiation at the altar, which, for the present purpose, is the wife. At the same time, the priest specifically referent to the Deity is bound to Him ceremonially which qualifies the priest as the bride individually; the priest, performing sacrifice, is included as the head of the congregation who constitutes the bride collectively. The priest's sex must of necessity be male, since he officiates at the altar that indicates femininity, but his ceremonial designations are, by figure, androginous; this arrangement means that, in a sense, the masculine priest is also partially feminine; however, the sex of the matter is not the issue since the gender-roles are illustrative microcosmically and macrocosmically. The micro-macro-nature being male and female respectively served as both an illustration to the priest himself and to his congregants that unification with the Deity is compatible with both sexes and glorifies the specific designations of the family, for designation (not ability) is the goal that signifies types held in harmony as all-encompassing aspects of the One Who designed every aspect of unfallen family. Eliminating the specific designations in preference for the simple ability to pour libation or pull a bloody blade forces a type of unnatural union that mocks the precise design of untainted worship, and, when applied conjugally, does not respect both sexes, but wholly prefers one to the other in a type of homosexuality. As such, we can perceive why Adam was the father, brother, and husband of his wife, for the priest, the sacrificer, was the intermediary between God and man and therefore represented the one to the other. The sacrificer represented the Deity to the worshippers by being a spiritual husband and father who unified the bride to the Giver of life. The sacrificer represented the worshippers to the Deity by being a constituent of the spiritual bride in that he, leading the congregation, was to bring forth the fruit of the Spirit. Offering life upon the altar is of the incarnate masculine ability and therefore the priestly designation representative of the Divine Father. Yielding life up from the altar is of incarnate feminine ability and therefore bridal designation representative of maternity who recognizes God as the giver of both the sire and the offspring. In the delicate harmony of sacrificial worship, the priest was physically male and spiritually illustrative of all humanity. We can, therefore, see why the title אדם *Adam* means a male specifically and humanity *generally*, and observing that the whole is accounted for in this man, we can understand that Adam was not simply the first human, but the first priest among the eventual human race. It is for such a reason that a male, not a female, be the sire of humanity because the male pours out life physically whereas the female unites by first receiving physically and then birthing. Since there was none found for the priest prior to the creation of his wife, it was necessary that the man pour out his life in a libation which was expressed tenderly in that his bride was crafted from his own circumcised heart. That the fruit of the vine flowed from the first human priest's heart meant, of necessity, that there must be an altar to receive the libation in order for it to be yielded up to the God who gave it, and this is why the altar represents femininity generally and the union of male and female specifically, for איש *man (as male)* was probably spelled originally as the feminine noun אש *fire*, and אשה *woman* also means both *gift* and *fire offering*. The fiery union of the sacrifice with the altar, as being representative of holy conjugation, explains why the letters חם spell both the noun *father-in-law* and the adjective *heat*, and why adding א spells חמא *to curdle*; that is, the father-in-law is a covenantal father prior to the consumation of offspring, the marital union is heat since the altar who is the wife is the fire-offering, and the husband's libation can be expressed as milk that will curdle poetically within the womb in order to form the fruit of the sacrifice: "Your hands have made me and fashioned me, an intricate unity... remember, I pray, that You have made me like clay... Did You not pour me out like milk, and CURDLE me like cheese clothe me with skin and flesh, and knit me together with bones and sinews? You have granted me life and favor, and Your care has preserved my spirit" (Job 10:8-12). Adam was indeed made "like clay," and Adam, by God, did indeed pour out like milk so that his offspring could be curdled, solidified, in the womb; and, after sin, when man was in need of rebirth, God, in His intricate mercy, did clothe them with skins and granted them life by proclaiming, "He shall crush your head," to the enemy in order to preserve the spirit of man.

Confusing or reversing the spiritual and ceremonial roles of the sexes is errant and destructive. Genesis 2: 22 states that God ויבן *built* the woman from the man's pruned heart which distinguishes between קרבן *sacrifice* (from the root קרב *to draw near*) and זבח *sacrifice* (from the root זבח *to slaughter*). Sacrifice did not involve death originally for it was rather the conduit to life, by God, through man, back to God. Inverting the true original sacrificial process of *drawing near* indicates the horrid history of death, by man, through Satan, back to man, a pattern otherwise termed "damnation" that makes sacrifice analogous to a destructive womb and converts the beauty of conducive maternity into a crumbling mausoleum.

"THE LAW"

T HE desire to reduce grand complexities into simple categories is a common human tendency because it apparently simplifies a difficult program into something easily handled. At this point, the easy program gives power to its handler, and a reduced copy is taken as representative of a complex, older original. The reduced copy becomes confused with the complex original until the original and the copy are no longer distinguishable. The copy then replaces the original in the eyes of the handler who produced it. The handler thus becomes the master who mandates jurisdiction over the fruit of his own creation, having unintentionally cast off the original in his own mind by intentionally attempting to simplify something that cannot be made simple because it is itself intrinsically complex. The end result is reasoning about something that has no real existence beyond the real feelings, philosophies, theologies, and lifestyles spawned from a lifeless mirage.

For churchgoers, "The Law" often has but historical significance that leads chronologically up to their "faith" but is a system of rules and regulations they no longer find applicable to their daily lives, let alone to the interpretation of the so-called "New Testament." It has been long asserted that "The Law" is synonymous to "works" and is opposed to "Grace" which is synonymous to "faith"; these categories, when put at odds with each other, compute the equation that "The Law" is antithetical to Grace and that "work" is antithetical to "faith"; from here, theological wranglings ensue regarding which components of Scripture are binding and what is to be understood upon the fracture of that bond. Such assertions claim to have their basis in passages likc Romans 11:6 ("...and if by grace, then it is no longer of works; otherwise grace is no longer grace. But if it is of works, it is no longer grace; otherwise work is no longer work...") and Galatians 3:2: "Did you receive the Spirit by the works of the law, or by the hearing of faith?" In short, "The Law" is put at odds with "Faith" by many churchgoers, and these simple categories are easy constructs that serve as building-blocks for various philosophies, theologies, and lifestyles that I will now challenge directly.

When we say "The Law," we can recognize its grammatical qualification of being definite ("The" as opposed to "A") and singular ("Law" as opposed to "Laws"), but the conclusion that we can only be discussing one entity *because* of the grammatical designation of one entity is incorrect. For instance, Genesis 2:9 discusses " עץ החיים THE *Tree of Life*" and " ורע עץ הדעת טוב THE *Tree of the Knowledge of Good and Evil*" that were both "in the midst of the garden," but Genesis 3:3 displays the bride discussing simply " העץ אשר בתוך הגן THE *Tree that is in the middle of the garden*" as if there were only one. The grammar is fine, but the category in which it is placed is not. There were two trees in the center of the garden, but the bride discussed only one. The question here is, "To which 'tree' do you refer?" and the question I ask of you, reader, is "To which 'Law' do you refer?" In the same way that the Woman seemed only to see one tree, it seems as if the Bride is only currently able to see one corpus of "Law."

The stance that "The Law" is opposed to "Grace" functions on the proposition that there is only one "Law" under discussion, and such a proposition mandates that God effectually changed His mind over time in spite of the fact that God says in Malachi 3:6, "I DO NOT CHANGE," that Titus 2:13 calls Jesus Christ "our great God and Savior," that Christ Himself says in John 10:30, "I and My Father are One," and Hebrews 13:8 states plainly that "Jesus Christ is THE SAME YESTERDAY, TODAY, AND FOREVER," for Christ is God. Since Jesus is God, since God does not change, since Jesus is eternally the same from of old and forever, what then gives any churchgoer the right to claim that God changed His mind about "The Law" other than the churchgoer only seeing one Law? The most "Scriptural" answer I have heard regarding my question is a quotation from Hebrews 7:12: "For the priesthood being changed, of necessity there is also a change of the law," and this response functions on the assumption that the "changed" priesthood is from Aaron to Christ when a simple reading of the Torah (i.e. "The Law") reveals that Exodus 4:22 designates all of Israel as priests by using the specifically priestly title of "Firstborn" but that, after the majority of Israel ironically slew the firstborn at the base of Sinai, and after the Levites stood up for life by putting to death those who took part in innocent blood, it was then that the priesthood was "changed" from all Israel to only part of it even though it remained in Israel (as was the case with Christ Who was physically of Israel) to the effect that God said in Numbers 3:12, "Now behold, I Myself have taken the Levites from among the children of Israel instead of every firstborn who opens the womb among the children of Israel. Therefore the Levites shall be Mine, because all the firstborn are Mine." That is, after the Levites slew the slayers of the firstborn, they received the right of Firstborn and were signified accordingly by shaving their entire bodies so as to resemble babies (Numbers 8). The priesthood, that is, the Firstborn status, did "change" from the whole people to one-twelfth of it without departing from the people, and so the "Scriptural proof" of the priesthood "changing" to Christ based on Hebrews 7:12 is a simple misapplication of a quotation because it functions in a relative vacuum by disregarding the reference to which it is bound, for the very section this "proof" is found within compares Levi to Melchizedek who was before (not after) Levi. Merely quoting Scripture "proves" nothing as to Scripture's application, for Psalm 14:1 says plainly, "...there is no God...." and one may reflect on why "The Serpent" asked the bride "Did God say...?" in a morbidly successful effort to persuade the woman to condemn herself by misquoting God as the bride continues to do.

Regarding the bride misquoting God, it has long been asserted that "The Law" is opposed to "Grace," therefore "legalism" is wicked because it focuses on the adherence to a standard which is, by its own nature, opposed to Grace. It is also commonly stated that Christ contradicted Moses. Both of these assertions are flagrantly errant. Let us observe an example of this term "The Law" relative to Caiaphas. Caiaphas, the "High Priest" during the time of Christ's crucifixion, made it a specific point to have Christ crucified according to "The Law." The reader must, however, understand that Caiaphas craftily tried to unite The Torah's (i.e. The Law's) "Law" with Rome's "Law" by inducing Pilate to crucify Jesus. Rome crucified insurrectionists, for the term "thief" (like one next to whom Christ was crucified) was a legal term denoting someone who had stolen from Rome (possibly by killing a tax-collector); so, with respect to Rome, Caiaphas desired for Christ to be understood as defying the Roman government who would then, accordingly, hang Him on a tree. Since the High Priest (i.e. Firstborn) Caiaphas did not want the people to believe that Christ was the true High Priest (i.e. true Firstborn), the accomplishment of Christ's crucifixion would seem to mandate that Christ was cursed by God based on Deuteronomy 21:23 which states, "...he who is hanged is accursed of God"; the reasoning here would be that, if Christ were The Messiah, God would not curse His own Messiah. The Text does say that "...he who is hanged is accursed of God," but the application to which Caiaphas applied this passage to his own mind functioned on the proposition that he could induce God to "curse" Christ in the same way that he could induce Pilate to hang Christ. In other words, Caiaphas' errant reading of The Torah (The Law) caused him to believe that it is man who can determine the will and subsequent actions of God based on collective agreement and Scripture knowledge much in the same way churches today vote on the will of God following collective prayer. The reference to which Deuteronomy 21:23 is tethered can be found in the slaughter of the innocent(s) recorded in Numbers 25. Those who sacrificed through the improper copulative union along with the followers of Baal Peor (a child sacrificial deity) "joined [themselves] to Baal of Peor" (v. 3) through child sacrifice celebrated by the collective display of fertility's conduit. The punishment for having slaughtered the innocent was as follows: "Take all the leaders of the people and HANG THE OFFENDERS before the Lord, out in the sun, that the fierce anger of the Lord may turn away from Israel" (v. 4). The result of Israel's offense was the innocent death of children, and the punishment for taking the life of the innocent was hanging or stoning. That is, the hanging did not cause the curse of God, but the hanging was the result of the curse of God. How could man possibly force God to curse anyone? Thus, the innocents who were slain died because of the sins of others and not because of their own sins. The perversely ironic hanging of Christ necessitated a situation that literally displayed One dying for the sin of others even though, in plain view, others thought He died for his own sin as determined by Rome and as "proved" by Scripture. The Torah ("The Law") also states in Deuteronomy 27:26, "Cursed is the one who does not confirm all the words of this law by observing them" which is echoed by Christ in Matthew 5:17, "Do not think that I came to destroy the Law or the Prophets. I did not come to destroy but to fulfill." That Christ kept the whole "Law" but died without sin (and sin comes by breaking the "Law" Christ kept) indicates plainly that Christ died for a reason other than His own sin since He did not sin at all; He died on account of and for the sins of others whereas solely human children who are killed by others die on account of (but not for) the sins of others. Christ lay down willfully like Isaac. As in Numbers 25, Christ was as the Innocent who was killed on account of the sins of others.

The legal situation of Christ can now be seen as follows: Christ died for sins that were not His own; He had no sin of His own, which means that He kept the whole "Law"; keeping the whole "Law" means that one cannot die since "the wages of sin is death" (Romans 6:23); therefore, Christ could not legally remain dead, hence His resurrection. Likewise, in an oath to the death, the covenant can only be broken correctly by innocent death; therefore, if we die in covenant with One Who is alive eternally, we cannot legally remain dead, hence our resurrection: "For if we have been united together in the LIKENESS of HIS DEATH [not ours, for His sealed a perfect life (as opposed to ours)], certainly we also shall be in the likeness of His resurrection..." (Romans 6:5). Salvation is accomplished legally, not in spite of legality, but this fact would only be recognizable if the Bride committed "The Law" to memory so as not to confuse it with what Romans 6 calls "another Law" as was the case with the two "Trees" in Eden. A covenant contains both a blessing and a curse: a blessing in keeping it, and a curse to police or guard the agreement if it is not kept. To be redeemed from the curse means to be called back from the penalty of breaking an oath which is, of course, death. This very situation is discussed in Galatians 3:

O foolish Galatians! Who has bewitched you that you should not obey the truth, before whose eyes JESUS CHRIST WAS CLEARLY PORTRAYED AMONG YOU AS CRUCIFIED?... For as many as are of the works of the law are under the curse; for it is written, "Cursed is everyone who does not continue in all things which are written in the book of the law, to do them [which Christ did continue in them]." But that no one [other than Christ] is justified by THE LAW in the sight of God is evident, for "the just [Who is Christ] shall live by *faith* = πιστεως = אמנה *covenant*." Yet THE LAW is not of *faith* = πιστεως = אמנה *covenant*, but "the man who does them shall *live* by them." Christ has redeemed us from the CURSE OF THE LAW, having become a curse [= a guardian] for us, for it is written, "CURSED IS EVERYONE WHO HANGS ON A TREE," that the BLESSING of Abraham [who preceded Levi] might come upon the Gentiles [who preceded the Jews] in Christ Jesus [Who "precedes all things" (Colossians 1:17)], that we might receive the promise of the Spirit through *faith* = πιστεως = אמנה *covenant* [i.e. through One Who lives eternally].

The immediate connundrum here regards "The Law," for the same passage says that "The Law is not of *faith* [or *covenant*]" and also "Christ has redeemed us from the curse of the *law* [or *covenant*]"; ergo, the question could be, "Is 'The Law' of covenant or not?" — but the problem with this question is that it assumes there to be only one "Law" discussed. How could the very same "Law" be of covenant and not of covenant? The reader should ask, "Which 'Law' and which 'Covenant'?" I ask the reader, "How could one claim to be saved by faith, i.e. covenant through a Law that was simultaneously of faith and not of faith? Here is the union of unlike entities! — an inherent contradiction! — a melding of opposites! "The Law" and the "The Law" are not the same! These two are not one! For centuries upon centuries, the bride has unified two diametrically opposed entities that go by the same designation as the "The Law" as if these two were in any possible way the same. Genesis 2:9 discusses " עץ החיים THE *Tree of Life*" and " עץ הדעת טוב ורע THE *Tree of the Knowledge of Good and Evil*" that are "in the midst of the garden," but Genesis 3:3 displays the bride discussing simply " העץ אשר בתוך הגן THE *Tree that is in the middle of the garden*" as if there were only one. There were two trees in the midst of the garden, just as there are two "Laws" in the midst of our discussion. That the bride cannot, does not, or refuses to see two and not one does not change the fact that there are two and not one.

The English word "Law" we are examining is a translation of the Greek word νομος *custom, usage, law, ordinance, statute, principle, rule, maxim, tune, mode of singing, song, melody.* The "New Testament" does not use the word θεμις *divine right, law, custom, prerogative, privilege, judicial sentence, tax.* The main difference, relative to our examination, is that the one connotes divinity while the other does not necessarily; in this, we are probably dealing with something programmatic that is not necessarily Greek in its entirety. This Greek word νομος is often a translation of the Hebrew word תורה *Torah, torah instruction, teaching, law counsel.* Instruction or teaching carries a much different connotation in English than the word *law,* as we can observe readily in an English translation of Proverbs 1:8: "My son, hear the מוסר *instruction, discipline* of your father, and do not forsake the תורה *instruction, law* of your mother," for here the same English word *instruction* is two different Hebrew words, the one also meaning *discipline,* the other also meaning *law.* The word we often read in the "New Testament" as *Law* is often the translation of the Hebrew word תורה *Instruction, Teaching.* In parallel, the Hebrew word עצה *tree* (Jeremiah 6:6) also means *counsel, instruction* (Deuteronomy 32:28). The final ה is often an artificial articulation aid, and so we can see more clearly that the word עץ *tree* in the Eden account can also mean *counsel* and *instruction,* which should now point obviously to the fact that both God and Satan gave *counsel* regarding the same location in the garden, which is, on this level, how two *trees,* that is, *two bodies of law,* were in the midst: "Moreover I saw under the sun: In the place of judgment, wickedness was there; and in the place of righteousness, iniquity was there" (Ecclesiastes 3:16). Consider,

> I find then a law, that evil is present with me, the one who wills to do good. For I delight in THE LAW OF GOD according to the inward man. But I see ANOTHER LAW [i.e. OF SATAN] in my members, warring against the law of my mind, and bringing me into captivity to the LAW OF SIN which is in my members. O wretched man that I am! Who will deliver me from this body of death? (Romans 6:21-24).

How can the reader possibly think that Scripture only speaks of one "Law" to be avoided when Scripture Itself discusses that "another Law" is to be avoided? There is one and there is another. "The Law of God" is an Entity about which to be merry while the "Law of Sin" is an entity in which to be sorrowful; to mingle these two is to mingle the Hebrew words טוב *good, vital,* **merry (2 Samuel 13:28)** and רע *evil, injurious,* **sorrowful (Genesis 40:7)**. The Hebrew word דעת *knowledge* also means *unification* (Genesis 4:1) as opposed to its synonym בינה *knowledge,* which means the opposite of unification, that is, *discernment (i.e. the ability to separate).* The Tree of the Knowledge of Good and Evil can be literally translated in this sense also as The Tree of the Unification of Merriment and Sorrow; this fact can be observed in that Ecclesiastes 3:4 makes sorrow antithetical to dancing while Job 41:22 describes Satan as a contradictory union of sorrow and dancing. If one only saw the first half of this diametrically opposed unification, one would only see the Merriment and confuse it with the Sorrow or only see the Sorrow and confuse it with the Merriment it parasitically imitates. Since תורה Law means *Counsel*, and since עצה *tree* means *counsel* also, one can perceive how *Law, Counsel, and Tree* can all be descriptions or types of the same entity. The Woman discussed "The Tree" like the Bride discusses "The Law," both being incorrect and neither accounting for two Laws, that is, two trees. The reader will see that that logic can only be denominated precisely in Hebrew, hence the importance of naming entities first displayed in the Garden account. The Text is plain that one tree is to be avoided and that it opposes the Tree of Life, for it was the bride who confused the two trees by speaking of them as though the two were one rather than account for the fact that the two were merely in near proximity to each other. It is the bride today who can only see one discomforting "Law," and her eyes are *blinded, gouged, opened* (פקח) so that she does not see the Tree of Life by which she can be saved. The wisdom described here is in the naming of things, for this was the responsibility of Adam. The word שכל means both *name* and *wisdom*, just as the word שם can be pronounced to mean both *name* and *begetting*, which parallels the fact that בות means *house, temple, womb, wisdom, and dwelling*.

How can the reader, on account of the Book of Leviticus, think that God commanded burnt offerings when He delivered the people from Egypt when Jeremiah 7:22-23 states, "I did not speak to your fathers, or command them in the day that I brought them out of the land of Egypt, concerning burnt offerings or זבח *slaughter*. But this is what I commanded them, saying, 'Obey My voice, and I will be your God, and you shall be My people. And walk in all the ways that I have commanded you, that it may be well with you'"? Specifically, the "ways that I have commanded you" are here put in contrast to "burnt offerings or slaughter." When it says, "sacrifice," this word is literally זבח *slaughter*, which is why it is placed in contradistinction to the constructive preparation of a body as so interpreted by the Septuagint and Hebrews 10:5; furthermore, "זבח *slaughter*" is placed opposite the words "to do your will" by Hebrews 10:7. That blood is called "life" in Genesis 9:4, that "Sacrifice and offering You did not desire" (Psalm 40:6), that the slaughter of animals was the "reminder of sins" (Hebrews 10:3), and that sin "gives birth to death" (James 1:15), means that the priests who received bloody sacrifices literally ate death on account of the sins of others and themselves since they could not eat the meat with its *blood* (its *life*). That is, the Levitical priesthood was designated to eat the barbebque that resulted as a reminder of sin (not as a reminder of righteousness) and that this fleshly and bloodless reminder of sin was a carnal and demonstrative signification of the consumption of death of which our first human parents partook, for it is plain that the first bloody sacrifice discussed in Leviticus is bovine as a direct reminder of the child-sacrifice that took place regarding the golden calf. The Levites who used the blade against the child-sacrificers of the firstborn were subsequently honored by God with the Right of Firstborn, and these living Firstborn were designated to use the blade first against the very animal whose image was used to slay the firstborn. The animal, being innocent of sin, served as a meal of death since it could not be eaten with its "life" or blood, but this fleshly meal of death was eaten by the righteous priests first on behalf of the sinful people who were themselves compelled to eat a mingling of the metallic and fleshly sacrifice they concocted with the golden calf, for it would appear that the gold they used for the calf was "טוב *good*" (Genesis 2:12) and that it was mixed with the רע *injury or evil or sorrowful practice of child-sacrifice* that they practiced conversely as a celebratory rite in much the same way secularly legal rights are celebrated today. Tersely put, the Levitical priesthood was to eat death for the people as a sign of laying its life down for the people who chose death, and this self-sacrifice was con- ducted with the hope of restoring the people to life. Conversely, Adam ate death for the bride as a sign of laying his life down for the bride who chose death, and this suicide was conducted with the knowledge of sin, for Adam "was not deceived" (1 Timothy 2:14). At the same time, because the Leviti- cal Priesthood too was composed of flawed humans, the Priesthood, like the First Adam, ate death on account of its own sins as well: "Jesus, Who was made a little lower than the angels, for the suffering of death crowned with glory and honor, that He, by the grace of God, might TASTE DEATH FOR EVERYONE" (Hebrews 2:9) since He is the true High Priest.

Christ quoted Deuteronomy 6:5 and Leviticus 19:18 when He said, "'You shall love the Lord your God with all your heart, with all your soul, and with all your mind.' This is the first and great commandment. And the second is like it: 'You shall love your neighbor as yourself.' On these two commandments hang all the Law and the Prophets" (Matthew 22:37-39). "The Law" of God (as distinguished from "The Law" of Satan) is love. "The Law" of Satan (as opposed to "The Law" of God) is hate. The confusion of the Standard with its opposite seems to have produced this comment: "... whether love or hate, the man does not know all their faces" (Ecclesiastes

9:1), that is, their reflections, for "The Law" is reflective of its adherents whereby reciprocity proves the affiliation. Consider the fact that the ancient easterners conceived of the bride as the female reflex or mirror or double or "face" of her husband. "The Law" of God requires mutual selflessness, and it can be seen that God upheld His end of the covenant by dying for us on account of our sinful suicide by which we reflect the error in Eden. "The Law" of Satan requires mutual selfishness, and that can be seen in that Satan conversely persuaded us to die for him by sinful suicide. Remember that תורה means *law* and *instruction* just as עץ means *tree* and *instruction*. Both "Laws," both "Trees," both "Instructions" were present in the midst of Eden, but "eating" of the forbidden "tree" implanted within man "ANOTHER LAW in my members, warring against the law of my mind, and bringing me into captivity to the LAW OF SIN which is in my members." Surely, God did not give us "The Law of Sin," and, surely, the "Law of Sin" is not the "Tree of Life." Again, the bride has confused the two trees by speaking of them as if they are one. Scripture names the two "Laws":

(1) "The Law of God" and
(2) "The Law of Sin" (Romans 7:22-23)

(1) "The Law of the Spirit of Life" and
(2) "The Law of Sin and Death" (Romans 8:2)

(1) "The Perfect Law of Liberty" (James 2:12) and
(2) "Enmity" (Romans 8:6).

(1) "The Law of Truth... IN HIS MOUTH" (Malachi 2:6) and
(2) "deceitful LIPS" (Psalm 17:1), the "injustice" on the "LIPS" described in Malachi 2:6.

James 2 continues the distinction by stating that the "royal law" is "You shall love your neighbor as yourself" (Leviticus 19:18), and the opposite would be *You shall not love your neighbor as yourself.* Again, the "royal law" is selflessness, the "Law of God" which is the "Law of the Spirit of Life," the "Law of Liberty [from death]" and the "Law of Truth." The opposite of the "Law of God" would be the Law of Satan which is the Law of the Spirit of Death, the Law of Liberty from Life, and the Law of Deceit. Turning away from The Law of God is analogous to both adultery and murder, thus James continues the argument by stating, "For whoever shall keep the whole LAW [i.e. of God], and yet stumble in one point, he is guilty of all. For He who said, 'Do not commit ADULTERY [i.e. breaking an oath to the death and thereby wishing death],' also said, 'Do not MURDER [i.e. inducing death].' Now if you do not commit adultery, but you do murder, you have become a transgressor of the law. So speak and so do as those who will be judged by the LAW OF LIBERTY. For judgment is without mercy to the one who has shown no mercy. Mercy triumphs over judgment." James, therefore qualifies "The Law of God" which is the "The Law of the Spirit of Life" as "The Law of Liberty" from sin, which makes God's Law antithetical to a "Law of Liberty" FROM life, which then induces death. The question is, "The Law of Liberty from what captivity?"

Christ said in Matthew 6:24, "No one can serve two masters; for either he will hate the one and love the other, or else he will be loyal to the one and despise the other." Consider Romans 7:1-6 in light of the fact that בעל (transliterated as *Baal*) means *Lord* (Numbers 21:28), *Husband* (Exodus 21:22), and *Master of a covenant* (Genesis 14:13) and that it is used of both God (Hosea 2:16) and Satan (Numbers 25:3) in Scripture:

> Or do you not know, brethren (for I SPEAK TO THOSE WHO KNOW THE LAW), that the law [of God or of Satan] has dominion over a man as long as he lives? For the woman who has a husband [God or Satan] is bound by the law [of God or of Satan] to her husband [God or Satan] as long as he lives. But if the husband dies [God or Satan], she is released from the law of her husband [God or Satan, and therefore participates in either the death of Christ or the death of Satan]. So then if, while her husband [God or Satan] lives, she marries another man [i.e. God or Satan], she will be called an adulteress [by God or by Satan]; but if her husband [God or Satan] dies, she is free from that law [of God or of Satan], so that she is no adulteress [either to God or to Satan], though she has married another man [God or Satan]. Therefore, MY BRETHREN [in Christ], you also have become DEAD TO THE LAW [of Satan] THROUGH THE BODY OF CHRIST, that you may be married to another—TO HIM WHO WAS RAISED FROM THE DEAD [Christ], that we should bear fruit [i.e. of The Spirit of Life"] to God. For when we were in the flesh, the sinful passions which were aroused by the law [of Satan, i.e. of "sin and death"] were at work in our members to bear fruit to death. But now we have been delivered from the law [of Satan], having died to what we were held by, so that we should serve in the newness of the Spirit and not in the oldness of the letter (Romans 7:1-6).

Had we lived correctly in the Spirit, the letter would not have to be used to remind us of our sins. We can see, therefore, that the letter of God is good and it points out that we are not. We can be bound either to Christ by participating in the death of the Enemy, or we can be bound to the Enemy by participating in the death of Christ: "No one can serve two masters;

for either he will hate the one and love the other, or else he will be loyal to the one and despise the other" (Matthew 6:24). The word עבד *service, servitude, slavery, work* is often confused with the race slavery (like that of the American Civil War) and is not recognized as the servitude of one who is higher (whether for good or for evil). This *service* can be understood as θρεσκεια *religion, ceremonial worship*, and the first overt mention of this עבד *service* in Genesis is positive, as it is used to parallel the cultivation of wisdom through tilling the soil and making love to one's spouse in easy fertility (Genesis 2:15, keeping in mind that *womb* and *wisdom* are synonymous and that Song of Songs 4:12 calls a *woman a garden*), for the letters we are discussing as *service* can also be read as *servant* or עבד *son*. The opposite of this facile siring is the wearisome service which can be understood as the laborious religion, and the second mention of this toilsome service in Genesis (3:23) is the result of negativity as it is used in parallel to the clearing of thorns through tilling the soil and making love to one's spouse through the difficulties of infertility that characterize the family line from Adam until Mary, who is the ultimate example of fertility in that her garden was only cultivated by God directly and not through man (as was the case in the circumcision of Adam's heart). The reader can see that Genesis 2:15 uses עבד *work, slavery* in a positive sense with regard to the One Whose "yoke is easy" (Matthew 11:30), but, in rejecting God by adulterating with Satan, man assumed the difficult yoke whereby this same word עבד *work, slavery* made us "slaves of sin" (Romans 6:17). Consider Romans 6:16-19:

> Do you not know that to whom you present yourselves slaves to obey, you are that one's slaves whom you obey, WHETHER OF SIN LEADING TO DEATH, OR OF OBEDIENCE LEADING TO RIGHTEOUSNESS? But God be thanked that though you were slaves of sin, yet you obeyed from the heart that form of doctrine to which you were delivered. And having been set free from sin, you became slaves of righteousness. I SPEAK IN HUMAN TERMS BECAUSE OF THE WEAKNESS OF YOUR FLESH. For just as you presented your members as SLAVES of uncleanness, and of lawlessness leading to more lawlessness, so now present your members as SLAVES of righteousness for holiness.

Just as there were two trees that were antithetical to each other, there are two laws and two slaveries or servitudes that are antithetical to each other. Congruently, many have mandated that "works" are a form of "legalism" and that "legalism" is bad. Yet, we can see that slavery requires work, that work is according either to faith (covenant) in God or faith (covenant) in

Satan, and this is why Scripture discusses two "works" as opposed to one:

> "Good Works" (Ephesians 2:10);

> "Unfruitful Works of Darkness" (Ephesians 5:11).

The reader can easily see that the very same Book discusses two works that are antithetical to each other, and it discusses these works as "fruit" which should point the reader back to the two trees that have long been, likewise, discussed as one. The Hebrew עבד *works* or *service* also spells *son*, and this fact makes it easier to see why 1 Thessalonians 5:5 says regarding the "Unfruitful works of Darkness" that "You are all SONS OF LIGHT and SONS OF THE DAY. We are not [SONS] OF THE NIGHT nor [SONS] OF DARKNESS." Likewise, Jonah 4:9 calls הקיקיון *the kykeon* vine a בן לילה *son of the night.* Satan himself was once a *priest*, a *firstborn*, a *son of righteousness*, though now he is a priest of perversity, and this priesthood can be seen in his title "Leviathan."

The title לויתן **Levi**athan is from the same root as *Levi*, and this root (לוה) means *to be joined* and is synonymous with the root ענב *to be joined* that produces the word ענב *grape cluster.* The binding of types seen among notions of a *serpent* and a *vine* are retained well in the Latin word *draco,* which not only means a *serpent* and a *vine* but also *a boiling pot,* Job 41:31 says that Leviathan makes the "depths churn like a boiling pot." It would seem that לויתן *Leviathan* is formed by unifying the לוי *levi* with נתן *child sacrifice*; we can here perceive more of why the high priestly armor of righteousness in Exodus 18 is the same as that described in Ezekiel 28 that was worn by Satan prior to his expulsion from the Heavenly Paradise. Likewise, Scripture discusses how vines can "שכל *abort*" their fruit "in the field" (Malachi 3:11) like a "משכיל *miscarrying* womb" (Hosea 9:14); ironically, if the sibilant of the words משכיל *miscarrying* and שכל *abort* are hissed differently, these same letters produce the words משכיל *wisdom poem* and שכל *wisdom.* In other words, the same letters, articulated with different "s" sounds can indicate either life or death. Like the "Unfruitful Works of Darkness," like the "Law of Sin and Death," and like "The Tree of the Knowledge of Good and Evil," the vocabulary is obscured if the names are not defined. Simply using the words "works," "law," and "Tree of Knowledge" can induce the mistake of confusing life and death by somehow thinking perversely that the forbidden "Tree" gave "wisdom" even though Ecclesiastes 7:11 states that "the excellence of knowledge is that WISDOM GIVES LIFE to those who have it." Since the forbidden "Tree of Knowledge...," gave death, it is good for one to recall the full title of the forbidden tree so that one does not see only one tree and actually believe that God somehow restricted שכל *wisdom* when His first directive to man was to "Be fruitful and multiply..." which is the opposite of שכל *miscarriage, abortion* even though these antithetical entities were originally spelled the same (שכל) but pronounced differently. God could not have restricted wisdom if He does "not change" (Malachi 3:6) and gives *wisdom* "liberally and without reproach" (James 1:5).

The reader is here encouraged to begin at Revelation and to trek towards Genesis in an effort to distinguish between the two counsels throughout Scripture in order to see himself as a constituent of the Bride who, like the man, Adam, has accused God for the works of Satan and has accidentally worshipped Satan by rejecting the Law of God, His Works, and His Tree of Life in freeing himself from the love of Life as is evidenced by the fact that we die. Furthermore, the dire mistakes regarding "The Law" can be observed here in that freeing ourselves indiscriminantly from "The Law" has eventuated in our own demise, which means that what is more recent is not "newer" (as the world would have us think), but what is original is what is "new" which is why a "newborn" ages with subsequently "recent" birthdays. Chronology hurls us away from the source which is why we grow older, not younger. This headlong fall is mocked by the fact that our decrepit end grimly realigns us with the weaknesses that typified us in our helpless state of newness (but in antithetical order); in this fall, we might be reminded that we too, like our first human parents, partook of the forbidden "Works," "Law," and a "Tree" as is seen at the Cross or Tree of Christ Who tasted death for everyone (Hebrews 2:9) as it is written, "So WHEN JESUS HAD RECEIVED THE SOUR WINE, He said, 'It is finished!' And bowing His head, He gave up His spirit" (John 19:30).

It shall furthermore be noted that Scripture equates the "Law of God" with "The Law of My Mind" and contrasts these two with "Another Law" and "The Law of Sin" in Romans 6:21-24. This comparison and contrast would, of course, equate the "Law of God" and the "Law of My Mind" with the "Tree of Life" which means that the Tree of Life is the one that gave שכל *wisdom*, but that the Tree of Death gave שכל *abortion (death)* even though the point of origin, the womb, is the same.

The accidental synthesis of the two trees can be seen in the new name the bride devised (The Tree אשר *that is* in the middle of the garden), for the word אשר *that is* can also be pronounced to mean אשר *happiness* (Genesis 30:13), which is a synonym of טוב *happiness* that is more commonly translated as *good* as in The Tree of the Knowledge of טוב *Good* and Evil. The bride spoke of only one tree, and she renamed it by simplifying and synthesizing so that her invention was The Tree אשר *of Happiness* in the middle of the garden or The Tree אשר*that is* in the middle of the garden. That the woman regarded the forbidden tree as a Tree of Happiness functions on the proposition that God desired to restrict happiness and therefore calls into question the character of God; this poor assumption seems very much evidenced by the "Serpent's" question, " אף כי אמר*Did God say…*" which can be rendered also as "…אף *angered* that God said…?" If one vocalizes the word אשר as *happiness*, then one can see that the woman thought the forbidden tree would bring happiness and that Satan perceived this by asking if she was *angered* without it. As in a mirror, the word אף *anger* is also the word *brow*; after eating of the forbidden tree, Adam was condemned to work by the sweat of his *brow*, to work angrily and discontentedly since he allowed his bride who was made from his own heart to assume a happiness that did not exist in reality but that was agreed upon collectively and falsely.

The doctrines that claim that works are not a requirement of good conduct or evidence of salvation are incorrect because they do not discriminate between good works or evil works. The teachings that state that "The Law" is now abolished which is why we are no longer held to a moral standard after the admission that we are abject is wrong because they do not point out that there is more than one "Law" discussed in Scripture and that the two "Laws" are opposites. The convictions that assume the forbidden tree to have imparted wisdom are false because they disregard that Scripture connects wisdom to life and folly to death. Since the forbidden tree caused death, it was of folly, not wisdom. The assumption that the forbidden tree gave increased intellect because of the word "knowledge" in its name is wrong because it does not take into account that Genesis 4:1 employs this word to mean unification in distinction of a synonym like בינה *knowledge (that discerns or discriminates)*. The forbidden tree was only one of two trees that were in the midst of the garden, and "The Law" is the definite, singular name of two separate and antithetical teachings, judgements, and requirements that function like mirrors. When deciding between two, the Greek of Matthew 27:17 states that the choice was between Jesus, Son of the Father and Jesus the Anointed. There were two men named Jesus, both were the "son of the Father"; one was the Christ or Anointed of God, while the other was chosen by man incorrectly. There were two people named Jesus, two laws, two works, and two trees; the people are antithetical to each other, the laws are antithetical to each other, the works are antithetical to each other, and the trees are antithetical to each other. Not discerning between the two causes an apparent merger that is reflected in the grim title of The Tree of the דעת *Knowledge/Union* of Good and Evil, for it was this corrupt mixture alone that the Woman saw like the perverse Law alone that the Bride sees.

As there are two bodies of "Law," there are two antithetical entities called " בשר *flesh*." This word בשר *flesh* does not describe sinfulness, but sinfulness can be applied to the term בשר *flesh*. Consider Romans 8:1-8:

> There is therefore now no condemnation to those who are in Christ Jesus, who do not walk according to the flesh, but according to the Spirit. For the law of the Spirit of life in Christ Jesus has made me free from the law of sin and death. For what the law could not do in that it was weak through the flesh, God did by sending His own Son in the LIKENESS OF SINFUL FLESH, on account of sin: He condemned SIN IN THE FLESH, that the righteous requirement of the law might be fulfilled in us who do not walk according to the flesh but according to the Spirit. For those who live according to the flesh set their minds on the things of the flesh, but those who live according to the Spirit, the things of the Spirit. For to be carnally minded is death, but to be spiritually minded is life and peace. Because the carnal mind is enmity against God; for it is not subject to the law of God, nor indeed can be. So then, those who are in the flesh cannot please God.

At first glance, it seems apparent that "flesh" is opposed to "spirit," but this cannot be the case. Christ came in the "likeness of sinful flesh," but there was flesh before there was sin as is evident in that neither Adam nor his wife were created sinful. God is without sin and "tempts no one" (James 1:13), and God placed "flesh" over Adam's circumcised heart in Genesis 2:21, so to speak, for He created Adam a fleshly being. Christ came in the "likeness of SINFUL flesh" and in the flesh Himself; so, the "flesh" that Christ came in was sinless and was the "likeness" of the "flesh" that was sinful. Since there was a sinless flesh before there was a sinful flesh, the sinless flesh Christ came in must be as the sinless flesh the preceded sinful flesh. Therefore, "flesh" is not sinful inherently even though it can become sinful, as was the case with our first human parents. The "things of the flesh" that are sinful are the things of "sinful flesh," not sinless flesh. The things of the flesh that are sinless, it would seem, are "according to the spirit" and are "things of the Spirit." The "carnally minded" is of "sinful flesh," not sinless flesh. Sinless flesh is not "enmity against God" but is "subject to The Law of God." The ones who "please God" are those of the sinless flesh of Christ, the Law of God, the Gospel, and the word בשר *flesh* also means *good news (Gospel)* with specific reference to *successful birth*, i.e. the *proclamation of good news* (Jeremiah 20:15) evidenced in Holy Communion as opposed to unholy communion. Christ came according to the *proclamation of good news* in a *successful birth* which proves that Christ came in *flesh* that was sinless and was therefore in perfect union with the *Spirit* as evidenced at His baptism.

There is a sinlessness called "flesh" and a sinfulness also called "flesh." It can be seen, therefore, there is a sinlessness that is the "gospel" and a sinfulness that is the "gospel." The sinfulness that is called "The Law" is specifically "The Law of Sin and Death" (Romans 8:2) as opposed to "The Law of the Spirit of Life" (Romans 8:2). This "Law of Sin and Death" is called "another Law" (Romans 7:23) just like the sinfulness that is the "gospel" is called a "different gospel" (Galatians 1:6). The Law that is righteous is The Gospel that is righteous, and this Gospel is the Flesh that is righteous, the righteous and successful birth of The Son of Man through Mary. The "other Law" that is unrighteous is the "different gospel," and this "different gospel" is the flesh that is unrighteous. The "Bride," that is, "The Church," has, like Eve, unified the two trees, the two laws, the two fleshes, in her own sight, and this unification has resulted in the blindness, the eye-opening, the eye-gouging this chapter has sought to identify. "The Law" or laws that Christ broke were merely the customary, oral innovations that drew their apparent strength from the name of Moses. The situation regarding the law-breaking of which Christ was accused can be compared to the growth of absolutism in 17th Century Europe that progressively ignored customary laws, diminished local autonomy, and superceded traditional manners; for, in this, it can be seen that Christ's defectless adherence to Moses exposed the customary, local, and orally traditional values of the various, competing Jewish sects to be innovative, internally inconsistent, and ultimately against Moses even though they drew their apparent strength from Moses' name.

Christ kept "The Law" of God, and the fact that he broke "The Law" His adversaries discussed should point out quite simply that their "Law" was something other than what Moses wrote. A written law establishes uniformity, but oral laws are typically regional. The imposition of a written standard within a local, oral society establishes a revolution that changes whole ways of life; likewise, Christ referred to the written Law within His local, oral society (in which Hebrew was, essentially, a dead language) in an effort to change whole ways of life. The written "Law" of Moses preceded the oral "Law" of the Pharisees and the Septuagint of the Sadducees; the situation of Christ pointing this out before the Romans caused tremendous fear for the Second Temple and for the lay Pharisees in that they would be realized as clandestinely schismatic revolutionaries who disagreed even amongst themselves. So, the formerly divided professional and lay revolutionaries banded together in a uniform cause to accuse Christ of being the revolutionary they themselves were collectively, hence the capital and extreme Roman punishment of crucifixion He received. This punishment reflected Numbers 25 that states that hanging is the penalty for taking innocent life, and the reverse accusations of revolution can be seen neatly and luridly to have played out in the scenario where Christ received His accusers' punishment.

Hebrews 10:1 states that "The Law," i.e. of Moses, has only a shadow "and not the very image," and Genesis 1:27 states, "So God created האדם the man בצלמו *in/with/by His image*; in the image of God He created him; male and female He created them." This word צלם *image* also means a *shadow, an illusion, a likeness, a covering*, so a shining *likeness* could, with respect to this word, create the linguistic paradox of a *bright shadow* as is the case in a solar eclipse. The mountain Moses, whose face shined as it reflected God's face, died upon was Nebo or the *Mountain of the Moon* in the literary typification of a solar eclipse. This "Law of Moses" that has only a "shadow" should show the reader that the reader is beholding a dark reflection of human misconduct recorded now on paper in a manner comparable to the shadow cast by the moon obscuring the sun. It is the human misconduct, not "The Law" of God, that is the obscurant that produced the shadow recorded in "The Law" of Moses, that shadow revealed in regulations like "Thou shalt not..." for the articulated restriction admits silently a commission regulated against. The reader, without knowing this, is, thus, reading, at best, only half of the Text. The command "Thou shalt not commit adultery" describes the shadow cast by the obscurant lust produces when it blocks the light of God on the earth. The Law against adultery is the darkness cast by lust, so eliminating lust eliminates adultery. Merely addressing adultery does not eliminate lust. What Moses wrote concerning adultery was but the reflection of unspoken lust, and the covenantal love that bound Moses to God through "The Law" of God is the very Image, is Christ Who is Love. As Jeremiah 7 points out, keeping "The Law" of Moses does not necessitate animal slaughter. Instead, keeping "The Law" of Moses means acting in such a sinless manner so as not to require the "reminder of sins" (Hebrews 10:3) illustrated by animal slaughter, and it is for this reason that, even though Christ is "High Priest forever," we never read of Him slaughtering animals because He was sinless, i.e. He had no need to remind Himself not to sin. The Levitical slaughtering of animals is the shadow cast by the obscurant of sin, and it is for such a reason that James 1:15 states that sin gives birth to death. Death is the reminder of sin. Accordingly, Adam sinned first, and then he died. Not recognizing more than one Law, like not recognizing more than one tree, violates the covenantal love and eventuates abortively. The "New Testament," like the "new wine," is not good, nor should it be the title of the blessed Books of Matthew through Revelation as is evidenced by the abortion described in Revelation 12 that reflects, as though in a shadow, Genesis 3.

THE "FAITH" OF THE SO CALLED "NEW TESTAMENT"

In order to discuss the word πιστις *faith* in Scripture, I think it necessary to discuss the concept of falsification. By falsification, I mean confrontation with fact. A falsifiable statement may come into contact with facts that either support or oppose it to the extent that corroboration or invalidation of the statement occurs. If a discourse cannot be proven to be either true or false, it can be considered unfalsifiable and therefore unverifiable. Obviously, in order for correct verification to occur, the right facts have to be in place in order to make a comparison.

The word "faith" is something that has accidentally come to be restricted to the meanings of "belief" and "trust." "Faith" is commonly viewed as something that does not necessarily oppose the factual but is itself unprovable and therefore unfalsifiable. If something is not open to falsification, then it is also closed to verification; this errant definition of πιστις *faith* has been accidentally related to the idea of μυθος *myth* as opposed to the λογος *(logos) rational explanation. Myth* is often set in a time that disallows a remaining eye-witness account within an antiquity that can but be imagined and not perceived physically. Conversely, John 1 describes Christ as the *Logos*, and he finishes his Narrative by stating specifically that, "this is the disciple who testifies to these things and who wrote them down [i.e. an eye-witness account]. We know that his testimony is true" [i.e. this account is not set in remote antiquity that is physically imperceptible to the narrator]. Furthermore, 1 John continues to describe validatable faith by stating,

> That which was from the beginning, which WE HAVE HEARD, which WE HAVE SEEN WITH OUR EYES, which WE HAVE LOOKED UPON, and OUR HANDS HAVE HANDLED, concerning the *Logos* [Λογου] of life — the life was manifested, and we have seen, and BEAR WITNESS, and declare to you that eternal life which was with the Father and was manifested to us — that which WE HAVE SEEN AND HEARD we declare to you, that you also may have fellowship with us; and truly our fellowship is with the Father and with His Son Jesus Christ,

which is opposed to fellowship with some unvalidatable entity who existed, or at least manifested himself, in a setting detached from the person telling the story. It follows that the word πιστις *faith* is used by Scripture to describe provability, thus:

> Now πιστις *faith* is the SUBSTANCE of things hoped for, the EVIDENCE of things not seen. For by it the elders obtained a good testimony. By faith we understand that the worlds] were framed

by the ρηματι *action-inducing word* of God, so that the things which are seen were not made of things which are visible.

Prior to Plato, μυθος *myth* was used to indicate simply *something someone says, advice, a saying, a word, and a story*, and it was rather indistinct from λογος *(logos)*, which is commonly translated in the Bible as *word*. The Presocratics seemed not to make the distinction that Plato made between myth *(mythos)* and validatable *discourse (logos)*, but it is important to recognize Scripture's reference to Plato when Paul was tried by the Roman Court that had outlawed Christianity in his time. It is plain that Scriptural employments of Greek and Roman pagan authors (either referentially or by direct quotation) were crafted in order that Christians might "always be ready to give a *defense* [= απολογια, *apology, legal defense*] to everyone who asks you a *reason* [= *loγoς, logos*] for the hope that is in you, with meekness and fear" (1 Peter 3:15) for Paul himself stated in Philippians 1:12-21,

> But I want you to know, brethren, that the things which hap-pened to me have actually turned out for the furtherance of the gospel, so that it has become evident to the whole palace guard, and to all the rest, that my chains are in Christ; and most of the brethren in the Lord, having become confident by my chains, are much more bold to speak the word without fear. Some indeed preach Christ even from envy and strife, and some also from goodwill: The former preach Christ from self-ish ambition, not sincerely, supposing to add affliction to my chains; but the latter out of love, knowing that I am appointed for the *defense* [= απολογια, *apology, legal defense*] of the gospel. What then? Only that in every way, whether in pretense or in truth, Christ is preached; and in this I rejoice, yes, and will rejoice. For I know that this will turn out for my deliverance through your prayer and the supply of the Spirit of Jesus Christ, according to my earnest expectation and hope that in nothing I shall be ashamed, but with all boldness, as always, so now also Christ will be magnified in my body, whether by life or by death. For to me, to live is Christ, and TO DIE IS GAIN.

Paul, who had to give a legal defense (*apology*) for having broken the law by preaching a banned religion, utilized a reference to Plato's Apol-ogy where Socrates said in his own legal defense, "Now if death be of such a nature, I say that TO DIE IS GAIN." The employment of this reference displays the specific erudition Paul utilized to defend himself before a judg-ment seat that understood legality in the language of Plato. Furthermore, the fact that this Classical reference, as well as a host of others, were written down for Christians was a step in providing legal legitimacy before their governmental accusers, a legitimacy that led ultimately to the Faith becoming the official religion of the Roman Empire. Rome had outlawed new religions, but it had no problem with ancestral religions. A specific point is made by Christ in Luke 5:39 that the religion soon to be called "Christianity" is the "old wine" as opposed to the "new wine" or innovation betrayed by the various *Judaisms* that claimed falsely to be ancestral on the pretended strength of the names of Abraham and Moses; thus, Christ identified Himself, in John 8, as the "Son of Adam," who preceded even Abraham who, in turn, preceded Moses. It is not often taken into account that Rome had banned what became called "Christianity" because Rome assumed it to be an innovative and new religion based partially on the false testimony of the Judaisms of the time, a problem somewhat induced by the new title ("Christianity") that the religion acquired in Antioch. At the same time, the so-called "New Testament's" argument (as well as that of the early Church) was that "Christianity" was an ancestral religion that explains, through falsification, what the Hebrew Scriptures mean and that also proves what became known as "Judaism" to be, in fact, the innovative, new, and therefore illegal religion evidenced by the obviously observable schism between Hellenistic Sadducees and the Babylonish Pharisees. The eventual recognition of the various Judaisms to be a fractured and inconsistent group of innovation that grew in its resistance to Rome led ultimately to the destruction of the Second Temple as predicted in Matthew 24:2. The prediction of the Second Temple's destruction would be an example of a *logos, falsifiably and therefore verifiably true discourse proven true by being confronted with fact.* Christ is called *The Logos,* and it is Christ Who prophesied the razed Temple and His raised body, both of which were proven in time and could not, therefore, fall under the category of "cunningly devised μυθοις *myths* when we made known to you the power and coming of our Lord Jesus Christ, but [we] were EYEWITNESSES of His majesty" (2 Peter 1:16)....

The πιστις *faith* of Paul was not something closed to falsification but something he morally and legally set himself to prove concretely and abstractly through the Hebrew Scriptures — the ancestral religion that the Roman Empire had not deemed illegal. That is, the government that tried Paul was initially unaware that the Gospel was the fulfillment of, and not a variation of, the Hebrew Scriptures; so, through the Apostles explaining the Hebrew Scriptures in Greek, the early Church was provided with a legally defensive proof, not an unverifiable myth, of how Christ fulfilled the expectation of the Hebrew Scriptures absolutely. Ignorance of these facts has accidentally compelled people to view the word πιστις *faith* or *trust* as something unprovable though correct, even though such a stance is blatantly contradicted by Hebrews 11:1 that states, "Now FAITH is the SUBSTANCE of things hoped for, the EVIDENCE of things not seen." The current view of the word πιστις *faith* has accidentally mirrored Plato's definition of *myth* somewhat in the sense that it is unverifiable, and this mistake has dire consequences that contradict the remainder of the Scriptures; this arrangement allows for any belief, no matter how ridiculous, to be considered fact, and it diminishes the value of the word "faith" to the extent that the True Religion appears pocked with error and potentially manipulative deceit, the very same deceit employed by those who crucified Christ, and very same deceit employed by those who today "...crucify again for themselves the Son of God, and put Him to an open shame" (Hebrews 6:6) in what pretend to be Christian "churches."

Faith is something that has more to do with *logos* than *mythos* since Hebrews 11:1 states that faith is substantial and evidential. The point being discussed is explained in Romans 12:1 where "spiritual act of worship" is literally "λογικην λατρειαν *logical service*," i.e. substantially evident and therefore verifiably open to falsification so that the whole passage reads, "I beseech you therefore, brethren, by the mercies of God, that you present your bodies a living sacrifice, holy, acceptable to God, which is your LOGICAL SERVICE," for it is illogical to think that Paul was beseeching believers to light themselves on fire upon altars while he himself remained uncooked. Faith has to do with what is verifiable and therefore what is open to falsification, not what is unverifiable and potentially erroneous. It would seem that it is partially for this reason that the Greek word πιστις *faith* was used in the so-called "New Testament" as a direct translation of the Hebrew word אמנה *covenant* in Galatians 3:10 and Hebrews 10:38. As is true regarding a covenant, *faith* is something substantial and evidential which makes it, therefore, validatable.

The Greek word πιστις *faith* is equivalent to *trust*, and this trust is *placed in* something substantial, not that this trust *makes* something substantial. In other words, many mandate that they have firm faith in something and, therefore, that thing is true... which, when restated, communicates that believing something fervently enough proves the belief to be factual if it is believed in earnest... and such a stance is never true and is always ridiculous. Believing in something fervently proves the validity of the fervor, not the verity of the thing believed to be true! Trusting in something honestly proves the substance of the honesty, not the thing upon which the honest trust is exerted. In other words, many apply the word πιστις *faith* in a manner against concrete reality in hope of concrete reality whereas faith is actually a belief in a validatable verity that preexisted one's faith in it. One can believe in the concrete reality of a rock, but the rock is not physically constituted by someone's observation and subsequent belief; the rock is only recognized by someone's observation and, if the observer so chooses, can be trusted (whether accurately or inaccurately) to provide a substantial foundation. The Greek word πιστις *faith, trust* also means *a pledge* and is used as a translation of a Hebrew word אמנה*covenant* in the so-called "New Testament." The Hebrew word אמנה *covenant* is from the root אמן *to support* which is synonymous to the root עמד *to support* which can also mean *to bind*. The "New Testament" plays upon the translation of אמן *to support* and עמד *to support* by the Greek πιστις *faith* in Hebrews 11:17: "By faith [πιστις *faith* = אמנה *covenant*] Abraham, when he was tested, offered up Isaac..." for אמנה *covenant* is from the root אמן *to support,* which is synonymous to the root עמד *to support, to bind,* which is the conjugated verb used by Genesis 22:9 that describes how Abraham "bound" Isaac. Succinctly, πιστις *faith* is a Greek translation of the Hebrew אמנה *covenant;* it is the "binding" aspect of a covenant that describes the "faith" of Abraham, the same "binding" (δεω) we read of Christ in Matthew 27:2, and the Hebrew; it is the "supporting" aspect of a covenant that describes how they "crucified" Christ in Matthew 27:35. The reader may note the proximity with which Matthew places these two words to each other in the 27th chapter. Furthermore, the word "crucify" is but a verb form of σταυρος *wooden stake* that used synonymously with the word ξυλον *wood, tree,* and העצים*the woods* Abraham laid upon his son in Genesis 22:9 also can mean *the trees, the gallows, the crosses, the stakes,* etc.

Again, the Greek word πιστις *faith* is often (but not always) a translation of the Hebrew word אמנה *covenant.* For instance, James 2:18-24 plays upon the idea of "believing" as opposed to the fact of "covenanting" by employing the Greek "faith":

> But someone will say, "You have faith, and I have works."
> Show me your πιστιν *faith, belief* without your works, and I will show you my πιστιν *faith, covenant* by my works. You πισευεις *believe* that there is one God. You do well. Even the demons πισυουσιν *believe* and tremble! But do you want to know, O foolish man, that πιστις *faith* without works is dead? Was not Abraham our father justified by works [i.e. through a covenant] WHEN HE OFFERED ISAAC HIS SON ON THE ALTAR? Do you see that πιστις *faith* was working together with his works [i.e. with

the vindication of his faith, his covenant], and by works πιστις *faith, covenant* was made complete? And the Scripture was fulfilled which says, "Abraham believed God, and it was accounted to him for righteousness." And he was called the friend of God. You see then that a man is justified by works [i.e. of a covenant which is vindicated by works], and not by πιστεως *faith* [i.e. the belief and trust that precedes the works] only.

We can see that the Greek word πιστις *faith* is played upon in translation that regards Hebrew so that context is the only way to decipher the truest meaning, and this facet of the "New Testament" aligns it seamlessly with the ancient eastern intrinsic vagueness found within religious texts that deliberately exempt facets of writing in order to demand the repetition necessary for the inculcation and memory of the devout. Why else would the Gospels focus so much explicit attention on the disciples "remembering" what Christ formerly said after various events came to pass by repeating forms of the word "remember" so often?

A reasonable question could arise as to why the word πιστις *faith* would be utilized along with the common word διαθηκη *covenant* to indicate essentially the same thing. The answer is simple and straight-forward: The more common Hebrew word for *covenant* is ברית which is translated as the more common Greek word for διαθηκη *covenant*, while the less common Hebrew word for *covenant* is אמנה, which is translated as the Greek word for πιστις *covenant, faith, a trust, a pledge*. A similar situation can be seen in Psalm 110 where the Hebrew word שבע *to swear*, to enter into a covenant is interpreted by the Greek Book of Hebrews as ορκωμοσια *the act of taking an oath, an oath* in 7:21. Synonyms for "covenant" in Hebrew are translated by synonyms for "covenant" in Greek in such a manner as to rely on context which, in turn, relies on one's memorization of the Text in order to contextualize words according to the referential intentions of the Narrative. Perhaps the most blatant example of the principle being asserted here can be found in how Galatians 3:11 and Hebrews 10:38 translate אמנה *covenant*:

> "Behold the proud; his soul is not upright in him; but the righteous/just shall live באמונתו *by his covenant*" (Habakkuk 2:4).

> "But that no one is justified by the law in the sight of God is evident, for 'the righteous/just εκ πιστεως ζησεται *shall live by faith*'" (Galatians 3:11).

"But my righteous/just one εκ πιστεως ζησεται *shall live by faith*" (Hebrews 10:38).

Again, the Greek word πιστις *faith* also means *a pledge, a covenant* and is employed by Galatians 3:11 and Hebrews 10:38 as a translation of the Hebrew word אמנה *covenant;* thus we may read Galatians 3:11 and Hebrews 10:38 as "...*Just/just* shall live by *His/his covenant/faith*..."— not merely by One's/one's belief and hope but by One's/one's confidence in something that is preexistent, factual, and provably feasible in which to place trust that is brought into existence by actions that cause the work to remain in a completed state as in the case of Biblcally righteous marrriage. Again, the Greek word translated as "faith" here is also a word for "covenant" (which is why it is used in translation for the Hebrew word "covenant"), and this means that salvation is by covenant and not simply belief, for the covenant is vindicated by works that exemplify the faith that produces them. Since Christ died in covenant with the Father, He therefore lives eternally with the everlasting Father. Since Christ died in covenant with the Father and with us, combined with the fact that His followers also die in covenant with Him, means that those who die in Christ must, of necessity, live everlastingly as well with Christ who is with the Father. Since "My Just One shall live by His covenant," then My just one shall live by his covenant" as well:

> Yet indeed I also count all things loss for the excellence of the knowledge of Christ Jesus my Lord, for whom I have suffered the loss of all things, and count them as rubbish, that I may gain Christ and be found in Him, not having my own righteousness, which is from the law, but that which is through πιστεως *faith* = אמנה *covenant* in Christ, the righteousness which is from God by πιστει = אמנה *covenant*; that I may know Him and the power of His resurrection, and the fellowship of His sufferings, being CONFORMED TO HIS DEATH, IF, BY ANY MEANS, I MAY ATTAIN TO THE RESURRECTION FROM THE DEAD (Pilippians 3:8-11).

Again,

> But now the righteousness of God apart from the law is revealed, being witnessed by the Law and the Prophets, even the righteousness of God, through πιστεως *faith* = אמנה *covenant* in Jesus Christ, to all and on all who believe. For there is no difference; for all have sinned and fall short of the glory of God, being justified freely by His grace through the redemption that is in Christ Jesus, whom God set forth as a PROPITIATION [covenantal sacrifice] by His blood, through faith, to demonstrate His righteousness, because in His forbearance God had passed over the sins that were previously committed, to demonstrate

at the present time His righteousness, that He might be just and the justifier of the one who has πιστεως *faith* = אמונה cov-enant in Jesus (Romans 3:21-26).

Again,

For we know that if our EARTHLY HOUSE, THIS TENT [mortal body], is destroyed, we have a building from God, a house not made with hands [eternal body], eternal in the heavens. For in this we groan, earnestly desiring to be CLOTHED with our habitation which is from heaven [i.e. GESTAIONAL "body" as "clothing" to agree with Job 10:11: "Clothe me with skin and flesh, and knit me together with bones and sinews"], if indeed, having been clothed, we shall not be found naked. For we who are in this tent groan, being burdened, not because we want to be unclothed, but further clothed [and thus BORN AGAIN with an eternal body, an eternal clothing], that mortality may be swallowed up by life. Now He who has prepared us for this very thing is God, who also has given us the Spirit as a guaran-tee. So we are always confident, knowing that while we are at home in the body we are absent from the Lord. For we walk by πιστεως *faith* = אמנה *covenant*, not by sight. We are confident, yes, well pleased rather to be absent from the body and to be present with the Lord. Therefore we make it our aim, whether present or absent, to be well pleasing to Him. For we must all appear before the judgment seat of Christ, that each one may receive the things done in the body, according to what he has done, whether good or bad. Knowing, therefore, the terror of the Lord, we persuade men; but we are well known to God, and I also trust are well known in your consciences. For we do not commend ourselves again to you, but give you opportunity to boast on our behalf, that you may have an answer for those who boast in appearance and not in heart. For if we are beside ourselves, it is for God; or if we are of sound mind, it is for you. For the love of Christ compels us, because we judge thus: that IF ONE DIED FOR ALL, THEN ALL DIED; AND HE DIED FOR ALL, THAT THOSE WHO LIVE SHOULD LIVE NO LONGER FOR THEM-SELVES, BUT FOR HIM WHO DIED FOR THEM AND ROSE AGAIN. Therefore, from now on, we regard no one according to the flesh. Even though we have known Christ according to the flesh, yet now we know Him thus no longer. Therefore, if anyone is in Christ, he is a NEW CREATION [Hebrew: חדש *renewed* creation," i.e. born *again*]; old things have passed away; behold, all things have become new [Hebrew: חדש *renewed*]. Now all things are of God, WHO HAS RECONCILED US TO HIMSELF THROUGH JESUS CHRIST, AND HAS GIVEN US THE MINISTRY OF RECONCILIATION, THAT IS, THAT GOD WAS IN CHRIST RECONCILING THE WORLD TO HIMSELF, not imputing their trespasses to them, and has committed to us the word of reconciliation. Now then, we are ambassadors for Christ, as though God were pleading through us: we implore you on Christ's behalf, be reconciled to God. For He made Him who knew no sin to be αμαρτιαν = חטא *sin offering*] for us, THAT WE MIGHT BECOME THE RIGHTEOUSNESS OF GOD IN HIM.

The way that we, as sinners, could be called "the righteousness of God" is if we live in eternal covenant (and therefore blamelessly) with Christ after earthly death as a result of living in the recognition of our guilt in breaking covenant with God on earth but in the hope and steadfast faithfulness of doing our best to maintain the stipulations of His renewed covenant through His Son.

> Behold the proud; his soul is not upright in him; but the righteous/just shall live באמונתו *by his faith* (Habakkuk 2:4).

> But that no one is justified by the law in the sight of God is evident, for "the righteous/just εκ πιστεως ζησεται *shall live by covenant*" (Galatians 3:11).

> But my righteous/just one εκ πιστεως ζησεται *shall live by covenant* (Hebrews 10:38).

If "my Just/Righteous One shall live by His covenant," then His just/righteous one shall live by his covenant" as well in the resurrection. Job 29:14 describes "righteousness" as a garment following Job 10:11 that describes our earthly body as a garment. Isaiah 59:17 describes "righteousness" as a war garment, and we can observe that Christ died temporally to live again eternally after making war on Satan following the sacrifice of His flesh; thus,

> In Him you were also circumcised with the circumcision made without hands, by putting off the body of the sins of the flesh, by the circumcision of Christ, buried with Him in baptism, in which you also were raised with Him through faith in the working of God, who raised Him from the dead. And you, being dead in your trespasses and the uncircumcision of your flesh, He has made alive together with Him, having forgiven you all trespasses, having wiped out the handwriting of requirements that was against us, which was contrary to us. And He has taken it out of the way, having nailed it to the cross. Having DISARMED

PRINCIPALITIES AND POWERS, He made a public spectacle of them, TRIUMPHING OVER THEM IN IT.

It is beneficial to remember that some of the oldest forms of armor were leather hides placed upon the body. Furthermore, when a battle involving animal hides and animal skulls utilized for armor and helmets was viewed from afar, and while a common Eastern mirage took effect from the perspective of the viewer, it appeared to the spectator as though gigantic warriors with animal faces battled each other in the heavens in a fashion similar to the cherubs described by Ezekiel. Likewise, Christ, the Lion of the Tribe of Judah, put on the battle-garments of flesh in order to make a sacrifice that would allow Him to wage war as mortal in the eternal realm; having conquered to the extent of eternal life after mortal death — and thus a renewal to His former state — He has given us an example whereby we may also put on spiritual battle-garments while in the flesh, make a sacrifice in our flesh that allows us to participate victoriously against the routed foes in the eternal realm, and, having shared in the victory to the extent of life after mortal death, we can "... put on the new man [Christ] which was created according to God, in true RIGHTEOUSNESS and holiness" (Ephesians 4:24) and, as Christ did, "put on the breastplate of RIGHTEOUS-NESS" (Ephesians 6:14). We might then reconsider the words, "my Just/Righteous One shall live by His covenant," and His "just/righteous one shall live by his covenant." A covenant is an oath (often to the death). Such oaths were often sworn immediately prior to war, and ancient eastern war was initiated by sacrifice. To break the covenant is to side with the enemy.

A covenant is something substantial and is symbolized by physical reality that is often sacrificial. The word אמנה covenant is from the root אמן to support, to stay, to nurse, to bring up, to be firm, faithful, and true, and it produces the words אמון child (even adopted child), אומונה steadiness, truth, faithfulness, אמנה a beam, lintel, אמנה education, nursing, אמת truth, as opposed to deceit, and אמן Amen. By raw definition and etymology, it is glaringly obvious that a mother's and father's obligation to their child is as much a product of their covenant as the child himself; therefore, a couple cannot participate in reproduction rightfully without an oath to the death that is carried out in both signification and application through the care of their fruit. To slay the fruit that God clothed in the woman's house is, so to speak, to initiate war upon heaven through the sacrifice of a child, which breaks the oath to the death pledged through gestation and to make an oath with death conversely:

> As they departed, Jesus began to say to the multitudes concerning John: "What did you go out into the wilderness to see?

A reed shaken by the wind? But what did you go out to see? A man clothed in soft garments? Indeed, those who wear soft clothing are in kings' houses. But what did you go out to see? A prophet? Yes, I say to you, and more than a prophet. For this is he of whom it is written: 'Behold, I send My messenger before Your face, Who will prepare Your way before You.' "Assuredly, I say to you, among those BORN OF WOMEN [which exempts Adam and his wife] there has not risen one greater than John the Baptist [who wore leather, like ancient eastern armor]; but he who is least in the kingdom of heaven is greater than he. And from the days of John the Baptist until now THE KINGDOM OF HEAVEN SUFFERS VIOLENCE, AND THE VIOLENT TAKE IT BY FORCE. For all the prophets and the law prophesied until John. And if you are willing to receive it, he is Elijah who is to come. He who has ears to hear, let him hear! But to what shall I liken this generation? It is like CHILDREN sitting in the marketplaces and calling to their companions..." (Matthew 11:7-16),

for,

Jesus called A LITTLE CHILD to Him, set him in the midst of them, and said, "Assuredly, I say to you, unless you are converted and BECOME AS LITTLE CHILDREN [i.e. are born again, are clothed again], you will by no means enter the kingdom of heaven. Therefore whoever humbles himself as this little child is the greatest in the kingdom of heaven. Whoever receives one little child like this in My name receives Me (Matthew 18:2-5),

and

Jesus said, "Let the little children come to Me, and do not forbid them; for of such is the kingdom of heaven" (Matthew 19:14).

A covenant is something substantial and is symbolized by physical reality. The word אמנה covenant is from the root אמן to support, to stay, to nurse, and it produces the word אמון child. The word אמנה covenant is the synonym of the word ברית covenant, which is a binding oath; it is from the root ברה to cut, to eat, to choose; it is related to the root ברא to create. The Latin translation of "covenant" is often "testamentum," but "sacramentum" (mystery) explains the Hebrew terms ברית covenant and אמנה covenant more explicitly since sacramentum means an oath sworn by both parties to action in vindication of their claims as it also means the sum of money staked by them in support of those claims and forfeited in the case of the losing party. Consider how, in Greek, Christ said, "τετελεσται paid *in full, it is finished,*" which, in Hebrew, can be understood as "כי עשה *for He produced,*" He vindicated His claim — thus we must vindicate ours. The error of the common usage of "belief" and "faith" is that, though an oath is sworn, the vindication of the claim is viewed as entirely one sided.

אמנה, ברית *covenant:* "And it is yet far more evident if, in the likeness of the King of Righteousness/Justice, there arises another priest who has come, not according to the law of a fleshly commandment, but according to the power of an endless life. For He TESTIFIES: 'You are a priest forever according to the order of the King of Righteousness/Justice'" (Hebrews 7:15-17).

אמה *a beam, lintel:* "You know that after two days is the Passover, and the Son of Man will be delivered up to be CRUCIFIED" (Matthew 26:2). "And you shall take a bunch of hyssop, dip it in the blood that is בסף *in the threshold,* and strike the LINTEL and the two doorposts with the blood that is בסף *in the threshold...*" (Exodus 12:22).

אמן *to support, to nurse, to bring up;* אמון *child (even adopted child);* אמנה *education, nursing:* "My LITTLE CHILDREN, for whom I LABOR IN BIRTH again until Christ is formed in you..." (Galatians 4:19).

אמן *to be faithful and true:* "And he showed me a pure river of water of life, clear as crystal, proceeding from the throne of God and of the Lamb. In the middle of its street, and on either side of the river, was the tree of life, which bore twelve fruits, each tree yielding its fruit every month. The leaves of the tree were for the healing of the nations. And there shall be no more curse, but the throne of God and of the Lamb shall be in it, and His servants shall serve Him. They shall see His face, and His name shall be on their foreheads. There shall be no night there: They need no lamp nor light of the sun, for the Lord God gives them light. And they shall reign forever and ever. Then he said to me, 'These words are FAITHFUL AND TRUE.' And the Lord God of the holy prophets sent His angel to show His servants the things which must shortly take place. 'Behold, I am coming quickly! Blessed is he who keeps the words of the prophecy of this book'" (Revelation 22:1-7).

אומונה, אמת *truth, faithfulness:* "If we confess our sins, He is FAITHFUL AND JUST to forgive us our sins and to cleanse us from all unrighteousness" (I John 1:9). Jesus said to him, 'I am the way, THE TRUTH, and the life. No one comes to the Father except through Me'" (John 14:6).

The examples above show that the seemingly various positive aspects of Christ are not mere accurate compliments regarding the unwavering character of God; rather, the they are the literal definitions and ramifications of the Hebrew concept, an oath to the death, whereby death is the curse or vengeance should one reject the covenant and life is the blessing should one uphold it. Covenants involve a blessing and a curse (or vengeance), a blessing for vindicating your agreement, and a curse (or vengeance) for violating your agreement, life inside of the covenant and death outside of the covenant.

> Blessing of the Covenant: "Then God blessed them, and God said to them, "Be fruitful and multiply; fill the earth and subdue it; have dominion over the fish of the sea, over the birds of the air, and over every living thing that moves on the earth.... See, I have given you every herb *that* yields seed which *is* on the face of all the earth, and every tree whose fruit yields seed; to you it shall be for food" (Genesis 1:28-29).

> Curse or Vengeance of the Covenant: "Of every tree of the garden you may freely eat; but of the tree of the knowledge of good and evil you shall not eat, for in the day that you eat of it you shall surely die" (Genesis 2:16).

A covenant is a type of threshold whereupon one side is death and the other side is life. The covenanting parties are to pass into life in union under penalty of death should either or both be deceitfully willing to cross back into death. Ancient Eastern thresholds were concave delineations that were filled with life (blood) by way of death, thereby simultaneously offering a thriving unity under penalty of a divorcing death. Neither life nor death were abstract beliefs that one could create by a certain, fervent conviction. Life and death existed prior to personal conviction in them. Life and death are physical, substantial, evidential realities that are the reward or penalty alotted to an individual based on his personal conviction: "I call heaven and earth as witnesses today against you, that I have set before you life and death, blessing and cursing; therefore choose life, that both you and your descendants may live..." (Deuteronomy 30:19). One's faith does not create the life that preceded the covenant, but one's faith cocreates life that proceeds from the covenant by the power of the life that preceded it. In other words and in fleshly terms, a man's son does not create his own father, but a man's son is the product of procreation or adoption that, through the son's procreation or adoption, a man's son can become another's father. The πιστις *faith* under discussion must, of necessity, be activated through works, for one cannot make and keep a covenant without continual works. The works proceed from the covenant as substantial evidence of the covenant, thus "... πιστις *faith* [= אמנה *covenant*] is the substance of things hoped for, the evidence of things not seen" (Hebrews

11:1). Things can occur obviously, but the reasons they occur may not be obvious at all and may be the result of an unknown covenant made by parties who are themselves yet to be known and understood fully; as such, we may interpret Hebrews 11 as follows:

> Now COVENANT is the substance of things hoped for, the evidence of things not seen. For by it the elders obtained a good TESTIMONY. By COVENANT we understand that the worlds were framed by the word of God, so that the things which are seen were not made of things which are visible. By COVENANT Abel offered to God a more excellent SACRIFICE than Cain, through which he obtained WITNESS that he was righteous, God TESTIFYING of his gifts; and through it he being dead still speaks. By COVENANT Enoch was taken away so that he did not see death, 'and was not found, because God had taken him'; for before he was taken he had this TESTIMONY, that he pleased God. But without COVENANT it is impossible to please Him, for he who comes to God must COVENANT that He is, and that He is a rewarder of those who diligently seek Him. By COVENANT Noah, being divinely warned of things not yet seen, moved with godly fear, prepared an ark for the saving of his household, by which he condemned the world and became heir of the righteousness which is according to COVENANT. By COVENANT Abraham obeyed when he was called to go out to the place which he would receive as an inheritance. And he went out, not knowing where he was going. By COVENANT he dwelt in the land of promise as in a foreign country, dwelling in tents with Isaac and Jacob, the heirs with him of the same promise; for he waited for the city which has foundations, whose builder and maker is God. By COVENANT Sarah herself also received strength to conceive seed, and she bore a child when she was past the age, because she judged Him FAITHFUL who had promised. Therefore from one man, and him as good as dead, were born as many as the stars of the sky in multitude—innumerable as the sand which is by the seashore. These all died in COVENANT, not having received the promises, but having seen them afar off were assured of them, embraced them and confessed that they were strangers and pilgrims on the earth. For those who say such things declare plainly that they seek a homeland. And truly if they had called to mind that country from which they had come out, they would have had opportunity to return. But now they desire a better, that is, a heavenly country. Therefore God is not ashamed to be called their God, for He has prepared

a city for them. By COVENANT Abraham, when he was tested, offered up Isaac, and he who had received the promises offered up his only begotten son, of whom it was said, 'In Isaac your seed shall be called,' concluding that God was able to raise him up, even from the dead, from which he also received him in A PARABOLIC SENSE. By COVENANT Isaac blessed Jacob and Esau concerning things to come. By COVENANT Jacob, when he was dying, blessed each of the sons of Joseph, and worshiped, leaning on the top of his staff. By COVENANT Joseph, when he was dying, made mention of the departure of the children of Israel, and gave instructions concerning his bones. By COVENANT Moses, when he was born, was hidden three months by his parents, because they saw he was a beautiful child; and they were not afraid of the king's command. By COVENANT Moses, when he became of age, refused to be called the son of Pharaoh's daughter, choosing rather to suffer affliction with the people of God than to enjoy the passing pleasures of sin, esteeming the reproach of Christ greater riches than the treasures in Egypt; for he looked to the reward. By COVENANT he forsook Egypt, not fearing the wrath of the king; for he endured as seeing Him who is invisible. By COVENANT he kept the Passover and the sprinkling of blood, lest he who destroyed the firstborn should touch them. By COVENANT they passed through the Red Sea as by dry land, whereas the Egyptians, attempting to do so, were drowned. By COVENANT the walls of Jericho fell down after they were encircled for seven days. By COVENANT the harlot Rahab did not perish with those who did not COVENANT, when she had received the spies with peace. And what more shall I say? For the time would fail me to tell of Gideon and Barak and Samson and Jephthah, also of David and Samuel and the prophets: who through COVENANT subdued kingdoms, worked righteousness, obtained promises, stopped the mouths of lions, quenched the violence of fire, escaped the edge of the sword, out of weakness were made strong, became valiant in battle, turned to flight the armies of the aliens. Women received their dead raised to life again. Others were tortured, not accepting deliverance, that they might obtain a better resurrection. Still others had trial of mockings and scourgings, yes, and of chains and imprisonment. They were stoned, they were sawn in two, were tempted, were slain with the sword. They wandered about in sheepskins and goatskins, being destitute, afflicted, tormented— of whom the world was not worthy. They wandered in deserts and mountains, in dens and caves of the earth. And all these, having obtained a good TESTIMONY through COVENANT, did not receive the PROMISE, God having provided something better for us, that they should not be made perfect apart from us.

Now that we understand that the so-called "Faith" section of Scripture discusses covenant, we might also observe how the specific examples given deal with the threshold that demarcates between life and death sacrificially. Again, Hebrews 11 says,

Now covenant is the substance of things hoped for, the evidence of things not seen. For by it the elders obtained a good testimony. By covenant we understand that THE WORLDS WERE FRAMED BY THE WORD OF GOD, SO THAT THE THINGS WHICH ARE SEEN WERE NOT MADE OF THINGS WHICH ARE VISIBLE. By covenant Abel OFFERED TO GOD A MORE EXCELLENT SACRIFICE than Cain, through which he obtained witness that he was righteous, God testifying of his gifts; and through it HE BEING DEAD STILL SPEAKS. By covenant ENOCH WAS TAKEN AWAY SO THAT HE DID NOT SEE DEATH, 'and was not found, because God had taken him'; for before he was taken he had this testimony, that he pleased God. But without covenant it is impossible to please Him, for he who comes to God must covenant that He is, and that He is a rewarder of those who diligently seek Him. By covenant Noah, being divinely warned of things not yet seen, moved with godly fear, prepared an ark FOR THE SAVING OF HIS HOUSEHOLD, by which he condemned the world and BECAME HEIR of the righteousness which is according to covenant. By covenant Abraham obeyed when he was called to go out to the place which he would receive as an INHERITANCE. And he went out, not knowing where he was going. By covenant he dwelt in the land of promise as in a foreign country, dwelling in tents with Isaac and Jacob, THE HEIRS WITH HIM OF THE SAME PROMISE; for he waited for the city which has foundations, whose builder and maker is God. By covenant Sarah herself also RECEIVED STRENGTH TO CONCEIVE SEED, AND SHE BORE A CHILD WHEN SHE WAS PAST THE AGE, because she judged Him faithful who had promised. Therefore from one man, AND HIM AS GOOD AS DEAD, WERE BORN AS MANY AS THE STARS OF THE SKY IN MULTITUDE—innumerable as the sand which is by the seashore. These all DIED IN COVENANT, not having received the promises, but having seen them afar off were assured of them, embraced them and confessed that they were strangers and pilgrims on the earth. For those who say such things declare plainly that they seek a homeland. And truly if they had called to mind that country from which they had come out, they would have had opportunity to return. But now they desire a better, that is, a heavenly country. Therefore God is not ashamed to be called their God, for He has prepared a city for them. By COVENANT Abraham, when he was tested, OFFERED UP ISAAC, and he who had received the promises OFFERED UP HIS ONLY BEGOTTEN SON, of whom it was said, 'In Isaac your seed shall be called,' concluding that God was able to RAISE HIM UP, EVEN FROM THE DEAD, from which he also received him in a parabolic sense. By covenant Isaac blessed Jacob and Esau concerning things to come. By COVENANT Jacob, WHEN HE WAS DYING, BLESSED each of the sons of Joseph, and worshiped, leaning on the top of his staff. By covenant Joseph, WHEN HE WAS DYING, made mention of the departure of the children of Israel, and GAVE INSTRUCTIONS CONCERNING HIS BONES. By covenant Moses, when he was BORN, was hidden three months by his parents, because they saw he was a beautiful child; and they were not afraid of the king's command. By COVENANT Moses, when he became of age, refused to be called the son of Pharaoh's daughter, choosing rather to suffer affliction with the people of God than to enjoy the passing pleasures of sin, esteeming the reproach of Christ greater riches than the treasures in Egypt; for he looked to the reward. By covenant he forsook Egypt, not fearing the wrath of the king; for he endured as seeing Him who is invisible. By covenant he KEPT THE PASSOVER AND THE SPRINKLING OF BLOOD, LEST HE WHO DESTROYED THE FIRSTBORN should touch them. By covenant they passed through the Red Sea as by dry land, whereas the EGYPTIANS, ATTEMPTING TO DO SO, WERE DROWNED. By covenant the walls of JERICHO FELL DOWN after they were encircled for seven days. By covenant the harlot Rahab DID NOT PERISH with those who did not COVENANT, when she had received the spies with peace. And what more shall I say? For the time would fail me to tell of Gideon and Barak and Samson and Jephthah, also of David and Samuel and the prophets: who through COVENANT SUBDUED KINGDOMS, WORKED RIGHTEOUSNESS, OBTAINED PROMISES, STOPPED THE MOUTHS OF LIONS, QUENCHED THE VIOLENCE OF FIRE, ESCAPED THE EDGE OF THE SWORD, OUT OF WEAKNESS WERE MADE STRONG, BECAME VALIANT IN BATTLE, TURNED TO FLIGHT THE ARMIES OF THE ALIENS. WOMEN RECEIVED THEIR DEAD RAISED TO LIFE AGAIN. OTHERS WERE TORTURED, NOT ACCEPTING DELIVER-

ANCE, THAT THEY MIGHT OBTAIN A BETTER RESURRECTION. STILL OTHERS HAD TRIAL OF MOCKINGS AND SCOURGINGS, YES, AND OF CHAINS AND IMPRISONMENT. THEY WERE STONED, THEY WERE SAWN IN TWO, WERE TEMPTED, WERE SLAIN WITH THE SWORD. THEY WANDERED ABOUT IN SHEEPSKINS AND GOATSKINS, BEING DESTITUTE, AFFLICTED, TORMENTED— of whom the world was not worthy. They wandered in deserts and mountains, in dens and caves of the earth. And all these, having obtained a good testimony through covenant, did not receive the promise, God having provided something better for us, that they should not be made perfect apart from us.

We can see, obviously, that Hebrews 11 is discussing a covenant, the threshold between life and death, that is constituted by a blessing (life) and a curse (death) signified by sacrifice; this chapter is not one of mere "belief" or what is loosly called "faith," but it is one of "covenant", that is, "faith," in other words, the vindication of an oath. Consider the 89th Psalm:

I will sing of the mercies of the Lord forever; With my mouth will I make known Your FAITHFULNESS to all generations. For I have said, "Mercy shall be built up forever; Your FAITHFULNESS You shall establish in the very heavens." "I have made a COVENANT with My chosen, I have sworn to My servant David: 'Your seed I will establish forever, and build up your throne to all generations.'" Selah. And the heavens will praise Your wonders, O Lord; Your FAITHFULNESS also in the assembly of the saints. For who in the heavens can be compared to the Lord? Who among the sons of the mighty can be likened to the Lord? God is greatly to be feared in the assembly of the saints, and to be held in reverence by all those around Him. O Lord God of hosts, Who is mighty like You, O Lord? Your FAITHFULNESS also surrounds You. You rule the raging of the sea; When its waves rise, You still them. You have broken Rahab in pieces, as one who is slain; You have scattered Your enemies with Your mighty arm. The heavens are Yours, the earth also is Yours; The world and all its fullness, You have founded them. The north and the south, You have created them; Tabor and Hermon rejoice in Your name. You have a mighty arm; Strong is Your hand, and high is Your right hand. RIGHTEOUSNESS AND JUSTICE ARE THE FOUNDATION of Your throne; Mercy and truth go before Your face. Blessed are the people who know the joyful sound! They walk, O Lord, in the light of Your countenance. In Your name they rejoice all day long, and in Your righteousness they are exalted. For You are the glory of their strength, and in Your favor our horn is exalted. For our shield belongs to the Lord, and our king to the Holy One of Israel. Then You spoke in a vision to Your holy one, And said: "I have given help to one who is mighty; I have exalted one chosen from the people. I have found My servant David; With My holy oil I have anointed him, with whom My hand shall be established; Also My arm shall strengthen him. The enemy shall not outwit him, Nor the son of wickedness afflict him. I will beat down his foes before his face, and plague those who hate him. "But My faithfulness and My mercy shall be with him, and in My name his horn shall be exalted. Also I will set his hand over the sea, and his right hand over the rivers. He shall cry to Me, 'YOU ARE MY FATHER, My God, and the rock of my salvation.' Also I will make him My FIRSTBORN, the highest of the kings of the earth. My mercy I will keep for him forever, and My COVENANT shall STAND FIRM with him. His seed also I will make to endure forever, and his throne as the days of heaven. "If his sons forsake My law and do not walk in My judgments, if they break My statutes and do not keep My commandments, then I will punish their transgression with the rod, and their iniquity with stripes. Nevertheless My lovingkindness I will not utterly take from him,Nor allow My FAITHFULNESS to fail. My covenant I will not break, nor alter THE WORD THAT HAS GONE OUT OF MY LIPS. Once I have SWORN by My holiness; I will NOT LIE to David: His seed shall endure forever, And his throne as the sun before Me; It shall be established forever like the moon, Even like the faithful witness in the sky." Selah. But You have cast off and abhorred, You have been furious with Your anointed. You have renounced the COVENANT of Your servant; You have profaned his crown by casting it to the ground. You have broken down all his hedges; You have brought his strongholds to ruin. All who pass by the way plunder him; He is a reproach to his neighbors. You have exalted the right hand of his adversaries; You have made all his enemies rejoice. You have also turned back the edge of his sword, and have not sustained him in the battle. You have made his glory cease, and cast his throne down to the ground. The days of his youth You have shortened; You have covered him with shame. Selah How long, Lord? Will You hide Yourself forever? Will Your wrath burn like fire? Remember how short my time is; for what futility have You created all the children of men? What man can live and not see death? Can he deliver his life from the power of the grave? Selah Lord, where are Your former lovingkindnesses, Which You swore to David in Your truth?

REMEMBER, Lord, the reproach of Your servants — How I bear in my bosom the reproach of all the many peoples, with which Your enemies have reproached, O Lord, with which they have reproached the footsteps of Your anointed. Blessed be the Lord forevermore! AMEN and AMEN.

Without knowing that the faith under discussion is not a mere belief but a provable covenant, it might appear that faith and works exist in a confusing symbiosis that manifests itself in a kind of peaceful non-action of goodwill, and this insipient stance constitutes what many claim to be a righteous conviction when it was formerly and rightfully deemed as slothful cowdardice.

Again, one of the most obvious examples of the Greek πιστις *faith* being used to translate the Hebrew אמנה *covenant* is the Septuagint's version of Genesis 15 where the actual covenant was made prior to its signification (which is a typical pattern in Scripture). We see that Abraham's πιστις *faith* is a translation the Hebrew word אמנה *covenant* (Genesis 15:6) while the sign of Abraham's διαθηκη *covenant, pledge* is a translation his ברית *covenant, pledge* (Genesis 15:18). Abraham's bloody sacrifice at sundown was the physically antithetical and conceptually mirrored sign of the bloodless sacrifice at the sunrise of Isaac's birth — both of which nearly merge atop Mount *Moriah*. A covenant is the mingling of two natures to effect a new creation that, in turn, would require renewal in order to maintain the covenant. Genesis 2:7 states that, "...the Lord God formed man of dust from the ground, and breathed into his nostrils the breath of life; and man became a living being." There are several Hebrew words that can be translated as "covenant," and the Greek word we often only translate as "faith" or "trust" is actually a direct translation of the Hebrew "covenant." A difficulty with notions of "covenant" is that English uses this word today synonymously with contract. A contract leans more towards legal terms that revolve around rendered services as stipulated in a written document whereas a *covenant* is better viewed Biblically as *a union separable only by death* or *an oath to the death*, and such a binding does not necessarily have to be written with letters. Contrary to this life-long binding is the fracture of it, and it is this fracture (not the binding) that is contractual and stipulated by a legal document: "Thus says the Lord: 'Where is the CERTIFICATE OF YOUR MOTHER'S DIVORCE, whom I have put away? Or which of My CREDITORS is it to whom I have sold you? For your iniquities you have SOLD yourselves, and for your transgressions your mother has been PUT AWAY" (Isaiah 50:1). The marriage is covenantal, but the divorce is contractual. More blatant passages regarding the divorce contract can be found in Deuteronomy 24, but when Christ was questioned about divorce, He quoted the Creation account as though it was readily understood that the first two humans were being described as married by God — for when they practiced iniquity, they sold themselves and received the divorce that was consequent to their choice, for the Hebrew states directly, "therefore the Lord God שלחהו *divorced him* from the garden of Fertility to till the ground from which he was taken. So He גרש *divorced* the man; and He placed cherubim מקדם *at the entrance* of the garden of Fertility," (Genesis 3:23-24). We may observe that cherubs are connected with the marital covenant and fertility, and this divorce was proposed by "The Anointed Cherub who Guards with Outstretched Wings" (Ezekiel 28:14) whom Genesis 3 calls in Hebrew "הנחש *The Shining One*" whom we call in English *"The Serpent"* (Genesis 3:1), the one whom the Apostle Paul translates as a masquerading *"angel of light"* i.e. *Shining One* in 2 Corinthians 11:14. Thus, Satan would seem to stand for infertility as opposed to the unfallen cherubs who guard fertility. Remembering the bloody leathers that adorned our first human parents in the process of their exile (their divorce), we can see a grim reflection in the retelling of Malachi where it is written, "For the Lord God of Israel says that He hates divorce, For it covers one's garment with violence" (2:16) as was true of Adam and Eve. Such hairy garments are what English often transliterates (not translates!) as "sackcloth" or mourning clothes. To clothe with skin describes gestation (Job 10:11). Following the Fall, Fertility (= עדן Eden) was linked to mourning: "I will greatly multiply YOUR SORROW AND YOUR CONCEPTION; in pain you shall bring forth children" (Genesis 3:16). If the punishment involves fertility, the crime must have involved fertility, especially when considering that the garden's name is "Eden, Fertility" and Satan is connected with infertility. In short, marriage is a covenant, that is, a union until death. Divorce is a type of living death signified contractually. The concept of skin-clothing indicating both gestation and war is accomplished in the Hebrew word גבור *strong man, warrior* that also means *male baby*, for it is in this word that the name *Gabriel* (Warrior/Male Baby) finds its root. It was Gabriel who announced the Holy Child to Mary, and it was the Holy Child with Whom Herrod sought to make war through his soldiers in the slaying of Bethlehem's innocents. "Faith" in Christ is, literally, an "oath to the death," that is, a "covenant for life" with Christ, for "even the demons believe — and tremble" (James 2:19).

As a result of not recognizing Scripture as a riddle, the terms "Old Testament" and "New Testament" are the standard when discussing the Hebrew Scriptures and their Greek complement; but, I object to the terms "Old Testament" and "New Testament." When it is written, "Behold, the days come, says the Lord, when I will make a διαθηκην καινην *new covenant* with the house of Israel and with the house of Judah" (Hebrews 8:8), we are viewing a Greek translation of Jeremiah 31:31 where "new covenant" is actually ברית חדשה *renewed and reaffirmed covenant* — not that this covenant is something different, but something original. Here we have the so-called "Old Testament" renewed and reaffirmed, not something new in spite of the "Old Testament." As to the term "Old Testament," 2 Corinthians 3:14 states, "But their minds were blinded: for until this day remains the same veil untaken away in the reading of the παλαιας διαθηκης *Old Testament*; which veil is done away in Christ." The unveiling, the revelation, the rolling away (of the stone) occurs in Christ. This "παλαιας διαθηκης *Old Testament*" is the Hebrew ברית העולם*Hidden, Eternal Covenant* of Jeremiah 50:5. The point is that The Eternal Covenant is also The Renewed Covenant, for this renewal keeps it Eternal. It can, therefore, be seen that what is called "The Old Testament" is exactly the same as what is called "The New Testament," for these titles are but translations of something eternal as evinced through its renewal. The damage that has been done to beliefs concerning Scripture is paramount here, for the majority of believers have actually assumed that there is an "old" half and a "new" half to Scripture without realizing that the "new" half actually only constitutes one-fourth of the Bible and that it is an exposition and commentary on Genesis through Malachi. It is for this reason that Acts 17-18 discusses proving Christ from the "Scriptures" in a time when "The New Testament" did not exist, for these Scriptures are what is called "The Old Testament." Flatly, the words עולם *ancient, hidden, eternal* and חדש *renewed* are essentially synonyms, and this can be seen plainly in that the further back (or more ancient) one proceeds on a timeline, the closer one gets to the origin (or newness) of the matter; thus, "The Old Testament" (Eternal Covenant) and "The New Testament" (Renewed Covenant) are one and the same. A preference for one over the other is a proof for poor reading and false doctrine. The word עולם is from the root עלם *to hide, conceal*, and it can mean *a time hidden, indefinite or unlimited, from ancient times* and *everlasting*; furthermore, the noun עלםa *male youth* (like גבור *male child, man-child, strong man, warrior*) is derived from this root and is synonymous to טליא *a male youth, a lamb*. Reviewing 2 Corinthians 3:14 in this light, we have the following: "But their minds were BLINDED: for until this day remains the same VEIL untaken away in the reading of the παλαιας διαθηκης = עולם ברית HIDDEN COVENANT; which VEIL is done away in CHRIST [The MALE CHILD, The LAMB, the "Holy CHILD" of Acts 4:30]," so their minds were blinded: for until this day remains the same veil untaken away in the reading of the Hidden Covenant; which veil is done away in The Holy Child. It would seem that there was an original, hidden covenant, regarding a male child who was at once as a Lamb and as a Warrior, that was renewed in Christ — not something previous that was replaced by something more recent. Proverbs 3:13-18 calls "Wisdom" a "tree of life" (a counsel of life): "Happy are those who find wisdom, and those who get understanding, for her income is better than silver, and her revenue better than gold. She is more precious than jewels, and nothing you desire can compare with her. Long life is in her right hand; in her left hand are riches and honor. Her ways are the ways of pleasantness, and all her paths are peace. She is a tree of life to those who lay hold of her; those who hold her fast are called happy"; again, "...wisdom gives life to the one who possesses it" (Ecclesiastes 7:12). Surely the forbidden tree did not impart wisdom, for it brought death. "Womb" and "wisdom" are both understood in the letter ב, and a womb is meant to bring life, not death. As such, we cannot ignore this enigmatic Scripture: "How can you say, 'We are wise, and the law of the Lord is with us,' when, in fact, the false pen of the Scribes has made it into a lie?"(Jeremiah 8:8). Where can we find evidence of this false pen? Where did the Scribes transmit lies? — perhaps in the accepted tradition that the forbidden tree imparted wisdom, for this teaching is in direct opposition to the Text itself. The forbidden tree caused sorrow, not happiness; it caused death, not life. Again, "And Adam was not deceived, but the woman being deceived, fell into transgression" (I Timothy 2:14). It would, therefore, be a mistake to assume that humanity obtained righteous wisdom through the deception and transgression regarding the forbidden tree that caused death when ב wisdom, the בhouse, the בtemple, the ב womb, is a "tree of life."

The knowledge of the Hebrew language and its recondite references are a consistent barrier regarding the logic of the Torah. Knowledge of Hebrew roots is essential to our study. Let us consider the root נחש. The root נחש is the third person, singular, masculine, perfect *he shined, he perceived*; it can also mean *he whispered, he hissed, and he used enchantment, he divined*; to consider the root as an infinitive may make for easier compatibility with English thought, thus *to perceive, etc.* From the root נחשto shine, *to perceive*, both the common noun "serpent," and the proper nouns " נחשNahash" and " נחשון Nashone" are derived. In other words, a נחש serpent is etymologically derived from conceptions of perception (consider: ב wisdom, the בhouse, the בtemple, the בwomb). It can be seen that a *womb* and a *serpent* are linked by way of wisdom, but the term "womb-serpent" indicated, in the ancient East, the cause of an abortion, the opposite of Fertility or "Eden."

This word serpent is also the name of the Amonite Nahash (נחש of I Samuel 11:1) and of the leader of the tribe of Judah (נחשון of Numbers 7:12). Therefore, the English-reader may see that I Samuel 11:1 says, "Then, Serpent, the Ammonite, went up and besieged Jabesh-gilead...." and Numbers 7:12 says, "The one who brought his offering on the first day was Serpent, son of Amminadab, of the tribe of Judah." The "serpents" in the two preceding passages above are men, not reptiles. Furthermore, the Chaldee נחש copper, brass is the same as Hebrew "serpent," which is etymologically related to נחשת fetter, chain, money. That a "serpent" would be related to "money" makes sense, in Hebrew, for the root נשך means to bite and to exact interest, to lend on usury. The point is this: even a genius, without some knowledge of the Hebrew tongue, would have no initially practical reason to link any of these ideas innately and would be able to perceive but patterns and trends throughout the overlapping themes of the Text as opposed to direct references and specific circumlocutions (such as "chain," "whip," "rope," or "vine," for "serpent"). Even the etymological links under discussion must be complemented with the historicity that surrounded the Text in the time it was written in order to grasp fully the timeless implications and allusions of the Text. That is, a translation can be a good place to start, but it cannot be, by nature, definitive. That the translated Text has been considered definitive unveils the reason why many devout believe in talking reptiles who, by nature, have no organs of speech.... Hebrew words written with the exact same consonants in the exact same order can be pronounced to render different, but related, definitions and parts of speech; nevertheless, these offshoots share the same root that is a concentration of the ideas that ramify from it.

> "naw-khash" (verb) = נחש = "to hiss, whisper a (magic) spell, to prognosticate, to observe, learn by experience"
>
> "nakh-ash" (noun) = נחש= "an incantation, augury, enchantment"
>
> "naw-khawsh" (noun) = נחש = "a serpent"

In the Hebrew number-system of Gematria, a serpent, incantation, augury, enchantment, to whisper, and hissing all compute to the number **358** (נחש = נ + ח + ש = 50 + 8 + 300 = 358). The number 358 numerically defines the root חשן to be beautiful, to adorn [similar to כוט beauty, good] (from where the word חשן breastplate is derived); this root is a transposition of the letters that compose the word serpent which, therefore, makes its gematria (numeric equivalency) the same as נחשserpent. Consider the fact that this breastplate was a vestment of the High priest, and the first Levitical High Priest was Aaron. Aaron means Shining One, and the Hebrew word

נחש serpent also means Shining One. To consider the allusion expressed numerically and linguistically here, observe that the description of Aaron's breastplate in Exodus 28 is similar to Satan's in Ezekiel 28. Notice that John the Baptist called the Pharisees and Sadducees a "brood of vipers" in Matthew 3:7, for the head Sadducee of that time was the כהן ראש High Priest, Head Priest, which can also be translated negatively as Priest of Venom, i.e. Serpent Priest (as opposed to כהן גדול Great Priest, High Priest). The Gematria of the Hebrew language is not the mere recognition of mathematically symmetrical words. Gematria, it would seem, is an illustration that runs parallel to the content of Scripture by tersely reflecting linked stories through numerically joined words.

1 Samuel 11, Nahash (Serpent), the King (Counsellor) of the Amonites desired to bore out the eyes of the men of Jabesh-gilead... that is, the Serpent desired to open the eyes of these men — literally. When the "Serpent" of Genesis 3 told humanity " ונפקחו עיניכם and your eyes will be opened," he must have used "פקח to open" in the sense of Exodus 23:8 that reads, "Do not accept a bribe, for the bribe will BLIND פקחים the open [i.e. the open of eye, the wise] and corrupt the words of the just." "The open" of eye will be blinded by a bribe, and the very fact that blindness and open eyes are juxtaposed (riddled, parabled) here explains what the Serpent of 1 Samuel 11 meant physically by intending to bore out the eyes of his victims. It would therefore seem that a consequence of the Fall was the loss of spiritual sight, not an increase in wisdom (!) since evil is connected to "madness" in Ecclesiastes 9:3. "And Adam was not deceived, but the woman being deceived, fell into transgression" (1 Timothy 2:14); since he chose to rebel with open eyes (for wisdom), the punishment of open eyes (for blindness) appears sorrowfully fitting. The riddle Satan propounded in Eden challenged an oral recounting of God's Word. Such oral recounting opened the door to sin by the flawed recounting of the bride. Psalm 119:18 discusses the opening of eyes, the unveiling of eyes (miraculous spiritual discernment), while Genesis 3:5 discusses the opening of eyes, the boring out of eyes (disastrous spiritual blindness). How eye-opening it is to observe that the word "נקבה female" in Genesis 1:27 comes from the root נקב to bore through, for His followers are the bride who was deceived and fell into transgression, thus decreasing her spiritual sight: "And even if our gospel is veiled, it is veiled only to those who are perishing. In their case the god of this world [Satan] has BLINDED the MINDS of the unbelievers, to keep them from seeing the light of the gospel of the glory of Christ, who is the image of God. For what we proclaim is not ourselves, but Jesus Christ as Lord, with ourselves as your servants for Jesus' sake. For God,

who said, 'Let LIGHT shine out of darkness,' has shone in our HEARTS to give the LIGHT of the knowledge of the GLORY of God in the face of Jesus Christ" (2 Corinthians 4:3-6). Again, reviewing 2 Corinthians 3:14: "But their minds were BLINDED: for until this day remains the same VEIL untaken away in the reading of the παλαιας διαθηκης = ברית העולם HIDDEN COVENANT; which VEIL is done away in CHRIST [The MALE YOUTH, The LAMB, the "Holy CHILD" of Acts 4:30]. "Unveil my eyes that I may behold the wondrous things in Your Torah" (Psalm 119:18). Accordingly, since "נקבה female" comes from the root "to bore through," since such a boring can indicate both the opening of the womb and the opening of the eyes, it would follow that the "serpent" opened the eyes of the inhabitants of Eden (The Fruitful Womb) in a perverse mockery of the Holy Communion, in a wretched overturning of Marriage in such a manner "...that sin, when it is fully grown, gives birth to death. Do not be deceived, my beloved," (James 1:14-16). Do not have your eyes opened (bored out spiritually) by Satan, but have your eyes opened (unveiled for the Marriage) by God. The letters עור spell to dig out, to make blind, to awake, to be raised up, to be made bare, and skin, flesh — the story of the open eyes in Eden, the naked humans, and the coats of skin provided them. The Hebrew ברית העולם Hidden Covenant, it would seem, conceals the story of our first parents and reveals it in Christ through His renewing of the Covenant through rebirth, i.e. conversion, i.e. washing, i.e. baptism. The open eye must be considered in baptism, for the word עין eye also means surface, appearance, and fountain. The Renewed and Reaffirmed Covenant is an explanation of the Hidden Covenant, and באר to engrave (as upon a tablet), to expound, to explain produces the word בבאר well, cistern. Consider that rocks were used to cover wells and that rolling such stones away would also open the eyes so that explanations would flow forth.

"To unveil" is, in Hebrew, to גלל to roll away, from which the word גלה fountain is derived as well as גלגלת Golgatha, Skull, where Christ was crucified. The metaphor is clear: to roll the stone from the mouth of the well is to open the eye so that the water, the explanation, flows forth. Accordingly, the root גלה (spelled consonantally identically to גלה fountain) means to make bare, to open, to uncover, to inform, to reveal a secret.

> But if the ministry of death, WRITTEN AND ENGRAVED ON STONES, was glorious, so that the children of Israel could not look steadily at the face of Moses because of the glory of his countenance, which glory was passing away, how will the ministry of the Spirit not be more glorious? For if the ministry of condemnation had glory, the ministry of righteousness exceeds

much more in glory. For even what was made glorious had no glory in this respect, because of the glory that excels. For if what is passing away was glorious, what remains is much more glorious. Therefore, since we have such hope, we use great boldness of speech— unlike Moses, who put A VEIL OVER HIS FACE so that the children of Israel could not look steadily at the end of what was passing away. But their MINDS WERE BLINDED. For until this day the same veil remains unlifted in the reading of the Old Testament, because THE VEIL IS TAKEN AWAY IN CHRIST. But even to this day, when Moses is read, a veil lies on their heart. Nevertheless when one turns to the Lord, THE VEIL IS TAKEN AWAY (II Corinthians 3:8-17),

i.e. the covering is rolled away as was the rock before Christ's tomb. It is for these reasons that I object to the terms "Old Testament" and "New Testament." Instead we are beholding the glorious Hidden Covenant and its explanation, the Renewed and Eternal Covenant, the Spirit of the words penned darkly in the Hidden Covenant. It would appear as if spiritual insight was lost as a result of the Fall that opened (blinded) the (spiritual) eyes of humanity and the Covenant became hidden. It would also appear that the rebirth flowed forth from the עץ *Tree* on גלגלת *Golgatha* (*Counsel of the Head*) that opened (gave wisdom) the (spiritual) eyes of revivified humanity who became washed in the water by the Word. The very notion of a Renewed and Reaffirmed Covenant points back to an original covenant, thus our Savior's words: "Do not think that I came to destroy the Law or the Prophets. I did not come to destroy BUT TO FULFILL" (Matthew 5:17). The forbidden tree did not, and could not, give edifying perception, for it blinded the spiritual discernment that was formerly within the sight of our first human parents, and we can see this very fact in Genesis 3:8:

> And they heard the sound of the Lord God walking in the garden in the cool of the day, and Adam and his wife hid themselves from the presence of the Lord God בתוך עץ הגן *in the midst of the tree/trees of the garden.*

The word עץ means both *tree* and *trees.* God was in the midst of the tree of the garden. God was right in front of them, but they could not see Him with their "opened" (spiritually gouged eyes) until He made His triumphal entry that was but perceptible with human physical senses. The very mention of God "in the midst" refers to a threshold, for this boundary is the sword in the ground that separates the blessing of the covenant from the curse or vengeance of the covenant. When the humans "knew that they were naked," they unified with death directly before God in the midst of the tree, directly before the King of Kings Whom they could no longer recognize in the same way as though they were on the road to Emmaus, for the "flame of the sword" guarded the דרך *way, road, right* of the Tree of Life, the Right of the Firstborn. We might behold the connections made by Hebrews 4:12-13:

> For the Word of God is living and powerful, and sharper than any two-edged sword, piercing even to the division of soul and spirit, and of joints and marrow, and is a discerner of the thoughts and intents of the heart. And there is NO CREATURE HIDDEN FROM HIS SIGHT, but all things are NAKED and OPEN TO THE EYES of Him to whom we must give account,

for we must account for the sin of our "opened" (gouged) eyes once our eyes are opened (enlightened) in the Judgement. The place where the two ways meet, i.e. the fork in the road, is called the " פתח עינים *opening of the eyes*" (which is translated often as "the *entrance to Enaim*" in Genesis 38:14). The logic of a fork in the road being called the "פתח עינים *opening of the eyes*" is that one eye begins to be directed to the right while the other begins to be directed to the left beginning from where the two divergent ways meet; in this sense, the opening of the eyes demands and reflects a choice. The choice under discussion is covenantal. The Word of God, compared to a two-edged sword, would seem to be illustrated by the division or fork called "the opening of the eyes" that reflected the covenant humanity cut with death. Since a covenant anticipates and requires the production of fruit, it would also seem that a covenant cut with Death is a covenant reflected by infertility. Numbers 25 tells us that the child-sacrifice it describes was punished by hanging, and the cross was called, among other things, in Latin, the *infelix lignum* or *unfruitful wood*.

THE APOLOGY OF THE RENEWAL

THE oldest recorded employment of the word "theology" is found in Plato's *Republic* out of the mouth of Adeimantus, and it was only adopted (like the word "exegete" from Plato's *Euthyphro*) by early Christian scholars, many of whom were trained in Plato prior to being trained in the Scriptures. So profound was the influence of Platonism and Neoplatonism upon Biblical scholarship that, in my opinion, Plato is much closer to traditional "Christian" doctrine than the Bible. The program of Plato often served inadvertently as the sieve of Biblical scholarship to the extent that the philosophical model became the standard by which Biblical scholarship received its mark; however, the problem with such a development is that it assumes Scripture to be constructed to fit into a Platonic mold when it does not. Such an assumption seems to have stemmed in part from the recognition of a plentitude of Classical references in the so-called Greek "New Testament," but the reason for these quotations is something deliberate and unknown to the various "theologies" of the disparate factions that unite uncommunicably under the title "church."

Paul was educated in the Western Classics and he penned in Greek, and so it can be easily (albeit incorrectly) assumed that the Hebraic world of the so-called "Old Testament" was being synthesized and reinvented with a Hellenistic model; yet, this opinion is proven false when one realizes that such a synthesis had already occurred with the Sadducees (of whom a large quantity of the Second Temple Levites were a part); John the Baptist, cousin of The Lord, denounced openly this hybrid's brood. Even prior to Paul's conversion, he was not a Sadducee. Instead, Paul was a Pharisee. Ironically, after the destruction of the Second Temple, the Pharisees hybridized Platonic ideas with Babylonian practices, and this graft appeared (albeit incorrectly) parallel to the oral and written aspects of Biblical Hebrew to the extent that Plato's concept of speech's position above writing became reworked as the "Oral Law" of the Pharisees, the ancestors of the Rabbis, and this stance was displayed in what became known as "Orthodox Judaism" well over a thousand years after Moses penned the Torah.

Without knowing the history of the words "theology" and "Oral Law," it is both easy and false to claim that "Christianity" was a development of "Judaism" that was primed by Classical writers who never anticipated the so-called "New Testament" and who knew nothing of the so-called "Old Testament." Even the title of "Christianity" is an unoriginal name given by outsiders at Antioch to the followers of "The Way," "The Way" being the name of the religion Paul professed in Acts 24:13-14, the faith Malachi defended in 2:8 and the covenant Moses discussed as "guarded" in Genesis

3:24, for Paul said, "...The Way which they call a sect, so I worship the God of my fathers, believing all things which are written in the Law [Moses] and in the Prophets [Malachi, specifically 2:8]." The fact that "The Way" was called Christianity by outsiders at Antioch (Acts 11:26) placed the faith found first in Eden in the difficult position of being a new religion when it was not only ancestral but the first religion in the history of the world. When Nero outlawed Christianity in 64 AD, he outlawed a religion whose name had not appeared until recently, a name given by those outside the faith who served to provide for themselves power over those inside. Rome tolerated ancestral religions but not new religions, and the task of the "Christian" in 64 AD was to prove that this religion was that same faith penned by The Law and The Prophets that derived from Eden itself, not some recent innovation that departed from The Law and The Prophets. Even the term "New Testament," which is discussed in passages like Matthew 26:28, Mark 14:24, Luke 22:20, 1 Corinthians 11:25, 2 Corinthians 3:6, and Hebrews 8:3, is a Greek translation of Jeremiah's ברית חדשה *re-newed* covenant (31:31), i.e. original covenant revitalized, which is why Christ specifically said, "And no one, having drunk old wine, immediately desires new; for he says, 'THE OLD IS BETTER'" (Luke 5:39). Paul, like the other followers of "The Way," had to defend himself legally with respect to the ancient character of his religion that appeared to be "new" based on the outside name "Christianity" being superimposed upon it.

Considering that the artificial usage of Attic Greek was the court-language of the eastern portion of the Roman Empire, and considering that Paul was tried by the Roman Empire that had outlawed Christianity in his time, it is plain that Scriptural employments of Classical authors (either referentially or by direct quotation) were crafted in order that Christians might "always be ready to give a *defense* [= απολογια, apology, *legal defense*] to everyone who asks you a *reason* [= λογος, *logos*] for the hope that is in you, with meekness and fear" (1 Peter 3:15) for Paul himself stated in Philippians 1:12-21,

> But I want you to know, brethren, that the things which happened to me have actually turned out for the furtherance of the gospel, so that it has become evident to the whole palace guard, and to all the rest, that my chains are in Christ; and most of the brethren in the Lord, having become confident by my chains, are much more bold to speak the word without fear. Some indeed preach Christ even from envy and strife, and some also from goodwill: The former preach Christ from selfish ambition, not sincerely, supposing to add affliction to my

> chains; but the latter out of love, knowing that I am appointed
> for the *defense* [= απολογια, *apology, legal defense*] of the
> gospel. What then? Only that in every way, whether in pretense
> or in truth, Christ is preached; and in this I rejoice, yes, and
> will rejoice. For I know that this will turn out for my deliverance
> through your prayer and the supply of the Spirit of Jesus Christ,
> according to my earnest expectation and hope that in nothing I
> shall be ashamed, but with all boldness, as always, so now also
> Christ will be magnified in my body, whether by life or by death.
> For to me, to live is Christ, and TO DIE IS GAIN.

Paul, who had to give a legal defense (apology) for having broken the law
by preaching a banned religion, used a Classical reference to Plato's Apology where Socrates said in his own legal defense, "Now if death be of such
a nature, I say that TO DIE IS GAIN." The employment of this reference
does not in any way show a melding of "Judaism" with the Classical world,
but displays the specific erudition Paul utilized to defend himself before a
judgment seat that understood legality in the language of Plato. Furthermore, the fact that this Classical reference as well as a host of others were
written down for Christians was a step in providing legal legitimacy before
their accusers that led ultimately to the Faith becoming the official religion
of the Roman Empire. Once such beliefs were adopted officially, however,
it was at this point that Platonic ideas became accidentally intermingled
with the Greek "New Testament," and such a mingling (as apposed to the
unalloyed "New Testament") found itself at odds with the "Old Testament"
that was not Platonic at all. From here, "theology" became the Platonic
strainer of "Christianity" to the extent that ideas and explanations of ideas
became the rule, and substantial evidence became replaced by conceptual ethereality. Here, then, we can see that "theology," which is a Platonic
term, is inadvertently more influenced by the conceptual program of Plato
than by the unmixed program that is internally consistent from Genesis to
Revelation.

Language is the sieve of thought. Thought is received and transmitted through language, and language is a program. Every language possesses its own scheme and reacts to other types of thoughts initially by its
own program until a graft occurs, and such a graft is capable of producing
a hybrid. The advantage of dead languages is that they no longer change
as the result of grafting; however, dead languages are studied through the
lenses of living languages, and the conclusions drawn about the meaning
of dead languages are often superimposed accidentally and produce a lens
that does not accurately reflect the original being studied. For instance,
Biblical Hebrew was not a spoken language during the time of Christ; it

was, instead, liturgical. The terms "Hebrew," "Israelite," and "Jew" were confounded, and the remaining Judean sect beside Christianity was Rabbinic Judaism. Rabbinic Judaism developed its own form of Hebrew, but it superimposed innovative definitions upon Biblical words so that the interpretation of Biblical Hebrew became alloyed with Rabbinic Hebrew under the errant assumption that the "Jewish" religion was that of the Hebrew Bible necessarily. Accordingly, later Christian scholars received the flawed teaching that a "Hebrew" was an "Israelite" and therefore a "Jew," and they consulted Jewish sources in an attempt to understand "Christianity" as though it had developed from a system that was rather different from the Hebrew Scriptures. Such a situation can be observed in the Book of Hebrews where the King James Version translates the word αιωνας as "worlds" so that Hebrews 1:1-2 reads in English, "God, who at various times and in various ways spoke in time past to the fathers by the prophets, has in these last days spoken to us by His Son, whom He has appointed heir of all things, through whom also He made the worlds." I find this translation to be ingenious even though I find it to be incorrect. The translator must have been learned in Rabbinic Hebrew and Biblical Hebrew, and it seems that he viewed the Greek of the Book of Hebrews through the lens of "Judaism" (i.e. Rabbinic Pharisaism) which is described by Rabbinic (not Biblical) Hebrew; thus, the word, which is a translation of the Biblical Hebrew word עולם eternity (from the root עלם to hide) was reinterpreted in Rabbinic Hebrew as world; Christianity was assumed (falsely) to have developed from Rabbinic Judaism which was, in turn, assumed (falsely) to be synonymous with the religion of Moses; therefore, the early Christian Book of Hebrews was assumed (falsely) to reflect Rabbinic Hebrew's interpretation of Biblical Hebrew being discussed in the Greek text of the Book of Hebrews. Sagastically, the King James translator must have accounted for all of this when he translated into English the Greek word αιωνας as worlds, and this translation displays a level of understanding far above most — but it functions on the (false) premise that equates the terms "Hebrew," "Israelite," and "Jew" because people have thought for nearly two millennia that these three are necessarily one when they necessarily are not. Such an equation was crafted by "Orthodox" Jews who are but the blended descendants of the "Rabbis" who are, in turn, the descendants of the "Pharisees" who were bitter religious adversaries of the Christians. In short, the language used to describe the Biblical personalities has been strained through a filter that disallows a complete view of history even to the extent that early Christianity was the spiritual descendant of its most bitter adversary which is, of course, incorrect.

Let us then probe together why there are apparently three different terms that designate today a single group of people (and I stress the word "apparently"); but, in order to do this, we must accept the proposition of a single people, and this acceptance leads to questions like, "Aren't the Hebrew Scriptures Jewish?" "Isn't Judaism the religion of the 'Old Testament'?" "Don't the Jews still follow 'Old Testament' Law?" The answer to these questions is resoundingly negative on all counts, and this is so largely because of the confusion of the terms "Hebrew" "Israelite" and "Jew."

The term "Jew" appears nowhere in the Torah of Moses, and the errant assumption that Moses was Jewish causes the Torah to appear Jewish in a time when no Jews walked the earth. Moses was both an Israelite and a Hebrew, but he was not a Jew. An Israelite is a descendant of Jacob who was renamed "Israel," and Moses descended from Israel through Levi; so, Moses' tribal affiliation was that of Levi, and Levi issued from Israel. Israel, who was formerly called Jacob, descended from Isaac, and Isaac descended from Abraham who was formerly called Abram. If one were to call Abraham "Jewish" by accident and then claim that Abraham's descendents are therefore "Jewish," then one would, of course, have to call all Ishmaelites "Jewish" as well, since they issued from Abraham (prior to Isaac). Surely this nomenclature is mistaken. The first overt mention of the name "Hebrew" concerns Abraham in Genesis 14; however, this by no means indicates that Abraham was the first Hebrew simply because he was the first overtly qualified as such. Genesis 14:13 calls Abraham a "Hebrew" when his name was still "Abram" immediately after he moves his tents to the terebinths of Mamre in Hebron. The word עברי *Hebrew* comes from the root עבר *to pass* over which is a synonym of the root פסח *to pass over* from which "Passover" is derived. Abraham is called a "Hebrew" (One Who Passes Over) immediately after he passes from one location over to another and constructs an altar, a type of threshold. Abraham is designated as One Who Passes Over, and then locomotes. Abraham locomoted immediately after God articulated His covenant; this relationship is repeated in the very next chapter where Abram carves a physical deliniation of blood flanked by halved animal corpses, and it is here that the Pillar of Cloud and Pillar of Fire passes over into covenant with Abram towards the consumation of the covenant: Isaac, the eventual father of Israel. We may see in this a multifaceted typification of the ancient threshold covenant in that the first altar was a threshold, Abram passed over geographically and built an altar, God passed over Abram's encrimsoned threshold, Abraham sat bleeding from his midst into his own threshold, and God produced life from Abraham's threshold, i.e. Sarah, who was the altar upon whom

God chose Abraham to yield up life that draws near to God (sacrificial life) named Isaac, the one whom God commanded Abraham to offer upon the mountain for life, not for death — which should explain boldly to the reader that original sacrifice did not involve death at all and that death was but the destructively bloody outcome of sin as opposed to the constructively bloody outcome of unsullied birth. According to Job 7:21, a "Hebrew" is a "Forgiven One."

The term "Hebrew" means "One Who Passes Over" into covenant with God, not one of a physical lineage, for why else would the Book of Hebrews be written to Christians who can be of any nationality whatsoever? A Hebrew is one who covenants with God and vindicates this covenant with the duration of life, not with the suddenness of destruction, for it is written, "I beseech you therefore, brethren, by the mercies of God, that you present your bodies a LIVING SACRIFICE, holy, acceptable to God, which is your reasonable service" (Romans 12:1) and, "Coming to Him as to a LIVING STONE, rejected indeed by men, but chosen by God and precious, you also, as living stones, are being built up a SPIRITUAL HOUSE, a holy priesthood, to offer up SPIRITUAL SACRIFICES acceptable to God through Jesus Christ" (1 Peter 2:4-5). Since a ברית covenant is related to the word ברא to create, we can easily observe why a "spiritual house," a womb, is critical to our understanding of a "Hebrew," for covenants anticipate the blessing which is fertility, and this is exactly what we see in Abraham's story. The very fact that God told Abraham to sacrifice his own son and yet prevented the slaughter should be proof enough that sacrifice was meant to be a spiritual declaration enacted through a life of servitude to God and not a physical destruction enacted through a death opposite the very blessing God gives through covenant. It has been often assumed and asserted that God somehow changed His mind concerning the life of Isaac, and this mistake derives from the misconception that sacrifice is inherently destructive when, in fact, the destructive side of sacrifice is but the result of sin, not obedience: "Abraham believed God, and it was accounted to him for righteousness" (Romans 4:3). It is also in such a way that Communion is a sacrifice yet the participants live. The word קרבן sacrifice is from the root to draw near, not necessarily to die, and the fact that so-called "Orthodox Jews" claimed previously that sacrifice eventually necessitated slaughter is a mistake in accordance with their own religion called "Talmud," the woeful "Oral Law" that is assumed to explain the Torah. A Hebrew is one who passes over into covenant with God and can therefore be of any race or nationality. An Israelite — by flesh — is one who descended physically from Israel who may or may not have chosen to adhere to God's covenant: "For they are not all

Israel who are of Israel, nor are they all children because they are the seed of Abraham" (Romans 9:6-7). Let us examine the term "Israelite" further.

As stated by Romans 9:6-7 above, there are at least two types of "Israelites," otherwise the Apostle could not have said "they are not all Israel who are of Israel." "Israel" means ישראל *he wrestles with* אל *el*; the question is, "Who is 'el'?" "El" can mean "God" (Genesis 14:18), "power" (Genesis 31:29), or a false "deity" (Exodus 34:14). Many have assumed incorrectly (and translated as such) that Jacob wrestled with God and, because he prevailed over the One Who created the entire universe, he was given the name "He wrestles with God." How flagrantly outrageous! No human is capable of such a feat. God, the One who made the sun that has a core of 27 million degrees Fahrenheight that fuses 700 million tons of protons into helium nuclei each second and releases energy equivalent to 10 billion hydrogen bombs, lost a wrestling match? The absurdity propounded here would then teach that, when one is in the midst of trouble, he can literally throw God around, make Him submit, and then succeed in his endeavors by putting God in the dust. Is this not what Satan wanted the Christ's adversaries to think as He was put into the tomb? Is there anyone so arrogant as to assume that Christ was feable and could not control His own path when He guards The Way of the Tree of Life and is flanked by His cherubs at the threshold of Eden? How could it be that Jacob wrestles God when it is plainly stated, "The Lord also brings a charge against Judah, and will punish Jacob according to his ways; according to his deeds He will recompense him. He took his brother by the heel in the womb, and in his strength HE STRUGGLED WITH אלחים ELOHIM. YES, HE STRUGGLED WITH THE ANGEL and prevailed; he wept, and sought favor from him. He found him in Bethel, and there He spoke to us — that is, the Lord God of hosts. The Lord is His memorable name" (Hosea 12:2-5). Surely Jacob wrestled an angel in Genesis, and certainly God cannot be the "angel" mentioned in this Hosea reference. The confusion has surfaced because the word אלהים *elohim* can mean "God" (Genesis 1:1) and "angels" (Psalm 8:6) just as אל can mean "God" (Genesis 14:18), "power" (Genesis 31:29), or a false "deity" (Exodus 34:14). It can be seen that Tradition has confused God with Satan.... for God said, "If you do well, will you not be accepted? And if you do not do well, sin lies at the door. And its desire *is* for you, but you should rule over it" (Genesis 4:7), for Jacob did do well in subduing sin, and he was therefore given the name "Israel = ישראל *he strives with elohim (spirits) and prevails*," for one cannot prevail against God as Satan has disastrously proven for us. Knowing then that Jacob prevailed over a wicked spirit, we can observe that the word נחש *serpent* is related to the verb נחש

to prognosticate, to tell the future. The evil spirit being prognosticated to Jacob after losing and weeping, "Your name will no longer be Jacob, but Israel, because you have struggled withאלהים *angels* and with men and have overcome" (Genesis 32:28). Later, God Himself tells Jacob of his name-change in Genesis 35:10, for Satan knew beforehand that, if Jacob won the fight against darkness, then Jacob would become Israel, i.e. a Hebrew like Abraham, one who overcomes by adhering to God's covenant as we observe Jacob building an altar on the very place he descended into darkness following the trickery of his own brother regarding the birthright, the right to officiate at God's altar. That is, at the very threshold from which Jacob fled, he built an altar, and a threshold is a type of altar; this doorway was where he passed over into sin, and also where he passed from death to life after overcoming sin: "...sin lies at the door. And its desire is for you, but you should rule over it" (Genesis 4:7). Surely Jacob overcame sin by defeating an evil principality signified by the dreamy ascent of the heavenly host, for why else would the unvictorious, wicked angel insist that he be released because "it was day-break" (Genesis 32:26)? The shepherds received an angel and the Magi received the star on account of the infant Christ, and the parallel of the angelic host to the starry host has long been grasped. As the appearance of stars evanesces when overwhelmed by the sun, the spiritual messenger of wickedness was compelled to depart at dawn like a morning star which seems to point us in the direction necessary to see in this parallel Venus, Lucifer. It would also seem that this struggle against the wicked host warring in the heavens, as we see in Job, is paralleled in Revelation 12 and explained in Ephesians 6:10-12:

> Finally, be strong in the Lord and in his mighty power. Put on the full armor of God, so that you can take your stand against the devil's schemes. For our παλη *wrestling* is not against flesh and blood, but against the rulers, against the authorities, against the powers of this dark world and against the spiritual forces of evil in the heavenly realms. Therefore put on the full armor of God, so that when the day of evil comes, you may be able to stand your ground, and after you have done everything, to stand.

The word παλη *wrestling* used here is the same as the Septuagint's rendering of Jacob's encounter with this wicked spirit, but the very notion that Jacob caused God to submit is incomprehensable. That Jacob saw the face of spiritual divinity does not mean he saw God's face; furthermore, even if he did see God's face, it would be more likely that he beheld the judge of the wrestling match Who used a mere mortal to defeat a familial defecter from the "sons of God," the Great King's familial court. Surely Jacob stood against the schemes of Lucifer and not against flesh and blood since Esau, though flanked by an army, did not war with his brother. Certainly, Jacob prevailed against the dark spiritual forces in this world and stood his ground in protection of his wives and children, in protection of his marital altar on the threshold where he would pass from death back to life and where he would erect an altar as a victorious one who passes over into covenant with God, that is, as a Hebrew and as a Firstborn. Jacob did not wrestle with flesh and blood, for a Hebrew is neither qualified nor bound by flesh and blood.

A Hebrew is a strictly spiritual term, but "Israel" has the dual meaning of someone physically descended from Jacob (secondarily) and someone in covenant with God (primarily). Knowing that "Israel," in the spiritual sense, is a synonym of "Hebrew," we can observe why, through God's covenant and the daily adherence to it, "For they are not all Israel [spiritually] who are of Israel [physically], nor are they all children [spiritually] because they are the seed of Abraham [physically]" (Romans 9:6-7); therefore, we may comprehend why it is written, "For I do not desire, brethren, that you should be IGNORANT OF THIS MYSTERY, lest you should be wise in your own opinion [by claiming superiority by physical descent], that blindness in part has happened to Israel until the FULLNESS OF THE GENTILES HAS COME IN. AND SO ALL ISRAEL will be saved...." (Romans 11:25-26), for "...you will be hated by all for My name's sake. But he who endures to the end will be saved" (Matthew 10:22). Remember, "If you do well, will you not be accepted? And if you do not do well, sin lies at the door. And its desire is for you, but YOU SHOULD RULE OVER IT" (Genesis 4:7) and "He who has an ear, let him hear what the Spirit says to the churches. To HIM WHO OVERCOMES I will give to eat from the tree of life, which is in the midst of the Paradise of God." (Revelation 2:7). "All Israel," not "all Jews," will be saved, and this should point explicitly to the fact that the religion of Abraham later came to be called "Christianity" by outsiders looking in at Antioch (Acts 11:26) and why, once Christianity was outlawed in 64 AD, the Christians protested vehemently that they were not a new religion but an ancestral one... and that it was the varying Jewish sects who were falsely innovative and not ancestral at all. After the destruction of 70 AD, the two remaining sects of the Judean province were the "Christians" and the "Pharisess" (who currently adhere to their roughly 2,000-year-old title of "Rabbis"). A "Hebrew" has only one sense, and that sense is spiritual. An "Israelite" has two senses, the first spiritual, and the second physical. Both of these terms preceded the term "Jew" since neither the kingdom of Judah nor the later provinces of Judah (as controlled by Babylon and Rome respectively) existed in the time of Abraham: "But when he saw many of the Pharisees and Sadducees [who certainly were Judeans, i.e. "Jews"] coming to his baptism, he said to them, 'Brood of vipers! Who warned you to flee from the wrath to come? Therefore bear fruits worthy of repentance, and do not think to say to yourselves, 'We have Abraham as our father.' For I say to you that God is able to raise up children to Abraham from these stones" (Matthew 3:7-9). We can see clearly that the Jewish sects denounced above were not considered to be of the covenant of Abraham, but only of the physical line of Abraham, which means that these Jewish sects were not Hebrews of God. If something that is not original is thought to be primary, then the design of the mistake will evolve (or, at least, grow) into something that is not itself in total accordance with what preceded it. If what preceded the growth is unknown, the growth cannot thrive optimally relative to an original design that remains unapprehended. What then of this term "Jew"?

A "Jew" is a "Judean," that is, one of the province of "Judah" as qualified by the Romans and the Babylonians when they occupied what was formerly the land of Israel. When Israel became a monarchy in the time of Saul, all 12 tribes existed in geographic harmony. When the monarchy divided under Rehaboam, Judah and Levi (the regal and priestly tribes) remained unified in the south. Once the northern 5/6 of the former unified monarchy was disassembled by Assyria, the kingdom of Judah remained; these people were termed יהודים *Judahites, Jews* (2 Kings 25:25) and were, in time, exiled to Babylon. Their religion became known as the Judahite or Jewish religion; in other words, their Sacred Texts, what came to be the Hebrew Bible, was the religion of the people formerly of the southern Kingdom of Judah that had been reformed into a foreign province by successive captors. At the time of Christ, no normative "Judaism" existed; rather, there were competing sects (princibly the Qumran communities, their relatives the Sadducees who were the Second Temple Levites, and the influential lay-group called the Pharisees). After the destruction of 70 AD, the Qumran and Sadducean sects were wiped out, and the Pharisees crafted the Babylonian Talmud that came to solidify the eventual (and chronologically inadmissable) title of "Orthodox Judaism" by default since all of their competitors (except the Christians) had been eliminated. Even a swift reading of the magnitudinous Babylonian Talmud juxtaposed to Plato's Phaedrus obviates the reality that so-called "Orthodox Judaism" is neither orthodox nor Hebrew because it is but a Jewish take on the Platonic stance that the written word is insufficient and potentially promiscuous without an oral word that serves both to protect and explain it. The Jewish religion, so called, is termed by its adherence as the "Oral Law" and the "Talmud" which explains why, if one searches the entire Pentateuch, one cannot find a single Pharasaic rule contrary to Christ contained within it; but, if one reads the Talmud, every Pharasic argument put to Christ can be found, thus proving that the Pharisees were not, in any sense of the words, conservative or legalistic relative to Moses, but were liberal and plastic just as the Qumran sect had accused them of being during the time of Christ: "But when he saw many of the Pharisees and Sadducees coming to his baptism, he said to them, 'Brood of vipers! Who warned you to flee from the wrath to come? Therefore bear fruits worthy of repentance, and do not think to say to yourselves, 'We have Abraham as our father.' For I say to you that God is able to raise up children to Abraham from these stones" (Matthew 3:7-9).

"All Israel," not "all Jews," will be saved, and this should point explicitly to the fact that the religion of Abraham later came to be called "Christianity" by outsiders looking in at Antioch (Acts 11:26) and why, once Christianity was outlawed in 64 AD, the "Christians" argued vehemently that they were not a new religion but an ancestral one and that it was the varying Jewish sects who were falsely innovative and not ancestral at all. After the destruction of 70 AD, the two remaining sects of the Judean province were the "Christians" and the "Pharisees." A "Hebrew" has only one sense, and that sense is spiritual. An "Israelite" has two senses, the first spiritual, and the second physical. Both of these terms preceded the term "Jew" since neither the kingdom of Judah nor the later provinces of Judah existed in the time of Abraham. Again:

> But when he [John the Baptist] saw many of the Pharisees and Sadducees [who certainly were Judeans, i.e. "Jews"] coming to his baptism, he said to them, "Brood of vipers! Who warned you to flee from the wrath to come? Therefore bear fruits worthy of repentance, and do not think to say to yourselves, 'We have Abraham as our father.' For I say to you that God is able to raise up children to Abraham from these stones" (Matthew 3:7-9),

as God did with Jacob (Israel) when he overcame the spiritual warrior of wickedness and built an altar whereby he received the same blessing of the covenant that Adam was given. Adam was given this covenant, this Way: "...be fruitful and multiply" (Genesis 35:11) which elucidates that Adam was a "Hebrew" and that his religion in Eden is rightly to be identified with true "Christianity"; this explains Jesus' titles of "Son of Man (Adam)" and "The LAST Adam" in particular light of this: "I am the Alpha and the Omega, the Beginning and the End, THE FIRST AND THE LAST" (Revelation

22:13). The religion of the Bible, from Adam until Christ is called "The Way," and it is expressed in this directive: "...be fruitful and multiply." This directive called "The Way" (Genesis 3:24) was penned by Moses, thus we read that "...death reigned from Adam to MOSES..." (Romans 5:13) instead of something like "Death reigned from Adam to Christ." In other words, the Books written through Moses overcame death. Consider the Book of Life (Revelation 3:5) about which Moses spoke (Exodus 32:32).

Since the first Adam sinned in eating and thus sired the sacrifice of sin (i.e. sinful destruction), it is apparent how the Last Adam renewed and reaffirmed the Hebraic covenant (through a threshold, an altar, a table) in eating and thus sired the sacrifice of righteousness. Adam was not "Jewish," but he was a "Hebrew." Christians have not replaced Jews because the first "Christians" were Judeans (Jews). In order to prove this point, let us reflect on the fact that Christians are Hebrews with particular attention paid to the fact that the Levitical mandates given through Moses the Levite were dismissed by the Second Temple Levites (the Sadducees) in Christ's days as was the case in the time of Malachi historically. The Book of Luke is "Christian," and it addresses the fruit of the Levitical covenant by discussing Hebrews who are Israelites and Jews but not Sadducees or Pharisees.

The beginning of Luke is jaw-droppingly confrontive. If one were to end after the first chapter, the Book of Luke would appear beyond inflammatory. Nearly every notion of truth regarding the Temple Priesthood in the days of Christ was challenged blatantly in only the beginning of this Book, and it is astounding to read the piercing boldness mingled with Scriptural subtlety recorded therein.   Essentially, it looks as if the first chapter of Luke applies the Book of Malachi, in sequence, to the Sadducees' errors regarding the Second Temple Officiation, and the Book of Luke does this by highlighting a Levite who is officiating correctly in the midst of a corrupt church, a defiled temple. Unless repentance was involved on the part of the specific priesthood of Luke's day, it would be shocking if the first chapter of Luke would have been taken as anything other than intensely audacious by the one to whom it was written: Theophilus, the High Priest of the time (*Encyclopedia Judaica, Volume II*, p.1131).

> Luke 1:1-5 Inasmuch as many have taken in hand to set in order a narrative of those things which have been fulfilled among us, just as those who from the beginning were eyewitnesses and ministers of the word delivered them to us, it seemed good to me also, having had perfect understanding of all things from the very first, to write to you an orderly account, most excellent

> Theophilus, that you may know the certainty of those things in which you were instructed. In the time of Herod king of Judea there was a priest named Zechariah who belonged to the priestly division of Abijah [Jehovah is My Father]; his wife Elizabeth [Oath of My God] was also a descendant of Aaron [Shining One, Enlightened].

The parents of John the Baptist were not only Levites but descendants of the first High Priest in the Levitical Order, Aaron.

> Malachi 2:4-15: "And you will know that I have sent you this warning so that my covenant with Levi may continue," says the LORD Almighty. "My covenant was with him, a covenant of life and peace, and I gave them to him; this called for reverence and he revered me and stood in awe of my name. True instruction was in his mouth and nothing false was found on his lips. He walked with me in peace and uprightness, and turned many from sin. For the lips of a priest ought to preserve knowledge, because he is the מלאך *angel* of the LORD Almighty and people seek instruction [*Aaron* or *Shining One*, Enlightened] from his mouth...." Has not the one God made you? You belong to him in body and spirit. And what does the one God seek? GODLY OFFSPRING.

> Luke 1:6-7: Both of them were righteous in the sight of God, observing all the Lord's commands and decrees blamelessly. But they were childless because Elizabeth was NOT ABLE TO CONCEIVE, and they were both very old.

We can see a parallel in "GODLY OFFSPRING" and "NOT ABLE TO CONCEIVE." If the reader reviews Malachi 2:4-15, the negative aspects of this Text fit, historically, with what was happening in the Second Temple during the days of John the Baptist's parents, and the positive aspects certainly apply to John the Baptist's parents. In His reference to God's covenant with Levi, *Malachi* or מלאכי *My Angel* states that God desires godly offspring, and here we have descendants of Aaron who are apparently too aged to have children, too aged to pass on the priestly covenant of Levi; however, God's desire, as recorded by *Malachi* or מלאכי *My Angel* , would come to fruition as it did with Adam, the first human High Priest.

> Luke 1:8: Once when Zechariah's division was on duty and he was serving as priest before God, he was chosen by lot, according to the custom of the priesthood, to go into the temple of the Lord and burn incense. And when the time for the burning of incense came, all the assembled worshipers were praying out-

side. Then an ANGEL of the Lord appeared to him, standing at the right side of the altar of incense. When Zechariah saw him, he was startled and was gripped with fear.

Again, מלאכי Malachi means *my angel*. In Zechariah's day, The Second Temple was Sadducean. That is, the Sadducees were the Levites at that time. "The Sadducees say that there is no resurrection, and that there are neither angels nor spirits..." (Acts 23:8). Certainly, the church Zechariah was amidst did not revere the Text enough to conduct its life by it; but, certainly this church enjoyed the Scriptural provision of the tithe enough to grow wealthy by it.

Malachi 2:8-14: "But you have turned from The Way and by your teaching have caused many to stumble; you have violated the covenant with Levi," says the LORD Almighty. "So I have caused you to be despised and humiliated before all the people, because you have not followed my ways but have shown partiality in matters of the law." Do we not all have one Father? Did not one God create us? Why do we profane the covenant of our ancestors by being unfaithful to one another? Judah has been unfaithful. A detestable thing has been committed in Israel and in Jerusalem: Judah has desecrated the sanctuary the LORD loves by marrying women who worship a foreign god. As for the man who does this, whoever he may be, may the LORD remove him from the tents of Jacob — even though he brings an offering to the LORD Almighty. Another thing you do: You flood the LORD's altar with tears. You weep and wail because he no longer looks with favor on your offerings or accepts them with pleasure from your hands. You ask, "Why?" It is because the LORD is the witness between you and the wife of your youth. You have been unfaithful to her, though she is your partner, the wife of your marriage covenant.

Luke 20:27-40: Some of the Sadducees [the Levites of that time], who say there is no resurrection, came to Jesus with a question. "Teacher," they said, "Moses wrote for us that if a man's brother dies and leaves a wife but no children, the man must marry the widow and raise up offspring for his brother. Now there were seven brothers. The first one married a woman and died childless. The second and then the third married her, and in the same way the seven died, leaving no children. Finally, the woman died too. Now then, at the resurrection whose wife will she be, since the seven were married to her?"

The scenario of the seven husbands is from the Book of Tobit (3:8) found in the Apocrypha. The Levites were an aristocratic group who attempted to Hellenize the Torah, and one of their most enduring marks in this matter is the Greek version of the Hebrew Scriptures, accompanied by the Apocrypha, thus the Tobit scenario. By the time of Christ, the Sadducees (Levites) discarded beliefs in the spirits, but they retained the scenario of the seven husbands for the purposes of their argument. Ironically, Christ responded also with a reference to the Apocrypha and reasserted the reality of angels:

> Jesus replied, "The people of this age marry and are given in marriage. But those who are considered worthy of taking part in the age to come and in the resurrection from the dead will neither marry nor be given in marriage, and they can no longer die; for they are like the angels. They are God's children, since they are children of the resurrection. But in the account of the burning bush, even Moses showed that the dead rise, for he calls the Lord 'the God of Abraham, and the God of Isaac, and the God of Jacob.' He is not the God of the dead, but of the living, for to him all are alive." Some of the teachers of the law responded, "Well said, teacher!" And no one dared to ask him any more questions (Luke 20:27-40).

4 Maccabees 7:19 states,

> But perhaps some might say, "It is not all who conquer passions, as all do not possess wise reasoning. But they who have meditated upon religion with their whole heart, these alone can master the passions of the flesh: they who believe that to God they die not; for, as our forefathers, Abraham, Isaac, Jacob, they live to God."

It would seem as if Christ caught the reference to the Apocryphal book of Tobit regarding marriage and the resurrection, and He responded with an Apocryphal allusion after, it would seem, denouncing the Apocrypha as Scripture.

Mark 12:18-27 states,

> Then the Sadducees, who say there is no resurrection, came to him with a question. "Teacher," they said, "Moses wrote for us that if a man's brother dies and leaves a wife but no children, the man must marry the widow and raise up offspring for his brother. Now there were seven brothers. The first one married and died without leaving any children. The second one married

the widow, but he also died, leaving no child. It was the same with the third. In fact, none of the seven left any children. Last of all, the woman died too. At the resurrection whose wife will she be, since the seven were married to her?" Jesus replied, "Are you not in error because you do not know the Scriptures or the power of God? When the dead rise, they will neither marry nor be given in marriage; they will be like the angels in heaven. Now about the dead rising — have you not read in the Book of Moses, in the account of the burning bush, how God said to him, 'I am the God of Abraham, the God of Isaac, and the God of Jacob'? He is not the God of the dead, but of the living. You are badly mistaken!"

The point is that Levi was in covenant with God regarding the Right of the Firstborn, i.e. the privilege to officiate at the altar, and the profanation of this covenant is, of course, directly analogous to adultery, as is observed in the fact that the penalty for abusing the Eucharist is penalized the same as the Torah's prescription for adultery. A wife is her husband's alter upon which life is poured out in holy libation. The Levites of John the Baptist's Father's time had profaned the Temple and divorced their wives indiscriminantly; they were adamantly denounced by the Qumran sect for doing so. The religious profanation of the Levitical mandates is a type of marital pollution, and so we have observed above the Levites (Sadducees) ironically challenging the resurrection from the dead by using a marital illustration. Fittingly, the unvowelled letters עלה spell *to ascend* (the resurrection of which Christ spoke) and *burnt offering* (for which the Levites/Sadducees were commissioned). Zechariah was surrounded by a church who did not regard the written Word of God as it should have, even to the extent that it did not believe in the very angel who appeared in it to Zechariah; "When Zechariah saw him [the angel], he was startled and was gripped with fear" (Luke 1:8). "'Behold, I send My מלאך *angel*, and he will prepare the way before Me. And the Lord, whom you seek, will suddenly come to His temple, even the מלאך *angel* of the covenant, in whom you delight. Behold, He is coming,' says the LORD of hosts. But who can endure the day of His coming? And who can stand when He appears? For HE IS LIKE A REFINER'S FIRE AND LIKE LAUNDERERS' SOAP [I.E. HE IS SHINING, RE-SPLENDENT, ENLIGHTENING, the very definition of "Aaron" and "serpent"]" (Malachi 3:1-2).

Luke 1:13-14: But the angel said to him: "Do not be afraid, Zechariah; your prayer has been heard. Your wife Elizabeth will bear you a son, and you are to call him John. He will be a joy and delight to you, and many will rejoice because of his birth, for he will be great in the sight of the Lord."

Zechariah, it would seem, was practicing the faith of Abraham as a Levite by praying that, even though his wife's body and his body were "as good as dead" (Hebrews 11:10-12), he would be able to sire a son in order to pass on the priestly inheritance. Zechariah, a Levite, practiced the faith of Abraham (Levi's great-grandfather before any "Jews" walked the earth), and thus, "Even Levi, who receives tithes, PAID TITHES through Abraham, so to speak" (Hebrews 7:9).

> Malachi 3:3-12: He will sit as a refiner and a purifier of silver; He will purify the sons of Levi [as we see with Zechariah and his eventual son, John the Baptist] and purge them as GOLD AND SILVER, that they may offer to the LORD an OFFERING IN RIGHTEOUSNESS. Then the OFFERING of Judah and Jerusalem will be pleasant to the LORD, AS IN THE DAYS OF OLD, AS IN FORMER YEARS... [as in the time of Melchizedek and Abraham]. "... Yet from the days of your fathers you have gone away from My ordinances and have not kept them. Return to Me, and I will return to you," says the LORD of hosts. "But you said, 'In what way shall we return?' Will a man rob God? Yet you have robbed Me! But you say, 'In what way have we robbed You?' In tithes and offerings. You are cursed with a curse, for you have robbed Me, even this whole nation. Bring all the tithes into the storehouse, that there may be food in My house, and try Me now in this," says the LORD of hosts, "if I will not open for you the windows of heaven and pour out for you such blessing that there will not be room enough to receive it. And I will rebuke the devourer for your sakes, so that he will not destroy the fruit of your ground, nor shall the VINE fail to bear fruit for you in the field," Says the LORD of hosts; "And all nations will call you blessed, for you will be a delightful land," Says the LORD of hosts.

We may observe the paralleling of "vine" and "wine":

> Luke 1:14b-17: He is never to take WINE or other fermented drink, and he will be filled with the Holy Spirit even before he is born. He will bring back many of the people of Israel to the Lord their God. And he will go on before the Lord, in the spirit and power of Elijah, to turn the hearts of the parents to their children and the disobedient to the wisdom of the righteous—to make ready a people prepared for the Lord.

Malachi 4:4-6: Remember the Law of Moses, My servant, which I commanded him in Horeb for all Israel, with the statutes and judgments. Behold, I WILL SEND YOU ELIJAH the prophet before the coming of the great and dreadful day of the LORD....

Zecariah was promised the miraculous conception and birth of his son, John the Baptist, and Malachi prophesied this pointedly when he penned, "Behold, I will send you Elijah":

Matthew 3:7-15: As they departed, Jesus began to say to the multitudes concerning John: "What did you go out into the wilderness to see? A reed shaken by the wind? But what did you go out to see? A man clothed in soft garments? Indeed, those who wear soft clothing are in kings' houses. But what did you go out to see? A prophet? Yes, I say to you, and more than a prophet. For this is he of whom it is written: 'Behold, I send My messenger [מלאכי my angel, Malachi] before Your face, who will prepare Your way before You [Malachi 3:1].' Assuredly, I say to you, among those born of women there has not risen one greater than John the Baptist; but he who is least in the king- dom of heaven is greater than he. And from the days of JOHN THE BAPTIST until now the kingdom of heaven suffers violence, and the violent take it by force. For all the prophets and the law prophesied until John. And if you are willing to receive it, HE IS ELIJAH who is to come. He who has ears to hear, let him hear!'"

Christ Himself quoted Malachi's reference to Elijah regarding John the Baptist, and the Book of Malachi seeks to revive the Levitical covenant that had been disregarded, and this revival, it would seem, came about through Elijah (John the Baptist) who proclaimed the בשר *successful birth, proclamtion of good news, Gospel, flesh* of the abeyant טליא *Lamb, Male Child* of Abraham's utterance (Genesis 22:8) prior to the living sacrifice of Isaac (Genesis 22:11) and the dead sacrifice of the Ram wearing the crown of thorns (Genesis 22:13) on the very location that became the threshing floor (2 Samuel 24:18-25) upon which the Temple was constructed: "In those days John the Baptist came preaching in the wilderness of Judea, and saying, 'Repent, for the kingdom of heaven is at hand!' For this is he who was spoken of by the prophet Isaiah, saying: 'The voice of one crying in the wilderness: Prepare the way of the Lord; Make His paths straight.' ... But when he saw many of the Pharisees and Sadducees coming to his baptism, he said to them, 'Brood of vipers! Who warned you to flee from the wrath to come? Therefore bear fruits worthy of repentance, and do not think to say to yourselves, 'We have Abraham as our father.' For I say to you that God is able to raise up children to Abraham from these stones. And even now the ax is laid to the root of the trees. Therefore every tree which does not bear good fruit is cut down and thrown into the fire. I indeed baptize you with water unto repentance, but He who is coming after me is mightier than I, whose sandals I am not worthy to carry. He will baptize you with the Holy Spirit and fire. His WINNOWING FAN IS in His hand, and He will thoroughly clean out His THRESHING FLOOR, and gather His wheat into the barn; but He will burn up the chaff with unquenchable fire.'" The Lamb Abraham anticipated said, "Your father Abraham rejoiced to see My day, and he saw it and was glad" (John 8:56), and a "ram," not the "Lamb" was sacrificed upon the location that became a threshing floor that, eventually, founded the First Temple where "... David lifted his eyes and saw the angel of the Lord standing between earth and heaven, having in his hand A DRAWN SWORD stretched out over Jerusalem" (I Chronicles 21:16). Similarly,

> Malachi 4:4-6: Remember the Law of Moses, My servant, which I commanded him בחרבב *in Horeb* [or בחרב *with a sword*] for all Israel, with the statutes and judgments. Behold, I will send you Elijah the prophet before the coming of the great and dreadful day of the LORD. And he will turn the hearts of the fathers to the children, and the hearts of the children to their fathers [Luke 1:17: "He will also go before Him in the spirit and power of Elijah, 'to turn the hearts of the fathers to the children,'"], Lest I come and strike the earth with a curse.

as it happened in David's day when he violated the Law by taking the census and by inducing the plague against the land. Consider: "Remember the Law of Moses, My servant, which I commanded him בחרב *in Horeb* [or בחרב *with a sword*] for all Israel, with the statutes and judgments," for the reader may observe that the celestial lights played a part in Salvation's war in Joshua 10 and the Commander of The Lord's צבא *Host (Celestial Bodies, Heavenly Luminaries, Army)* appeared to Israel's commander in Joshua 5. The illustration discussed previously concerning the "silence" of the sun (a shining one) appears to be paralleled by Zechariah's silence:

> Luke 1:18-20: Zechariah asked the angel, "How can I be sure of this? I am an old man and my wife is well along in years." The angel said to him, "I am Gabriel. I stand in the presence of God, and I have been sent to speak to you and to tell you this good news. And now you will be silent and not able to speak until the day this happens, because you did not believe my words, which will come true at their appointed time..."

time, of course, being kept by the celestial luminaries, the shining ones that "speak" despite the fact that humanity struggles to "hear," or comprehend, the message: "The heavens declare the glory of God; and the firmament shows His handiwork. Day unto day utters speech, and night unto night reveals knowledge. There is no speech nor language where their voice is not heard. Their voice goes out through all the earth, and their words to the end of the world..." (Psalm 19:1-4). Zechariah's silence was probably mandated as protection for both Zechariah and particularly John so that his own astonishment did not jeopardize John's birth from the indignance of the Sadducees who did not believe in the miracle Zechariah was about to receive; this explains why Elizabeth, "hid herself five months" (Luke 1:24-25), for when Herod discovered that Jesus, John's cousin, had been proclaimed King by Judea's former captors, he sought to kill Christ. The parallel births of John and Christ show how both sets of parents had to flee the Levites and the Judahites (for John descended from Levi and Christ descended from Judah) on account of the rulers of the Levites specifically and the Judean province generally. Judea was once the Kingdom of Judah, and this kingdom comprised 1/6 of the tribes: Judah and Levi. Both Elizabeth and Mary went into hiding to have their children born successfully, and both of these righteous ladies had their sons killed by the elite of Judea. Zechariah's compelled silence was probably a provision to secure John's successful birth, and the letters אדם mean both *Adam* and *I will be silent*. Again, time was kept by the celestial luminaries, the shining ones that "speak" despite the fact that humanity struggles to "hear" the message; the Magi received the star, and Zechariah received the angel, though he did not initially receive the angel's message. Remember that "Eden" is also related to "time" in Chaldee, for, in the Book of Daniel, a form of the letters that spell "Eden" is rendered "time"; it may prove beneficial to consider "gestation" as a parallel to "time" regarding the fulfillment of God's Word.

> Luke 1:59-64 " On the eighth day they came to circumcise the child, and they were going to name him after his father Zechariah, but his mother spoke up and said, 'No! He is to be called John.' They said to her, 'There is no one among your relatives who has that name.' Then they made signs to his father, to find out what he would like to name the child.' He asked for a writing tablet, and to everyone's astonishment he wrote, 'His name is John.' Immediately his mouth was opened and his tongue set free, and he began to speak, praising God. All the neighbors were filled with awe, and throughout the hill country of Judea people were talking about all these things. Everyone who heard

this wondered about it, asking, 'What then is this child going to be?' For the Lord's hand was with him."

Eyes can easily be blinded by confusing the symbol and its subject so that the symbol takes on a life it was only intended to reflect. Surely, we humans struggle to understand since we allowed our spiritual eyes to be opened (gouged out) by the Shining One (Satan). Surely the only remedy for the plight we unleashed upon ourselves is to have the veil lifted by Christ, i.e. to have our spiritual sight restored. How hilarious it is to consider the fact that the people "made signs" to Zechariah since he was mute, not deaf.... At this point, we may observe Zechariah, with positively spiritually opened eyes.

> Luke 1:68-79: His father Zechariah was filled with the Holy Spirit and prophesied: "Praise be to the Lord, the God of Israel, because He has come to his people and redeemed them. He has raised up a horn of salvation for us in the house of His servant David (as he said through his holy prophets of long ago), salvation from our enemies and from the hand of all who hate us — to show mercy to our ancestors and to remember His holy covenant, the oath he swore to our father Abraham: to rescue us from the hand of our enemies, and to enable us to serve Him without fear in holiness and righteousness before Him all our days. And you, my child, will be called a prophet of the Most High; for you will go on before the Lord to prepare The Way for him, to give His people the knowledge of salvation through the forgiveness of their sins, because of the tender mercy of our God, by which the rising sun will come to us from heaven to shine on those living in darkness and in the shadow of death, to guide our feet into the path of peace."

At this point, in the narrative of Luke, one would naturally expect that Zechariah's flowing praise and exultation would come to completion by his son assuming his Levitical inheritance and serving in the Temple proper. One would expect the Temple proper to be cleansed immediately with the teaching of John, son of Zechariah, descendant of Aaron—but no! We read a breath-taking, explosive statement:

> Luke 1:80: "And the child grew and became strong in spirit; and he LIVED IN THE WILDERNESS until he appeared publicly to Israel."

He lived among the Qumran sect? After an angel appeared in the Temple, in a church who did not believe in angels, after a notable miracle concerning birth, like that of Abraham and Isaac occurred before the Temple community, after Zechariah finally was given his heart's desire by siring an heir to the inheritance of Levi, Zechariah sent his son as spiritually far away from the Temple and its order to the Temple's most bitter detractors, the desert communities of Qumran. What disregard for the Temple order! What boldness this must have been when put in writing and addressed to the High Priest, Theophilus! Amazingly, the name Gabriel means both Warrior of God and Male Infant of God. When *Malachi* (which means *My Angel, My Messenger*) states that the priest "is the מלאך *messenger/angel* of the Lord" (2:7), we can understand how Zechariah (an old man) was a priest (angel) of the Lord who conversed with *Gabriel (Strong Man, Male Baby of God)* who was an angel (priest) like Zechariah; they were reflections of each other; Gabriel prophesied concerning the future Male Infant of God (John, Zechariah' future son) and thus served as a reflection of time (in that time was reversed) for Zechariah whose elderly countenance beheld the Male Infant/Warrior of God (Gabriel) speak of his own image and likeness (John). To tell the Temple Levites of this would be to violate their lack of belief in angels which would be apparently substantiated to the public if they eliminated Elizabeth or her fruit, John. It would therefore seem that Gabriel, in order to protect John, silenced Zechariah long enough for his wife to go into seclusion, give birth, and deliver John to the other Levites at Qumran who were the familial hostiles of a Temple that was hostile to its own infant family who was miraculously sired.

Leviticus provides the directives for the priesthood, and Malachi chastised the Levites after they became polluted — a pollution that nearly permeated from the time of Malachi until the time of Zechariah and then to Theophilus. Since the Qumran community comprised many disposessed Levite priests, it may be that Zechariah sent John to live with relatives who would protect John's life so that the Temple Levites did not assasinate the child in order conceal the notable miracle that occurred, which they refused to accept doctrinally — for the very same situation occurred regarding Christ's miracles in Matthew 12 and Mark 3 when the Pharisees sought to "destroy" Jesus because of his miracle. Again,

> ...Therefore EVERY TREE WHICH DOES NOT BEAR GOOD FRUIT IS CUT DOWN AND THROWN INTO THE FIRE. I indeed baptize you with water unto repentance, but He who is coming after me is mightier than I, whose sandals I am not worthy to carry. He will baptize you with the Holy Spirit and fire. His winnowing fan is in His hand, and HE WILL THOROUGHLY CLEAN OUT HIS THRESH- ING FLOOR [His Temple, for the Temple was built upon a thresh-

ing floor], and gather His wheat into the barn; but He will burn up the chaff with unquenchable fire" (Matthew 3:8-12).

Seeing that an unfruitful tree being razed is compared to the Temple being cleansed, we notice the same pattern in Mark 11 where Christ curses the fig tree, cleanses the temple, and then returns to behold the dead tree; this pattern is preceded by little children proclaiming Christ as king; consider the proclomation of Christ as king when He Himself was a child and had His life threatened because of that very proclamation.

It would seem that the inspired writer of Luke took the Book of Malachi on one hand, and the history of John the Baptist on the other, observed how they aligned prophetically, and wrote an enlightening invective, but hopeful defense and witness, to the highest religious order of Judea at the time. Such a denunciation documented how one of their own gave his only son for the sake of humanity, an only son who had eyes open enough to say "Behold the Lamb of God Who takes away the sin of the world!" (John 1:29). The Aramaic word טליא(Hebrew: טלה *lamb*) can mean both a *child* and a *lamb*; "And Abraham said, 'My son, God will provide for Himself the lamb for a burnt offering.' So the two of them went together" (Genesis 22:8). Our English word "resurrection" is a translation of the Greek αν–αστασις *a raising up* and is equivalent to the Hebrew עלה *to ascend* from where עלה *burnt offering* is derived. Genesis 22:8 can also be rendered, " 'My son, God will provide for Himself a Lamb for resurrection.' And the two of them proceeded as one," i.e. the Sacrificer and the Sacrifice proceeded as an Offering and the Resurrection, for Christ is blatantly identified as the Sin Offering in 2 Corinthians 5:2: "For He made Him who knew no sin *to be* αμαρτιαν = חטא *Sin Offering* for us, that we might become the righteousness of God in Him"; thus, "Behold the טליא*Lamb, Male Child, Son of God* Who takes away the חטא *sin* of the world!" (John 1:29). That is, the word חטא can mean both *sin* and *sin offering* (i.e. antithetically both *sin* and its *remedy*). We, therefore, see that John was probably saying, "Behold the Holy Child of God (who is the αμαρτιαν = חטא *Sin Offering*) Who takes away the αμαρτιαν = חטא *sin of the world*." Yes, it would seem as if the so-called "Greek New Testament" is really a Greek riddle concerning the Hebrew Renewal of the Hidden Covenant (regarding a Holy Male Child) that was renewed in Christ — which is why the Greek Narrative seems to be employing Hebrew linguistic concepts. After Christ was baptized, the Title of the "Holy Child" (Acts 4:30), the "Son of God," was affirmed: "And the Holy Spirit descended in bodily form like a dove upon Him, and a voice came from heaven which said, 'You are My beloved Son; in You I am well pleased'" (Luke 3:22).

John, a Levite who called his own Levite brethren "vipers" (Matthew 3:7), identified the Sin Offering Who Is Himself the High Priestעולם *forever, of old, hidden* [~ Male Child], according to the order of Melchizedek to whom Abraham tithed, just before he baptized Him in the River. The term "baptism" simply means "to immerse," but it was employed by the Judeans to signify conversion and ritual purity which they made synonymous with the term "born again" or regeneration, renewing, i.e. the Renewed Covenant (errantly called the "New Testament"). The term "Gospel" was employed to announce the new reign of a ruler and to declare royal birthdays. Accordingly, Psalm 110 says,

> The LORD said to my Lord, "Sit at My right hand, till I make Your enemies Your footstool." The LORD shall send the rod of Your strength out of Zion. Rule in the midst of Your enemies! Your people shall be volunteers in the day of Your power; in the beauties of holiness, from the womb of the morning, You have the dew of Your youth. The LORD has sworn and will not relent, "You are a priest forever according to the order of Melchizedek." The Lord is at Your right hand; He shall execute kings in the day of His wrath. He shall judge among the nations, He shall fill the places with dead bodies, He shall execute the heads of many countries. He shall drink of the river by the wayside; therefore He shall lift up the head.

Again,

> The LORD said to my Lord, "Sit at My right hand, till I make Your enemies Your footstool." The LORD shall send the rod of Your strength out of Zion. Rule in the midst of Your enemies! Your people shall be volunteers in the day of Your power ["And the Holy Spirit descended in bodily form like a dove upon Him, and a voice came from heaven which said, 'You are My beloved Son; in You I am well pleased'." (Luke 3:22).]; in the beauties of holiness, from the womb of the morning, You have the dew of Your youth [baptism, being born again]. The LORD has sworn and will not relent, "You are a priest forever according to the order of Melchizedek." [The Gospel of the New/Renewed Ruler] The Lord is at Your right hand; He shall execute kings in the day of His wrath. He shall judge among the nations, He shall fill the places with dead bodies, He shall execute the heads of many countries. He shall drink of the river [Christ was being baptized in the river] by the wayside; therefore He shall *lift up the head* [an Egyptian expression meaning *to resurrect* that is rendered in the Hebrew of the Book of Numbers as *take a census* – irony,

considering the Infant Christ came to Bethlehem on account of a census].

John the Baptist, a Levite, a descendant of Aaron, proclaimed the Son of God, the Lamb of God, as the One who takes away the חטא *sin* of the world, חטא *The Sin Offering*. John's father, Zechariah, gave his son by removing him from the false Levites, the Sadducees, the Brood of Vipers along with the Pharisees. When we consider the corrupt Temple in Zechariah' time, the fact that Zechariah' wife's name, Elizabeth, means "Oath of My God," and the Sin Offering followed by the Guilt Offering and the עלה *Burnt Offering, the Resurrection*, we may observe the parallel, the parable, the riddle in Leviticus 5:21-26:

> And the Lord spoke to Moses, saying: "If a person sins and commits a trespass against the LORD by lying to his neighbor about what was delivered to him for safekeeping, or about a pledge [oath], or about a robbery [Malachi 3:8; Luke 19:46], or if he has extorted from his neighbor, or if he has found what was lost and lies concerning it, and swears [oath] falsely—in any one of these things that a man may do in which he sins: then it shall be, because he has sinned and is guilty, that he shall restore what he has stolen, or the thing which he has extorted, or what was delivered to him for safekeeping, or the lost thing which he found, or all that about which he has sworn [oath] falsely. He shall restore its full value, add one-fifth more to it, and give it to whomever it belongs, on the day of his trespass offering. And he shall bring his trespass offering to the LORD, a ram without blemish from the flock [Consider the ram crowned with thorns that Abraham and Isaac sacrificed in Genesis 22 instead of the Lamb whom God provided and whom John the Baptist announced], with your valuation, as a trespass offering, to the priest. So the priest shall make atonement for him before the LORD, and he shall be forgiven for any one of these things that he may have done in which he trespasses.'"
> "Then the LORD spoke to Moses, saying, 'Command Aaron and his sons, saying, 'This *is* the law of the עלה *burnt offering* [= αναστασις *ascending, resurrection*]: The burnt offering shall be on the hearth upon the altar all night until morning, and the fire of the altar shall be kept burning on it. And the priest shall put on his linen garment, and his linen trousers he shall put on his body, and take up the ashes of the burnt offering which the fire has consumed on the altar, and he shall put them beside the altar. Then he shall take off his garments, put on other gar-

ments, AND CARRY THE ASHES OUTSIDE THE CAMP TO A CLEAN PLACE." "For I *am* the LORD, I do not change; therefore you are not consumed, O sons of Jacob, (Malachi 3:6)." "Jesus Christ *is* the same yesterday, today, and forever. Do not be carried about with various and strange doctrines. For it is good that the heart be established by grace, not with foods which have not profited those who have been occupied with them. We have an altar from which those who serve the tabernacle have no right to eat. For the bodies of those animals, whose blood is brought into the sanctuary by the high priest for sin, ARE BURNED OUTSIDE THE CAMP. Therefore Jesus also, that He might sanctify the people with His own blood, suffered OUTSIDE THE GATE. Therefore let us go forth to Him, OUTSIDE THE CAMP, bearing His reproach. For here we have no continuing city, but we seek the one to come. Therefore by Him let us continually offer the sacrifice of praise to God, that is, the fruit of our lips, giving thanks to His name. But do not forget to do good and to share, for with such SACRIFICES God is well pleased." (Hebrews 13:8-16).

Zechariah, the father of John the Baptist, chose to proceed in direct opposition to the religious (and antibiblical) expectation and authority of his day in order to follow the Written Word of God. The first chapter of the Book of Luke is both a bold and a subtle account against the highest officially religious order of that time. A Judean of Luke's time had to confront the possibility of being entirely incorrect regarding all that he was taught concerning religious devotion and Scriptural thinking... and he was provided with a Book that begins with an example of a Levite who was faced with similar circumstances and who overcame by the grace of God. Concluding this brief discussion of fruitful wombs, children, serpents, and Eden, it is advantageous to observe the following:

> Nebuchadnezzar the king of Babylon has devoured me, he has crushed me; he has made me an empty vessel, he has swallowed me up like a serpent; he has filled his stomach with מעדני *my Eden, my delicacies*, he has spit me out (Jeremiah 51:34).

Notice that Jeremiah 51:34 discusses a "serpent" eating, destroying "Eden," for the name "Eden" indicates "Fertility." The Fertility of Elizabeth and Mary was divinely protected, the one concerning a father's silence, the other concerning the Son of Adam. Again, the letters אדם can mean both *Adam* and *I will be silent*. After beholding the tangled mess of the conflicting Judean sects and their constant wrangling to the point of innocent bloodshed, we can grasp firmly the fact that normative or "Orthodox" Judaism did not exist at this time, but the term "Orthodox Judaism" came to designate the remaining Pharisees following 70 AD. At this point, it should be more than clear that "Christianity" did not derive from "Judaism," so the term "Judeo-Christian" is altogether fallacious and henceforth inadmissable. Let us review one final example of why "Hebrew," "Israelite," and "Jew" are not synonymous terms.

The word עברי *Hebrew* comes from the root עבר *to pass over, to forgive, to enter, to shave (i.e. to appear as a child reborn),* and *to become pregnant*. The word הר *mountain* or הרה *mountain* is, consonantally, spelled the same as הרה *pregnant with child,* which is from the root הרה *to conceive, to implant with seed,* and relates to the idea of teaching just as the root לקח *to take, to marry* produces the word לקח *doctrine, instruction.* In short, a mountain is a physical illustration of a womb, and it is spelled similarly to words denoting conception both mentally and physically as can be seen unified in the root לקח. To a Hebrew, marriage and doctrine (with respect to training) were two sides of one face, for even the term "Hebrew" derived from the threshold covenant of pregnancy. Particularly with respect to what we English-speakers call a "vine" and what in Hebrew may be called a גפן *vine,* a עץ גפן *vine-tree,* or a עץ *tree,* we may understand how both a mountain and a tree are linked to "conception" both mentally and physically: the letters עצה can mean both *tree* and *counsel,* which are synonymous to the root לקח *to marry,* which produces the word לקח *doctrine, instruction,* and vines were trained (instructed) upon fruit-trees or trellises and on the sides of terraced mountains. It can be seen that a mountain and a tree can both indicate fertility in that one is illustrative of fruitful convection that ensconses riches to be mined while the other is physically generative regarding fruit to be harvested. Furthermore, the process of training vines to other fruit-trees or to crosses, stakes, and other forms of trellises is called, in the end, a "wedding" or a "marriage," which illustrates more of why Christ designated Himself the "True Vine" following His wedding-supper of Holy Communion just prior to being united to the cross covered with the blood of grapes. Surely Abraham's constructive sacrifice of Isaac, followed by his destructive sacrifice of the ram, are prefigurations of both types of sacrifice being united in Christ, The Lamb God provided.

Abraham was a type of vine, for he was pruned in order to bear positively covenantal fruit. As vines bind trees, so Abraham bound Isaac. We can comprehend why Christ discussed the bindings of death when, regarding Lazarus, He said, "Loose him, and let him go," (John 11:44), for such bindings were once understood as illustrations of death negatively. We may grasp the death/binding (pythonic) figure when we notice that Hebrews 11:19 refers to such a binding as death itself: God "...was able to raise him [Isaac] up, even from the dead; from whence also he received him in a παραβολη *parable*" (Hebrews 11:19). "Binding," like "sacrifice," can be both positive and negative — negative as in the example described immediately above, positive in that a priest (a sacrificer) was said to be "bound" (לוה) to God in a union that can be illustrated by marriage (whether man and a woman, God and humanity, or two trees provided that one is what we call a "vine" in English). Working backwards, we can see that circumcision is a type of pruning since the word ערל *unpruned* also means *uncircumcised*; in fact, this word can further mean *forbidden*, so an unpruned vine is, by definition, a forbidden tree... for we must keep in mind that vines can unify with other trees maritally, and such a union is called דעת *knowledge* (Genesis 4:1) just as the root לקח *to marry* yields the word לקח *instruction*. Vines left unpruned luxuriate themselves and strive for height against other trees; however, circumcised vines are humbled by the blade that causes them to consider their perpetuity threatened and subsequently induces them to produce fruit. "Abram" means "Father of Height" (like an unpruned vine) and this was his name prior to Isaac. "Abraham" means "Father of Multitudes" (like a fruitful and therefore pruned vine), and he was only told to circumcise his foreskin after he knew Hagar, the Egyptian. Having accorded with the human law and custom of his time and geography, his physical firstborn was not to be the ceremonial Firstborn, the one who possessed the right to officiate at the altar; as an indicator of this human misconception, Abraham had his vine pruned as a sign of the fruitful multiplicity that would extend through Isaac. The vine-science hidden throughout Abraham's story climaxes upon a mountain, and a mountain (an illustration of a womb) was used to epitomize the spiritual pruning, with the fire and the blade (like a gimlet and like the "flame of the sword" at Eden's gate) of Abraham, that necessarily prefigured the Lamb and the thicket twined about His own head like a Roman victor's crown that indicated symbolically the rewardable exploit which is in this case the triumph over the "thorns and thistles" that resulted from the accursed soil of bloody sacrifice as opposed to unbloody sacrifice. The Book of Galatians provides ample examples of these principles.

What we now call the third chapter of the Book of Galatians, we may observe what many consider to be a dichotomy of "faith" and "law," though I find this apparent dichotomy incorrect. We have already noted that that the Greek πιστις *faith, trust, pledge* is often a translation of the Hebrew אמנה *covenant, pledge*; so, the problem exists that the Greek "pledge" is often forgotten in favor of a "belief" alone, and this is flagrantly errant since James 2:19 plainly states, "...Even the demons πιστευουσιν *believe* — and shudder." Since the demons have πιστις *faith*, that is, since the demons "believe" but work opposite of God's אמנה *covenant, pledge*, they are not in God's אמנה *covenant, pledge* but outside of it despite their belief in Him and shuddering reverence for Him. James 2:26 states, "As the body without the spirit is dead, so πιστις *faith* without works is dead," which, when translated back to Hebrew, would communicate, "As the body without the spirit is dead, so covenant without vindication is dead," and this makes the body the covenant and the spirit the vindication of the pledge. Covenants anticipate and require fruit production; with respect to gestation, blood is spilled into the threshold in order to provide a vitalizing sign of the anticipated offspring. Works are here paralleled to the animation of the oath to the death which is itself a body, and the image constructed here makes perfect sense when the referential threshold is kept in mind since sacrifices were cut over the threshold altar in covenant. Again, the animated and animating works of the body are the fruits, the children, for "wisdom is justified by her εργων *works*" (Matthew 11:19) and "wisdom is justified by her τεκνων *children*" (Luke 7:35). We can see that *a work is a child, a work is a fruit*. A fruit is a work and a work is a child, for the noun עבד *servant, slave* also means *son*, and it is translated by the Greek εργον *works* in Matthew 11:19 that is clarified by the word τεκνων *children* in Luke 7:35. The body is the sign of the oath to the death (Greek "faith," Hebrew "covenant"), and the spirit is the vital principle that animates it (the works, the children, the fruit necessary to validate the covenant) as the first command to "Be fruitful and multiply" demands: "Therefore a man shall leave his father and mother and BE JOINED ב *with / through* his wife, and they shall become ONE flesh" (Genesis 2:24); "But did He not make them ONE, having a remnant of the Spirit? And why ONE? He seeks godly offspring" (Malachi 2:14-15). The covenant is kept alive through the sustentation of its stipulations, just as the body is kept alive through the sustentation of its spirit, particulary as expressed through children. Such sustentation is expressed in the fruit that the covenant anticipates, for the covenant of a man and wife clinging to God in marriage produces a mountain (womb) and a threshold (altar, ziggurat) upon which one may receive the blessing (the child). Again, the word הר *mountain* or הרה *mountain* is, consonantally, spelled the same a הרה *pregnant with child* which is from the root הרה to *conceive, to implant with seed*, and relates to the idea of teaching just as the root לקח *to take, to marry, which* produces the word לקח *doctrine, instruction*: "Now Hagar stands for mount Sinai in Arabia and corresponds to the present city of Jerusalem, because she is in slavery with her children" (Galatians 4:25), for Sinai is where Moses received the Torah, and "Torah" means "instruction." That is, since a "mountain" is related to "pregnancy," and these two are related to "marriage" and "instruction," we may understand why Sinai corresponds to Hagar and the fruit of Hagar's covenant was Ishmael, not Isaac – an argument that makes the "Law of Sin and Death" identified on Sinai analogous to Ishmael, not Isaac who stands as symbol of the "The Law of the Spirit of Life." The veiled face of Moses reflected the "Law of Sin and Death" (Romans 8:2) whereas his unveiled face reflected "The Law of the Spirit of Life in Christ Jesus" (Romans 8:2):

> But if the ministry of death ["Law of Sin and Death"], written and engraved on stones, was glorious, so that the children of Israel could not look steadily at the face of Moses because of the glory of his countenance, which glory was passing away, how will the ministry of the Spirit ["The Law of the Spirit of Life in Christ Jesus"] not be more glorious? For if the ministry of condemnation had glory, the ministry of righteousness exceeds much more in glory. For even what was made glorious had no glory in this respect, because of the glory that excels. For if what is passing away was glorious, what remains is much more glorious. Therefore, since we have such hope, we use great boldness of speech– unlike Moses, who put a veil over his face so that the children of Israel could not look steadily at the end of what was passing away. But their minds were blinded. For until this day the same veil remains unlifted in the reading of the Old Testament, because the veil is taken away in Christ ["The Law of the Spirit of Lie in Christ Jesus"]. But even to this day, when Moses is read, a veil lies on their heart. Nevertheless when one turns to the Lord, the veil is taken away. Now the Lord is the Spirit; and where the Spirit of the Lord is, there is liberty. But we all, with unveiled face, beholding as in a mirror the glory of the Lord, are being transformed into the same image from glory to glory, just as by the Spirit of the Lord (2 Corinthians 3:7-18).

The Sinai Code of Law, the Torah, the Instruction, anticipated the fruit of its fulfillment in the same way that Ishmael stewarded the office of Firstborn physically until the ceremonial Firstborn, designated prior to the birth of Ishmael, was birthed into the right of office: "...the Law was our schoolmaster to bring us unto Christ that we might be justified by πιστεως = אמנה = covenant. But after that πιστεως = אמנה = covenant has come, we are no longer under a schoolmaster," for one requires training and instruction before entering an oath, just as one needs the Sinai Law before entering into communion with Christ. Once we were given Isaac for a teacher, there was no longer a need for Ishmael as our teacher; however, Ishamael was not rendered obsolete, for he was present with Isaac in order to bury Abraham. One must understand Moses in order to understand the covenant of Abraham that continues to point back to the covenantal communion of bread and wine offered up in constructive sacrifice by Melchizedech.

Genesis 15:6 states that Abraham "והאמן *covenanted with, believed in* God, and it was accounted to him for righteousness." It was not simply Abraham's understanding, but his covenant, that was credited, that was vindicated, that was vitalized by the fact that the Messiah would come through his genealogy; this acreditation of righteousness came immediately after God brought Abram out to behold the starry heavens, but it is often taken that it was only God who told Abram that his descendants would be as the stars despite the fact that a covenant has at least two partners, two halves, of which Abram was only one. Literally, Genesis 15:5 reads "He took him outside and said, 'Look up at the sky and count the stars — if indeed you can count them.' ויאמר לו*Then he said to him*, 'So shall be זרעך *your seed*." It has often been assumed singularly that " ויאמר לו *Then He [God] said to him [Abram]*, 'So shall be זרעך *your [Abram's] seed*"; this rendering is not wrong, but it cannot account for the dual meaning of both halves expressed here. Since Hebrew makes no written distinction between upper-case and lower-case letters, this passage could also communicate, " ויאמר לו*Then he [Abram] said to Him [God]*, 'So shall be זרעך *Your seed [God's Seed]*," for Abram was indeed beholding the stars, and the Magi, who came from Abram's original home, sought God's Seed by also beholding the stars: "The promises were spoken to Abraham and to his Seed. Scripture does not say 'and to seeds,' meaning many people, but 'and to your/Your seed/Seed,' meaning one person, who is Christ" (Galatians 3:16). It would seem that Abram said to God what God said to Abram, and these two covenanting parties, these two halves (so to speak), both were anticipating the fruit, the blessing of the covenant, first through Isaac, then through Christ in the fullness of time; thus, "your/Your seed/ Seed" must have referred to Isaac and Christ simultaneously at the time of the covenant and sequentially relative to their respective gestations. We can observe the exact same scenario, even the exact same word (זרעך *your seed*), in 1 Chronicles 17. Nathan communicated that God said, "You are not the one to build me a house to dwell in" (I Chronicles 17:4) and, "I declare to you that the Lord will build a house for you" (1 Chronicles 17:10) i.e. the Lord will give you offspring as is so stated in Exodus 1:21, for He continues, "When your days are over and you go to be with your fathers, I will raise up זרלך *your seed* to succeed you, one of your own sons, and I will establish his kingdom. He is the one who will build a house for me, and I will establish his throne forever. I will be his father, and he will be my son. I will never take my love away from him, as I took it away from your predecessor. I will set him over my house and my kingdom forever; his throne will be established forever" (1 Chronicles 17:10-14). In 1 Chronicles 22, David announces that he took God's oracle to mean Solomon, so he charged Solomon to construct the Temple, and he makes this proclamation public in 1 Chronicles 28. It can be seen, however, that 1 Chronicles 17:10-14 could also be read as "When your days are over and you go to be with your fathers, I will raise up זרעך *your seed* [Christ] to succeed you, one of your own sons ["The Son of David, the Son of Abraham" (Matthew 1:1)], and I will establish His kingdom. He is the one who will build a house for me, and I will establish His throne forever [for Solomon's throne was not forever]. I will be His father, and He will be my son. I will never take my love away from him, as I took it away from your predecessor. I will set Him over my house and my kingdom forever; His throne will be established forever," as it is so stated in Hebrews 1:5-9: "For to which of the angels did God ever say, 'You are my Son; today I have become your Father [Psalm 2:7]'? Or again, 'I will be his Father, and he will be my Son[2 Samuel 7:14; 1 Chronicles 17:13]'? And again, when God brings his firstborn into the world, he says, 'Let all God's angels worship him [Deut. 32:43]' ... about the Son he says, 'YOUR THRONE, O GOD, WILL LAST FOR EVER AND EVER; a scepter of justice will be the scepter of your kingdom. You have loved righteousness and hated wickedness; therefore God, your God, has set you above your companions by anointing you with the oil of joy' [Psalm 45:6,7]." The point being asserted about Abraham's "Seed" is the same as the point concerning David's "Seed," for both references to זרעך *your/Your seed/ Seed* meant immediately Abraham's and David's children, but ultimately Abraham's and David's Savior: "The book of the generation of Jesus Christ, the son of David, the son of Abraham" (Matthew 1:1). Abraham (who was not a Jew) and David (who was a Jew) both can claim that they served in Christ's family line, and so the Gentile and the Jew are united in Christ as it is written, "Abraham will surely become a great and powerful nation, and all גויי הארץ *nations, gentiles on earth* will be blessed through him" (Genesis 18:18). The "blessing" of a covenant is its Fruit born for all regardless of nationality: "Many nations shall be joined to the Lord in that day, and they shall become My people. And I will dwell in your midst. Then you will know that the Lord of hosts has sent Me to you" (Zechariah 2:11). Relative to Abraham, the term "Gentile" is as anachronistic as the term "Jew." The word גוים meant *nations* in Abraham's day and *gentiles* in Paul's day. To speak anachronistically, Abraham was a "gentile" (if you will) since no Jews yet walked the earth BECAUSE THEY HAD NOT YET DESCENDED FROM HIM.

Since we know that the blessing of a covenant is its fruit, let us consider Galatians 3:10: "For all who rely on the works of the law are under a curse, as it is written: 'Cursed is everyone who does not continue to do everything written in the Book of the Law,'" which is a reference to Deuteronomy 27:26. The blessing of a covenant is the fruitful union established by covenant, and the curse of a covenant is the unfruitful separation opted by transgression against the covenant. The covenant is the body, and the works of the covenant constitute the body's spirit, its fruit, its children — as was the case with the covenant that begat Ishmael and the covenant that begat Isaac. When the covenant is in tact, the body is alive and fruitful, but when the covenant is fractured, the body is dead and unfruitful. As such, the curse of the Law indicates the defensive punishment for the transgression against the works, the fruits, and the children of the covenant so that the transgressor necessarily dies; this death would be necessary because breaking a covenant (a pledge of life, for life, with the purpose of perpetuating life) is a silent admission that the transgressor wishes the other covenantor to be dead, which legally breaks an oath to the death. A transgressor breaking covenant is a transgressor wishing death upon the one with whom he is in union so that, in justice, the transgressor is killed for his injustice. Since the covenant is the body, then the covenant being broken is as a body being killed, though, ironically, a ברית *covenant* made necessarily admits a cutting. The "curse" of the Torah takes effect in that no one, other than Christ, has kept "everything" in it, so all, except for Christ, are bound to its curse of death. Since we broke the Law of the Spirit of Life in Christ Jesus, it is as if we made a silent statement that we wish Christ would die in order that we might be free from our oath to the death; אדם means "Adam" and "I will be silent," and Christ died in order to give Adam/humanity hope. The Law of the Sprit of Life is not accursed, but a curse of death awaits one who breaks The Law of Liberty, The Law of the Spirit of Life. Since all of humanity, except Christ, has broken the Law of the Spirit of Life, we are all under the curse and therefore must die because we silently wished Christ's death (and received our bloody wish). The works that the Torah demands are good: "We know that the law [of the Spirit of Life] is good if one uses it properly" (1 Timothy 1:8). Since we are not perfect in keeping the Law of the Spirit of Life (and therefore bear the sentence of death upon us), the only way for us to be saved is to be in covenant with One Who was perfect in keeping it:

As for you, you were DEAD IN YOUR TRANSGRESSIONS and sins, in which you used to live when you followed the ways of this world and of the ruler of the kingdom of the air, the spirit who is now at work in those who are disobedient. All of us also lived among them at one time, gratifying the cravings of our flesh and following its desires and thoughts. Like the rest, we were by nature deserving of wrath. But because of his great love for us, God, who is rich in mercy, made us alive with Christ even when we were DEAD IN TRANSGRESSIONS — it is by grace you have been saved. And God raised us up with Christ and seated us with him in the heavenly realms in Christ Jesus, in order that in the coming ages he might show the incomparable riches of his grace, expressed in his kindness to us in Christ Jesus. For it is by grace you have been saved, through πιστεως = אמנה *covenant* — and this is not from yourselves, it is the gift of God — not by works, so that no one can boast. For we are God's handiwork, CREATED IN CHRIST JESUS TO DO GOOD WORKS, which God prepared in advance for us to do (Ephesians 2:1-10),

for it is evident that "not by works" communicates that our deeds fell short since we were originally "created in Christ to do good works" unfailingly. Since we failed to live perfectly just lives, the covenant would have to be renewed through death (the curse of breaking the covenant) and new life (the blessing according to the vivifying of the covenant). We cannot do enough good works (we cannot have enough children) to be saved without Christ (Who is the Holy Child) because the very fact that we require salvation means that we require "Jesus" whose name means "He saves." We cannot do enough good works (have enough fruit) to be saved without Christ (the "True Vine") since the very fact that we need salvation is evidence that we have already broken the Law (of the Spirit of Life), for it is written that 'Cursed is everyone who does not continue to do everything written in the Book of the Law" (Deuteronomy 27:26) and "For whoever keeps the whole law and yet stumbles at just one point is guilty of breaking all of it" (James 2:10). In order to be the "body" of Christ, we must be His "bride," and in order to be the "bride" of Christ, we have to be the altar upon which He is to officiate as Firstborn for the purposes of renewing and reaffirming His covenant perpetually as can be seen in the succession of offspring, that is, fruit: "...For it is by grace you have been saved, through πιστεως = אמנה *covenant* — and this is not from yourselves, it is the gift of God [being officiated upon] — not by works, so that no one can boast..." [of themselves since they should boast in Christ (1 Corinthians 1:31)] (Ephesians 2:1-10). Christ gave us His body first, which means that He also gave us to be His bride, and this necessitates that we have to become His bride in order to be His body. Christ's gift IS NOT FROM OURSELVES, but TO OURSELVES by His officiation through us. "...For we are God's handiwork, created in Christ Jesus to do good works, which God PREPARED IN ADVANCE for us to do" (Ephesians 2:1-10). Being in covenant with Christ, as His bride, makes us His body. Since Christ's body was cut in covenanant before and after human sin, it was sacrificed destructively (זבח) once but raised in sacrifice constructively (קרבן) forever; as such, we are to be a "living sacrifice," which mandates a constructive sacrifice otherwise considered a "drawing near" to God or a life spent in devotion to God (and this devotion is evidenced by our works, our fruit, our children who are to, in turn, spend their lives in devotion to God). Christ offered us His body in destructive and construc- tive sacrifice, and, if we accept the terms of His covenant, we must be will- ing to lay our lives down in order for Him to raise us up, which elucidates Colossians 1:24: "Now I rejoice in what I am suffering for you, and I fill up in my flesh what is still lacking in regard to Christ's afflictions, for the sake of His body, which is the church," for since Christ offered His flesh to us in order to perpetuate life then, by accepting His covenant, we must offer our flesh to Him in order to vindicate the covenant and receive perpetual life. The husband and the wife are used by God to create the child, and the child is the insignia of perpetuity; in the same way, Christ and the bride are employed by the Father to create rebirth, and this rebirth is the sign of eternity. "Now if we are children, then we are heirs — heirs of God and co- heirs with Christ, if indeed we share in his sufferings in order that we may also share in his glory" (Romans 8:17). "For just as we share abundantly in the sufferings of Christ, so also our comfort abounds through Christ" (2 Corinthians 1:5). "I want to know Christ — yes, to know the power of his resurrection and participation in his sufferings, becoming like him in his death, and so, somehow, attaining to the resurrection from the dead" (Philippians 3:10-11).

> By πιστις = אמנה covenant Abraham obeyed when he was called to go out to the place which he would receive as an inheritance. And he went out, not knowing where he was going. By πιστις = אמנה covenant he dwelt in the land of promise as in a foreign country, dwelling in tents with Isaac and Jacob, the heirs with him of the same promise; for he waited for the city which has foundations, whose builder and maker is God... By πιστις = אמנה covenant Sarah herself also received strength to conceive seed, and she bore a child when she was past the age, be- cause she judged Him faithful who had promised. Therefore from one man, and him AS GOOD AS DEAD, were BORN as many

as the stars of the sky in multitude — innumerable as the sand which is by the seashore. By faith Abraham, when he was tested, offered up Isaac, and he who had received the promises offered up his only begotten son, of whom it was said, 'In Isaac your seed shall be called,' concluding that God was able to raise him up, even from the dead, from which he also received him in a parable (Hebrews 11:8-19).

Abraham believed in, that is, covenanted with God. The children of faith are the children of the covenant, even the children of a non-Jewish man: "Therefore know that only those who are of πιστις = אמנה covenant are sons of Abraham. And the Scripture, foreseeing that God would justify the Gentiles by πιστις = אמנה covenant, preached the gospel to Abraham beforehand, saying, 'In you all the גוים nations, gentiles shall be blessed.' So then those who are of πιστις = אמנה covenant are blessed with believing Abraham" (Galatians 3:6-9). Abraham covenanted with God 430 years prior to Moses receiving the Law (in Isaac) and its reflection (in Ishamel); therefore, covenanting as Abraham did precedes Moses (who recorded or reflected the life of Abraham) and necessitates correct action prior to the necessary realignment for (and therefore reflection of) wrong action. In such an arrangement, we see the initial promise of Isaac prior to Sarai offering Hagar (Sarai's reflection) for the purpose of Ishmael (the reflection of Isaac who was prophesied before Ishamel was born), but Ishmael was born before Isaac (although after the prophecy). The argument, at this point, revolved around the term "firstborn" relative to what could be seen physically, even though the physical is secondary. Since Isaac was promised first, Isaac was intended to assume the ceremonial title of "Firstborn," which is the priestly designation often, but not always, given to the physical firstborn male in a family. Not fully according with or understanding God's Word, Abram and Sarai produced a firstborn according to the flesh through Hagar. The argument, at this point, also revolves around the term "flesh." Since בשר can mean *flesh, good news (gospel), and successful birth*, the question arises as to whom belonged the nomination of "Firstborn of the Flesh." A Firstborn according to the Flesh could be either the first male to emerge from the womb physically or the priest who is to proclaim the Gospel by signifying the sacrifice at the altar ceremonially. Since Hagar (the reflection of Sarah) is identified with Sinai by Paul, then Ishamael (the reflection of Isaac in mirrored chronology) is being tacitly connected to the "ministry of death" or "Law of Sin and Death" that is reflected by Moses's veiled face, the covenant that was "added because of transgressions" (Galations 3:19). The veiled face of Moses, like the situations surrounding the birth of Ishmael, was given in reaction to human error (the negative reflection of the standard), and this fact explains why, "the law, which was four hundred and thirty years later, cannot annul the covenant that was confirmed before by God in Christ, that it should make the promise of no effect" (Galatians 3:17) since Isaac was promised before Ishmael (Isaac's reflection) was born even though, in a second reflection, Ishmael was physically born before Isaac. The veiled face of Moses, like the birth of Ishmael, "was added because of transgressions, till the Seed [Christ, reflected by Isaac on Moriah] should come to whom the promise was made" (Galatians 3:19); in the same way, Ishmael awaited Isaac just as the veiled face of Moses awaited the unveiling or "revelation" of Christ Who was prophesied in the Law of Liberty itself. Accordingly, one cannot believe in Moses and not believe in Christ, for the contention between Hagar and Sarah was the struggle between whose son would officiate at the altar of God Who made the promise. Since Christ died and rose for conciliatory purposes, it is auspicious for one to consider the reconciliation observed between Ishmael and Isaac at the tomb of Abraham and the reconciliation of Esau and Jacob at the tomb of Isaac. We know that the promise was for Isaac, and we also know that both Ishmael and Isaac buried Abraham together (Genesis 25:9), just as both "Jews" and "Christians" (who were originally from the seed of Israel who was of the seed of Abraham) are guilty of the death of Christ Whom the Law anticipated: "... the law was our tutor to bring us to Christ, that we might be justified by πιστις = אמנה covenant" (Galatians 3:24). The reader will notice that such a declaration equates "Jews" with Ishmael and not Isaac. The issue is the spiritual as opposed to the physical, for Isaac was the Firstborn regarding the spiritual designation of being the familial sacrificer, just as Ishmael was the firstborn respecting the physical lineage of Abraham.

Ishmael sired 12 sons as did Isaac's son, Jacob. Of Jacob's 12 sons, Joseph was the 11th by the time he received the Right of Firstborn as signified by the special garment his father gave him. Judah, the man whose name would later be applied collectively as "Judea" from where the term "Jew" is derived, devised the plan to sell his own brother Joseph into Ishmaelite slavery that became Egyptian bondage. Judah (along with all of his brothers excepting Reuben, the physical firstborn) exhibited jealousy in part because Israel had given the Right of Firstborn to his youngest son at the time, Joseph; for Benjamin (Son of My Right Hand) had not yet been born, and we know this because Joseph's dream and Israel's interpretation of it accounted Rachel as alive while leaving Benjamin unaccounted (Genesis 37:9-11). Joseph was the last born at that time, but was given the

Right of Firstborn; in this, Joseph was first and last, a fact that should direct the reader to the title of Christ: "The First and The Last" (Revelation 1:11). Joseph was a type of Christ. Reuben, who was the physical firstborn, had lost hope for the Right of Firstborn for having violated Israel's wedding bed, which can be thought of as Jacob's altar. Thus, with Reuben's misconduct, the betrayal of Joseph, and the birth of Benjamin, we can see 10 sons of Israel separated from two. Reuben acknowledged his error and attempted to save Joseph who currently held the ceremonial title, but was preempted by Judah's plan to sell Jospeh. When considering the 10 sons of Israel, we can see in this a dark prophecy of the 10 tribes who would defect into the northern kingdom while two, the priestly and the kingly, remained in the southern kingdom. The southern Kingdom of Judah would become the mere province of Judea, the land of the "Jews." Since "Judas" is but a Greek rendering of "Judah," we can behold the connection in that both Judas and Judah sold their "Firstborn" brother. Moses was of the stock of Israel physically but was raised both Egyptian and Hebrew culturally. Joseph, of the stock of Abraham and Sarah, was not physically half Egyptian like the Ishmaelites who were physically half Chaldean and half Egyptian; however, Joseph was deported to Egypt and was compelled to adopt Egyptian customs, thus making him, in a sense, half Egyptian in the land of his eventual descendant, Moses, who was in turn raised both Egyptian and Israelite culturually. In the deportation of Joseph, we see the literary mingling of the Hebrews and Egypt, a union from which Moses sprung forth. Hagar was an Egyptian slave and Abraham was a Chaldean Hebrew; Joseph became a Hebrew slave under Egypt, and the roles became reversed as though in a reflection. The mingled Hebrew-Egyptian cultural aspects of Moses regarding the Hebrew Torah express themselves in the mingled Hebrew-Egyptian physicality of Ishmael, and as the Torah was "added because of transgression" (Galatians 3:19), so Ishmael was born after the promise of ceremonial firstborn was given regarding Isaac. Since Hagar, Ishmael's mother, was Egyptian, and since the Law was given after the Israelites were יצא *birthed out of* Egypt (Exodus 20:2), we can understand why Paul equated Hagar with Sinai, which then means her son is as the covenant written through Moses at Sinai that hints darkly at The Law of the Spirit of Life by recording its reflection, The Law of Sin and Death:

> I call heaven and earth as witnesses today against you, that I have set before you life and death, blessing and cursing; therefore choose life, that both you AND YOUR DESCENDANTS may live (Deuteronomy 30:19).

The father of the covenant with Hagar is also the father of the covenant with Sarah, and Sarah was his wife first. Nevertheless, the Father cared for Ishmael and his 12 sons as He provided for Israel and his 12 children, each set of 12 being separated by one generation. Since Rachel, who gave her life for Benjamin, was buried in the territory of Benjamin in which is Bethlehem, since Benjamin was a child yet to be as signified celestially in Joseph's dream, and since "Benjamin" means "Son of My Right Hand," we can notice how Benjamin is also a type of Christ since we read of "Rachel weeping for her children and refusing to be comforted, because they are no more" (Matthew 2:18) when, antithetically to her example (as in a mirror), babies were murdered for the sake of an adult where Christ was born, since Christ was signified celestially, and since The Father says of His Son, Christ, "Sit at My *right hand* [the Hebrew hints at "Benjamin"]" (Psalm 110:1). As Joseph and Benjamin were brothers, one being an innocent sold into doom but raised in glory, the other being the one who bound Joseph's brothers to him for righteousness, we can see that these two were types of the Son of Adam, Christ. The union discussed here occurred after Abraham and before Moses even though the Messiah of Deuteronomy 18 was prophesied during the time of Moses. Ishmael (which means *He Comprehends*) is as the *work* or *fruit* or *child* of The Law of Sin and Death since Hagar (Fugitive) is as Sinai (Thornbush); Ezekiel 2:6 calls wicked people "thorns," and the wicked people at the base of Sinai who slew the firstborn were as the thorns who refused to participate in The Law of the Spirit of Life, The Law of Liberty from sin and death.

We can see how Isaac was the child of promise in that his elder brother was his steward chronologically awaiting the succession of the ceremonial Firstborn status to be conferred to his younger brother, as was the case with Joseph. As Ishmael persecuted Isaac, so the non-"Christian" Judeans ("Jews") persecuted the "Christian Jews" (Judeans), which means that the non-"Christian" Judeans ("Jews") represented the physical firstborn, whereas the "Christians" represented the child of promise (Isaac/Christ) Who was the ceremonial "Firstborn" (Hebrews 1:6). Christ was persecuted (like Isaac was by Ishmael) as a fugitive ("Hagar" means "fugitive") and had a thornbush ("Sinai" means "thornbush") placed upon His head, for when He cried out the prayer of Psalm 22 while under the thornbush, while under Siani, that is, while under the Law of Sin and Death, He was heard ("Ishmael" means "God Comprehends"), which is why the first "Christians" were "Jewish" converts from spiritual Ishmaelitism (called "Judaism"). Again, Christ died under the thorns and thus under the wicked people and under the mountain of Sinai (Thornbush):

Also the high places of Aven, the sin of Israel, shall be destroyed. The thorn and thistle shall grow on their altars; they shall say to the mountains, "Cover us!" And to the hills, "Fall on us!" (Hosea 10:8).

Then they will begin 'to say to the mountains, "Fall on us!" and to the hills, "Cover us!" (Luke 23:30).

As we read of the reconciliation of Ishamel and Isaac at the grave of their father (Genesis 25:9), we may note this reference:

Therefore remember that you, once Gentiles in the flesh — who are called Uncircumcision by what is called the Circumcision made in the flesh by hands— that at that time you were without Christ, being aliens from the commonwealth of Israel and strangers from the covenants of promise, having no hope and without God in the world. But now in Christ Jesus you who once were far off have been brought near by the blood of Christ. For He Himself is our peace, who has made both one, and has broken down the middle wall of separation, having abolished in His flesh the enmity, that is, the law of commandments contained in ordinances, so as to create in Himself one new man from the two, thus making peace, and that He might reconcile them both to God in one body through the cross, thereby putting to death the enmity (Ephesians 2:11-16).

Isaac was offered up and a thornily crowned ram was also offered up with him, the one constructively, the other destructively, for the word עלה to ascend can indicate a lifting up, a burnt offering, and a resurrection. Isaac, a type of Christ, ascended a mountain crowned with a thornbush and was offered up to God by his own free will since his father surely did not overpower him; Abraham was past 100 years old and Isaac was an adult, for Isaac was strong enough to carry wood abundant enough to burn an entire human body. The flame and the sword of his father were as present atop the Mountain of Vision ("Moriah" or Mirror) as they were at Sinai (that burned with fire and was called "Horeb" = חרב = Sword), as they were at Golgatha, and as they were at Eden's entrance after man was exiled. Let us recapitulate the main points regarding the distinguishing factors that delineate a Hebrew, an Israelite, and a Jew.

A "Hebrew" is one who passes over (as the title implies) into covenant with God in order to obtain forgiveness and rebirth that allows for correct action in accordance with the will of the Father. The title of "Hebrew" admits no physicality as a constituent of its title but does suggest spiritual fruit-production that can be validated physically through a child and the spiritual education necessary to bring the child to Christ.

An "Israelite" is originally one who strives in spiritual warfare and prevails (as the title implies) thus accomplishing, by the grace of God, the status of a Hebrew in order to obtain admittance into the intended design of the Father. The title of "Israelite" admits physicality in that it can be physically applied to the fleshly lineage of the man Israel secondarily in hopes of the primary and spiritual denomination regarding the valid, spiritual success of the divine struggle against sin. Accordingly, an Israelite is a title of dual meaning, for it is both spiritual and physical: the spiritual title can exist without the physical, and the physical title can exist without the spiritual.

A "Jew" is a shortened rendition of a Judahite or a Judean. The title of "Jew" admits physicality in that it can be applied to the people of the tribe of Judah initially, the people of the Kingdom of Judah secondarily (which included Levites), the people descended from this kingdom thirdly, the relocated Judean peoples in Babylon fourthly, the people who returned to Judah fifthly, and the people under the province of Judah subjugated by Rome sixthly. A "Jew" could also be a spiritual title in that it implies one who practices the religion of the Judeans or the Judahites, which was originally the religion of the Israelites, and this faith was that of the Hebrews. The major difficulty with the title "Jew" today is that it is used promiscuously as a simple national name and incorrectly as the name of the descendents of the Rabbis, that is, the Pharisees, who errantly assumed the title of "Orthodox Judaism" after the Qumran community, the Sadducees, and the remaining Judean religious persuasions were either destroyed or dispersed into dissolution by Rome in 70 AD. It is therefore provable that it is absurd to equate Orthodox Judaism with the so-called "Old Testament" because it was originally a mostly lay view of the vowell-lacking Torah pushed through the filter of the Platonic ideal that viewed the oral word as superior to the written word and that hybridized the oral and the written into documented argumentation that seeks to answer questions and challenges to the doctrine as the document progresses, as would be the case in a live conversation. The term "Jew" is today utilized as a gross misnomer that has birthed the doctrinally, chronologically, and thematically impossible term "Judeo-Christian" that assumes Christianity to be an offshoot of Judaism despite the fact that non-Christians invented the term "Christian," just as non-Pharisees invented the term "Pharisee."

The confusion of names is both reflected and anticipated by the garden story: Adam, in his pre-sinful wisdom, was empowered to denominate beings. The letters שם can be pronounced to indicate *name* and can also be pronounced to indicate a *covenant* (compare Genesis 2:8 to 2:15) by the parallel term לקח that can mean *to marry* and *to instruct*, both of which revolve around the Hebrew concept of *wisdom* doctrinally and gestationally. Another word for "name" is "שכל" (Proverbs 22:1) which can be pronounced to indicate both *wisdom* (Genesis 3:6) and *folly* (Ecclesiastes 1:17: שכלות). Ultimately, we can see in these thematic relations a link between naming and wisdom regarding authority, for humanity was to rule (Genesis 1:28) and to name (Genesis 2:19). The word משל means both *to rule* and *to riddle*, so losing power is as failing to answer the riddle — which is exactly what happened when Satan propounded his riddle to the bride. Accepting the outsider's terms is to accept his designations, and to accept these is to accept his rule and his covenant through unification with him.

Abraham was the father of two principal sons (not counting the children of his concubines as related in Genesis 25:6). Abraham's physical firstborn came from an Egyptian slave, but his ceremonial firstborn came from his free wife. Similarly, the Torah of Moses came out of Egyptian bondage, while the freedom from slavery was found in the Promised Land; Ishmael was the product of bondage, but Isaac was the child of promise. Again, Ishmael is the innocent issue of this bondage as the Torah is the righteous progeny of sin's slavery. The freedom from "the curse of the law" (the condemnation mandated for breaking covenant with God) is anticipated in the Law and was vitalized through the life of the ceremonial Firstborn Creator, Who Himself initiated and descended through Isaac and not Ishmael who both were knit by one father and One Father. Abraham sired Ishmael as the Law through Hagar as Mount Sinai; Abraham sired Isaac as the Gospel through Sarah as the Mount of the Beatitudes; there is the "Law of the Spirit of Life" (Romans 8:2) "another law" (Romans 7:23) just as there is the Gospel and "a different gospel" (2 Corinthians 11:4) like there is the "likeness of sinful flesh" (Romans 8:1-8) and sinful flesh. In the case of Abraham, his sinful flesh sired Ishamel and his sinless flesh sired Isaac for, being human, he was affected by the Tree of the Union of Good and Evil. The Father, however, is not subject to the ruinous hybrid, for even though Mary was sired by her human father, her Son, Jesus, was sired by no human at all. In this way, Mary was unified to the Everliving Half of the Divine covenant and was revitalized eternally by her Husband, God, as should be the case with the bride who is supposed to "labor in birth again until Christ is formed in you" (Galatians 4:19). God is not composed of good and evil as we humans are, and our hope can reside in that our dead half will be cut off in order to unite with God in covenant so that our works, our fruits, will be viable expressions of the perpetuity in which we were designed to live. Both mountains, both wombs, were sired by one father and One Father. Beginning from Sinai, the Beatitudes can be mined from the mountain of the Law and birthed forth like riches as can be seen in the dictum, "You shall love your neighbor as yourself" (Leviticus 19:27). The birth of such love shows that Sinai is not the original but is secondary relative to the mandates of Eden; therefore, Eden is the standard, Sinai is the womb instituted as the hope of rejuvination after sin, and the Gospel (as designed before, within, and after the Torah) is both as the Sire and the Son of a covenant that exists on either side of man's fall. As such, we see that Moses died on a mountain outside of the Promised Land but was raised on the mountain of transfiguration inside the Promised Land. The mountain Moses died upon was Nebo, which means the *Mountain of the Moon*. A Hebrew word for "moon" is the same as "month" (ירח), and "month" (חדש) also means "renewal" but is translated into Greek limitedly as "καινος *new*." In the death of Moses, we see one mountain anticipating another... one womb anticipating another... one covenant anticipating another, for Moses died on the Mountain of the Moon which, when conceived of in Hebrew, is the Mountain of Renewal, the Renewing Womb, and we see his renewed birth on the Mount of Transfiguration in the Renewed and Reaffirmed Covenant that Moses anticipated where Moses, Elijah, and Christ were changed into shining glory of which the Apostle wrote, "Listen, I tell you a mystery [Hebrew סוד *secret, base of an altar*]: We will not all sleep, but we will all be changed — in a flash, in the twinkling of an eye, at the last trumpet. For the trumpet will sound, the dead will be raised imperishable, and we will be changed" (I Corinthians 15:51-52) where the Text discusses resurrection. That Moses died on a mountain figuratively means that Moses died on a womb, for the Moses story begins and ends with the issue of the womb dying. Moses' covenant written within the perameters of death issuing from a womb anticipates a viable womb that animates the covenant perpetually... a situation that can be understood as a Renewed and Reaffirmed Covenant or, as is commonly and limitedly named, "New Testament." The vital womb issuing after the abortive womb is not secondary but tertiary since a womb is only intended to be vital and not abortive; this means that the abortive womb is not primary but secondary and that both the end and the beginning of a womb, as intended originally, is vitality. It was secondary when God said, "Increasing I will increase your sorrow and your conception" (Genesis 3:16) because He said primarily "Be fruitful and multiply" (Genesis 1:28). The word עברי *Hebrew* comes from the root עבר *to pass over, to forgive, to enter, to shave (i.e. to appear as a child reborn),* and *to become pregnant.* The word הר *mountain* or הרה *mountain* is, consonantally, spelled the same a הרה *pregnant with child,* which is from the root הרה *to conceive, to implant with seed,* and relates to the idea of teaching just as the root לקח *to take, to marry,* produces the word לקח *doctrine, instruction.* "Torah" means "Instruction," and the reflection at Sinai was designed chronologically following the advent of sin in order to teach us how to enter again into the womb so that we can be birthed again according to the original design. The secondary design is sin. The passing over back to rebirth designates someone as a "Hebrew," for a "Hebrew" is singularly a spiritual title that necessitates life as is true of the womb's design. As Xenophon's *Anabasis* depicted Cyrus' troops passing over the river as a sign of their oath to the death with him in war, so our covenant with Christ signifies something similar (and something higher). The sin in Eden was secondary to the primary perfection. "Eden" means "Fertility," and the word הפך *to turn, to move back and forth,* used of "the flame of the sword" in Genesis 3:24, is also a term denoting abortive birth (I Samuel 4:19). Sin, like a destructively sacrificial womb, "gives birth to death" (James 1:15), and the righteous, highly polished, "flaming" sword refected in its blade the destructively sacrificial womb to which man secondarily adhered as displayed by his work, his fruit, his aborted child whom he cut off from the land of the living by defecting from The Law of the Spirit of Life and adhering to The Law of Sin and Death.

THE WORD "DAY"

TRANSLATIONS are marvelous tools that allow a reader to see the observations of diligent minds as they attempted to grasp the Text, and the subtleties observed are of inestimable value, particularly with respect to allowing immediate access to Scripture. Consider the fact that the word translated יום *day* was spelled ים originally and can also be pronounced to render the translation of ים *sea*; Zondervan's *Interlinear NIV Hebrew-English Old Testament* notes that this word could be read as "day" or as "sea" in Job 3:8. At the same time, translations (like the available multi-form traditions) are not definitive, and dissecting Scripture to the point of individual words is not altogether possible in translation; yet, simply being a master of Biblical languages has its limits as well, and such a mastery is itself incapable of being definitive when the references alluded to by Scripture are not themselves known. "Joshua" and "Jesus" are essentially the same name, and they both mean "Salvation." Let us consider Joshua 10 regarding the sun "standing still." Joshua 10:12-14 states,

> Then Joshua spoke to the Lord in the day when the Lord delivered up the Amorites before the children of Israel, and he said in the sight of Israel:
>
>> 'Sun, stand still over Gibeon; and Moon, in the Valley of Aijalon.' So the sun stood still, and the moon stopped, till the people had revenge upon their enemies.
>
> Is this not written in the Book of Jasher? So the sun stood still in the midst of heaven, and did not hasten to go down for about a whole day. And there has been no day like that, before it or after it, the Lord heeded the voice of a man; for the Lord fought for Israel.

Though it is understood that the sun and moon stopped moving along their lines across the heavens, Joshua literally said, "Sun, דום be silent in Gibeon, and moon in the Valley of Aijalon." The lack of movement is equated with silence; therefore, movement is connected to sound. Here, the stilling of the celestial movements is equated with silence; therefore, the activity of the celestial movements can be understood not only as sound, but as speech or communication that requires discernment... for Psalm 19:1-7 states,

> The heavens DECLARE the glory of God;
> And the firmament SHOWS His handiwork.
> Day unto day UTTERS speech,
> And night unto night REVEALS knowledge.

There is no SPEECH nor LANGUAGE
Where their VOICE is not heard.
Their LINE has gone out through all the earth,
And their WORDS to the end of the world.

In them He has set a tabernacle for the sun, which is like a bridegroom coming out of his chamber, and rejoices like a strong man to run its race. Its rising is from one end of heaven, and its circuit to the other end; and there is nothing hidden from its heat.

The reader may observe that the celestial lights played a part in Salvation's war in Joshua 10, and Psalm 19's description compares the sun to both a groom and warrior. It is interesting to note that a warrior, the Commander of The Lord's צבא Host *(Celestial Bodies, Heavenly Luminaries, Army)* appeared to Israel's commander in Joshua 5. The tacit decisiveness of the illustration concerning the "silence" of physical stillness is obscured easily in translation. Consider how differently the so-called "Old Testament" would be read if its employments of the words "salvation" and "deliverance" were read as "Jesus" since these are the same word:

"And Moses said to the people, 'Do not be afraid. התיצבו *Stand still*, and see the Salvation of the LORD, which He will accomplish for you today. For the Egyptians whom you see today, you shall see again no more forever" (Exodus 14:13).

Notice that, again, we have a reference to physical stillness and silence with respect to warfare.

The instance of Salvation commanding the sun to stand still (to be silent) is a physical illustration of a spiritual truth. Such a physical reality is called a παραβολη *parable (a placing beside, a juxtaposition, a parallel)* in Hebrews 11:17-19:

By faith Abraham, when he was tested, offered up Isaac, and he who had received the promises offered up his only begotten son, of whom it was said, 'In Isaac your seed shall be called,' concluding that God was able to raise him up, even from the dead, from which he also received him in a παραβολη *parable.*

Notice that the word "parable" is being used here as a physical illustration and not exclusively a moral teaching. A "parable" and a "riddle" are the same words from Greek to Hebrew, and the Greek παραβολη *parable (a placing beside, a juxtaposition, a parallel)* is the Septuagint's משל

riddle (a smilitude, a comparison). Scripture is a Library of Riddles discernable by a faithfully guided and probing mind.

A clue to the meaning of the word יום *day* can be found in Genesis 40 where Joseph compares the word "day" to branches and basins. The object that has both branches and basins is the menorah.

> You shall also make a lampstand of pure gold; the lampstand shall be of hammered work. Its shaft, ITS BRANCHES, ITS BOWLS, its ornamental knobs, and flowers shall be of one piece (Exodus 25:31).

The fact that the word "day" is compared to branches and basins (i.e. the menorah or tree of life) is consistent with the fact that "Day" is the name given to "light" in Genesis 1:5. The menorah is a signification of a plant that is ablaze and is yet unconsumed by the fire. The menorah is, of course, a symbol of the Tree of Life. When Joseph interpreted the three baskets and the three branches as three days, it would seem as if he was not making a simple metaphor through divine wisdom but that he was speaking according to Hebrew etymology. The word יום *day* is from the root יום *to ascend* (literally "*he ascended*"); according to its root, it can be reasonably thought of as an *ascension* substantively, i.e. a rising or an *exaltation* (as with a גביע *cup,* which is from the root גבע *to be high*, when raising a cup in an oath, or like the "cups" on the menorah).

> And they said to him, "We each have had a dream, and there is no interpreter of it." So Joseph said to them, "Do not interpretations belong to God? Tell them to me, please." Then the chief butler told his dream to Joseph, and said to him, "Behold, in my dream a vine was before me, and in the vine were three BRANCHES; it was as though it budded, its blossoms shot forth, and its clusters brought forth ripe grapes. Then Pharaoh's CUP was in my hand; and I took the grapes and pressed them into Pharaoh's CUP, and placed the cup in Pharaoh's hand." And Joseph said to him, "This is the interpretation of it: THE THREE BRANCHES ARE THREE DAYS. Now within three days Pharaoh will LIFT up your head and restore you to your place, and you will put Pharaoh's CUP in his hand according to the former manner, when you were his butler. But remember me when it is well with you, and please show kindness to me; make mention of me to Pharaoh, and get me out of this house. For indeed I was stolen away from the land of the Hebrews; and also I have done nothing here that they should put me into the dungeon." When the chief baker saw that the interpretation was good, he said

to Joseph, "I also was in my dream, and there were three white BASKETS on my head. In the uppermost basket were all kinds of baked goods for Pharaoh, and the birds ate them out of the BASKET on my head." So Joseph answered and said, "This is the interpretation of it: THE THREE BASKETS ARE THREE DAYS. Within three days Pharaoh will LIFT off your head from you and hang you on a tree; and the birds will eat your flesh from you." Now it came to pass on the third DAY, which was Pharaoh's birthday, that he made a feast for all his servants; and he LIFTED up the head of the chief butler and of the chief baker among his servants. Then he restored the chief butler to his butlership again, and he placed the CUP in Pharaoh's hand. But he hanged the chief baker, as Joseph had interpreted to them. Yet the chief butler did not remember Joseph, but forgot him (Genesis 40:8-23).

According to its root, the word "day" can be reasonably thought of as an *ascension* substantively, i.e. a rising or an *exaltation* (as with a גביע cup, which is from the root גבע *to be high*, when raising a cup in an oath); the cup given to Pharaoh seems to provide a neat example here. Likewise, the menorah has both "branches" and "bowls" according to Exodus 25:31, and the lights in its basins are the fires atop its branches: "You shall make seven lamps for it, and they shall arrange its lamps so that they give LIGHT in front of it" (Exodus 25:37). The word "light" is named "Day" in Genesis 1:5, and the remainder of the Creation account employs the name "Day" for its substance "light." Seven "Days" are seven lights like those seen atop the menorah and like the stages of a ziggurat or temple. If one keeps in mind the basins that hold the lights of the menorah along with the steps of a ziggurat, then one can see an illustration of how the word יום *day* is from the root יום *to ascend* (literally "*he ascended*"). It seems that the usage of the name "Day" for the word "light" dos not confine "Day" to time, particularly when one considers that the first three "Days" of Creation were without celestial time-keepers, which forces a situation where it is impossible to account for the arrow of time. The usage of the name "Day" for the word "light" in the creation account seems to be describing the steps of God's Temple and the Tree of Life at its center and apex that blazes light and life down upon and up to all of Creation as the nexus of Heaven and Earth; this proves easy to conceive of since the tops of mountains and towers are burnt readily by lightning. The very fact that Hebrew does not express grammatical tense with respect to the time-periods it sometimes discusses makes sense with respect to the eternity designed for the sinless creation. The tiers on a temple and the lights on the golden Tree of

Life or menorah are more analogous to an eternal flame than a temporal measure.

The word יום *day* is spelled with the long ו, which is not original; its original spelling must have been ים, and this spelling seems to be the key to the truest definition of the word. The letters ים spell both *day* and *sea* consonantally according to their respective pronunciations. Though *sea* is nearly the uniform translation of ים, it is properly a *basin* capable of holding water as we read in 1 Kings 7:23-26 where Solomon " יועש את הים מוצק *made the molten sea*" that had " ושפתו כמעשה שפת כוס פרח שושן *a rim like the rim of a cup, like a lily blossom...*" that held 2,000 units of water. Obviously, the water did not hold 2,000 units of water. Instead, the word translated ים *sea* is more precisely the vessel that held water. Solomon made a "cast" or "molten" sea, for he did not cast or melt water to hold water; Solomon cast metal to hold water, and the cast object was the word that we call a ים *sea* that is truly a *basin*, for Scripture itself states it is like a "כוס *cup*" which from the root כסה *to cover*, the overturning of the גביע *cup* that is from the root גבע *to be high*. If we know that the letters ים can spell both *day* and *basin*, then we can understand clearly that the word we often translate as "day" has the possibility of relating to or hinting at an exalted *basin* or *altar*; so, like the seven altars (so to speak) or fires of the menorah, we can observe the seven altars of Balaam in imitation (Numbers 23). Consider that many ancient eastern temples had an open-air precinct, a court. In the center of this court, there was a sacrificial altar. Next to the altar was a "sea" or basin of water that derived its name through the notion that it was a symbol of the primeval "deep," and this water was used for ablution. At the same time, temples were also used for astronomical observation, and so "seas" were sometimes filled with oil, which is less tremulous than water and serves to preserve the reflection of the sky better (*Natural Questions*, Seneca), in order to watch the heavens. An oil-filled-sea could be set ablaze, like a large lamp, until the fire lapped up the last drop of oil.

There exists another good reason to suspect that the definition of the word "day" has to do with a *basin*. A ceremonial cornerstone was the threshold to the house, and the word סף means both a *threshold* and a *basin* literally, an *altar* by implication, and a *womb* by metaphor — all of these being connected through libation (like the masculine libation poured upon the feminine altar) that necessitates אור *light, life, fire, wisdom,* and *happiness*. Libation can be understood as a type of sacrificial lustration utilized for ritual purity. As such, the first instance of the word "day" used in the Creation narrative is in reference to "life," "light" and "water" and is reflected by the sequence of the Narrative itself, so one can see in this a cleansing and kindling of an altar as the אור *light, life, fire, wisdom,* and *happiness* break forth over the threshold of the dark horizon. It would seem then that the name "Day" or "Basin" was given to "Light," "Life," or "Fire" with reference to water (or, at least, its container); these relationships are all bound in one word: אאגן*basin, belly (womb), cup, bowl.* Consider Job 38:8: "Or who shut in the םי*basin* with doors, בגיחו *when it burst* and מרחם יצא*issued from the womb.*" Who or what "burst forth and issued from the womb"? — אור *light, fire, wisdom, happiness,* and this light was named "Day" in Genesis 1:5. If light is named "Day," and "Day" is a basin, then light is understood as a basin, or, more specifically, along with a basin like the fire upon the oil contained in the basins atop the menorah. If a "Day" is light, a basin, and a threshold (that is analogous to a womb), then the round horizon can be understood thus: "...in the DAY of Your power; in the beauties of holiness, from the WOMB OF THE MORNING, You have the DEW of Your youth" (Psalm 110:3). We may surmise that the word "Day" is a reference to a womb metaphorically, and we know that a womb is symbolized by an altar, a threshold, and a basin, all of which are understood in the word סף *threshold, basin,* (metaphorically, *womb*), the very vessel that contained the blood, which is the life of the Passover. As in birth, light (or life) issued forth following a flow of water out of the basin (or womb). It is interesting to note that, in the ancient east, birth stars were anticipated once pregnancy was perceived based on the knowledge of gestation's timing relative to the seasonal change indicated by the stars. Basins of water, oil, and pitch were used to reflect the heavens for observational purposes (in this case, in order to calculate when a pregnant woman would give birth, as was also the case concerning the calculation of agricultural periods). Here we have the basin (womb), the light (fire, stars), and the water or oil ("dew of youth") all contained in one harmonious and anticipatory whole of happiness that connects the productivity of inanimate and animate nature, which constitutes the substance of Creation. It can be seen that the "day" (basin, threshold, altar) is the strand that binds material creation to the works done in and through it, for "Day" is the name of אור *life, light.* The seven thresholds are easily accomplished in the seven tiers of a ziggurat. Consider the fact that the ziggurat at Borsippa had the name of "The House of the Seven Bonds of Heaven and Earth." The seven lights are easily accomplished upon the basins of the menorah. The agriculture-womb-water-altar in relation to the light-life-wisdom-fire link is blatantly observed in 1 Corinthians 3:5-15:

> Who then is Paul, and who is Apollos, but ministers through
> whom you believed, as the Lord gave to each one? I PLANTED,

Apollos WATERED, but God gave the INCREASE. So then neither
he who PLANTS is anything, nor he who WATERS, but God who
gives the INCREASE. Now he who PLANTS and he who WATERS
are one, and each one will receive his own reward according to
his own labor. For we are God's fellow workers; you are God's
FIELD, you are God's building. According to the grace of God
which was given to me, as a WISE master builder I have laid
the foundation, and another builds on it. But let each one take
heed how he builds on it. For no other foundation can anyone
lay than that which is laid, which is Jesus Christ. Now if anyone
builds on this foundation with gold, silver, precious stones,
wood, hay, straw, each one's work will become clear; for THE
DAY WILL DECLARE IT, because it will be REVEALED BY FIRE; and
the FIRE will test each one's work, of what sort it is. If anyone's
work which he has built on it endures, he will receive a reward.
If anyone's work is BURNED, he will suffer loss; but he himself
will be saved, yet so as through FIRE.

Similar links can be observed in 1 Thessalonians 4:16-5:5:

For the Lord Himself will descend from heaven with a shout,
with the voice of an archangel, and with the trumpet of God.
And the dead in Christ will rise first. Then we who are alive and
remain shall be caught up together with them in the clouds to
meet the Lord in the air. And thus we shall always be with the
Lord. Therefore comfort one another with these words. But
concerning the TIMES and the SEASONS, brethren, you have
no need that I should write to you. For you yourselves know
perfectly that the DAY OF THE LORD so comes as a thief in the
night. For when they say, 'Peace and safety!' then sudden destruction comes upon them, as LABOR PAINS UPON A PREGNANT
WOMAN. And they shall not escape. But you, brethren, are not
in darkness, so that this DAY should overtake you as a thief.
You are all SONS OF LIGHT AND SONS OF THE DAY. We are not of
the night nor of darkness.

A Hebrew יום day must be, or allude to, a י basin, threshold, altar
(that holds the light or fire), which is why the "day" (altar) is testing works
by fire. More specifically, it would appear that the word "day" is a lit altar,
a fiery basin, a burning threshold that has already been cleansed through
water. The linguistic mingling for fire and water is understood in the word
שמים *heavens* that is composed of the symbol for *fire* (ש) and the word for
מים *waters:* "And I saw something like a SEA of glass mingled with FIRE..."
(Revelation 15:2). The upside-down basin of the sky upon which the stars

appear painted mingles water with fire during thunderstorms. A סַף *thresh-old* (which is from the root סָפַף *to expand*) was a basin. Furthermore, a מִפְתָּן *threshold*, which is from the root פָּתַן *to twist*, produces the word פֶּתֶן *asp, snake*). We can see a hint at how a יָם *basin* is related to the root פָּתַן TO TWIST in the account of the molten sea (molten basin): "It took a LINE of thirty cubits to measure AROUND it" (I Kings 7:23). The word רָקִיעַ, which is often translated as *firmament*, is from the root רָקַע *to expand*, and the word *threshold* is from the root סָפַף *to expand*. The firmament is understood as a type of doorway by illustration, and such an analogy can be observed in 1 Corinthians 3:5-15 quoted above in terms of the fiery threshold that tests by fire.

A סַף *threshold* (which is from the root סָפַף *to expand*) is a synonym for the word רָקִיעַ *firmament* by way of its root. The firmament or basin of the heavens can easily be viewed as a mirror and a threshold simultaneously if one considers a ziggurat being reflected in a mirage whereby the sight of the substance and its reflection are united by the light of the altar at the pointed summit of the one and the upside-down pointed base of the other. Thus, the altar atop a ziggurat would be the gateway to heaven (as the name Babel implies), for such a structure was seen by Jacob when he said, "How awesome is this place! This is none other than the house of God, and this is the GATE OF HEAVEN!" (Genesis 28:17). The word רָקִיעַ *firmament* could be translated easily as *mirror*, for its root רָקַע *to expand* also means *to stamp, tread down, to beat into thin plates, to cover with metallic plates*; ancient eastern mirrors were sheets of polished metal, and this so called "firmament" is described explicitly in Job 37:18: "...like Him, can you SPREAD OUT the skies, hard as a MIRROR OF CAST BRONZE?" — and the words "you... spread out" are the Hebrew תַּרְקִיעַ, a form of the word otherwise translated as רָקִיעַ *firmament*. Both the "molten sea" or "cast sea" and the "firmament" or "mirror of the Heavens" have in common the idea of reflection, and we can now comprehend the manner in which the heavens are here being described.

The heavens are being described in terms of an ancient celestial globe, and the "day" is being described in terms of a basin since basins, when filled with water, oil, or pitch were used for celestial observations. The sky appears as a bowl overhead, and this point can be easily understood when one views the stars from the eastern horizon to the western horizion. By observing the conceptual concave basin overhead in the liquid of a concave basin below one's head, one can see, as though in a mirror, how there would appear to be liquid below and liquid above delineated by the reflection of one's face in the midst. Another related way to understand the apparent celestial sphere is by means of representing celestial cartography on a polished ball in reverse so that the observer must imagine himself within the sphere looking out as though in a mirror.

Some cast celestial spheres were as two equally-sized basins (two hemispheres) put together to form a sphere. When God commanded (on "Day Second") that the waters be divided above and beneath the רקיע *firmament, mirror,* it would seem as if we are reading about an image of opening a celestial globe to form a terrestial globe within it; for, when using a standard celestial globe, you have to understand that you are beholding the heavens as through a mirror from the opposite perspective assumed when standing on the earth that resides conceptually within the celestial sphere. In other words, a celestial globe compels its user either to imagine himself within this sphere looking out at it from the inside or viewing the starry heavens from a perspective on the opposite side of a viewer standing on earth. In effect, a celestial globe is a type of mirror functionally, and cast globes were reflective physically. Describing the firmament as a mirror is a riddled analogy to a physical and static representation of the starry skies used for astronomical calculation.

I contend that there is no "ancient cosmology" intended in the Creation account, nor do I believe that the Hebrew Bible speaks from the standpoint of assuming the sky to be an actual bronze bowl. Rather, the Hebrew Bible is discussing the heavens as they exist in reality but through the lense of a tool used to observe the heavens, for it is this observational tool (not the heavens) that is the bronze bowl. When Job 26:7 states that God "hangs the earth upon nothing," we might consider the fact that we call this "nothing" by the term "space." When Job 26:10 states that God "drew a circular horizon on the face of the waters," we might consider the fact that sailors then certainly knew that the earth was round by the simple observation that land was sighted by a man above the deck of a ship faster than a man on the deck of a ship because of the earth's curvature. The very same effect happens when climbing a mountain, for, the higher one ascends the mountain, the more sky can be seen due to the curvature of the earth. One standing on a plane might only see six Zodiacal constellations, while one standing upon a mountain can see seven. Strabo, some two millennia ago, discussed how one will wind up east if one travels west long enough because the earth is round. If one observes the clouds directly, one will notice that they travel in an arc. If one, however, observes the clouds indirectly through a bronze basin filled with water, one will see the clouds in water that appears overhead and that seems to be contained in a bronze basin that holds the water upside-down. A reason one would actually think that the ancient Hebrews laughably conceived of the sky as a metal bowl is that the Hebrews' observational tools were not known to the one who degraded the Hebrew Text by assuming it to be simple. The Hebrew Bible is not simple.

Ancient celestial spheres were often cast globes. The hand-held celestial globes were fastened atop a handle such that the apparatus resembled a scepter, and the larger standing models were supported by corner spindles with the globe in the midst (thus the four corners of the earth were understood as conceptually spherical and not physically flat). The ball itself was sometimes covered with leather upon which the constellations were painted. The *Enuma Elish* describes Tiamat (a sea monster) who is cut in half like "a fish for drying" and whose flesh is stretched out above the earth to form the dome of the heavens. At first glance, the description seems strange without the ability to associate it with a reference. It can be seen, however, that celestial observation was conducted with reflecting pools and celestial calculation with globes that often had painted skins stretched over them. A sea monster (water) whose skin is stretched (like the leather on a celestial sphere) is used to describe the heavens by way of the instruments used to observe and calculate the heavens. Such descriptions are as riddles that rely upon the receiver's knowledge of substance and reflection whereby the antitype is described as the type. The handle of a hand-held celestial globe served as an axis (like a tree or the center of a tent), and, depending on the sophistication of the device, various calculations could be made as though looking in a mirror since viewing the device from the outside put the user of the tool in God's perspective, that is, on the other side of heavens as though looking through them down on the earth. It makes sense that the so-called רקיע *firmament* would be described as literally a "mirror" if it were compared to a tool used to calculate the real and apparent motions of the heavens; the Hebrew Scriptures use the word רקיע *firmament, mirror* in the second-oldest Book, Genesis, and a circumlocution for it ("mirror of cast bronze") in the oldest Book, Job. If God were viewed as the One holding His own celestial sphere, then, quite literally, He would see both His image in the cast ball and an earthly reflection in the skin stretched over it with its reversed depictions. Even the idea of something heavenly placed within flesh makes perfect sense when considering the reflective and cast sphere (a symbol of eternity) ensconced beneath perishable flesh, for, after enough time elapsed, the skins of celestial spheres degenerated, leaving the enduring reflective metal sphere that awaited a new body to clothe it. In essence, a hand-held celestial sphere could be understood as something heavenly, hidden in flesh, and fastened atop a pole, and such an image was probably conceived of illustratively in conjunction with the Hebrew ראש *head* in Colossians 1:15-20:

> He is the image of the invisible God, the firstborn over all creation. For by Him all things were created that are in heaven and that are on earth, visible and invisible, whether thrones or dominions or principalities or powers. All things were created through Him and for Him. And He is before all things, and in Him all things consist. And He is the head of the body, the church, who is the beginning, the firstborn from the dead, that in all things He may have the preeminence.

Furthermore, when it is written, "... He is the head of the body, the church, who is the beginning, the firstborn from the dead, that in all things He may have the preeminence," this is every rendering of the first word of Genesis 1:1, "בראשית *in the beginning*." The word בראשית *in the beginning* is formed from ראש *head, beginning, firstborn, preeminence*, as Colossians 1:15-20 above translates in Greek. Such a translation therefore states that Christ is the first Word of the Creation Narrative if He is described in translation as every possible rendering of that first Word. The Hebrew ראש *head* translated exhaustively here by itself encompasses meanings that are applicable to a hand-held celestial sphere in that the entirety of Creation can be understood within this word as it could be represented with the tool under discussion; whichever way, the depiction of the heavens as a mirror of bronze is certainly an illustration reflecting a celestial sphere and not a crude depiction of an ill-understood cosmos by primitive poets with childlike assertions. If Paul was grasping a hand-held celestial sphere while recieveing his inspiration for penning the Colossians passage above, it would seem as if he was describing Christ (according to the Hebrew of Genesis 1:1) through a mirrored model that reflected the hand of the Father Who saw His image in His Son, the Creator of the cosmos (but this particular image is only an conjecture on my part). Let us return to the evidence.

Knowledge of the heavens was immediately connected to wisdom in the ancient east, and Scripture even designates "wise men" as those who understood the heavenly movements, for we see this fact in the Magi and also in Esther 1:13 among other places. In the story of the Fall, God, the wisest of all, says, "He shall crush your head, and you shall bruise His heel" (Genesis 3:15) which seems to be a direct reference to the constellation of the Kneeler with his upturned heel stepping on the head of the constellation Draco, these two being reflected as in a mirror by Ophichus wrangling with Serpens while treading the head of the Scorpion; even the notion of treading is accomplished in the word רקיע *firmament, mirror,* since it is from the root רקע *to expand, to stamp, tread down, to beat into thin plates, to cover with metallic plates,* from which the heavenly mirror is derived. The brass, copper, or bronze related by the word נחשת is serpentine in construction since נחשת *brass, copper,* or *bronze* is related to the word נחש *serpent.* In false imitation, the adversary is described in reptillian fashion as both Job 41:15-17 and Genesis 3:1 literally imply scales, which is probably a metaphor that compares the Adversary's armor to the animals after which it was patterned (crocodile, serpent, etc.), for we see a type of Satan in Goliath and his scaled armor. That is, Goliath was a type of antichrist resembling Nehushtan (the serpent on the pole) for the Hebrew Text literally says, " וכידון נחשת בין כתפיו *and a spear of bronze* BETWEEN HIS SHOULDERS," (I Samuel 17:6) regarding this scaly adversary. Furthermore, God told Moses to make a נחש *serpent* on a pole, but He did not tell Moses what material to use. The word נחשת *bronze, copper, brass* is constructed by adding the ת *cross* to the נחש *serpent* (ת + נחש = *bronze, copper, brass*). We must also consider the fact that armor was polished like a mirror in order to blind an opponent while fighting: "But even if our gospel is veiled, it is veiled to those who are perishing, whose minds the GOD OF THIS AGE [Satan] HAS BLINDED, who do not believe, lest the LIGHT of the gospel of the glory of Christ, who is the image of God, should SHINE on them" (2 Corinthians 4:3-4). Keep in mind that "opening eyes," as Satan deceitfully stated in Eden, has both a positive and negative application, the negative being a type of blinding analogous to gouging (opening) eyes. Furthermore, since a fork in the road is called "the opening of the eyes" in Hebrew, then an observer who could find the North Celestial Pole relative to the North Ecliptic Pole (that is always in the constellation of the Dragon) would be standing at the "opening of the eyes" or the fork of the two North Poles. Satan acted as a wise man, a *magos,* for the root of the word נחש *serpent* can mean נחש *to shine* and *to prognosticate* as was done truly astronomically and falsely astrologically. When God "divided the waters that were under the רקיע *firmament, mirror* from those that were מעל *above* the רקיע *firmament, mirror*" (Genesis 1:7), it should be noted that the word מעל *above* is from the root עלה *to ascend* that is not only a synonym of the root of the word "day" but also produces the word תעלה *channel (of water),* which happens to be what is divided in this segment of the story. It would seem as if the division of the waters is illustrated by a liquid-filled hemisphere constructed of reflective metal that figuratively mirrors the heavens in order to complete the illustration of a hemisphere of waters in the upper hemisphere conversely reflected by the tangible hemisphere of waters being observed; this illustration links the ים *day, basin* to the רקיע *firmament, mirror,* by the fact that ancient wise men used metallic reflecting pools to observe the heavens (as in a mirror) just as they used celestial spheres (as in a mirror) to calculate the celestial paradigms. Simply put, all the reader must do is to regard the tangible world as the perishable reflection of Heavenly reality, and the astronomical reflecting pool becomes the lower, tangible constituent necessary to complete the sphere in a fashion that places the beholder's perspective within the sphere like a child within the womb. It would seem as if this very image is described in Genesis 1:2.

Genesis 1:2 states that the Earth, "היתה *she became* תהו *barren, unformed.*" The relation to an impregnable and wasted womb is obvious since Earth is regarded as even the mother of Adam in Genesis 2:7. Adam was יצר *formed,* and this technical potter's term is the antonym of תהו *barren, unformed,* as is related in Isaiah 45:18, for Isaiah 45 compares the potter's craft to the creation of man and to the formation of earth and thus explains "formation" to be gestationally related to people and the earth from which our first human father sprang. The celestial lights were made "FOR SIGNS AND FOR SEASONS AND FOR DAYS AND YEARS" (Genesis 1:14), and the same metaphor that relates gestational formation to astronomical observation can be observed in Galatians 4:10-19:

> You observe DAYS AND MONTHS AND SEASONS AND YEARS. I am afraid for you, lest I have labored for you in vain. Brethren, I urge you to become like me, for I became like you. You have not injured me at all. You know that because of physical infirmity I preached the gospel to you at the first. And my trial which was in my flesh you did not despise or reject, but you received me as an angel of God, even as Christ Jesus. What then was the blessing you enjoyed? For I bear you witness that, if possible, you would have PLUCKED OUT YOUR OWN EYES [opened your eyes] and given them to me. Have I therefore become your enemy because I tell you the truth? They zealously court you, but for no good; yes, they want to exclude you, that you may be zealous for them. But it is good to be zealous in a good thing always, and not only when I am present with you. My LITTLE CHILDREN, for whom I LABOR IN BIRTH AGAIN UNTIL CHRIST IS FORMED IN YOU....

Again, reflecting pools, made by watery basins, were used for astronomical observations, and birth (formation, gestation) was anticipated by the rising of the celestial lights. The celestial lights are compared to tree fruit by the fact that the North Celestial Pole was understood as a conceptual trunk that ramified into branches holding fruit that is illustrated by the stars, a point that is made apparent by naming the light "Day, Basin" in connection with having seven lights. The tree of seven lights is the menorah that has גבעיה *her uplifted cups,* פרחיה *her blossoms,* and her מנרה קני *branches of the lampstand* (Exodus 37:17-18). The גבעים *uplifted cups* were משקדים *like almonds,* and almonds are from the root שקד *to wake, to watch*; that is, an *almond* was, linguistically, a type of *eye and fruit that opened,* and Aaron's (Shining One's) rod became a serpent (shining one) and also budded almonds, i.e. it became a serpent with open eyes. The menorah is as a tree whose branches are aflame but are not burnt, and the fires are as both budded fruit and opened eyes, which is a situation analogous primarily to Christ as He described Himself in John 3:14 and Satan's imitation of Him in Eden. When considering the North Celestial Pole and the North Ecliptic Pole as trees, we can observe two trees in the midst that influence not only the earth, but the entire cosmos relative to gestation, and it seems as if the utilization of a celestial sphere's imagery is manifold. The celestial globe is merely a fashioned ball, but conceiving of the heavens as such compels the one gazing into the reflective waters of celestial observation basins (like the molten sea) to be in the imaginary midst of two hemispheres, i.e. within a womb. In this way, the Christ Child "...is the image of the invisible God, the FIRSTBORN OVER ALL CREATION. For by Him all things were created that are in HEAVEN AND THAT ARE ON EARTH, visible and invisible, whether thrones or dominions or principalities or powers. All things were created through Him and for Him. And He is before all things, and IN HIM ALL THINGS CONSIST. And He is the head of the body, the church, who is the beginning, THE FIRSTBORN FROM THE DEAD, that in all things He may have the preeminence" (Colossians 1:15-20). A simple observation of the movements of clouds reveals that they travel in an arc from one part of the horizon to the other. Likewise, the stars, when viewed from one part of the horizon to another appear to be within a hemisphere in the heavens.

The waters, contained above the firmament on "Day/Basin/Altar Second," were used to house the מארת *fires* on "Altar/Basin/Day Fourth," and we can see in this fire and water mingled thematically as a description of the stars. Interestingly, the fire/water mingling (originally utilized as a poetic description of the stars and as a natural description of a thunderstorm that, of course, obscures stars) is utilized in the description of the volcanic hail used to destroy Sodom ("Flaming"), Gomorah (Bondage), Admah ("Sterile"), and Zeboriim ("Shining") that is paralleled by the stars falling from heaven, "as a fig tree drops its late figs when it is shaken by a mighty wind," in Revelation 6:13. In other words, the Tree of Light/Life, with its seven fires, drops its light upon the earth destructively in reaction to the sterility Earth's inhabitants have chosen. (Consider the fact that the ancient Babylonians retained the idea of "fire" by two ideographs which meant literally "the wood of light.") As Leviticus 18 says of both Egypt and the Promised Land, the inhabitants who resided there prior to the Israelites practiced unfertile and unholy unions entwined with child sacrifice, which was typically conducted with fire; they "burned in their lust for one another," as the name "Sodom" implies, and they also burned the fruit (the children, the eyes) that they did have; thus, in perfect justice, the Heavenly Tree of Light/Life dropped its fiery fruit upon them:

> For the WRATH OF GOD IS REVEALED FROM HEAVEN against all ungodliness and unrighteousness of men, who suppress the truth in unrighteousness, because what may be known of God is manifest in them, for God has shown it to them. For since the CREATION of the world His invisible attributes are clearly seen, being understood by the things that are made, even His eternal power and Godhead, so that they are without excuse, because, although they knew God, they did not glorify Him as God, nor were thankful, but became futile in their thoughts, and their foolish hearts were darkened. Professing to be WISE, they became fools, and changed the glory of the incorruptible God into an image made like [1] corruptible man—and [2] birds and [3] four-footed animals and [4] creeping things [like the constellations in Day/Basin/Altar Fourth for (1) "signs" and for (2) "seasons" and for (3) "days" and (4) "years"]. Therefore God also gave them up to uncleanness, in the lusts of their hearts, to dishonor their bodies among themselves, who exchanged the truth of God for the lie, and worshiped and served the creature rather than the Creator, who is blessed forever. Amen. For this reason God gave them up to vile passions. For even their women exchanged the natural use for what is against nature. Likewise also the men, leaving the natural use of the woman, BURNED in their lust for one another, men with men committing what is shameful, AND RECEIVING IN THEMSELVES THE PENALTY OF THEIR ERROR WHICH WAS DUE" (Romans 1:18-27).

Consider:

> Beloved, I now write to you this second epistle (in both of which I stir up your pure minds by way of reminder), that you may be mindful of the words which were spoken before by the holy prophets, and of the commandment of us, the apostles of the

> Lord and Savior, knowing this first: that scoffers will come in
> the last days, walking according to their own LUSTS, and say-
> ing, 'Where is the promise of His coming? For since the fathers
> fell asleep, all things continue as they were from the beginning
> of creation.' For this they WILLFULLY FORGET: that by the word
> of God the heavens were of old, and the earth standing out of
> water and in the water, by which the world that then existed
> perished [the first world where both the skies and the earth
> were both lost], being flooded with water. But the heavens and
> the earth [only the earth was destroyed in Noah's flood] which
> are now preserved by the same word, are reserved for fire until
> the day of judgment [by fire, according to Zechariah 14] and
> perdition of ungodly men [like the Sodomites]" (2 Peter 3:1-7).

The fiery destruction from on high of the earth is called "The יום Day of the
Lord," i.e. the Basin, Threshold, or Altar of the Lord that mirrors in opposing
and correcting justice the wickedness done on the earth:

> "For behold, the DAY [altar, basin] is coming, BURNING LIKE
> AN OVEN, and all the proud, yes, all who do wickedly will be
> stubble. And the DAY which is coming shall BURN them up,"
> says the Lord of hosts, "That will leave them neither ROOT NOR
> BRANCH [a tree consumed by fire as opposed to the menorah,
> another description of the word "day" like that which Joseph
> utilized in Genesis 40]" (Malachi 4:1).

Consider a destructively sacrificial fire, for this "Day/Basin/Threshold/Al-
tar is described frightfully in Zephaniah 1 with vivid descriptions of the
fiery destruction awaiting the worshippers of the stars who practice child-
sacrifice (v. 4-5) as was the case with the Egyptians and the Cannanites.

    If the conclusions asserted above are correct, then the יִם day, ba-
sin, is a bowl used for libation and lustration so that fire and water are
contained in the same realm. Such a conclusion is made clearer when
one recalls that רקיע firmament, mirror was the name given to שמים heaven,
for, again, the word שמים heaven is formed by adding the Hebrew signification of fire and tooth (ש) to the Hebrew word for waters (מִים) — for fire
and water coexist in the heavens during a storm, and thunderstorms were
considered illustrations of fertility since they impregnated the soil for crop
production. Fertility is necessarily understood on account of a basin since
an altar was understood as femininity, since the altar and the threshold
were held synonymously, and since the word סף means both threshold and
basin. A synonym of סף threshold, basin is מפתן threshold which is from the
root פתן to twist that produces the word פתן asp, snake; ancient eastern-

ers often depicted the world as a snake encircling a disc, for the snake symbolized the water surrounding the dry land on all sides; this snake was associated with "the deep" in a way similar to Homer's Okeanos, though it was also compared to a "bond" or "rope of the world" by the Babylonians. The Accadians associated the primordial deep with notions of "wisdom." According to the Hebrew Bible and language, the serpentine connection to water can be seen in that the word נחש *serpent* is from the root נחש *to shine*, and the word נהר *river* is also from the root נהר *to shine*. The word יום *day*, it would seem, is more properly the word ים *basin*, and this basin is probably utilized in the Creation narrative as a threshold and as an *ascent* which is the substantive form of its root יום *to ascend*. As there were six "days" or basins and one of "rest" or covenant regarding Creation, we can see how there are seven basins of destruction prophesied in Revelation 15:7 as administered by a cherub: "Then one of the four living creatures gave to the seven angels SEVEN GOLDEN BOWLS FULL OF THE WRATH OF GOD who lives forever and ever." The seven golden bowls would seem to be as the seven golden uplifted cups (גביע) atop the Heavenly Tree of Life, the Menorah, the same seven "days" in which the earth is destroyed by overturning these "days," these "basins" (כוס) like the dome or basin that appears to contain the stars and that seems to expand above us.

It is written, "...ויהי ערב ויהי בקר יום and he was evening and he was morning day..." One, Second, Third, etc. Samuel Shuckford, in his *Sacred and Prophane History of the World Connected*, proposed that the Text is actually communicating, "and the evening and the morning were *day*...." Consider: "and the evening and the morning were *threshold*..." One, Second, Third, etc. In other words, the "day" or the "threshold" is *the evening and the morning*, i.e. *the boundary, the delineation, the demarcation* touching death and life, darkness and light, evening and morning. That the word ים *day, basin* is a *threshold* would seem apparent in that it is described by regarding the demarcation of light in Job because Job 26:5-10 says,

> The dead tremble, those UNDER THE WATERS and those inhabiting them. Sheol is naked before Him, and Destruction has no covering. He STRETCHES OUT the north over empty space; He HANGS THE EARTH ON NOTHING. He binds up the water in His thick clouds, yet the clouds are not broken under it. He covers the face of His throne, and SPREADS His cloud over it. He drew a CIRCULAR HORIZON on the face of the waters, at the BOUNDARY OF LIGHT AND DARKNESS. The pillars of heaven [as on a standing celestial globe] tremble, and are astonished at His rebuke. He stirs up the sea with His power, and by His understanding

He breaks up the storm. By His Spirit He adorned the heavens; His hand pierced the fleeing serpent. Indeed these are the mere edges of His ways, and how small a whisper we hear of Him! But the thunder of His power who can understand?

The "boundary of light and darkness" harkens back to "Day One" of Creation, or rather "Altar One" or "Basin One" or "Threshold One," since we are speaking of a "boundary," a demarcation, a delineation, etc. That we are even discussing "creation" admits a demarcation since the word ברא to create means literally to cut out or to carve out, for the word ברית covenant is from the root ברה to cut, and this root is a synonym of the root ברא to create. That the word "day" is "boundary of light and darkness" would of necessity make it an ignescent altar as opposed to a flameless one, which explains the fiery destruction of earth by these same seven "days" or "basins" or "altars" of which an ancient eastern threshold is a type. The rendering "and the evening and the morning were the day/basin/threshold" seems more than admissable with respect to the "boundary of light and darkness," for a יום day is a ים basin, and a סף means both basin and threshold, a threshold being a boundary; however, there is yet an observation concerning the altar/threshold aspect of the word "day" relative to both astronomical observation and sacrificial fire. The word "day" is from the root "to ascend" which makes a "day" and "ascension" by definition. An ascent and a threshold are accomplished easily in a step. A step in relation to an altar and astronomical observations is accomplished easily when considering a ziggurat, the pyramidal structure illustrated by Jacob's "ladder," ziggurat, or סלם ascending thing (Genesis 28:12).

Ziggurats served as temples and astronomical observatories. Ziggurats also resembled terraced mountains. In Jacob's dream, we can subtly observe the comparison to a temple and a mountain terraced for vines. The Seraphim are angels that can be compared to serpents, for the word "seraph" means "serpent," and "seraph" is from the root שרף to burn, making a seraph literally a burning one. Isaiah 6 describes these angelic beings as having wings, and the word כנף wing also means corner (as of a garment). These angels can be viewed as serpents with wings and as robed men offering sacrificial fire, i.e. as priests. Isaiah 6:2 states that these angels were עמדים ממעל attending above or standing upon ascents (raised platforms). The image of flying, fiery serpents is a literarily literal description of priests with flowing, flapping robes ministering upon a ziggurat with incense basins burning and proffering smoke, and this is probably why Isaiah envisions one of them taking a burning coal in order to purify him. Furthermore, the Seraphim are written of in connection with the "doorposts of the thresholds" (Isaiah 6:4), and סף *threshold* also means *basin*, like the *bowls* with which they minister; Jacob states that the House of God is the "Gate of the Heavens" (Genesis 28:17), i.e. the heavenly *threshold*. The very fact that Jacob describes the "ladder" as a "Gateway" points to the description of a structure similar to Babel (which means "Gateway" in its original language). A יוֹם*day* is as a ים *basin* and *an ascent*, a *basin* is a *threshold*, and an ascending threshold is a step; all of these definitions are accomplished in a ziggurat, which was a temple and an observatory. The womb is called a בית *house, temple*, and it is physically illustrated by a mountain as can be seen in the letters הרה, which can be pronounced to mean *mountain* and *to conceive (mentally or with respect to pregnancy)*. Mountains were terraced in order to plant vineyards, and such terracing resembled ziggurats. The similarity between a terraced mountain stocked with rows of vines and a ziggurat officiated at by "serpents" (priests with burning coals) is unmistakable. Both the mountainous vineyard terraces and the ziggurat are literary and physically parabolic illustrations of a womb, as can be understood by the words בית *house, temple, womb*, הרה *mountain* and הרה *to conceive*; thus, we may see in these relations a womb and a mountain, vines and serpents, along with mental conception and physical conception, for Jacob's encounter at the foot of the ziggurat concerned a prophecy regarding his "seed/Seed" (Genesis 28:14) — and the word ים *sea, basin*, is even stated overtly in verse 14 to indicate the ימה *westward sea* based on Jacob's geographical location. Seven "days" are seven "ascents," and the seventh ascent or day is the top of the ziggurat where the altar resided. The top tier was used to light the sacrifice and to view the celestial lights. Both an altar and the stars have obvious gestational relations, and, when considering both atop a makeshift mountain vineyard, one cannot ignore the reference to a serpent and the Seed Who would one day crush His adversary's head. Jacob's Seed can be understood relative to the ziggurat that Jacob beheld when He said, "Most assuredly, I say to you, hereafter you shall see heaven open, and the angels of God ASCENDING AND DESCENDING upon the Son of Man" (John 1:51); compare this to Genesis 28:12: "Then he dreamed, and behold, a ladder *was* set up on the earth, and its top reached to heaven; and there the angels of God were ASCENDING AND DESCENDING on it." The parallel would seem to indicate that Christ was as the Head of the temple Jacob beheld, thus, "Jesus answered and said to them, 'Destroy this temple, and in three days I will raise it up' (John 2:19), for the word סוי *day* is derived from the root יום *to ascend (literally he ascended)*.

The sunrise is understood as an altar of constructive sacrifice that brings life, and such a life-giving altar is as the womb that conceives upon the marriage, the union, of heaven, earth and water (with respect to the *sea, basin*) — for the threshold of this womb is where heaven meets water and earth in order to kindle the אור *light, life*: "...but a אוד *stream* (or אד *firebrand*) WENT UP from the EARTH and WATERED the whole face of the ground. And the Lord God FORMED man of the dust of the ground, and breathed into his nostrils the breath of life; and man became a living being" (Genesis 2:6-7). This "forming (יצר)," having already been understood as being the antonym of "barrenness (תהו)," seems here to unify fire, water, and earth (clay), and we can see why יצר was used as a technical potter's term since pottery unifies earth, water, and fire. Furthermore, ancient eastern potters were also book-makers, and their books were impressed upon clay tablets and fired in ovens. Connecting the potter's craft to gestation and writing explains why Ephesians 2:10 states, "For we are His ποιημα *poem, workmanship,* created in Christ Jesus for good works, which God prepared beforehand that we should walk in them." Eating words, as Ezekiel and John use the expression, makes sense when considering that ancient eastern books were baked like bread, for, in so doing, one eats unleavened bread so that the words do not distort in the oven or belly (אכל *to eat* also means *to burn*). The letters מצות spell both *unleavened breads* and *commandments* that Paul translates as αζυμος *unformed,* as was also the case with Plato's expression "αζυμος σαρξ *unformed flesh*" found in the *Timaeus.* Eating "the unleavened bread of sincerity and truth" (I Corinthians 5:8) was as consuming the manna or Communion, Christ, the "Bread of Life"; the unleavened manna tasted like " כזרע גד *Seed of Good Fortune*" (Exodus 16:31). Consuming The Seed, that is The Word, indicated an implantation that situationally places the consumer into the role of the bride while Christ gestates within in order that His Church might bear good works, good fruit, His Image: "For we are His ποιημα *poem, workmanship,* created in Christ Jesus for good works, which God prepared beforehand that we should walk in them," as the Israelites did covenantally: "Thus says the Lord: 'I remember you, the kindness of your youth, the love of your betrothal, when you went after Me in the wilderness" (Jeremiah 2:2). As with Mary, God is both the Sire and the Son of His bride, and this realization joins the man and wife together as a constituent of the bride through whom God births His Righteousness: "My little children, for whom I LABOR IN BIRTH again until Christ is FORMED in you..." (Galatians 4:19). Birth requires a temple, an altar, a basin, a womb, a threshold, or, for our purposes, a *day.*

The Molten Sea, or Molten Basin, was a cauldron used for priestly lustration, and such watery baptism was commanded for ritual purity.
"Baptism" is simply a common Greek word for "immersion," and, as it applies to water, is but the sign of the true baptism (1 Peter 3:21), which is a
clean conscience as a result of Wisdom pouring out its Spirit or Heart ("רוחי
אביעה לכם" Proverbs 1:23), as was the case when Christ's circumcised heart
poured forth. "Wisdom" and "Womb" are essentially the same idea in Hebrew as expressed in the letter ב and the word בית *house, temple, womb*.
"Spirit" and "Heart" are synonymous in Hebrew as expressed in the word
רוח, which can also mean perception. Thus, humanity collectively can produce: the woman through her womb and the man through his heart, for
Adam was, in this sense, the human father of his bride. That "light" is
synonymous with "wisdom" in the word אור light (as in, "Let there be light,")
is plain in 2 Corinthians 4:5-6: "...in whom the god of this world blinded
the minds of them which believe not, lest the LIGHT of the glorious GOSPEL
[= בשר of which we already understand as *successful birth*] of Christ, Who
is the IMAGE of God, should SHINE unto them. For it is the God who commanded LIGHT to shine out of darkness, Who has shone in our HEARTS to
give the LIGHT of the KNOWLEDGE of the GLORY of God in the face of Jesus
Christ"; however, those who have a "veil that covers their HEARTS" (2 Corinthians 3:15) cannot perceive such light. Again, understanding that heart,
spirit, light, wisdom, womb, and successful birth or "gospel" are all tinc-
tures of the same base color, we can comprehend the word "day" relative
to Christ as the "Image" of God in this particular thematic relationship. The
celestial lights were often studied in reflection basins (parabolic wombs)
in order to calculate fertility relative to both agriculture and people. One
who gazed into the midst of the basin saw his image reflected in a basin
whereby the reflection of his face was encapsulated by an apparent dome
of the heavens. As such, the celestial lights were before him in reflection
and behind him in reality as was also true of his image: "As in water, face
reflects face; so, the heart of the man to man" (Proverbs 27:19). Christ is
called "The Man," and, contrary to many English translations, it is written,
"God created את האדם *the man* ב *in/with* His Image" (Genesis 1:27). Such
a reflection, when beheld in a celestial basin, conceptually placed the image within the midst of a watery sphere that had the apparent motion of a
potter's wheel because of the apparent spinning of the celestial lights. In
this sense, the state of being static and in motion united as it does with a
child in the womb before the eyes of others. In the ancient east, life was
indicated by movement; since the womb appears outwardly to be stationary within the mother, but we know life to be beating inside of it, the image

of a potter's wheel spinning gyroscopically served well as a metaphor for the unborn, and this very metaphor is used to describe the creation of man by the word יצר *to form* in Genesis 2:7 (which is the antonym of the תהו *barren* world in Genesis 1:2 as is explained in Isaiah 45). When Christ prayed Psalm 22 from the tree, we must remember that this Psalm says, "many bulls surround me," which would seem to be a reference to the prophetic design of the Molten Sea/Basin/Day that sat atop the backs of 12 bulls and that was used for baptisms and for astronomical calculations. The Molten Sea/Day explains why the "Day of the Lord" is one of fire (2 Peter 3:10), for this day is molten. Since "day" is also the word for "west," we can behold the sunset of Christ's morning and evening sacrifice that marked the boundary of Christ's time on the tree. Beholding prophetically such an image, as in the Molten Sea, would then place Christ in the midst of the watery basin of what is under the earth, on the earth, and above the earth, an image accomplished perfectly by a tree with its roots, its trunk from which He hung, and His branching arms. Joseph compared a "day" to both branches and basins, and we can see, in this sense, the "day" of the Lord in that His branches were on the cross and His cup was accomplished by a poisonous sponge. Knowing that Christ died on a tree but specifically by poison (John 19:30), the image becomes terrifying: The Son of Man (Adam) on the axis (tree) that binds all of creation together dying of poison in the midst of a sphere (womb) where the opposites of water and fire ("lake of fire") are *mingled* (Hebrew: "*known,*" from ידע). The cross reenacted an innocent death by poison on account of a tree that mingled opposites, and this horrific deed shook Heaven, Earth, and what lies beneath, thus the earthquake following Christ's death. The crucifixion was a type of abortion wherein the aborted One received the punishment of the aborters.

THE MIRROR

THE root ראה to see, to observe, to visit, to choose, to understand produces the words ראי mirror, ראי revelation, vision, מראה appearance, form, and מראה vision, and mirror. A mirror can be, literally, a place of vision and choice that is revelatory and instructive. We can see such relationships in Ezekiel where a מראה mirror is rendered appearance in chapter 1 (as in the appearance of the cherubs) and a vision (8:4) as in Ezekiel's understanding of the appearance, the mirrored revelation. This word מראה mirror is a synonym of רקיע beaten out sheet of metal, mirror, firmament, which explains why visions are seen in the שמים heavens (heavens being the name given to the רקיע firmament or mirror in Genesis 2:8). Again, this word מראה mirror is used synonymously in Numbers 8:4 with the word תבנית pattern in Exodus 25:9 and 25:40, and it is from the root בנה to build, construct that produces the word בן son, pupil, descendant; it is connected to דמות likeness, pattern in 2 Kings 16:10 (that is from the root המד to be silent, to resemble) and which is connected to צלם image, likeness, shadow, illusion, idol in Genesis 1:26 (that is from the root צלם to be dark, to be obscure, to delineate, to cover). The word תבנית pattern is made synonymous with משפט pattern, judgement by Exodus 26:30. If we behold all of these words simultaneously, it appears as if a dark reflection is related to revelatory instruction that is connected with a child and that leads to a choice, a judgment. Let us consider Moses' veil in such a light. Let us also consider that a dark reflection and revelatory instruction are bound up in an eclipse, for this is the very prophecy of Joel (2:31) concerning the Messiah that Peter uses as proof of Christ's Divinity (Acts 2:20).

Scripture shows us manifestations of the Holy Spirit in the form of fire and a dove. Scripture shows us Christ in the flesh. Yet, John 1:18 states, "No one has seen God at any time. The only begotten Son, who is in the bosom of the Father, He has declared Him," and 1 John 4:12 says, "No one has seen God at any time." If we have seen the Holy Spirit and Christ in the Bible, if we know that the Bible was written by "The Spirit of Christ" (1 Peter 1:11) Who is called "The Holy Spirit" (2 Peter 1:21), if we know that Christ is "our great God and Savior" (Titus 2:13), if God said to Moses, "you cannot see my פני face" (Exodus 33:20), but if Moses spoke with God "face to face, as a man speaks to his friend" (Exodus 33:11), then it is God the Father Who is invisible since Christ and His Holy Spirit are visible; hence, Christ "is the image of the invisible God, the firstborn over all creation" (Colossians 1:15) Who said, "He who has seen Me has seen the Father" (John 14:9), and this sight is equated with knowledge, perception in John 14:7. *Sight* and *knowledge* are equated in the Greek of John 14, and we see the same connection in Hebrew between Genesis 4:1 and 6:2.

That God made "האדם *the man*" " בצלמו *in/with His image*" means that He made the woman in man's image and the child in the parents' image "since he is the image and δοξα *glory, brightness* of God; but woman is the glory of man" (1 Corinthians 11:8). Now we see a paradox. If man is the צלם *image, likeness, shadow* of God while, at the same time, man is also His δοξα *glory, brightness*, it would seem as if the reflection is in one way dark and in another way bright; this situation (the dark brightness) occurs naturally during a total solar eclipse, for the land and sky are darkened to the point that stars emerge, yet the eclipsed sun remains too brilliant to be viewed directly. A similar situation, by way of reflection, occurred when the ancients used basins filled with pitch in order to observe solar eclipses, for pitch is dark and yet reflects the brightness of the eclipse's phases. The Hebrew word דעת *knowledge/union* can be conceived of as generative in the conjunction of a solar eclipse, for this conjunction only occurs at new moon, i.e. the moon (woman) reflecting the sun (man) and then joining the man (as in fecundity) produces the corona of the eclipse (as in a newborn with a CROWN): "She bore a male Child who was to RULE all nations with a rod of iron. And her Child was caught up to God and His THRONE" (Revelation 12:5).

In a mirror, the right hand of the substance is the left hand of the reflection; so, in this sense, a mirror displays both a congruence and an opposition simultaneously. For instance, when Moses put the מסוה *veil* (from the root סוה TO COVER) over his face, it should be remembered that צלם *image, likeness, shadow, illusion* is from the root צלם *to be dark, to be obscure, to delineate,* TO COVER; thus, Moses' *covering* projected an *image* that was dark to the humans with whom he spoke; however, when this priestly (and therefore bridal) veil was withdrawn before God, His image was reflected upon the face of Moses in the fruit the bride brings forth, i.e. in the face of a child. In this sense, Moses was as an old man to Israel but as a newborn to God (depending on which way he faced). Moses face, like the moon, reflected the One Whose face is "like the sun shining in its strength" (Revelation 1:16), and the conjunction of a solar eclipse only occurs at new moon and, thus, the birth of a new month (like the birth of a child). The *conjunction* (Hebrew: דעת *Knowledge*) of the sun and moon produces this dark glory, this mirror of day and night unified in anticipation of eventual light, this birth; in the case of Moses, The Law, The Way, was birthed in writing. Since בית *house, dwelling place* means both *womb* and *wisdom*, it can be seen that "Moses indeed was faithful in all His house as a θεραπων NURSING *and healing servant*" (Hebrews 3:5), which is indicated by the fact that Moses asked, "Did I conceive all these people? Did I beget them, that You should say to me, 'Carry them in your bosom, as a guardian carries a NURSING child,' to the land which You swore to their fathers?" (Numbers 11:12). Thus, Moses was male and, as a worshipper, was a constituent of the bride, and the bride is to bring forth the fruit of her husband Who, in this case, is God. When Moses faced the people, the bride, he was as the husband, the male whose face was obscured by his wisdom. When Moses faced God, the Husband, he was a constituent of the bride, the wife whose bridal veil was pulled back and whose procreational veil was drawn aside that the face of the infant could shine forth. Since בית *house, dwelling* place means both *womb* and *wisdom*, one can look to the ancient threshold covenant as analogous to marriage in that the אור *fire* (*light, life, wisdom*) of the בית *house* (*womb, wisdom*) was kindled at the דלת *door* (*opening of the house*) where the SMOKE is emitted as the life of the womb is also emitted at the opening — for in this we may comprehend why God manifested Himself in a pillar (or tree) of SMOKE at the opening to the Tent where Moses spoke to Him (infant) face to (infant) face — for this is the same God Who manifested Himself in blinding light to Paul "last of all as τω εκτρωματι *the aborted one*" (I Corinthians 15:8). Again, as we have examined above, a dark reflection is related to revelatory instruction that is connected with a child and that leads to a choice and a judgement. Stephen, the man whose murder Paul participated, accused his soon-to-be murderers of being of the same ilk as the transgressors in the wilderness during Moses' day, and he specifically quoted Amos 5 in Acts 7 where the Golden Calf at the foot of Sinai is identified explicitly as Molech (a child-sacrificial image/idol). It should be recalled that, just before Stephen's accusation, "all who sat in the council, looking steadfastly at him, SAW HIS FACE AS THE FACE OF AN ANGEL" (Acts 6:15). That Stephen looked like an angel to his murderers, and that his murderers appeared as Molech, it would seem as if the angels being discussed have the faces of children (in a sense), and we see this reflected in the name גבראל *Gabriel* which means גבר *Warrior/Male Child* אל *of God*, i.e. Gabriel is, like Moses, at once old and young: "Moses was one hundred and twenty years old when he died. His eyes were not dim nor his natural vigor diminished" (Deuteronomy 34:7).

The Father is invisible, Christ is His Image, that is, His Son, and the Spirit of Christ completes the circuit as in libation. In libation, the father or priest cleanses the altar with water, heats it, pours out the wine, and the vapor or spirit ascends like a living bird. Bloody sacrifice is the opposite of this original libation, for the original sacrifice was not bloody but was a קרבן *drawing near* as a husband *approaches* his bride. Thus, the father or priest cleansed the altar and poured out a life-giving spirit in order to perpetuate life by completing the cycle: "Husbands, love your wives, just as Christ also loved the church and gave Himself for her, that He might sanctify and cleanse her with the washing of water by the word" (Ephesians 5:25-26). Similarly, The Father sanctified Mary as a cleansed altar in order to pour His Holy Libation or Holy Spirit upon her as a blessed approach or sacrifice in order that the Son could ascend from her; the mirrored opposite occurred at the cross where the Son ascended on the tree in a bloody and destructive sacrifice whereupon He gave up His Spirit before His mother by committing it to the Father Who gave it. The priest is the father, the altar is the bride, the libation becomes the child: "Did You not POUR ME OUT like milk, and curdle me like cheese, clothe me with skin and flesh, and knit me together with bones and sinews? You have granted me life and favor, and Your care has preserved my spirit" (Job 10:10). When we consider that gestation is described as "clothe me with skin and flesh," we can understand our fleshly garments as a covering, that is, an צלם *image, covering* that is designed to promote life and not to destroy it. For example, God gave Adam and his wife "clothing" of skin and flesh to house their spirit, and Adam was to be a *life-giving spirit* (that is, *he was to have children* by participating with God in pouring libation at the altar God provided). However, once man sinned, man was covered with a coat of skin derived from death that is commonly called "sackcloth," the fleshly garment of mourning. The word *to atone* is, in Hebrew, כפר *to cover*, and so our atonement is accomplished through Christ's blood when we "put on the Lord Jesus Christ, and make no provision for the flesh" (Romans 13:14), for many ancients wore armor of hide (as opposed to metal), and it is this armor that seems to be the imagery described in 1 Corinthians 15:4: "So when this corruptible has put on incorruption, and this mortal has put on immortality, then shall be brought to pass the saying that is written: 'Death is swallowed up in victory.'" As warriors once wore the heads and hides of lions for armor, the soldiers of Christ are to have Him as their head and covering as is depicted in the constellation of the Kneeler who crushes the head of the Draco the serpent while smashing grapes. Consider that the "...truth is in Jesus: that you PUT OFF, concerning your former conduct, THE OLD MAN which grows corrupt according to the deceitful lusts, and be renewed in the spirit of your mind, and that you PUT ON THE NEW MAN which was created according to God, in true righteousness and holiness" (Ephesians 4:21-24).

It seems plain as to why the Book of Hebrews discusses how the earthly priests who served in the tabernacle and temples of God enacted, in signification, what is called "a copy and shadow of the heavenly things" (Hebrews 8:5) when one realizes that a law like "You shall not kill" admits that people have already partaken of murder. That is, "The Law" of God is only reflected by, as though in a shadow or mirror, the command "You shall not kill" since "The Law" of God involves loving God and your neighbor as yourself. The term "The Law of Moses" has been incorrectly applied to only commands like "You shall not kill" when both "The Law" of God and "The Law" of Satan are spoken of simultaneously in Moses to show, like a parasitic wild vine and like an opposing mirror, how "...sin, taking opportunity by the commandment, produced in me all manner of evil desire. For apart from the law [of Satan] sin was dead" (Romans 7:8). The departure from "The Law" of God resulted in reminders like "You shall not..." and violating such a command was often reminded by the bloodshed of an herbivore (for such are all the sacrificial animals of Leviticus) as a statement that innocent blood was to be protected and not shed; thus, continuing to sin after the reminder signified in herbivore bloodshed and the subsequent EATING of death (bloodless flesh) results in this predicament: "For if we sin willfully after we have received the knowledge of the truth, there no longer remains a sacrifice for sins, but a certain fearful expectation of judgment, and fiery indignation which will DEVOUR the adversaries" (Hebrews 10:26-27). "The Law" of God is selfless love. The departure from selflessness is signified by animal bloodshed and the subsequent eating of bloodless death that is roasted in flames whereby further sin results in the sinner, not the animal carcass, roasting in flames. Since Christ's body was preserved, and since He descended into the flames for us, then Christ died instead of us in this respect; therefore, further willful sin that follows THE KNOWLEDGE OF THE TRUTH that is called "The Law of Truth" (Malachi 2:6) is tantamount to wishing Christ back in the flames. Consider:

> Therefore, leaving the discussion of the elementary principles of Christ, let us go on to perfection, not laying again the foundation of repentance from dead works [as opposed to living works] and of faith toward God, of the doctrine of baptisms, of laying on of hands, of resurrection of the dead, and of eternal judgment. And this we will do if God permits. For it is impossible for those who were once ENLIGHTENED, AND HAVE TASTED THE HEAVENLY GIFT, AND HAVE BECOME PARTAKERS OF THE HOLY SPIRIT, and have tasted the good word of God and the powers of the age to come, if they fall away, to renew them again to

repentance, since THEY CRUCIFY AGAIN FOR THEMSELVES THE SON OF GOD, AND PUT HIM TO AN OPEN SHAME. For the earth which drinks in the rain that often comes upon it, and bears herbs useful for those by whom it is cultivated, receives blessing from God; but IF IT BEARS THORNS AND BRIERS, IT IS REJECTED AND NEAR TO BEING CURSED, WHOSE END IS TO BE BURNED. But, beloved, we are confident of better things concerning you, yes, things that accompany salvation, though we speak in this manner. For God is not unjust to forget your [living] work [as opposed to "dead works"] and labor of love which you have shown toward His name, in that you have ministered to the saints, and do minister. And we desire that each one of you show the same diligence to the full assurance of hope until the end, that you do not become sluggish [which means you must work], but imitate those who through faith and patience inherit the promises (Hebrews 6:1-12).

Genesis 1:27: "So God created האדם the man בצלמו *in/with/by His image*; in the image of God He created him; male and female He created them." The word צלם means a *shadow, an image, an illusion, a likeness, a covering*, so a shining *likeness* could, with respect to this word, create the linguistic paradox of a shining *shadow*. The link between *shadow* and *likeness* here is in the idea of reflection, and, a shining mirror can at once be a *dark reflection* in Hebrew, thus, "For now we see in a *mirror, darkly*, but then FACE TO FACE" (I Corinthians 13:12). Moses, seeing that "He has set a TABERNACLE for the sun, which is like a bridegroom coming out of his chamber" (Psalm 19:4-5) was instructed by Him in this manner: "And let them make Me a sanctuary, that I may dwell among them. According to all that I show you, that is, THE PATTERN of the TABERNACLE and THE PATTERN of all its furnishings, just so you shall make it" (Exodus 25:8-9) and "... see to it that you make them according to THE PATTERN which was shown you on the mountain" (Exodus 25:40; Hebrews 8:5). It can be seen, accordingly, that the Tabernacle of Moses (specifically its veil), like the veiled face of Moses, was a copy, shadow, or reflection of the reality, for this man-made Tabernacle and this man-penned Law was "substance of things hoped for and the evidence of things not seen" (Hebrews 11:1) which explains more of why God used people indirectly to make what He could otherwise make directly. Likewise, even though Moses' countenance shined with "the knowledge of the truth," Christ being "The Truth" (John 14:6), the people "...heard the sound of the words, but saw no form" (Deuteronomy 4:12) as Christ indicated when He said, "For if you believed Moses, you would believe Me; for he wrote about Me" (John 5:46) as was reflected by Moses' shining countenance since Christ's "countenance was like the sun shining in its strength" (Revelation 1:16); thus, when we recall that "He has set a tabernacle for the sun, which is like a bridegroom coming out of his chamber" (Psalm 19:4-5), we can see how the veil Moses put over his face, when removed before Christ on Sinai, reflected the Heavenly tabernacle's veil that Christ drew aside when speaking face-to-face with Moses:

> But if the MINISTRY OF DEATH [like a *shadow* in the sense of *reflection*], written and engraved on stones, was glorious, so that the children of Israel could not look steadily at the FACE OF MOSES BECAUSE OF THE GLORY OF HIS COUNTENANCE [shadow, reflection], which glory was passing away, how will the ministry of the Spirit not be more glorious? For if the MINISTRY OF CONDEMNATION HAD GLORY [shadow, reflection], the ministry of righteousness exceeds much more in glory. For even what was made glorious had no glory in this respect, because of the glory that excels. For if what is passing away was glorious, what remains is much more glorious. Therefore, since we have such hope, we use great boldness of speech—unlike Moses, who put a veil over his face so that the children of Israel could not look steadily at the end of what was passing away. But their minds were blinded. For until this day the same veil remains unlifted in the reading of the Old Testament, because the veil is taken away in Christ. But even to this day, when Moses is read, a veil lies on their heart. Nevertheless when one turns to the Lord, the veil is taken away. Now the Lord is the Spirit; and where the SPIRIT OF THE LORD IS, THERE IS LIBERTY. But we all, with UNVEILED FACE, BEHOLDING AS IN A MIRROR THE GLORY OF THE LORD, ARE BEING TRANSFORMED INTO THE SAME IMAGE FROM GLORY TO GLORY, JUST AS BY THE SPIRIT OF THE LORD (2 Corinthians 3:7-18).

Again, "The Law" of God is "The Law of THE SPIRIT OF LIFE" and "The Perfect Law of LIBERTY" and not something negative to be avoided. "The Law" that reflects the Spirit of Life is, of course, the spirit of death, and it is this law, this mirror, that people are to avoid. When we view Genesis 3:16 that says, "In pain you shall bring forth children," we can understand that we are looking at a reaction to childbirth wherein pain was not such as it was after the sin in Eden; when we view this declaration, we are looking at a reaction to the sin of אכל eating, *destroying* "fruit"; when we view this pronouncement, we cannot escape that it darkly mirrors the imperative, "Be fruitful and multiply" (Genesis 1:28). Furthermore, when we view Genesis 1:28 that says, "Be fruitful and multiply," we must understand that it was said to people who had yet to be fruitful and yet to multiply, and it is for such a reason that eating fruit instead of multiplying it was a direct attack upon the Image of God by Whom that fruit was given — for why else would the womb be punished for what the mouth did? Like the two Laws, like the two Trees, the root מלך *to counsel* produces the word מלך *king, counselor*, as well as *Molech, the child sacrificial deity (typically represented as something bovine, i.e. an herbivore like the first sacrificial animal listed in Leviticus in direct reaction to the golden calf).* A *king* was a *counselor* in Hebrew, and *Molech* was understood as a *king.* Since both a *king* and *Molech* are literally *counselors*, then we can understand the immediate connection to תורה *law, counsel* and עצה *tree, counsel*; Malachi 2:6 speaks of the "תורה אמת *instruction [law, counsel] of Truth*," and we may consider the false opposite in the forbidden tree.

To say that the first humans "ate" "fruit" from a forbidden "tree" is not incorrect, but it is a way of reflecting a larger reality that is "the evidence of things not seen." In every Creation "Day," excepting the third, we read of God saying something, doing something, and the result of the deed (for the third "Day" exhibits the earth doing); however, after the conclusion of the seven-tiered refrain of Creation, the catalysts for many of the results of which we read are no longer stated until the story ends with what appears, at first glance, to be confusion until we realize that the confusion is ours and that we have inverted cause and effect and have expected to see in writing that which is but reflected by it. Instructing not to eat of the forbidden tree must have been in reaction to the desire to eat from it. The fact that there was a tree qualified as רע *evil, injury, sorrow*, in light of the fact that everything God made was "good," must mean that someone other than God was responsible for inducing the רע *evil, injury, sorrow*. That "pain" became mingled with childbirth explains why the word for physical "evil" (רע) was used to name the forbidden tree as opposed to moral "evil" (רשע) which is a different word. The physical evil was the reflection of moral evil as the mixture of sorrow and birth is the reflection of moral evil as signified by the gestational sackcloth given to man after sin. In a mirrored sense, there are two laws, two trees, two counsels, and two kings, and the morally evil "king" introduced physical evil to those who accepted his counsel by proclaiming him "Firstborn" as was physically illustrated at the base of Sinai with the golden Molech that acted in opposition to the reflectively golden Tree of Life or menorah.

Let us consider the ideas of a "tree" and a "mirror" being one, as James seems to indicate.

> Therefore lay aside all filthiness and overflow of wickedness, and receive with meekness the implanted word, which is able to save your souls. But be doers of the word, and not hearers only, deceiving yourselves. For if anyone is a hearer of the word and not a doer, he is like a man observing his NATURAL FACE IN A MIRROR; for he observes himself, goes away, and immediately forgets what kind of man he was. But he who looks into the PERFECT LAW OF LIBERTY and continues in it, and is not a forgetful hearer but a doer of the work, this one will be blessed in what he does (James 1:21-25).

A עצה *tree, instruction, counsel* can be thought of as a תורה *law, instruction, counsel*, and James 1:23-25 calls "law" a "mirror." James 1:23 is often translated as discussing a "natural face" being reflected in a mirror, but it literally says, "το προσωπον της γενεσεως αυτου *his infant face at birth*." Obviously, no one forgets what he looks like immediately after turning away from a mirror, otherwise daily shaving would be a daily surprise. The face one can forget is how one once was as an innocent child which is how one is supposed to be morally, for everyone forgets what he looked like at birth; when reminded, few adhere to that reminder in order to become again like that child by receiving the birth from above as we have seen on the face of Moses when he turned towards Christ on Sinai. James connects "The Law" of God with a mirror and an infant face at birth. A עצה *tree, instruction, counsel* can be thought of as a תורה *law, instruction, counsel* (both of which are compared to a mirror), and the letters מלך can spell *king, counselor*, and *Molech*; thus, a tree, a law, a king, and a child can all be perceived here, and the difference between the two trees, the two laws, the two mirrors, the two kings, is whether or not the baby's face is of life or of death, whether the birth is successful or not. Numbers 8 discusses the golden tree of life, the menorah, that was made "according to the pattern" God showed Moses. This reflective tree is followed by the Levites being commanded to shave their bodies whereby grown men resemble newborns, that is, grown men signifying a reversal or "redemption" (Ephesians 5:16) of time like Naaman's cleansing from living death whereby his skin appeared as a babe's, Hezekiah's sundial, Joseph's release from prison, Sarah's womb, Christ on the road to Emmaeus, etc. Genesis 38:14 calls the fork in the road or the place where the two "ways" meet the "פתח עינים *opening of the eyes*" (which is translated often as "the entrance to Enaim"). The logic of a fork in the road being called the "עינים

פתח *opening of the eyes"* is that one eye begins to be directed to the right while the other begins to be directed to the left beginning from where the two divergent ways meet; in this sense, the opening of the eyes demands and reflects a choice. I Samuel 11 describes the Amonite King called "Serpent" (or, in English, Nahash — the same as in Genesis 3:1) offering to cut a covenant in which he gouges out or opens the eyes of the other side of this pact. 2 Chronicles 6:40 discusses opened eyes in terms of attentiveness. Psalm 119:18 uses the figure of open eyes to indicate enlightenment. All of these examples of open eyes can be seen to be uniform if one knows that the "opening of the eyes" is the place where the path bifurcates, for this divergence necessitates a choice that will result in the inability to see the other path whereby (if one path is good and the other is evil) one's eyes will either be enlightened as he continues to walk away from the evil path or one's eyes will be blinded as he continues to walk away from the good path. Either way, the fork or "opening of the eyes" demands a choice; this choice is described as covenantal by the "Serpent" of 1 Samuel 11, which seems to be the opposite of the covenantally righteous choice provided in Deuteronomy 29:29 "to do all the things of this Law."

When James discusses a grown man beholding an infant face in the mirror, the congruent opposite being reflected in the mirror is a reflection of the arrow of time, for it is the illusory quality of time that is captured in the word צלם *image, likeness, shadow, covering, illusion.* The righteous mirror, the righteous law is the "Law of the Spirit of Life" (Romans 8:2) that is, the Law of God, the Tree of Life. The unrighteous mirror, the unrighteous law is the "Law of Sin and Death" (Romans 8:2) is the Law of Satan, the Forbidden Tree, the Tree of the דעת *Knowledge/Mixture* of Good and Evil. A righteous and wise adult is one who typifies the command "do not be children in understanding; however, in malice be babes, but in understanding be mature" (I Corinthians 14:20) while upholding the teaching that "unless you are converted and become as little children, you will by no means enter the kingdom of heaven" (Matthew 18:3). Since "a tree is known by its fruit" (Matthew 12:33), we are known by our works which are a proclamation of our parental guidance. That is, "wisdom is justified by her εργων *works"* (Matthew 11:19) and "wisdom is justified by her τεκνων *children"* (Luke 7:35) whereby we can see that *a work is a child, a work is a fruit*; thus, "once you were darkness, but now in the Lord you are light. Live as children of light — for the fruit of the light is found in all that is good and right and true" (Ephesians 5:9-10), and this fruit is opposed to the *"unfruitful works* of darkness" (Ephesians 5:11) as is evidenced by 1 Thessalonians 5:5: "You are all sons of light and sons of the day. We are not of the night nor of darkness." A fruit is a work and a work is a child, for the noun עבד *servant, slave* also means *son,* and it is translated by the Greek εργον *work* in Matthew 11:19 that is clarified by the word τεκνων *children* in Luke 7:35. A verb form of εργον *work, son* is utilized by the Septuagint to translate the Hebrew עבד *work,* till in Genesis 2:15; we understand that "ויקח and He took, covenanted with the man and He placed him in the Garden of Fertility לעבדה *to perform work in her, to sire a son in her,* and to guard her." That a son is even discussed in Fertility explains the original design that was inverted on account of sin that resulted in Sarah's barren womb, Joseph's imprisonment, Naaman's leprosy, Hezekiah's disease that was healed by the same plant Adam attempted to use to heal his own loins, etc. This sin was introduced by the unrighteous mirror, the unrighteous "Law of Sin and Death" (Romans 8:2), the negatively reflective Law of Satan, the abortive Forbidden Tree, the Tree of the דעת *Knowledge/ Mixture* of Good and Evil that induced the notion of "coats of skin" (which should be the mark of gestation) being used as symbols of mourning and slaughter. We have already understood that the letters עצה can be read as *trees* (Jeremiah 6:6) and as *counsel* (Deuteronomy 32:28) which is a synonym for תורה *counsel, instruction, law, torah, Torah.* James 1:23-25 calls "law" a "mirror." When we consider that acient eastern mirrors were polished metal, the menorah could at once be seen as both a tree and a mirror.

Again, the root ראהto *see, to observe, to visit, to choose, to understand* produces the words ראי *mirror,* ראי *revelation, vision,* מראה *appearance, form,* מראהvision, *and mirror.* A mirror can be, literarily, a place of vision and choice that is revelatory and instructive. We can see such relationships in Ezekiel where a מראה *mirror* is rendered *appearance* in chapter 1 (as in the *appearance* of the cherubs) and a *vision* (8:4) as in Ezekiel's understanding of the *appearance,* the *mirrored revelation.* This word מראה *mirror* is used synonymously in Numbers 8:4 with the word תבנית *pattern* in Exodus 25:9 and 25:40, and it is from the root בנה *to build, construct* that produces the word בן *son, pupil, descendant* (and in this we can understand a *son* as *fruit*); it is connected to דמות *likeness* (as was the creation of humanity in Genesis 1:26) and *pattern* in 2 Kings 16:10 (that is from the root דמה *to be silent, to resemble*) and which is connected to צלם *image, likeness, shadow, illusion, idol* in Genesis 1:26 (that is from the root צלם *to be dark, to be obscure, to delineate, to cover*). The word תבנית *pattern* is made synonymous with משפט *pattern, judgement* by Exodus 26:30. If we behold all of these words simultaneously, it appears as if a *dark reflection* is related to *revelatory instruction* that is connected with a *child* and that leads to a *choice*, a *judgment*. After God's judgement, we read that "He drove out the man; and He placed cherubim at the east of the garden of Eden, and a flaming sword which turned every way, to guard the way to the TREE OF LIFE" (Genesis 3:24), the מראה *mirror* or *appearance* of life and its אור *light, fire* or *life* (named "Day" in Genesis 1:5) that displayed the cherubs to Ezekiel in chapter 1:

> ...each one's work will become clear; for the DAY will declare it, because it will be revealed by fire; and the fire will test each one's work, of what sort it is. If anyone's work which he has built on it endures, he will receive a reward. If anyone's work is burned, he will suffer loss; but he himself will be saved, yet so as through fire (I Corinthians 3:12-15).

Consider:

> For you yourselves know perfectly that the DAY of the Lord so comes as a thief in the night. For when they say, "Peace and safety!" then sudden destruction comes upon them, AS LABOR PAINS UPON A PREGNANT WOMAN. And they shall not escape. But you, brethren, are not in darkness, so that this Day should overtake you as a thief. YOU ARE ALL SONS OF LIGHT AND SONS OF THE DAY. WE ARE NOT OF THE NIGHT NOR OF DARKNESS... (1 Thessalonians 5:2-5).

We can here observe the mirror of the two kinds of sons, the reflected fruit, the mirrored work, and the two trees from which they spring and of which they are: light and darkness, life and death. Let us consider reflections in order to illustrate the assertion further.

Consider Jacob and Esau. Malachi 1:2-3 displays God saying, "Yet Jacob I have loved; but Esau I have hated." "God our Savior... desires ALL men to be saved and to come to the KNOWLEDGE OF THE TRUTH" (1 Timothy 2:3-4); therefore, God desired Esau to be saved. Esau was the physical firstborn who had the Right of Firstborn, i.e. the privilege of serving God by serving the congregation at the altar; hence, "the elder will דבע *serve* the younger" (Genesis 25:23) as Firstborn since this word דבע *serve*, as a noun, means *servant* and *son*. By functioning as a Son or Firstborn of God, Esau exhibited the right of sonship, the Right of Firstborn for God to others, but "Esau הזבי *despised, spurned, hated* The Firstborn Status" (Genesis 25:34). Since Esau hated his birthright, Esau hated God. "If we deny Him, He also will deny us" (2 Timothy 2:12). Since Esau hated God,

God reflected Esau's (not God's) choice, and such a reflection would appear to admit that it is God who is typified by the Tree of Life, especially with respect to the fact that ancient eastern monarchs often named trees after themselves. The hatred was initiated by Esau by his rejection of the altar, and, since the *altar* is analogous to *womb* in Scripture, we can understand more of why Hebrews 12:14-16 says, "Pursue peace with all people, and holiness, without which no one will see the Lord: looking carefully lest anyone fall short of the grace of God; lest any root of bitterness springing up cause trouble, and by this many become defiled; lest there be any fornicator or πορνος (pronounced **porn**os) *sexually immoral* person like Esau, who for one morsel of food sold his birthright." Copulative impropriety, eptiomized by the child-sacrifice that so often accompanies it, spurns the birthright, and it is for this reason that we read that Esau had a wife named *Aholibamah*, which means *Tent of the High Place, Tent of the Child Sacrificial Altar* (Genesis 36:6), for she was a Canaanite. It would seem that this was the reason that "Isaac called Jacob and blessed him, and charged him, and said to him: 'You shall not take a wife from the daughters of Canaan'" (Genesis 28:1) and that for "Esau then realized how רעות *physically injurious* and *emotionally sorrowful* the Canaanite women were to his father Isaac" (Genesis 28:8). The word *physically injurious* here is the plural of the word "Evil" in "The Tree of the Knowledge of Good and רע *Physical Injury.*"

When Genesis 26:25 states that the wives of Esau "were a grief to Isaac and Rebekah," it literally states that they " ממרת רוח ליחק ולרבקה *cut the spirit of Isaac and Rebekah.*" To "cut the spirit" seems to be a reference to child-sacrifice also, for Malachi 2:14-15 says, "...yet she is your companion and your wife by covenant. But did He not make them one, having a REMNANT OF THE SPIRIT? And why one? He seeks GODLY OFFSPRING" (Malachi 2:14-15). The "remnant of the spirit" is for procreation. To "cut the spirit" would seem to be the termination of procreation. One of Esau's wives was named *Aholibamah*, which means *Tent of the High Place, Tent of the Child Sacrificial Altar* (Genesis 36:6). That Esau spurned his birthright means that he hated his office to God, and Esau's hatred was expressed through the destruction of his offspring, the very fruit or work for which God gave a "remnant of the Spirit." The consistent expression in the Torah, to "cut off from his people," can be observed in the "cut" spirit regarding Esau's slain offspring who, like the Servant of Isaiah 53:8, was "cut off from the land of the living." Consider the words of Jeremiah 11:19: "But I was like a docile lamb brought to the slaughter; and I did not know that they had devised schemes against me, saying, 'Let us destroy the tree with its fruit, and let

US CUT HIM OFF FROM THE LAND OF THE LIVING, that his name may be remembered no more.'" Remember that Genesis 30:1 equates childlessness with death while Isaiah 56:3 calls childlessness a "dry tree." Esau "hated" God by killing God's children; and, since he was willing to have his own children die, we can see why Jacob feared for his own children at the hands of Esau when he prayed, "Deliver me, I pray, from the hand of my brother, from the hand of Esau; for I fear him, lest he come and attack me and THE MOTHER WITH THE CHILDREN" (Genesis 32:11).

Esau "hated" his birthright and sold it for food, for Esau was called אדם *Edom,* which is the same consonantal spelling as *Adam* both of whom sold their firstborn for red food. God only hated Esau in reaction to Esau hating God by spurning his birthright to the extent that he participated in effacing the image of God through the slaughter of his child and His fruit, that is, through the "eating" of his own "fruit." How can God be blamed for wrongful hatred when He gave life to His children who, in turn, took the life of His children? Since "God is Love" (1 John 4:8), God loves His children to the point of punishing their murderers who exempted themselves by forsaking their familial ties to God through cutting a covenant with death as evidenced by the פרי *fruit, children* they אכל *eat, destroy.* It would seem as though the tradition that claims that God created Esau to be rejected came from equating the statement, "the elder will עבד *serve* the younger" (Genesis 25:23) and "Yet Jacob I have loved; But Esau I have hated" (Malachi 1:2-3) and by equating the servitude under discussion with that of Genesis 9:25 where Canaan is cursed by being a עבד *slave.* Only accounting for one kind of *slavery* or *servitude* (and the negative one at that), allows a retroactive superimposition of Malachi 1:2-3 onto Genesis 25:23 which would, in this case, make Canaan the victim and not the victimizer. Esau rejected the עבד *religion, service, slavery* of God (and thus liberation from sin) by electing the religion, service, slavery of sin (and thus liberation from God by rejecting the birthright). The rejection of God through the rejection of the Birthright can be seen in the rejection of his own fruit in that he married into child sacrifice, which is against the first imperative given to man. The reflection or the "evidence of things not seen" is that God hated Esau, but the substance being reflected is that Esau hated God as was evidenced in his marriages that were seen and the resulting fruit that was hidden. God "hated" Esau, for "the wicked and the ONE WHO LOVES VIOLENCE His soul HATES" (Psalm 11:5).

Again, It has been assumed that God rejected Cain without cause or by some expression of predestination. It is, however, evident that we are but beholding the reflected image of Cain who rejected God without cause. Cain offered a מנחה *gift* to God, and the offering of a gift brings with it the possibility of rejection. When God rejected Cain's gift, Genesis 4:5 states that God did not שעה *look* at it, i.e. He did not turn towards it. Psalm 73:28 discusses the constructive sacrifice or " קרבת אלהים*nearness of God*" in connection with "trust in the Lord God," while Zephaniah 3:2 states that "not drawing near (לא קרבה)" is in connection with "not trusting in the Lord." It can be seen then that God turning away from people is the result of people turning away from God: "Yet from the days of your fathers you have סרתם *turned away* from My ordinances and have not kept them. שובו *Turn* to Me, and אשובה *I will turn* to you" (Malachi 3:7), and this is echoed by James 4:8 where it says, "Draw near to God and He will draw near to you." That "evidence of thing not seen" wherein we read of God not turning to Cain is the reflection of Cain not turning to God. In not giving legitimately, Cain received rejection regarding his gift, and "his face fell" on account of his own shame and not God's favoritism since "It is not good to show partiality to the wicked, or to overthrow the righteous in judgment" (Proverbs 18:4-6) and "It is not good to show partiality in judgment" (Proverbs 24:22-24) and "To show partiality is not good, because for a piece of bread a man will transgress" (Proverbs 28:20-22) for "... there is no partiality with God" (Romans 2:11) and "knowing that your own Master also is in heaven, and there is no partiality with Him" (Ephesians 6:9) and "But the wisdom that is from above is first pure, then peaceable, gentle, willing to yield, full of mercy and good fruits, without partiality and without hypocrisy" (James 3:17). This fullness of mercy and good fruits without partiality seems to be in contrast to Cain's gift, for God offered repentance in His mercy towards Cain (Genesis 4:7), but Cain practiced the opposite of what is "peaceable" and "gentle" and "willing to yield" in that he offered a sacrifice (a slaughter) that could not be refused and that was not to God but to His enemy, and this Satanic offering of murder is evidenced in that Cain attempted to hide his deed to God by lying. Cain further mocked God in that, after offering a sacrifice that could not be refused, he punned the word שמר *guardian* that was the title of his brother's occupation; that is, his brother was the guardian of sheep, but Cain displayed his disdainful dominance over his brother by proving that Able could not guard himself but only the sheep of his offering. In this way, Able's flock was guarded to the point of acceptance by God, and Cain's bloody sacrifice was guarded by Able's inability to return. The sickening irony here is that God rejects what Satan accepts, for Satan's acceptance is a demand for the opposite of the standard to the extent that he is a mirror of one's own misconduct that is a mirror of its coercer. It can be seen, through the dark mirror, that

Cain was already wicked prior to our advent in the Narrative concerning him, and we are thrust into the scene following something not seen but in the midst of the "evidence of things not seen," for it is this fact, it would seem, that is revealed in 1 John 3:11-12: "For this is the message that you heard from the beginning, that we should love one another, not as Cain who was of the wicked one and murdered his brother. And why did he murder him? BECAUSE HIS WORKS WERE EVIL AND HIS BROTHER'S RIGH-TEOUS," as it is written, "And he who is upright in the way is an ABOMINA-TION TO THE WICKED" (Proverbs 29:27). Cain did not turn towards God, and, prior to the words of Genesis 4, Cain was already living unrighteously. The Narrative of Cain's gift begins with the reaction to the unrighteousness that preceded the gift and the lack of sincerity produced in this admixture. Cain publically humiliated himself by having acted in such a manner as to disregard the Birthright (i.e. rejecting God) whereby God rejected Cain's gift in favor of the one who was not Firstborn. Rather than turn back to God, Cain, as Firstborn, caused death intentionally in reaction to the con-viction of his own sin, whereby it can be seen that a man, not an animal herbivore, was slain as a reminder of sin, and that the reminder was nei-ther to God or prescribed by God but was to God's enemy and according to his prescription. The inversion of a Firstborn being murdered was, with Cain, overturned by God in that God refused to allow Cain to be murdered in like, and this refusal for the Firstborn to be slain, it would seem, was for the purpose of Cain begetting offspring who would surpass the righteous-ness Cain refused. It is this point upon which I shall conclude concerning Cain: Esau's marriages made his children invisible to the reader, Cain's murder of his brother temporarily stifled righteous offspring, and God's refusal to allow capital punishment to be exacted against the Firstborn, in this case, resulted in Cain's offspring Enoch's disappearance on account of righteousness and not on account of evil in that "Enoch walked with God and was no more..." (Genesis 5:24), for he was "seventh from Adam" (Jude 1:14) and the letters that spell שבע covenant also spell seven. Since rest is a Scriptural circumlocution for covenant, it can be seen that Cain drove himself from God in being a "restless wanderer" (4:12) as opposed to the Firstborn he was intended to be.

Since John 8:44 designates Satan as "a murderer from the begin-ning," the reader should ask, "Who then did Satan murder?" Satan, hav-ing formerly been Firstborn as evidenced by the fact that his high priestly armor (Ezekiel 28) is the same as Aaron's (Exodus 28), was a "murderer," and his fallen state can be seen to be reflected in Cain's fallen state. The written Word, I assert, is a reflection of the Mind Who wrote it and was composed in reaction to circumstances from which we have otherwise blinded ourselves in our fallen states by having our eyes "opened" by the blinding נחש *Nahash, Serpent, Shining One* (I Samuel 11:1). "The Law" of God must be distinguished from "The Law" of Satan, otherwise one can be induced to think, abjectly and absurdly, that Satan's murder is a Godly act of mercy. "In pain you shall bring forth children" (Genesis 3:16) is a reaction to a sin that upset the ease that was intended to bring forth children. "Fruit" was "eaten."

THE PHYSICAL & VIRTUAL WORLDS OF GARDENS

THE main factor that divides the various traditions regarding Scripture is the context under which the Text is viewed. There is a thematic strand that underlies the chronologically sequential sub-contexts of Scripture. The thematic strand is that of the ancient eastern monarchies described so beautifully by George Rawlinson. The ancient eastern kings were gardeners called "shepherds" who planted kingdoms unified by a royal road or way. The Great King's palace, paradise, and garden were modeled in miniature throughout the monarchy, and these miniatures were provided as domiciles for provincial governors whose privileged duty it was to defend the kingdom. The ancient eastern kings often lived a veiled existence, and their ancestrally cultivated and private trees were, as Pliny the Elder describes, capable of producing a medicinal and life-sustaining diet superior to those on the outside. The monarchs of old were approached with prostration. When their wars were won, they exacted a Day of Judgement wherein they pronounced sentences upon their live, defeated foes. Their adversaries were often stripped naked, prostrated, had their limbs bound, and had fishing hooks pierced through their groveling lips; when they were pulled forward to their doom and forced to locomote as a serpent on account of their bondage, they had their heads crushed by the victorious monarch. In this brief description, one cannot mistake the substance and reflection projected in the first three chapters of Genesis. It was such a "serpent" whose defection was accomplished with a humanity who accepted an unoriginal nature made through covenant and solidified by habit. It was such a King Who saved this fallen humanity from the "Serpent" and will restore the original nature that resulted from a covenant that conforms through the consistency of the primary design.

The intricacies and distinctions among the ancient eastern monarchies do not appear to be a mere almagamation induced by borrowing; they appear as fractions of an original whole that was not entirely seen in any one human kingdom but that is consistently observable in every human mind with adequate background knowledge. The various false deities called "Molech" or "Baal (Lord, Husband, Master)" "Milcom," "Chronos," etc. are all shadowy conduits of the same horror: child sacrifice. The specifics of Molech worship seem to be but parts of the mechanism used to describe something far older and larger, and this sub-context seems to reinforce the underlying and overall context of absolute rule typified by fruit and described as a tree.

The aesthetic cultivation of nature can be, among other things, a method of preserving a message. Such a subtle method of communication and preservation can be observed even as late as in 18th Century English gardens for, over time and geography, the rudiments of this form of speech remain in some fashion or another (even if relatively diminished). In essence, picture-making, sculpture, and literary composition can coincide with trained nature whereby the organic dynamically expresses the static; however, such dynamism and station can only coexist with respect to plant life if the cultivator transmits both the message and its signification to a successor, for, if he does not, his neglect or death will result in the reversion of nature to its wild state to the effect that the message will deliquesce into extinction. The verdent parks that were crafted in the fashion of an admired painting or in accordance with a literary work point back towards the age-old inclination to unite aspiration with reality in a communicable whole. Consider the famous Hanging Gardens of Babylon, for surely the very name given to this terraced, planted ziggurat assumes it to be viewed from afar in a land where mirage is common; when viewed through a mirage, one would believe to see a magnificent Heavenly garden dipping downward through the sky in gleaming daylight with all its lushness hanging (instead of standing) and kissing the apex of the earthly stepped pyramid that appeared as though it were the gateway to Heaven itself. Even the very idea of a garden ziggurat typifies mountains terraced for vineyards, for, in this, the very idea of serpentine life attempting to "... sit on the heights of the North..." (Isaiah 14:13) can be clearly seen with special respect to the fact that the summits of such gardens were utilized for astronomical observations as well as ritual slaughter. Considering that Eden was a both a garden planted by God Himself, and that its account was placed as the historical premise of Scripture, why would it be reasoned that we are reading of some commoner's unadvanced landscape? An opulent garden, as such, was a mark of nobility.

It was common for gardens to have a secretive, or at least private, intention. Outside walls or gates hedged off internal groves that could be entered by a single path obscured visually by surrounding obstruction. Similar to the menorah, a grove proposed by Louise de La Valliere had, at its center, a pool that contained a metal tree that was a fountain capable of spouting water from its branches and leaves. In this, one can see a connection between gardening and art, for gardening is an art. The enigmatic and emblematic qualities of communicative natural cultivation seem to admit the necessity of auxiliary education in order to interpret the message no differently than one must be skilled with letters before one can interpret a book. Emblematic gardens are intended to be read and Scripture provides us emblematic reading about a garden; in this, we should anticipate a literary reflection that is analogous to the "Hanging Gardens" of the sky that are, conversely, the image of a standing garden on the earth; Genesis, instead, tells us of a terrestrial garden that is the reflection of a celestial garden, and Hebrews 9 calls what is earthly a "copy." Statues, temples, and other objects of signification were sometimes arranged inside gardens in a manner that resembled what are called "emblem books," which are static literary productions utilized to help interpret the dynamic message of cultivated nature. That Isaiah 34:4 refers to the starry "host" as a scroll, a vine, and a fig tree is evidence of a conceptual link between trained nature and a message as reflected by the stars. On account of vast distance, beholding the light of the stars is seeing the light of the past.

Emblem books, like those common in the 1500's, fused images with words in a clandestine manner. Such books were deliberately crafted to provide artists and speakers with inspiration, and it is easy to see why each book subsequent to the Torah and Job contains the exact same conceptual framework. Regarding emblem books, educated people, when encountering a certain image or phrase, would be able to see its connection to a preexisting source in a veiled and riddled respect that gave them an advantage beyond that of others who viewed the garden. The significations that gardens and their corresponding books portrayed could be of a moral nature, a scientific nature, or of an interlacement of several disciplines that functioned in unison to produce an overarching message. The constellations serve as perfect examples of such a method in that groupings of stars do not physically represent the pictures that signify them, but they are remembered along with the pictures. The reason for this remembrance can be found in the names of the stars. That is, the stars were given names whereby the individual constituents of the celestial clusters bore related names that could be categorized and recalled by drawing a picture over a given cluster that was emblematic of the similarity of the group's collective denomination. Psalm 147:4 and Isaiah 40:26 discuss God calling the stars by name while Genesis 2:20 describes Adam naming animal life. Since the majority of the celestial emblems are animals, it can be conjectured that Adam was instructed to imitate his Maker's activity on the earthly satrapy that was a copy of the heavenly paradise; on top of this, the life-span of Adam was long enough to witness the subtle shift called the Precesion of the Equinoxes. Furthermore, it can be understood, by the signification of the garden having been planted in the east of Eden, that the union of Heaven and Earth was typified conceptually by the horizon at sunrise from where both the day begins and the starry pictures of the heavenly beings rise:

> The heavens declare the glory of God; and the firmament shows His handiwork. Day unto day utters speech, and night unto night reveals knowledge. There is no speech nor language where their voice is not heard. Their line has gone out through all the earth, and their words to the end of the world (Psalm 19:1-4).

It would seem as if the starry host is as an emblem book arranged to interpret Eden and that Eden currently exists on the earth in the mind as set forth by the pages of Scripture. Thus, in order to interpret the Eden account, one must have background knowledge in order to associate the words of the Text with the pictures they recall and the meanings those pictures convey. For instance, when Genesis 3:15 says, "He shall crush your head, and you shall bruise his heel," this is an emblematic reference to the constellations of Draco and the Kneeler that seem to recall how, again, adversaries of The Great King were often stripped naked, prostrated, had their limbs bound, and had hooks pierced through their lips in order to pull them to their judgement and demise. Since parks and gardens could be, and were often, constructed to resemble paintings, it follows that Eden and its garden could very well have been patterned after the conceptual pictures drawn out (so to speak) by astronomical cartography, thus making Adam's home both a reality and an imitation. The exact same scenario played itself out historically in the satrapies of ancient Eastern Monarchs who provided the *satraps* or *defenders of the kingdom*, i.e. *provincial governors* with copies of the royal palace, paradise, and garden (but in miniature). Eden, considered in these respects, is a literary composite.

Literarily, the deliberate arrangement of nature through cultivation and placement for the purpose of telling a story harkens back as far as the home of our first human parents. It has been long understood that the art of gardening parallels arts like poetry and picture-making. The cross-fertilization of representation and reality is apparent in the fashioning of nature into shapes for purposes unattainable in an untamed state. In a sense, the dynamic and the static are intertwined when nature is organized beyond its free inclinations. One who is educated in botanical arcana as such would understand a garden as a living picture or as an organic poem constructed with hints back at an idealized and pristine past. Relative to the account of the first humans, it can be noticed that the planting of Eden began, from the perspective of the reader, in the direction of the sunrise (Genesis 2:8) which, when thought of equinotically, would be what Genesis 18:14 calls the עת חיה *time of life*. Humanity, however, is expelled out of the east of the garden (Genesis 3:24) thus placing humanity, and the reader, in a perspective that sees Eden in the direction of the sunset which, when thought of equinotically, would be the opposite of the "time of life." Furthermore, when considering the cherubs and the "flame of the sword," it was this same scenario that Moses saw with respect to Egypt, that was "like the garden of the Lord" (Genesis 13:10), when he led the Israelites to Sinai before him while the "pillar of cloud" remained behind the Israelites to separate them from their Egyptian persuers (Exodus 13:19); it was this same scenario that Ezekiel saw when he looked west towards Jerusalem from where he was exiled and saw the pillar of fire or fire tornado, like a tree that is ablaze but is not consumed by its fire, that walked back and forth, turning itself, amidst the enflamed city. Here is a living picture: Jerusalem, according to Ezekiel, was a type of Eden from the perspective of the exile just as it was, according to the Gospels, from the perspective of death on a tree. Contrariwise, the fertilizing, watering, pruning and hybridization that produces varieties crafts the highest capability of plant-life: medicine.

Medicine promotes life, and the very idea of a Tree of Life is readily acceptable when one considers sustentation through medicine in light of the fact that Revelation 22:2 states that the "leaves of the tree were for the healing of the nations." As Pliny the Elder said in the 19th Book of his *Natural History*, "There still remains indeed a most important operation of nature... the true nature of each plant can only be fully understood by studying its medicinal effect, the vast and recondite work of divine power, and the greatest subject that can possibly be found." He goes on, in his 25th Book to discuss how he used to visit a man's "special garden in which he would rear a great number of specimens even when he passed his hundredth year, having suffered no bodily ailment and, in spite of his age, no loss of memory or physical vigor. Nothing else will that aroused greater wonder among the ancients than botany." The importance of this statement can be observed in that the extremely long life-spans the Bible discusses only occurred prior to the flood of Noah. From a literary standpoint, a flood of 365 days wherein all humans excepting eight people were destroyed would have reversed or eclipsed the cultivation handed down from remote antiquity to the extent that the potency acquired in plantlife through the collective memory that had perished would not be enabled to be reproduced on account of the ages of Earth's survivors. In congruence with the Eden story wherein Adam was expelled, we read of Noah planting a vineyard on a mountain (like a ziggurat) and, like Adam, experiencing a type of nudity and expulsion by way of a serpentine plant that did not promote healthy fructification.

The association of pictures and words can be seen, for example, in the work of the artist Nealces who painted a donkey standing on the

shore drinking while a crocodile lay in wait for it which was a symbolic depiction to the battle in the Artaxerxes III Ochus' conquest of Egypt in 350
BC, for the Egyptians called him "Ass" on account of an allusion to the
donkey-shaped Seth Typhon who represented the enemy and the likness
between the Greek word for ass (onos) and Ochus became a jest amongst
the Greeks who fought on either side. The point being asserted here is
that such a painting can be appreciated by many and understood by few
simultaneously because it used common subject matter to depict a story
the subjects in and of themselves do not innately represent. In order to
grasp the significance of such a painting, one would have to know that a
political war between people and not a natural war amongst animals was
the subject, that a man was represented by a one of the animals because
of a slight semblance of sound based on the Greek pronunciation of his
name combined with Egyptian religious associations. If such a method
were written rather than painted, we might consider it a complicated parable or riddle. If insignias were crafted by the manipulation of landscapes,
watercourses, and plantlife in a garden, the same result would be achievable. If actions were carried forth symbolically by live participants, yet another similar example would be perceptible. It is probably for such reasons
that the two times the Book of Hebrews uses the word παραβολη parable
(a placing beside, a juxtaposition, a parallel), it discusses a physical reality that has conceptual meaning and historical reference beyond the mere
tangibility it describes. The narration of Scripture can be likened to a gardener conducting the reader around his estate in order for the reader to
receive the correct reading of His sculpted and trained world.

The picturesquely instructive unions that were utilized in the construction of gardens and their interpretively inspirational emblem books
(be they the actual printings in Europe or the night sky as conceived by
the ancient dwellers between the Tigris and Euphrates) also served as
microcosmic models of the known world. Ancient rulers planted gardens
that represented, in scale, their own empire. A rock placed strategically
in a garden could represent a certain mountain, an irrigation ditch a certain river, and a shrub a certain forest. Such a mimetic miniature was a
simultaneously natural and synthetic stage whereupon the monarch could
walk through his empire all at once, figuratively, and, in this sense, be
omnipresent, omniscient, and omnipotent. Labyrinthine, brain-like paths
allowed the possibility to move about a garden's geography in all directions in order to keep an eye on all. The grand parks of ancient royalty were
often stocked with both animate and inanimate life that originated from
the breadth of the known world, and this was especially true of the east-

ern rulers who, like the Persians, prided themselves as "gardeners." The transplantation of plants and animals from disparate locations to within the walls of a royal park fashioned an environment where seemingly all the soil or lands of the earth, all the trees, all the birds, fish, and beasts of the known world existed harmoniously with the capability of engendering further varieties through cross-fertilization. It is probably such a situation described concerning Adam's home and Noah's ark (which would be especially possible with seeds, plant cuttings for nurseries, pregnant animals, eggs, and young rather than actually thinking that such a quantity of life could be placed within the limited boundaries described). Such a situation would be the synthesis of a real and virtual world, and this union would compel its ruler to have a considerable amount of expansive knowledge in order to unite the nonindigenous entities with a singular home.

The assimilative conception of nonvisual relationships is accomplished easily through metaphor provided that the nonvisual references are understood. The relationship between a garden and the arts (composition, painting, music, etc.) is subtle but substantially proven by the vast array of evidence that appears to exist irrespective of time and geography. Especially in the ancient world, pleasure gardens or garden parks (as opposed to our small versions of private farms) served as physical illustrations for virtual realities and therefore had to be interpreted in order for the virtual concept to be comprehended. Effectually, gardens spoke, they told a story, and they encapsulated some reflection of the mind of their cultivator in the same way a literary work reflects its author, a painting reflects its creator, and music reflects its composer. Scripturally, the pattern is reversed: The Text serves as a virtual illustration for physical realities and therefore has to be interpreted in order for the physical realities to be comprehended. It is within the first three chapters of Genesis that the known world receives its physical reality by way of Creation, and the liturgical refrain "and there was evening and there was morning" hints at the formulaic nature of a story told through obliqueness: the evening and the morning are the times for watering a garden. The very notion of superimposing an exclusively empirical method upon the Eden Narrative betrays a detrimental disregard for the cultural context in which the Text was written and is akin to judging the scheme of basketball by the rules of baseball. Similarly, the very notion of idyllic idiots meandering nude through a petting zoo hardly fits the account of The King of King's personal cultivation that was penetrated by death itself... for the very fact that death is even discussed relative to a garden should trigger the notion of a tomb garden or mausoleum... for why else would this be but one of a comparatively miniscule number of places that the Cherubs are mentioned, particularly in light of the fact that Eze-kiel 28 states that Satan was a Cherub himself? The question that arises from this notion is "Whose tomb would be in Eden if it is plain that Adam and his wife died outside of Eden?" Consider when Jeremiah 20:17 states disparingly, "...that my mother might have been my grave...." Even the very notion that the death of one man necessitates the mass death of others is surely a reference back to the mass death and suicide that accompanied the funerals of ancient eastern monarchs; like Adam, many members of such mass mortality died through the suicidal ingestion of poison.

Let us consider that the Torah was written by Moses. Moses was raised as an Egyptian, and Scripture makes it a special point to put into the mouth of a man about to die, a man who has relatively few words in Scripture, to specify that Moses was "... learned in all the wisdom of the Egyptians, and was mighty in words...." (Acts 7:22). The natural question to ask is, "What is the 'wisdom of the Egyptians'?" Samuel Shuckford states in his *Sacred and Profane History* that the ancient Egyptians did not DISCLOSE their physiological knowledge through writing but instead ENCLOSED it through writing. That is, regarding certain aspects of their knowledge, they taught it first by instruction in common letters, then their sacred character, and finally in hieroglyphic. After mastery was proved, a student was allowed to inspect the ancient literary productions in or-der to decipher their inner meaning, for such writings were indeed written as though enciphered. As opposed to instructing through argumentation and reasoning, the art described here is the skill of concealing ancient knowledge from the common man by discussing such knowledge through mystical, intricate, and uncommon language. The student's task was "to learn to read what was written, and to be able to explain a dark an enig-matical sentence, and give its true meaning" (p. xlvi). When considering King Solomon's close contact with Egypt, we see a very similar explanation of his Proverbs provided in 1:1-6. Even the very stress laid upon the אדמה *red land*, in terms of the ground from which Adam was taken and the ter-ritory to which he was expelled, points to the Egyptian concept of sterile and foreign soil in direct contrast to "the black" and fertile soil of Egypt. It would seem that the contrast intended between the land without and the land within Eden, as described in Genesis 2 and 3 is between the אדמה *red land* or *unfruitful land* as opposed to עדן *Eden* or *Fertility*. It is the same contrast revolving around the words ערומים *naked ones* and יתבששו *they felt shame* in Genesis 2:25, for the word עריר *naked* also means *childless* and בשש means *shame* and *dryness* like the *sterility of a desert* or the "*dry tree*" metaphor used to describe a *childless* man in Isaiah 56:3. In other words, the contrast is between the nudity that leads to fertility versus the nudity of infertility, and it such an illustration to which Job refers when he discusses his grave as a womb after the *death of his children*: "Naked I came from my mother's womb,and naked shall I return there" (Job 1:21). Likewise, Nicodemus asked, "How can a man be born when he is old? Can he enter A SECOND TIME INTO HIS MOTHER'S WOMB and be born?" (John 3:4). As was the case in Adam's expulsion, the אדמה *red land* or *unfruitful land,* that is, *the desert* or *wilderness,* is where Moses was expelled following his act of slaying where he similarly hid the corpse in the חול *sand* (sterile ground) which is, ironically, from the root חול *to turn, to bring forth (as through birth)*; for Adam was brought forth from אדמה *red land* or *unfruitful land* and was subsequently commanded to be fruitful; Adam received the *curse against the soil* or *the infertile soil,* from which he was birthed, as his punishment in expulsion; Moses was expelled to the *sterility* of *the accursed land* in which, typically, he hid the corpse. In short, notions of empirical deductivity and inductivity for the purposes of disclosure do not form the cultural context for the Eden Narrative, nor should they be superimposed upon such a Narrative that aims towards enclosure as the Hebrew word גן *garden* intimates (for this word גן *garden* is from the root גנן *to protect, defend, hedge in*). The very premise of Scripture is protected as by thorns and thistles from those who expelled themselves through sin, and reentry can only be perceived through the Mind encompassed by those thorns and thistles with respect to His status relative to the focal trees of Eden and Golgotha. Considering that the soil was cursed in Genesis 3, let us turn to consider a physical illustration whose remnants may help to understand symbolically what happened in Eden

Fenced enclosures are spread over the Negev that could have, presumably, belonged to the Amalekites who lived there at the time of the Exodus, that is, at the time Moses was writing of Eden. The desert of El Tij contains similar remnants, circular camps surrounded by walls composed of boulders fashioned together but whose height has been reduced by time. The ancient peninsula was probably much more verdant before neglect translated the green to the dry. A composition called "Our Work in Palestine" states that "The barrenness of the peninsula is due to neglect. In former times it was more richly wooded; the wadys were protected by walls stretching across, whch served as dams to resist the force of the rushing waters; the mountains were terraced and clothed with gardens and groves. The fertility lasted till (comparatively) modern times. The monks — there was formerly a large Christian community in the peninsula — carried old traditions of cultivation (traditions perhaps as old as the Amalekites) and terraced, protected, and planted. Then came the bad times of Mohammedan rule, which let in the Bedouin to waste and destroy. The protecting walls were broken down; the green terraces along their sides were destroyed; the trees were cut down, or carried away by the winter torrents." Warfare can convert lushness into infertility by putting a geography to fire and sword, and the lack of knowledge necessary to maintain the fructification offered by tapping underground water sources can curse the soil in a manner analogous to beholding the remains of a decaying corpse. Consider the "Flaming Sword" here. It may have been structures similar to what was described above that Moses passed in his journeys in exile and in the wandering that served as physical reminders of past harmony that once stood as the home of our first human parents. Let us now consider Egypt, the land that both birthed and exiled Moses and was itself brought under a curse on account of slain infants.

Egypt was gifted by a great diversity of plants through what was indigenous to it and through trade and conquest. Pleasure gardens, temple gardens, and tomb gardens were planted near the Nile and required much labor to maintain; furthermore, the spring can bring with it the dreaded Khamsin storm that usually lasts for 50 days. The walls of a garden are important for, among other things, defending against sandstorms which could otherwise immediately reduce lush cultivation into a sandy grave. These gardens were often planted atop raised ground in order to escape flooding, but the near proximity to the Nile allowed for the importation of trees from other gardens. The botanical precincts of the Egyptians were areas for sacred worship as was true of other civilizations. Gardens, as such, also often held vineyards, and tombs sometimes had their roofs adorned with grapevines whereby life and death were connected in a central core that showcased the forerunner of wine hanging over the ארון *ark* or *coffin*. The Egyptians held that certain types of trees were religiously significant, for the pharaoh was believed to be reborn with the sun every morning from a tree whereas Christ was reborn after dying on a tree by poisonous wine (John 19:30). Though I do not believe that The Ark of The Covenant mimicked Egyptian art, The Ark probably looked similar to Egyptian religious arks that (instead of cherubs) had figures of Truth personified covering the emblems of their gods and these litters were carried, as well, by poles on the shoulders of men, for the Ark's relationship to gardens can be seen in that it is a representation of the Eastern Gate of Eden from which Adam was expelled. Egyptian gardens and culture serve as a rich physically contextual backdrop for the Eden Narrative, but so do the gardens that were set within the boundaries of what were later recalled by the Persians as "paradises."

Xenophon described a palace of Cyrus that had a large park or παραδεισος *paradise* in his book *Anabasis*. He stated that it was stocked with animals (as is related in Genesis 2:19) and that it had a river that flowed through the middle of it (compare to Genesis 2:10) whose source was beneath the palace (which is similar to the descriptions of Ezekiel 47:1). Xenophon further described how such paradises were stocked with vegetation that contained all the products of the seasons, i.e. year-round fruit. When considering the fruit trees as related in the Genesis 1-3, a relationship can be seen to Revelation 22 that describes a river proceeding from the throne of God and watering The Tree of Life "yielding its fruit every month." The royal parks or paradises were also utilized for the assemblage of armies (consider the "host" that was finished in Genesis 2:1) and, fittingly, they were connected as though in a circuit by a royal road (like "The Way" spoken of in Genesis 3:24) that the peripatetic Great King could travel to receive tribute, inspect his empire, and gather troops. Provincial paradises had gardens and were stewarded by *satraps* or *defenders of the kingdom* who had the duties of collecting taxes and providing troops for the Great King, and we must recall that Adam was set in the garden to "cultivate and to *defend*" (Genesis 2:15). In this area of the world, the thresholds to gardens and paradises were guarded, and statues of winged bulls or what we might call cherubs stood imposingly as constituents of the wall-doorway connection. In warfare, paradises were often looted and then set ablaze through fire and sword. A conflagration large enough to decimate an entire paradise and the garden within it could engender a fire tornado, the flaming vortex that walks back and forth amongst the fire and, from the perspective outside of the threshold of the burning paradise, can be seen as though passing in and out near the entrance flanked by cherubic statues of what was once a zoological orchard. It would seem as if such a scene is remembered in Genesis 3:24 where it is written, "He placed cherubim at the east of the garden of Eden, and a flaming sword which turned every way, to guard the way to the Tree of Life," and it would also seem more than probable that the war described in Revelation 12 harkens back to this scene. Lastly, the Persians retained a custom that would seem to extend from the earliest antiquity, for they termed their Kings as "Gardeners." Let us now move to Jerusalem.

Centuries before Xenophon, King Solomon wrote in Ecclesiastes 2:4-9,

I made my works great, I built myself houses, and planted myself vineyards. I made myself gardens and פרדסים *paradises*, and I planted all kinds of fruit trees in them. I made myself water pools from which to water the growing trees of the grove. I acquired male and female servants, and had servants born in my house. Yes, I had greater possessions of herds and flocks than all who were in Jerusalem before me. I also gathered for myself silver and gold and the special treasures of kings and of the provinces. I acquired male and female singers, the delights of the sons of men, and musical instruments of all kinds. So I became great and excelled more than all who were before me in Jerusalem. Also my wisdom remained with me.

In Song of Songs 412-13, King Solomon compares a woman both to a garden and a paradise:

A גן *garden* enclosed Is my sister, my spouse, a spring shut up, a fountain sealed. Your plants are a פרדס *paradise* of pomegranates with pleasant fruits, fragrant henna with spikenard....

It can be seen that gardens and paradises, that is, walled enclosures that encompass vegetable and animal life, are employed by Solomon in relation to a woman. Since עדן *Eden* means *Fertility*, we can understand Eden as a fertile woman in that God planted a garden within her. Jerusalem is likewise referred to as a woman in Lamentations 1:1. In other words, Genesis 2:8 states that "the Lord God planted a garden IN Eden, in the east..." for the garden was IN Eden, and this explains why the man was "alone" even though he was created after the animals. Since both a garden and a paradise are enclosures, Adam was inside the garden that was inside the precinct of the animals. If this arrangement is thought of anatomically, then a garden is as a non-pregnant woman and a paradise is as a pregnant woman since what distinguishes a paradise from a garden is that a paradise houses animate life (aside from the caretaker). Impregnation converts a garden into a paradise and compels the borders to expand in order to perpetuate the process through successive enclosures that increase in size, for it was probably the horizon that was conceived of in the command "Be fruitful and multiply and FILL THE EARTH and subdue it" (Genesis 1:28). It would seem as though the horizon is the physical illustration for the entire earth and that Matthew 24:14 is a parallel to "Be fruitful... and fill the earth..." when it says, "And this gospel of the kingdom will be preached in all the world as a witness to all the nations, and then the end will come."

What we now call a "zoological garden" or "zoo" is as a labora-
tory where cognitive interaction with animate and inanimate life occurs
at the nexus of the tangible and the conceptual. The garden described in
Genesis 2 seems to bring to mind a vivarium where a menagerie existed
amongst orchards in vegetarian peace. Genesis 3 seems to decline towards a seraglio of combating animals (so to speak) by the introduction of
the term חית השדה often translated *beast of the field*, literally, *living creature*
or *life of the cultivated field* to describe the mental inferiors of the so called
"serpent" or literally נחש*shining one*, i.e. *one who is brilliant*. In other
words, this word "field" is, in Hebrew, a cultivated field (for agriculture or
the removal of obstacles on the plain of battle) and the hunting territory
described regarding Esau in Genesis 27:27. Esau, like Nimrod's kingdom,
hunted both animals and infants for the purposes of ritual slaguther. The
word for "demons" in Deuteronomy 32:17 bears a resemblance to the
word "field" regarding the "beasts of the field" in Genesis 3:1. It would
appear that a subtle reference is made that the "Serpent" was the most
cunning of all the warrior demons. It would further seem that Satan was
"hunting" a sacrifice to initate his war, as was the custom of ancient eastern warfare. If this is so, then the gate of Heaven, the top of the Ziggurat
of Eden, was stormed through child-sacrifice, the child being the sacrifice
acceptable to Satan and his demons; for it is upon this altar, this threshold, that war is made upon the Kingdom of Heaven that "belongs to such
as these" children (Luke 18) and that "suffers violence" (Matthew 11:12).
Lastly, it would say much to the war described in Revelation 12 that would
point back to the rebellion in Eden.

Zoological gardens are enclosures of collective memory that con-
stellate disparate forms of understanding and practice into an amalgamous
whole; this facet of botanical menageries was understood well enough by
the Emperor Wen-Wang (9th Century BC) who called his 375-hectare zoo
the *Garden of Intelligence*. We may here consider the Garden of Eden with
its central trees. In royal gardens as such, animals could serve as tribute,
and major efforts were undertaken to tame them, even to the extent that
some (who were capable) trained lions to sleep at their feet in peace like
dogs. The grand amalgamation of plants and animals was a sign of luxury,
power, and intelligence. Parading exotic and otherwise threatening creatures was as much a display of power as the parading of defeated foes in
public triumph, and we may read of a perverse account of Molech worship
(infant sacrifice) in Job 18 where Satan is called the "King of Terrors" who
receives a charred child as trophy; this situation is described with references to understanding (v. 2), beasts (v. 3) captivity (v. 10) roots (v. 16)

and the knowledge of God (v.21). Since the control of sexual reproduction was an aim of many a zoo, one can see in this sordid reference a glance back at Eden when it became adulterated as revealed by the punishment against the womb. The gory, induced fights between various animal types in zoos of old was common and was symbolically imitative of duels between people among more than one culture, for zoological gardens were, essentially, proclamations of subjugation of humanity over wildlife as much as the gladiatorial provocation of beasts against each other served to display man's bloodthirsty and sin-imbued power. Similarly, viewing a human war from afar as reflected by a mirage over a plane or field would appear as a war in the heavens where the combatants would look part human and part animal if the soldiers wore animal hides as armour and animal heads as helmets. Such may be illustrative of the cherubs. Since Satan was a cherub (Ezekiel 28) who is called a "Shining One" in Hebrew and a "Serpent" in English, reflective scale armor would appear in a lofty mirage as the flesh of a bronze dragon warrior celestially. Gardens were even crafted for the purposes of hunting, which was, of course, contrary to the vegetarian diet mandated in Genesis 1. In short, the hunting-grounds, animal-combat circuses, and laboratories that became grimly enmeshed in the once peaceful vivariums of old resulted in collections like a cabinet of curiosities wherein taxidermied death hung suspended from ceilings in dark imitation of the constellations.

What we might call (anachronistically) zoos or zoological gardens have a history so ancient that it dates back to Eden. Death could not have been part of the originally intended design of the first zoological garden that existed prior to sin (since "the wages of sin is death"), so seraglios of fighting animals, hunting-grounds, and other places of suffering cannot be an accurate description of mankind's primacy but are defective offshoots that reveal the overturning of nature in the midst of an effort to elevate it. Yet, it is quite believable that Eden's timeless message, told within the arrow of time, utilizes imagery after the advent of iniquity to describe, as though in a mirror, what the original design of cultivated nature was before transgression so that one can observe that the reflected opposite comprising our present knowledge is actually the substance of which we truly are the mirrored antithesis. In the preparations of man's various habitations, wars have been made against animals considered to be detrimental to the advancement of man. In a sense, the enclosures and bars of zoos contain snapshots of man's relationship to the creation over which he was placed and his relation to Satan to whom he gave dominion. The mastery of exotic, toxic, and ferocious nature of both the inanimate and animate kinds was a mark of might as much as it was of intellect. Zoos and botanical gardens mesh the artificial with the natural in an entangled symbol of collective memory that displays triumph along side of failure, for the very attempt to preserve endangered species is often the conservatory effort of the creation that spawned the endangerment. For instance, exotic animals and plants were (and are) considered luxury items and were often among the captives taken in warfare to be relocated and recultivated on the soil of the victor. The relocation of animals, like that of people, was often the result of conquest, and the newly acquired animals, like the newly acquired people, were also often used for warfare on the side of their new master.

Innumerable expeditions were launched through war, opulence, and scientific inquiry to procure rare species for private purposes. A common technique for the capture of live animals was to kill suckling females and a herd's leaders so that the infant or juvenile animals would be left defenseless; these young animals were subsequently welcomed into the hands of their captors who would be surrogates or the conduits to adoption in a foreign environment. Zoological specimens were contained in all sorts of manners (pits, enclosures, large jail cells), and were often used for amusement via bloody combat; this situation exuded a complete disregard for both money and life since it was costly to procure, contain, and feed the very creatures whose sole purpose was to be extinguished violently to the slavish pleasure of earthly, belicose regency. One can also see that forcing animals to battle both animals and people could easily be converted into the observations of experimental science that would provide subjects for dissection that would eventuate into surgical techniques and other practices otherwise employed positively. The positive employments would be retroactively thrown upon the former atrocities in order to justify the means, for such was the case with vivisection. In fact, natural inquiry, when confusing the value of life with what simply can be derived from it, went so far as to attempt to graft foreign limbs onto animals that were not of the same species in an effort to study botanical grafting techniques thought to be compatible with animate nature. The ability to fell a beast with a blade and the attempt to modify one were unbridled exertions of power concentrated upon subjects incapable of cognizing such horror, and that this ability to dominate massaged the ego of the "victors" is evidence of a new nature not yet present prior to human error when it is plain, according to Genesis 1:26-31, the dominion of man was coupled with a vegetarian diet and the aspect of death was yet to be introduced as a modification of God's zoological garden. "Wisdom gives life" (Ecclesiastes 7:12), for animals were raised and bred for educational purposes within menageries; in a fallen world, they are raised and bred for food; wisdom and food can be seen unified here against the original design when the blood of animate beings is involved.

With the systematic slaughter of hunting, experiment, vivisection, and dissection came "cabinets of curiosities" which were rooms or houses constructed to display a vast and disparate array of lifeless biological specimens. Eventually, the scholar spent more time among the dead than the living, exploring the depths of what could be discerned within lifeless bodies. Like grand gardens, cabinets were as a microcosm of the world's four corners, a still photograph of a past preserved in silence. Like grand gardens, cabinets were part of the realm of nobility. Collectors would display their knowledge of arcane and foreign nature in conglomeration of motionless beings, be they taxidermied animals or dried plants. Artificial constructions crafted by human ingenuity were sometimes a component of these cabinets in order to heighten the imagination of viewers who could be entertained at the prospect of anomaly wherein the distinction between natural and supernatural was blurred. Accordingly, the curiosities engendered by the manipulation of nature resulted in a fascination with the increasingly exotic to the point where deformed creatures became prized for their rarity. Ultimately, embryos were coveted supremely. Nascent biological specimens were often preserved in alcohol as though floating in an artificial womb only capable of birthing interest in knowledge that served little more than morbid intrigue.

Books, like garden emblem books, containing drawings of both live and dead animals were produced to preserve memory of nature's inhabitants. The descriptions of exotic animals were often comparative so that individual portions of an otherwise unknown creature would be described as similar to the individual portions of a known one. For instance, a camel was once described as having an elephant's eyes, a rhinoceros's ears, a snake's neck, a beaver's tail — and the head of a Russian! (see Zoo, by Baraty and Hardouin-Fugier). Though the last description is insultingly comical, one can see a very serious resemblance to the descriptions of the cherubs in Ezekiel 1 and the zoa (from where we derive our word for zoo) in Revelation 4: "The first living creature was like a lion, the second living creature like a calf, the third living creature had a face like a man, and the fourth living creature was like a flying eagle. The four living creatures, each having six wings, were full of eyes around and within." It is difficult not to see in this principal constellations (three of which being zodiacal) preserved in the celestial cabinet full of the blinking eyes of the scintillating stars. Cabinets were microvolumed mirrors of nature's breadth, and they would commonly be ornamented by flowerbeds and other botanical delights, all synthesized to stimulate curiosity through mysterious knowledge.

It would seem that botanically adorned menageries and cabinets were the dynamic and static reflections of each other, both of which could be used to harness the knowledge of the world by centralizing portions of nature into a convergent, ocular feast of learning comparable to a library, museum, or academy. The master of these schools was a master who held the power of life and death, a power usually relegated to kings alone; thus, the master of a menagerie or a cabinet was the absolute monarch of both the living and the dead within his sphere that centered around the acquisition of knowledge. In both the seraglio of moving creatures and the cabinet, nature could be manipulated to serve the master as far as his knowledge and might serve him. It is for such reasons that zoological gardens were often carved out for the purpose of glorifying the king who possessed them, a glory that was perpetuated emblematically; the dwellers within his nature were the epistles themselves who perpetuated the preservation of a message that preceded them.

In Genesis 2:8, we read that God planted a "garden in Eden, in the east"; this word "east" is קדם and is from the root קדם to go before, precede, to anticipate, which also produces the meaning מקדם of old; we may understand that God planted a garden in former times. The name Eden means Fertility, and the fact that it is in the east is further clarified by Psalm 110:4 that describes the direction of the sunrise as the משחר מרחם womb of the dawn. As such, we may see that God planted the garden of Fertility in the womb of the dawn, hence the voluptuous command, "Be fruitful and multiply... and rule...." The womb of the dawn Is described in connection with the word קרב midst in Psalm 110:2, and this is especially important since this word קרב midst also means womb which is from the root קרב to draw near, approach, to offer a gift which produces the word קרבן offering, oblation, and sacrifice; it is obvious here that the sacrifice cannot be one involving death but rather what Paul later calls a living sacrifice. A living sacrifice is a life dedicated to God until death as was the case with Samuel and his mother's dedication; the opposite of this would a be a נתן (=**NaTHaN**) child sacrifice to Molech through sinful union which is why it is **Nathan** who proclaims the death of David's son (Solomon's nameless older brother) after David hung the crown of Molech that he looted from the son of נחש Serpent (= NaHaSH) over his royal throne and stole Bathsheba (= בת שבע Daughter of the Oath). The point is that east, womb of the dawn, and midst are all synonymous; the reader will notice that Fertility was planted in the east that is, in a sense, the midst, and that the two principle trees of Eden were also בתוך *in the midst* of the garden (Genesis 2:9; 3:3). The word לבב *heart, mind, life* is also a word for *midst,* and the word לבב means *to become wise.* The *east* is the *womb* that is the *midst,* which is the place of *life* and thus the *heart* and *mind,* for these associations allow us to see that Adam *bore* his wife from his circumcised *heart* which is analogous to a fruitful *womb.*

Typically, a garden where the focal point is in the middle is a maze or labyrinth, for the goal of this serpentine construction is its central core. Since the letters לבב can mean *heart, mind, life, midst* and *to become wise,* we can understand (at least thematically or conceptually) that the garden was patterned after the brain, i.e. was a maze garden, for both the Tree of *Life* (Genesis 2:9) and the word להשכיל *to make one wise* (Genesis 3:6) are discussed in *Eden's (Fertility's) midst* or *womb.* The ideas of womb and wisdom are linked in the letter ב which is spelled fully as בית *dwelling place* (as in a garden) or commonly *temple, house* (but this word is applicable to open-air precincts as well), i.e. *location wherein life resides.* A labyrinth resembles the intestines (womb) and the brain (wisdom), and between these two anatomically is the לבב *heart, mind, life, midst* through which one can לבב *become wise.* The fact that the directional perspectives of Eden before and after sin change from east to west places Eden at the threshold of the account, and the word פתן *asp, snake* is related to the word מפתן *threshold.* Since Satan is called a "serpent" in Genesis 3 and a "cherub" in Ezekiel 28, and cherubs are doorkeepers or threshold guardians, we can see the connection between a threshold and an asp. What must be remembered is that a maze is a type of mirror in two ways: (1) a maze can be constructed according to strict symmetry whereby all things double against each other; (2) the entry to a maze's core is reflected by the exit from that core.

The Eden account in the Book of Genesis seems to contain aspects of all of the gardens we have observed above. It may be, perhaps, that the Eden account of Genesis is a conceptual composite of many different types of gardens, and that such a composite was crafted in order to discuss the sin that spread through the entire earth in an emblematic or symbolic way in order to discuss an existence that the Author knew would become remote to later readers. It also may be that the Eden account of Genesis is a conceptual composite of the world during Moses' time used mechanistically to describe something long before by way of deliberate motifs that only a uniquely educated readership would comprehend. The possibility exists that Eden contained all of the qualities discussed above (and more) and that it was a physical concentration in miniature of the four corners of the earth that was intended to spread through reproduction in order to restore new rulership over the earth to which Satan was cast. Possibilities upon possibilities exist, but one truth remains: the Eden account is told programatically, emblematically, symbollically, and conceptually by way of deliberate motifs that require extrabiblical background knowledge to coincide with a memorization of Scripture. It is here that I would like to begin addressing some of the accusations against the geneaologies of Genesis in order to prove how the type and antitype work harmoniously to craft a narrative that I believe was intended to be read as though in a mirror, and it is my conviction that this mirror is what we call the *firmament* but what Genesis 1:6 calls רקיע *a beaten out sheet of metal* that Job 37:18 defines as a כראי מוצק *cast metal mirror*.

The arrangement of the stars themselves is not symmetrical, nor do the stars themselves (though they are in motion) spin around our heads 360 degrees per day. The earth itself spins though we do not feel this motion physically, and the motion of earth gives the mirrored impression that the heavens are in more motion than they are; thus, it is the apparent motion of the sky wherein observable patters occur as though repeated in reflection. The apparent motion of the stars, not their groupings, is symmetrical. These patterns are reflected in the geneologies of Genesis in a manner like that of an emblem book. The recognition is obscured by the illegitimate study called astrology (which is but a cheap imitation of astronomy) that deals itself a fatal blow in that it does not know of the celestial motion known as The Precessionof the Equinoxes; astrology ignorantly assumes that the solstices and equinoxes do not shift with time.

The earth rotates on the axis of the North Celestial Pole 360 degrees per day and revolves around the sun 360 degrees per year; however, even though the angle of Earth's North Celestial Pole remains fixed, its direction changes to the extent that it slips backwards one degree in about 72 years, which is difficult to observe in a single lifetime today. What this means for celestial cartography is that the entire grid of the stars appears to move in a complete circuit about every 25,800 years in a motion called The Precession of the Equinoxes. Functionally, this precession indicates why the equinoxes and solstices appear in different zodiacal constellations over vast quantities of time. The pattern is counted from the vernal equinox or what Genesis 18:14 calls the עֵת חיה *time of life*. For instance, today, the vernal equinox resides in the fish of the constellation Pisces that is closest to Aquarius; however, at the time of the Crucifixion, the vernal equinox was in the other fish of Pisces and, during the Passover of the Israelite Exodus, the vernal equinox was in the Lamb. In the Exodus, the followers of God ate the lamb, and, after the Resurrection, His followers at the fish, for it was this emblem (the Icthus) that came to signify the superior knowledge of the early Church, a knowledge that the current, official establishment did not have. The constellation insignias are used as literary motifs throughout Scripture, and they aid in tethering the events described in the Text with the time-periods in which they happened both historically and thematically.

Genesis tells us that Adam died 930 years after his expulsion from the garden. If one reckons the amount of years the Torah counts from Adam's death to the present, one will arrive in about 2,800 BC. In this century, the vernal equinox resided in Taurus the Bull (**Image 1**), and this means that the summer solstice was in Leo the Lion (**Image 2**), the winter solstice was in Aquarius the Water-pouring Man (**Image 3**), and the autumnal equinox was in the Scorpion (**Image 4**).

Immediately, one can see the three of the four faces of the cherubs described in Ezekiel 1,10 and Revelation 4 (but the four faces described in these two books should be compared). Ezekiel 10:14 lists the faces as those of a cherub, a man, a lion, and an eagle while Revelation 4:7 lists the faces as those of a calf, a man, a lion, and an eagle. Since no other type of animal is listed in Scripture relative to the cherubs, it would seem as if the "face of a cherub" is that of the calf, and we can begin to observe a link between the Molech statue אהרון *Shining One, Aaron* crafted at the base of סיני *Thorny, Sinai*. The cherubs are called חיות *living creatures* in Ezekiel 1, and English versions of Genesis often translate this word as *beasts*; living creatures are not necessarily live beasts, but live beasts are necessarily living creatures. Since Ezekiel 28 calls Satan a cherub, it is prudent to view him as a living creature but connected with a bovine insignia and not as such a beast physically. Revelation 4 translates the cherubic חיות **living creatures** as ζωα **living creatures** also often translated into English simply as *beasts*. It is helpful to note here that, according to *The American Heritage Dictionary of the English Language*, the word *zodiac* comes to Middle English from the Old French *zodiaqu*, from Latin *zodiacus*, from Greek *zoidiakos (kuklos)*, "(circle) of carved figures," from *zoidion, carved figure, sign of the zodiac*, dimiutive of **zoion, living being, animal**; similarly, the word *zoo* is short for *zoological garden* and is from the Greek **zoion, living being, animal**. E.W. Bullinger believed that the word zodiac is from the Greek ζωδιακος *zodiakos* which is from the Hebrew סודי *sodi, confidant* which in Sanscrit means *a way*.

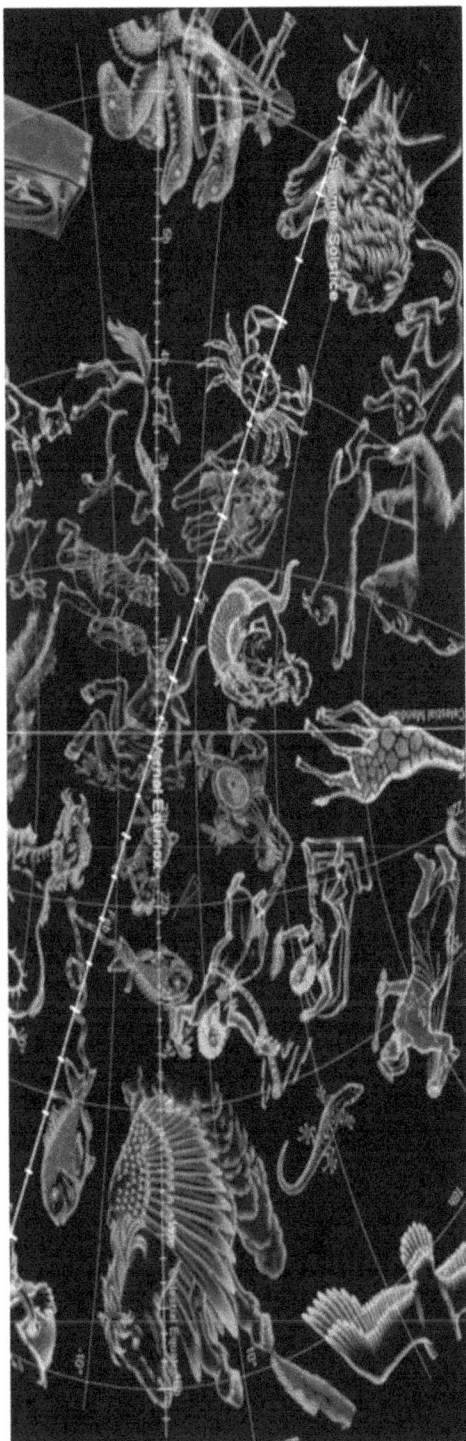

Image 1

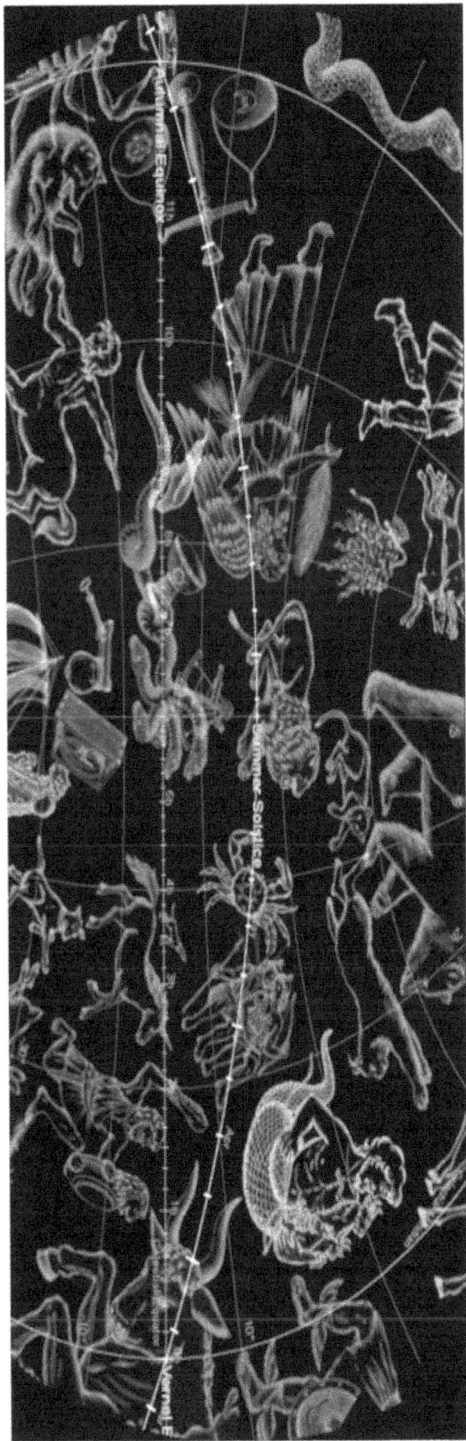

Image 2

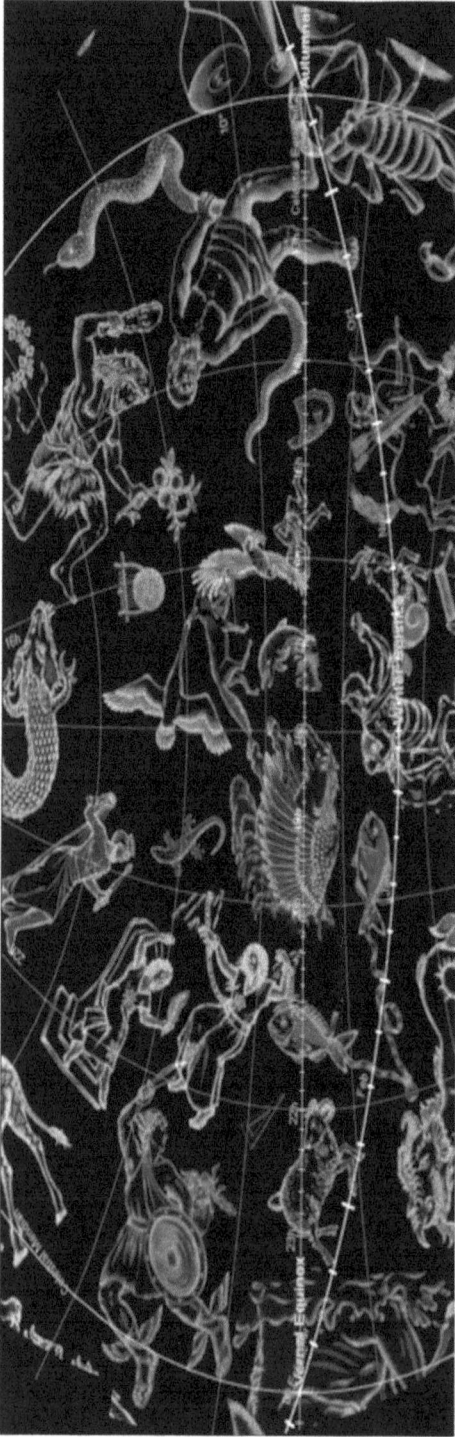

Image 3

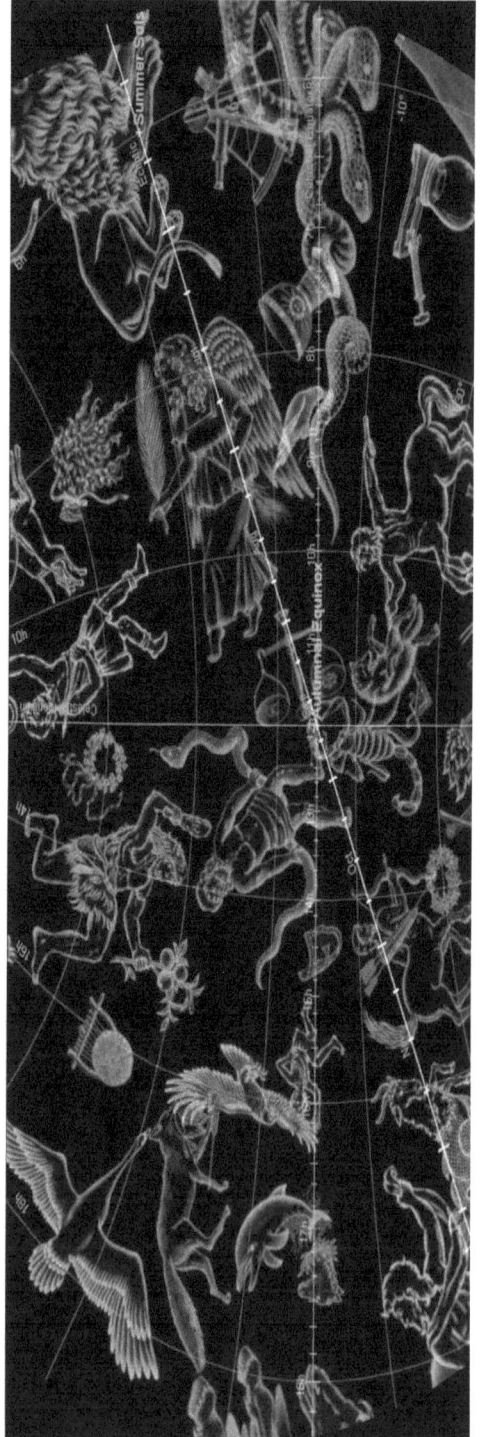

Image 4

Again, in 2,800 BC, the vernal equinox resided in Taurus the Bull, and this means that the summer solstice was in Leo the Lion, the winter solstice was in Aquarius the Water-pouring Man, and the autumnal equinox was in the Scorpion. None of the cherubic descriptions mention a scorpion; since all of the other emblems are accounted for, we can observe that the odd figure in the group is the eagle because the other three are constituents of the zodiac while Aquilla the Eagle is not. The natural question to ask is, "Why would a non-zodiacal constellation be tethered to the equinoxes when such a constellation could never hold an equinox?" The answer is that the constellation of the Scorpion, which can hold an equinox, is being deliberately avoided here, and the reason for it necessitates that the reader not only conceive of the celestial symbols but to think of them in Hebrew diction according to the Hebrew Scriptures. The arrangement of the zodiac in 2,800 BC shows the autumnal equinox to be in Scorpio, which is 180 degrees opposite (as in a mirror) from the vernal equinox in Taurus. Again, the vernal equinox is the "time of life" that leads the living creatures through the circuit of the year beginning with the sun's equinotical ascent towards the summer solstice. Thinking as though in a reflection, the autumnal equinox would then be the "time of death," the time when the sun descends towards the winter solstice. If the year is conceived of as a macrocosm of a 24 hour microcosm, then the vernal equinox would be as the sunrise of the year and the autumnal equinox would be as the sunset. The Scorpion would be the draconic insignia of death. When we recall that Genesis 3:15 states, "He will crush your head and you will strike His heel," we can observe that the ancient celestial engravings depict a man, who wrestles a snake, crushing the head of the Scorpion; furthermore, this man is reflected 180 degrees north by a man, with a wounded heel, crushing the head of the constellation of Draco, the Dragon, while smashing a vine (a serpentine plant).

Scripturally, an eagle is a sign of fertility that is placed in contradistinction to the ostrich, for Job 39 discusses how the ostrich (with its wings that are useless for flight) is harsh towards her young and forgets that a foot may crush her eggs while Revelation 12, after the Dragon destroys the woman's newborn, discusses how she is revitalized with wings of an eagle (as opposed to those of an ostrich: **Image 5**). On the other hand, the word *scorpion* is, in Hebrew, עקרב which is from the root *to uproot, to pluck up, to extirpate, to destroy,* and which produces the critical word עקר *barren, sterile.* The zodiacal Scorpion, the symbol of sterility, is avoided and replaced by the non-zodiacal Eagle, the symbol of fertility. It is important that the Eagle is non-zodiacal and is above the zodiac. The zodiac, the wall of the

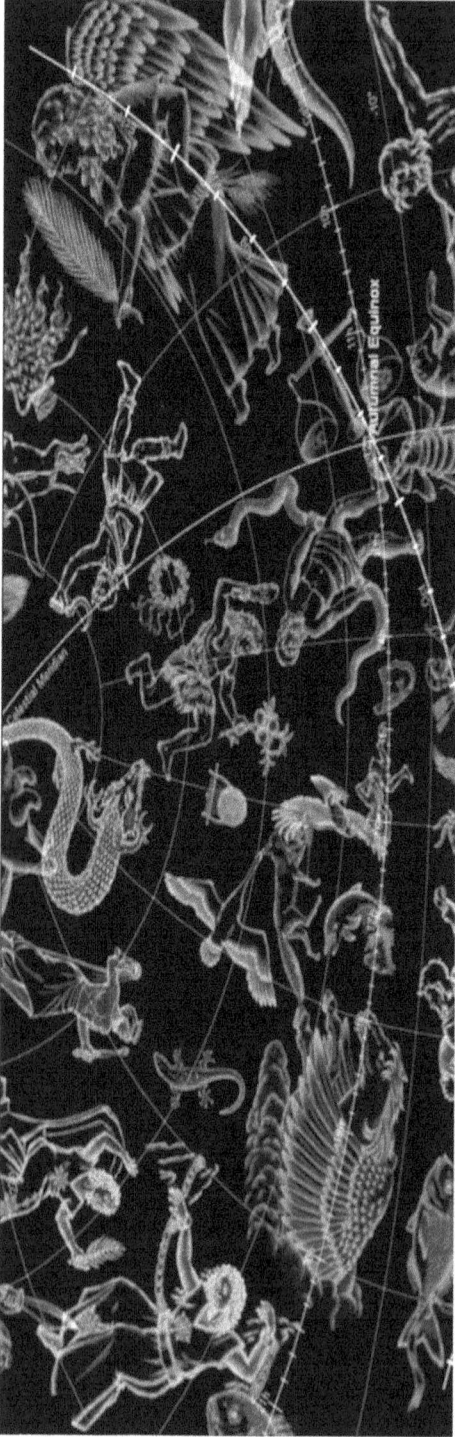

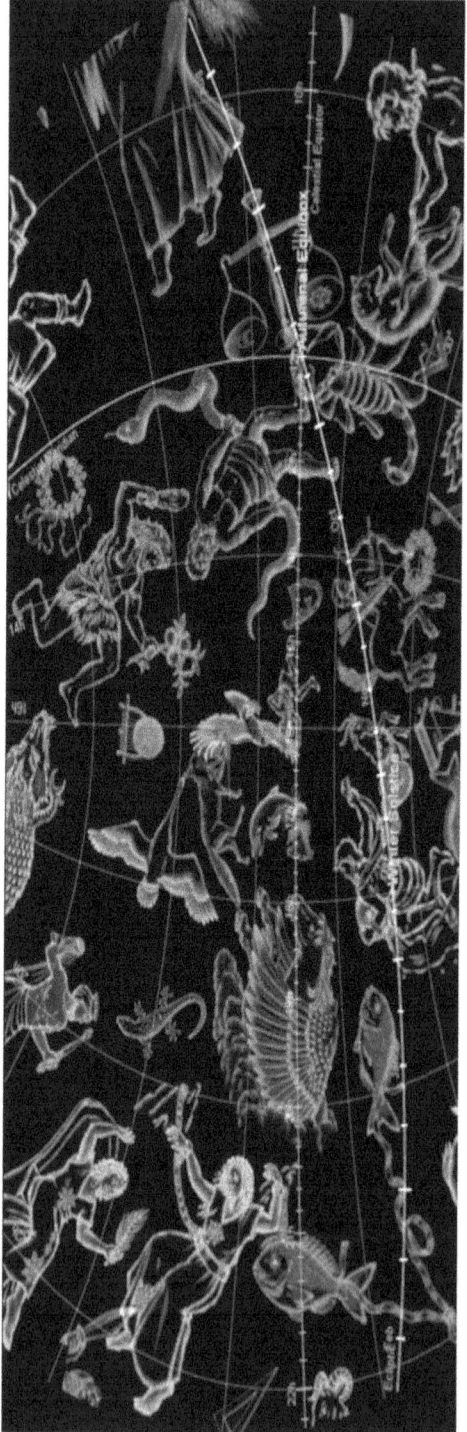

Image 5

Image 6

celestial zoological garden, is below the insignia of the Eagle (**Image 6**), an animal that can leave the precincts of a garden, in this case, of the celestial Eden. That is, after the woman in Revelation 12 was bereaved by the "Dragon," she was lifted out of the Dragon's territory: "...the woman was given two wings of a great eagle, that she might fly into the wilderness to her place, where she is nourished for a time and times and half a time, from the presence of the *serpent*" (Revelation 12:14), i.e. the *womb-serpent*.

The woman who suffered sterility (the draconic figure of the Scorpion) was given wings capable of flight (the transcendently fruitful figure of the Eagle). In other words, the Scorpion, in the 29th Century BC, held the point of the annual sunset (the time of death) while the Eagle is fixed above the path of the sun. We must keep in mind that the sunrise is called by Psalm 110 "the WOMB of the dawn" which, if conceived of as in a mirror, would make sunset as the womb of the dusk, i.e. an abortive or barren womb here typified by the sterile Scorpion. The Scorpion is the emblem of sterility, and the eagle is listed in its place as an emblem of fertility (**Image 6**). The Hebrew word שכל, depending on how it is pronounced, can mean *name* (Proverbs 3:4), *wisdom* (1 Samuel 25:3; Genesis 3:6), and *abortion* (Genesis 31:38). It is the naming of the creatures wherein the wisdom lies, and we can begin to recognize the wisdom of Adam.

The solstices and equinoxes in 2,800 BC place the North Celestial Pole in Thuban. Bullinger notes that the name *Thuban* means *Subtle*. The two critical markers that define the celestial alignment of which we have been discussing are the North Celestial Pole and the Vernal Equinox. In this alignment, the North Celestial Pole rotated in the (1) constellation Draco the DRAGON around the (2) Pole Star Thuban the SUBTLE and thus beginning the "time of life" or Spring season with (3) Taurus the BULL; at the same time, Genesis 3:1 states, "Now the (1) SERPENT was more (2) SUBTLE than any (3) BEAST of the field...."

Since the word "beast" here is literally of the "living creatures" or cherubs we have been discussing, we can understand why Ezekiel 28:14 explains that Satan was ordained כרוב ממשח הסוכך *The Anointed Guardian Cherub* but was cast down, and we see listed among the cherubs the Eagle instead of the Scorpion; thus, Satan was the most subtle of the cherubs. That cherubs are threshold guardians is now obvious because the threshold of which we speak here is the horizon that determines the "morning stars." Job refers to the horizon accordingly: "He drew a circular horizon on the face of the waters, at the BOUNDARY OF LIGHT AND DARKNESS" (26:10).

This word "boundary" is the Hebrew תכלית which is from the same root as כליה *inward, secret parts* which would be a synonym of the word קרב *inner part, womb*; thus, the eastern horizon, the eastern portion of the "boundary of light…" can be understood easily as the רחם משחר *womb of the dawn*. At this boundary, there can be seen a phenomenon of zodiacal light known today as the "Green Flash" that is a faint, green, hazy cone (or ziggurat) of light visible in the east just before sunrise and in the west right after sunset. It is probably this occurrence that astronomically signifies the directional perspective of the garden between man's induction to and expulsion from Eden. That is, Genesis 2 speaks of Eden as being "in the east" relative to the perspective of the reader and prior to the introduction of sin in the garden; however, after man's sin, he is cast east of the garden which places the reader (who is man) in a position where the garden is in the west. That this celestial green is seen before sunrise and after sunset almost certainly is the motif utilized to discuss the creation of Eden and man's banishment from it. Literarily, it is the man and not the garden that has moved… it is man who has bonded himself to the arrow of time and not to the eternal garden. The astronomical phenomenon taken into account here would likewise speak tacitly of the fact that it is the earth and not the sun that moves in order to create the ephemeral and yet eternal verdure of a simultaneously former and future place, i.e. a hidden and eternal abode. The Hebrew root עלם *to hide* produces the words עולם *antiquity, of old, ancient* which is the same Hebrew word as עולם *eternity, forever, without beginning,* both of which are related to the word עלם *a male youth*. It is this word עולם *without beginning* that is translated in Hebrews 7:3 in its connection of Melchizedek to Christ. This same word is used in Psalm 110:

> The Lord said to my Lord, "Sit at My right hand, till I make
> Your enemies Your footstool."The Lord shall send the rod of
> Your strength out of Zion. Rule in the MIDST of Your enemies!
> Your people shall be volunteers in the day of Your power; in
> the beauties of holiness, from the WOMB OF THE DAWN, You
> have the dew of Your youth. The Lord has sworn and will not
> relent, "You are a priest סלועל *forever* according to the order of
> Melchizedek…."

for it is this word *forever* that is related to the word עלם *a male youth*, the Child of which the passage speaks… the One Whose "…countenance was like the sun shining in its strength…" (Revelation 1:16).

The check and balance of this study of the cherubic faces can be easily summarized as follows. On a common celestial sphere all four of the faces can be found once one discerns the relationship between the zodiacal Scorpion and non-zodiacal Eagle. What makes the faces notable amongst all of the other emblems is that they exist 90 degrees apart from each other provided that any one of these faces holds an equinox or a solstice; however, since 90 degrees in The Precession of the Equinoxes accounts for about 6,500 years, we are restricted to finding a time-period that fits within the Biblical Narrative. The geneologies of Genesis account for about 6,000 years from the first mention of a date until now, but the last time an alignment of these four faces occurred within that span was the in the 2,800's before Christ. **Immediately, one can see that this is achievable precisely by subtracting the years of Adam's life from the remaining years for which the Text accounts in the genealogies of Genesis until now.** This alignment would force the Pole Star to be found in the Dragon on the star called Subtle whereby the Spring or "time of life" would be in the Bull, and Genesis 3:1 states all three of these. Furthermore, the Hebrew definite article (ה the) is usually used to indicate the intended familiarity with the characters of the stories; Genesis 3:1 says ה the נחש serpent, shining one and Genesis 3:24 says ה the כרבים cherubs as if the reader knows who they are upon their introduction. If the reader understood the astronomical references discussed by the introduction of the serpent, then the reader would grasp that he was more subtle than all of the cherubs, and that this subtlety was signified by the star called Subtle which, when possessing the North Celestial Pole, aligns the faces of the cherubs described throughout the remainder of Scripture. Genesis 3:24 states that these Cherubs are set לשמור to guard, to preserve, which is what these relatively static insignias do when they are compared to the sun that circuits through them. The main thing, however, that the reader must keep in mind is that the geneologies only reveal this pattern by subtracting the years of the life of Adam from them which means Adam saw the cherubs' faces as they would be at his death, which was 930 years following his expulsion from the very doorway those cherubs guarded. Adam saw into the future, so to speak, in that these cherubic faces were to be aligned as such 930 years following his expulsion. When one beholds the light of a star, one sees the star as it once was. The alignment of the stars, however, is something that can be predicted because of their patterned apparent progression through the sky. As the ancient Mesopotamian dwellers used to prognosticate birth by stars, it seems as though, in a mirror, the Text prognosticated Adam's death by stars. It is here that we have a conundrum and an immediate exposure of the limits of translation.

It has been so often commented on that God said to Adam in Genesis 3:17 that "in the day that you eat of it you shall surely die" but that Adam lived 930 more years. The first problem is that Biblical Hebrew, technically, has no tense, for *tense* indicates *time*. Instead, Hebrew has states: imperfect and perfect, i.e. unfinished or finished. God literally said, "in the day you eat of it מות תמות *dying you shall begin the process of dying*," that is, you begin to age towards death. Once Adam ate, he began to age mortally to the extent of 930 more years. Since English sentences are forced by grammar to express time, one can see the instant difficulty (or impossibility) of translating the more hair-splitting aspects of the Hebrew Bible. What further complicates the matter is that it is a common custom to consider what is more recent in chronological progression to be, somehow, "newer" when chronological progression makes one older. The so-called "New Testament" translates מות תמות *dying you shall begin the process of dying* in 2 Corinthians 1:9: "...we had the *sentence of death* in ourselves, that we should not trust in ourselves but in God who raises the dead..." and, in this, we may see that Adam gave himself a death-sentence when he ate the forbidden fruit. The mirror now becomes clearer in that the cherubs described later by Ezekiel and Revelation were as those guarding the threshold from which Adam was driven, and being described as such means that Adam saw the time of his death in a figure by the cherubic countenances that reflected his own recently acquired mortality that drove him on the arrow of time towards death, which could only be reversed, in a sense, through procreation that eventuated in Christ being born through man. Such a premonition follows in suit with regard to the fact that he was driven east, which is away from his origins, for the his origins were found in Eden, which was in the east; being driven further east means that he was compelled to continue on the line of chronology away from his origins in the process we all experience called "aging." No matter how resiliantly one attempts to return to his youth, the transient Green Flash can only be seen after the sun has sunk beyond the western horizon or before the sun rises at its eastern gate; it would seem that this is a daily reminder of man's introduction to and expulsion from Eden, a daily reminder of man's sin. Similarly, I Corinthians 15 recounts the astronomical observations recorded here to the extent that it states that the physical body cannot reenter Eden:

> Moreover, brethren, I declare to you the gospel which I
> preached to you, which also you received and in which you
> stand, by which also you are saved, if you hold fast that word
> which I preached to you—unless you believed in vain. For I

delivered to you first of all that which I also received: that Christ died for our sins according to the Scriptures, and that He was buried, and that He rose again the third day according to the Scriptures, and that He was seen by Cephas, then by the twelve. After that He was seen by over five hundred brethren at once, of whom the greater part remain to the present, but some have fallen asleep. After that He was seen by James, then by all the apostles. Then last of all He was seen by me also, as τω εκτρωματι THE ABORTED ONE. For I am the least of the apostles, who am not worthy to be called an apostle, because I persecuted the church of God. But by the grace of God I am what I am, and His grace toward me was not in vain; but I labored more abundantly than they all, yet not I, but the grace of God which was with me. Therefore, whether it was I or they, so we preach and so you believed.... But now Christ is risen from the dead, and has become the FIRSTFRUITS of those who have fallen asleep. For since BY MAN CAME DEATH, BY MAN ALSO CAME THE RESURRECTION OF THE DEAD. FOR AS IN ADAM ALL DIE, EVEN SO IN CHRIST ALL SHALL BE MADE ALIVE. But each one in his own order: Christ the firstfruits, afterward those who are Christ's at His coming. Then comes the end, when He delivers the kingdom to God the Father, when He puts an end to all rule and all authority and power. For He must reign till He has put all enemies under His feet. *The last enemy that will be destroyed is death...*"

for this anticipates the translation of *"you shall surely die"* not only as *"dying you shall begin the process of dying"* but מות תמות *Death, you shall die* whereby מות is interpreted substantively as *Death*. Paul continues,

I affirm, by the boasting in you which I have in Christ Jesus our Lord, *I die daily*. If, in the manner of MEN, I have fought with BEASTS at Ephesus, what advantage is it to me? If the dead do not rise, "Let us eat and drink, for tomorrow we die!" Do not be deceived: "Evil company corrupts good habits." Awake to righteousness, and do not sin; for some do not have the knowledge of God. I speak this to your shame. But someone will say, "How are the dead raised up? And with what body do they come?" Foolish one, what you sow is not made alive unless it dies. And what you sow, you do not sow that body that shall be, but mere grain — perhaps wheat or some other grain. But God gives it a body as He pleases, and to each seed its own body. All flesh is not the same flesh, but there is one kind of flesh of men, another flesh of animals, another of fish, and another of

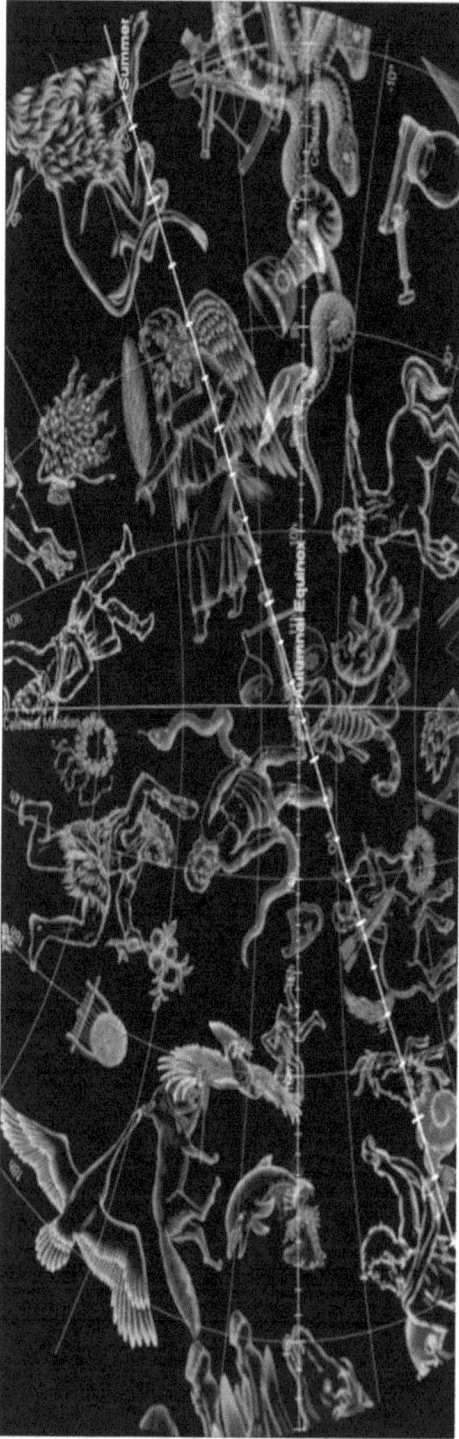

Image 7

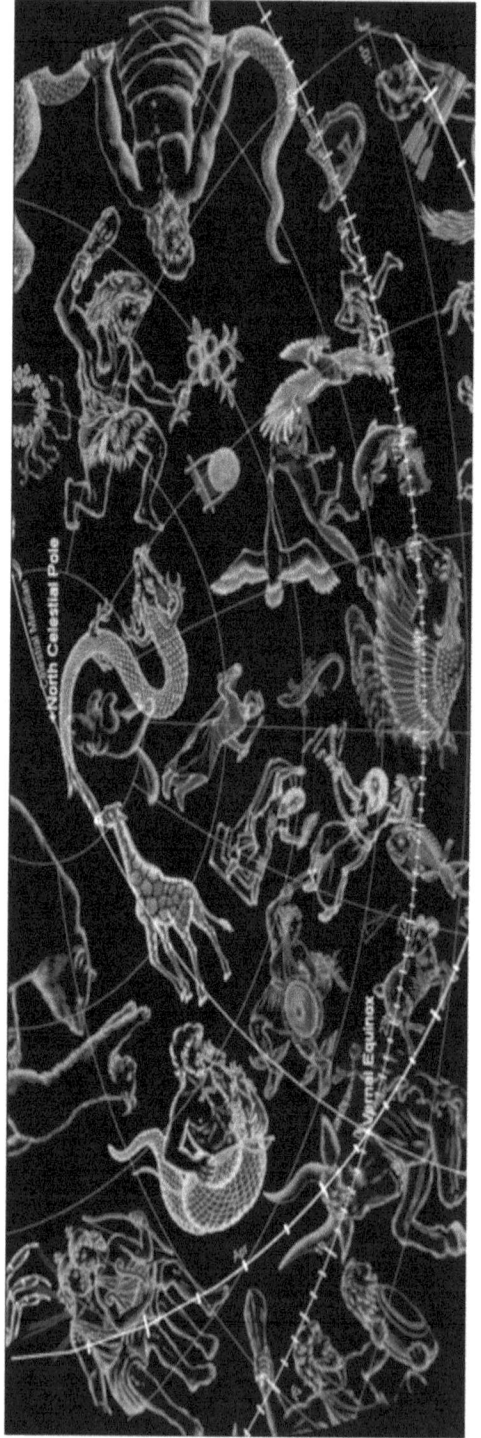

Image 8

birds. There are also celestial bodies and terrestrial bodies; but the glory of the celestial is one, and the glory of the terrestrial is another. There is one glory of the sun, another glory of the moon, and another glory of the stars; for one star differs from another star in glory. So also is the resurrection of the dead. The body is sown in corruption, it is raised in incorruption. It is sown in dishonor, it is raised in glory. It is sown in weakness, it is raised in power. It is sown a natural body, it is raised a spiritual body. There is a natural body, and there is a spiritual body. And so it is written, "The first man Adam became a living being." The last Adam became a life-giving spirit. However, the spiritual is not first, but the natural, and afterward the spiritual. The first man was of the earth, made of dust; the second Man is the Lord from heaven. As was the man of dust, so also are those who are made of dust; and as is the heavenly Man, so also are those who are heavenly. And as we have borne the image of the man of dust, we shall also bear the image of the heavenly Man. Now this I say, brethren, that flesh and blood cannot inherit the kingdom of God; nor does corruption inherit incorruption. Behold, I tell you a mystery: We shall not all sleep, but we shall all be changed — in a moment, in the twinkling of an eye, at the last trumpet. For the trumpet will sound, and the dead will be raised incorruptible, and we shall be changed. For this corruptible must put on incorruption, and this mortal must put on immortality. So when this corruptible has put on incorruption, and this mortal has put on immortality, then shall be brought to pass the saying that is written: "Death is swallowed up in victory." "O Death, where is your sting? O Hades, where is your victory?" The sting of death is sin, and the strength of sin is the law. But thanks be to God, who gives us the victory through our Lord Jesus Christ. Therefore, my beloved brethren, be steadfast, immovable, always abounding in the work of the Lord, knowing that your labor is not in vain in the Lord.

"The heavens declare the glory of God" (Psalm 19:1). It is also true that "The heavens will reveal his iniquity" (Job 20:27), for it was in these very heavens that Christ appeared to Paul on the road to Damascus as "τω εκτρωματι the aborted one" (I Corinthians 15:8), for it was the Autumnal emblem that signified the Time of Death, the sterile Scorpion (**Image 7**), whose head is crushed like the reflected Dragon in the North Ecliptic Pole (**Image 8**), the false vine in opposition to the "True Vine" of John 15:1 Who described Himself as Moses' serpent on the pole in John 14:1. The starry host's individual pictures do not appear to move independently, but they do appear to move collectively in unison; death and life appear mingled by the apparently stationary procedure of celestial light. The very instant the *process of dying began*, the record of the sin that induced aging towards death was imprinted for all the earth to see hanging in the simultaneously black and fiery heavens, as though in a cabinet that reflects a once-thriving world, as though in a mirror darkly.

We may also consider the arrow of time in Adam's death in spite of the grammatically tenseless Hebrew that describes Adam's demise. Genesis 30:1 describes childlessness as death itself. Adam certainly died on the very day he ate of the forbidden tree if his wife was pregnant (like the woman in Revelation 12) and gave birth abortively. In other words, if the son of Adam/Man (the very name Christ chose for Himself) died on account of the forbidden tree, then the day Adam's son died was, in the sense of Genesis 30:1, the day Adam died also — and Adam's death that day would be signified by the aging towards his demise for his deeds. Since the cherubic faces are signified by the four corners of the heavens in a specific era, the cherubic faces are emblematic of time. The cherubs were created good, and it is from this goodness that Satan fell. Satan, having been the anointed cherub, would necessarily be connected to time and the specific direction of its arrow. Even in the eternal state of goodness in which humanity was originally placed, humanity was endowed with the ability to procreate; therefore, even in an eternal state, humanity was blessed with the arrow of time proceeding from one person to another relative to gestation and birth, which is a situation that pronounces a definite beginning but utters no end. The fact that humanity also fell from this goodness by covenanting with death is a fact that illustrates the sorrowful revolution that forced a definite end to a definite proceding from a definite beginning. It can thus be seen that Satan's role as a cherub, Satan's role as a time-keeper, focused on the womb to the extent that the definite beginning of an individual's gestation and life would be reversed within the very vessel created to house viability. This reversal, pronounced in abortive birth, subjected the external world to the same reversal. This futile birth, articulated in deathly birth, subjected the remaining creation to relative futility. The ability to procreate, after man's fall, is, in a sense, a reversal of the arrow of time in that matter constellates into another origin of the same type that preceded it. It can be seen here that successful birth wars back at the time-keeping serpent who initiated his war on heaven through the awful sacrifice of unsuccessful birth.

Summarily, if one subtracts the years of Adam's life outside of Eden from the years the Torah reckons until now, one will arrive at an astronomical alignment that fits perfectly the descriptions of Eden as preserved by the faces of the cherubs. The genealogies are not incomplete, nor are they the pathetic remnant of a primitive and unrefined cosmology of fools. The genealogies preserve a message timelessly by using a circuit to discuss a segment on it so that wherever anyone finds himself along the arrow of time he is provided with a way to look into the past in order to grasp the emblematic program preserved in celestial cartography. Due to its distance from us, the light of the stars we see compels us to view the stars as they used to be and not as they are. We are, thus, in the stars' future while we presently behold the stars' past. Even due to the processing speed of our brains, we all experience the "present" slightly after it has happened. Even observing a flattened sun when it is setting is observing but a mirage of the sun that has already sunk below the horizon so that the sun we think we see is but a reflection of a sun we cannot see.

I repeat that subtracting the years of Adam's life from the Torah's family tree until the present brings us to a celestial alignment that reveals the sin in Eden emblematically preserved by the cherubic faces. Adam saw the faces of the cherubs in a celestially symbolic way that mirrored his death (930 years later). That is, the cherubs and the Flaming Sword described at Adam's expulsion prognosticated Adam's physical death outside of Eden that was a reflection of his "death" or childlessness (Genesis 30:1) inside of Eden. Adam's vision of Eden's Eastern Gate upon his expulsion was an astronomically systematic way to describe Adam's new journey onto the arrow of time towards his physical demise. The Scorpion, that is so carefully avoided in the Eden Narrative, is none other than the emblem of the "Serpent" who, like a "Beast of the Field" or cherub, was the most able warrior on the side of the demons. It is this "serpent," this king, who waged war on Heaven at Heaven's gate through the child-sacrifice and by his forbidden tree as described in Revelation 12. It was the Advocate of this slain child, The Son of Adam, The Son of Man, Who returned and initiated war on Satan through his deathly tree in order to claim victory in eternity that seemed, on the arrow of time, to be but three "days," for it was on the third "Day" of creation that the trees were created. The descriptions of Eden's inhabitants are literary, not literal. The death of Adam is put in astronomical terms and calculated to this particular time for literary purposes. A child died, and his history is preserved, not literally, but literarily.

"FOLLY" & THE FORBIDDEN TREE

IT is often the case that the two trees in the garden's midst are regarded merely as of "Life" and of "Knowledge," but the second denomination ("Knowledge") is insufficient. Calling the forbidden tree merely "Knowledge" pits "Life" against "Knowledge" to the extent that one must be ignorant to adhere to morality or that immorality is advantageous and part of God's overall design. Such thinking is flawed, and it is flawed because its premise focuses on "Knowledge" isolated from the remainder of the name "Knowledge of Good and Evil" without knowing that the Hebrew word דעת *knowledge* also means *unification* (Genesis 4:1) as opposed to, say, בינה *knowledge* that also means *discernment*, i.e. understanding through *discrimination* and not inclusion. If "Knowledge" were opposed to "Life," and since Christ, Who is "Life" (John 14:6) was not ignorant, then "...our Savior, Who desires all men to be saved and to come to the KNOWL-EDGE of the truth" (1 Timothy 2:4) must want us to sin as the means of necessitating salvation? — for this conclusion is blasphemous since Christ is "the power and the WISDOM of God" (1 Corinthians 1:24) Who "committed no sin" (1 Peter 2:22). Often, a translated mistake is perpetuated in 2 Corinthians 5:21 that states, "For He made Him who knew no sin TO BE SIN FOR US, that we might become the righteousness of God in Him." Christ did not become "sin." The Greek word αμαρτια *sin* is the translation of the Hebrew חטא, which can mean either *sin* or *sin offering*, and it is this fact that is reflected in 1 John 2:2: "And He Himself IS THE PROPITIATION FOR OUR SINS, and not for ours only but also for the whole world." Sin was never a component of the original design, let alone a constituent! There was a Tree of Life and its negative reflection that was functionally a Tree of Death (Genesis 2:17). The Tree of Death's name was "The Tree of the דעת *Knowledge/Union* of טוב *Good/Beauty/Wealth* and רע *Physical Injury/ Emotional Sorrow*." The unification of what was attractive with what was detrimental led to death. Eating from the union of wealth and physical injury is stated in Job 20:15 that recounts Adam partaking of the forbidden Tree of Death: "He swallows down RICHES and vomits them up again," as was the case with the Golden Calf. The death that was eaten worked as a slow-acting poison to the extent that life and death were unified in a sentence of doom that we call *aging*, for the Hebrew states not "in the day you eat of it, you will surely die" but literally "in the day you eat ממנו *from him*, מות *dying*, תמות *you will begin to die*," that is, *you will start aging towards death*, for Adam lived 930 more years. Paul seems to translate "dying, you will begin to die" as "the sentence of death" in 2 Corinthians 1:9. The Law of God was broken through the adherence to "another law" (Romans 7:23) called "The Tree of the Knowledge of Good and Evil," for the word עץ/ עצה

tree also means *instruction,* just as תורה *law* also means *instruction.* There were two laws in the midst of Eden, and humanity broke God's oath to the death by adhering to Satan's tree, which is why humanity died by the "tree" of death or the "law of sin and death" (Romans 8:2). Christ is the "True Vine" (John 15:1) Who died while hanging on the Tree of Death in order to reverse the effects of the False Vine who murdered by hanging on The Tree of Life. Why then did God plant such a poisonous tree in the midst of Eden? — God did not.

I have already written an entire book on the subject of the forbidden tree's origins called *Did God Plant the Forbidden Tree?*; what follows is a very brief summary of the main points of that book. (1) Genesis 1:11-12 states that the vegetation God made "seeded seed according to its kind," but the forbidden tree was according to two kinds that are diametrically opposed: good and evil. If God was responsible for making vegetation according to its kind, but vegetation existed otherwise, then God could not be responsible for making discordant vegetation. God did not plant the forbidden tree, and this fact is apparent in that Christ said, "Every plant which My heavenly Father has not planted will be uprooted" (Matthew 15:13). Since there are plants that God did not plant, but the plants God did plant were according to their kind, then a plant that was not according to its kind is a plant other than what can be attributed to God. (2) The only "Day" that God did not qualify as "good" was the second "Day." Everything, otherwise, was "good." The Tree of the דעת *Knowledge/Union* of Good and Evil was something other than "good" as is evidenced by its very name containing the word "evil." Since vegetation was created on a "Day" qualified as "good," since "everything" God made was not only "good" but "very good" (Genesis 1:31), the forbidden tree was, by its very own name, a container of "evil" and cannot therefore be attributed to the "very good" creation of God. (3) The vegetation that God made "seeded seed" (Genesis 1:11-12). The first diet for both animals and man was vegetarian, and people were specifically given "every" plant that was "seed-bearing" and that was on the face of the "whole earth" (Genesis 1:29). The usage of superaltives here necessitates that any plant that was seed-bearing was fit for man's diet, and any plant that did not have seed could not be fit for man's diet. Since the forbidden tree was not fit for man's diet, and since "every" plant that was "seed-bearing" was given man to eat, the forbidden tree could not have been fit for man's diet, nor could it have been "seed-bearing." The utilization of superlatives here also necessitates that since every seed-bearing plant on the "whole earth" was given to man, and since the forbidden tree was on some part of the earth, the restriction of this tree points to its sterility, which is diamatrically contrary to the first command given to man which was to "be fruitful." The employment of superlatives here further forces the issue that the forbidden tree, being on the earth, being restricted from man, and being seedless, would be the unholy mingling of opposites that results in sterility, which is often the case of grafts and other kinds of unifications that can coexist but do not reproduce through their co-existence naturally, thus the name "The Tree of the דעת *Union* of Good and Evil" or the Tree of unified opposites that resulted in the sterility restricted from humans who were to be fruitful. (4) The vegetation that God made "seeded seed" (Genesis 1:11-12). The first diet for both animals and man was vegetarian, but people were specifically given "seed-bearing" plants while animals were given "every green plant" (Genesis 1:29-30). If all vegetation created by God was seed-bearing (for plants are not naturally sterile), and if the specific diet intended for man was further marked by be-ing specifically seed-bearing (for plants are naturally seed-bearing), then the forbidden tree could not have been natural but an unnatural mingling of discordance evinced by sterility, which is itself unnatural. The Tree of the דעת *Union* of Good and Evil is a unification of antithetical components that is analogous to the unnatural mingling typified by the King of Sodom as opposed to the King of Salem. Since people were commanded first to "be fruitful," since their diet was naturally "seed-bearing," and since the forbidden tree was unnatural by the fact that it was a mixture of opposites, it would have been disagreeable for God to construct a plant that would be the opposite of the diet He gave to man and the fruitful product He awaited from the womb, which is directly linked thematically to the stomach; it is here that we may note that the womb is punished in connection with a stomach that sinned (Genesis 3:16). It should be asked where the child of this sterilized womb was buried since the ground was cursed on account of a gardener (Genesis 3:17): "If I have כסיתי *covered* my transgressions as Adam..." (Job 31:33) and "...I say that a STILLBORN CHILD is better than he — for it comes in vanity and departs in darkness, and its name is יכסה *covered* with darkness" (Ecclesiastes 6:4).

The very notion that God planted the forbidden tree in the midst of the first humans' home that God Himself gave them is the complete op-posite of the fact that God "...Himself tempts no one" (James 1:13). The design intended by coercing people into thinking that God crafted a plant that ruined humanity is truly a slander against God's character (as if His character should even be called into question at all). God did not plant the forbidden tree, and it is unwise for one to attribute the unnatural graft-ing of Satan to the natural fertility that God commanded of man as the standard from which deviations fall. All of the theology dealing with the purpose of the forbidden tree is false if it is founded on the premise that God planted it in the first place and if one actually thinks that such a tree granted "wisdom" when it was a horrible mistake to partake of it. Are hideous crimes like murder, incest, and rape derived from the simple eating of fruit? — hardly! The degradation of guilty mankind came by the destruction of an innocent man, and the salvation of guilty mankind came by the resurrection of an innocent Man. The question that should be asked here is, "What innocent man was killed in Eden?" and the answer is the גבר *strong man, warrior, male child* who was *bound* in his *house* or womb as Isaac was *bound* to his *altar*. Christ, the Innocent, can be linked seamlessly to the problem of sin by way of the forbidden tree when one examines the miracles He wrought in direct reaction to the plant called Hellebore. Hellebore, it would seem, was a constituent of the forbidden tree, and its Latin name *Veratrum* or *Truth* retains part of this hideous concoction's irony. Consider the reference Seneca makes to the "medical treatment" of insanity through hellebore (Epistle XCIV).

    The ancients practiced what we can call helleborism, for helleborism was utilized medicinally as a cure for chronic diseases. Hellebore was also used ordinarily for the purposes of study and comprehension. Hellebore was thought, through the body's violent reaction to it, to effect radical cures that were seemingly miraculous. The doctors or augurs who practiced helleborism were remedy workers who were experts in medicine and poison; this is reflected in the Hippocratic Oath where Hippocrates says, "...I will give no deadly medicine to anyone if asked, nor suggest any such counsel; and in like manner I WILL NOT GIVE TO A WOMAN A PESSARY TO PRODUCE ABORTION. With purity and with holiness I will pass my life and practice my Art...." During the time of Hippocrates, the words "Hellebore" and "vomiting" were synonymous. Samuel Hahnemann states that "The word *Hellebore*, the name of the sole and uiversally known emetic, received by use such an extended signification that it was applied to the operation itself and sometimes signifies *vomiting*" (*On the Helleborism of the Ancients*). Hellebore was a purgative, and the vomiting it caused can be observed in Job 20:15-16: "He swallows down riches and VOMITS them up again; God casts them out of his belly. He will suck the poison of COBRAS; the VIPER'S tongue will slay him," for this vomit-producing plant was commonly linked to snakes. The 14th Book of Pliny's Natural History states, "Similarly in Thasos also Hellebore is planted among the vines, or else wild cucumber or scammony; the wine so obtained is called by a Greek name denoting miscarriage, because it produces abortion." We may see the link between a purgative, a snake, a vine, a poison, a remedy, and an abortion. The destruction of children, as we have already examined at length, is very often linked to something bovine in Scripture, and Helleobre was associated with cattle, oxen, sheep, and goats (προβατα), for these quadrupeds eat Hellebore and purge themselves on it. There is a white Hellebore and a black Hellebore, but they both bear the name "Hellebore" and have been found difficult to discern in antiquity's records; however, it can be safely said that the Hellebore used so widely by the ancients causes the following effects:

> (1) The throat and stomach become heated and burn but dissuade one from drinking. The throat constricts and can cause suffocation if the amount ingested is too severe. Vomiting or dry-heaving occurs. The face becomes red. Vertigo ensues. There is a loss of breath and subsequently a loss of voice. The senses are lost to delirium;
>
> (2) A loss of vision can occur;
>
> (3) Teeth begin to gnash;
>
> (4) Consciousness is lost.

Hahnemann states that one who ingests this plant, "As if strangled... falls down with his teeth clenched like a strangled victim" (*On the Helleborism of the Ancients*). Surely, the suffocation was envisioned as an incorporeal python, and the burning was compared to a venomous serpent. Hellebore was utilized to cure malady, and so it became a source of profit: "He swallows down RICHES and VOMITS them up again; God casts them out of his belly. He will suck the poison of COBRAS; the VIPER's tongue will slay him" (Job 20:15-16). Furthermore, the roots, when brought near the nose, cause sneezing. Hahnemann again tells us, "Good Hellebore has at first a sweetish taste, which then becomes acrid for a short time, and afterwards excites a great heat in the mouth, causes a great flow of saliva and deranges the stomach.... Others condemn that kind which produces a copious flow of saliva, because it causes too easily the strangulating sensation in the throat; but they are wrong, for this is only a sign of the greater medicinal virtue of the Hellebore, and indicates that a smaller dose should be given." Hellebore was also considered as a type of fire based on the burning sensation it ultimately produced, and it was conceived that the power of this plant was concentrated in its seeds that induced such heat that water was given to a patient immediately after ingestion which often led to the patient's prostration. Vinegar was also ingested during Hellebore treatments (even though the patient may not have desired it) in order to delay premature vomitting. Hellebore was used to treat the following:

> (1) melancholia;
>
> (2) fever;
>
> (3) insanity;
>
> (4) chronic pain;
>
> (5) epilepsy;
>
> (6) mental insufficiency;
>
> (7) unconsciousness;
>
> (8) lethargy/paralysis;
>
> (9) leprosy.

Hellebore was mingled with various substances and fruits, but the most important for our study is the fact that it was mixed with grapes. Outwardly, an eater of Hellebore (in one form or another) exhibited a flow of saliva, dry heave, a swollen face, protruding eyes, apparent asphyxiation, a projected tongue and/or chattering, gnashing teeth, bodily sweat, and, ultimately, mental dementedness. Conversely (if not insanely), this plant was commonly used to facilitate the learning process. It was ingested frequently in conjunction with study since it was thought to induce wisdom even though it was simultaneously considered to be a severe remedy and even a poison. Hellebore was utilized in an attempt to increase wisdom. The reasoning behind this attempt was that Hellebore was actually thought to cure mental deficiency in the impaired person; so, if Hellebore were taken by an unimpaired person, mental ability should increase (though this is impossible). Lastly, Hellebore caused abortion in pregnant women. In fact, Hellebore was avoided by children, women, and the elderly since even the ablest of men could kill themselves simply by ingesting too much. In short, Hellebore was thought to give wisdom (but did not) and was used to produce abortion in pregnant women. The notion of wisdom and the reality of abortion were thus intertwined in the usage of this plant, and the positive association of these two opposed qualities is diamentrically opposed to Hebrew Scripture since Hebrew equates "wisdom" with the *womb* and with *life* (not *death*).

We can now, finally, understand why the same essential spelling of one word in Hebrew (שכל) can mean both "wisdom" and "abortion": one plant was thought falsely to be capable of producing both! — and these very letters (שכל) were used to describe the forbidden tree in Genesis 3:6.

At once, we can observe conceptions of wisdom (life) and folly (death) simultaneously and from a unified source as in "The Tree of the דעת Union/Knowledge of Good and Evil." Furthermore, when the Text states "a tree desirable להשכיל *to make one wise*," the word להשכיל *to make one wise* can also be read as להשכיל *to make one abort* by pronouncing the letter ש as *sh* instead of as *s*, i.e. by varying the serpentine hiss of the sibilant (ש). The original Hebrew Text admits both readings since the mark that distinguishes the *sh* from the *s* is not original but is a latter invention devised to facilitate oral reading, which, by its own nature, limits definitions to one traditional rendering and thus disallows the decipherment of understatement and simultaneous comprehension. The root letters שכל (scl) can mean *to be wise (s)* and *to abort (sh)*, and the only difference between their respective spellings is the sibilant ש that is today distinguished as either שׂ(s) or שׁ(sh) but was originally left to context. In the case we are discussing, the letters להשכיל can be read simultaneously as *to make one wise* and *to cause abortion*, and these two are *opposites unified* in the same word like the two trees that were unified in the midst of Eden.

Being a master of language can only get one as far as his knowledge of references are concerned, for no translation or tradition accounts for the reference to Hellebore that is bound up in the letters שכל (scl) that can be pronounced with respect to *wisdom (scl)* or to the *eating of fruit, i.e. the consumption of a child in abortion (shcl)*. Hellebore was taken foolishly by the erudite in a vain attempt to increase *fertility of cognition*, and Hellebore was taken murderously by the selfish in a successful attempt to decrease their family tree. How could scholars yesterday or today actually believe that a tree with bark could give man wisdom upon eating it, and why would God restrict man from the wisdom He requires? — by knowing the words without their references. In large part, confusion has come about by accidentally adopting the Babylonian notion that (1) the Tree of the Knowledge and the Tree of Life were the same and (2) associating the Babylonian Tree of Knowledge with the Hebrew Tree of the Knowledge *of Good and Evil*. The Tree of Life was the Tree of Wisdom in Eden, whereas the forbidden tree was a tree of folly whose full name included "the *Knowledge* (Hebrew: *Union*) of Good and Evil." In other words, the "Knowledge/ Union of Good and Evil" was not a wise splicing and was opposite The Tree of Life that was the true Tree of Knowledge. The letters עצה can be read as *trees* (Jeremiah 6:6) and as *counsel* (Deuteronomy 32:28) which is a synonym for תורה *counsel, instruction, law, torah, Torah*; the letters מלך can mean *a king, counsellor* and also *Molech, a child-sacrificial false deity*; the letters אכל can mean *to eat, to destroy to understand, to unite with oneself, and to copulate*; the letters שכל can indicate *wisdom, folly,* and *abortion*;

thus, to say that *eating of the tree of a king grants wisdom* (Job 12:13) can also in Hebrew be read as *understanding the counsel of a counselor grants wisdom* (Proverbs 15:22) or *destroying the law of the king produces folly* (Proverbs 1:25) or *making oneself a part of Baal or Molech through copulation causes abortion* and the subsequent capital punishment of hanging or stoning the offenders, which is the exaction of the curse of the covenant, i.e. the defense of life counteracting the offense against life (Numbers 25). The consistent word-play regarding the letters שכל *wisdom, folly, abortion* can be observed in Ecclesiastes.

The letter ש can be pronounced either as "s" or as "sh," and the difference between the two is literally the difference between life and death. The word שכלות (pronounced *seeklooth*) appears one time in Scripture (Ecclesiastes 1:17) and it is rendered *folly*. The word סכלות, which is pronounced the same way (*seeklooth*) is also rendered *folly* in Ecclesiastes 2:3, 2:12, 2:13, 7:25, 10:1, and 10:13. The orthographical difference between the two words under discussion regards the sibilants, for the first word utilizes the ש as "s" while the second word uses the ס as "s". It is peculiar that "folly" (*seeklooth*) is penned seven times in Ecclesiastes, but that it is spelled alternately once and that the alternate spelling only occurs in Scripture once and only in the very book where it is repeatedly spelled otherwise. It is difficult to believe that the Biblical writer misspelled the word *seeklooth* in the first instance and then amended his orthography six more times consecutively throughout the course of his book without noticing, for it is more likely that something paradigmatically understated is at work here. In Ecclesiastes 7:12 states that "חכמה *wisdom* gives life," and so we can understand the opposite principle in that folly gives death. The irony here is that a synonym for the feminine noun חכמה *wisdom* is the masculine noun שכל *wisdom* (with the "s" letter), but it is a form of the word translated as *folly* (pronounced with the "s" letter). It would at first seem that the one word שכל can be interpreted as either *wisdom* or *folly*, but there may be more involved here. If the word שכל *wisdom* is pronounced not with the "s" sound but with the "sh" sound, it means *abortion* and *bereavement*; this fact opposes life since wisdom gives life. If wisdom is as life, then folly is as death; the death this word spells is abortion; therefore, wisdom is analogous to a fertile womb as folly is analogous to an infertile womb. "Eden" means Fertility, and infertility was allowed to penetrate the garden.

Since בית means *dwelling, house, temple, wisdom,* and *womb*, we can understand *life*: "wisdom gives life" (Ecclesiastes 7:12) as a womb gives life, for, "Through wisdom a house is built" (Proverbs 24:3). The giving of life through regeneration and procreation is the "building up" of life as though a house were being discussed, and we can see this imagery in that Genesis 2:22 says literally in Hebrew that God "יבן *built up*" the "צלע *side*" of the man to make the woman, in that Genesis 16:2 discusses literally family "built up" through Hagar, and 1 Peter 2:5 discusses "you also, as living stones, are being built up a spiritual house." That Christ is called the "Author of Life" (Acts 3:15) agrees with the fact that He was a carpenter, "for by Him all things were created that are in heaven and that are on earth" (Colossians 1:16). Circumcision occurred on the eighth day (Leviticus 12:3), and it was eight days after (John 20:26) Thomas discussed putting his hand "into His side" (John 20:25) that we read of Thomas grafted into the "True Vine" (John 15:1) by touching the circumcised heart of Love Incarnate. We can see that, like the first Adam, the Last Adam had His heart circumcised after He slept so that His bride could be born through His opened side, for the man's heart is analogous to the woman's womb, while both are connected to the mind, as we observe in that *womb* and *wisdom* are בית, *heart* and *mind* are לב, and "*wisdom* gives *life*." The opposite of a life-giving house is an abortive womb, and the word שכל can be read as with an "s" (indicating *wisdom* and *life*) or as with an "sh" (indicating *abortion* and *bereavement*). The serpentine sound distinguishes between wisdom and folly, between life and death. When we consider that King Solomon the *Wise* facilitated the *child-sacrifice* of his own fruit on account of his foreign wives (1 Kings 11:7), we can understand, perhaps, why Ecclesiastes 1:17 states that " ואתנה *I gave* [נתן = NTN] my לב *heart/mind* לדעת *to understand/unify* **[1] wisdom and knowledge, [2] madness and folly/destruction of offspring or fruit**, and I learned that this is רעיון *feeding* on a חור *spirit/wind/perception*." The word "אתנה *I gave*" is from the root נתן that can be used to indicate *child-sacrifice*. It is plain that the woman was first "built up" from the man's exposed heart (so to speak), so the Man Adam did not permit his wife to do anything beyond what he permitted his own heart to do. That King Solomon the Wise *gave his heart (wives) to unify* polar opposites (as can be seen in the letters שכל which can mean **[1] life and wisdom** or **[2] abortion and folly**) seems to hint that the "feeding on wind" is the *consumption of the spirit, the eating of false perception, the breakdown of the implantation of God's image into man*. Consider: "I will greatly multiply your sorrow and your conception; in pain you shall bring forth children" (Genesis 3:16). What else would consumption of fruit have to do with the womb? Perversely, the ancients used to practice a type of threshold covenant wherein a child was slain sacrificially and buried beneath the cornerstone or doorway of the house, and the internal fire as seen from outside of the doorway was supposed to be the dwelling of the child who stood at the door to guard the way into the dwelling. Of course, such repulsive thinking is but the grim opposite of Genesis 3:24, where we see the "flame of the sword" guarding the way of the Tree of Life, and this guardianship is in direct reaction to the sin in עדן *Fertility, Eden.*

Here is The Great Secret, the greatest secret in all of human history: The first sin in Eden resulted in the abortion of Adam's firstborn whose "name is covered in darkness" (Ecclesiastes 6:4). The sin of Eden was remedied by The One Who is both The Last Adam (I Corinthians 15:45) and the Son of Adam (Matthew 11:19) Who has "a name written that no one knew except Himself" (Revelation 19:12). Christ died willfully as an Innocent in order to cancel the unwillful death of an innocent.

The first human infant was aborted!

There was a human being other than Christ who lived and died in perfection, and that manchild was the Son of Man. In Hebrew, the word נפל means both a *fallen* one and an *abortion.* The simple title of "The Fall of Man" is accidentally remembered Platonically through the philosophical ponderings of the early Christian Platonists who knew nothing of The Great Secret. Christ, however, referred to a בית *house, temple, womb* that *fell* because of, it would seem, an UNWISE builder in Matthew 7. Christ spoke darkly of the first human fruit by calling Himself after the same name: The Son of Man, that is, The Son of Adam. In the seventh Chapter of Matthew, Christ strings many of these references together into a seamless whole that has yet to be discovered in written history outside of the Bible, for He spoke consecutively of seeking the narrow way, knowing a tree by its fruit, those who think they follow Him but who are damned, and the house that fell. After the disciples and their immediate circle, "Christian" writings did not know that the firstborn human was a male baby who was cast abortively from the womb. During the time of Christ, only the early Church could have known The Great Secret of The Son of Adam, The Son of Man:

> "And I, brethren, when I came to you, did not come with excellence of speech or of WISDOM [scl] declaring to you the testimony of God. For I determined not to know anything among you except Jesus Christ and Him crucified. I was with you in weakness, in fear, and in much trembling. And my speech and my preaching were not with persuasive words of human WISDOM [scl], but in demonstration of the Spirit and of power, that your faith should not be in the WISDOM [scl] of men but in the power of God. However, we speak WISDOM [scl] among those who are mature, yet not the WISDOM [scl] of this age, nor of the rulers of

this age, who are coming to nothing. But we speak the WISDOM [scl] of God in a mystery, the hidden WISDOM [scl] which God ordained before the ages for our glory, which NONE OF THE RULERS OF THIS AGE KNEW; FOR HAD THEY KNOWN, THEY WOULD NOT HAVE CRUCIFIED THE LORD OF GLORY. But as it is written: 'Eye has not seen, nor ear heard, nor have entered into the heart of man the things which God has prepared for those who love Him.' But God has revealed them to us through His Spirit. For the Spirit searches all things, yes, the deep things of God. For what man knows the things of a man except the spirit of the man which is in him? Even so no one knows the things of God except the Spirit of God. Now we have received, not the spirit of the world, but the Spirit who is from God, that we might know the things that have been freely given to us by God. These things we also speak, not in words which man's WISDOM [scl] teaches but which the Holy Spirit teaches, comparing spiritual things with spiritual. But the natural man does not receive the things of the Spirit of God, for they are FOOLISHNESS [scl] to him; nor can he know them, because they are spiritually dis-cerned" (I Corinthians 2:1-14).

It is quite clear that the Temple Levites did not grasp who Christ was, for their Septuagint, being a translation, knew nothing of the Son of Adam and therefore could not point them towards The Son of Adam clearly. The Pharisees had their own oral interpretation of the vowel-lacking He-brew Text, but their oral tradition was a sloppy invention that eventuated into what is now called "Orthodox Judaism" that was not and is not ca-pable of discerning that there are only two laws, two trees, two mirrors, two infant faces in the midst. Why then did Christ take on the name of Adam's son? — the answer can be found easily through the sickening knowledge of Molech, the bovine altar upon which children were slaughtered to Satan.

Molech is explicitly discussed in passages like Leviticus 18:21, Jer-emiah 32:35, and 2 Kings 23:10, but he is, in connection with or under the title of, the נחש Serpent, *Shining One* of Genesis 3, the שטן *Satan, Resister* of Job, and the Leviathan of Job, which is a name that appears to be formed by uniting the words לוי bound *one, priest (Levi)* and נתן *child-sacrifice (Nathan)*, for it was the Levites who defended innocent, infant life at Sinai, and it was Nathan who prophesied the death of the *son of David* (which is a title of Christ in Matthew 1). One can see that Satan is a priest of child-sacrifice, the former high priest who preceded Adam (Ezekiel 28) and the one from whom Adam learned to destroy the fruit of the womb by consuming the fruit of the Leviathan's tree/law/mirror that reflects the infant's countenance. *Molech* is spelled consonantally the same as *king* and *counsellor* (מלך) and the synonymous term מלכם *Milcom* can be read also as *Their King* whose crown King David hung over the throne of Israel (2 Samuel 12:30; 1 Chronicles 20:2) after vanquishing the Son of *Nahash*, the *Shining One*, The *Serpent*... for it was soon after that his own infant son, the elder and nameless brother of Solomon died. Ironically, Solomon built a child-sacrificial grove to this Milcom for his wives on the very mount Christ was apprehended. This Satan or king Molech was worshipped absolutely by igniting children upon a metal altar. Molech was, by his own misguided and death-worthy followers, equated with or held in parallel to God (as though in a mirror). Remnants of this atrocious mistake can be observed in the backwards theologies that actually believe that God commanded Abraham *to cause to burn* (והעלהו) his son rather than *to cause him to ascend* (והעלהו) symbolically in the reality of the sacrosanct office of Firstborn in Genesis 22:2. *To cause to burn* and *to cause to ascend* are the same word in Hebrew, for the one is to death and the other is to life (as though beholding opposites in a mirror). The letters that spell Molech are מלך and are understood commonly to indicate simply *offering* or *sacrifice* that, when applied to Molech personally, imply human sacrifice. Molech was connected with the *Tophet* (2 Kings 23:10, Isaiah 30:33, Jeremiah 7:31-32, Jeremiah 19:6,11-14) which is spelled תפת and is from the root תוף *to spit* that is synonymous to the letters ירק that produce the root *to spit* and the noun *green herb*, the very word used for the diet of the animals in Genesis 1:30 that was not qualified as seed-bearing, which is probably referenced by Ecclesiastes 3:18: "God tests them, that they may see that they themselves are like animals." This place of child-sacrifice, this Tophet, is connected with the Aramaic word for *stove, fireplace,* and *pot*, the Syriac word for *bake-house, oven, kettle,* and *cauldron*, the Arabic *stone* whereupon the cauldron is placed for cooking that becomes an ash-heap. The ash of the Tophet is connected intimately to pottery, for the charred remains of sacrificed children were placed in pots (often with the ashes of rams), sealed, and buried beneath tombstones inscripted with the child's family tree. Here, one can see clearly the imagery that instigates the premise of the Book of Job, for Job offered animal sacrifice in an attempt to cover the sins of his firstborn and remaining children; however, his attempt failed as his firstborn's and subsequent siblings died in the *house* and were mourned by their father's *nakedness* (1:21) who then sat upon *ash* with *pottery* (2:8) and describes himself as a תפת *Tophet* or a contemptable *spitting* (17:6).

Molech, Milcom, Baal, Chronos, and Saturn are all variations on the united theme of child-sacrifice, for Isaiah 57 describes Molech or Satan as the one who received the gift of incinerated innocents provided by those who found themselves "naked" (childless) because of their morbid offerings. This very same theme is apparent in Job 18 where Bildad describes the horrors of killing children as the consuming fire is envisioned as a personified death eating fruit or devouring a baby followed by roots drying up in shame (יבשו *they are ashamed, dried up*), and Eliphaz precedes this horrific description by stating that the "godless will be barren, and fire will eat the אאהלי שחד *tents/wombs of bribe* (i.e. a price paid for destroying the fruit of the womb in abortion). They conceive trouble and give birth to evil; the womb fashion's deceit" (15:34-35). The idea of Death eating skin is, of course, linked to leprosy, which was understood as a type of living death in which a decaying corpse was animate. The imagery of a walking death placed in mirrored contrast to innocent life can be noticed in 2 Kings 5 where Naaman, who was leprous, was cleansed in a mirror (the Jordan River) "and his flesh was restored like the flesh of a LITTLE CHILD, and he was clean." Sacrificing a child to Molech, Satan, or whatever name suits, was literally a covenant with Death himself. A covenant is an oath and must be ratified by actions that anticipate and require fruit production; thus, consuming the fruit of the womb was a covenant wherein the fruit production and subsequent butchery ratified the oath to the death permanently and instantly by sealing the life in flames and connecting the sacrificer to a new king, lord, husband, and god; it is this "covenant with death" of which Isaiah 28 speaks, for it is upon this altar, this threshold, that war is made upon the Kingdom of Heaven that "belongs to such as these" children (Luke 18) and that "suffers violence" (Matthew 11:12). The Canaanites and later Carthaginians practiced the *mlk* (as in MoLeK) sacrifice, and the Punic *mlk* was a sacrificial term derived from the root הלך *to go, to proceed, to locomote, to walk,* for it was after Adam and his wife ate the fruit that they "heard the Voice of the Lord מתהלך *proceeding* through the garden" in direct response to their proceeding with Satan in the first *mlk* sacrifice, which is, of course, why the womb was punished on account of eating fruit. Molech-worship also contained the formula "because he heard his voice." It is this horrid and condemned practice that serves as the plan for Hell's design, for Isaiah 30 explicitly describes Hell as a "Tophet" (v.33); this was the fittingly accursed abode God made for Satan as though in a mirror: a child-sacrificial domain for a child-sacrificer.

As in the case of the two trees of Eden, Molech-worshippers were depicted sometimes in antiquity at a tophet, i.e. a sacrificial garden or grove, standing between two columns. The remains of the incinerated infants were often buried head-down in clay urns. The charred remnants of the babies' bodies were often accompanied by the remains of sheep and goats (but especially lambs). An ancient stele depicts a priest with a raised hand (which probably indicates a covenant) about to transfer through flame the life of a child to Satan. If the parent of the child shed a tear in such a transfer, the sacrifice would be invalid. Typically, noble children were slaughtered for this necromantically communal meal with the dead; however, in more lax and common situations, children were often purchased and nurtured for the purpose of ritual slaughter. The solemn and formulaic words "because he heard his voice" were uttered by the sacrificer who colored himself with red ochre. We can see the irony of the audibility of the "voice" when Adam (the Red Man) "heard the voice" of God proceding at the time of the evening breeze in Genesis 3:8 after he ate the "fruit." It seems that infant life, new life, was the object of extinguishment primarily, for the tophet gardens were chiefly planted with babies both born live and stillborn along with children who were fetuses and thus the result of some manner of abortion (which, in my opinion, was probably induced since stillbirths did not complete such a sacrifice and necessarily required an older advocate to receive the flames of death to seal the covenant).

Animals were an integral component in tophets since children could have a lamb sacrificed in place of themselves, for in this respect one may notice that the Aramaic word טליא (Hebrew: טלה *lamb*) means both *lamb* and *child*. The child is a reflection of the parents genetically to begin with, and a person can declare himself the pupil or child of a teacher by his own reflective actions. The reddish copper or bronze religious mirrors, like those of the Carthaginians, had faces of the infernal deities marked into them, and it is my estimation that this object allowed one to see himself in the image of the one he worshipped though the "gift" of his child whom he sadistically sent to the underworld as a messenger or angel to Death (Isaiah 57:9), for the child was often buried in an urn head-down as though in a reflection of his former viability. Deuteronomy 12:31 states that the most detestable practice man can perform is שׂרף *to burn* his "sons and daughters in the fire," and it is this root שׂרף *to burn* that produces the word שׂרף *serpent, burning one* that is used synonymously with the word נחש *serpent, shining one* (Genesis 3:1) in Numbers 21:6. It would seem as if such incendiary practices were conducted in conjunction with divine funerary feasts, particularly royal banquets, wherein the reigning monarchy communed with its dead ancestors in order to procure favor and information, for this would explain much as to the desperate and dispicable practices to which Saul reduced himself near the end of his life. Furthermore, it would also seem that this was but the putrid and parasitic opposite of Holy Communion wherein one remembers that his Maker is his Father and Feeder Who unites with His family as though through a kiss, that is, through wine and food. Sphinxes or cherubs adorned the carved rock of tophets, and we must recall that Satan was a cherub (Ezekiel 28). The worship of false deities like Baal, Molech, Chronos, etc. typically linked fertility and death whereby the object was to procure fertility of womb and land by offering the fruit of the womb's life invertedly into the land as though in a mirror of sympathetic magic often thought to be accomplished by religious orgy and other vomitous forms of concupiscense which can be seen in Leviticus 18 that links incest, homosexuality, adultery, bestiality, child-sacrifice, and Molech-worship (v.21) in an unlawful group to be punished capitally. The symbolic triangle was used in times past to communicate both femininity and fire: the Sumerian pictogram that denoted *woman* is a triangle with a line dividing it at one of its points; ancient cylinder seals depict a bull (bovine altar) upon which was a small human figure (thought to be an infant) over which was a pyramid or triangle (interpreted as fire). In this diacritical comprehension of the triangle, one can discern why Leviticus 18 places the prohibition of Molech worship (v.21) in connection with the command "A woman must not present herself before an animal..." (v.23), for, it seems, the copulation between man and beast is analogous to sacrifice of the womb's fruit whereby both incediary unions reduce fertility in type and antitype. At Ur, the land from which Abraham hailed and which is spelled אור as are the words *light* (Genesis 1:3) and *fire* (Isaiah 10:17), infant burial jars were set into the floor near the family altar or before a pillar next to it. It was often the case that a single child was buried apart from the remainder of the family as in the *foundation sacrifice* where the remains of the child were thought to guard the doorway to the house recalled typically in the Passover in which we see, again, the link between a baby and a lamb... for the Israelites painted their doors with the blood of a lamb and, soon afterward, they "...went out with boldness in the sight of all the Egyptians. For the Egyptians were burying all their firstborn..." (Numbers 33:3-4). Again, the ritual slaughter of infants in a feast with the dead usually involved the objectives of gaining fertility and knowledge from a spiritual realm of Death who would not and could not refuse the humanly and demonically irreversable instance of murder, for the irretrievable condemnation of death against another in ritual slaughter was a sacrifice that was insured to be received. Burying an infant body into the earth was as forcing a child back into the very womb from which his first human father was delivered.

Since a womb was understood as a house, the light that proceeded from the fire within the house was understood to represent the child viably proceeding from his birthing mother, and this symbolic relationship was possible according to the ACQUISITION OF KNOWLEDGE. The triangle was understood to represent *fire* as well as the *womb*; all one had to do was to confuse one meaning for the other or splice the two meanings together incorrectly and the burning of the womb (i.e. its fruit) would ensue through a LACK OF KNOWLEDGE. Since the womb was understood as an altar, since libation was poured onto it and subsequently ascended in a gas as through flame, and since the word עֹלָה can indicate both *an ascension* and *a burnt offering*, it can be grasped how the dark mirror of Satan inverted human fecundity into human sacrifice. An altar was heated and the fruit of the womb was placed upon it. Libation (understood as a type of kiss) was poured onto the victim or the victim was kissed prior to being placed upon the altar. The exhaled spirit of the child ascended in the flame as his body was eaten by the flame of burnt offering. The very imagery of life's conduit in divine worship and of divine reciprocity was inverted completely so that the fruit offered was not living but dead, was not ascending in holy consecration but ascending in unholy consumption, was no longer capable of siring the future but was remembered in the pallid declaration of "to dust you shall return" (Genesis 3:19). Child-sacrifice and abortion can be understood clearly as the same practice. When, in the ancient world, a mother consumed toxicity (like Hellebore, too much wine, etc.), she was pouring an unholy libation upon the altar of God and her husband, and the fruit offered up was cast from the womb slack and deformed. Such an image is uttered in terror by Aaron at his sister's punishment of leprosy when he cried, "Please do not let her be as one dead, whose flesh is half consumed when he comes out of his mother's womb!" (Numbers 12:12). How much more sickening when today's "wise men" butcher children with knives and suction in the womb for income! Consider: "...come, let us deal shrewdly with them, lest they multiply...." and "When you do the duties of a midwife for the Hebrew women, and see them on the birthstools, if it is a son, then you shall kill him...." (Exodus 1), for it was on account of this serpent that Solomon referred to Egypt as the "iron furnace" (1 Kings 8:51), the Tophet that was "...like the GARDEN OF THE LORD, like the land of Egypt...." (Genesis 13:10). It was child sacrifice that expelled the people of Judah during the time of Jeremiah, and, when the city was set ablaze, Judah doubtlessly became the domain of the fire tornado, that fearsome cyclonic blaze that walks within great conflagrations; it was child sacrifice that expelled the people of Eden during the time of humanity's primacy, and, when man and

Molech were judged and expelled, Eden believably became the domain of the Flaming Sword that turned every way, that fearsome storm of light Who walked within Nebuchadnezzar's fiery furnace with Daniel's unharmed compatriots; in both instances, the cherubs flanked the Lord Jesus who will be "...revealed from heaven with His mighty angels, IN FLAMING FIRE taking vengeance on those who do not know God, and on those who do not obey the gospel of our Lord Jesus Christ" (2 Thessalonians 1:7-8). He exists unburned in the flames, in the fires of Molech, and those in covenant with Christ will be saved, even if it is "...as through fire" (1 Corinthians 3:15).

Christ, our "Advocate" (1 John 2:1) became flesh in order to complete the sacrifice so that Molech or Satan did not acquire the whole of mankind, and this can be readily grasped in a complication of the Molech offering: a child could be dedicated from the womb to die for Molech; if, however, the child was stillborn, the child's ashes were placed in an urn that anticipated another child in order to complete the viability required in a covenant. The parents, therefore, were obligated to have yet another child and to offer him as the advocate of the first child in order to complete the pact made with Death. Once that child was born, the murder and reduction to ashes of that child (so that their brethren dust might be mingled eternally) sealed the oath. In this sense, the two victims became as one flesh that had been transformed by fire into ash. The parents became as one flesh copulatively in order to sire children who would become as one flesh covenantally, provided the first child was stillborn. The pattern is now clear: Man and woman became as one flesh in order to produce the fruit of God; man poured upon this holy fruit the unholy libation and mingled life and death; man united himself to Satan and thereby wished the death of God by breaking his covenant with Him; God gave man his wish and died so as to mingle with the innocent Son of Adam and the guilty sons of Adam; God could rise and resurrect the innocent Son of Adam and purify the guilty sons of Adam as through fire whereby saved-man's flesh is united with Christ's in an eternally purified form. Since the model is that man and wife constitute the bride who is united with God (the Husband), and since this Husband slept and had His heart circumcised in order that His bride could live again, we can understand more clearly this statement:

> For it is shameful even to speak of those things which are done by them in secret. But all things that are exposed are made manifest by the light, for whatever makes manifest is light. Therefore He says: "Awake, you who sleep, Arise from the dead, And Christ will give you light." See then that you walk circum-

spectly, not as FOOLS but as WISE, redeeming the time, because the days are evil. Therefore do not be unwise, but understand what the will of the Lord is. And do not be DRUNK WITH WINE [which is destruction], in which is dissipation; but be FILLED WITH THE SPIRIT [which is construction], speaking to one another in psalms and hymns and spiritual songs, singing and making melody in your heart to the Lord, giving thanks always for all things to God the Father in the name of our Lord Jesus Christ, submitting to one another in the fear of God. Wives, submit to your own husbands, as to the Lord. For the husband is head of the wife, as also Christ is head of the church; and He is the SAVIOR OF THE BODY. Therefore, just as the church is subject to Christ, so let the wives be to their own husbands in everything. Husbands, love your wives, just as Christ also loved the church and gave Himself for her, that He might sanctify and cleanse her with the washing of water by the word [as though cleansing an altar prior to offering upon it], that He might present her [the altar, the bride] to Himself a glorious church, not having spot or wrinkle or any such thing, but that she should be holy and without blemish. So husbands ought to love their own wives [altars] as their own bodies [through which they sire the offering of life]; he who loves his wife loves himself. For no one ever hated his own flesh, but nourishes and cherishes it, just as the Lord does the church. For we are members of His body, of His flesh and of His bones [which is the name of Eve in Genesis 2:23]. "For this reason a man shall leave his father and mother and be joined to his wife, and THE TWO SHALL BECOME ONE FLESH." This is a great mystery, but I speak concerning CHRIST AND THE CHURCH. (Ephesians 5:12-32).

The consumption of alcohol during pregnancy is unnatural, and an expecting mother's physiology instinctively repels her from substances like wine. Since libation was poured destructively upon victims of the altar, one can see (with respect to the altar being analogous to the womb) that a pregnant mother drinking wine is as pouring an unholy libation destructively upon the God-made altar whose object is to yield up life but is instead converted to a state typified by the tomb-altars of mausoleums. The "תפלה folly, repulsive thing" of Jeremiah 23:13 is the child-sacrifice that eventually expelled Judah back to the land of Adam where a fiery furnace awaited them, for the people rejected God's Sabbath, i.e. His Rest, i.e. His Covenant, i.e. His Image who appeared in the midst of Babylon's furnace to deliver the three who stood for His Name. The Tree of Life was of wisdom, and the Tree of the Knowledge of Good and Evil was of folly. God did not plant the lethal tree, nor should Adam have allowed the enemy into his domain to fashion it. The forbidden tree was a tree of mingled opposites that formed an antithesis to life by internal contradictions. Since grapes can ferment on the vine, the consumption of the forbidden tree's fruit was as drinking wine of a covenant with Death in an impossible and contradictory attempt to gain knowledge and favor when the two humans already possessed both grandly.

It is likely that the physical constitution of the forbidden tree was a perversion of an original design. That is, in the ancient east particularly (but by no means exclusively), grape-vines were trained onto fruit trees, and it takes little imagination to see in this a snake in a tree or a bifurcated vine resembling a crucified man. When we read the words "Tree of Life," they are in Hebrew "עץ חיים" which can be read as *Tree of Lives, Trees of Life, Trees of Lives, Living Tree, Living Trees,* etc., and the ancient east often equated life with motion, which probably explains the imagery behind following the pillar of fire (like a menorah, like a tree of light or life) around the wilderness as the Israelites received manna, the Bread of Life, which is the natural product of trees in that region. I stress this point about manna because manna is not supernatural but natural and can be found today on the trees of that region; the supernatural or miraculous aspect of what seems to be Scripture's description of this heavenly bread is that there was enough of it to feed the whole of the freed Israelites, which would suggest a tree of proportions we have not yet seen; further, it is my conviction that this tree was signified in cloud and fire, for it was this pillar that descended before the Tent maritally and spoke with infant face to Moses. This childlike face, it would follow, was the face of the "True Vine" (John 15:1) signified by Nehushtan, the Serpent on the Pole who healed with His life-giving wisdom. Thus, the image of a vine trained upon a fruit tree would appear to have no necessary negative associations.

At the same time, infusing Hellebore by the artificial means of some poker into a fermenting grape-cluster would signify the union of two disparate entities thought falsely to give wisdom but understood clearly to produce abortion. It is probably the case that the two trees in the midst of Eden were the craft of God, but a craft that Adam allowed Satan to inject with an antithesis that mingled viability with a ruinous substance as though in an adulterous penetration of fruit; if this was the case, then the forbidden tree was a modification of the original and true vine that was the sign of the "True Vine" (John 15:1) Who does not change, and this modified vine became, essentially, a sign of the antichrist. If one considers the vast quanity of times Daniel describes the antichrist by using the word "wisdom," then one will see that the antichrist is defined by the destruction of the family to the extent of the whole human race as was the case with Satan in Eden.

Genesis 49:11 refers to wine as the "blood of grapes," and Genesis 9:4 refers to blood as "life," so one can easily understand that wine was originally analogous to life which explains what is called Holy Communion and why it was offered PRIOR to the horrible bloodshed of Christ. Since Jeremiah 11:19 calls tree *fruit* לחם *bread*, we can see that consuming a grape that fermented on the vine is, in Hebrew, literally eating bread and wine in unison. This unison, being the fruit of the vine, would then be a figure of a Serpent (John 3:14) or Hanging Man (John 3:16) producing *offspring* or *fruit* or *bread and wine* or *flesh and blood* or *children* out of his circumcision or pruning, for it is such an image we read of when the first Adam's heart was circumcised in order to produce the bride and when The Last Adam's heart was pierced in order to reproduce His bride. The grape then appears to be an image of the heart which is, in Hebrew, analogous to the womb since both are analogous to the mind (for "wisdom gives life"). Penetrating the womb, piercing the heart, and pruning the mind are one idea; connecting the mind, heart, and womb with a piercing, penetrating, and pruning divides the body into halves constructively, and these halves were illustrated destructively in the animal sacrifice of Abram that the Pillar of Smoke and Fire passed between. The word ענב *cluster* (of grapes) is from the root ענב *to bind together*. If we consider what is being said here in a dark mirror of sinful history, then the image would be as follows: "The Serpent" pierced the grape/heart destructively in order to reconstitute negatively the bride of God in order to make her his own through the whoredom of sin, and Satan accomplished this by piercing the heart/wife of Adam by the grape in order to bind him in a covenant of destructive bloodshed evidenced by the nonviable fruit of the womb. In a manner of speaking, God, the Priest and Husband of man, poured holy libation into Adam in their communion; Adam poured holy libation into his bride in their communion; the fruit of the altar began to grow as seed within the garden of the womb. In a manner of speaking, Satan, the new priest and husband of man's election, beheld man's wife pour unholy libation onto her husband's altar where the growing fruit was trampled with its seed into a newly converted wilderness or desert, a disaster that was then followed by Adam joining in this unholy communion, this new testament, when he ate as well. Having planted seed before, Adam planted his seed, so to speak, and putrified the soil to the extent that it too would become a wilderness described as "accursed ground." Since 1 Timothy 2 tells us that Adam was not deceived but that his wife was, we can see how she thought that the infusion typified literarily as Hellebore could give wisdom (which it cannot) when it only gave folly, that is, abortion (which is a well-known effect); this mingling of opposites is bound up on the letters שכל to make wise, to cause abortion, which appears to indicate the remembrance of the Helleborism of the ancients and their folly.

The venom of snakes is called in Hebrew ראש, which also means the head. The High Priest is called the כהן גדל Great Priest or כהן ראש Head Priest, which can also be translated negatively as Priest of Venom, i.e. the so-called "serpent" of Genesis 3 that Ezekiel 28 describes as a former high priest with vestments like Aaron's in Exodus 28. Satan, the priest of poison, induced abortion by persuading man's heart, that is, man's bride, to eat a fruit that was bread and wine infused with poison by piercing. This destructive piercing, when ingested, resulted in the piercing of God's heart to the extent that His image was marred upon the altar of His union with mankind; correctively, God became a man, maintained His Image, and had man pierce His heart again destructively whereby He, constructively, grafted man into His heart through His blood as is seen in Thomas' hand grasping the heart of Love Incarnate Who is the "True Vine."

Copulative license is itself a mockery of Holy Communion as was the consumption of the forbidden tree, for Holy Communion is supposed to produce the "fruit of the Spirit" which is signified in one's righteous deeds sealed communally in a generative meal of truce and covenant, that is, bread and wine, flesh and blood, i.e. incarnation or viable children who will perpetuate the wisdom of God. It can, therefore, be seen that the context of the trees in the midst of Eden is one of regality and that man was intended to be as The King's cupbearer, for a basin, stomach, and a womb are one idea in Hebrew (בטן). Man, drinking from the cup of The King, staked his life for his King Who is Life Incarnate and Who lives eternally, for this covenant was an oath to the death with Eternal Life which qualifies it as a perpetually fruitful union. Man, drinking from this same cup with the additive of poison by the hand of the "king of all the children of pride" (Job 41:34) staked his life for this king who is as Death Incarnate and who dies eternally, for this covenant was an oath to the death with Eternal Death, which qualifies it as a perpetually unfruitful union that is described as a tophet or child-sacrificial garden by Scripture; it is the exact opposite, as though in a mirror, of the Garden of Eden's original design. The woman was the altar, the child in her womb was the offering, Hellebore was the fire, the man was the priest, and "The Serpent" was the king whom man elected and whose image he now bore as in a mirror. Mankind was the altar, Christ was the Holy Child Who was offered, the poison He drank on the cross was the fire, Ciaphas was the priest, and Caesar was the king whom man elected, whose image he now bore as mirrored on coins.

Surely the forbidden tree was a vine whose fermented grapes were infused with Hellebore, for this would seem to be the very reason ONLY CERTAIN MIRACLES of Christ are recorded in Scripture. Hellebore was used to treat many maladies. In Mark 1:34, Jesus heals "many who had various diseases." John 21:25 states that some, but not all of Christ's works are recorded in Scripture because "the whole world would not have room for the books that would be written," and this means glaringly that the works that are recorded are not recorded randomly but are preserved in writing for a specific purpose. The question is, "What is the purpose for recording only these works if there were comparatively innumerable works to recount?" The answer is: Each of these works is recorded to reveal that Hellebore, a mere creation, was thought to accomplish what only the Creator Himself can accomplish. Consider the maladies to which Hellebore was prescribed.

(1) **melancholia** (All physical maladies produce this effect to some degree.): Matthew 9 records that referred to Himself as a "doctor."

(2) **fever**: Matthew 8 records that Christ healed Peter's mother-in-law of a fever.

(3) **insanity**: Luke 5 records that Christ put a man "in his right mind."

(4) **chronic pain**: Matthew 9 records that Christ healed a woman who had a chronic disease and then He raises a girl from the dead.

(5) **epilepsy**: Luke 9 records that Christ healed a convulsing boy.

(6) **mental insufficiency**: Luke 8 records that Christ put a man "in his right mind." Mark 10 displays Jesus opening the eyes of the blind.

(7) **unconsciousness**: Matthew 9 records that Christ raised a girl from the dead.

(8) **lethargy/paralysis**: Matthew 9 and Mark 2 record that Jesus healed a paralytic.

(9) **leprosy**: Matthew 8 records Christ healing a man with leprosy.

Hellebore caused these reactions:

(1) **The throat and stomach become heated and burn but dissuade one from drinking. The throat constricts and can**

cause suffocation if the amount ingested is too severe. Vomiting or dry-heaving occur. The face becomes red. Vertigo ensues. There is a loss of breath and subsequently a loss of voice. The senses are lost to delirium: Mark 9 records that Christ healed a boy who was "foaming at the mouth." A convulsing boy was healed in Luke 9 by Christ.

(2) **A loss of vision can occur:** Mark 10 records that Jesus opened the eyes of the blind.

(3) **Teeth begin to gnash:** Matthew 8 records that Christ healed a man with leprosy and follows it by discussing the "gnashing of teeth."

(4) **Consciousness is lost:** Matthew 9 records that Christ raised a girl from the dead.

People "...worshiped and served the creature rather than the Creator..." (Romans 1:25) by giving credit to a plant as opposed to the Gardener. Mary was "thinking He was the gardener" (John 20:15) since "At the place where Jesus was crucified, there was a garden, and in the garden a new tomb..." (John 19:41). In Eden, the bride actually thought that the forbidden tree "נחמד *was desirable* להשכיל *to make one wise,*" which is what Hellebore was thought to be capable of doing, but it was instead "נחמד *covetous* להשכיל *to cause abortion,*" which is the same spelling (respecting the serpentine distinction of the diaphonous sibilant שׁ) as though in a mirror that reversed morality. Thus, the reason only these miracles are recorded is that Hellebore was thought to be the answer to the human maladies Christ's miracles fixed.

The miracles are deliberately recorded, it would seem, to show "The True Vine" (John 15:1) Who gave His blood in contradistinction to the false vine who gave but Hellebore in a fermented grape. Hellebore was thought to increase wisdom, but it produced abortion, and both definitions are accounted for in the letters להשכיל that Genesis 3:6 describes; for, the True Vine gives wisdom in His parables, but the false vine gave death to the innocent fruit of the womb by his riddles. *Poison* and *venom* are called ראשׁ in Hebrew, and this word also means *head*. Hellebore, which is also called "Snake Vine," deals with the head, that is, with the mind, and it would seem as if we are given repeated clues to this Hebrew definition when reading in Greek that the root חמץ means *to be sour, to be leavened* (thus combining sour wine and bread) and produces the words חמוץ *splendid and dazzling scarlet* (like wine), חמץ *vinegar;* the same letters transposed (and thus the same gematria: 138) spell מצח *forehead,* which is synonymous to ראש *head, poison, venom*: "And they... platted a crown of thorns, and put it about His *head*," (Mark 15:17); "And they smote Him on the HEAD..." (Mark 15:19); "And they that passed by railed on Him, shaking their HEADS..." (Mark 15:29); "Over His HEAD they put the charge against Him, which read, 'This is Jesus of Nazareth, the King of the Jews," (Matthew 27:37); "...Then He bowed His HEAD and gave up His Spirit," (John 19:30). We may see pieces fitted when we consider that the title כהן ראש can indicate *High Priest* or *Priest of Poison* or *Priest of Venom*, for "The Serpent" or Shining One is an ersatz priest who fell from glory and burned the image of God on the altar of God's bride by pouring Hellebore, which was thought of as liquid fire by the ancients, to a deceived bride who thought she would acquire something that only God, and not a mere plant, can give. "If any of you lacks wisdom, let him ask of God, who gives to all liberally and without reproach, and it will be given to him" (James 1:5), for Satan, being as Death himself, cannot give wisdom but only folly, that is, abortion. The first word of Genesis is בראשית *in the beginning* which is from the root ראש which produces the word *head*. The word *in* used here is the prefixed particle ב *the house, the womb*; this particle (ב) can mean *in, with,* and *by.* The next part of the first Word of Scripture is ראשית; this word can mean *beginning, firstborn,* and *first-fruits*, and it comes from the root ראש which produces the word *head chief, foremost*, that is, something or someone exhibiting *preeminence*. Therefore, the first word in Scripture can be understood in these ways:

> He is the image of the invisible God, the FIRSTBORN over all creation. For BY HIM all things were created that are in heaven and that are on earth, visible and invisible, whether thrones or dominions or principalities or powers. All things were created through Him and for Him. And HE IS BEFORE all things, and IN HIM all things consist. And HE IS THE HEAD of the body, the church, who is the BEGINNING, the FIRSTBORN from the dead, that in all things HE MAY HAVE THE PREEMINENCE (Colossians 1:15-20).

When Christ, the Innocent Firstborn, gave up His Spirit, I believe that the poison He drank was actually the poison of *herba Sardonia* that produces the infamous *sardonic smile*, not Hellebore. That is, Christ's miracles answered the false suppositions credited to Hellebore and pointed back to the death in Eden of the son of Adam. Christ's healing miracles, thus, remedied the destruction administered to the son of Adam. At the same time, the "altar" upon which the son of Adam died was his mother's womb (and thus his father's false "wisdom," i.e. abortion). Kleitarchos (3rd

Century BC) records that child sacrifice on an altar appeared this way:

> Out of reverence for Chronos [the Greek equivalent for Baal], the Phoenicians, and especially the Carthaginians, whenever they seek to obtain great favor, vow one of their children burning it as a sacrifice to the deity, if they are especially eager to gain success. There stands in their midst a bronze statue of Chronos, its hands extended over a bronze brazier, the flames of which engulf the child. When the flames fall upon the body, the limbs contract and the OPEN MOUTH SEEMS ALMOST TO BE LAUGHING, until the contracted [body] slips quietly into the brazier. Thus it is that the "grin" is known as "sardonic laughter," since they [the children] die laughing.

Hellebore was thought to bring happiness, but it brought abortion to pregnant women. The accidental synthesis of the two trees can be seen in the new name the bride devised: "The Tree אשר *that is* in the middle of the garden" (Genesis 3:3). The word אשר *that is* can also be pronounced to mean אשר *happiness* (Genesis 30:13), which is a synonym of טוב *happiness* that is more commonly translated as *good* as in The Tree of the Knowledge of טוב *Good* and Evil. The bride spoke of only one tree, and she renamed it by simplifying and synthesizing so that her invention was The Tree אשר of *Happiness* in the middle of the garden or The Tree אשר*that is* in the middle of the garden. That the woman regarded the forbidden tree as a Tree of *Happiness* functions on the proposition that God desired to restrict happiness and therefore calls into question the character of God; this poor assumption seems very much evidenced by the "Serpent's" question, " אף כי אמר*Did God say...*" which can be rendered also as "...אף*angered* that God said...?" If one vocalizes the word אשר as *happiness*, then one can see that the woman thought the forbidden tree would bring happiness and that Satan perceived this by asking if she was *angered* without it. Again, Hellebore was thought to bring happiness, but it brought abortion to pregnant women. The Sardinian Herb was known to bring a sorrowful death, but it made the dead appear to be smiling, just as this herb made the burning child sacrificed to Satan appear to be smiling. The Son of Man's miraculous remedies overturned the satanic maladies of the son of Adam emblematically, symbolically, and typically regarding Hellebore. The Son of Man dying with a smile induced by Herba Sardinia would have indicated emblematically, symbolically, and typically a child burning on an unholy altar where wood and fire were used morbidly. Recall that Numbers 25 prescribes hanging upon a tree as the punishment for burning children to Baal. What then is the symbolic union of Hellebore and the Sardinian Herb?

Both Hellebore and the Sardinian Herb are poisons, so both would be called ראש *head, poison, venom* in Hebrew; that is, both of these poisons would be named similarly in connection with a serpent. Since this word for "venom" or "poison" is also the word for "head" (like the top of a ziggurat where children were sacrificed as though in the mind of a single body and as though on the female counterpart known as the "womb" or "altar") Christ "bowed His head" when He died, which means that He must have openly displayed considerably emphatic strength in that He held His head up during His agony. Accordingly, we can understand why Colossians 2:15 does not depict a weakened, woeful Christ:

> Having disarmed principalities and powers, He made a public spectacle of them, triumphing over them in it.

Christ made a public spectacle of evil (not the converse) since He held His head aloft, drank the sardonic poison and died with the sardonic smile. Furthermore, *The Oxford Dictionary of of Byzantium* states (page 555) that the earliest survinging representations of the crucified Christ depict Him with open eyes and that it is only later in history that He is depicted with slumbering eyes. Christ, it would seem, died with open eyes, for Balaam prophesied correctly in his fourth riddle, or parable (משל) — the word רבע *four* being from the root רבע *to copulate* — that he uttered "the נאם *oracle* of the גבר *warrior, strong man, male baby* whose eyes see clearly, the oracle of One Who obeys God, Who has דעת *knowledge of/union with* The Most High" and that he sees "An abortion, fallen one with unveiled eyes": (Numbers 24:15-17). It is this prophecy that immediately precedes the child-sacrifice at Moab to Baal that necessitated the punishment of hanging the offenders who combined orgy with infanticide, thus mirroring the fourth (copulative) riddle that Balaam uttered and thus connecting with the murder of the "Holy Child" as Christ is described in Acts 4. Christ died on the *infelix lignum* or *unfruitful wood*. As Christ hung on the infertile scorpion-like tree (signified by His crown of thorns), we can recall Mount Sinai or Thorny Mountain, i.e. that Christ died under "The Law":

> Also the high places of Aven, the sin of Israel, shall be destroyed. The thorn and thistle shall grow on their altars; they shall say to the mountains, "Cover us!" And to the hills, "Fall on us!" (Hosea 10:8).

> Then they will begin 'to say to the mountains, "Fall on us!" and to the hills, "Cover us!" (Luke 23:30).

While Christ hung on the infertile wood, He said, as it is recorded in Greek, the word τετελεσται PAID *in full, it is finished,* which quotes the Hebrew

כי עשה *it is finished, He converted, He produced*. The Last Adam slept and had His heart pruned so that His bride could be born through conversion that was made possible through ransom to mirror how the first Adam slept and had his heart circumcised so that his wife could be produced through his exposed heart, his grape. It was the blood of grapes that birthed the first human mother by the "True Vine," and it was the blood of grapes that made her barren once her "eyes were opened" and spiritually gouged. Christ, it would seem, died with His eyes open. The fork in the cross (whether it was a Y-shape, X-shape, or a T-shape) would have been the tree's "opening of the eyes," and it is here where Christ held high His head with open eyes and here where Christ hung His head with open eyes — smiling.

> Having disarmed principalities and powers, He made a public
> spectacle of them, triumphing over them in it (Colossians 2:15).

The early followers of Christ were not disenchanted fools who attempted to turn an ugly defeat into a victory; rather, they understood that Christ (as though in a perfect mirror) reversed Satan's attempt to destroy man through human sacrifice by offering Himself as a human sacrifice in order to initiate the war that crushed Satan's head in a manner similar to treading a winepress. This war was unseen and was accomplished, it would seem, in the space of three "days" as are counted on earth. This war was unseen like that which took place in Eden. We see the conclusion of that war by the great day of judgement in Eden and the expulsion of man from God's holy mountain as was the case with Satan in Isaiah 14.

Hellebore was understood as liquid fire that gave *wisdom* and *abortion* simultaneously, as is encapsulated in the letters שכל. The fire of wood was used to incinerate infants who then exhibited a smile that was understood to mimic that of the lethal Herb of Sardinia. Christ was seen as "נפל *An Abortion, A Fallen One*" Who had "open eyes" in Numbers 24 immediately before the child-sacrifices and subsequent crucifixions in Numbers 25. It would seem perfectly fitting for Christ to have displayed, as though it were a Roman victory crown signifying the nature of the conquest, on his head (the place of wisdom) the very thorns that typified the curse wrought through the abortion in Eden, for this symbol of abortion was found in blood on the Head Who is the Wise Master Builder. As was the case in ancient eastern warfare, acceptable sacrifice was essential to initiate a campaign. Christ, who is both the High priest (Firstborn) and the Sacrifice (Firstborn), which is a situation that is only possible in child-sacrifice, passed through the flames to the tophet of Hell in order to crush the head of The Serpent, The Shining One. The fire of His translation, it would seem, was analogous to Hellebore in that it bore the same Hebrew title of ראש *snake venom, poison, head,* and this He signified by bowing His head, with open eyes, in the triumphant defiance of evil that looks down on defeated adversaries from on high while smiling.

> The LORD said to my Lord, 'Sit at My right hand, till I make Your enemies Your footstool.' The LORD shall send the rod of Your strength out of Zion. Rule in the midst of Your enemies! Your people shall be volunteers in the day of Your power; in the beauties of holiness, from the womb of the morning, You have the dew of Your youth. The LORD has sworn and will not relent, "You are a priest forever according to the order of Melchize-dek." The Lord is at Your right hand; He shall execute kings in the day of His wrath. He shall judge among the nations, He shall fill the places with dead bodies, He shall execute the heads of many countries. He shall drink of the river by THE WAY; therefore HE SHALL LIFT UP THE HEAD (Psalm 110).

The word מלך *king* is derived from the root *to counsel,* the word עצה *tree* also means *counsel,* and the word הרות *law* also means *counsel.* In the midst of Eden, there were two laws, two trees, two counsels, and two counselors: Christ and Satan. In the ancient east, the cultivators or dis-coverers of plants often named the plants after themselves as a type or double. Materialistic symbolism (wherein names cannot be severed from the substance they qualify) can be understood as a common facet of an-cient religion and can, for example, be readily referenced in the Egyptian and Babylonian religious records. Unfortunately, time and the temporary disappearance of records led to a situation where representation was tak-en for the substance it reflected, while the substance became obscured and ultimately forgotten to the extent that people actually believe the Fall Narrative discusses a simple story of trees and animals and fools who were too insipid to realize that they were without garments. The name was a facet of the reality of the entity it qualified. Since we know that a name is a progeny, then the progeny also possessed the face of the one from whom it descended as though in a mirror, a law, a tree, a counsel, a coun-sellor, a king... and it is in this way that we may understand the reflected "προσωπον της γενεσεως *infant face, face of genesis*" that James 1:23 describes and that Moses typified. The Menorah is a mirrored tree that is ablaze but unconsumed by flame, and Christ is the Holy Child Whose face does not change and remains the same yesterday, today, and forever.

The Shining One's face will burn forever as will the fruit, the progeny, the name, who elected him in life unto death and who will burn with him in an eternal death described as a tophet, an inferno of unceasing self-abortion, evidenced in the "old man who grows corrupt" whose face shrivels with the flames of insistantly iniquitous age that eats away at the innocent and humble child he once was but unwisely chose not to be.

THE WAY

LIKE the name "Judaism," "Christianity" is the incorrect name for the religion the Bible professes. Referring to the Hebrew Scriptures as the "Old Testament" and "Judaism" is errant, for we have already observed how the term "Old Testament" is actually, in Hebrew, the "Hidden/Eternal Covenant"; we have seen how a "Jew" is not necessarily a Hebrew; and, we have percieved how what we now call "Judaism" is simply a modified form of Rabbinic Pharisaism. Since no "Jews," and definitely no Pharisees, existed in the days of Moses, the Pentateuch was not and cannot be a "Jewish" book because "Judaism" is an anachronism that exists on account of equating "Jews" with Hebrews uniformly and absolutely. The name "Old Testament" was embraced, it would seem, by a raw Greek reading of 2 Corinthians 3:14 that discusses Moses as of the παλαιας διαθηκης *old covenant*; but, considering this term in Hebrew would render it the עולם *hidden, eternal* covenant, and it seems that Hebrews 13:20 translates this *hidden, eternal* covenant as "διαθηκης αιωνιου *everlasting covenant,*" which is understood in Latin as *testamenti aeterni*. This covenant is *hidden*, which is why Paul states, "Indeed, to this very day whenever Moses is read, A VEIL LIES OVER THEIR MINDS..." (2 Corinthians 3:15). Matthew 26:28 and Mark 14:24 are often translated as, "...this is My blood of the *new* covenant," but other ancient authorities lack the word "new" so that they would read, "this is My blood of the covenant." At the same time, however, Luke 22:20 communicates Jesus saying "καινη διαθηκη *new covenant*" which is a Greek rendering of Jeremiah 31:31 that says "חדשה ברית *renewed covenant*"; in this, one can grasp that the religion of Christ was the religion about which Moses wrote so that, if one were to describe glibly the Bible consisting of "Old" and "New" covenants or testaments, it should be understood that Christ was renewing that which preceded what we now call "Judaism" and that is the religion of Eden prior to Moses' life but in accordance with Moses' pen, thus: "Blessed are those who do His commandments, that they may have the εξουσια *right, authority* to the tree of life, and may enter through the gates into the city" (22:14). In other words, the bloody injunctions that were given at Sinai occured in Moses' lifetime, but after a lot of the history of which Moses wrote. Consider Moses' history of Abraham. Abraham was a fallen human, but, unlike Jacob, insisted on no particular stipulations regarding his covenant with God. Jacob insisted on food and clothing in his covenant:

> Then Jacob made a vow, saying, "If God will be with me, and
> keep me in this Way that I am going, and give me bread to
> eat and clothing to put on, so that I come back to my father's
> house in peace, then the Lord shall be my God."

The religion Jacob discussed was called The Way, and Jacob was willing to proceed on it under the terms that God gave him food and clothing. Moses reminds Jacob (Israel), in Deuteronomy 8, that God provided food and clothing for 40 years while Israel trekked the labyrinthine Way in the wilderness and sired the next generation. Here, one should see that The Way has much to do with fertility, that is, with "Eden." Furthermore, one should see that The Way is the Hidden/Old/Eternal Covenant that Hebrews 13:20 discusses as the "Everlasting Covenant" that was renewed by Christ according to Luke 22:20 in reference to Jeremiah 31:31 as stated above. The Way, the religion expressed in the terms "Be fruitful and multiply," was renewed by Christ as declared by the fact that he came through successful gestation into the world. Jacob (Israel) was provided with food and clothing by God in The Way. God provided food for Adam and Eve; but, when they found themselves naked on account of forsaking God's food, God "clothed them with skins," which is gestational terminology according to Job 10:8-12, and which reflects God's pronouncement, "I will increase your sorrow AND YOUR CONCEPTION" (Genesis 3:16). The intended clothing of man is spiritual. Consider: "...yet she is your companion and your wife by COVENANT. But did He not make them one, having a REMNANT OF THE SPIRIT? And why one? He seeks GODLY OFFSPRING" (Malachi 2:14-15); Luke 24:49 compares being filled with the Holy Spirit to being "CLOTHED with power from on high," thus 2 Corinthians 5:4 states, "For we who are in this tent groan, being burdened, not because we want to be unclothed, but further CLOTHED, that mortality may be swallowed up by life." The vital "clothing" that "swallows" death is spiritual as it enfolds unviability in order to renew life, and this principle probably hints to the fact that the words גלם *embryo,* גלמוד *sterile, barren* and גלום *cloak* are derived from the root גלם *to wrap together.* The pronouncement of increased conception and the provision of "clothing" are followed by the cherubs and the Flaming Sword "to guard The Way of the Tree of Life" (Genesis 3:24), this Way being the religion that was discussed in the Old/Hidden/Eternal Covenant and restablished in the New/Renewed Covenant by Christ through gestation from Heaven into the world and then into death, and rebirth from death into the world and back to Heaven.

The Greek words "εξουσια *right* to the Tree of Life" are but a translation of the Hebrew words " עץ החיים דרךway *of the Tree of Life*" (Genesis 3:24). The proof is in the fact that the Greek "εξουσια *right, authority*" is a translation of the Hebrew "דרך *way*" as can be seen by Amos 2:7 that uses "דרך *way*" to discuss *justice* and *rights*. It seems much more consistent that "The Way," not "Christianity," is the name of the religion of the Savior, for this is the name Paul defended in Acts 24. Christ Himself said, "I am THE WAY, the truth, and the life. No one comes to the Father except through Me" (John 14:6). "Christianity" is the label that "The Way" acquired in Antioch (Acts 11), and this "Way" is the same as that which Malachi defended (2:8). When Malachi 4:4 tells us to "Remember The Law of Moses," it should be understood that the Torah or Pentateuch only introduces Moses in its second Book. Moses writes about two "Laws" or "Trees" or "Teachings": one of life, the other of death; thus, the final Book of Moses states plainly, "I call heaven and earth as witnesses today against you, that I have set before you life and death, blessing and cursing; therefore choose life, that both you AND YOUR DESCENDANTS may live" (Deuteronomy 30:19), for "descendents" (seed) are a constituent of The Way. Life and death are symbolized by the two trees in Eden within the Book of Genesis (that preceded Moses' birth and was written through Moses hand). The Tree of Life symbolizes the Way just as Zechariah 11 shows how a wooden staff symbolizes the covenant, the covenant of life and peace (Malachi 2:5), the "peace" that Christ offered as described in Ephesians 2:14-17. The Tree of the דעת of Good and Evil is the tree that *mingled* good and evil, life and death, into a ruinous mixture; the forbidden tree was The Tree of Death and The Way of Death "the enmity, that is, the law of commandments contained in ordinances" (Ephesians 2:15) that are not necessary if we adhere to The Tree of Life, The Way of Life, The Covenant of Life and not death "that made nothing perfect" (Hebrews 7:19) wherein "those sacrifices there is a reminder of sin every year" (Hebrews 10:3). Thus, when Christ said that He did not come to abolish the Law or Prophets (Matthew 5:17), and when Ephesians 2:15 says that Christ abolished the Law, it should be understood that Christ upheld The Law of Life proclaimed by Moses and the Prophets that preceded Sinai (according to Jeremiah 7 and Hebrews 10). Christ put to death The Law of Sin and Death. There are two diametrically opposed entities that go by the same name, and one is parasitic upon the other.

(1) "The Law of God" and
(2) "The Law of Sin" (Romans 7:22-23)

(1) "The Law of the Spirit of Life" and
(2) "The Law of Sin and Death" (Romans 8:2)

(1) "The Perfect Law of Liberty" (James 2:12) and
(2) "Enmity" (Romans 8:6).

Genesis 31:49 discusses a covenant by signifying it with the erection of a material symbol by the use of the word המצפה *the watch-place* or *watch-tower*. This "tower" was not an actual tower in which one could climb and look out from its apex, but it was a stone signification of the "watching" or guarding or preserving of the covenant it signified, like the stone pillar Jacob erected when he entered covenant with God in Genesis 28 and like the pillar of fire and cloud that God erected that led Israel through the wilderness in Exodus through Deuternomoy. Likewise, a tree can be a signification of a watching or guarding or preserving of a covenant like the one Abraham planted in Genesis 21:33 where he "called on the Name of Jehovah, the Everlasting God." This word "Everlasting" is the same translated in Greek as "Old" in the term "Old" Testament. The point is not that God is "old," but that He is "everlasting" and "hidden," as the Hebrew term implies, for Romans 1:20 discusses God's "invisible attributes" just as Colossians 1:15 says that Christ is the "Image of the invisible God." Accordingly, Christ would be as that stone signification of an invisible covenant as we read of Him: "For they drank of that spiritual Rock that followed them, and that Rock was Christ" (1 Corinthians 10:4). A rock was often used as the foundation of a planted tree, and the common Biblical "rock and tree" metaphors would seem to indicate strongly the symbols of unseen, hidden covenants man has made for good and for evil. The Tree of Life bears viable fruit, and The Way of Death "gives birth to death" (James 1:15). Both "Ways" appear to point to gestation, fertility, fecundity, etc. The Way of Life is the standard from which The Way of Death deviates since death is parasitic to life (but not the other way around). That is, since the wages of sin is death, and since death came because of sin, it can be seen clearly that life preceded death and that death had no place in the sinless creation God made. The deviation from life resulted in a humanity that "...defiled the land and committed adultery with stones and trees" (Jeremiah 3:9), i.e. killed children whose bodies were hidden in a covenant that was signified by rocks and plants. Such innocent death according to a horrific covenant was overturned on the tree in which Christ died and out of the rock from which He rose. Consider: "Of the Rock who begot you, you are unmindful, and have forgotten the God who fathered you" (Deuteromony 32:18), and this indictment, it would seem, is the opposite of what Christ accomplished when He rose again.

"The Way" of Christ is "life" and "blessing," and the first mention Genesis gives us of "blessing" is Genesis 1:22, 28 regarding offspring, thus, "...that both you AND YOUR DESCENDANTS may live" (Deuteronomy 30:19). Opposite to The way "of life and peace" (Malachi 2) is the mirrored and antithetical "Way" of child sacrifice Jeremiah 2:23 names. It can be seen here that "The Way" (of Life) is the standard that is negatively reflected by "The Way" (of Death), both of which involve seed, offspring, descendants, etc. who either live or die. It should be seen clearly now that the two trees in Eden were two trees whereby offspring lives or dies. Since we have already understood that the forbidden tree did not have seed, the dead seed was not of the tree but of the humans who ate of it, and Christ our "Advocate" (1 John 2:1) is called "The Seed" (Galatians 3:16; Genesis 15:5). God offered "The Way" of the Tree of Life, and Satan offered "The Way" of the Tree of Death. God offered offspring from the Seed He gave, and Satan offered seedlessness from the seedlessness he gave. For thousands of years, only one "Law," one "Way," and one "Tree" were discussed, and they were all thought to give death because it was not realized that the same name qualified the standard of Life that was imitated falsely by death as though in a mirror that reflected moral antitheses.

The title "Christian" given as a label to those who followed "The Way" (of life) in Acts 11 ultimately served to sire persecution that probably could have been avoided. Rome restricted innovative religions while it gave leeway to many ancestral religions. One of the chief arguments of the "New Testament" (i.e. the Renewed Covenant) is that "The Way" is the most ancestral religion and dates back to Eden, which is why so many powerful parallels are drawn between Christ and Adam and why so many illustrations Christ discussed have to do with gardening. Once the label of "Christian" became known, a *new* name (instead of the *renewed* name of "The Way") circulated and gave the accidental appearance of a new religion (instead of an ancestral and thus *renewed* religion). This new name gave Nero an opportunity to brand "Christians" with the fire he set to Rome; it would seem that, concerning this fire and this innovative and unoriginal label, Peter said in 1 Peter 4:12-16,

> Beloved, do not think it strange concerning the FIERY TRIAL which is to try you, as though some strange thing happened to you; but rejoice to the extent that you partake of Christ's sufferings, that when His glory is revealed, you may also be glad with exceeding joy. If you are reproached for the name of Christ, blessed are you, for the Spirit of glory and of God rests upon you. On their part He is blasphemed, but on your part He is glorified. But let none of you suffer as a murderer, a thief, an evildoer, or as a busybody in other people's matters. Yet if anyone SUFFERS AS A CHRISTIAN, let him not be ashamed, but let him glorify God in this matter.

Suffering as a "Christian," it would seem, was suffering under a label that gave one the appearance of being innovative and new as opposed to ancestral. In Acts 24:10-16, Paul said,

> "Inasmuch as I know that you have been for many years a judge of this nation, I do the more cheerfully answer for myself, because you may ascertain that it is no more than twelve days since I went up to Jerusalem to worship. And they neither found me in the temple disputing with anyone nor inciting the crowd, either in the synagogues or in the city. Nor can they prove the things of which they now accuse me. But this I confess to you, that according to THE WAY [the true name of the Faith or Covenant] which they call a sect, so I worship the God OF MY FATHERS [ancestral], **believing all things which are written in the Law and in the Prophets**. I have hope in God, which they themselves also accept, that there will be a resurrection of the dead, both of the just and the unjust. This being so, I myself always strive to have a conscience without offense toward God and men.

Paul and Peter both worshipped according to "The Way" of God that Paul identified under this title (explained from those inside to the outside world) and to which Peter responded under accusation (accused by the outside world against those inside). "And he who is upright in THE WAY is an abomination to the wicked" (Proverbs 29:27).

As we have seen, there are two trees, and the woman, the bride, only saw one. We have already observed the connections amongst the terms "tree," "law," and "way" in that the same terms are used to discuss antithetical entities whereby the reflection or reversal is given in both morality and the arrow of time. As a further example, we may note that Genesis 19:31 uses the term "דרך כל הארץ *the way of all the earth*" to indicate copulation that leads to fruit-production, but 1 Kings 2:2 uses the same term to indicate death. "The Way" is the standard of life and fruit-production, and its parasitic opposite reflects this title both morally and chronologically. In other words, the standard counts down to birth, while its opposite counts down to death. Jeremiah 21:8 describes "דרך החיים *The Way of Life*" and "דרך המות *The Way of Death*," and he illustrates The Way of Death, in 21:9, by "sword," "famine," and "plague"; woes like these are linked to "childlessness" in 18:21. One should consider here the flaming sword and the curse against the soil in Genesis 3.

The place where the two "laws" or "trees" or "ways" meet is called the "פתח עינים *opening of the eyes*" (which is translated often as "*the en-*

trance to Enaim" in Genesis 38:14). The logic of a fork in the road being called the "פתח עינים *opening of the eyes"* seems to be that one eye begins to be directed to the right while the other begins to be directed to the left beginning from where the two divergent ways meet; in this sense, the opening of the eyes demands and reflects a choice. Accordingly, Judah could not see that it was Tamar (whose name means "Palm Tree") to whom he went carnally (Genesis 38) according to *the way of all the earth.* When this "Way" was about to be the death of Tamar, i.e. the death of this Tree, she revealed the father and this "Way" became one of life in that Matthew 1:3 lists Tamar in the line of Christ, "The Way" Himself. Since Colossians 1:16 states that Christ is the Creator, we can, through this tree, this Tamar, observe a demonstration of how "I and My Father are One" (John 10:30), which explains how both the first human and His creator are both called "Adam." It can, therefore, be understood that the first man was the image or reflection of his Creator so that, when Christ took on flesh, He did not look like us but revealed how we were created to look like Him. According to the bifurcation called "the opening of the eyes," one may perceive that a choice is essential, and that choosing one way places the other way progressively further away from the chooser. Eyes can, accordingly, be "opened" to sight or "opened" (gouged) to blindness as one proceeds along the singular choice that was initiated at the fork in the road. Genesis 28:6-8 uses "sight" to discuss perception, and it was the forbidden tree that both initiated and continued to reproduce a lack of perception by "opening the eyes" to a ruinous choice and then continuing to "open the eyes" by perceptual blinding. Opening the eyes to the two "Ways" would begin at the antithetical union of copulation and death; the mingling of these two would be abortion or child-sacrifice which is how Jeremiah 2:23 qualifies "The Way" antithetically. Congruently, "The Way" of death, following copulation, was suffered by Solomon's nameless older brother, and the "The Way" of life birthed Solomon in his place. When Solomon asked for the wisdom to discern between good and evil while in a process usually called "incubation" or inspired dreaming, it should be recalled that he was between the high place and the Tabernacle or the "opening of the eyes" that pointed towards the death of child-sacrifice and the image of the life-giving bride, the Tabernacle of Moses. Likewise, Solomon validated his wisdom by choosing between the two "Ways" regarding a dead and a live infant just after worshipping at the infant coffin of The Son of Man called The Ark of the Covenant, the very same seen in Christ's tomb and at the gate of Eden. It was this same Solomon who said in Proverbs 14:12 and 16:25 that "There is a way that seems right to a man, but its end is the ways of death." Solomon opened his own eyes positively when he threatened to open the eyes of the two women by the two potential halves of the baby who, according to The Way (of life), was restored to the rightful mother.

Genesis 30:1 describes childlessness as *death* (מתה אנכי). Genesis 15:2 describes childlessness as *nudity* (ערירי). Isaiah 56:3 calls childlessness a "dry tree" i.e. a dead and naked tree which is what the cross is called in Latin: *a naked tree.* After Job lost his children, he described himself as "naked." We may see in these connections that one who makes himself childless is as one who makes himself without clothes, a tree without water, and dead. 2 Corinthians 5:4 states, "For we who are in this tent groan, being burdened, not because we want to be unclothed, but further clothed, that mortality may be swallowed up by life." Since a "dead" person is a childless person, and since Adam lived 930 years following his expulsion, we can understand that Adam did die the very day he ate of the forbidden tree because, on that very day, he became childless and naked on account of a tree he chose at the "opening of the eyes." Abraham and Lot separated at the opening of the eyes, Lot towards Sodomites and Abraham towards the fertility expressed in Isaac — and it would seem that the antithetical reflection concerning the opening of the eyes is hinted at when Genesis 13:10 describes Lot "lifting his eyes" towards the same direction where Abraham saw "smoke rising" from Sodom's fiery destruction.

"The Way" is discussed in Genesis 24:27,40,42; Psalm 1; Psalm 25:9; Isaiah 40:27; 1 John 2:6; 1 Peter 2:2. Volumes upon volumes could be written about "The Way" as the name of the Bible's religion, for, with this realization, one can understand that the religion of Jesus was the religion of Eden and of Adam. For instance, 1 John 2:6 states, "He who says he abides in Him ought himself also to walk just as He walked," and the expression to "guard the way" (Geneis 3:24) is defined in Genesis 18:19 as "doing what is right and just." "Abiding in Christ" is "doing what is right and just" and "guarding the way." When the cherubs and the Flame of the Sword were set "to guard The Way" to the Tree of Life, it can be seen that the blade that proceeds from the mouth of Christ is his Word (Revelation 1:6) that is "right and just" which means that it "guards The Way" to The Tree of Life as opposed to a "dry tree" of "nudity" and "death" understood as "childlessness." Since this Sword was set at Eden's gate in reaction to man's sin, we can see how man suffered "death" the very "day" he ate of the forbidden tree that caused his nudity and dryness and that revealed that man's eyes were "opened" towards the way of sin and death that subsequently blinded him to The Way of Life and Liberty to the extent that he could not see the omnipresent God before him: "For the WORD OF GOD is living and powerful, and sharper than any TWO-EDGED SWORD, piercing even to the division of soul and spirit, and of joints and marrow, and is a discerner of the thoughts and intents of the heart. And there is NO CREATURE HIDDEN FROM HIS SIGHT, but all things are NAKED and OPEN TO THE EYES of Him to whom we must give account" (Hebrews 4:12-13).

Since "the wages of sin is death" (Romans 6:23), we can assume safely that our first human parents were to live forever in their untainted flesh prior to their sin regarding the forbidden tree. Time, then, would be of no detriment if death was of no reality. Time, however, would be of extreme benefit insofar as gestation is concerned. Parents who lived in eternity could count time on account of sowing seed agriculturally and anatomically to a positive effect with no possible detriment if perfection was the constant. Declining with age could not be a function of time in a sinless world; measuring growth incrementally could be a function of time-keeping in a sinless world. I bring up this point, relative to this discussion of "The Way," to say that a sinless existence would subject time itself to be the servant of eternity, for time's progress would serve to multiply nature. How a terminal velocity in perfection would be reached is a mystery insofar as the physical limits of Earth's geography are concerned. Yet, since sin and death entered the earth, it is, perhaps, a point not worth considering. Sin and death did enter the earth, and this entrance caused earth's inhabitants to be subject to the arrow of time through the declination of age. The only way to offset the constancy of death and to exhibit a growth instead of a stasis is through bearing fruit in larger quantities than the current population. Such a situation seems to have been the case with the wandering Israelites. God emancipated His people in order to bring them into the Promised Land, but the people killed their children and did not want to enter the Promise, the Covenant, the Rest, the Sabbath, the Fertility, the Eden, which is the same rejection of the Sabbath committed by the Israelites who became the subjects of Babylon (that was situated geographically where Eden had been formerly). Had God allowed Israel to be destroyed utterly, He would not have accomplished the repopulation of the Promised Land with Israel. As though in a mirror, the Israelites were marched for four decades in the pattern of a labyrinth. A labyrinth is a type of mirror. They were marched in a land where mirage was common, and a mirage is a type of mirror. The Israelites produced children in their physical image and according to their physical likeness, but children who mirrored or reversed their parents' misconduct and who were willing to inherit the Promise, the Covenant, the Rest, the Sabbath, the Fertility, the Eden.

When the first generation of wandering Israelites died off, it died by leaving behind a positive copy of itself, and it was this copy, this image, who entered into the Promise, the Covenant, the Rest, the Sabbath, the Fertility, the Eden. Israel, through childbirth, entered the Promised Land even though Israel, on account of killing children, was utterly destroyed. Time's subjugation of the creation was reversed through fertility, and it is this fertility that revealed that creation was designed to subjugate time. Time serves the purposes of fertility absolutely in a world where all is good and nothing dies, whereas fertility is checked by time in a world where all have sinned and have fallen short of the glory of God. The reader of Scripture can notice that the infertility that marked Abraham and Sarah, Isaac and Rebecca, as well as the constant threats to this family line were overcome by being made fertile by God in spite of circumstance to the extent that the entire pattern that threatened life was completely reversed through a Virgin Birth. This Virgin Birth revealed a Man. The first human was not the product of copulation, and, in this, we may grasp that the marital union is a physical reflection of the Right of Firstborn wherein life is poured out prior to its sign. Adam was made from the ground and Psalm 139:15 describes human gestation as being "skillfully wrought in the lowest parts of the earth"; after Christ died, Ephesians 4:9 says that He "descended into the lower parts of the earth." The depth of earth is described in terms of gestation as well as death (Psalm 63:9), thus Christ was reborn after death "early in the morning" (Mark 16:2) in accordance with the "womb of the dawn" (Psalm 110).

The letters שבע spell both *seven* and *covenant*. The seven covenantal colors of the rainbow are dispersed in the morning and are reversed in the evening so that midday is the mirror of the light. The opposite can be observed in that *midnight* is called "חצת הלילה *the halves of the night*" (Exodus 11:4) so that there is a conceptual mirror defined by noon and midnight wherein morning is reflected by evening and sunrise is reflected by sunset. Sunrise disperses the covenantal colors while sunset consumes them. Consider Jeremiah 33:20-23:

> If you can break My covenant with the day and My covenant with the night, so that there will not be day and night in their season, then My covenant may also be broken with David My servant, so that he shall not have a son to reign on his throne, and with the Levites, the priests, My ministers. As the host of heaven cannot be numbered, nor the sand of the sea measured, so will I multiply the descendants of David My servant and the Levites who minister to Me.

In this passage, the concept of covenant is combined with "day" and "night" relative to gestation and multiplication. Viewing a star is peering into the past because of the distance between the star and the observer. The viewer stands at the "opening of the eyes" when he regards the North Celestial Pole and the North Ecliptic Pole, the axis of Earth's rotation and the axis of Earth's precession. Precession is difficult to see because it requires a vast amount of time in order to be discerned. There are two trees or two poles in the midst, and one of them is difficult to see moving in a single human lifetime. The Eden story is written in the stars, the very Tabernacle where Salvation was prophesied.

The "green flash" that occurs near sunrise and sunset is the effect of a mirage. The root אבב to bear fruit produces the words green, verdure, fruit, father, advisor, and author along with the name of the first Hebrew month, Abib. Consider the fact that the Accadians denoted "the daybreak" with the ideograph of a leaf. It is my opinion that this green flash was conceived of as a sign of Eden in the east and in the west, at sunrise and at sunset, which is why the Eden story begins with its human inhabitants in the east and ends with man being cast out of the eastern gate so that Eden is west of him. The letters בשר can mean to bring, declare, tell and announce good tidings and can also mean flesh, and Jeremiah 20:15 discusses this good news, this gospel, with these letters referring to proclamation of a successful birth. The Gospel is called "The Way," and "The Way" is of life proclaimed by successful birth. Psalm 19:1 states that "the Heavens declare the glory of God," for those heavens were utilized to count down to the birth of Christ following the sin in Eden. Originally, time was subjected to eternity in that it was used to count down to birth in perfection. The pattern was reversed when the fruit of the womb was consumed so that intended eternity was subjected to time that was then used to count down to death in degradation. The pattern was again reversed and set aright by Christ Who came up from the ground in the manner in which the Creation is described in Genesis 1-2, and these facts are perhaps hinted at by Paul's description of "The Way" in Acts 24:14-14:

> But this I confess to you, that according to THE WAY which they call a sect, so I worship the God of my fathers, believing all things which are written in THE LAW and in the Prophets. I have hope in God, which they themselves also accept, that there will be a RESURRECTION OF THE DEAD....

The Law, The Teaching, The Way, The Tree, The Flesh, and The Gospel of Christ seem to be synonymous terms, and they are mirrored in morally and viably antithetical terms by The Law, The Teaching, The Way, The Tree,

The Flesh, and The Gospel of Satan described as "a different gospel" (2 Corinthians 11:4) and as "another law in my members, warring against the law of my mind, and bringing me into captivity to the law of sin which is in my members" (Romans 7:23). The Law that is The Gospel of Christ births children who are the signification of an invisible covenant expressed through perpetual life. The Law that is the Gospel of Satan kills children who are the signification of an invisible covenant expressed through perpetual death, which is why Hell is called a "Tophet" (Isaiah 30:33), a place of child-sacrifice, wherein the temporary killers of children are themselves killed eternally.

REFLECTIONS

SCIENCE has proven beautifully that the brain is plastic. The brain is like a tree. The letters עצה spell both *tree* and *counsel*, and it is such a fact that can help one understand the choice between the two trees in Eden. The brain can be conformed to an image, for it is a mirror of one's choices. Sin is the result of a choice, and one's choice will begin to mold one's brain so that one's mind will tend more towards that choice and grow in it; in this we see a departure from the original intention; in this we can see a new nature, a sinful nature. The "spirituality" of the matter can be understood also as the "perception" of the matter. That is, the Hebrew word רוח *spirit* means breath and wind, but it is from the root רוח *to smell, to perceive,* which means that accurate spirituality is accurate perception. Just as "...sin, when it is full-grown, GIVES BIRTH TO DEATH" (James 1:15), Hosea 4:6 says, "My people are destroyed for LACK OF KNOWLEDGE. Because you have rejected knowledge, I also will reject you from being priest for Me; because you have forgotten the law of your God, I also will forget your CHILDREN." Innacurate perception, improper spirituality, is sin, and sin is abortive. The only remedy is Christ:

> But you have not so learned Christ, if indeed you have heard Him and have been taught by Him, as the truth is in Jesus: that you put off, concerning your former conduct, the old man which grows corrupt according to the deceitful lusts, and be RENEWED IN THE SPIRIT OF YOUR MIND, and that you put on the new man which was created according to God, in true righteousness and holiness (Ephesians 4:20-24).

> And do not be conformed to this world, but be transformed by the RENEWING OF YOUR MIND, that you may prove what is that good and acceptable and perfect will of God (Romans 12:2).

The arrow of time compels choices to produce sequential affects on our lives. The time one spends as the result of one's choices proves one's values based on the elective chronology that defines one's time on earth. What one chooses to do with his own time is who one is. What one chooses to do with his own time shapes his brain into the labyrinthine garden that ultimately produces the fruit of his will. It is for this reason that I claim the religion of what is called the "Church" is fundamentally no different than the religion of those who reject the "Church," for both sides spend an equal portion of their elected time dedicated to a Screen that wages war on the purity of Scripture, a Screen that gives a new nature to a brain that was not intended to make the connections the Screen makes. The "Church" is not the Church. Associating one entity with another, unifying one thing with another, affects how a person thinks about both entities, both things. The Screen glamorizes the sale of that which cannot be repurchased, for it gloats in celebration of a lost virtue's price. This shining Screen promotes the means to gold as an end and thus inverts nature to effect a mindset that prefers possessions to people, bodies to hearts, vessels to contents, and, ultimately, the lifeless to the living. Our national culture no longer knows much of shame, only of difference. The inebriation induced by the abandonment of self-control has severed the sign of the covenant from the covenant itself to the degree that the oath to the death is no longer seen and the sign is viewed for hire as an art manufactured to inculcate a population into national and social policy that began at the point of forbidden sensuousness and will end upon the dispassionate edge of infertility.

The insubstantial and nonevidential proclamations of "Faith," like the outright rejection of an authority higher than human license, has produced the fading of holy divinity in the very minds originally patterned after a forgotten primacy. Such a ruinous admixture, the "knowledge" of good and evil, disallows the ability to bear the very fortune it seeks in order to persuade one to vanquish himself with the unsounding smile of a sick mind that calls failure "success." On account of this ruinous admixture, the "Wisdom of God" willfully bore the very suicide of mankind upon Himself with the sound smile of a sober mind that recalled the failure and destroyed it successfully through His victorious rebirth. As Plato said of the general humanity he called "Atlantis,"

> They despised everything but virtue, caring little for their present state of life, and thinking lightly of the possession of gold and other property, which seemed only a burden to them; neither were they intoxicated by luxury; nor did wealth deprive them of their self-control but they were sober, and saw clearly that all these goods are increased by virtue and friendship with one another, whereas by too great regard and respect for them, they are lost and friendship with them. By such reflections and by the continuance in them of a divine nature, the qualities which we have described grew and increased among them; but when the divine portion began to fade away, and became diluted too often and too much with the mortal admixture, and the human nature got the upper hand, they then, being unable to bear their fortune, behaved unseemly, and to him who had an eye to see, grew visibly debased, for they were losing the fairest of their precious gifts; but to those who had no eye to see the

true happiness, they appeared glorious and blessed at the very time when they were full of avarice and unrighteous power.

The English that bordered the 19th and 20th centuries, written with Greek and Latin sources in mind, cannot be easily understood by the average "English" reader today who reads with only English sources in mind. As the ancient, three-dimensional writing on clay is regarded by the "Church" today, so one can see that simply reading English from a century ago, watching a film made during WWII, or listening to songs from less than a century ago requires so much explanation to Today's mass-media-infected mind that it proves almost useless to attempt to convey a beauty that is deemed nearly indecipherable and practically valueless by an uninitiated populace. As such, how can anyone actually believe that today's man, without serious training, can understand Moses — who lived thousands of years ago and thousands of miles away, who wrote in a language no longer spoken or written as it was, who was educated in disciplines now only vaguely recalled, who rejected sullied royalty to embrace sootless eternity — by a simple referencing of a translation often not read with the objective of memorization in mind?

Consider what Vergerio said in his "Character and Studies": "For those who read books in a disorderly way, now beginning from the end, now dipping into the middle, learning second what they should have learned first — the only profit such people take from their reckless reading is the appearance of having read nothing at all." The record of Christ's victory has become recounted through diluted methods that believe they can simplify in order to edify, but they too often provide excuses for the unseemly to the extent that the deliberate selection of isolated passages is used with a contradictory permissiveness and with the goal of attracting the largest, and thus most profane, crowd. Uncontextualized quotations such as "Judge not" are employed to overturn other uncontextualized quotations such as "Drive out the wicked from among you," and a false humility that equates killing an ant by an accidental step in public with killing a child by an intentional stabbing in private pervades in a spectrum that colors everyone identically to the effect that sin itself can no longer be seen easily. Consequently, the difference between the inside and the outside blends into an ignored past that sinks into literary waters soon to be counted as seemingly unnavigable as the shoal mud produced in Atlantis' destruction by its own father.

The reliance of the "believer" on the digitized clicks of flippant word-searches has been dubbed a technological "success" to the extent that foolish statements like "The Bible never specifically states..." are the imbecilic result of a failure to grasp a pattern discerned through mass-memorization within contextual chronology for an eternal purpose that reflects an original design. By such reasoning, one could claim that "The Bible never specifically talks about bananas" to the extent that such a fruit must be branded "unbiblical." The effects of the various statutes that are devised to regulate the viewing of artificial concupiscence for fiduciary purposes are called commonly by Scripture "harlotry," so relying on some electronic process to sift Scripture's pages to discover a "Biblical" world-view on today's rating-systems is as contradictory as the mind that enjoys such viewing in the first place. Even to question the biological constituents of legitimate nuptials on a Biblical basis shows not only poor reading but also the revulsion of all that is natural, positively fecund, and productively innate. The strange are called by Scripture בני בליעל *Sons of Belial* in Judges 19:22 (euphemistically translated as "wicked men") and 2 Corinthians 6:15 tells us that *"Belial"* is a name for *Satan*, for in this we can see why Satan was signified by the King of Sodom and the Tree of the דעת *Union/Knowledge* of Good and Evil, a tree of the unlike mixture of apparent likenesses that should not be joined. Likewise, 2 Samuel 5 uses the name *"Belial"* in synonymous parallel with "Death" with the image of deadly WATERS to indicate the idea of DESTRUCTION; thus, the practice of biologically lifeless unions, was destroyed: "...bringing in the FLOOD on the world of the ungodly; and turning the cities of Sodom and Gomorrah into ashes, condemned them to DESTRUCTION, making them an example to those who afterward would live UNGODLY..." (2 Peter 2:5-7). The "strange" (Jude 1:7) female counterparts of this absurdity are addressed adequately in Romans 1. "Believers" now make these children of *Belial* their pastors, teachers, role-models, and political leaders by rejecting the King of Salem and by accepting an unholy communion often fortified by mere celebrity that cannot distinguish fame from infamy. It is ironic to observe how impotent and infertile the libidinous mind is! Repetition is a form of persuasion. The continual intake of anti-Scriptural images, words, and ideologies sires an appetite that only increases with feeding to the point that all that is vomited out is the "Daily Bread" of Scripture while insipidity at the speed of light is grossly regurgitated and inversely breeds by making the eaters, not the food, the worms they were warned to avoid in the foreign desert that has become both their home and grave on the edge of a land promised to those who are willing to cut a venomous social umbilical cord. The willful inability to decipher the eternal emblems results in a defiantly smiling self-abortion.

The lethargic preference to take the bigger boy's word via simplified reduction and collective agreement proves woefully unsophisticated. Statements like "My pastor said… my father said… my teacher said…" are of no real importance if they cannot be verified in the entirety of Scripture. Jeremiah said: "Surely our fathers have inherited lies, worthlessness and unprofitable things" (16:19). The priests of Jeremiah's day sanctioned the infernal tophets for the people and for themselves; their entire city became a flaming tophet as a reflection of their deeds that violated a "Sabbath," i.e. that violated a covenant through extinguishing innocent life; for, the "priests and the people transgressed more and more, ACCORDING TO ALL THE ABOMINATIONS OF THE NATIONS, and DEFILED THE HOUSE OF THE LORD which He had consecrated in Jerusalem" (2 Chronicles 36:14). That some religious, familial, educational, or political leader makes provision for perversion does not decrease the illness of the perversion; rather, perverse provision increases the illness of a collective mind that conforms itself to communal doom only after "eating" its own "fruit" that otherwise anticipated nothing but tender love from the parents who pretended to stake their own lives for it. The sign has been mistaken for the substance. Today's society sneers at literature that challenges cognition, for it embraces writing that only strokes nerves. Fertile fields are traded for manured thoughts that are the biproducts of statistical digestion reinforced by the finances that fill today's bookstores. Prostitution and recorded malice are now called "art," and the profane is the substitute for the emphatic as much as the casual is the substitute for the familial. Cleverly abstruse insidiousness projected widely through cognitive degenerates has resulted in the most incompetent of slaves being regarded as the most inspired of artists, teachers, political leaders, and pastors. The notion that erotic love can exist without the familial covenant has resulted in the murderous and the dishonest, the broken and the dispersed.

The objective of this book is to proclaim that the Fall in Eden was what we now call "abortion," and this knowledge is linguistically and ironically the "wisdom" of Genesis 3:6 — as well as the remainder of Scripture and of Human history! This is the greatest secret of human history! The fact that this sin was great enough to plunge the whole world into darkness can be observed in the pronouncement of Deuteronomy 12:31. *Abortion* and *wisdom* are both the Hebrew שכל distinguished antithetically, as though in a mirror, by the serpentine letter (ש) and in relation to two different serpentine plants. The child was killed by the ingestion of a fermented grape that is described throughout with the characteristics of Hellebore infusion and the Sardonic smile. The liquid "fire" of Hellebore is described in reflection by the judgement of hellfire in Isaiah 30. Eden, like Jerusalem, was razed through fire and sword on account of the murderous tophets, the child-sacrificial gardens, of old typified by many wombs of today. The emblem of the fire and sword flanked by the cherubs at Eden's gate was preserved in the heavens by the starry faces of the ancient celestial cartography. The star-map was read by Moses on top of a mountain that symbolized a womb, and he obediently rendered the story of humanity's firstborn atop the Ark of the Covenant, which was the infant-sized tomb-altar used to signify propitiation. The propitiation was realized at the door of Christ's tomb that appeared as the Ark, the Heavens, and the Eastern Gate of Eden. When considering that a basin, BELLY, and womb are one word in Hebrew (בטן), it should be noticed that the basin of the heavens, the dome of stars above us, displays a huge dragon at its apex as though it were the "womb-serpent" of old.

> Do you not know this of old, since Adam was placed on earth, that the triumphing of the wicked is short, and the joy of the hypocrite is but for a moment? Though his haughtiness mounts up to the heavens, and his head reaches to the clouds, yet he will perish forever like his own refuse; those who have seen him will say, 'Where is he?' He will fly away like a dream, and not be found; yes, he will be chased away like a vision of the night. The eye that saw him will see him no more, nor will his place behold him anymore. His children will seek the favor of the poor, and his hands will restore his wealth. His bones are full of his youthful vigor, but it will lie down with him in the dust. Though evil is sweet in his mouth, and he hides it under his tongue, though he spares it and does not forsake it, but still keeps it in his mouth, yet his food in his stomach turns sour; it becomes cobra venom within him. He swallows down riches and vomits them up again; God casts them out of his בטן BELLY. He will suck the poison of cobras; the viper's tongue will slay him.... THE HEAVENS WILL REVEAL HIS INIQUITY....

In the ASTRONOMICAL work called "The Observations of Bel," we are informed that "on the high-places the SON is burnt"; a prescribed prayer (recorded by Sayce in his *Lectures on Babylonian and Assyrian Religion*) that accompanied child-sacrifice discusses the "establisher of *law*"; this word "*law*" is, literally, "*secret wisdom*." One can see in this gruesome word-picture that the ritualistic *slaughter of children* was related to *secret wisdom*. Likewise, the Hebrew letters שכל spell both *wisdom* and *abortion* (depending on how the sibilant ש is pronounced). One should consider the punishment against the womb of our first mother (Genesis 3:16) relative to the ability *"to make one wise"* discussed in Genesis 3:6. A high place had an altar. A womb was considered an altar. A child could be sacrificed on a fiery altar as a child could be aborted through burning poison. Such an abortive poison is, in Hebrew, called "venom" and is associated with a serpent.

The most glaring evidence, outside of Scripture, that points to the first human death to be that of an infant is found in the Sumerian cuneiform that describes defective birth as the result of the activity of what the ancients called a "womb-serpent." The very fact that there is a punishment against the womb incurred by Adam's wife on account of a "serpent's" inducement should hint strongly enough to the understanding that our first human mother bore dead fruit. Furthermore, she consumed a poison like Hellebore or "Snake Vine" which points us not only to the "serpent" of Genesis 3 but also to the Snake Vine that was specifically utilized to produce abortive birth in the ancient world. That the womb was punished in Eden, that marred birth was described as the result of a "womb-serpent" in the ancient east, that an abortive plant was called "Snake Vine" and was falsely thought to give wisdom, and that the Enemy is called a "serpent" who hinted falsey at the acquisition of wisdom through a plant should be a corpus of connected information evidential enough to lead one to the conclusion that the firstborn human was born a corpse as the result of toxic ingestion. This toxic ingestion was the fire of the sacrifice that initiated the war on Heaven, for a child is the substance and evidence of the union of Heaven and Earth. Christ, the Creator, is The Way. The Way is generative. The Creator passed between the sides of His creation and was thus born into the world according to the system He created; in this way, He is the beginning and the end. The Creator is The Light, human error is the obstruction, and the shadow of death was cast by this eclipse onto the flesh, or Gospel, of the first human infant (the only other person to live and die in moral perfection like Christ, the Creator).

It is my conviction that Adam's firstborn is essentially nameless and can be referred to as "The Son of Adam." Furthermore, I believe that it was this very title that Christ took upon Himself in order to reverse the covenant man cut with death and in order to restore the coveant with life. It is also my conviction that "Christianity" is not the name of the Bible's religion. The Bible's religion is called "The Way," and the same religion unwaveringly proceeds from Genesis until Revelation irrespective of its errant offshoots called today "Judaism" and "Christianity," both of which are later innovations comparable to "new wine." What is called "Christianity" I believe to be none other than Molech worship or child-sacrificial religion.

Molech worship is characterized by "sacrifice" that is destructive and sub-stitutional. Molech worshippers, as well as their child-killing counterparts as is seen in the religion of the Accadians, used to understand the slay-ing of a child to be "the child's head for his head, the child's neck for his neck, the child's breast for his breast." Furthermore, the formulaic words "because he heard his voice" were uttered by the ancient eastern child-sacrificer who colored himself with red ochre, and in this we can see the horror of when Adam (the Red Man) "heard the voice" of God, in contrast to the voice of Satan to whom he had recently bound himself through the "fruit" his wife gave him, proceding at the time of the evening breeze. I be-lieve that The Son of Adam and The Son of Man were the only two people ever to live and die in the flesh with moral perfection and that understand-ing Christ by this title and in this way explains the otherwise indecipherable punishments allotted to sinful man in Genesis 3 that led to the expulsion of humanity from Eden as well as the otherwise incomprehensible grace given to repentant man that leads to the reception of humanity back into Eden. "Christians" read Isaiah 53:12, "He bore the sin of many," to mean that The Father essentially dumped our sins onto His own Son as a form of substitution, and this situation means that blame can be shifted from the sinful to the sinless! They fortify this conclusion with 2 Corinthians 5:21 that appears to say "For He made Him who knew no sin to be αμαρ-τιαν sin for us, that we might become the righteousness of God in Him" without realizing that αμαρτιαν sin is but the Greek translation of חטא a sin offering called by 1 John 2:2 "the propitiation for our sins." In other words, "Christians" claim that Christ "bore" our sins by becoming "sin" which means, therefore, that Christ became guilty of our misconduct. I claim that this manner of substitution is not of The Way of God but is of the way or law "of sin and death" (Romans 8:2). "Christians" are reading the three-dimensional Word in the wrong light... as though Christ became guilty of our shortcommings. Christ did "bear" our sin and death, but in the same way that the children who died in Numbers 25 bore the sin and death of their parents. These horrid parents were punished by being hung (like crucifixion). The bizzare instance of an innocent Christ being hung forces the situation that the Victim bears the death of the sinners whom He allowed to put Him there, and this means literally that He died the death that was due them — but their part in placing Him in this situation is not made good by the situation! In fact, their part in this situation displays the highest level of insanity, an insanity that believes one can impute sin onto someone else *because* the intended receiver of the imputation is righteous. What kind of reasoning is this? How sick this truly is! Furthermore, the word "bore" used in Isaiah 53:12 ("He *bore* the sins of many") is from the root נשא *to lift up* and also means *to forgive, to pardon*. Thus, "He *forgave* the sins of many." Christ was the Innocent Firstborn of God. People participated in His death which means, according to Numbers 25, that people should have been hung on the cross for killing Christ. Christ, however, hung on the tree where His murderers should have been. Christ, then, "bore" their sin on the cross by the fact that He was hanging, and He "forgave" while He hung. The words "bore" and "forgave" are the same Hebrew words. The created Son of Man, i.e. Adam's firstborn, died in moral perfection but could not return in order to forgive; thus, the past was irrevocable in terms of forgiveness since, on earth, forgiveness was not possible to give by one who could not return. The Creator Son of Man, i.e. Adam's Father, died in moral perfection and could return in order to forgive; thus, the past was reversible in terms of forgiveness since, on earth, forgiveness became possible through a return to the land of the living.

Many claim that "The Law" of Moses is singular and that the Book of Leviticus is proof that God desired blood through the ritual slaughter of animals, especially since the Book of Hebrews says that forgiveness comes through blood. There is more than one "Law," and what Moses wrote down is a shadow cast by human obscurant of the shining face Moses beheld on Sinai, and that shining face is Christ's. The Sermon on the Mount does not "intensify" "The Law"; it restates "The Law of Moses." "Do not commit adultery" is the shadow cast by the light of God obscured through lust; so, for Christ to speak against lust is not an example of intensification but of clarification as to why Moses wrote as he did. Christ is The Light and sinful humanity is the obscurant that casts the shadow of sin upon the earth in a manner that is inseparable from the sinner. Righteous fidelity is "The Perfect Law of Liberty" (James 2:12) and "The Law of Truth" (Malachi 2:6). Sinful humanity obscures the truth, and a marred record or shadow is cast to the earth and proceeds upon its belly, like the accursed "serpent," to the extent that the obscurant of lust is proven by the shadow of adultery. "The Law" of God, I assert, never changed. Man changed by adopting "The Law of Sin and Death." "The Law of Sin and Death" demands that innocents should be harmed by the guilty, as is the case in adultery, and as is the case in child-sacrifice. "The Law of Truth" demands that no harm should be done to the innocent, and this is accomplished by all remaining innocent. To claim that The Father desired His Son to die is to impute Satan's guilt on to God's guiltless character and onto the innocence of His Son Who is Love Incarnate, the Creator. The Creator of The Way illustrated the ideal functionality of His own design by proceeding through it to the extent of His incarnation, and it is Christ's passage through The Way that revelas Him to be both the first and the last. On top of this, He is The Way, He is The Truth, and the fact that He is The Life was proven through His rebirth, His birth, and by the fact that He is the Creator. Fertility is a necessary function of The Way, and it is God's fruit that was Satan's target. Humanity joined hands with Satan so that, through fruit, God's fruit became man's target as well. The greatest trick ever played upon the "devout" can be seen in that, as in Eden and as at Golgotha, Satan convinced humanity to place guilt upon the innocent. The bride in Eden is the "Church." The child she killed originally was the son of Adam, and the Child she killed eventually was The Son of Man. The child she continues to blame for her guilt is Christ, and she smiles to think that all of her filth can be thrown onto Him in order to bury her transgressions! A Hope of "The Law of Truth" is that she, the Church, will receive her cleansing in order to become the pure and spotless bride she was intended to be as stated by Paul: "I labor in birth again until Christ is formed in you" (Galatians 4:19).

Moses wrote concerning "The Way" in a clandestine and mirrored manner, and it is for this reason that it does not say that death reigned from Adam to Christ but that "...death reigned from Adam to MOSES, even over those who had not sinned according to the likeness of the transgression of Adam, who is a type of Him who was to come" (Romans 5:13-14). When Christ returned from the dead, He came upwards as did His Creation in Genesis 1 and 2 in order to reverse an earthly womb that consumed and in order to restore the original earth that bore out its fruit as evidence of The Way, The Covenant, The Gospel, The Law, The Flesh that preceded it. The Law and the Gospel are the same Entity as evidenced by The Covenant in The Flesh according to The Way: the positive and original Law that gave life is reflected by the negative and new Law that gave death. The womb of the bride was punished because of the Son of Adam it consumed, and the womb of the bride was restored because of The Son of Man it birthed out. The ground was cursed because of the son of Adam who was buried in it, and the earth was restored because of The Son of Man Who rose from it. Innocent life was taken on account of the false vine, and this false vine produced a slow-acting poison that infected the line of humanity to an extent that disallowed eternal life but that maintained life through gestation counterbalanced by death. Innocent life was given on account of the "True Vine" (John 15:1), and this True Vine provided Holy Comunion as a sign of eternal life maintained through worshipful fidelity typified by gestation that overcomes death in a covenant with Life. Accordingly, it would not surprise me to discover that the reason Christ was difficult to recognize after His resurrection is because He appeared much younger than when He died, and that this hidden appearance was an expression of the reversal of death as evidence of rebirth.

Today, what is commonly called "prayer" is often but a mirage. People, without knowing the definition of "Amen," speak words that they have no intention of acting upon because they have believed a false teaching that assumes "prayer" to be but the utterance of man that initiates the actions of God when it is man who is, instead, supposed to act "in the Name" of God Who has already spoken. Consequently, the "faithful" make fools of themselves and butchered meat of children as they utter words to the ceiling while babies breathe their last in the womb. The greatest secret in all of human history is that the first human born of woman was born a corpse devoured by his parents' meal — and his story is remembered without him as a child's fairy-tale that concerns talking animals and magic fruit. The induced expiration of children is not merely a sin, it is the sin that condemned the world to doom.

To say "Amen" at the conclusion of a prayer is, essentially, to say, "I covenant," which necessitates the petitioner's participation in his request since a covenant requires more than one party. If God is thought to be the only one taking action following the utterance of prayer, the petitioner breaks his own covenant through ignorance entwined by sloth. When saying, "Amen," one is not punctuating a petition periodically. One is, instead, saying, "I covenant regarding my prayer." Prayer would, therefore, be covenantal, which means it involves an oath, a pledge. Prayer is, from the perspective of the one praying it, the responsive course of action understood to be initiated by the will of God Who first authorized the prayer. Similarly, the true binding of a covenant is the initiator of the oral binding of prayer that carries through to the product achieved by working toward the goal understood to be previously desired by God to Whom the prayer is directed. It can be seen, therefore, that praying against or ignorant of the will of God does not produce a desirable end.

In order for one to know God's will, one would have to study His Word diligently, for prayer could not be a substitute for study since, according to strict diction, a prayer has to be in sure congruence with His will as being finalized with the proclamation of "Amen," and His Word would be the check and balance that would determine the validity of prayer. Praying in opposition to His Word would be inevitable if one did not know God's Word and relied only on one's own heart: "Because the sentence against an evil work is not executed speedily, therefore the heart of the sons of men is fully set in them to do evil" (Ecclesiastes 8:11); because of this fact, we may grasp why James said, "Where do wars and fights come from among you? Do they not come from your desires for pleasure that war in your members? You lust and do not have. You murder and covet and cannot obtain. You fight and war. Yet YOU DO NOT HAVE BECAUSE YOU DO NOT ASK. YOU ASK AND DO NOT RECEIVE, BECAUSE YOU ASK AMISS, that you may spend it on your pleasures" (James 4:1-4). Prayer precedes the human action already anticipated to accomplish the prayer, for prayer is not the substitute for action. Uttering words in hopes that children are saved from professional butchers does not stop the professional butchers.

A covenant requires a relationship bound by oath, and participation is mutually expected in submission to the Divine Will that initiated the desire for the follower to make his petition. The prayer is not the action. The prayer is the initiation of the action, the sacrifice that precedes the war, and this can be seen in Scripture by the fact that Christ prayed the 22nd Psalm before waging war on the Tophet, on Hell. Praying and then waiting without intention of acting is like mustering all of the troops, offering the sacrifice, and then sitting down in order to wait for the charging enemy to fall over dead without a struggle — and it is for this reason that many devout meet demise with a lamentable smile that reflects a misunderstanding of duty.

I pray to be forgiven if I have spoken errantly in anything I have written. I hope that whatever I have discerned and articulated incorrectly will be forgiven and forgotten. I hope that whatever I have discerned and articulated correctly will be utilized zealously to defend innocent life for the glory of its Sire. God, I have done my best to speak well of You. If I have not accomplished the task, please look upon my intention.

In the mindset of the ancients who lived between the Tigris and Euphrates rivers, the ideas of animating clay or writing upon clay are essentially one and the same. Mesopotamian clay, three-dimensional writing was considered to be alive. Ancient tablets state how people "listened to the tablet" and discuss the "mouth of the tablet." When a tablet was made void, it was said to be "killed," but when a tablet was renewed it was said to be "brought back to life." Without understanding the way the ancient Mesopotamians described the world, we today can easily superimpose artificiality on top of the story of the first man, our first human father, who was created in Mesopotamia just as easily as we can, through habit, take on a new nature that is not original and that cannot understand the original. Christ, The Light, was incomprehensible to the "darkness," and

Christ is thus called "The Wisdom of God" (1 Corinthians 1:24). The Wisdom of God is the Creator (Colossians 1:16). We may say, in a manner of speaking, that the Creator took clay and animated it concerning the creation of Adam, thus, "...we are His ποίημα *poem, book, workmanship* created in Christ Jesus for good works, which God prepared beforehand that we should walk in them" (Ephesians 2:10). Christ, The Wisdom of God, the Creator, was "killed" by those who made void His word, for He accused them of "...making the word of God of no effect through your tradition which you have handed down" (Mark 7:13). Since what is "handed down" (i.e. tradition) perpetuates the name of its commissioner, then the tradition that rendered God's Word "of no effect," so to speak, can be considered abortive in that it sought to obstruct what God Himself handed down. Abortive birth was said to be accomplished by a "womb-serpent" in Sumerian cuneiform. The very fact that "Eden" or "Fertility" was penetrated by a "serpent" points straight to the "womb-serpent" and to infant mortality, the nauseating death of the Fall Narrative. In Genesis 3, it was the "Serpent" who challenged what God "said" orally. The fall of man resulted from departure from The Word of God, for man's testimony was found errantly distinct from God's Word. The tablet of man was "killed." When The Word of God came in clay to the earth in order to save, He was "brought back to life" through the renewal of a covenant that was once made void by man, that was once aborted by man; He came as an infant, and His Father brought Him back to life in accordance with the original design. Since the "priests and the people transgressed more and more, according to all the abominations of the nations, and defiled the house of the Lord which He had consecrated in Jerusalem" (2 Chronicles 36:14), one can see that this blasphemous violation of the Sabbath was induced by a "serpent" and accomplished through humanity's perverse covenant with him in the womb of the Lord, the house of the Lord, the temple of the Lord, the garden of the Lord, Eden.

The abominable desolation of God's House reflects the fact that a child's parents unified with the Adversary of the Creator, for such mutilation is an attempt to efface the image of God by blaspheming His Name in His temple. It is the union of Earth and Hell evinced by the destruction of the fruit of the womb that makes war on the gates of Heaven. Let it be understood that the union of Heaven and Earth is bound in the face of a newborn, and let it be remembered that such a face resembles the Creator.

THE WOUNDED HEEL

R<small>EADING</small> any text, regardless of how "timeless" its message might be, is looking at a standardized, time-specific, medium utilized for the purposes of an author exacted through the technology of writing. Writing graphically represents spoken language, and spoken language is subject to time. Spoken languages drift from any given point in time whether or not they have written counterparts, and writing graphically represents spoken language. It is, therefore, necessary to consider the milieu of the author of a text in real time, as well as the setting of a text, in its original language, relative to the time that the author wished to describe, discuss, or compare within the composition to a specific audience. For instance, one can write about a time in the remote past, but one does not have to do so in the language or style of that remote past (especially to an audience living at the time of the writer, not the narrative). If a narrative takes place in a time, language, and geography unknown to the readership, then simple, photographic descriptions tend not to be as efficacious as comparisons, comparisons to which the readership can link to the past setting of the narrative. Furthermore, the method of talking about a distant past may utilize artificial references that did not exist in the time of the narrative but, rather, in the time of the author in order for the author to discuss a past in terms his readership will comprehend. Consider the sentence, "The warrior read hatred in his opponent's eyes"; now consider the setting to be prior to the invention of writing (and therefore reading); we understand that the warrior interpreted meaning, but we understand his reception in terms of a technology that did not exist in his time; thus, the narrated world is related in terms of the milieu of the author, not the conceptual time of the narration — purposely — to the ones *reading* the narration.

Today's literary expectations are often imbued, almost totally, with literalistic descriptions of scenes that can be conjured photographically in the mind. The stylistic literary canopy that is nearly ubiquitous in terms of readership continuously discusses things with photographic realism in terms of description far more than essential realism in terms of comparison. The writing you are reading right now is English, and English is a complete alphabetic system, unlike the incomplete alphabetic system of Biblical Hebrew, more unlike the various systems of cuneiform, and even more unlike pictographic systems. Simply thinking today, and simply thinking in English, compels a wide gap between the first writing system developed in Mesopotamia, the setting used for Eden by the Hebrew of Genesis. Reading translations is reading interpretive traditions. Reading "original language" from the standpoint of being a native of another language is also, largely, reading from a tradition. Traditions have the tendency to admit anachronism, especially when considering a basis in a spoken language. Let us turn to consider, in the original language, the Biblical word שׁוּף: it only occurs in three Biblical passages (Genesis 3:15; Job 9:17; Psalm 139:11).

> "I will put enmity between you and the woman, and between your seed and her seed. He shall BRUISE (שׁוּף) your head, and you shall BRUISE (שׁוּף) His heel. TO THE WOMAN HE SAID: 'I WILL GREATLY MULTIPLY YOUR SORROW AND YOUR CONCEPTION; IN PAIN YOU SHALL BRING FORTH CHILDREN...'" (Genesis 3:15-16).

> "For He **crushes** (שׁוּף) me with a tempest, and multiplies my wounds without cause" (Job 9:17).

> "If I say, 'Surely the darkness shall **cover** (שׁוּף) me,' Even the night shall be light about me; indeed, the darkness shall not hide from You, but the night shines as the day; the darkness and the light are both alike to You. FOR YOU FORMED MY IN- WARD PARTS; YOU COVERED ME IN MY MOTHER'S WOMB. I WILL PRAISE YOU, FOR I AM FEARFULLY AND WONDERFULLY MADE; MAR- VELOUS ARE YOUR WORKS, AND THAT MY SOUL KNOWS VERY WELL. MY FRAME WAS NOT HIDDEN FROM YOU, WHEN I WAS MADE IN SECRET, AND SKILLFULLY WROUGHT IN THE LOWEST PARTS OF THE EARTH. YOUR EYES SAW MY SUBSTANCE, BEING YET UNFORMED. And in Your book they all were written, the days fashioned for me, when as yet there were none of them" (Psalm 139:11-16).

The word שׁוּף, rendered *bruise* (Genesis 3:15) and *cover* (Psalm 139:11), immediately precedes the description of human gestation. This word, ren- dered *crush* (Job 9:17), is used in terms of innocent suffering or "wounds without cause."

This word שׁוּף comes from the root שׁוּף *to wound*, and Psalm 139:11 uses it *to mean to cover (with darkness)*. Accordingly, it can be deduced easily as to why a *wound* that *covers* *with darkness* is translated as a *bruise*. Yet, such a wound does not necessarily mean a bruise, but it can be used to describe a bruise. In fact, Psalm 139:11 uses שׁוּף *to wound, to cover (with darkness)* in the context of "darkness" and "light" (v. 12) juxtaposed to a child developing in the womb (v. 13-16), and it compares this gestation to authorship (v. 16). It should be noticed, however, that humans have undergone gestation for uncountable years prior to author- ship since writing is a time-specific invention. So, to describe gestation in terms of authorship is to describe the cause of gestation (which originally preceded the first writing) through a lens following the cause of writing (which originally followed innumerable gestations). The conceptual time of the narration is viewed in terms of the real time of the one writing down the narration. It is this writer, using the technology of writing, who describes gestation (which is not a technology) that existed prior to writing itself and prior to the writer of this comparison.

Conceptually, the ideas associated with and by the word שׁוּף *to wound, bruise, cover with darkness* were applied Scripturally thrice: twice in the context of pregnancy, and once in the context of innocent suffering. "Job," which means "The Persecuted" and is etymologically related to the Hebrew word rendered "enmity" in Genesis 3:15, uses this word to discuss his **innocent suffering**, Genesis uses this word to discuss someone who will receive **wound** immediately prior to its description of birth, and the Psalm uses this word to describe **human gestation**.

A *bruised* heel can be understood literally as a *wounded* heel, and, in the context of Genesis 3, the description of a wounded head and a wounded heel is a blatant reference to the constellations of Draco and The Kneeler. At the same time, discussing a wounded heel in terms of gestation is also a blatant reference to the procurement of abortion.

The English word "abortion" is the Hebrew word נפל *a fallen one, untimely birth* and the Greek εκτρωμα *untimely birth*. It is this Greek word, εκτρωμα *abortion* (meaning the *baby*), that Philo uses to translate the Hebrew נפל regarding Miriam in Numbers 12:12 in his "Allegorical Interpretation" of Genesis. It is also this same Greek word for an aborted baby that Ignatius quotes from 1 Corinthians 15:8 in his work "To The Romans." Peculiarly, the Greek of the Septuagint translation of Numbers 12:12 and the Greek of 1 Corinthians 15:8 understand this word, *abortion*, to indicate a living adult; obviously, this situation is not descriptive but comparative. The Hebrew original is, again, a נפל *fallen one* and is also used in terms of child sacrifice, as in Numbers 5:22 where an adulterous woman who is impregnated by adultery (but who deceitfully maintained her innocence) would be administered a toxic drink that would produce spontaneous abortion. Such a situation would then, legally, place her child's blood on her own head and subject her and her adulterous partner to the death penalty while absolving her husband. In this sense, the adulterous mother is one who is willing to risk sacrificing her child in order to maintain her lie. A similar situation can be observed on page 162, footnote 16, of the I Tatti Journal of Studies in The Italian Renaissance (17 1 2014):

> In a 1569 case from Milan, thirteen-year-old Costanza Colonna was diagnosed as suffering from dropsy as her belly swelled after months of menstrual retention. Costanza was believed to

be a virgin even though she admitted to attempting although failing to have sexual intercourse with her seventeen-year-old husband Francesco Sforza. After a regime of medicines and therapies designed to open the blockage and expel the obstructed matter from her womb, Costanza delivered a dead male fetus.

Contrarily, the desire, at all costs, not to destroy the child, even in the case of marital infidelity (or supposed marital infidelity), can be seen in Joseph's treatment of The Virgin Mary in that he wished not to accuse her. Had Joseph accused Mary, the Virgin Birth would have been a secret that died with both Christ and Mary. Joseph is described as a "just man" in Matthew 1:19, even though the apparently "just" thing to do was to carry out the sentence prescribed in Numbers 5. That is, Joseph, although being initially humiliated in the eyes of others, must have had some faith in Mary's story initially as well, otherwise he could not have been considered "just" by Matthew for ignoring the very legal prescription put in place by Moses to guard against infidelity but then according with the legal prescription put in place by Moses (Luke 2:21-24) unless Joseph believed Mary to be a virgin even though she was visibly pregnant. In order to save her own life prior to being potentially executed, she could easily have bled herself or have drunk a purgative in order to conceal and eliminate her pregnancy. The fact she chose to face death on account of her Child explains much as to Joseph's willingness to listen to her and still marry her in spite of the apparent shame it would bring on him (who descended from David). Essentially, the Joseph-and-Mary narrative is the morally improved David-and-Bathsheba narrative: neither woman was willing to conceal her pregnancy, neither father accused the woman, neither couple was willing to abort, both couples' children died before the couples, and both had prophets discuss the "sword" involved with their child (Nathan in 2 Samuel 12:10 and Simeon in Luke 2:34-35).

In Soranus' *Gynecology*, a related word, φτοριον *abortion* (meaning the *procedure* that procures abortive birth) is the same word used in Hippocrates' "Oath": "...I will not give to a woman a pessary to produce φτοριον *abortion*." Soranus cites Hippocrates' Aphorisms XXXI: "A woman with child, if bled, miscarries; the larger the embryo the greater the risk." Scientifically, enough blood-loss of a pregnant woman will cause her body to abort in an effort to maintain the mother's life, however and from wherever the blood is lost. Yet, the texts we are examining all predate scientific methodology and carry associations along with them that are of a different system. The texts under discussion exist within the boundaries of empiricism, and the specific location from where the pregnant body is bled in order to induce abortion is a straight-forward marker of associative empiricism that looks back towards a tradition in order to predict forward towards a desired end. For instance, the *I Tatti Journal of Studies in The Italian Renaissance* (17 1 2014) contains an article by John Christopoulos called "Nonelite Male Perspectives on Procured Abortion"; this article examines a court case involving the procurement of abortion induced by the ingestion of a purgative and the cutting of the saphena vein in the heel (called *vena della madre*). Consider again *abortion* in terms of the Hebrew *fallen one*, and then consider the Hebrew *fallen one* in terms of the word שׁוּף, rendered *bruise* (Genesis 3:15), *cover* (Psalm 139:11) that immediately precedes the description of human gestation, and *crush* (Job 9:17) that is used in terms of suffering "wounds without cause" innocently. This particular Italian court case occurred in 1598 AD, Soranus lived until the 2nd Century AD, Paul lived in the 1st Century AD, The Septuagint was completed in the 3rd Century BC, Hippocrates flourished around 400 BC, and the Torah places Moses near 1,500 B.C.; all of these pieces of documentary evidence are chronologically before the world of Science and are within the realm of Empiricism.

Tradition, like language, carries with it associations understood at one time but that tend to be forgotten in a future time. The fact that an association may bring about a desired result reinforces adherence to the association whether or not the reasoning for the association is understood at all. "Science" is a method that makes predictions, whereas "Tradition" is a method that makes references that call to remembrance. Science depends heavily upon writing, whereas Tradition does not. Science existed after the invention of writing, whereas Tradition existed before the invention of writing. The practitioners of empiricism who produced a desired end consistently did not have to concern themselves with why the practice worked, but only that the practice worked and was remembered. Traditions that existed prior to writing, and that became written, eventually existed as the shadows of a milieu that had disappeared; this situation is greatly exacerbated when the spoken language the writing reflects dies, and the writing itself becomes obscured as a result. Again, the "wounded" or "bruised" head and heel of Genesis 3:15 recalls blatantly the constellations of The Kneeler and Draco. The fact that this is so is one matter, but the reason why it is so is another. Let us consider the Italian court case concerning procured abortion via the bleeding of the heel and the ingestion of a purgative.

In 1598 AD, a man was accused of raping a woman (who was impregnated as a result) and hiding his transgression by convincing her to abort so as to conceal the evidence of their physical union. The woman claimed that she was forced, and that, in order to hush the violation she claimed to endure, she feigned to suffer from dropsy (or congestive heart failure) in order to gain the prescriptive treatment for dropsy that would also cause spontaneous abortion. The treatment for dropsy was the ingestion of a purgative and controlled bleeding. The barber who bled the pregnant woman claimed to have bled her from the arm even though the standard therapy for dropsy suffered by a pregnant woman was to bleed her from the foot. It would seem as though the barber's claim of bleeding the woman from the arm was an attempt to maintain ignorance of procured abortion since abortion was also procured by the same procedure at the heel. The point is that abortion was associated with purgative ingestion and bleeding at the heel even though a potent enough purgative alone or significant bleeding alone are capable of accomplishing the same end. It is the association, specifically the *prescientific* association, that matters.

Job asks rhetorically in 31:33, "If I have covered my transgressions as Adam, by hiding iniquity in my **bosom**...." Again, the cure for congestive **heart** failure was the ingestion of a purgative (described as snake venom and Adam's sin in Job 20:14-15) and bleeding from the heel (described as the result of Eve's sin in Genesis 3:15). Since suffering from heart failure and early pregnancy appeared outwardly similar, and since 1598 was an empirical time like that of Genesis, the Septuagint, Hippocrates, 1 Corinthians, and Soranus, it can be seen here that bleeding a pregnant woman, specifically from her heel, was an association that indicated abortion itself. The association, not just the actual method, could indicate abortion throughout a timespan bound to a traditional understanding of how, but not why, to bring a result about.

The word שׁוּף to *wound, crush, bruise, cover with darkness* was used in Biblical Hebrew only three times to discuss (1) **innocent suffering**, (2) someone who will receive a **wound** immediately prior to a description of **birth**, and (3) **human gestation**. Throughout history, one of the most common ways to hide transgressions of concupiscence that resulted in pregnancy was abortion. In fact, abortion was viewed as a type of perverse salvation for the transgressors. That is, the deliberate hiding of the fruit of one's private deeds allowed for the suppression of suspicion. Likewise, the murder of Christ was an attempt to hide the transgressions of the corrupt Second Temple priesthood by suppressing Rome's suspicion of them, a suspicion that eventuated in the destruction of the Temple in 70 AD.

With respect to virginity, abortion was an easier means for men to cover their deeds than for women since the virginity of a man could not be proven beyond testimony whereas the virginity of a woman could be proven physically. Likewise, the "veil" of the Tabernacle and subsequent Temples is literally the פרכת breaking thing, the curtain that *separated* the Holy of Holies from the Holy Place. The Temple is understood in the same sense as the Tabernacle: a bride (Jeremiah 2:2) who eventually slew the offspring she bore her Husband (Jeremiah 2:34). The veil or "breaking thing" is the womb's opening or the "flesh" of Christ, i.e. His bride (Hebrews 10:20) through whom a "new and living way" was devised, i.e. rebirth. When Christ died, His death was coupled with the sign of a birth: the breaking or rending of the veil where the Ark or infant tomb was supposed to be atop the Foundation Stone. Christ's death was coupled with a signified birth. This event signified the rebirth from the dead, for it is the same scene observed at the entrance to the empty tomb of Christ flanked by the Cherubs. Abortion temporarily allowed men to cover their misconduct via false testimony, but the integrity of the Temple was challenged when the rent veil could be viewed openly.

In a case where adultery, incest, rape, or any other illegal transgression of the sort was evidenced by conception, men have often persuaded their victims to abort in order for men to save themselves; thus, from the perspective of male violator, the abortion was his personal salvation; the abortion preserved his life by keeping him from the penalty of his deeds. This twisted logic of secrecy is far more common than might be believed initially.

The connection between abortion and salvation can be understood from the perspective of a male violator considering only himself. This connection is a bit weaker from the perspective of a virgin female victim because her virginity could not be restored, and her violated status could only remain secret through words (or lack thereof) since her physicality was permanently altered. This connection disappears altogether from the perspective of the aborted... but the aborted disappeared with the transgression... the transgression was placed onto the abortion who essentially carried it away into darkness. Such reasoning allowed for an adult to be considered as an abortion if he died for the deeds of others and not for his own deeds. For instance, Uriah, the husband of Bathsheba, was a type of abortion from the perspective of David even though it was David's baby who died. David slept with Bathsheba, but this action resulted unintentionally as the fruit of the womb. If the pregnancy was known, David would have had to give his life for his sins. David attempted unsuccessfully to resolve the issue with deceit in order to preserve the child's life, for Uriah was away and his wife could easily have aborted in order to conceal her union with David. Neither David nor Bathsheba chose to abort, but David indirectly murdered Bathsheba's Husband, Uriah, and married her so that the child would not be born illegitimately, so there would be no contention with Uriah, so that David's status could be maintained, but, ultimately, so that David would not have to die on account of his own deeds. In this sense, David placed his guilt on Uriah and attempted to hide his guilt forever by hiding Uriah forever. Uriah, though he was an adult, was understood as an abortion because he hid the pregnancy that resulted from *misconduct*... he covered the misconduct with his death. After Balaam wounded his foot in Numbers 22, he devised a perverse covenant to be cut between the Moabites and the Israelites; subsequently, in Numbers 25, the punishment for child sacrifice was "hanging" on a tree (so that the dead transgressor symbolizes the dead fruit for which he was responsible). In short, (1) abortion, (2) child sacrifice, and (3) the death of the innocent are equated in the Bible. From the perspective of the transgressors, these three were considered a type of salvation. "Jesus" (the name essentially meaning "Salvation") died (3) an innocent death as the (2) "Holy Child" (Acts 4:27) of God like (1) an abortion in the sense of Uriah and in the sense that He is called in 1 Corinthians 15:8: "τω εκτρωματι" or *the aborted one.* The irony can be seen in that Christ died the death of the transgressors, for Numbers 25 orders the transgressors to be hung on trees. This compels the literary structure to place the sins of the transgressors onto their "Salvation" in order to hide their misconduct by covering it over in the darkness of the tomb. Again, the word שׁוּף comes from the root שׁוּף *to wound*, and Psalm 139:11 uses it *to mean to cover (with darkness)*. This word, when applied to the heel, is a direct reference to abortion or innocent death.

In a pre-scientific world, a common way to procure abortion was blood-letting. A significant loss of blood caused spontaneous abortion. It was, however, the loss of blood *from the heel* of a pregnant woman that was specifically linked to abortion by association. The word שׁוּף *to* **wound** is but translated *to* **bruise**. The saphena vein was opened in a deliberate attempt to induce abortive birth:

> "...He shall bruise your head, and you shall **bruise** (וְשׁוּף) **His heel**. TO THE WOMAN HE SAID: 'I WILL GREATLY MULTIPLY YOUR SORROW AND YOUR CONCEPTION; IN PAIN YOU SHALL BRING FORTH CHILDREN...'" (Genesis 3:15-16).

We can notice the "bruising" or wounding of the heel is connected to a description of "conception" and "pain," and this is the punishment for consuming "fruit." It is this word שׁוּף *to wound, to bruise,* that Psalm 139 uses to mean *to cover* just before describing human gestation in terms of AUTHORSHIP. The fact that we **read** about this bruised heel hints literarily to a procured abortion. As pointed out on page 155 in Volume 1 of the 2014 *I Tatti Journal*, "…procured abortion is difficult to access in the historical record." Since the procurement of abortion was usually a quiet attempt to avoid the hardship associated with the transgression, the written word on abortion is confined largely to legal and moral writings. The Bible is both legal and moral. By reading the rule that came about because of an unwritten transgression, the reader should be able to understand the nature of the transgression. Consider:

> "If I have covered my transgressions as ADAM, by hiding my iniquity in my bosom, because I feared the great multitude, and dreaded the contempt of families, so that I KEPT SILENCE and did not go out of the door — Oh, that I had one to hear me!" (Job 31:33-35).

The irony highlighted here is that "Adam" and "I kept silence" are spelled identically in Hebrew (אדם). Genesis 3 tells us that Adam ate of the forbidden tree, but Job 31 tells us that Adam hid iniquity in his heart in light of the legal and moral pronouncement concerning the wounded heel.

Of course, claiming rape was and is a common way for a woman to hide a blemish to her character. If a man and a woman consented to each other in a manner which, if discovered, could bring them both into difficulty, then a pre-agreed pact to procure abortion if conception occurred was a method of preserving apparent integrity in the eyes of others. If the woman turned on the man in a consensual union and did not want to become a mother as a result, she could maintain her apparent integrity by feigning illness; if that lie was ineffective, she could maintain her status by accusing the man. If a woman was in fact violated and simply wished no one to know of the matter, she could agree with her attacker that she would erase the evidence of his crime. Abortion was mostly a secret matter, and it was not often written about; it seems that for this reason the Bible takes this perspective into account in order to craft its narrative concerning "the beginning." Interestingly, The Targum of Onkelos' translation of Genesis 3:15 says, "He will remember thee, what thou didst to him from the beginning, and thou shalt be observant unto him at the end," whereby we observe "head" and "heel" considered as "beginning" and "end." The

Hebrew word for "head" used here does also mean "beginning" and is part of the single Hebrew word "In the beginning" in Genesis 1:1. The head, not the heel, is the normal beginning of birth.

The declaration of illness (particularly that of dropsy) was often a cover-up for pregnancy since bloodletting and the ingestion of purgatives both were prescribed to cure dropsy and procure abortion. A loose woman could often be "ill" without the general public realizing her secrets. Clandestine knowledge typified abortion, both in terms of the ambiguity surrounding conception and the female body and of the means by which to thwart procreation. In the astronomical work called "The Observations of Bel," we are informed that "on the high-places THE SON IS BURNT"; a prescribed prayer (recorded by Sayce in his *Lectures on Babylonian and Assyrian Religion*) that accompanied child-sacrifice discusses the "establisher of *law*"; this word "*law*" is, literally, "SECRET WISDOM." The astronomical aspect of abortion in the ancient, Eastern world can be understood particularly in the constellations of The Kneeler and Draco, both of which are physically and thematically reflected by the constellations of Ophiuchus/Serpens and Scorpio. The Speech from The Whirlwind in Job describes wisdom in terms of knowing the various times of gestation, and the measurement of time itself was accomplished astronomically within that setting (as is made plain in the comparison of Leviathan to the constellation Draco). The name "Leviathan" is a compound of לוי bound one, ie. priest and נתן child sacrifice; thus, "Leviathan" is a Hebrew rendering of "the establisher of law" who officiates "on the high places [where] the son is burnt." This "Leviathan" or priest of child sacrifice can be seen also in the fact that the vestments of Satan in Ezekiel 28 (described by a priest, concerning his accusations against the Temple on account of child sacrifice, who accused people of being "thorns" in 2:6) are the same as Aaron's priestly/warrior vestments in Exodus 28 (for, according to Amos 7:43, it was Aaron, The High Priest, who officiated over Molech-worship at the base of *Mount Sinai or* הר סיני *thorny pregnancy in Hebrew*). Consider the fact that the discussion of the "serpent" connected to the "wounded heel" is followed by the description of "thorns" in the legal proceedings of Genesis 3. All in all, it should be understood that the idea of a wounded heel was associated with procured abortion in the prescientific world. When Genesis 3 describes the wounded heel in relation to pregnancy, it is because abortion is the subject to which the punishments react. It is abortion that is signified celestially. It is this celestial signification of abortion that is recounted in Job 20:27: "The heavens will reveal his iniquity...." It was this same celestial signification that was accomplished when Christ was crucified as "The Aborted One" of 1 Corinthians 15:8.

After Balaam wounded his foot in Numbers 22, he devised a perverse covenant of orgiastic worship that eventuated, not in birth but, in child sacrifice to be cut between the Moabites and the Israelites. Subsequently, in Numbers 25, the punishment for child sacrifice is "hanging" on a tree. The association between the wounded heel and crucifixion can be understood in terms of the death of the innocent, for, without understanding the association, a foot appears to have nothing to do with crucifixion. Christ's tree pointed backwards to the abortion in Eden. Genesis 3:15-16 says, "I will put enmity between you and the woman, and between your seed and her seed. He shall **bruise** (שׁוּף) your head, and you shall **bruise** (שׁוּף) His heel. TO THE WOMAN HE SAID: 'I WILL GREATLY MULTIPLY YOUR SORROW AND YOUR CONCEPTION; IN PAIN YOU SHALL BRING FORTH CHILDREN...'" (Genesis 3:15-16). Birth, a heel, and a tree are all bound by abortion or the death of the innocent. The wounded head and heel here refer to the circumpolar constellations of The Kneeler and The Dragon. In terms of the sin in Eden, Adam and Satan are accounted for here. However, let us consider now the constellation of The Virgin.

Lunar eclipses (blood moons) can only occur on the 14th day of a lunar month, which means that Passover regularly experiences a lunar eclipse. Joel and Peter both indicated the time of Christ's death in relation to a lunar eclipse. If we use our calendar to look back at the crucifixion of Christ, then we will find this lunar eclipse on April 3, 33 AD. In Acts 2:20, Peter claims Christ's death to have been prophesied by Joel (2:31) when he quotes, "The sun shall be turned to darkness and the moon to blood." Since a solar eclipse can only occur at new moon and a lunar eclipse can only occur at full moon, both could not have happened at the same time. A clue to the meaning of this solar and lunar darkness is found in Matthew 27:46 where it says "about" 3pm in reference to Christ praying the 22nd Psalm and expiring. The word "about" is not an approximation because the lunar eclipse Joel wrote of and to which Peter referred began *about* 3pm (3:14 local time); this is important because, in Jerusalem, no one could have observed this since it occurred below the horizon hours before sunset. Sunset occurred near the end of the blood moon; this is important because Joel's statement that "The sun shall be turned to darkness and the moon to blood" indicates when the eclipse could be seen: at sundown, low on the eastern horizon, for this eclipse ended soon after (8:45pm local time). The lunar eclipse could only have been seen to be significantly red from Jerusalem's perspective as sun set in the constellation of The Lamb and as the bloody moon rose in the *heel of The Virgin*.

The Bible places Moses near 1,500 BC in Sinai, Joel centuries later, and Christ early in the 1st Century AD. What Moses wrote concerning the wounded heel was interpreted by Joel and validated by Christ according to Peter's quotation of Joel. Writing was invented by the Mesopotamians in roughly 3,700 BC, the astronomical pictures were devised around 2,800 BC, and Moses lived more than a millennium later. Moses *wrote* about a judgement told to the first human (that occurred before writing was invented) in terms of a traditional abortion technique understood in Moses' day forward, in reference to the star maps. Moses, using writing to connect a traditional abortion technique to star maps, must have assumed that those star maps would be present and discernable at the time of the fulfillment of his written prediction that communicated an abortion practice discernible to his future audience. The language Moses wrote in passed away from spoken usage long before the time of Christ. Moses tethered his written language to a traditional practice and to celestial pictographs, the star-maps interpreted by Peter concerning the crucifixion in reference to Joel (who lived centuries between Moses and Peter). Had Moses not tethered his written language to celestial cartography, then under the circumstances of Joel, and especially those of Peter, there would be no real way to validate or invalidate Moses' written prediction celestially. Peter observed the lunar eclipse that occurred as "the sun shall be turned to darkness" from a physical vantage point that Moses did not have when he predicted the traditional wounded heel in writing relative to the *stars, i.e. relative to a certain time and place.* In order for Moses' prediction to come true, concerning astronomy only, all that was required was for Moses to know was astronomy. Yet, in order for Moses' prediction to have been interpreted by Peter through Joel, Moses had to have the foresight to know that the *spoken* language he wrote would not endure until the time of Peter, and Moses had to have the foresight to anticipate that the astronomical pictures used cartographically in his day would be the same in Peter's day — in order for the astronomy to be observed from a geographical location that Moses never entered in his life. Furthermore, Moses and Joel would both have to anticipate a Man being born at the right time and in the right place, who would be officially executed on the very day Moses predicted, Joel interpreted, and Peter observed... an execution carried out by Romans who were a people who did not exist in the days or lands of Moses... an execution style that meant something different to the Romans in Peter's day than it did to the Israelites in Moses day... an execution of a

Man Who had to die at the very minute a non-visible blood moon occurred below the horizon, a Man Who had to be taken down from The Tree of The Knowledge of Good and Evil at the very time the blood moon became visible to Peter and then returned to an uneclipsed full moon for the rest of the night. Consider Paul's retelling of the event in Romans 5:6-19 through the lens of Moses' writing in Genesis 3:

> For when we were still without strength, **at καιρον the right time Christ died** for the ungodly. For scarcely for a righteous man will one die; yet perhaps for a good man someone would even dare to die. But God demonstrates His own love toward us, in that while we were still sinners, Christ died for us. Much more then, having now been justified by His blood, we shall be saved from wrath through Him. For if when we were enemies we were reconciled to God through the death of His Son, much more, having been reconciled, we shall be saved by His life. And not only that, but we also rejoice in God through our Lord Jesus Christ, through whom we have now received the reconciliation. Therefore, just as through one man [Adam] sin entered the world, and death through sin, and thus death spread to all men, because all sinned— (For until the law sin was in the world, but sin is not imputed when there is no law. Nevertheless death reigned FROM ADAM TO MOSES, even over those who had not sinned according to the likeness of the transgression of **Adam, who is a type of Him who was to come [Christ]**. But the free gift is not like the offense. For if by the one man's [Adam's] offense many died, much more the grace of God and the gift by the grace of the one Man, Jesus Christ, abounded to many. And the gift is not like that which came through the one who sinned {Adam}. For the judgment which came from one offense resulted in condemnation, but the free gift which came from many offenses resulted in justification. For if by the one man's [Adam's] offense death reigned through the one, much more those who receive abundance of grace and of the gift of righteousness will reign in life through the One, Jesus Christ.) Therefore, as through one man's [Adam's] offense judgment came to all men, resulting in condemnation, even so through one Man's [Christ's] righteous act the free gift came to all men, resulting in justification of life. For as by one man's [Adam's] disobedience many were made sinners, so also by one Man's [Christ's] obedience many will be made righteous (Romans 5:6-19).

Christ died, "at the right time," signified by the wounded heel about which Moses and Joel wrote. The reader may notice that the wounded heel of The Kneeler is of a man, but the blood moon occurred in the heel of The Virgin, which are not only two different constellations, but two different sexes. The Hebrew words "he" and "she" both were spelled originally "הוא," and so its translation is contextual, for "he" and "she" have the same Hebrew spelling (though differing pronunciation). It is for this reason that we can observe the Latin Vulgate stating,

> "I will put enmity between thee and the woman, and thy seed and **her** seed: <u>**she**</u> will crush thy head, and thou shalt lie in wait for **her** heel" (Genesis 3:15),

while the King James' version states,

> "And I will put enmity between thee and the woman, and between thy seed and **her** seed; <u>**it**</u> shall bruise thy head, and thou shalt bruise **his** heel,"

even though Hebrew has no neuter "it." The drift continues in the New King James version that states, "

> "And I will put enmity between you and the **woman**, and between your seed and **her** seed; <u>**He**</u> shall bruise your head, and you shall bruise **His** heel."

The bruiser or crusher of the head is contended to be "she," "it," and "He," all of which are obviously not the same. The one with the wounded heel is disputed to be "her," "his," and "His," all of which are different also. Add further the translation of Onkelos that says,

> "<u>**He**</u> will remember thee, what thou didst to him from the beginning [head], and thou shalt be observant unto **him** at the end [heel],"

and we will notice the "beginning," "head," or first days of Genesis (the Creation) and "these last [heel] days spoken to us by His Son" (Hebrews 1:2).

If the only possibility to untangle the apparent mess presented here were strictly through interpretive literary effort, the problems would never end. I wish to end these problems by stating that you cannot dispute eclipse cycles, any more than you can dispute the existence of the sun, moon, or earth, because they are regular; but the observations of eclipses are chronologically regular *according to specific geographic locations*. All of the above translations can be proven correct if you observe the sky, as Christ was taken down from the cross, on Passover, April 3, 33 AD, at sundown (but not much longer) in Judea no matter how far into the future or how far away on the earth you exist to read these words — as prophesied by Moses centuries before Christ, in Sinai, concerning Adam, in Mesopotamia, prior to the invention of writing (by the Mesopotamians) from where the Magi, who *read* the prophet Daniel, came to find Christ by observing the stars.

CONCLUSION

To conclude this book, I seek to elucidate the fact that the Bible, particularly the Book of Genesis, uses the history of writing itself as a parable for the history of humanity. It is literate humanity in Mesopotamia that is utilized as the literary model for the discussion of "Adam." That is, it is the first books that Genesis uses to describe the first people. The reason roughly six millennia can be calculated according to Genesis as to the origins of humanity cast out of "Eden" is because writing (not people) emerged roughly six millennia ago in "Eden" or Mesopotamia. The Bible, through the lens of writing, describes the first people as far back as written records (not people) can be traced. Genesis records literarily the time of the first people by describing the first records of the first literate people. Genesis is a written record that views people, who existed before written records, as written records themselves. A written record is a recreation of a time and place through the technology of writing; it is a lens through which a time and place can be seen. I assert that the Bible utilizes the history of written documents as the lens through which humanity is viewed. The longstanding debates regarding the belief and disbelief in the age of the world as related by the Book of Genesis have been undertaken by those unaware of the fact that the Book of Genesis does not attempt to disclose the age of the world or of humanity. Neither Science nor Theology has yet discovered that Genesis' timeline is a precisely verifiable parable that discusses the origin of time **through the origin of writing**. Furthermore, I seek to reveal the fact that the Hebrew word we translate "to create" also means "to author, to write about," and it is authorship specifically, writing itself, that is the lens through which the terminology of "Creation" finds its origin. A reason this method was taken to accomplish the story of "Creation" was that the ancient Eden-dwellers or Mesopotamians, who invented writing, understood writing as the pathway to invisible timelessness. That is, writing always looks to the future in terms of its readership. Writing conjures in the mind images that have passed away to people who are yet to be, a fact that parallels timelessness or eternity to its receivers; for, in this sense, the ancient Mesopotamians understood writing as a pathway to the divine; by this technology, readers far into the remote future could experience a form of divinity that was manifested in the remote past through a filter that recognized humans in preliterate times to be chronologically unaccountable to readers in literate times yet to be born. Finally, I seek to demonstrate that writing affects the brain neuroplastically to the extent that the fact we read about preliterate people means that our brains are related but different from preliterate people because their brains were unaltered by reading. Preliterate people's brains never crossed the senses of sight and sound as our brains do.

The Book of Genesis provides the age of human recording, not human existence. The chronology of Biblical genealogy stretches back to Mesopotamia or "Eden" around 3,700 B.C. because records themselves stretch back to the same time and place. "History" is the story of literate people, or at least a story told by literate people. Literate people emerged in Mesopotamia near 3,700 B.C. where and when the technology of graphic speech was invented. As it has been demonstrated previously in this book, the Hebrew "Eden" means "Fertility," and the letters that spell the Hebrew "Eden" also spell "time" in Chaldee (Daniel 2:8,9,21; 3:5, 15). "Fertility" and "Time" are understood together in terms of gestation. The Book of Genesis merges the story of the first humans with the story of the first literate humans in order to discuss wisdom, the production of an error, and the reproduction of that error in terms specific to a technological preservation of the original wisdom that preceded the error that marred its record. That is, the Book of Genesis describes people in terms of books, people who reproduce the same error in subsequent copies without knowing exactly what the error is.

Whatever year we reckon ourselves to live within, it is a year reckoned from some point of origin, be it a regnal year, a genealogical year, etc. We live today roughly 2,000 years from the time of Christ. The Book of Genesis counts time genealogically and in years. Looking backward in time and counting as such means that years must originate with a person, in this case, Adam. The reckoning of time, in this sense, is bound to the recognition of a person; people and time, under this rule, would be inseparable; however, the record of people could only go back so far as records (not people) go; thus, the reckoning of time with respect to people could only go back to the beginning of records and not to the beginning of time or people because it would require records to exist and people to make them. The point is that a human chronology established by genealogy must terminate with the beginning of records, but records were created after the advent of humanity.

The animal called the gastrotrich is born and dies of old age within seven days. If both the gastrotrich and the human were born on the same day and died of old age, they both would experience a comparable process but with a different number of Earth's rotations counting from their births to their deaths... but the human and the gastrotrich would seem little different from the perspective of an 80,000-year-old clonal colony of quaking aspen. Imagine if a person wrote a story to a gastrotrich about the life of a single aspen colony. Now, imagine if the existence of the gastrotrich depended on this story in order to maintain a portion of his species for the duration of that aspen colony. How would the person tell it, and how would one gastrotrich transmit it to another gastrotrich for the duration of the life of a single human, let alone for the duration of the life of the aspen colony about which he reads? Such considerations should be part of an approach to reading Genesis, for it speaks in human language to a distant future about a remote past in terms of eternity for readers who are bound to time.

The amount of narrative space utilized by an author affects a reader's perception of the real time about which the narration speaks — and the entirety of the origin of the material universe occupies about a page in the Hebrew Bible. When reading a narrative, it must be understood that a perspective is essential to the composition. Every detail of every event cannot be perceived and remembered by any one person at any time. We are bound to time, and so writing can only take so long, and there is a set amount of time possible for reading. Concerning a narrative, the perspective utilized must be chosen to focus attention in narrated (artificial) time concerning terrestrial (real) time. The amount of space devoted to any written topic demands an amount of time to read it, so two subjects that occupy the same amount of real time in history can occupy an unequal amount of time for a reader based upon the space allotted them in writing; this situation admits a deliberate purpose intended by the author. Why, then, does the creation of the material world described in Genesis occupy such a brief amount of narrated space in order to describe such a vast amount of real time? Moses' life occupies four entire books of the Torah, while Moses' "Creation" narrative spans about a page. The recollection of the past occurs by organizing a pattern methodically in order to arrive at a point of perspective. The "Creation" story is usually viewed as a record of material origins and, as such, has its detractors and supporters. What if, however, Genesis' "Creation" narrative never was intended to describe material origins and was organized into a map of time intended to serve a different purpose? — then it would be evident that it had been misrepresented by both its supporters and detractors who forwarded their views from the same premise.

As was stated earlier, the majority of books written about the Bible begin with an accepted theology and these books are theologically dependent on someone outside the Bible who developed the theological foundation accepted as a premise. The situation, then, is that a man penned his own thoughts about Scripture, and his followers patterned their thoughts after his; this then points to the fact that there are few original theologians relative to their adherents. If we consider roughly 2,000 years of original theologians, and if we allot 50 years to each of them, then time and strength-in-numbers take on a different aspect. Again, giving the first original theologian in our scenario a 50-year reign that is followed by another original theologian who began immediately after the end of the previous 50 years, etc., then the total number of original theologians would only equate to 40 over 2,000 years. It is not difficult to believe that only 40 people — over the span of two millennia — were mistaken about a single point; furthermore, it is not difficult to accept that all of the followers of the 40 originals were also mistaken regarding that single point since they began from a premise that did not anticipate or allow for that single point. Being mistaken at a single point does not necessitate that everything the "originals" said was wrong, but it does allow for nothing of what the originals said to have addressed the correctness of a single point of which none of them were aware. One such point regards the origin of writing itself. Writing first occurred in Mesopotamia and was mostly accomplished on clay. Theology began after the disappearance of Mesopotamian clay writing, and this clay writing was only rediscovered in the midst of the development of Evolutionary theory.

Now, instead of counting time by human, literary careers, let us consider counting time by the first human literature. The first human literature was invented roughly 3,700 B.C. in what the Bible specifically calls "Eden" and what we generally call "Mesopotamia." This writing, mostly crafted on clay, was last produced in the First Century A.D. shortly after the destruction of the Second Temple. It was not rediscovered until the 19th Century A.D. If one were to count time, that is, human history, not in terms of human literary careers in general but in terms of Mesopotamian clay writing specifically, then one would begin the reckoning of the first days about 3,700 B.C., one would stop about 100 A.D., and one would begin again in the 19th Century A.D. with two obvious and major exclusions: (1) all of the prehistory that existed before the invention of writing itself up until 3,700 B.C., and (2) all of the history that existed from the time of the death and burial of Mesopotamian clay writing until its resurrection in the 19th Century A.D. In essence, both prehistory and Theology as we currently conceive of them would be absent in our chronology. We simply would be viewing the birth of the first literate man who wrote in clay, the death of his clay, and the resurrection of his clay as one seamless beginning, middle, and end. This situation would not evince a deliberate exclusion; it would reveal a model utilized for a specific purpose that deliberately included only the subject to which it referred.

The term "Creation" carries with it a weighted history wherein various proponents and opponents wrangled, and continue to wrangle, vehemently. The contention revolving around the word "Creation" itself has displayed ironic twists over forgetful spans of time to the extent that popular opinion currently pits the "Big Bang" against Genesis' story of origins... even though it was the Belgian priest, Georges Lemaitre, who devised it under his belief in *Creatio Ex Nihilo* or *Creation Out of Nothing*. The popular mindset today that sees a possible unification between the Book of Genesis and the "Big Bang" does not realize that the *creation out of nothing* was assumed in the "Big Bang" because the man who devised it already believed Genesis to be correct (as he understood it). A further irony can be seen in the very name "Big Bang," an unsophisticated and cheap title for such a grand explanation. As is laid down in his lectures on *Science & Religion*, professor Principe of The Great Courses records how, originally, Lemaitre, who devised this explanation of origins, called his theory the "Primordial Atom Model" in 1927, and he claimed that expansion had initiated from a "single quantum." Since this model sounded so much like Genesis' declaration, "Let there be light," it was rejected as something too similar to Christian doctrine and was mocked with the ridiculous title "Big Bang" by its atheist opposition. In 1951, Pope Pius XII embraced what became known as the "Big Bang." The derisive title, "Big Bang," became remembered positively, in spite of its original intent.

It can be seen in this history of such a monumental model of the universe that only decades (not centuries, not millennia) of forgetfulness have resulted absurdly in a situation (1) where atheists not only adopted the model of the universe they once thought to be too theistic but even the very title they used to mock this model, (2) of Christians seeing in the doctrine of *Creation Out of Nothing* an opposition to the model that paralleled it, and (3) moderates who attempt to unify the Big Bang and *Creation Out of Nothing* without realizing that the unification occurred upon the Big Bang's appearance under its original title, "Primordial Atom Model." The main point here is that even a brief passage of time not only erased from the popular mind the foundations of a significant controversy, but created the exact opposite of the original fact in the minds of the masses. It can be argued that the masses are not the originators of such platforms and, therefore, have no significant voice in the matter; yet the masses (who make up churches and schools) are not scholars of the Bible or scientists.

If such error occurs over decades, then imagine the error that occurs over millennia. What is "remembered" in the future may never have existed at any point in the past.

As has been discussed previously, Theology is not the same as the Bible, which is why there is one Bible that the many different theologies claim to support. The Bible is one matter, but *all* of the various theologies cannot be correct. It is hardly taken into account (if at all) that Genesis' "Creation" story may not describe the origin of life, for a description is quite different from a comparison, and an explanation is different from a parable. Explanations often require more time to establish than the subjects they explain. The "Creation" story of Genesis comprises less than one percent of the written content of the Bible. Is the entirety of the material universe explained in a sliver of a collection of Books that continually describe temporal and eternal existence? Certainly not! The "Creation" story has been argued mostly from the standpoint of translation, doctrine, dogma, and culture. The "Creation Out of Nothing" dogma is a product of Bible translation and theology, not the Hebrew "Old Testament" or the Greek "New Testament." Human dogma asserts "Creation Out of Nothing"; the Bible itself is another matter in this regard. Defining, modifying, and redefining what the word "create" means in Genesis has fueled more problems than it has solved. The word "create" in Genesis is simply a translation, and it is a translation that was defined prior to the discovery of the material access necessary to grasp its Hebrew literary employment — not scientific employment, but *literary* employment. The Hebrew word "create" is a literary term, not a cosmological term. Genesis was not written in Latin or English but was translated so. Translations are not facsimiles; they are ways of looking at parts of things. For instance, the words of Genesis 1:26, "Let Us make man in Our image, according to Our likeness," can seem straight-forward; yet, the Hebrew word "make" here also means "convert" (Genesis 12:5), the Hebrew "in" is the same as "with," and the Hebrew word "likeness" here also means "parable" and "similitude" (Hosea 12:10); thus, "Let us make man in Our image, according to our likeness" can also be read in Hebrew as "Let us convert man with Our Image, according to Our parable."

The discussion of "conversion" according to a "parable" in writing should cause the reader to understand that he is reading a historical *parable*, not a historical account, a comparison and not a description. The reliance on translation, however, has hidden the very word "parable" from the readers who seek to explain or argue the "image" and "likeness" of God as to whether such an account of origins is reliable. By testing the parable, and not the very subject it elucidates through comparison, one can draw the conclusion that the origin of man as recorded in Scripture is unexplainable (but to be believed) or unreliable (and not to be believed). The various "Creation vs. Evolution" controversies have revolved around a premise that has not known the Scripture's telling of origins to be literally a "likeness" or "parable" whose subject is something yet to be encountered in the "Creation vs. Evolution" arena. Without knowing that the very Hebrew "Creation" story is of a parabolic construction, as it says of itself in Hebrew, many passionate claims have been forwarded to little accurate effect on any side of the issue.

Consider the difficulty of warning people 10,000 years from now by *writing* the warning down now. The spoken language 10,000 years later would not be the same, and it is almost certain that no one would understand the written language used in the warning or the warning itself unless it could be corroborated with or compared to something else in the distant future 10,000 years away. The warning would have to function within a frame of reference that accounted for at least two present time-frames: (1) the time in which it was written and (2) the time in which it is read. How would or could one anticipate the distant future with accuracy in this respect? Explanations often take more time and space than the things they explain, but parables, likenesses, similitudes, riddles, etc. economize time and space through comparison in order to provide a frame of reference that unifies the sender and the receiver of a message with a meaning common to them both. Moses described the first humans through writing, but the first humans existed prior to writing... this would be like describing the first bird in terms of an airplane. For the sake of argument, imagine a distant future where birds no longer exist but airplanes do. Now, imagine yourself attempting to write to this distant future about birds. You could only begin to talk about birds by describing a functional likeness or image, and it is this likeness that would be understood as a platform to begin understanding this ancient entity that mankind of old called a "bird." You would, essentially, have to speak in a parable whose relevance would open the door to the future by comparison rather than by explanation. You, having knowledge of both birds and airplanes because they both exist in your time, could write to readers 10,000 years later about birds but not in the same exact terms in which you understand them in your day. Your present time must meet your readers' present time through the constant of flight as compared to an airplane and not as explained as an entity they have no conception of or way to observe materially. The constant is flight, the example is an airplane, and the subject is a bird. If, however, your future readers had yet to discover that the subject of your writing is a bird, then all of their explanations would concern themselves only with your constant (flight) and your example (airplane). Likewise, those who attempted to explain the Hebrew Bible after the disappearance and before the rediscovery of Mesopotamian clay writing were masterfully able to describe flight and airplanes but not birds. The cognitive output of the written word can cause a physical reality lost to the passage of time to be virtually conveyed to a cognitive reception in a future time.

A 4,000-year-old Egyptian quotation is recorded in Fischer's sagacious *A History of Writing*: "A man has perished and his body has become earth. All his relatives have crumbled to dust. It is writing that makes him remembered." It is easy to appreciate the power of these ancient words. At the same time, it is beneficial to define "writing" in order to increase the accuracy of our appreciation. If by "writing" we mean *the graphic representation of a spoken language,* which is the crossing of two otherwise separate senses into *visual sound*, then we can comprehend in the Egyptian quotation above an echo, a voice solidified in external memory that once was internal with respect to the man who wrote it. Professor Marc Zender, in his *Writing and Civilization* lectures by The Great Courses, defines "writing" tersely as "visible speech." The quotation above is evidence of (1) a man's words living longer than (2) the man himself, and those words refer to (3) human life that preceded the writer's words and the writer himself. Writing always looks to the future in that it is to be read by one who exists after the writing occurs. As such, we understand, through reading, a man who lived before us who was capable of describing men who lived before him to us 4,000 years in his future through the lens of literacy. Without this lens, the specificity of the quotation above would be lost to the fading memory that characterizes oral tradition and myth. Writing, the invention that made the sound of spoken language visible, compels the standardization of a message. Printing, the invention that allowed the mass reproduction of a single message, standardized spelling and thus changed written language itself by reducing the scribal tendency to write a word according to how it sounded to an individual writer. The simplicity, facility, and efficiency of a given writing system do not determine the system's endurance. Instead, it is the potency and prestige of the users of a writing system that override the degree of difficulty in its employment, and this is easily seen in situations of conquest.

We today, who live in a world composed of literate and illiterate people, can tend to merge reading and writing in our minds through the singular label of "literacy," but it should be understood that

> ...reading and writing are separately processed cerebral activities. Writing is spelling, and many people who spell excellently read only poorly, while many who read excellently spell poorly. This is because these processes involve different learning strategies in the human brain. Writing is an active linguistic activity that demands both the visual and the phonetic component, appealing directly to phonological essentials. Reading is passive visual activity, linking graphic art directly to meaning....
> (A History of Writing, Fischer; p. 309).

The written word is speech that can be seen. Prior to writing, spoken language was only heard, remembered internally, and transmitted audibly instead of seen, remembered externally, and transmitted visually. It is easy to grasp this when one takes into account *disglossia* or *the situation revealed when a people's written language becomes so different from their spoken language that two separate languages emerge.* As an example in today's American English, the official language used in American court documents is distinct from the manner in which regular American English conversation occurs. Spoken vernacular shifts faster than standardized writing. Speakers of a given language who can read their ancient writings may not understand specifically what they are reading if even the same vocabulary, over time, has obtained a meaning within a domain the original could not have anticipated. Consider the English word "slave"; most American people today immediately connect this word to racial factors related to American history, but, factually, such slavery is not discussed accordingly in an English translation of the Bible; it is the word "slave" that the English Bible uses that, anachronistically, is connected mistakenly to the Bible's translated content and is confusedly received by the average reader. Simply learning Biblical languages is not the key to understanding the Bible's content because one can do so and still conceive of Scripture's content in a current, English sense with the sound of ancient, Hebrew words. Let us consider here a general history of writing.

In Fischer's book, he explains that writing was, initially, a tool of power that was wielded by a small number of elites who served deified kings (p.69). Writing became understood in close connection with wisdom itself (p. 68). Societies are significantly based on speech (p.7), although writing is not essential to civilization (p.35). Civilizations existed prior to the invention of writing. Writing systems and scripts die out less quickly than the languages they transmit (p.66). Most systems of writing that ever have existed are now extinct (p.7). Writing changes by human agency (p.13). Writing is the graphic counterpart of a spoken language (p.11).

What can be called a "complete" writing system is one wherein sound is the priority of the graphics (p.31). The original idea of graphically depicting sound emerged not quite six millennia ago in Mesopotamia (p.33). By about 2,500 B.C., nearly all graphic elements in the Sumerian writing system had become units of sound (p.49). Egypt seems to be the home of the first consonantal alphabetic writing system around 2,000 B.C. (p. 39). As in Egypt, scribes became a social class, mostly employed in agriculture (p.50). Near the time of Moses, Semitic scribes of Ugarit wrote entirely phonetic cuneiform, which is a mingling of the three-dimensional technique of Mesopotamia and the ultimately two-dimensional alphabetic conception of writing (p.55). It should be immediately apparent that the Bible is taking into account the history of writing itself as it forwards its message. It is not simply the case that the Bible is a written document along the timeline of history; the Bible is taking into account the history of the method of external memory it is using: writing. For instance, God is described as "King," the Edenic dispute regarding "wisdom" between the "Serpent" and the "Woman" hinges tightly on Hebrew grammar (though this aspect of the story is totally lacking in translation), the "Tower of Babel" account understands civilizations bound by speech, Moses writes down the very words he spoke for years and this writing is described as a counterpart or "shadow" (Hebrews 8), and, most importantly, the very place and time humanity's "creation" begins is Mesopotamia, the birthplace of the world's oldest complete writing system. These similarities cannot be ignored. They are too blatantly reflective of each other.

The written language of Scripture maintained itself longer than the spoken language of its various readers along the arrow of time. Something similar to (but more complex than) disglossia occurred. Consequently, subsequent readers spoke — **and therefore thought** — differently about Scripture to the effect that chronological progress impelled interpretive regress. New definitions of the Hebrew root ברא emerged and are currently settled in the agreed-upon translation of *created* without realizing that the Hebrew word meant something related but different when it was written originally. The idea of "creation" became defined by various groups that argue from various platforms for various reasons that have collectively resulted roundly in the "Creation vs. Evolution" debates of today. When reading the English Bible, or even when reading the Masoretic Text of the Hebrew Bible, we are reading more of a vestige than the foot that imprinted it, more of a shadow cast by an obscurant than the light source the obscurant blocks, more of a reaction than an action. To use an evolutionary model in an attempt to understand the history of writing does not work, for modifications to writing occur by human agency and not of themselves. As in the case of a vestige, the earth is changed into the shape of a foot; a foot print in the earth does not change the earth into a foot print.

A "complete" writing system, as opposed to an "incomplete" one, is a writing system wherein sound assumes priority. Art began to utilize human speech around 3,700 B.C. in Mesopotamia or "Eden." That is, the first complete writing system, where symbol became sign, appears to have been introduced around 3,700 B.C. — in the very time and place when and where Genesis describes the first man to have been "created."

This resounding fact is no accident.

The Book of Genesis places the first "created" man in Mesopotamia around 3,700 B.C. The first writing system was invented at the same time and in the same place. The arguments over Genesis' reliability have largely revolved around Genesis' chronology and genealogy. The reliability of Genesis' documentary evidence has not been viewed through the lens that understands Genesis to be a document that discusses a time when documentation did not exist. Of course, when looking backwards against the arrow of time, counting chronology by *genealogy through a written work* must of necessity terminate when writing itself historically terminates. Or, to look at the matter proceeding with the arrow of time, the record of human origins begins with a record as much as it does with a person, even if the two did not originate simultaneously.

Genesis discusses the topic of the first humans through the lens of the first writing. The reliability that is in question is the errant frame of reference that does not take into account the fact that writing did not originate at the same time as man; man preceded writing; man eventually used writing to talk to the future; writing and man merged into a single origin in Genesis deliberately to mark the *topic* of man's origin by the *time* of man's creation: writing. Writing is not necessary for civilization to exist. The genealogies of Genesis, as opposed to the stories of Genesis, do not count back to the first civilizations. The genealogies of Genesis count back to the first literate civilization, and the stories of Genesis look back to the first people. Two times are unified by the genealogical chronologies of Genesis: (1) the undisclosed quantity of time humans have existed, and (2) the disclosed quantity of time literate humans have existed.

An inevitable feature of writing is that the spoken language writing reflects changes faster than the writing itself. Over time, the writing can be misunderstood or not understood at all on account of the gradual shifting of speech. The ancient constellation pictures resemble pictographic writing and not cuneiform or alphabetic writing. Without writing, science cannot thrive and, within a relatively brief time, the inability to record and analyze records gives way to mere tradition. Writing allows for science to be cultivated to the extent that time aids scientific progress, whereas time diminishes scientific progress when there is no system that can preserve data collectively and externally. E.W. Maunder reasoned that constellation pictures were devised by people who lived around 2,700 B.C. (*Astronomy of The Bible*, p. 157-158); this observation is important relative to the history of writing because the constellation pictures resemble pictographic writing, and pictographic writing ceased to be a living system around the same time the constellation pictures were first crafted. The difference in the stars' appearance between 2,800 B.C. and 2,700 B.C. is almost unobservable to the naked eye. If we use the narrative chronology established by Genesis' genealogies, then pictographic writing (in real time) began when Adam was expelled from Eden (in narrative time), and it ended when he died (in narrative time). The chronology of Genesis has Adam expelled from Eden near 3,700 B.C., and it states that his death was 930 years later (in narrative time) or about the time that the constellation pictures were first developed (in real time). The constellation pictures were developed near the death of Mesopotamian pictographic writing and the birth of cuneiform writing (in real time); thus, cuneiform writing made pictographs obsolete even though the cartographic system of the constellation pictures reflected pictographic and not cuneiform writing. In a manner of speaking, the celestial writing system reflected the original terrestrial writing system, and the earthly system departed into cuneiform. This departure marked the death of clay pictographs that were but remembered in the celestial pictures of astronomy. "Adam," or clay pictographic writing, ascended to Heaven, or the realm of the stars.

Since the Hebrew Bible places Adam's "creation" near 3,700 B.C., and since by about 2,500 B.C. nearly all graphic elements in the Sumerian writing system had become units of sound, we can notice that Adam's lifespan of 930 years places his death near the solidification of the cuneiform script. In this manner, the stars themselves could be understood as the conveyers of sound.

> "The HEAVENS declare the glory of God; and the FIRMAMENT shows His handiwork. Day unto day UTTERS SPEECH, and night unto night reveals knowledge. There is no speech nor language where their VOICE is not heard. Their VOICE goes out through all the earth, and their WORDS to the end of the world..." (Psalm 19:1-4).

Job 20 says,

> "Do you not know this of old, since ADAM was placed on earth, that the triumphing of the wicked is short, and the joy of the hypocrite is but for a moment? THOUGH HIS HAUGHTINESS MOUNTS UP TO THE HEAVENS, AND HIS HEAD REACHES TO THE CLOUDS, yet he will perish forever like his own refuse; those who have seen him will say, 'Where is he?' He will fly away like a dream, and not be found; yes, he will be chased away like a VISION OF THE NIGHT. The eye that saw him will see him no more, nor will his place behold him anymore. His children will seek the favor of the poor, and his hands will restore his wealth. His bones are full of his youthful vigor, but it will lie down with him in the dust. Though evil is sweet in his mouth, and he hides it under his tongue, though he spares it and does not forsake it, but still keeps it in his mouth, yet his food in his stomach turns sour; it becomes cobra venom within him. He swallows down riches and vomits them up again; God casts them out of his belly. He will suck the poison of cobras; the viper's tongue will slay him.... THE HEAVENS WILL REVEAL HIS INIQUITY.... "

The Book of Genesis places Adam's death shortly before writing transitioned from the pictographic depiction of spoken language to the abstract depiction of spoken language and about when the constellation pictures were developed.

The judgment of when the Vernal Equinox precisely enters a constellation is a matter somewhat dependent on how the celestial cartography/pictography is depicted. The precision is more in the entirety of the cycle called The Precession of The Equinoxes. It is plain that the platform the Eden story uses celestially is a time when the Vernal Equinox was in Taurus, the "beast of the field" that qualified "The Serpent" or Draco, wherein the pole star resided, described in Genesis 3:1. The celestial reference Exodus makes to the Passover can be observed in the time-period afterward when the Vernal Equinox was in Aries, the lamb of Moses' departure from Egypt. The celestial reference to the birth of Christ's followers who used the Fish insignia to identify themselves can be observed when the Vernal Equinox was afterward in the first fish of Pisces. If one utilizes Biblical genealogy to establish Biblical chronology, and if one keeps in mind that such agrarian societies relied heavily upon celestial cartography in order to survive (as is particularly highlighted in the stories of Joseph in the Book of Genesis, Daniel in the Book of Daniel, and the Magi in the Book of Matthew), then one will observe fluidly that the movement and themes of the terrestrial stories in Scripture align with the celestial motions, both of which converge in the birth and death of Christ. The countdown to Christ's birth was literarily and historically mirrored by the countdown to Christ's death.

The destruction of the Second Temple in Jerusalem occurred during the same time-period as the death of Mesopotamian cuneiform writing. The Book of Hebrews 1:2 refers to the time after the death of Christ as "these last days." Christ is called "The Word" (Revelation 19:13). Christ was physically visible. The first physically visible word was accomplished in the same time and place that Genesis describes the "creation" of the first human, Adam. Christ is called "The Last Adam" (1 Corinthians 15:45) in the Resurrection section of the Book of 1 Corinthians. The point is that The First Adam is described according to the first writing (devised in Mesopotamia) and The Last Adam is described in "these last days" according to the death and burial of Mesopotamian clay writing. The "last days" here align with the first "days" Genesis discusses. The first and last days discussed here are of three-dimensional, clay, Mesopotamian writing. This frame of reference (clay writing) exists within the chronological progression of the Vernal Equinox through time, from Taurus, to Aries, and then to Pisces. Moses, who wrote of Eden according to the celestial reference to Taurus, lived during the time of Aries afterwards; likewise, Moses wrote of the "creation" of the first man according to the terrestrial invention of writing itself, which was also a time afterwards. The system used in Scripture being described here is the discussion of a topic in a previous time through the lens of a later time in order to preserve a present occurring at the time of composition for the future. The chronological line from Taurus to Pisces, or from the creation of Mesopotamian writing to its death and burial, is one and the same: the first and the last "Adam" are recorded from the Vernal Equinox proceeding from the *beast of the field* to the *icthus*. As the stars were used to count time for the purposes of agriculture, so books became utilized for the same purpose; stars, people, and books are unified here; however, on account of The Precession of The Equinoxes, the gradual separation of a written calendar from the celestial cycles is analogous to *disglossia* or *the situation revealed when a people's written language becomes so different from their spoken language that two separate languages emerge.* In this case, the language of the heavens (described overtly in Psalm 19 and Romans 1) became unheard by many based on a lack of understanding and not a lack of celestial "speech." As should be noticeable here, specialization in literature largely disregarded other disciplines that used to be understood along with literature, and a reference to astronomy will reveal a perfect conceptual alignment with Scriptural chronology and geography so that the real time of history and the virtual, narrated time of the first Adam converge with the real time of history and the real, narrated time of "The Last Adam," Christ. Utilizing the ancient, collective memory encapsulated in the pictographic constellation insignias as a key that fixes its chronological boundaries within nearly 26,000 years, one can take Scripture's accounts of the "Beginning" and its accounts of "these last days" and see prehistoric (and therefore preliterate) time unify with historic (and therefore literate) time. This system is fixed, and it hangs above us every night (whether or not we possess the skills to decipher it). Furthermore, this system accounts not for decades or centuries, but for millennia within roughly 26,000 years, and in this way is a recording device capable of greater permanence than most. It is not accidental that the Passover was to be conducted on the 14th day of the first month (in Spring, indicated by the Vernal Equinox) in Egypt, for it was on this very day, fifteen centuries later, that Christ died on Passover in Judea whose evening experienced a verifiable lunar eclipse (displayed in NASA's *Five Millennium Canon of Lunar Eclipses*, by Espenak & Meeus).

If one looks backwards or forwards in time at the circuitous zodiacal constellations, one will encounter an alignment that pictographically communicates a sequence directly analogous to the Garden of Eden story (if one accounts for the constellations' names in Hebrew). Thus, time and spoken language converge here by way of pictures. Spoken language represented by pictures is how writing began in Mesopotamia or Eden. The pictures became reduced to abstract graphic representations of the sounds of spoken language about a millennium later. The interval of time when Mesopotamia represented the spoken language with pictures until Mesopotamia's writing became more abstractly phonetic than pictographic in nature is the same time-period of the "creation" and death of Adam. It is at the time of Adam's death that the celestial alignment that pictographically reflects the literary Eden narrative that last occurred in history, about 2,800 B.C. (give or take). That is, the cherubs in Genesis 3 are described by Revelation 4 and Ezekiel 1 & 11 as the constellations at the solstices and equinoxes near 2,800 B.C. The life of Adam was, essentially, the life of pictures utilized to recall the sounds of spoken language long before the invention of the alphabet in Egypt. The lifespan of Adam was begun with the birth of writing and ended with the birth of the constellation pictures; for the pictographic constellation pictures emerged as pictographic writing died and gave way to cuneiform. It can be observed well here that, unlike the remainder of Scripture following the expulsion from Eden, the

Eden account discusses its characters not with elaborate descriptions but in specific pictures: "The Man, "The Woman," "The Serpent," "The Tree," "The Cherubs," etc., as if the reader already knows who these beings are. A similar fact is true of the first millennium of writing. When the zodiac was utilized to reflect the *Fall* in Eden, it is the *Autumnal* Equinox of about 2,800 B.C. that shows a man treading on a scorpion and wrangling with a serpent (who attempts to put his head into a crown); this cartographic situation is reflected by a wounded warrior who crushes the head of a serpent (who holds the Northern Pole Star or crown of the heavens). It is to this same celestial alignment, the Fall Equinox of about 2,800 B.C., that Luke 10:18-20 seems to refer *literally*:

> "...I saw Satan FALL LIKE LIGHTNING FROM HEAVEN. Behold, I give you the authority to TRAMPLE ON SERPENTS AND SCORPIONS [= the constellations of Ophiuchus and Scorpio reflected north by the constellations of The Kneeler and Draco], and over all the power of the enemy, and nothing shall by any means hurt you. Nevertheless do not rejoice in this, that the spirits are subject to you, but rather rejoice because your names are WRITTEN IN HEAVEN."

The narrative time of Adam's death is the real time when clay pictographic writing died and rose to become celestial pictographic cartography. It is this real time-period (2,800 B.C.) that Genesis uses to describe Eden. Genesis describes Eden as the constellation pictures were arranged when they were first invented, when clay pictographs were abandoned, and when cuneiform emerged. On earth, signs took precedence over pictures whereby the reduction in graphic marking increased the complexity of writing through the cuneiform script. Let us consider these chronologically historical steps in conjunction with The Hebrew Bible's account of history:

1)   *Visual speech*, or *writing*, emerged in Mesopotamia near 3,700 B.C., and Scripture states that Adam was "created" in this same time and place.

2)   The transition from more pictorially complicated writing to more abstract phonography via the complete cuneiform script occurred about one millennium later, and Scripture states that this is when and where Adam "died."

3)   The time of Mesopotamia's transition from pictographic writing into cuneiform is the same (and most recent) period when the constellations observable in Mesopotamia aligned in the order of "The Garden of Eden" Narrative (if one considers the constel-

lations' names in Hebrew). The Eden narrative is thus related in terms of the invention of the constellation pictures.

4) The sign superseded the picture in Mesopotamian writing at the same time as the constellations told the story of Eden, and the Hebrew אות used to describe the first quality of the celestial luminaries on the Fourth Day of "Creation" means *the communication of ideas* (as in Genesis 34:15). The fact that the celestial luminaries were for "sings" or "the communication of ideas" (Genesis 1:14) is a way of describing writing being used for astronomical cartography.

The account of Adam's "creation" is explained through the chronology of the creation of Mesopotamian writing, not the "creation" of the first human that Scripture itself says occurred in a place other than Eden (Genesis 2:7-8). The account of Adam's death is explained through the chronology of the demise of pictographic writing. The narrated chronology of Adam's death is the real time when pictographic writing ceased being used on clay and began being used to map the sky. The stars themselves were understood to contain the communication of ideas, and the Hebrew word often translated as "create" is literally from the root ברא *to carve out, to shape out,* and connotes *birth*. The disglossia implied thus far can be seen here to reveal that the Hebrew word we read in translation as "create" is actually "to carve or shape out," that is, *to write upon a three-dimensional surface,* which is how the Mesopotamians or Eden-dwellers wrote. Pictographic writing was raised to Heaven, so to speak. Joshua 17:15 uses the word usually translated *to create* to mean *to clear out a space:*

> "So Joshua answered them, 'If you are a great people, then go up to the forest country and CLEAR [= Hebrew "ברא *create*"] a place for yourself there in the land of the Perizzites and the giants, since the mountains of Ephraim are too confined for you.'"

The authorization of conquest and the razing of a territory are understood in miniature as authorship being carved into clay. As Adam was *written about* or *"created"* out of the dust following the flooding stream saturating that dust into clay (Genesis 2:6-7), so Genesis 41:2 uses the Hebrew root usually translated "to create" to describe the fatness of cattle in a dream:

> "Suddenly there came up out of the river seven cows, FINE LOOKING AND FAT; and they fed in the meadow." These "fat" or "created" cattle in the dream *ate* gaunt cattle; the root usually translated "to create" means "to eat" in 2 Samuel 12:17: "So

the elders of his house arose and went to him, to raise him up from the ground. But he would not, nor did he EAT [= Hebrew "ברא create"] food with them."

In Hebrew, to *comprehend*, to *eat*, to be *attractive*, to *clear* land, and to *carve* all derive from the same root that is usually translated "to create"; the reader will notice that all of these definitions are used together to form the narrative of Mark 6. The monumental declaration, "In the beginning, God *created* the heavens and the earth" is literally, "In the beginning, God *wrote about* the heavens and the earth." The next statement in Genesis tells of the earth's destruction by water, which is how clay writing tablets were commonly erased. The heavenly *book* (*so to speak*) remained intact, but the earthly *book* (*so to speak*) did not, and it can be seen here why Genesis says, "Be fruitful and multiply and REPLENISH the earth" (Genesis 1:28). Writing itself is the virtual lens Scripture uses, in writing, to convey the meaning behind the state of man's existence.

The Bible does not say that Adam was *physically created* some six millennia ago.

The Bible places Moses around 1,500 B.C.; Moses was Adam's biographer, and Moses places Adam more than two millennia before himself; the Biblical Adam is dated about 3,700 B.C., but he is used literarily to describe the first man who existed prior to the ability to date in any way discernable to us now. The written dating of the Biblical Adam goes back chronologically to written dating, not to Adam himself. This fact is the literary method that establishes the literary pattern that runs throughout the Books of the Bible, and this pattern ties each story together into a seamless thematic whole, not a seamless chronological whole.

.One cannot deny the fact that, long before Moses, the Sumerian Legends of The Kings of Uruk describe a man doomed to die who reappears three days later as the savior of his people. The word "create" in Hebrew has been misunderstood anachronistically as disglossia reveals, for the frame of reference to Mesopotamian three-dimensional clay writing disappeared with the death and burial of this writing during the First Century A.D., shortly after the destruction of the Second Temple, that was only rediscovered or reborn in the 19th Century A.D.

"Acknowledged to the pathway of wisdom itself, writing soon spread through the Middle East, its most active champions and innovators being the Semitic peoples," (*A History of Writing, Fisher; p. 68*). Moses' written account of Eden centers around the idea of wisdom while recalling that the history of Adam centers around the idea of writing. Moses was Semitic, but he was raised in Egypt. Again, a 4,000-year-old Egyptian said, "A man has perished and his body has become earth. All his relatives have crumbled to dust. It is writing that makes him remembered." Moses wrote of Adam, "In the sweat of your face you shall eat bread till you return to the ground, for out of it you were taken; for dust you are, and to dust you shall return" (Genesis 3:19). "Indeed, the alphabetic idea... was first elaborated more than four thousand years ago in Egypt, Sinai, and Canaan" (Fischer; p.69), and Moses was born in Egypt, received The Law at Sinai, and led the Israelites to Canaan. Fischer describes "the world's first alphabet" as "the most remarkable innovation of ancient Egyptian scribes," and it was created about 2,000 B.C. (p.39). The Hebrew Bible's chronology of Moses places his life around 1,500 B.C. It is at this time that the "Semitic scribes of Ugarit... wrote wholly phonetic cuneiform.... [t]heir writing is a hybrid creation: consonantal alphabetic using the physical technique of Mesopotamia's cuneiform" (Fischer; p. 55). It is such a hybrid that allows us to understand with more clarity the literary technique utilized by Moses.

We must understand that the nearly 1,700 years that Mesopotamian clay writing disappeared was the monumental disappearance of an entire world of comprehension. The burial of the ancient Mesopotamian tablets is analogous to a perceptual eye-gouge, for the disappearance of this manner of thought was followed by the entire history of the discipline that came to be called Christian Theology, which is a literary system that emerged independently of the world or lens Scripture provided to understand the pronouncement in Eden (the house of wisdom) that eventuated in Golgatha ("The Scull," the house of the brain). Ancient Mesopotamian clay writing was lost to oblivion for nearly two millennia. "The last trace we have recovered of these final representatives of the traditional culture is a cuneiform tablet dating from about AD 74 to 75: a stodgy astronomical almanac! It is the last word, the last breath we have of this admirable, 4,000-year-old civilization that changed our world," (*Ancestor of The West*, Bottero, Herrenschmidt, Vernant, Fagan; 17). The "Theological" model of Scripture became its own creation, and it is astonishing how far the theologians got in their learning without having any apparent material access to the knowledge of the lens Moses utilized to record the original encounter of God with the man He "created."

We can construct models that attempt to mirror our observations for the purposes of describing reality, and the best possible model in a certain time or place can act as the standard of reality's description. Moses can seem geographically and/or chronologically far removed from us who

read print or digital versions of his words in our native tongues. Nevertheless, Moses shares with us a major similarity: In Moses' day, as in ours, the
oldest known writing emerged from what Moses called "Eden" and what
we call "Mesopotamia." People existed prior to literacy. To be completely
fair, the possibility stands that writing existed prior to Mesopotamia, but
most probably not. Yet, even if writing certainly existed prior to Mesopotamia, we (like Moses) have no material access to it. People and writing
may have existed for much longer than we currently estimate, *but that is
beside the point*. The point is that Moses wrote in a time and place that
counts the oldest writing from Mesopotamia just as we live in a time and a
place that counts the same. The Hebrew Bible places Moses in a setting
around 1,500 B.C. and thus more than two millennia after the invention
of Mesopotamian writing, about one millennium after the dominance of
the cuneiform script, about half-a-millennium after the invention of the
consonantal alphabet, and at the time of the Ugaritic hybrid of three-dimensional Mesopotamian writing with two-dimensional alphabetic writing.
This Ugaritic reflection can be observed in that the Hebrew letters אשה that
can mean *fire offering* also mean *gift* as discerned by a Ugaritic cognate;
these same letters spell "woman"; that the name *woman* is connected
to a *gift* can be observed when Adam blamed God by stating, " האשהthe
woman, the gift whom נתתה *You* GAVE to be with me, she GAVE me of the
tree" (Genesis 3:12).

 Since the entirety of both the "Old" and "New" Testaments was
written down after the invention of Mesopotamian clay writing and before
its disappearance, then those who lived after this writing's disappearance
and before its rediscovery in the 19th Century A.D. must, of necessity, admit a gap in interpretive scope based not on a deficiency in their powers
but on the chance of having lived within a frame of time that did not allow
them to exercise their powers otherwise. For example, we cannot account
for what the world's greatest basketball player might have been in a time
prior to the invention of basketball any more than we can anticipate what
he would otherwise be in a time after the disappearance of basketball.
What we can say is that, within the frame of reference he found himself,
he was the greatest player of a game wherein his genotype and pheno-
type aligned with his choices in order to excel under a specific set of circumstances. Let us then consider the circumstance of literacy — for this
circumstance places us within the same frame of reference with Moses in
that the oldest identifiable form of literacy is identical to us both: Mesopotamian clay writing.

It might not occur to the modern reader that writing an accurate historical account would involve imagination. Yet, should we write down a physical description of a single person at a single moment in time, and should that person live 40 years longer than the completion of his written description, the reader of the description made 40 years before must, when facing the subject of the writing 40 years later, use his imagination to merge what he sees and reads about in order to understand the world that then was in light of the world that is now. The person whose description was frozen into words 40 years prior to the present observation of him by the reader is and is not the same person, as could be said easily of rivers, trees, and so forth. To behold a decrepit man unable to tend to himself and then to behold a description of his earlier years as a champion athlete requires imagination; both instances are true, and both are connected: the athlete existed then, the invalid exists now, and the same man connects these two realities. Similarly, the lushness of ancient Mesopotamia is now the sandiness of modern Iraq. The two rivers (Tigris and Euphrates) that hedge Mesopotamia in are described in Genesis as being only two of the four rivers in Eden; but, the other two have not been found, and the account of Eden's geography has been suspected of inaccuracy. This suspicion is short-sighted because it ignores the mindset of one looking to describe the essence of the past to a future afar off. The four rivers mentioned in Genesis 2 all have names with procreative meanings, and the fact that there are four of them in number tells the ancient Hebrew reader that the story is describing procreation because the Hebrew "four" derives from the root "to copulate." It is, therefore, myopic to look for these extra and non-existent *rivers* in order to validate the story when one should be looking for the *product of the copulation* in the story. "Eden" means "Fertility." The Eden story ends in death but it begins with the command, "Be fruitful and multiply." Again, the line that connects human origin to human death is the arrow of time. The consequence of sin was death in Genesis; this consequence introduced a negative application of time in that it counted down to demise instead of down to birth. Death itself is here paralleled to birth in this respect. The birth of a person was commanded, and the four rivers (based on their names and the fact that there were four of them), is the theme of the story whose book-ends are birth and death. Utilizing writing to describe the first birth and death in a time when writing did not exist necessitates a situation wherein imagination is to be used to push the point of the story since human written records terminated into a preliterate world about two millennia before Moses. In other words, Moses could only read backwards so far; and, as such, he penned in a manner that thematically wove written history into a parable that (as parables are designed to do) mirrored the essence of a reality it compared itself to more than it described. The essence of parables is found by way of comparison. For instance, Genesis 3:24 indicates that Adam was driven out of the east of Eden. The eastern river is the Tigris (meaning "Light, Swift") and the western river is the Euphrates (meaning "Fruitful"). Man was commanded to be fruitful, man departed from God's command, so man was driven east away from the Euphrates or "Fruitful" river. The situation of four rivers bearing procreative names is a comparison to the situation of human fecundity which, in the "Creation" story, is the reflection of a command; in this *literary* way, entities were *spoken* into existence.

In the laudable book, *Ancestor of The West*, the origin of writing is described in this way:

> Artists were not only accustomed to projecting and concretely fixing images, to composing small tableaux intended, I won't say to explain, but at least to suggest something in the realm of feelings rather than that of clear vision; but they acquired mastery over drawing, learning to plan out and sketch things in a few strokes.... Writing was born the day when someone... understood systematically using a given number of sketches in a design that was uniform enough to be recognizable everywhere, one could, like artists, not only give birth to emotion, evoke a state of mind, but also transmit a message in plain language. The most ancient documents employing this writing, small clay tablets covered with pictograms... indeed offer us a thousand different such sketches, all clearly traced, easy to distinguish from each other, and easy to recognize. This was no longer the fantasy and freedom of artists: it was by all evidence a fixed system (*Ancestor of The West*, Bottero, Herrenschmidt, Vernant, Fagan; p. 20-21).

The first fixed system of writing revolutionized the world by converting the world from *preliterate* to *literate and illiterate*. The literate brain is physically different (demonstrably, measurably, and provably) than the preliterate brain. For the purpose at hand, the literate brain uses human sight differently than the preliterate brain. A neuroplastic conversion that results from deliberate practice over time causes us to see the sounds of a spoken language rather than merely to hear the sounds. In this sense, our sight is partially converted to the faculty otherwise reserved for our ears and vice-versa. It is likely that this grafting of brain regions (observable in a manner different than by our methods) that was taken into account when it was written, "Let us make man in Our image, according to our likeness," which can also be read in Hebrew as "Let us convert man with Our Image, according to Our parable." An observation of such a conversion can be accomplished without high-tech tools simply in that a message forwarded by spoken language without writing is only external when it is told to another person who retains it internally, whereas writing standardizes the external transmission and allows the message to outlive and outdistance the people who receive it. Speech alone involves internal memory, but writing is external memory. Certainly, man was converted by writing itself, and certainly man was further converted by a specific message that was put in literary terms even though it did not begin that way. If one considers the same story first to have been recorded on film, then converted to DVD, and then finally to a computer file, one will easily realize that it is ridiculous to assert that the story on the computer file is unoriginal by the fact that it was first recorded prior to the invention of the computer. It is the format (not the message) that differs, of course. Once sight and sound are crossed, two obviously different objects distinguished by sight become unified mentally if they both bear the same sounds in their names.

Consider the word "flight." Watching a man run away is watching the "flight" of the man. Watching a bird fly in the sky with wings is watching the "flight" of the bird. After the invention of airplanes, watching a passenger jet move across the sky is watching the "flight" of the machine. Even in our own language, should we write down an account of a man's "flight" in the year 2014 that is to be read 6,000 years later, the time-period of that word indicating a running man and the time-period indicating a flying machine would appear relatively close together, and this closeness is fertile ground for serious interpretive error. The problem is further exacerbated when a different language system 6,000 years from now attempts to decipher the same message, for that different language almost certainly will not connect a running man to a flying bird and then to the essential hybrid of the two in the case of the passenger jet. Seeing the word "flight" demands interpretive energy that is reliant on contextual correctness. The brain that uses this one word to talk about human and bird locomotion prior to the invention of airplanes easily views human swiftness in light of birds instead of, say, a cheetah. The brain that uses one word to talk about human and cheetah locomotion, but distinguishes both from the flight of birds, will not immediately see a bird in his mind while seeing a running person with his eyes. The mental model of the world a person has within his skull depends largely on the language he wields. Over a long enough span of time, specific description simply does not work well. As an example, the extinct thylacine looks to us like a species of dog when, in fact, it was a marsupial related to the kangaroo and koala. Koalas are commonly compared to bears. It can be seen here that to describe a thylacine, one could use descriptions of dogs, kangaroos, koalas, and bears and quickly realize that a dog looks nothing like a bear. The description does not work over a long enough period of time.

To recall fixed points along the zodiac with pictures of animals whose names are bound to a specific language system in a given time ingeniously allows for a permanence the zoological world on earth cannot provide on account of its gradual transformation; all one has to do is recall the exact same point on the zodiac in whatever language system he has and tether it to the language system utilized in a particular document and he will be able to establish a chronology that is fixed within a much larger scope of time. Since The Precession of The Equinoxes uses the North Ecliptic Pole as the axis for the cyclic motion of the North Celestial Pole, one can function within roughly 26,000 years; next, one can take into account the age of writing itself relative to whenever he finds himself; then, one can take into account the document he reads in its original language; finally, one can place himself back into his own time while reading the document in translation and construct a straight line back to whenever and wherever his purposes suit him within roughly 26,000 years. The deep time involved repeats itself 26,000 years forward or backward from a given point on the zodiac. Such time is not properly "historical" since "history" is the story of literate people. When accounting for literate people, one must account for the history of writing itself, not the history of time. Genesis describes the history of time through the lens of the history of writing, and it uses specific constellation pictographs to merge the world that then was with the world of the date of a particular literary composition. The animals' names and pictographs may change, but the points on the zodiac do not. What one person called a "lion" might be what another, in a different language, time, and place called a "fliblltyflop," but the point of time on the 26,000-year circuit is fixed. In this way of recording a message for posterity, one could use animal emblems as a method of establishing a fixed chronology that functions as a relatively time-sensitive key to unlocking a frame of reference for a message in one time to communicate to a later time about a meaning that predates the *written* record of time itself.

Even though writing was "born" in a specific time and place, it should be kept in mind that for "...the Mesopotamians the name was the object being designated, the vocalized thing when the name was uttered and the written thing when it was written. The person who wrote... while he formed the characters that represented and reproduced objects, thus made and produced those objects themselves" (*Ancestor of The West*; p.44). In the original sense of "writing" that the Mesopotamians themselves invented, writing was creating. The Hebrew "create" has been but partially remembered without its original frame of reference. The Hebrew word "created," as in the statement, "In the beginning, God created the Heavens and the Earth," primarily has God as its subject throughout the Hebrew Bible (see Joshua 17:15). God "creates," that is, "authors." Since both the Hebrew "Old Testament" and the Greek "New Testament" assert that God is only good, the truth of "create" meaning "author" or "write about" is resounding when one examines Isaiah 45:7: "I [God] form the light and *create* darkness. I bring prosperity and *create* evil; I, the Lord, do all these things." It can be seen here that God is the Biographer of good and evil, and the good flows from Him:

> "And I saw the dead, small and great, standing before God, and BOOKS were opened. And another BOOK was opened, which is the BOOK OF LIFE. And the dead were **judged** according to their works, by the things which were WRITTEN IN THE BOOKS" (Revelation 20:12).

> "For God will bring every work into **judgment**, including every secret thing, whether good or evil" (Ecclesiastes 12:14).

A similitude in name was a true similitude since the name of someone or something was that very person or thing to the ancient Mesopotamians. This model, it would seem, was used by Scripture to discuss the deeds of people upon the earth since writing itself was made upon soil or clay. Writing was understood to produce the subject of the writing; in this way, reading allowed a continual present in the mind of the reader. The continual present provided by a story is what we today might consider in the light of an eternal message. In other words, an analogue clock is just that: an analogy. The 12 hands on the clock represent the 12 zodiacal constellations of antiquity, but the 12 markers are not the regions in space themselves. To think, however, in an ancient Mesopotamian conception of writing, then the graphic representation of the 12 hands of the clock — if tethered to a spoken language — would be a reproduction of the heavens on clay that could be spoken into existence any time the document was read. By describing "Eden" or Mesopotamia as the scene of the first duel between man and Satan, the characters of the story would necessarily be spoken into creation (i.e. through the graphically indicated spoken word of writing) within the mind of the reader and cause a mental convergence of earth and heaven that resulted in the point of a cognitive continual present, and a history that was both virtual and real simultaneously. It is for this reason, it would seem, that every Bible story is, essentially, the same even though the various Books were written at different times, in different places, and in different languages. The Bible takes into account the gradual shift of language and perception by beginning its narrative time uniformly even though this narrative time actually merges multiple real times; this merger maintains throughout all the Books whose languages shift throughout their respective histories. For instance, the Hebrew of Ecclesiastes is grammatically different than the Hebrew of Genesis, and the Chaldee of Daniel is not Hebrew at all; though a uniform message binds them, their individual linguistic features are not uniform. Likewise, the various constellation pictographs along the zodiac differ in shape and size; though a uniform circuit binds them, their individual physical depictions are not uniform.

The source of the Biblical accounts is the Eden story. As each Book was subsequently produced in time, it remained tethered to a single, cyclic story: "Eden" or Fertility. Similarly, as each zodiacal constellation subsequently holds the Vernal Equinox, it remains tethered to the single, cyclic zodiac. The creation of writing itself was the creation of taking an audible entity (spoken language) and converting into a visible entity (graphic markings), and this fact demonstrates why the ancients viewed writing as the pathway to the invisible. The visual past becomes the invisible future. The audible past was invisible because audibility was not visible at all. By crossing the audible past with the visible past through a presently visible technology, namely writing, writing itself partook of a type of timelessness that relied upon a skillset to view and to hear the past. In this light, the idea of an invisible God Who speaks in a continual present, eternity, is not hard to grasp. Writing was understood as the visible pathway to hearing the otherwise invisible past for an undisclosed present and, therefore, the future. Writing on a durable surface is a type of eternity within time. Fired clay has proven itself as the world's most durable writing surface, and the use of fired clay as such was the invention of the ancient dwellers of Mesopotamia who were used as the model for the first recorded humans in a story that concerns itself with "wisdom." The first recorded humans and the first recording humans were merged literarily in Genesis by uniting real time with narrated time.

The ancient Mesopotamians believed that writing itself involved the invisible in that it was capable of capturing things themselves that would be otherwise outside of our immediate experience. It is such thinking that allows for a facile transition into understanding writing as a medium for divine communication, communication able to transcend time and space far beyond any individual human lifespan. Again, sound alone is audible, not visible; however, the invention of writing caused sound to be "heard" visually, and thus comprehended. Someone from centuries or millennia ago can still be "heard" through our eyes insofar as reading is concerned. As long as one connected flesh to clay in his mind, then a word could become flesh through writing on clay. A voice could be seen — the invisible became visible with respect to writing. When the Mesopotamians used clay to encapsulate writing, the clay was the visible medium of the formerly invisible voice; the visible earth received invisible breath; the soil became literally inspired in that it received the message formerly carried only upon the *wind, the breath, the spirit (all of which are the same word in Hebrew and Greek respectively)*. By understanding this parlance and thus model of thinking, the physical production of writing allowed an invisible spirit from a once visible person to be received into a clay vessel that, by being read, would transmit that very spirit into a new person; this process would be from person, to clay, to person whereby one person essentially lived within another subsequent to himself in a new, yet at the same time original, form. It is easy here to understand how writing and gestational fertility were understood as being related.

Again, the Hebrew word translated "create" is literally from the root ברא *to carve out, to shape out,* and connotes birth (as its passive form suggests). The word בשר can mean, ***good tidings, flesh, Gospel*** *(as Luke 4:18-19 translates Isaiah 61:1-2),* and also ***successful birth*** (Jeremiah 20:15). It is this "flesh" that is used to describe humanity and its capability of reproduction in Genesis 2:24, and its definition is provided in the Greek of Luke 2:10 regarding the birth of "The Son of Man," i.e. The Son of Adam, "The Word" Who "became flesh and dwelt among us" (John 1:14). We must recall that, through his reading of and obedience to the Scriptures, the Apostle Paul called his students in The Word "My little children, for whom I labor in birth again until Christ is formed in you" (Galatians 4:19). Writing makes speech (that was once only audible and therefore invisible) able to be seen over great distances of time and space. It is the illustration of writing itself that the Bible uses to describe God's activity in humanity. God's activity in humanity is the reality Scripture describes through the lens of writing itself, and so humanity and writing are melded together in Scripture's explanation of deeds that, at first, can seem bizarre when, in fact, the communication of those deeds is simply foreign to our current conventions.

Conventionally, we today who read complete alphabetic writing can forget (or even not realize) that we read a system that accounts for all of the spoken components of our language. Not all alphabets do so, and the first alphabet did not. The first writing was not even alphabetic. The most important point here is that accounting for all the spoken components of a language means accounting for vowels also, and vowels are breaths. A writing system that does not account for vowels is as a body without a spirit, a matrix without the visible additive that allows the complete graphic production of the message it intends to convey. Writing without vowels is writing that is only partially seen and only partially heard; consonantal writing is a graphic mnemonic aid to a message intended already to be held within the mind. Since writing partook of the invisible world, and since the first alphabetic writing did not (like Hebrew) graphically represent the vowels of the language it made visible, it was the wind, breath, or spirit that was invisible, i.e. it was the correct vowelization of the message that was invisible. The man capable of correctly supplying the vowels of consonantal writing contained the invisible wind/breath/spirit within himself literally. This inspiration required memory, and the ancient Mesopotamians viewed the memory of a person as the person's ghost. The memory of a person, when written down, was therefore a reformation of that person whereby his works were sealed for eternity. It is probably for this reason that Adam is called זכר (from the root "to remember") that is usually translated as *male* (Genesis 1:27). God *"creating"* the *"male"* is literally God *writing about the memory of Adam*. Consider the words of Diodorous Siculus:

> What man, indeed, could compose a worthy laudation of the knowledge of letters? For it is by such knowledge alone that the dead are carried in the memory of the living and that men widely separated in space hold converse through written communication with those who are at the furthest distance from them, as if they were at their side; and in the case of covenants in time of war between states or kings the firmest guarantee that such agreements will abide is provided by the unmistakable character of writing. Indeed, speaking generally, it is writing alone which preserves the cleverest sayings of men of wisdom and the oracles of the gods, as well as philosophy and all knowledge, and is constantly handing them down to succeeding generations from the ages to come. Consequently, while it is true that nature is the cause of life, the cause of the good life is the education which is based upon reading and writing," (*Library of History*, Book XII).

The ability to make copies of writing from a former piece of writing was, then, procreative. The Hebrew word for "male" used to describe Adam in Genesis 1 is from the root "to remember," and since Adam was made of clay, one can see here the writing of Adam's Father onto the clay He prepared for His son.

The life of Adam was the life of the first writing: Mesopotamian pictographs. The life of Adam was, essentially, the life of concrete pictures utilized to recall the sounds of spoken language. The virtual constellation pictures remembered along with the visible points in the sky, the domain of the winds/spirits/breaths/vowels, can be understood easily as the heavenly territory of the inspired book, i.e. the constellation pictographs are as the correct vowels required to comprehend the incomplete (or vowel-less) Hebrew of the Bible. The constellation pictographs were derived from clay pictographs, and this literary juncture of writing and time was utilized as the chronology of Genesis, it would seem, for the purpose of uniting the consonantal message to the correct vowelization, breath, or spirit necessary to perceive the intended message. Revelation 4 and Ezekiel 1 & 11 describe the cherubs in terms of the constellation pictures that held the four corners of the heavens (the equinoxes and solstices) of about 2,800 B.C., about when Scripture states Adam died (literarily). Unlike the remainder of Scripture following the expulsion from Eden, the Eden account discusses its characters not with elaborate descriptions but in specific pictures: "The Man, "The Woman," "The Serpent," "The Tree," "The Cherubs," etc., as if the reader already knows who these entities are; yet, the story of Eden is written in an alphabetic system that does not write its vowels, and it is for this reason that the specific characters of, "The Man," "The Woman," "The Serpent," etc. are the same in each Bible book but are qualified by more elaborate descriptions. Consider: Christ is called "The Man" in John 19:5 as well as "Adam" in 1 Corinthians 15:45; the Hebrew word "woman" is the same word as "wife," and Christ's followers are called His "bride" in Revelation 22:17; Christ's antagonists are called a "brood of vipers" in Matthew 12:34, etc. Likewise, in the "Old Testament," God is called a "man" in Genesis 18:2; God's followers are referred to as his collective bride in Jeremiah 2:2; and God's antagonist is called a "Serpent" in Genesis 3:1, etc. The Eden story is the model of the remaining stories, and it is told in a system that lacks graphic vowels, i.e. a system that lacks breath. Should one read the vowels correctly, then one unites the matrix of the Text with the breath essential to animate it... and, in this way, a person can speak into existence what preceded him as though adding seed to the ground or adding seed to the womb or adding breath to a clay body... for in this way one displays the union of man and God described in Genesis 2:7 where God "breathed into his nostrils the breath of life"... thus, in this way, every reader is part of Adam, and every reader is linked to God in some way through His Word. It is this very Word that "The Serpent" used to concentrate his attack on "The Woman" in the Eden story, for the woman herself being called "Adam" (Genesis 5:2) received the "breath of life" or the understanding and, having been "deceived and fell into transgression" (1 Timothy 2:14), lost her life, her understanding, her breath, and the proper way to read the Text. The reader, being "The Woman" and "Adam," should note that Adam's death is described in Genesis 5:5, but, specifically "The Woman's" death is not: "But even if our gospel is veiled, it is veiled to those who are perishing" (2 Corinthians 4:3). "The Woman" is still dying, so to speak.

Vowels are breaths. Spoken vowels are audible breaths and written vowels are visual breaths. Alphabetic writing was invented roughly 4,000 years ago in Egypt, but the type of alphabet used there (as is the case with Biblical Hebrew) was consonantal and did not represent vowels. We can call a consonantal alphabet "incomplete" with respect to the fact that it does not include all the sounds of a spoken language. Specifically, consonantal alphabets do not represent breath. The breathing necessary to read consonantal writing aloud must directly follow the perception of what is only being cued mnemonically by the consonants. The articulation of what is written is only capable of being heard audibly by first knowing what the correct vowels are and then including them with the visual consonants. A correct reading of consonantal writing is not so much evidence of being able to articulate what is on the graphic medium as it is perceiving beforehand what the graphic medium was devised to reflect. Reading the words of a "complete" alphabetic writing system (1) does not demand understanding content in order to articulate the actual sounds being represented graphically and (2) moves the reader in a single direction only over time which also progresses in a single direction only. For example, the meaning of the letters "NDNGR" can be guessed at but not in a single direction; each letter must be observed in connection to what follows and/or precedes in order for contextual perception to reveal what these letters were written (without breath) to recall. These letters could mean "eNDaNGeR" or "No DaNGeR," which have essentially opposite meanings. Within an entire sentence or even text, the same principle applies on increasingly larger levels so that the reader who first encounters the written message must keep in mind what follows and/or precedes a given letter, word, and sentence in order to understand the correct meaning of the stream of letters whereas the reader who already has the message committed to memory simply receives his cue from "NDNGR" and exhibits his perception by evincing it with his breath, his spirit, that is, his vowels. Complete alphabetic messages can be read aloud correctly without the requirement of any perception of the message's content whereas incomplete alphabetic messages only can be read aloud correctly by the perception of the message's content. The contemplation necessary to read complete alphabetic messages aloud moves only in the same direction as time whereas the contemplation necessary to read incomplete alphabetic messages moves as far backward as it does forward simultaneously. The interpretation of "NDNGR" could be fatal to one reader but not to another based solely on the perceived content and not on the letters themselves; it is in this sense that the letters can kill but the correct breath gives life to the meaning of the message (reconsider here 2 Corinthians 3:6: "...for the letter kills, but the Spirit gives life...."); it is in this sense that correct inspiration causes correct comprehension. A significant contribution of incomplete alphabetic systems is that they mingle reading with comprehension intrinsically whereas complete alphabetic systems do not necessarily. It is the potential definitions of the Hebrew word "LHSCL" that the reader must choose between as though she were between two trees, for these letters originally spelled both "to make one wise" and "to suffer abortion"; the former choice is the uniform translation of both "Judaism" and "Christianity," in spite of the fact that Ecclesiastes 7:12 states plainly that "wisdom gives life" while Genesis states plainly that the forbidden tree gave death, or, as James says, "sin... gives birth to death" (James 1:15). The invisible became visible through writing. To one system of writing, and therefore one system of thought, one reader sees a tree while another reader sees a man. For example, Exodus 3 states that the "Messenger of the Lord appeared to him in flames of fire from within a thorny bush," but proceeds to state how Moses was awe-struck by the fact that the bush was not burned and not that he was awe-struck that the angel of the Lord was not only in the thorns but within the very fire at which Moses marveled. It is only after being taught by God that Moses states in Deuteronomy 33:16 that this Messenger "dwelt in the burning bush"; it is with such a reference that Christ, "The Word" (who dwelt in the midst of thorns and in the midst of a tree), described resurrection:

> "The people of this age marry and are given in marriage. But those who are considered worthy of taking part in the age to come and in the resurrection from the dead will neither marry nor be given in marriage, and they can no longer die; for they

are like the angels. They are God's children, since they are children of the resurrection. BUT IN THE ACCOUNT OF THE BURNING BUSH, EVEN MOSES SHOWED THAT THE DEAD RISE, for he calls the Lord 'the God of Abraham, and the God of Isaac, and the God of Jacob.' He is not the God of the dead, but of the living, for to him all are alive." Some of the teachers of the law responded, 'Well said, teacher!' And no one dared to ask him any more questions" (Luke 20:27-40).

In a manner of speaking, Mesopotamian clay, three-dimensional writing was considered to be alive. Ancient tablets state how people "listened to the tablet" and discuss the "mouth of the tablet." When a tablet was made void, it was said to be "killed," but when a tablet was renewed it was said to be "brought back to life." The personification of writing is understood easily if one considers the function of a stop sign to have been held formerly by a police officer. A written governmental warning is, essentially, the same as the government that (and the governor who) issued the warning.

Again, the Mesopotamians understood that the invisible became visible through the art of writing since it cognitively produced the objects the writing portrayed. The message of writing was thought to be encoded and therefore discernable only to those skilled in its system, its way of viewing the subject it contained. Writing, therefore, contained the invisible, and the person reading the writing also contained the invisible within himself. Writing could easily be made labyrinthine (i.e. serpentine) in the mind by wordplay that necessitated foreknowledge to solve the graphic puzzle that gradually constructed the intended, visible/audible picture. Sound and sight materialized into the singular world of a subsequent mind through writing, and consonantal writing allowed for a precise model for literal *divine inspiration* or *the ability to articulate the holy message through the union of visible consonants and invisible vowels.* Recall that the Hebrew word בשר can mean *flesh, good tidings, Gospel,* and also *successful* **birth** and that the Hebrew word translated "create" is literally from the root ברא *to carve out, to shape out,* and connotes **birth** (as its passive form suggests). To "create the flesh" is the same as "to write the Gospel" in Hebrew. The ability to articulate the correct vowels of Hebrew is the subject of the tension between the "New Testament's" Greek renderings of "The Old Testament" since these differ from the Septuagint, which was the Second Temple's official text in the time of Christ, "The Word." The Book of Hebrews consents to the Septuagint, since it speaks to the official establishment of the Second Temple through the medium of its text while also speaking to followers of Christ who certainly rendered the Hebrew Scriptures differently. The point is that the Hebrew "create" indicates a message contained in writing and in birth just as the Hebrew "flesh" indicates the Gospel and birth. Both the Hebrew "creation" and "flesh" are merged to describe Christ and Adam since some of the oldest writing states that when a tablet was made void, it was said to be "killed," but when a tablet was renewed it was said to be "brought back to life."

> "You are our EPISTLE WRITTEN IN OUR HEARTS, known and read by all men; clearly you are an EPISTLE OF CHRIST, ministered by us, written not with ink but BY THE SPIRIT OF THE LIVING GOD, not on tablets of stone but on TABLETS OF FLESH, THAT IS, OF THE HEART," (2 Corinthians 3:2-3).

The person, like the Book, was inspired and alive when unified with the original intention recalled by the frame that anticipated the breath, so to speak. The ancient inventors of writing thought that their gods resided in the images or "statues for worship" that were placed in temples, but the readers and followers of Scripture were understood to be the very temples that The Image of God, Christ, The Word resided within. The idea of personifying writing can be easily understood in the case of a stop sign: the sign takes the place of the person who formerly performed the function of the sign. Furthermore, to write about a person is to speak to the future about a person in the past, and a future far enough removed from the writer and the person serving as his subject will experience a glimpse of that person, according to the author, in the form of writing; thus, in this sense, the writing and the person are as one (through the lens of writing itself and the author himself who, in this sense, are as one also).

The word תחבולה *wise counsel* comes from the root חבל *to twist, to bind*, and this root produces the word חבל *birth pangs*. The word מליץ *translator, interpreter* is from the root לוץ *to turn, to twist, to speak obscurely*. The idea of "twisting" could call to mind the visual writing of birthing and the translation of language. In this sense, flesh was spoken into existence. The proper interpretation of the Hebrew original, which lacked vowels, was the proper breath or spirit or the proper wise counsel. Again, quite literally, the words, " נעשה אדם בצלמנו כדמותנו *Let Us make man in Our image according to Our likeness*" could just as well be translated, " כדמותנו נעשה אדם בצלמנו *Let Us convert man with Our image according to Our parable*." Christ is consistently depicted as speaking in parables in the Greek Scriptures of the "New Testament." Four centuries before Christ, in Greek, the "...prohibition of individual speech and the renunciation of the empire in the language are symbolized in the exclusion of the aspirated *h* from the writing system: the writing down of the laws in 403 [B.C.] pushed both the individual and the empire out of the field of action of the new democracy" (*Ancestor of The West*, p. 143). The official Roman court language in Judea, in the time of Christ, was Greek, and it is from this Greek where the counsel or *ecclesia* (translated "church") finds its origin. The Greeks called the aspirated *h* the *pneuma*, or what the English "New Testament" translates as *wind, breath, or spirit*. Neatly done, the "New Testament" uses a writing system whose history ceased writing with "the spirit" (the aspirated "h") as a way to describe and translate the Hebrew Scriptures that did not represent vowels and thus required "the spirit" and The Spirit to interpret the obscure wise counsel properly through its parabolic lens of writing itself. In short, the Greek of the "New Testament" took into account the history of a writing system that lost its written "spirit" or "breath" in order to give "breath" or vowels to the Hebrew Scriptures that did not graphically represent "spirit" or "breath," i.e. vowels, and it is the Hebrew Scriptures that took into account the first writing that was shaped into clay to describe the first human made animate by "the breath of life" of The Living God, the invisible God Who became flesh.

Unlike alphabets that depict vowels, the Hebrew alphabet is consonantal, which means that reading is only accomplished by beholding each letter in the context of what surrounds it. In other words, one has to go backward to see forward and forward to see backward... and doing this correctly demonstrates the original inspiration in mind when its shadow or unanimated body (i.e. its letters) was put down in consonantal writing. By the function of a consonantal alphabetic system (particularly one like Hebrew that grammatically does not account for time), eternity, that is, a continual present, is easy to imagine. It is this imagination that was used to describe Eden, a literal place of origin in a literal time that existed prior to the ability to record it chronologically, that is told through a virtual lens in order to imprint a real message to real minds by way of a virtual picture that was recorded chronologically in a time after its subject but ever present to its reader. Scripture uses language such as "breath of life," "spirit," "resurrection," and the like to describe the physical world fixed and encapsulated within its words. This language is not physically descriptive simply of a world put down in literature, but it is literarily descriptive of a world put down on earth. It was Mesopotamian clay that received "the breath of life" that could be "killed" and "brought back to life." It is such terminology that Scripture uses in order to relay a message that is more real than for that which it has been given credit. It can be seen, therefore, why saved humanity is said to be in the "Book of Life" (Philippians 4:3), so to speak.

According to Charpin's masterful book, *Reading and Writing in Babylon*, Mesopotamian writing was invented in the late Fourth Millennium B.C. and became extinct in the First Century A.D. Currently, the last datable cuneiform text is from about 75 A.D. (Charpin, p.7). Mesopotamian writing first appeared as a complete system from the beginning and eventually developed into cuneiform. Alphabetic writing that only represented consonants graphically (like Hebrew) followed cuneiform chronologically. Alphabetic writing that represented all the sounds of spoken language (like Greek) followed consonantal writing chronologically. Let us, at this point, narrow our scope to cuneiform and alphabetic writing. Cuneiform emerged at the time that the Hebrew Bible states that Adam died, which we have already noted was the time when the constellation pictures were first devised. The hybrid of cuneiform and alphabetic writing emerged at the time that the Hebrew Bible states that Moses wrote. The Greek "New Testament" states that "death reigned from Adam to Moses" (Romans 5:14). It would seem that Moses remembered the original story, and he revitalized it through his writing so that the death of Adam was reversed.

The cuneiform artificers saw, in the invention of alphabetic systems, their eventual demise. The facility and rapidity with which alphabetic writing could be learned and utilized forced a situation where the cuneiform men of old knew that the more recent technology would overcome the existent one. Reactively, instead of simplifying their writing even further, they intentionally complicated it in order to obscure information and secure a position for themselves that claimed they possessed knowledge that predated The Flood. The particular method of obscuration and complication they chose was the deliberate addition of more values to the signs of their written language in order to play upon potential alternate readings; thus, the cuneiform artificers knew what their own texts said by way of remembrance, while subsequent alphabetic readers had to guess and therefore were reliant upon their older literary brothers, so to speak. In essence, the history of cuneiform displays a situation where the elder persecuted the younger he would eventually serve, which is a consistent theme throughout the Bible. Cuneiform, at first, did retain knowledge from the preliterate world, but only through the lens of the pictographically literate world that preceded cuneiform by about a thousand years. The only pictographs that remained for *all* to see were those imagined in the stars (the constellation pictures), and it appears that the cuneiform scholars could innovate celestially in their interpretations without altering the star-pictures, which is similar to adding more values to the signs of their written language. The inventors of Mesopotamian pictographic writing, not cuneiform, were from the preliterate world and became hybrids of preliteracy and literacy themselves; the cuneiform artificers were their younger brothers, for they represented the preliterate world of their older brothers to a new type of man who looked to the future also by way of his invention: the alphabet. If one accounts for the "Creation" or "Authorship" story of Eden in Hebrew, then it is clear that "The Serpent" is as the cuneiform man who guards a celestial knowledge (Ezekiel 28:13-19) on account of the fact that cuneiform emerged near the time of the development of the constellation pictures and the death of pictographic writing that was but remembered in the "signs" of celestial cartography. Genesis 3 first mentions the Cherubs as if the reader already knows their identity, but the description of the Cherubs in Ezekiel makes it obvious that their faces are those of the equinoxes and solstices as indicated by the constellation pictures during the time that (1) pictographic writing died and was translated to star-maps and (2) cuneiform writing displaced pictographic writing. "The Serpent" is represented at the Autumnal Equinox, along the autumnal colure, and at the North Celestial Pole during this time. The Bible seems to speak of "The Serpent" in terms of a wise man who knows the stars (the constellation pictographs; see Revelation 12) and a scholar who is adept at word-play (cuneiform; see Genesis 3) because both the celestial pictographs and cuneiform emerged at the death of pictographic writing or Adam, "the man of dust." In other words, Adam's creation and demise were described in such terms... terms that would be able to be discerned in the distant future.... "The Serpent" is as the cuneiform scholar and astrologer who knows he is going to be ruled over by the alphabetic man and the astronomer being written about in the alphabetic system of Biblical Hebrew that describes things in "heavenly" or celestial terms. It would seem that these reasons are why "The Serpent" carries out his warfare in the Bible through the deliberate use of Hebrew words that have more than one possible meaning — an aspect of the Text completely lost in translation. It would also seem that these reasons are why "The Serpent's" military defeat is described in terms of the constellation *pictures* (when they were first devised) in Genesis 3:14-15 and Revelation 12. Adam is as the pictographic man who rose after death to become the celestial man. The Serpent who twists words is as the shifty cuneiform man who attempted to hide the meaning of the constellations from those in the future but was thwarted by men like Daniel. Moses is as the hybrid of cuneiform and the consonantal alphabet, a descendant of Mesopotamian Abraham and of royal Egypt. The Bible uses the history of writing as a parable for the history of humanity.

When one looks at something of a tangible reality, one beholds it in a certain frame of reference that understands the reality in a way but not necessarily in all ways or even the best way. Accordingly, we have examined previously that one people-group, on account of language, perceived color differently than another group. Let us here consider the word "reading." When we discuss "reading," we often specifically mean the action that allows you to receive the words you are currently beholding, and we often generally mean the act of receiving and interpreting meaning in, say, a facial expression, a marker, a pattern, etc. If, however, we narrow our frame of reference to *reading* by discussing *a system of graphic markings that represent the words of a spoken language system*, then we can understand two systems: (1) a spoken language and (2) graphic markings that represent the spoken language. It can be seen here that there are two systems, one that functions as a mirror of the other: (1) a system that is audible and (2) a system that is visible (based on the audible system). *Reading*, within the frame of reference provided here, is a connection of two different senses working in unison. This system only dates back to about 3,700 B.C. It should be taken into account that *reading* about the origins of man involves a *technology* that postdates the origins of man: *a system of graphic markings that represent the words of a spoken language system*, i.e. *writing*.

The term "neuroplasticity" refers to the brain's ability to change over time. Neuroplasticity is a proven fact that was, in former times, understood differently through outputs like propensity and habit. The brain can be compared to a tree that either can grow and proliferate into fertility or wither into a skeletal winter of fruitlessness, depending on to what it is applied over time. The brain can remap its connections when learning new things; as a result, new maps are created while old maps are altered. The brain allows one increasing ease in the repetition of a given practice by structurally organizing itself to accommodate choices, circumstances, environments, and so forth. Stanislas Dehaene states in the book *Reading in The Brain: The New Science of How We Read*:

> Learning to read involves connecting two sets of brain regions
> that are already present in infancy: the object recognition
> system and the language circuit. Reading acquisition has
> three major phases: the pictorial state, a brief period where
> children 'photograph' a few words; the phonological stage,
> where they learn to decode graphemes into phonemes; and the
> orthographic stage, where word recognition becomes fast and

> automatic. Brain imaging shows that several brain circuits are altered during this process, notably those of the left occipito-temporal letterbox area. Over several years, the neural activity evoked by written words increases, becomes selective, and converges onto the adult reading network (p. 195).

You are reading. To assume that man always utilized a system of graphic markings that represent the words of a spoken language system is only an assumption based on a literate frame of reference. Getting past the first "Week of Creation," so to speak, a basic assumption remains: the genealogies of Genesis claim that humanity is around 6,000 years old. On whatever side the reader here finds himself presently, I think I have proven sufficiently that Genesis does not date Time near 6,000 years, but it does look at time through the lens of the ability to record Time graphically in the terms of a spoken language, which is a technology that is around 6,000 years old. When the Hebrew Bible describes the first man in Eden, it is precisely identifying, **for a distant future**, the location and date of the emergence of literate humanity within the scope of the Biblical narrative. Moses lived significantly after the creation of writing. Moses described the first Edenic man in terms of the first Mesopotamian writing, and this point can be tested, proven, and reproduced with great clarity and ease.

We must acknowledge again that the cuneiform tablets of ancient Mesopotamia were not discovered and utilized from roughly the late First Century A.D. until the 19th Century A.D.—which is a bubble or timeframe that contains within it nearly the whole of Judeo-Christian Theology. That is, the various Judeo-Christian theological disciplines had no material access to Mesopotamia apart from what the Western Classical world wrote with ink; therefore, they could not have known the modes of speech and methods of the artificers of three-dimensional clay words who lived between the Tigris and Euphrates. Today, however, we can expand our chronological frame of reference to include the knowledge of the first Mesopotamian writing and grasp what the Bible did to preserve a world we would have lost otherwise. Traditionally, the ancient Mesopotamians, according to one Berossos in the early Third Century B.C., conceived of the origin of writing as something that "descended from" heaven and was given to humanity who was "without discipline and order, just like animals." According to the epic of Enmerkar and the Lord of Aratta, writing was a human invention brought about through a series of challenges that took the form of riddles too complex to be transmitted orally "because the messenger's mouth was too heavy, and he could not repeat it" (*Reading and Writing in Babylon*, Charpin). A "heavy" mouth can here be comprehended as one endowed with a message too complicated to be transmitted without the handiness of external memory, i.e. writing.

The ancient Mesopotamians considered all disciplines to be "wisdom," as opposed to the various categories of our current, Western specialization. The term "the one gifted with ear" meant "the one gifted with wisdom" and was identical to the term "beloved child." "Wisdom" was linked to the "ear," and Mesopotamian writing used expressions that described people who "listened" to the tablet. The "mouth" of the tablet was the functional equivalent of the "word" of the tablet; thus, clay (or metal or stone) writing, three-dimensional writing, was personified and considered to be alive, in a manner of speaking; this can be seen readily in that the writing medium froze a living man's word for a duration held longer than oral communication alone permitted. Essentially, words lived on within the tablet, and, as such, when a tablet was made void, it was said to be "killed," but when a tablet was renewed it was said to be "brought back to life." Oaths, covenants, contracts, etc. were recorded on tablets, and the expression "to swear an oath" was "to eat an oath." The act of "washing" the mouth of divine statues was understood as "opening" the mouth of the statue; therefore, washing the eyes could mean opening the eyes; likewise, the term "blind men" signified "garden workers." A woman who "went away naked" could be understood as a woman who was sent away without her dowry or property. The first man is called "Adam," which is, in Hebrew, "Red Ground," a term used by the Egyptians to discuss sterile ground, the very soil that the Mesopotamians used for writing. Moses, raised in Egypt, wrote about man's origins in Eden or the Mesopotamia of the patriarch Abram. "Adam" is here compared to a clay writing tablet, a man of dust (Genesis 2:7; 1 Corinthians 15:47). Adam, the "man of dust" (Genesis 2:7), turned away from God, and his very title foreshadows his rebellion; consider Jeremiah 17:13: "O Lord, the hope of Israel, all who forsake You shall be *ashamed* [literally: *dried up*]. Those who depart from Me shall be WRITTEN IN THE EARTH, because they have forsaken the LORD, *The Fountain of Living Waters*." If we understand Adam in the context of a tablet, then he was God's "beloved son" who was carved out (i.e. "created," that is, "authored" or "written about") and gifted with wisdom by receiving the "breath of The Almighty" (i.e. "words on clay," that is, "life," or "wisdom") in order to be born; he returned to dust after he was "killed" and was "brought back to life" (so to speak) when he as excavated, reread, and remembered (ultimately in the "signs" of celestial cartography). The manner in which clay writing was conceived serves as the model for life, death, and resurrection... for however life and death can be related with scientifically descriptive words and however "resurrection" occurs is one matter, while the literary parallels involved are another matter that is related but distinct. Literarily, human life was understood as dust receiving breath (clay receiving words), death was understood as dust being scraped or washed anew to the extent that the words were erased, and resurrection was understood in terms of the first writing (that was pictographic) being used for celestially cartographic purposes while this same system disappeared from earthly usage (i.e. the original "life" in clay being transferred to the winds of the night sky). Knowledge of the night sky was a mark of wisdom itself (Esther 1:13).

The story of the first man revolves around the acquisition of "wisdom" and makes Adam, the man of dust, the clay writing tablet, a direct "creation" of God (1:27). The Hebrew word translated "create" is literally from the root ברא *to carve out, to shape out,* and connotes birth (as its passive form suggests). "Adam" can be seen here as the result of "carving out," which makes sense within the frame of reference that recognizes clay being "carved" for the purpose of writing since "carving" does not occur with ink. Carving does occur with statues, but, more specifically for the particular purpose at hand, the very fact that "wisdom" is related to "dust" and "carving" is certainly a reference to the most common writing material within the very location in which the story is set: Mesopotamia. Since "wisdom" was contained in clay writing, we can see how the term "the one gifted with ear" meant "the one gifted with wisdom" and was identical to the term "beloved child" in that Adam was the direct offspring of God Who "created" or "carved out" His Word: "Adam, the son of God" (Luke 3:38). Genesis 2:6-7 describes water covering the ground in connection with the fashioning of the man of dust, for water mixed with such dust is the origin of clay utilized for writing that was also kept in pottery made of the same substance. Genesis 2:7 states that God breathed "the breath of life" into "Adam," but Job 32:8 and 33:4 says "there is a spirit in man, and the **breath of The Almighty** GIVES HIM UNDERSTANDING," and "The Spirit of God has made me, and the **breath of The Almighty** GIVES ME LIFE." Job equates "understanding" with "life" by connecting them both to "The Breath of The Almighty" and "The Spirit of God," which is the very "breath" that gave "Adam" life. The "mouth" of the tablet was the functional equivalent of the "word" of the tablet. Clay writing was personified and considered to be alive, in a manner of speaking. Consider Job 33:6: "Truly I am as your spokesman before God; I also have been formed out of clay." The man Elihu describes himself as a book (which might explain his sudden appearance for consultation).

The story of the first man involves man's doom for rejecting God's word. "Adam," the man of clay or the writing tablet, estranged himself from God by making the word of God void in his own heart. Likewise, words were thought by the Mesopotamians to live on within a tablet; as such, when a tablet was made void, it was said to be "killed," but when a tablet was renewed it was said to be "brought back to life." Adam was "killed," but he committed suicide in that he deliberately ate of the forbidden tree (1 Timothy 2:14). Oaths, covenants, contracts, etc. were recorded on tablets, and the expression "to swear an oath" was "to eat an oath." Since "tree" and "counsel" can be spelled identically in Hebrew, and since "Torah" means "Counsel," it is now plain that Adam "ate" (covenanted) of or according to the forbidden "tree" (counsel, law). Adam thus swore an oath to the death with Death, and "killed" himself by breaking an oath to the death with Life; the reverse of this process would be being "brought back to life" by breaking a covenant with Death by "eating" (swearing) a covenant with Life. Consider the fact that "the two syllables of the Sumerian word for 'grapevine', GESHTIN, mean 'tree' and 'life'" (*The Babylonians*, Saggs). "Eating" from the "Tree of Life" would mean being in covenant with "The True Vine" (John 15:1) whereas swearing a covenant with the opposite of the Tree of Life would mean "eating" from The False Vine, "The Serpent," so to speak. When a tablet was voided it was "killed," and when it was renewed it was "brought back to life"; "Adam" was driven in the direction of the rising, not the setting, sun (Genesis 3:24). The rising sun is called "the womb of the morning" (Psalm 110:3) in the very Psalm that discusses a priest whose *genealogy* is not recorded *in writing*: Melchizedek. It is worth noting here that, to a Roman (or, at least, Romanized) audience, Melchizedek could be viewed as a *novus homo* or *new man*, that is, a ruler who formerly had no recognized elite line from which he descended. It is in such a sense that Hebrews 7:1-16 seems to describe the Melchizedek of Genesis:

> "For this Melchizedek, king of Salem, priest of the Most High God, who met Abraham returning from the slaughter of the kings and blessed him, to whom also Abraham gave a tenth part of all, first being translated 'king of righteousness,' and then also king of Salem, meaning 'king of peace,' WITHOUT FATHER, WITHOUT MOTHER, WITHOUT GENEALOGY, having neither beginning of days nor end of life, but MADE LIKE THE SON OF GOD, remains a priest continually. Now consider how great this man was, to whom even the patriarch Abraham gave a tenth of the spoils. And indeed those who are of the sons of Levi, who receive the priesthood, have a commandment to receive tithes

from the people according to the law, that is, from their brethren, though they have come from the loins of Abraham; but
he whose GENEALOGY is not derived from them received tithes
from Abraham and blessed him who had the promises. Now beyond all contradiction the lesser is blessed by the better. Here
mortal men receive tithes, but there he receives them, of whom
it is witnessed that he lives. Even Levi, who receives tithes,
paid tithes through Abraham, so to speak, for he was still in
the loins of his father when Melchizedek met him. Therefore,
if perfection were through the Levitical priesthood (for under it
the people received the law), what further need was there that
another priest should rise according to the order of Melchizedek, and not be called according to the order of Aaron? For the
priesthood being changed, of necessity there is also a change
of the law. For He of whom these things are spoken belongs
to another tribe, FROM WHICH NO MAN HAS OFFICIATED AT THE
ALTAR. For it is evident that our Lord arose from Judah, of which
tribe MOSES SPOKE NOTHING CONCERNING PRIESTHOOD. And it
is yet far more evident if, in the likeness of Melchizedek, there
arises another priest who has come, not according to the law
of a fleshly commandment, but according to the power of an
endless life."

The fact that Genesis does not record Melchizedek's genealogy allows the
reader of Psalm 110 to understand a comparison: the lack of written genealogy is used here literarily to describe perpetuity (an earthly example of a
heavenly eternity) as is made apparent in Hebrews 7:1-16 above. It is the
absence of a written record that is used as a literary parallel for timelessness, and such a parallel only makes sense in a literate world. However
eternity was perceived in the preliterate world is another matter. Referring
to the man, Adam, and understanding "Adam" as humanity in general ac-
complishes the same task.

Again, *Adam*, the *writing tablet*, can be seen as the result of "carving out" or "shaping out," which makes sense within the frame of reference that recognizes clay being "carved" for the purpose of writing. Carving does occur with statues, and the ancient Mesopotamians did carve
writing onto their statues. The Hebrew word "image" recorded in Genesis
1:27 can also mean "statue." The act of "washing" the mouth of divine
statues was understood as "opening" the mouth of the statue; therefore,
washing the eyes could mean opening the eyes; likewise, the term "blind
men" signified "garden workers." Adam was a garden worker. Having
"eaten" of or "covenanted" with The Serpent, the "blind man" had his eyes

"washed" or "opened," to his own demise. The "opening," or rather goug-ing, of Adam's eyes would explain much as to why he attempted to hide from the omniscient God.

Humanity in covenant with God is referred to collectively as a *bride* in Scripture. Consider how Genesis 2:23 describes woman as "bone of my bones and flesh of my flesh," Jeremiah 2:2 describes the wandering Israel-ites as "betrothed" to God, and 2 Samuel 5:2 describes how "all the tribes" came to Israel and said to David, "we are your bone and your flesh." The description of sharing "bone and flesh" is a symbol of a covenant that is compared to a marriage. Humanity, "male and female," is called "Adam" collectively in Genesis 5:2, and this humanity (both male and female) is symbolically as a *bride* to the one with whom it is in covenant. Similarly, when Satan challenged by afflicting Job's *"bone and flesh"* (Job 2:5) it was immediately afterward that we read of Job's *wife* attempting to convince Job to curse God and die (Job 2:9). We might also consider the bride, *bone and flesh*, in terms of a *stylus and clay tablet*.

A woman who "went away naked" could be understood as a woman who was sent away without her dowry or property. Adam and his wife found themselves "naked" in Eden. Their nudity can be understood as the re-sult of exile on account of the "whoredom" of sin so commonly expressed in Scripture whereby their dowry and property were forfeited upon their departure from Eden (towards the rising sun). In Hebrew, though, "naked-ness" and "childlessness" are the same word, thus, "I will GREATLY MULTI-PLY your sorrow and YOUR CONCEPTION" (Genesis 3:16). "Adam," "writing material" who was "carved" by God's "breath" that gives "life" or "under-standing," was God's "beloved son" "gifted with wisdom" who made "void" The Word of God and was "killed." "Adam" killed God's "beloved son." "Adam" killed "the son" of "Adam" or Man, for had God not multiplied his "conception," he would have remained "childless" or "naked." After Job's children died, he cried, "Naked I came from my mother's womb, and naked I shall return there" (Job 1:21). It can therefore be grasped why God "... made TUNICS OF SKIN, AND CLOTHED THEM" (Genesis 3:21) since Job 10:8-12 describes human gestation in this way:

> "Your hands have made me and fashioned me, an intricate unity... Remember, I pray, that You have MADE ME LIKE CLAY. And will You TURN ME INTO DUST AGAIN? Did You not pour me out like milk, and curdle me like cheese, CLOTHE ME WITH SKIN AND FLESH, and knit me together with bones and sinews? You have granted me life and favor, and Your care has preserved my spirit."

As we have already seen, it is the "spirit" and the "breath" of God that gives "life" and "understanding." Gestation and writing are, of course, paralleled, which can be observed in the fact that the Hebrew word translated "create" is literally from the root ברא *to carve out, to shape out,* and connotes BIRTH. The Job passage above describes man as being made "like clay" that can turn "into dust again" and thus looks at man through the lens of clay writing as if man were God's book; this passage also views making man "like clay" in the same light as "clothing" man with "skin and flesh." Since the Hebrew word "flesh" can also mean "good news" and "successful birth," and since writing was understood to be the breath of life of inspired clay, it can be noticed that the reception of the message is as the writing of a book, the clothing with skin, and the gestation of a person, for with these connections in sight, the granting of "life" that "preserve[s] my spirit" is true of both birth and writing. The birth of copied writing was accomplished sometimes by the Mesopotamians by making a matrix or a block of protruding letters in a mirrored fashion (like a stamp) that, when pressed into clay, shaped out an indented, female copy of writing. The two sides of the impressed and the impression were as the protruding male and the impressed female; it should be recalled that Adam's wife was taken from "one of his sides" as copies of writing were taken from the side of a Mesopotamian writing matrix.

The first man, "Adam" in Eden, is described exquisitely in Genesis in terms of the first writing, articulatory "shaping out," or verbal "carving" in Mesopotamia. Charpin says that Mesopotamian literature appears highly pedagogical, for it contained "...myths; epic narratives of the great deeds of legendary kings such as Gilgamesh; lamentations for destroyed cities; hymns to the gods and temples; and debates on antithetical realities, such as 'the palm tree and the tamarisk' or 'summer and winter'" (Charpin, p. 39). The categories described above are, macrocosmically, the categories of the Bible as a whole and, microcosmically, the categories in the Eden Narrative. The "myth" we can consider here is the literary framework of the description of the first man. The "epic narratives" we can consider here are the Fall of man, the wanderings of the Israelites led by Moses, etc. The "lamentations" we can consider here are the Book of Lamentations regarding the fall of Jerusalem to the Babylonians (from Mesopotamia, Eden) and the exile from Eden when man fell. The "hymns" we can consider here are the Psalms, Genesis 1, etc. The "debates on antithetical realities" regarding "trees" can be easily linked to the two trees in the midst of Eden. The connections between what Charpin says of Mesopotamian writing and what I am naming Biblically can be seen, within this frame of reference, as straightforward. Furthermore, Charpin points out that Mesopotamian writing appears **pedagogical**, "Torah" means "Instruction, Counsel," and the Apostle Paul states literally that "...The Law [i.e. Torah] was our **pedagogue** to bring us to Christ..." (Galatians 3:24). Furthermore, in Hebrew, "tree" and "counsel" can be orthographically identical, and since they are spelled the same, it can be seen here that "Torah" can, by definition, be a synonym for "Tree." The Torah begins with a story where man defected on account of a "Tree" in connection with the counsel of The Serpent. The two trees are, of course, as two counsels, and the debate regarding antithetical trees is recorded in Genesis 3 as a result of The Serpent questioning The Bride as to the two apparently antithetical counsels of God regarding what was and was not permissible. The story concerning "wisdom" (Genesis 3:6) used the classic Mesopotamian (Edenic) method of instruction (Torah) that involved debates regarding antithetical realities (The Two Trees) in order for the reader to understand an Edenic message that predates the invention of writing through the first Mesopotamian writing itself. Mesopotamian writing, which was three-dimensional, was used referentially in Moses' alphabetical writing, which was two-dimensional, to describe the first man through the lens of the first book by writing a book to literate man long after literature was invented. Consider, likewise, that the 1611 King James version deliberately used antiquated English that predated the speech of the English speakers of 1611, and you can grasp immediately the intention: a stylistic method of portraying antiquity was used to connect two different segments on the arrow of time with the same essential message.

The story Moses scribed for "Adam" or "Humanity" was a story wherein the reader is always in the midst so that "Eden" is always *now* for the literate person. The motif of people described as writing always looks to the future as much as it does to the past, and the frame of reference only terminates laterally when time cannot be accounted for (either prior to the ability to record it or in the unknown future). It can be understood here why Evolutionists and Creationists are incorrect in their mutual assertion that the Bible counts material existence within a scope of six millennia, for the "Creation" Story of Genesis 1 is written deliberately to prevent the calculation of time. Consider:

1) What is taken for the sun, moon, and stars, the standards by which earthly time is kept and that were created as late as the "Fourth Day," should cause the reader to wonder what constituted a "Day" prior to the creation of the very standards by which earthly time is kept. If one cuts the sun's circuit into 24

hours, what then is an hour before the sun was created? Obviously, the very middle of the Week of Creation disallows the first three "Days" to be reckoned according to any timeframe whatsoever and only permits them to be viewed in an order or sequence.

2) People read the description of "evening and morning" and assume a 24-hour circuit, but we have already seen that such a circuit, according to how the story is written, could not have occurred when there was not yet a sun to determine "evening and morning." So, even neglecting the word "Day," the "evening and morning" are formulaically determined by something other than the sun, moon, or stars that will not be created until later. Furthermore, the frame of evening-to-morning never accounts for 24 hours. Morning-to-morning or evening-to-evening account for 24 hours.

3) People read the description of "Light"; however, just like the descriptions of "evening and morning" and "Day," whatever constituted this "Light" was determined by something other than the sun, moon, or stars, as Ecclesiastes 12:2 indicates: "While the [1] sun and the [2] LIGHT, the [3] moon and the [4] stars, are not darkened, and the clouds do not return after the rain...."

4) The "Seventh Day," though it follows the creation of the sun, moon, and stars, has no description of "evening and morning" to conclude the cadence. The cadence of "evening and morning" proceeds from the First to the Sixth, but not to the Seventh "Day." Thus, the middle of the Creation Week, the "Fourth Day," bars the reader from counting time prior to it. The final "Day" of the Creation Week has no conclusion and therefore bars the reader from counting after it (until the exile). Recall the fact that "covenant" and "seven" are etymologically related in Hebrew and that "rest" is a consistent circumlocution for "covenant":

> "Therefore the children of Israel shall keep the SABBATH, to observe the SABBATH throughout their generations as a PERPETUAL COVENANT. It is a sign between Me and the children of Israel FOREVER; for in six days the LORD MADE THE HEAVENS AND THE EARTH, AND ON THE SEVENTH DAY He RESTED and was refreshed."

All in all, even a straight-forward English reading of the "Creation" "Days" designedly disallows the reader from counting time. Furthermore, Hebrew (as opposed to English) does not express grammatical time, for its verbs (unlike English that depends on a verb to constitute a sentence) express either a finished or unfinished state of being, not time, which makes discussing eternity in Hebrew as easy as basic grammar. Even modern science is neglected by the "Evolutionist" and the "Creationist" alike in terms of how they read the "Creation" story on their own GPS-linked devices. Einstein's Relativity is proven by GPS regarding the relativity of time and specific frames of reference. The celestial clocks of GPS run at a different rate than their corresponding terrestrial clocks so that, using Einstein's equations that account for a change in gravity, the correspondence aligns for terrestrial navigation to be conducted successfully. From our frame of reference on the earth, beholding something 10 billion light-years away is beholding something presently as it was 10 billion years ago, and this quality of light creates a convergence of two differing segments along the arrow of time at the same instant. Defining that instant depends on the frame of reference. Likewise, the composition of words and the interpretation of them depend greatly on the time and circumstances under which they are produced. Words themselves can refer not just to what is in front of us directly but to things that are not present or entities that are not fully observable at any one period of time. It would seem that Ecclesiastes 8:16 comments on the deliberate prevention of time-calculation relative to the record of the "Creation" in Genesis 1:

> "When I applied my heart to know wisdom and to see the business that is done on earth, even though one sees no sleep day or night, then I saw all the work of God, that a man cannot find out the work that is done under the sun. For though a man labors to discover it, yet he will not find it; moreover, though a wise man attempts to know it, he will not be able to find it."

The "Creation" described in Genesis is not descriptive of *what* but deliberately programmatic concerning *why,* which means that the "Creation" has a purpose other than for what it is commonly used by today's man. If one reads the word ברא *created* as *authored* or *wrote about,* then God wrote about the stars on the Fourth Day. Whenever and however the physical universe specifically came about, Genesis would then be understood as conveying that the material universe was written about in seven stages or in seven parts, not that it was materialized in seven stages. The description of the celestial luminaries being used for "signs" (Genesis 1:14) is a literary technique that records the event of pictographic clay writing being translated into the constellation pictures. Thus, God wrote about the stars in the heavens through man who wrote about God in Heaven (a situation that recalls the story recorded in Genesis 15).

Cuneiform writing followed pictographic writing chronologically. Cuneiform, being three-dimensional, can in some sense be compared to English being carved into rock; but a major contrast between the two is that cuneiform requires light to come from the correct direction in order to read it, as it is the interplay between light and shadow that allows one to read it properly. The tablet is the intercessor between the light and the writing: the writing is, itself, a mingling of light and shadow. If one were to study a tablet by taking 12 hours to memorize it, one would have to move according to the sun's course lest the shifting shadow obscure the writing. Again, the Hebrew word translated "create" is literally from the root ברא to carve out, to shape out, and connotes BIRTH. Considering a clay medium for "creation," we may understand that to "create" means essentially "to write" in Hebrew. Now, it can be argued well that no English translation reflects the understanding that "to create" can mean "to write," but let us consider the Septuagint and the so-called "New Testament" otherwise.

The Septuagint version of Genesis 1:1 says, "In αρχη beginning εποιησεν created...." The Greek word αρχη beginning is pronounced **arkee** and is utilized to translate the Hebrew "בראשית in the beginning." This Greek **arkee** is related to the Greek word **arkee**gos or author (that is understood as founder in Olympus and Demosthenes, head in Lucian, and creator in Susarion). The Greek word εποιησεν created is from ποιεω to produce something, to bring about something and is utilized to translate the Hebrew word ברא to create, which literally means to carve out, to shape out, and connotes birth as well as writing. This word ποιεω **poeo** that means to produce something, to bring about something is related to the word ποιημα **poema** that means workmanship, instrument, book, poem (see Ephesians 2:10). It can be seen that the Greek words used to translate "in the beginning" and "created" both can have something to do with authorship; but, it can be seen that the Hebrew word "created" does mean writing by virtue of being literally "carved out," as we have just observed at length regarding the "creation" of "Adam." Likewise, the Book of John begins by stating, "Εν αρχη beginning o the λογος word." The first words of the Septuagint and of John are identical: "Εν αρχη beginning"; however, what the Septuagint translates as "εποιησεν created," John translates as "o the λογος word"—which explains the Hebrew "create" meaning literally "to carve out," i.e. to write (on a three-dimensional medium).

Both the Septuagint and John use **arkee**, which *can* imply authorship, but John uses "The Word," which *does* imply speech to translate the Hebrew "to carve out, to create." As in the case with "Adam," visible speech was carved out or shaped out by impression into clay; clay was the material used to compare to human flesh; therefore clay writing was used in the sense of the incarnate word; hence, "The Word became flesh" (John 1:14). The Hebrew of Genesis 1:1 can be understood as "In the beginning/By The Author, God created/wrote about the heavens and the earth" just as the Greek of John 1 can be understood as "By The Author was The Word." Recall that cuneiform was the script that emerged at the time of literary Adam's death. In narrated history, Adam is described as pictographic writing prior to there being any. Cuneiform is three-dimensional and requires a proper orientation to a light-source in order to make the words readable since it uses the tablet as the medium wherein the correct interplay of light and shadow reveals the word — which is not true of the pictographic writing that preceded it. It is after the death of fallen man (in narrated time) that writing (in real time) became the mingling of *light and darkness* like The **Tree (or Counsel)** of *Good and Evil*. Consider Hebrews 10:1-4:

> "For the law, having a SHADOW of the good things to come, and
> NOT THE VERY IMAGE of the things, can never with these same
> *sacrifices* [shadows], which they offer continually year by year,
> make those who approach perfect. For then would they not
> have ceased to be offered? For the worshipers, once purified,
> would have had no more consciousness of *sins* [obscurants].
> But in those *sacrifices* [shadows] there is a reminder of sins
> [obscurants] every year. For it is not possible that *the blood of
> bulls and goats* [shadows] could take away sins."

It is evident that, here, God is compared to the light, humanity is the clay, the sin is the obscurant, and the shadow is the "reminder of sins" or the reflection of the obscurant. The shadow is a two-dimensional entity with no depth, and it would seem that linking Moses' Law to the shadow is a literary reference to the fact that what Moses wrote was the reaction to what man did that obscured the "Light" in Day One. Moses wrote after Adam died; hence, Moses hybridized alphabetic writing with cuneiform descriptions so that his letters (in a literary sense) were as the shadows essential to read cuneiform; that is, Moses wrote the reaction to an unwritten stimulus or the shadow cast by the obscurant of sin and death (the "shadow of death"). The reader will notice the subject of child-bearing in connection with the eating of the forbidden fruit in Genesis 3:16; it is therefore evident that the forbidden consumption was the obscurant and fertility was cast in shade. To speak anachronistically, it is as if Moses wrote something comparable to the negative of a photograph; it is from the negative that one, as though in a dark mirror, can interpret the actual picture. If one were to conceive of the necessary shade cast by cuneiform's three-dimensional impressions as though the entire surface were two-dimensional, then one can see how two-dimensional ink writing could be conceived of in the context of the ink representing the shade cast in three-dimensional cuneiform; this is similar to Paul's Epistles in that they are responses, reflections of a stimulus, halves of conversations, the gloriously instructive shadows cast opposite the human misconduct they address. Consider 2 Corinthians 3:7-18:

> "But if the ministry of death [SHADOW], *written and engraved* [Hebrew: "ברא *created, carved out, shaped out"]* on stones, was glorious [LIGHT], so that the children of Israel could not look steadily at the face of Moses [LIGHT] because of the glory [LIGHT] of his countenance, which glory [LIGHT] was passing away [SHADOW], how will the ministry of the Spirit not be more glorious? For if the ministry of condemnation [SHADOW] had glory, the ministry of righteousness exceeds much more in glory. For even what was made glorious had no glory in this respect, because of the glory that excels. For if what is passing away [SHADOW] was glorious, what remains is much more glorious. Therefore, since we have such hope, we use great boldness of speech — unlike Moses, who put a veil [SHADOW] over his face so that the children of Israel could not look steadily at the end of what was passing away. But their minds were blinded [SHADOW]. For until this day the same veil [SHADOW] remains unlifted in the reading of the Old Testament, because the veil [SHADOW] is taken away in Christ [LIGHT]. But even to this day, when Moses is read, a veil [SHADOW] lies on their heart. Nevertheless when one turns to the Lord [LIGHT], the veil [SHADOW] is taken away. Now the Lord [LIGHT] is the Spirit; and where the Spirit of the Lord [LIGHT] is, there is liberty. But we all, with unveiled face [LIGHT], beholding as in a mirror the **glory** [LIGHT] **of the Lord** [LIGHT], are being transformed into the same image from **glory to glory** [LIGHT TO LIGHT], just as by the Spirit of the Lord."

Cuneiform is three-dimensional writing that must balance light and shadow in order to make itself readable. The quotation above seems to compare Moses to having encapsulated a message with two-dimensional ink that formerly was understood in some way three-dimensionally. The ink is here paralleled to the two-dimensional shadow; this causes the ink to be viewed as a type of reaction to the story it describes in a manner similar to how cuneiform required both shadow and light in order to convey its message. Consider the two-dimensional *sfumato* of Leonardo being translated into the thee-dimensional *non-finito* of Michelangelo: the same idea on two different mediums of differing dimensions. God is here paralleled to the light; this causes the reader to interpret that the Word or message is as God, the "FATHER OF LIGHTS, with whom there is no variation OR SHADOW OF TURNING (James 1:17). Thus, if one beholds God directly, shadow is not required to interpret God; but, if one turns away from God, the shadow cast by one's own sin only obscures the very God to which one turned his own back. It would seem straight-forward that Moses wrote a story concerning man turning his back to God, and that he wrote it in a way that formulaically demonstrates the substance of the story in a peculiar and perfectly-fitting literary method where ink is comparable to shade. Man is as the clay book that preceded the ink-version of the story; the ink-version of the story is as the shadow necessary to read the clay writing; from the shadow, one can infer the obscurant by the illumination it blocks; both the ink writing and the clay example post-date the story itself.

Since we have already understood the deliberate comparison of the first man in Eden to the first writing in Mesopotamia, we must remember that God said "Let us make man" and then God "created" man whereby we observe that this "making" is paralleled to "creating" or "writing." Consider how the Book of John is framed by the comparison of (1) Man to books and (2) God to The Author of the books, for the references only make sense regarding Mesopotamian clay writing:

> "In the beginning [/By THE AUTHOR] was THE WORD, and THE WORD was with God, and THE WORD was God. He was *in the beginning* [/by THE AUTHOR] with God. All things were MADE [WRITTEN] through Him, and without Him nothing was MADE [WRITTEN] that was MADE [WRITTEN]. In Him was life, and the life was THE LIGHT of men. And the LIGHT SHINES IN THE DARKNESS, AND THE DARKNESS DID NOT COMPREHEND IT. There was a man sent from God, whose name was John. This man came for a witness, to bear witness of THE LIGHT, that all through him might believe. He was not that LIGHT, but was sent to bear witness of that LIGHT. That was THE TRUE LIGHT which gives LIGHT TO EVERY MAN [CLAY TABLET] coming into the world. He was in the world, and the world was made through Him, and the world did not know Him. He came to His own, and His own did not receive

Him. But as many as received Him, to them He gave the right to become CHILDREN of God, to those who believe in His name: who were BORN [WRITTEN], not of blood, nor of the will of the flesh, nor of the will of man, but of God. And the WORD BECAME FLESH and dwelt among us, and we beheld His GLORY [LIGHT], the GLORY [LIGHT] as of the only begotten of the Father, full of grace and truth" (John 1:1-14).

"And there are also many other things that Jesus did, which if they were WRITTEN one by one, I suppose that even the world itself could not contain the BOOKS THAT WOULD BE WRITTEN. Amen" (John 21:25).

God is The Author Whose Light or Wisdom is reflected in man who is His book if man "repents" or "turns the other way" so as to cause the interplay of light and shadow to reveal, not to obscure, The Word: "And the light shines in the darkness, and the darkness did not comprehend it." If we understand "Adam" in the terms of a clay writing tablet that Genesis 2 provides, then Ecclesiastes, like John, begins and ends with a description that hybridizes man and writing:

"What **profit** has ADAM from all his **labor in which he toils** under the sun?" (Ecclesiastes 1:3).

"Of making many BOOKS there is no end, and much study is **wearisome to the flesh**." (Ecclesiastes 12:12).

Again, the Book of John is framed by the comparison of Man to books and God to The Author of books, for the references only make sense regarding the three-dimensional writing created at the death of Adam: cuneiform, the writing technology whose emergence occurred when the constellations were first marked out pictographically. The "Creation" and Fall of Man account is told through the masterful lens of the composition of clay writing and of that writing's erasure. The Redemption and Ascension of Man account is told through the masterful lens of the rewriting of humanity and that writing's preservation, for the very word σωτηρια *salvation* means also *preservation* and is, by definition, a translation of the name "Jesus" or "Savior" in Hebrew. Accordingly, both Heaven and Hell are described in terms of gardens and books in Scripture. The "Garden" of Eden is, of course, a garden, but its domain is described in literary terms by the words, "*Book of Life*" (Philippians 4:3; Revelation 3:5; 13:8; 17:8; 20:12; 20:15; 21:27; 22:19). Hell is described likewise as an antithetical entity of death; it is called a "Tophet," a child sacrificial garden (2 Kings 23:10; Isaiah 30:33; Jeremiah 7:31) and as an erased book (Exodus 32:32-33). By describing Hell as a place for forgotten names and of slaughtered children (the bearers of their lineage's name), one can understand what is called *"Damnatio Memoriae"* or "Condemnation of Memory." Writing could be "carved out" or "shaped out" on stone, metal, wood, clay, wax, etc. The Condemnation of Memory was the literal erasure or recarving of inscriptions used as punishment to blot out the remembrance of an individual. The name of a wicked person could be carved out from an inscription and a new name could be carved atop the remaining space. We can therefore understand why God delivered Daniel's three friends unharmed from Babylon's (Eden's) furnace because He remembered them just as we can understand God baking His writing on a clay tablet in order to solidify carved names for posterity. Unbaked clay writing was easily erased with water, as was the case with Noah's flood, and it is for this reason that the names provided genealogically from Adam to Noah are descriptive titles that formulaically anticipate The Flood. That is, Noah's flood is described in terms of earthen writing being erased and the earthen book being rewritten.

In the beginning, God **wrote about** the heavens and the earth. The Hebrew Bible paints God as "The *Author* of Life," to use the Greek translated expression of Acts 3:15, 5:31, and Hebrews 2:10, 12:2. The word **author** here is the Greek **arkee**gos that is related to the word **arkee** or *beginning,* which is but a Greek rendering of the Hebrew "בראשית *in the beginning*" of Genesis 1:1. Recalling that the ב is ablative, Genesis 1:1 can read simply as, "With The Author, God wrote about The Heavens and The Earth," which explains Proverbs 8:22-31:

> "The Lord possessed Me at the beginning of His way, before
> His works of old. I have been established from everlasting,
> from the beginning, before there was ever an earth. When
> there were no depths I was brought forth, when there were no
> fountains abounding with water. Before the mountains were
> settled, before the hills, I was brought forth; while as yet He
> had not made the earth or the fields, or the primal dust of the
> world. When He prepared the heavens, I was there, when He
> drew a circle on the face of the deep, when He established
> the clouds above, when He strengthened the fountains of the
> deep, when He assigned to the sea its limit, so that the waters
> would not transgress His command, when He marked out the
> foundations of the earth, then I was beside Him as a אמון male
> youth,**an *artificer [writer]*;** and I was daily His delight, rejoic-
> ing always before Him, rejoicing in His inhabited world, and *My
> delight was with the sons of men [see the translation in John
> 1:4 here]*."

The "Us" of "Let Us make man..." appears to be explained, by Proverbs 8 above, as the literary depiction of a King dictating to His Scribe — both united by The Word.

The word ברא to *create*, *to author, to write*, that connotes **birth** explains why the Greek **arkeegos**, *Prince*, **Author** can be used to discuss the **head of a family**. We must recall that Adam was told to "**rule**" in Genesis 1:28. Writing in ancient Mesopotamia was spoken of in personified terms and was understood to bestow life or wisdom upon the material on which it was written. Ancient Mesopotamian tablets state how people "listened to the tablet" and discuss the "**mouth** of the tablet." Likewise, the Septuagint uses the word **arkeegos**, *Author* to translate the Hebrew פאה *mouth* or *prince, ruler, edge of a blade* (Numbers 24:27), which is from the root פאה *to breathe*, for the "**mouth**" of a tablet was connected to an "**edge**" or the instrument used to carve out and shape out the words on clay. Such imagery was understood by the "New Testament" scribe who wrote, "For the **Word of God** is living and powerful, and sharper than any **two-edged sword**, piercing even to the division of soul and spirit, and of joints and marrow, and is a discerner of the thoughts and intents of the heart" (Hebrews 4:12). Written language in Mesopotamia ("Eden") was the product of an impressing or cutting instrument (depending on the mediums of stone, metal, or clay). Consider here the imagery in Greek:

> "He had in His right hand seven stars, out of His MOUTH went a sharp **two-edged sword**, and His countenance was like the sun shining in its strength" (Revelation 1:16).

> "And to the angel of the church in Pergamos WRITE, 'These things says He who has the sharp **two-edged sword**'" (Revelation 2:12).

In Hebrew, a sword has a "mouth," whereas in English it has an "edge." The "Old Testament," and the subsequent Chaldee and Greek Writings of the Hebrews, discuss One about Whom the Heavenly Voice commanded "This is My BELOVED SON, in whom I am well pleased. HEAR Him!" (Matthew 17:25); for, in Sumerian cuneiform, a "BELOVED CHILD" was the equivalent term for "the one gifted with EAR [= wisdom]." It will be noticed that Christ is called "The Wisdom of God" (1 Corinthians 1:24), "The Word" (John 1:1), and "The Word of God" (Revelation 19:13) and is said to possess "the words of eternal life" (John 6:68). Furthermore, Revelation 22:19 recalls the "*Book of Life*" in Exodus 32:32.

The two-dimensional word קרא means *to call, to invoke*, and also **to read**, but the manner in which this particular word is understood is contextual. The context depends on time. That is, what was once "called" became "read," and the same word was used to indicate both a time preceding and following the invention of writing. The verb *sitassum, to read* means primarily *to call out*, as is reflected in the Hebrew קרא *to call, to invoke, to read*. Genesis 4:25-5:1 seems to discuss the origin of reading:

> "And Adam knew his wife again, and she bore a son and named him Seth, "For God has appointed another seed for me instead of Abel, whom Cain killed." And as for Seth, to him also a son was born; and he named him Enosh. **Then men began קרא *to call, to* READ **on/in the** שם *name/progeny* **of the** LORD. This is the BOOK **of the genealogy** of ADAM [= Writing Tablet]. In the day that God CREATED [= wrote about] man, He made him in the likeness of God. He CREATED [= wrote about] them male and female, and blessed them and called them ADAM [= Writing Tablet] in the day they were CREATED [= recorded with the invention of writing].

When an invention is made, the language that preceded it can be given a new domain that becomes applied to that invention until a new name is coined; it is probably for this reason that the term "call" is also the term "read." It is only after this statement of "calling" or "reading" that we are given dates. These dates, when taken together, bring us back to the very time and place of the creation of Mesopotamian writing and of Mesopotamian literate man.

Recall that when the cuneiform man (who put pictographic man to death) saw that he was to be excelled by the alphabetic man, the cuneiform man complicated his writing in order to obscure information and secure a position for himself that claimed he possessed knowledge that predated The Flood. The method of obscuration and complication cuneiform man chose was the deliberate addition of more values to the signs of his written language in order to play upon potential alternate readings. To one who reads a translation of Hebrew, it should be known that the names of people he reads are transliterations and not translations, and this ignorance probably stems from the current practice of naming children according to some self-determined euphony instead of a preceding meaning. For instance, Cain attempted to blot his brother's name from existence. Cain attempted to erase God's *book, poem, or workmanship* (Ephesians 2:10). Surely no one can believe that our first human mother named her own child "Abel" or "Nothingness" (the "Vanity" of Ecclesiastes); rather, the lens used to look into a preliterate past is the *writing and erasure* of a book in order to understand the creation and destruction of life.

The description of Noah's Flood by Moses is a deliberate reference to the erasure of clay writing with water. Whatever the physical reality of the flood was, the perceptual picture Moses wrote called to mind the baptism that cleansed away evil and that was signified by water as much as a rewriting of a story that grew too corrupt to fix without erasing most of it. Moses concealed the duration, not the nature, of The Flood by providing dates in an intricate manner. As we have already observed in a previous chapter, The Flood consisted of two water-sources: the "FOUNTAINS OF THE GREAT DEEP" and the "WINDOWS OF HEAVEN." That it rained 40 days and 40 nights says nothing to the duration of the fountains surging forth. The Text then states that "THE FLOOD WAS ON THE EARTH FORTY DAYS," but it does not say that The Flood ended after 40 days only; instead, it is written, "THE WATERS PREVAILED ON THE EARTH ONE HUNDRED AND FIFTY DAYS." Immediately, one cannot state that Scripture discusses a flood that lasted 40 days when the very Scripture in question states that the waters prevailed for 150 days. The Flood began in the 600th year of Noah's life, but it ended in the 601st year of his life; so, if Noah was 600 years old before the 150 days under discussion, and he was 601 years old on the other end of the 150 days, then the years of Noah's life also indicate a flood that lasted longer than 40 days. The Flood began "IN THE SECOND MONTH, THE SEVENTEENTH DAY OF THE MONTH," but the earth was dried "IN THE SECOND MONTH, ON THE TWENTY-SEVENTH DAY OF THE MONTH"; therefore, the flood would have lasted longer than 150 days based on the dates of its beginning and ending. It would seem fitting that 12 moons comprising 354 days are accounted for here, thus a surplus of 11 days (in order to account for the seasonal harmonization of lunar and solar time) would mark neatly that the account of Noah's Flood lasted the duration of a solar year: 365 days. Noah was a descendant of Adam who lived prior to The Flood. The Flood occurred prior to the invention of writing. The Egyptian-educated Moses (who physically descended from the Mesopotamian Abraham) described "Adam" according to the terminology used to describe Mesopotamian writing. The cuneiform artificers crafted a writing-system that *claimed to retain* the knowledge of the world prior to The Flood but that *did retain* the knowledge of the world before cuneiform writing. The *literary* frame of reference is Mesopotamian *writing*, not The Flood, and the *geographical* frame of reference is *Egypt*, not Mesopotamia. It must be remembered that Noah's righteous life was saved in a wooden box just as Moses' infant life was saved in a wooden box, and Moses' writing about Noah was also saved in a wooden box: The Ark of The Covenant. When we reflect upon the dates provided for the rising and the setting of The

Flood, it will be noticed that they correspond with the flooding of the Nile. Humphrey Milford records in his book, *The Language of the Pentateuch in Its Relation to Egyptian*, that the 150 days of Noah's flood correspond to the rise of the Nile (at the beginning of May) and the highest water level (at the beginning of October). The sequence of rising and draining waters described in terms of Noah's flood mirrors the sequence of the rising and recession of the Nile in Egypt. The literary method used to describe a cataclysm prior to the invention of writing was written initially to a people-group who existed after the cataclysm and after the invention of writing, a people group exiting Egypt. Egypt was described by Moses in comparison to Eden: "...like the GARDEN OF THE LORD, like the land of Egypt...." (Genesis 13:10). It will be noticed that this comparison is provided in Genesis, through Moses, who was not born until the narrative timeframe of the Book of Exodus that followed it. Moses provides clues to his references regarding Edenic or Mesopotamian writing itself by precisely recording titles of people that fit the theme of Narrative.

> "And RED MAN OF STERILE GROUND [i.e. WRITING MATERIAL] *knew [unified with]* his wife again, and she bore a son and named him REPLACEMENT, "For God has appointed another seed for me instead of ABEL [literally NOTHINGNESS], whom CAIN [literally POSSESSION] killed." And as for REPLACEMENT, to him also a son was born; and he named him INCURABLE. **Then men began** קרא *to call, to read* **on/in the name of the LORD.** This is the BOOK OF THE GENEALOGY OF ADAM [WRITING MATERIAL]. In the day that God created man, He made him in the likeness of God. He created them male and female, and blessed them and called them ADAM [WRITING MATERIAL] in the day they were created. And ADAM [WRITING MATERIAL] lived one hundred and thirty years, and begot a son in his own likeness, after his image, and named him SETH [REPLACEMENT]. After he begot REPLACEMENT, the days of ADAM [WRITING MATERIAL] were eight hundred years; and he had sons and daughters. So all the days that ADAM [WRITING MATERIAL] lived were nine hundred and thirty years; and he died." *Replacement* lived one hundred and five years, and begot *Incurable*. After he begot *Incurable, Replacement* lived eight hundred and seven years, and had sons and daughters. So all the days of *Replacement* were nine hundred and twelve years; and he died. *Incurable* lived ninety years, and begot *Possessor.* After he begot *Possessor, Incurable* lived eight hundred and fifteen years, and had sons and daughters. So all the days of *Incurable* were nine

hundred and five years; and he died. *Possessor* lived seventy years, and begot *Praiser of God*. After he begot *Praiser of God Possessor* lived eight hundred and forty years, and had sons and daughters. So all the days of *Possessor* were nine hundred and ten years; and he died. *Praiser of God* lived sixty-five years, and begot *Descendent [possibly Ruler, Crusher]*. After he begot *Descendent [possibly Ruler, Crusher]*, *Praiser of God* lived eight hundred and thirty years, and had sons and daughters. So all the days of *Praiser of God* were eight hundred and ninety-five years; and he died. *Descendent [possibly Ruler, Crusher]* lived one hundred and sixty-two years, and begot *Initiate*. After he begot *Initiate*, *Descendent [possibly Ruler, Crusher]* lived eight hundred years, and had sons and daughters. So all the days of *Descendent [possibly Ruler, Crusher]* were nine hundred and sixty-two years; and he died. *Initiate* lived sixty-five years, and begot *It [The Flood] Shall Be Sent When He is Dead*. After he begot *It [The Flood] Shall Be Sent When He is Dead*, *Initiate* walked with God three hundred years, and had sons and daughters. So all the days of *Initiate* were three hundred and sixty-five years. And *Initiate* walked with God; and he *was* not, for God took him. *It [The Flood] Shall Be Sent When He is Dead* lived one hundred and eighty-seven years, and begot *Powerful Destroyer*. After he begot *Powerful Destroyer*, *It [The Flood] Shall Be Sent When He is Dead* lived seven hundred and eighty-two years, and had sons and daughters. So all the days of *It [The Flood] Shall Be Sent When He is Dead* were nine hundred and sixty-nine years; and he died. *Powerful Destroyer* lived one hundred and eighty-two years, and had a son. And he called his name *Rest [= Covenant]*, saying, 'This one will give us *rest* concerning our work and the toil of our hands, because of the ground which the LORD HAS CURSED.' AFTER HE BEGOT *Rest [= Covenant]*, *Powerful Destroyer* lived five hundred and ninety-five years, and had sons and daughters. So all the days of *Powerful Destroyer* were seven hundred and seventy-seven years ["seven" = "covenant"]; and he died. And *Rest [= Covenant; "grace" spelled backwards]* was five hundred years old, and *Rest [= Covenant; "grace" spelled backwards]* begot (1) *Name [i.e. Progeny or Increased Lineage, Renown]*, (2) *Inflamed*, and (3) *Enlargement, Beautiful*. Now it came to pass, when *men began to multiply* on the face of the earth, and daughters were born to them, that the sons of God saw the daughters of men, that *they were beautiful*; and they took wives for themselves of all whom they chose. And the LORD said, 'My Spirit shall not strive with man forever, for he is indeed flesh; yet his days shall be one hundred and twenty years.' There were *Fallen Ones, Defectors, Dissolved Ones [like erasing clay writing with water], Abortions [i.e. Child Sacrifices]* on the earth in those days, and also afterward, when the sons of God came in to the daughters of men and they bore children to them. Those were the *mighty men, warriors, male babies* who were of old, *incurable ones* of *Name [i.e. Progeny or Increased Lineage, Renown]*. Then the LORD saw that the *physical injuriousness and emotional sorrow* of man was great in the earth, and that every intent of the thoughts of his heart was only *physically injurious and emotionally sorrowful* continually. And the LORD was sorry that He had made man on the earth, and He was *sorrowful* in His heart. So the LORD said, 'I will destroy *Red Ground [Sterile Ground, i.e. Clay* or *Writing Material]* whom I have *created [Lit. carved out, i.e. wrote]* from the face of the earth, both man and beast, creeping thing and birds of the air, for I am sorry that I have made them.' But *Rest [= Covenant; grace spelled backwards]* found *grace* in the eyes of the LORD. This is the genealogy of *Rest [= Covenant; grace spelled backwards in Hebrew]. Rest [= Covenant; grace spelled backwards]* was a just man, perfect in his generations. *Rest [= Covenant; grace spelled backwards]* walked with God [as was the case with Enoch also]. And *Rest [= Covenant; grace spelled backwards]* begot three sons: **(1) Name [i.e. Progeny or Increased Lineage], (2) Inflamed, and (3) Enlargement, Beautiful.**

A "name" that is "inflamed" and "enlarged" would seem to be one that is written on clay that is baked. Adam was described as a clay writing tablet; "Adam" also means "Humanity"; humanity or Adam began anew with Noah. The genealogies from Adam to Noah are formulaic, and they use the lens of carved writing to explain a preliterate history. Noah "begot" names preserved (saved) on writing material that was erased through the Condemnation of Memory. The Hebrew word translated "create" is literally from the root ברא *to carve out, to shape out,* and connotes *birth* and *writing.* "Noah" or "Covenant" bound himself in an oath to the death with God, God saved him and preserved his name for posterity, and this relationship is told by the Torah in a parable whose mechanism is the invention of *writing.* The Hebrew "carving out" or "shaping out" that has been for so long translated as "creating" can be understood idiomatically as *writing* within the context and history it was written. Consider the fact that when today's man types or texts, he says often that he "writes."

The cuneiform artificers, the masters of the second type of writing (that followed clay pictographs) saw, in the invention of alphabetic systems, their eventual demise. The facility and rapidity with which alphabetic writing could be learned and utilized forced a situation where the cuneiform men of old knew that the more recent technology would overcome the existent one. Reactively, instead of simplifying their writing even further, they intentionally complicated it in order to obscure information and secure a position for themselves that claimed they possessed knowledge that predated The Flood. Moses wrote in the consonantally alphabetic system of Hebrew, and Deuteronomy records that Moses died on Mount Nebo. To the Chaldeans, Nebo was the planet Mercury. If we consider the name "Nebo" to be reflected in the root *nibbah* or *to prophesy*, we can understand why Moses is described as a unique *prophet* immediately after he dies on Nebo (Deuteronomy 34:10). George Rawlinson's *Chaldea* states that Nebo was "he who teaches," "he who instructs," and that he is symbolized by the arrowhead or wedge, the "primary and essential element of cuneiform writing, to mark his joint presidency with that God over writing and literature." Nebo is also called "the guardian over the heavens and the earth" and "the lord of the constellations." However the associations between Nebo and the mountain of Moses' death were received in Moses' day, the fact that Moses is ascribed prophetic knowledge regarding the stars as reflected in his writing is enough to see a deliberate literary link. Accordingly, let us consider the Chaldean account of The Flood. Rawlinson records that the Chaldean legend states,

> God appeared to Xisuthrus (Noah) in a dream, and warned him that on the fifteenth day of the month Daesius, mankind would be destroyed by a deluge. He had him bury in Sippara, the City of the Sun, the extant writings, first and last; and build a ship, and enter therein with his family and his close friends; and furnish it with meat and drink; and place on board winged fowl, and four-footed beasts of the earth; and when all was ready, set sail.... The flood came; and as soon as it ceased, [Noah] let loose some birds, which, finding neither food nor a place where they could rest, came back to the ark. After some days he again sent out the birds, which again returned to the ark, but with feet covered with mud. Sent out a third time, the birds returned no more, and [Noah] knew that land had reappeared: so he removed some of the covering of the ark, and looked, and behold! The vessel had grounded on a mountain. Then [Noah] went forth with his wife and his daughter, and his pilot, and fell down and worshipped the earth, and built an altar, and

> offered sacrifice to the gods; after which he disappeared from sight, together with those who had accompanied him. They who had remained in the ark and not gone forth with [Noah], now left it and searched for him, and shouted out his name, but [Noah] was not seen any more. Only his voice answered them out of the air, saying, "Worship God; for because I worshipped God, am I gone to dwell with the gods; and they who were with me have shared the same honor." And he bade them return to Babylon, and recover the writings buried at Sippara [the City of the Sun], and make them known among men; and he told them that the land in which they then were was Armenia.

It can be observed immediately that the reference to the City of the Sun here is referenced by Moses in the duration he provides for The Flood: 365 days. The books that were buried and then excavated are referenced by Moses in the names of Noah's **sons**: (1) **Name** [i.e. Progeny or Increased Lineage], (2) **Inflamed**, and (3) **Enlargement**, Beautiful; for, a "name" that is "inflamed" and "enlarged" would seem to be one that is written on clay that is baked; baked clay writing is not erased by water. Furthermore, the dimensions that Moses provides for the ark are more suitable for a library than a menagerie of all of the world's animals. Flooding a library of unbaked clay writing is functionally identical to burning a library of paper writing. The Bible states that the first destruction of man was by water, but the final destruction of man will be by fire — while the Bible compares man to books. It is the reduction of wisdom that summarizes the expulsion and death of man from his origins as described in the Eden story; is not the Noah story essentially the same? Water was used as a military weapon in the ancient East. The king of Babylonia between 1711 and 1684 B.C. (slightly before the narrative and/or real time of Moses) desired to control cities south of him (possibly Uruk); he blocked the flow of the Tigris River and redirected the water into a nearby irrigation channel; this orchestration subsequently caused a flood that covered the surrounding fields and thus impeded the movement of his enemy's forces. Surely, such a war tactic, when combined with the various religious purifications described by Moses, is the podium upon which The Flood story was composed. Whatever The Flood was, it seems to be described by Moses in terms of a flooded library, especially when one considers the term "breath of life." That is, regarding The Flood, God said, "And behold, I Myself am bringing floodwaters on the earth, to destroy from under heaven all flesh in which is the BREATH OF LIFE; everything that is on the earth shall die" (Genesis 6:17). Job 32:8 and 33:4 says "there is a spirit in man, and the **breath of The Almighty** GIVES HIM UNDERSTANDING," and "The Spirit of God has made me, and the

breath of The Almighty GIVES ME LIFE." It is the reduction of *wisdom* that is employed here to typify the reduction of *life*. Writing is external, collective memory that can transcend the time and geography of which a person is capable, and the loss of writing is as the loss of the person who wrote it. Likewise, the loss of the ability to comprehend a person's writing is also tantamount to the loss of the person who authored the misunderstood composition.

Consider the message forwarded concerning the "rock" that Moses "struck." Genesis 49 clearly states that "Judah is a lion's whelp," "Issachar is a strong donkey," "Dan shall be a serpent by the way," "Joseph is a fruitful bough," and "Benjamin is a ravenous wolf," yet no one struggles at all to see that Jacob did not sire animals and plants, but sons, whom he described emblematically as animals and plants. The end of the Book of Genesis describes people in terms of plants and animals, but the beginning of the very same Book does not? If Dan is a "serpent" according to Genesis 49, then one should ask who (not what) the "serpent" is in Genesis 3. If Joseph is a "fruitful bough" according to Genesis 49, then one should ask who (not what) the forbidden tree is in Genesis 2. In a similar manner, many actually believe that Moses "struck the rock" in order to give water to a multitude who were dying of thirst, and that this means he tapped a water-source that burst forth all at once to vitalize people and animals. It is ridiculous to assume that such a surge could happen without drowning the thirsty instantly. Surely, such an explosion of water did not happen. Moses struck "The Rock," i.e. he waged war on the well-watered and desert-fortified civilization we now call "Petra" ("The Rock"), when he could have negotiated for water through speaking — for he was commanded to "speak to 'The Rock'" instead. Perhaps this is why the story that immediately follows discusses the consequential failure of negotiation at Edom [spelled the same as "Adam" in unvocalized Hebrew] as a result of striking Petra, "The Rock" (Numbers 20). Likewise, recall that Zechariah 14:4 discusses how The Mount [like a rock] of Olives will be split open and that verse 8 states, "living waters shall flow from Jerusalem." The point is that the very same words, within a larger frame of reference, make more sense. Moses struck The Rock as he was first commanded. Petra had its own high place wherein the slaughter of innocents occurred, and the Torah is very clear that the peoples who were to be destroyed by the Israelites were uniformly practitioners of child sacrifice (Leviticus 18:24-25). Since Hell is compared to a child-sacrificial precinct and the result of a blotted-out book, it can be seen that Moses blotted out the blotters. Once they were destroyed, however, Moses was commanded to "speak" to The Rock, i.e. to negotiate with the humbled Petra; but, Moses instead struck Petra a second time and himself became guilty of the slaughter of the innocents. As a result, Moses was restrained from the terrestrial book of the Promised Land and he only entered it in the Transfiguration according to *The Book of Life*. As it was once actually believed that the entire world actually fell apart because of a single piece of "fruit," one can now understand the "rock" that Moses struck.

Again, the ancient Mesopotamians conceived of writing as a human invention brought about through a series of challenges that took the form of riddles too complex to be transmitted orally "because the MESSENGER'S MOUTH WAS TOO HEAVY, and he could not repeat it" (Charpin). We have already observed the written riddle of "The Rock" that was "struck," and it is here that we must consider the leader of Petra and the Leader of the Israelites. The leader of the Israelites was told to "speak to The Rock," a leader who formerly said to the LORD, "O my Lord, I am not a man of words, neither before nor since You have spoken to Your servant; but I am כבד פה וכבד לשון HEAVY OF MOUTH *and heavy of tongue*" (Exodus 4:10). The two Mesopotamian traditions do not differ in essence, for this Enmerkar was believed to be endowed with inspiration from a goddess. Moses was endowed with inspiration from God. The point is that the clay writing of Mesopotamia provided a literate but non-alphabetic frame of reference for Moses, and Moses provided a literate but alphabetic frame of reference to readers. Moses claimed formerly that his mouth was "too heavy," and in punishment for not participating with the פאה *Mouth or Prince or Ruler, Sword-edge* of God so that he would have his "mouth washed," his mouth "opened," Moses, acting as Mouth or Prince, or Ruler struck Petra, the Rock instead of speaking to the ruler of Petra. The manner in which "The Rock" is described by Moses is parabolic, that is, comparative and not definitive. The "rose-red" city of Petra, the rocky fortress that contains the "Springs of Moses," eventually housed the Nabatean people who practiced a ritual feast with the dead (a feast similar to that which became called "Holy Communion"). Psalm 105:41 recounts that the Rock's waters זוב*bled* forth waters; thus, the description of "bleeding" waters from the Rock describes the warfare that caused Petra to give forth its waters abundantly... but a Petra who, at the time Moses struck it the second time, was willing to give without going to war.

> "Jesus answered and said to her, 'Whoever drinks of this water
> will thirst again, but whoever drinks of the water that I shall
> give him will never thirst. But the water that I shall give him will

become in him a FOUNTAIN OF WATER SPRINGING UP INTO EVER-LASTING LIFE.'" (John 4:13-14).

"Moreover, brethren, I do not want you to be unaware that all our fathers were under the cloud, all passed through the sea, all were baptized into Moses in the cloud and in the sea, all ate the same spiritual food, and all drank the same spiritual drink. For they DRANK OF THAT SPIRITUAL ROCK that followed them, AND THAT ROCK WAS CHRIST. But with most of them God was not well pleased, for their bodies were scattered in the wilderness" (I Corinthians 10:1-5).

It would seem that the second encounter with Petra was an encounter where Petra did not resist.

The Hebrew root מלל means both *to circumcise* and *to speak*. In this root, we can observe speech that is inscribed. Recall that Mesopotamians tablets were "listened to" and "heard." The "Old Testament" expression "circumcised heart" used by Moses and Jeremiah (Deuteronomy 10:16, 30:6; Jeremiah 4:4) is the equivalent of the expression "engraved on the tablet of your heart" (Jeremiah 17:1) and is translated in the "New Testament" as "written on the heart" (Romans 2:15; 2 Corinthians 3:2-3) by Paul. Both the First and Last Adams had to sleep prior to having their hearts circumcised in order for their brides to live. The First Adam is described in terms of ancient clay books and the Last Adam is described in terms of The Word written upon His Creation. By the time Moses wrote the Torah down, writing itself was thousands of years old and the preliterate man was extinct. The age of the world — *of literate and illiterate man specifically*, not of the earth generally — is about 6,000 years old.

Leaving behind writings of former exploits expresses a hope to provide examples for the future. Moses did not "borrow" or "steal" information that preceded his own lifetime; for it should now be obvious that the very structure of the Torah, originally written on a scroll, looked as far forward to the end of time as it did backward to the beginning of time. The Torah itself functions as a whole in a similar fashion to the Week of "Creation" that initiated The Torah. When one reflects on the fact that the Hebrew word "four" (the first day where time could potentially be counted) is from the root "to copulate" and that the word "seven" (the day with no "evening and morning," no end) is from the same root as "to swear," it can be grasped that the copulation or juncture of creation produces a copy that counts down to birth and is capped by a covenant that has no end, i.e. eternity — provided the covenant is maintained. Charpin states that writing down agreements seems to protect the vulnerable by central powers that enforce the law (p. 170). For instance, those who witnessed a dowry were subject to forgetfulness provided a long enough period of time elapsed, thus a tablet (external memory) that recorded the dowry could validate or fortify the matter. A woman who "went away naked" could be understood as being a woman sent away without her dowry or property as a result of a broken covenant. In Hebrew, to be "naked" is the same word as to be "childless," for a child is not only the recipient of an inheritance but an inheritance himself. It can be seen here that books, like children, preserve the memory of their progenitors. Describing the first dweller of Eden as the first Mesopotamian writing causes the reader to understand that he is reading a book written by Moses, about a man who is as a book written by the Author who "created" or "wrote about" Moses, who wrote the book you are reading, *ad infinitum*.

The Book of Daniel, written in the land formerly called Eden, describes whole nations over time as individual animals engaged in conflict. Genesis 2:1, after describing the creation of the animals and man in Eden, states "Thus the heavens and the earth were completed with all צבאם *their armies*." Are not Daniel and Genesis speaking the same way? Was not the final conflict on earth begun with the initial Fall on earth — both described in terms of plants and animals in the same manner that Jacob spoke of his own sons? These descriptions are symbolic. Consider again the fact that "the two syllables of the Sumerian word for 'grapevine', GESHTIN, mean 'tree' and 'life'" (*The Babylonians*, Saggs). Scripture's references to "The Tree of Life" and "The True Vine" would have been understood well before Christ's physical advent, but only partially. The fulfillment of Christ, "The True Vine" (John 15:1) would have made a partial connection to "The Tree of Life" to the citizens of Judea. The Bible provides the connection between Christ's neighbors in Judea (who possessed the Book of Genesis that describes the Mesopotamian grapevine or Tree of Life) and the ancient Mesopotamians (who looked forward to a time after writing about The Tree of Life and whose Magi adored the Christ Child). Both people-groups are united through time and over space by the nexus of Scripture, each explaining the other to those who have the advantage of beholding both simultaneously by looking backward. Writing is as the nexus of different segments of time, and it can be comprehended easily that the Magi followed stars in accordance with writing in order to find them both unified in the birth of The Tree of Life, so to speak.

I said in an earlier chapter that the main factor that divides the various traditions regarding Scripture is the context under which the Text is viewed. There is a contextual strand that underlies the chronologically sequential sub-contexts of Scripture. The contextual strand is that of the ancient eastern monarchies described so beautifully by George Rawlinson. The ancient eastern kings were gardeners called "shepherds" who planted kingdoms unified by a royal road or way. The Great King's palace, paradise, and garden were modeled in miniature throughout the monarchy, and these miniatures were provided as domiciles for provincial governors whose privileged duty it was to defend the kingdom. The ancient eastern kings often lived a veiled existence, and their ancestrally cultivated and private trees were, as Pliny the Elder describes, capable of producing a medicinal and life-sustaining diet superior to those on the outside. The monarchs of old were approached with prostration. When their wars were won, they exacted a Day of Judgment wherein they pronounced sentences upon their live, defeated foes. Their adversaries were often stripped naked, prostrated, had their limbs bound, and had fishing hooks pierced through their lips; when they were pulled forward to their doom and forced to locomote as a serpent on account of their bondage, they had their heads crushed by the victorious monarch. This contextual backdrop explains much as to the language of Genesis 1-3, but we must also recognize the fact that the invention of writing by the Mesopotamians was utilized largely for regal purposes. Even describing Adam as a "man of dust" in Genesis 2:7 should be understood in the context of regality when reconsidered in 1 Kings 16:2: "Inasmuch as I LIFTED YOU OUT OF THE DUST and MADE YOU RULER over My people Israel...." In other words, the context of ancient eastern monarchy is also largely the context of ancient Mesopotamian writing, hence the "dominion" given to man in Genesis 1. The descriptions of God in the "Creation" and "Eden" sequences are that of The Divine King and the descriptions of Adam are that of a provincial satrap while, at the same time, the descriptions of God are also that of The Divine "Author of Life" and the descriptions of Adam are that of God's composition. The link between ancient eastern regality and ancient eastern writing is that Mesopotamian writing was primarily used for governmental purposes. Thus, describing "Adam" as a Mesopotamian book necessarily assumes Mesopotamian regality and its "dominion." The royal nature of Heaven brought to earth in man is communicated with a method that describes man as both royalty and royal literature itself. One may observe that Genesis' genealogies bear a stunning resemblance to the Sumerian King Lists, particularly with respect to the extremely long life-spans that precede The Flood. The Redemption and Ascension of Man account is told through the lens of the rewriting of humanity and that writing's *preservation*, for the word σωτηρια *salvation* means also *preservation* and is, by definition, a translation of the name "Jesus" or "Savior" in Hebrew. In the time of Alexander, kingship was not tied to a particular territory, but, instead, to a particular man whose origins lay in the acclamation that typified him. Such a king's *philoi* or *companions*, his *friends* or *nobles*, who were to run his kingdom, and his fellow heirs were those who ate and drank wine with him; such an arrangement of description can be found in John 15. Such a king's voluntary gift-giving was a lifeline to the survival of his cities, and this gift-giving is described in terms of "grace" and "spiritual gifts" in the Greek of Ephesians 2 and 1 Corinthians 12. The system of expenditure that was used on behalf of the community was called a *liturgy*. Over time, the specific regality of the Hellenistic Age that was used to describe the ancient Eastern Monarchies was lost with the disappearance of Mesopotamian clay writing, and the borrowing of what were once regal and literal terms for the use of ecclesiastical and literary things has obscured the grandeur of the translated message we might read mistakenly as myth.

Describing the first, preliterate man as writing, to a literate man, both of whom the Text claims are the writing of a single Author, is a *literary* method of portraying eternity, not a physical description of the origins of the universe. However, such an intended eternity could be disrupted if the tablet was "killed" (rendered void); and, the disruption could be erased if the tablet was renewed by being "brought back to life" after it was dug up and revitalized through adherence to the original design of the words. The invention of writing is capable of preserving externally (i.e. outside of our brains), over time and space, a message concerning divinity (and therefore regality), and the duration of a written document that exceeds individual lifespans and travels apparently ubiquitously is an illustration of Fertility, Eden, Timelessness. Since we have in previous chapters observed thoroughly that "gospel" can mean "successful birth" in Hebrew, and that the Book of Daniel (written in Babylon, formerly called "Eden") discusses entire nations over time as individual animals, consider "Fertility" in these two passages in juxtaposition:

> "Then God blessed them, and God said to them, 'Be fruitful and multiply; replenish the earth and subdue it; have dominion over the fish of the sea, over the birds of the air, and over every living thing that moves on the earth'" (Genesis 1:28).

> "And this gospel of the kingdom will be preached in all the world as a witness to all the nations, and then the end will come" (Matthew 24:14).

The two discuss the beginning of time from the unique perspective of original Mesopotamian literacy and the end of time from the equally unique perspective of the end of Mesopotamian clay writing being accomplished through cuneiform as it gave way to two-dimensional, alphabetic Aramaic, the spoken language of Judea in the earthly days of Christ. In other words, the ability to represent segments of time in graphic accordance with spoken language seems to be the literary framework in which Scripture's parables function, i.e. parables that explain a parable that refers to some other time and some other understanding not bound to time. The entire collection of "Old" and "New" Testament Books extends from the time of Moses (about 1,500 B.C.) to "these last days" (near 75 A.D.). Ending with "these last days," the entirety of Mesopotamian clay literacy extended from about 3,700 B.C. to about 75 A.D. Moses wrote about the beginning of time from the perspective of the beginning of literate time, and he fused together past time and space immemorial with 3,700 B.C. and Mesopotamian clay. The "New Testament" fused together the end of time and space with the end of Mesopotamian clay writing. The Bible begins and ends time at the beginning and ending of a particular invention of Eden: writing, the pathway to wisdom that precedes and postdates the person who reads it.

The human brain, through what we call "neuroplasticity," can create new maps and alter old ones so that, over time, the same human brain can be converted from one structural model to another. The first man, who lived before writing, was explained to a subsequent man who was literate. Writing is visible speech, so what the literate man could no longer hear one way he could hear through his eyes by reading. A new nature, cultivated in the absence of the knowledge concerning the former nature, could (and often does) blind one to the past. Remember that in the introduction to the book you are reading, I wrote, "keep in mind the ancient term 'womb-serpent' throughout your reading of this book. This 'serpent' is to be understood emblematically... Ancient inscriptions, like the Stela of Vultures (about 2,400 B.C.) paired iconography with text in order to account for illiteracy: the literate understood the words; the illiterate understood the pictures. Iconography, however, was often emblematic." Literate man displays a markedly altered physicality relative to preliterate man, for this new and different physicality can be observed through the tools of current neuroscience. Again, in the book *Reading in The Brain: The New Science of How We Read*, by Stanislas Dehaene, we are informed that

> [l]earning to read involves connecting two sets of brain regions that are already present in infancy: the object recognition system and the language circuit. Reading acquisition has

three major phases: the pictorial state, a brief period where children "photograph" a few words; the phonological stage, where they learn to decode graphemes into phonemes; and the orthographic stage, where word recognition becomes fast and automatic. Brain imaging shows that several brain circuits are ALTERED during this process, notably those of the left occipito-temporal letterbox area. OVER SEVERAL YEARS, THE NEURAL ACTIVITY EVOKED BY WRITTEN WORDS INCREASES, BECOMES SELEC-TIVE, AND CONVERGES ONTO THE ADULT READING NETWORK (p. 195) [emphasis added].

Writing is an invention and not a natural output of the human brain. Writing is the evidence of a neuroplastic connection accomplished through deliberate cultivation. People existed before writing was invented. A garden can be "read" if one thinks of *interpreting* non-linguistic communication as *reading* in the same manner as one "reads" the facial expression of another. Even though non-linguistic, graphic communication and linguistic, graphic communication both can share a graphic nature, they do not share a linguistic nature; they are not identical forms of communication since they both do not take into account the spoken word. To think linguistically, "reading" involves writing that precedes it, and writing is a visual reflection of speech. Writing is, thus, a shadow or copy of speech and is dependent upon speech. Speech does not depend on writing. Children speak before they read and write. Again, *Reading in The Brain: The New Science of How We Read*, by Stanislas Dehaene, states,

> If the neuronal recycling hypothesis is right, however, the brain pays a price for literacy. Reading invades the neuronal circuits destined for another use and probably brings about the loss of some of the cognitive abilities that were handed down.... This argument about the cost of reading rests on the observation that cortical reorganization is probably, at some level, a 'zero-sum game.' With some rare exceptions, the number of cortical neurons is fixed in infancy. The day some become dedicated to word recognition, they are probably no longer available for other purposes. Thus, reading acquisition possibly reduces the cortical space available for our other mental activities. The neuronal recycling hypothesis makes us wonder if our... ancestors had visual skills that we have now lost (211).

The fact that reading is the result of neuroplastically connecting the object recognition system and the language circuit means that we connect our senses of sight and sound literally in our brains through deliberate practice over time. In Biblical Hebrew, the word "spirit" derives from the root "to smell, to perceive." It is useful to consider the fact that English does not have unique names for smells as it does for colors or tastes. English likens smells to entities through adjectival terminology like "fresh-smelling" or "floral," and since language itself affects our perceptions and our ability to experience them, it proves difficult for us to appreciate fully the Hebrew term "spirit." Humans have their smell receptors located on a piece of tissue called the *olfactory epithelium* located out of the mainstream of inspired air. Smell receptors have direct connections with the cerebral cortex, and the sense of smell is linked to memory. The ancient Mesopotamians viewed the memory of a person as that person's ghost. In Biblical Hebrew, the very subject of "seeing" a "spirit" is linguistically tantamount to "seeing" a "smell" which, to us, can sound awkward, but is not any more awkward than the fact we can "see" a "sound" through the invention of writing which is "visible speech." Our ancestors may have seen smells just as easily as we see sounds even though they did not see sounds any more than we see smells. Perhaps, the link between the sense of smell and memory lies beneath the regulations concerning incense in the Torah. Consider the significance of incense in Luke 1, for it was while serving at the altar of incense that the angel Gabriel appeared to announce the birth of John the Baptist described through the remembrance of the Book of Malachi. A facile method of bridging the gap between our ancestors and ourselves would rely on our gift of sight in order to describe smells in terms of our sounds. Consider:

> "Now thanks be to God who always leads us in triumph in Christ, and through us diffuses the FRAGRANCE OF HIS KNOWLEDGE in every place "(2 Corinthians 2:14).

"Knowledge" can be connected to "fragrance" as easily as the Hebrew word "spirit" is derived from the root "to smell, to perceive." What Paul wrote down above might be more than mere figurative language and may point to an encounter with reality prior to the invention of writing that literate man can only begin to grasp through figurative language.

The book *The Mind & The Brain*, by Jeffrey M. Schwartz, MD. and Sharon Begley describes a map of cortical space devoted to processing tactile signals and states that "[s]ensitive regions such as the lips and genitals command a great deal of cortical space" (p. 170). This book displays a sensory map and a motor map of the brain to show how the brain feels and controls the body. The sensory map shows that the brain places the hand next to the face and the feet next to the genitals. (It is interesting to note that "feet" is a Biblical euphemism for "genitals.") The motor map shows how "Muscles involved in speech and hand movements receive a great deal of cortex, while less dexterous regions such as the shoulder receive very little" (170). The brain map seems, at first, to be an odd representation of the body it senses and controls until one considers the

> intriguing hypothesis... that it reflects the experience of the curled-up fetus: in utero, our arms are often bent so that our hands touch our cheeks, our legs are curled up so that our feet touch our genitals. Perhaps months of simultaneous activation of these body parts, with the corresponding synchronous firing of cortical neurons, results in those cortical neurons "being fooled" into thinking that these body parts are contiguous (pages 170-171).

In other words, the way our brain feels and controls our body is a mirror of what our body was doing while the brain was forming along with the body inside the womb. It is as if the child we were is physically imprinted in the brain of the adults we are, but the brain formed by the womb, following birth, makes reorganizational connections based on the world experienced outside the womb through neuroplasticity. Again, the letters that spell the Hebrew "Eden" or "Fertility" also spell "time" in Chaldee (Daniel 2:8,9,21; 3:5, 15; etc.) Consistency over time shapes our brains, as the neuroplastic changes our brain makes to connect our sight and sound prove. It is true that, when dealing with scientific hypotheses, or even what is deemed scientific "fact" in a given era, the science may be disproven or excelled by a better model of describing reality in a different era. The scientific hypotheses explained above are exquisitely compelling. What can be proven certainly is that the Book of James describes the "implanted word" (James 1:21). The Hebrew words "tree" and "counsel" can be spelled identically and are, by definition, synonyms of the word "Torah" or "Instruction." The Torah's seven feasts describe the Covenant or Way of Life the Torah proclaims. The Feasts were to be memorized through annual repetition. We know that repetition over time makes structural impacts upon brain maps and we may consider that the sensory and motor mappings original to the brain resemble in a way the physical positioning of a child in the womb. Likewise, if we consider an ideal Hebrew year (one that begins on the Spring Equinox or "time of life" in Genesis 18:14) in light of the duration of a pregnancy, then a typical pregnancy beginning on the Spring Equinox/"time of life" would result in a birth on Christmas. The egg appears on the 14th day of the first month (Passover). The sowing of man's seed must occur within 24 hours (Unleavened Bread). The fertilized egg implants within two to six days (First Fruits). Sticking to an average of 50 days from fertilization, at this point the embryo displays markedly visible human characteristics (Pentecost). On the first day of the seventh month, the tiny human's hearing capacity develops (the Feast of Trumpets). On the 10th day of the seventh month, the hemoglobin of the blood changes from that of a fetus to that of a self-sustaining human (Atonement). On the 15th day of the seventh month, a baby is equipped with two healthy lungs (Tabernacles). In other words, the very dates that the Torah mandates for the feasts of Israel are distinctly patterned to reflect the development of a child in the womb from the point of conception (*The Seven Feasts of Israel*, Levitt). The Hebrew word for the "appointed times (the feasts)" of Leviticus 20 comes from the root ידע *to betroth.* Similarly, Genesis 2:9 says, "And out of the ground the LORD GOD MADE EVERY TREE GROW THAT IS PLEAS- ANT TO THE SIGHT AND GOOD FOR FOOD." The Hebrew words "to the sight" can also literally be rendered "for a mirror"; thus God made every tree to grow that is *pleasant for a mirror.* The menorah is an obvious symbol of a mirror-tree. "Tree" and "counsel" can be spelled identically in Hebrew and are by definition synonyms of the "Torah" or "Law." God gave the Law and the Counsel that was pleasant for a mirror that the Book of James calls the "Perfect Law of Liberty"; consider a "mirror text" or advice book in the sense of self-reflective counsel. Consider the ideas of a "tree" and a "mir- ror" being one, as James indicates:

> "Therefore lay aside all filthiness and overflow of wickedness, and receive with meekness the IMPLANTED WORD, which is able to save your souls. But be doers of the word, and not hearers only, deceiving yourselves. For if anyone is a hearer of the word and not a doer, he is like a man observing his NATURAL FACE IN A MIRROR; for he observes himself, goes away, and immediately forgets what kind of man he was. But he who looks into the PERFECT LAW OF LIBERTY and continues in it, and is not a forget- ful hearer but a doer of the work, this one will be blessed in what he does" (James 1:21-25).

A עצה *tree, instruction, counsel* can be thought of as a תורה *law, instruction, counsel,* and James 1:23-25 calls "law" a "mirror." James 1:23 is often translated as discussing a "natural face" being reflected in a mirror, but it literally says, "το προσωπον της γενεσεως αυτου *his infant face at birth.*" Obviously, no one forgets what he looks like immediately after turning away from a mirror, otherwise he would not recognize himself initially upon seeing his own reflection to which he is accustomed daily; but, everyone forgets their infant origins (to one degree or another), hence,

> "...lay aside all filthiness and overflow of wickedness, and receive with meekness the IMPLANTED WORD, which is able

> to save your souls. But be doers of the word, and not hear-
> ers only, deceiving yourselves. For if anyone is a hearer of the
> word and not a doer, he is like a man observing το προσωπον
> της γενεσεως αυτου **his infant face at birth** in a mirror; for
> he observes himself, goes away, and immediately forgets what
> kind of man he was. But he who looks into the PERFECT LAW OF
> LIBERTY and continues in it, and is not a forgetful hearer but
> a doer of the work, this one will be blessed in what he does"
> (James 1:21-25).

The Torah (Law/Counsel/Tree) of God is compared to a mirror that reflects an infant's face; as such, a tree is connected to an infant here. The Torah is, among other things, a history, and history allows one to behold glimpses of those otherwise no longer seen. The face one can forget is how one once was as an *innocent* child, which is how one is supposed to be *morally*. The "infant face at birth" is synonymously paralleled by the term "perfect law of liberty," and so it is the Torah of God or Tree of Life that reflects this infant face to "the old man which grows corrupt" (Ephesians 4:22) as in the situation of Zechariah and Gabriel concerning John The Baptist. In opposition to the Tree of God, Adam aged towards death as a result of eating from the "Tree" of death. The sensory and motor brain maps suggest that the way our brain feels and controls our body is a mirror of what our body was doing while the brain was forming along with the body in the womb; it is as if the child we were is physically imprinted in the brain of the adults we are. The brain formed by the womb, following birth, makes reorganizational connections based on the world outside the womb. If one adheres to "another law" (Romans 7:23), that is, another "tree," another "counsel," or a "different gospel" (2 Corinthians 11:4), then the Bible seems to describe the propensity and habit exhibited by the "Law of Sin and Death" (Romans 8:2), the Tree of Death, i.e. the forbidden "Tree" described in Genesis. Writing was understood as something generative and was compared to birth, for writing is the exhibition of the neuroplastic modifications that bind sight to sound in the brain that is naturally organized in a manner that reflects an infant in the womb. The very "feasts" of the Torah, like the womb, are patterned according to human gestation and were intended to be "implanted" in the mind, like a cognitive "tree," which explains why the symbol (specifically, emblem) of a "tree" was utilized to discuss "wisdom" and "gestation" in the Fall of Man account. The tree is an emblem of a being and his words, for good or for evil; and, as such, the words and the being are essentially one and the same just as the Torah describes man as clay writing.

The words "to make one wise" and "to suffer abortion" were originally spelled identically in Genesis 3:6, and they were antitheses mirrored
by the different pronunciation of the same graphic markers, which is a
literary mechanism crafted to describe *why* man Fell prior to his ability to
create records we can *see* currently. Mesopotamians used clay to record
debates concerning antithetical realities, such as the palm tree and the
tamarisk; the Hebrew Bible records a debate concerning The Tree of Life
and its opposite or The Law of Life and its opposite. In the astronomical
work called "The Observations of Bel," we are informed that "on the high-
places the son is burnt"; a prescribed prayer (recorded by Sayce in his *Lectures on Babylonian and Assyrian Religion*) that accompanied child-sacrifice discusses the "establisher of *law*"; this word "*law*" is, literally, "*secret
wisdom.*" One can see in this word-picture that the ritualistic *slaughter of
children* was related to *secret wisdom.* This "secret wisdom" was folly that
destroyed innocents in the earth as it destroyed innocence in the mind: "I
will greatly multiply your sorrow and YOUR CONCEPTION" (Genesis 3:16).

In the ancient east, covenants, contracts, or formal agreements
were not primarily written; these were oral and were accompanied by symbolic gestures before witnesses who committed the agreement to memory.
One's word, spoken or written, was legally binding. The word was as the
person. When an individual acquired land, the acquisition was accompanied symbolically by a stake being driven into the ground, and this symbol
was a memory device that proclaimed ownership; in fact, the officials in
charge were called "stakes" themselves, and it was the witnesses who
drove in the stakes. (Consider crucifixion here.) A type of stake, a cone,
was used for the same purpose, and those who made a dishonest claim
to property had that cone, that stake, driven through their lying mouth
as a penalty. The penalty symbolically mirrored the crime. The symbolic
gestures that accompanied oaths or covenants that preceded writing can
be discerned from writing after the fact by the types of seemingly enigmatic expressions involved. To "swear an oath" was sometimes expressed
in writing as to "eat an oath," and it was understood that a violation of
this oath bore with it a curse (i.e. vengeance or retribution) understood
to be bound up within the ingested matter. Accordingly, covenants were
often accompanied by a ceremonial consumption, as in Holy Communion,
that also involved anointing the covenanters with oil. Being *anointed* was
understood as being *clothed.* Similarly, Luke 24:49 compares being filled
with the Holy Spirit to being "CLOTHED with power from on high," and John
20:22 parallels this by stating, "So Jesus said to them again, 'PEACE to
you! As the Father has sent Me, I also send you.' And when He had said

this, He BREATHED ON THEM, and said to them, 'RECEIVE THE HOLY SPIRIT'"; receiving the Holy Spirit is being converted or "reborn"; Job 10:8-12 refers to clothing of skin in terms of human gestation, whereby the flesh is formed in the womb; thus, "My LITTLE CHILDREN, for whom I LABOR IN BIRTH again until Christ is FORMED in you..." (Galatians 4:19). The protection, the oath, the rest, and the work are all as the Spirit and the Clothing from on high that covers (Hebrew: כפר *atones, covers*) the errors committed against the covenant. An example of such a covenant can be observed when one reflects on the ancient custom whereby a cup was poured out along with the words, "If we reject your oath, may our blood be spilt like the cup." The idea is that a covenanter swallowed down what are called "sweepings" (bread, wine, etc.) that would be converted into destructive forces should the covenant be broken by the "eater" or "swearer," as is the case in 1 Corinthians 11, Numbers 5, Job 20, and Genesis 3. In Genesis 3, we can observe both an accursed consumption and garments prior to the expulsion from Eden. The term *asakkum* was employed to indicate goods set apart for the king or deity and whoever unlawfully seized them suffered the destructivity within them, i.e. a curse. Covenants or oaths were often pronounced before divine symbols called "weapons," and it is facile to see here that the symbols, when converted to visible speech or written language, can be understood as weapons; thus, the Septuagint uses the word *arkeegos, author* to translate the Hebrew פאה *mouth, edge of a blade* (which is from the root פאה *to breathe*), for blades were thought to "devour" like a tooth. A sword could, therefore, indicate a covenant symbolically. Similarly, a mace signified the head of a family, and it was a symbolic object passed from father to son. The mace signified an inheritance, and when a mace was deliberately broken, it signified disinheritance. The gestures, it would seem, eventually became figures of speech set down in the invention of writing. The constellation called The Kneeler is depicted holding a mace, smashing a vine, and crushing the head of The Dragon. The stars became used for collective memory just as books became used for collective memory. "He shall crush your head, and you shall bruise his heel" (Genesis 3:15). The stars were also used to predict, according to the roughly 280 days of human gestation, the birth of a child, as is the case with the beginning of the Book of Matthew. The overarching point here is that the "Creation" story is a "Writing" story, a literary parable more true than the credit given to it commonly on either side of the Creation/ Evolution debate. Genesis' account of origins is a *way* of beholding the past in order to understand a *reason*. It remembers and anticipates a child, formed by the words it contains, and transmitted from mind to mind, womb to womb, conception to conception.... By the time Moses wrote the Torah down, the world of preliterate man was extinct. A new brain pattern had emerged. It was to this new brain pattern that Moses' pen was used to sketch the face of an ancient child to the distant future.

The knowledge of extinction was a new idea in the Western world only as recently as the 19th Century. Species had been thought (incorrectly) to be immutable for a substantial and influential amount of time. The same time period that discovered extinction also tried to harmonize science with a traditional (and incorrect) reading of the Bible. Science was modified and the traditional reading of the Bible was modified. The message of the Bible is not modifiable. Instead, it is the readers who are modifiable, sometimes for better and sometimes for worse. By not knowing that the verb "to create" can mean "to write," Isaiah 45:7 has been read as "I [God] form the light and *create* darkness. I bring prosperity and *create* evil; I, the LORD, do all these things." God "creates" evil? — No. "I [God] form the light and *write about* darkness. I bring prosperity and *write about* evil; I, the LORD, do all these things." Engraved cuneiform requires "glory" or light to mingle with shadow correctly in order to provide proper reading. The light, of course, has no shadow. The obscurant of the light casts the shadow. It is within this frame of reference that we read these passages:

> "This is the message which we have heard from Him and declare to you, that GOD IS LIGHT and in Him is no darkness at all." (1 John 1:5).

> "Every good gift and every perfect gift is from above, and comes down from the FATHER OF LIGHTS, with whom there is no variation OR SHADOW OF TURNING. Of His own will He brought us forth by THE WORD OF TRUTH, that we might be a kind of firstfruits of His creatures." (James 1:17-18).

> "But I saw no temple in it, for the Lord God Almighty and the Lamb are its temple. The city had no need of the sun or of the moon to shine in it, for the GLORY of God illuminated it. THE LAMB IS ITS LIGHT." (Revelation 21:22-23).

A reading of "I [God] bring prosperity and *create* evil" (Isaiah 45:7) does not square with "God is light and in Him there is no darkness at all" (1 John 1:5). Yet, if one knows that the Hebrew "create" can mean "write about," then the two passages can be read with a greater accuracy in order to see that there is no discrepancy at all. The Light, by definition, cannot be dark; rather, the light shines on an obscurant and the *mirrored effect* of the obscurant (i.e. *the shadow*) tells the message according to the obscurant. Without the obscurant, the message is entirely light and not bound to the time-frame of a shadow that moves with the sun or the reader. "But all things that are exposed are made manifest by the light, for whatever makes manifest is light" (Ephesians 5:3).

The family line from Adam to Christ consistently faced challenges to its reproduction, and the physically firstborn usually persecuted the physically younger who received the ceremonial title and significations of "First-born." Likewise, the Mesopotamian masters of cuneiform realized that they could not contend with the more recent alphabetical writing systems that offered greater expediency and plasticity with a comparatively lower taxation upon the memory. Alphabetic systems were easier to learn and easier to adapt to a given purpose over time than cuneiform. The seemingly incredible amount of learning it required to master cuneiform, the writing system that typified Adam's death, was not discarded immediately by its diminishing in the face of alphabetic systems. Instead, the complexity of cuneiform was intensified in order to make it even more exclusive, and this exclusivity brought with it a respected reputation for secret knowledge imparted to those with special expertise regarding the origin of writing (that was not accomplished with cuneiform) in the land we refer to as "Eden," i.e. Mesopotamia. Complexity often has the appearance of superiority, and concession is commonly made on account of an inability to understand. Because of competition with alphabetic writing (both of which were subsequent to the first writing accomplished in "Eden"), Mesopotamian scribes made their writing more esoteric, and diviners who initiated their sons in cunciform compelled the sons to swear not to divulge their learning. The acquisition of the "secret knowledge" that was "held" in clay writing was accompanied by a solemn swearing, oath, that is, a covenant. "[T]he decipherment of an omen text from the Old Babylonian period is much easier than that of the same text as it was written by scholars of the first millennium" (Charpin, p. 250). "The same text" was rewritten with more difficult language intentionally, and it is such rewriting that, today, gives Eden the appearance of a simple composite used as a semi-historical motif for the mere purpose of beginning the Narrative somewhere plausible... a supposition I hope I have proven false.

One cuneiform inscription reads, "I have examined stone inscriptions from before the flood, which are sealed, stopped up, mixed up" (Charpin, p.55). The manner in which the cuneiform writers increased the difficulty of their writings was by a "play on the different values of signs" (Charpin, p. 250), that is, *word-play*. Such word-play led to the concept of secret knowledge in Mesopotamian (Edenic) writing; in other words, such word-play led to the idea of restricted knowledge in Eden, hence the deception concerning the forbidden tree in Genesis 3. By using slippery language consistently and programmatically, both the initiated and the uninitiated could behold the exact same text and be able to read the exact same writing while only one saw the true meaning and the other saw an impossible labyrinth of mirrors (so to speak). More simply, a straight-forward message could be written precisely, but with a precise wordplay that disallowed a straight-forward understanding of a message without the "tradition" or prerequisite knowledge essential for the comprehension of the message immediately; it would require memorization and the trial of every possible variant for the uninitiated to begin to understand the reading made recondite by double-meanings and apparently nebulous circumlocutions. By the time of Aramaic's dominance, cuneiform was no longer used for communication but rather for the transmission of secret knowledge *that claimed to preserve wisdom from before The Flood.* As such, we have, in this chapter, examined Adam, The Flood, and the "New Testament" — the segment of time that used clay writing as the motif of the first human on one end and the period in history when clay writing died on the other end. Such a magisterial plan for writing the Bible is nearly incomprehensible! — but its purpose was intended to be comprehensible, for it used systems of alphabetic writing within a methodology that surpasses cuneiform's eventual complexity by describing the wisest created man of all. "...Adam was not deceived, but the woman being deceived, fell into transgression..." (1 Timothy 2:14). Adam was not deceived, and none of us can claim that status.

As we have observed, the Hebrew Bible's life of Adam is the time and place of Mesopotamian writing prior to the development and dominance of Mesopotamian cuneiform. Adam was not deceived, for he spoke the "pure language" of Zephaniah 3. The human immediately subsequent to him, his bride, was deceived by the intentionally complicated system of "The Serpent" who hid an invisibly twisted misreading in the visible view of Scripture's consonantal alphabetical Hebrew, the very tool "The Serpent" knew would destroy him, and the very "Word of God" he knew would eventually "crush [his] head." From pictography to cuneiform, from cuneiform to the consonantal alphabet, this seems to be the model of "The Man" (or the first "Adam") dying to "The Serpent," and "The Serpent" being crushed by "The Man" (or the "Last Adam"). The first man, Adam, as well as Christ, The Word, are both portrayed as writing in the Bible. Adam is himself compared to clay writing. Christ is compared to both "The Author" and the clay writing, i.e. God and Man. Both "Adam" and "Christ" are descriptive titles of real men who existed in time. Unlike Christ, Adam existed previously outside of *recorded* time, yet still exists in written form precisely waiting to be "brought back to life" or "remembered."

> "And I commanded the Levites that they should cleanse themselves, and that they should go and guard the gates, to sanctify the Sabbath day. REMEMBER ME, O my God, concerning this also, and SPARE ME ACCORDING TO THE GREATNESS OF YOUR MERCY!" (Nehemiah 13:22).

Now reflect on the segment of time when Christ hung on the tree:

> "'...we receive the due reward of our deeds; but this **Man** has done nothing wrong.' Then he said to Jesus, 'Lord, REMEMBER ME when You come into Your kingdom.' And Jesus [The Son of Man or **Adam**] said to him, 'Assuredly, I say to you this day, YOU WILL BE WITH ME IN PARADISE'" (Luke 23:41-43).

Recall that Christ came in a time where agriculture relied heavily on the stars. As we have examined in this chapter, the uses of astronomy, the invention of writing, and the message recorded in the Bible all converge into a single stream of thought with its own modes of eternal expression in time:

> "But someone will say, 'How are the dead raised up? And with what body do they come?' Foolish one, what you sow is not made alive unless it dies. And what you sow, you do not sow that body that shall be, but mere grain — perhaps wheat or some other grain. But God gives it a body as He pleases, and to each seed its own body. All flesh is not the same flesh, but there is one kind of flesh of men, another flesh of animals, another of fish, and another of birds. There are also celestial bodies and terrestrial bodies; but the glory of the celestial is one, and the glory of the terrestrial is another. There is one glory of the sun, another glory of the moon, and another glory of the stars; for one star differs from another star in glory. So also is the resurrection of the dead. The body is sown in corruption, it is raised in incorruption. It is sown in dishonor, it is raised in glory. It is sown in weakness, it is raised in power. It is sown a natural body, it is raised a spiritual body. There is a natural body, and there is a spiritual body. And so it is written, 'The first man Adam became a living being.' The last Adam became a life-giving spirit. However, the spiritual is not first, but the natural, and afterward the spiritual. The first man was of the earth, made of dust; the second Man is the Lord from heaven. As was

the man of dust, so also are those who are made of dust; and as is the heavenly Man, so also are those who are heavenly. And as we have borne the IMAGE OF THE MAN OF DUST, we shall also bear the IMAGE OF THE HEAVENLY MAN" (1 Corinthians 15:35-49).

This "image" is described through writing *as writing itself*. As far as the ultimate reality of the matter is concerned,

"Beloved, now we are children of God; and it has not yet been revealed what we shall be, but we know that when He is revealed, we shall be like Him, for we shall see Him as He is." (1 John 3:2).

The existence of Adam before recorded time is preserved for literate man through the method of recalling Adam's existence in the beginning of recorded time, and this sequence is merged into a whole that disallows the reader from counting the actual date of the first man altogether; this is the very reason that Genesis 1-5 tells the same story of man's origins three times in a sequence that moves the reader from timelessness to time. It should be clear now that there is only one "Creation" Story, and had "Creation" been understood as "Writing," the JEDP Theory would not have been accepted.

Again, the knowledge of extinction only became accepted by the educated West as recently as the 19th Century. Hunting tends to affect individuals as opposed to entire populations, whereas loss of habitat leads to the destruction of populations with far greater facility. By the time a species nears extinction, it has already lost far too many conflicts to reverse the process. Here, we should recognize that the postliterate man, the man of the screen, will furrow his brow at the words you are reading (if he even encounters these words at all). A large cause of extinction is hybridization, the dilution into obscurity. Preliterate man lost the dominion of truth, and literate man attempted to recover it; hence, "Death reigned from Adam to Moses" (Romans 5:14). Death, a loss of memory, reigned from the first man until a literate man solidified preliterate man's history in a way that literate man in the distant future could understand the *reason why* man suffers and dies. A record was crafted to counteract the damnation of oblivion, and this record was made capable of accounting for time before time could be counted within a durable system. When the truth of preliterate man was forgotten along with whatever methods he used to remember the past, it is of no value to attempt to stretch Scripture to include the "history" or "age" of the earth. Postliterate man must remember the world of literate man or else literate man will be blotted out of the memory of his children. Literate man, through his concessions, has lost too many battles to sustain himself, for his corruption was written by his own hands for a posterity he has sired and who might not observe the problem, even though it stands in the open displaying and proclaiming itself to a creation that can neither see nor hear it.

The book *Lost Animals*, by Fuller, records, "Gradually, all of Ezra's captive ducks died off and so too did their counterparts in France, but the date of the death of the last one remains something of a mystery. The year 1936 is probably correct. However, some authorities give a date of 1939 and others suggest 1945. Who knows which date is correct? But, of course, it no longer really matters" (p.36). The genealogies in Genesis have been thought to indicate Scripture's claim that the material creation of the world is about 6,000 years old. The genealogies in Genesis are perfect for their own purpose. It was the *purpose*, the *reason*, that was forgotten. Nevertheless, the *timeframe* of Genesis and its beautiful genealogies do not point to the origin of the material world or to the origin of man. Rather, the genealogies indicate precisely the time, place, and main material of literate humanity, a hybrid who could see the audible and hear the visible. The genealogies of Genesis tell us when and where writing began; and, using this time and location as a platform, the stage is set by this information to tell us (in writing) why man must die... why oblivion exists. Writing counteracts oblivion. Remembrance is preservation or salvation. Writing is as the salvation in this scenario, and so Salvation or "Jesus" is called "The Word."

E.W. Maunder reasoned that constellation pictures were devised by people who lived around 2,700 B.C. (*Astronomy of The Bible*, p. 157-158); this observation is important relative to the history of writing because the constellation pictures resemble pictographic writing, and pictographic writing ceased to be a living system around the same time the constellation pictures were first crafted. The difference in the stars' appearance between 2,800 B.C. and 2,700 B.C. is almost unobservable to the naked eye. If we use the narrative chronology established by Genesis' genealogies, then pictographic writing (in real time) began when Adam was expelled from Eden (in narrative time), and it ended when he died (in narrative time). The chronology of Genesis has Adam expelled from Eden near 3,700 B.C., and it states that his death was 930 years later (in narrative time) or about the time that the constellation pictures were first developed (in real time). The constellation pictures were developed near the death of Mesopotamian pictographic writing and the birth of cuneiform writing (in real time); thus, cuneiform writing made pictographs obsolete

even though the cartographic system of the constellation pictures reflected pictographic and not cuneiform writing. In a manner of speaking, the
celestial writing system reflected the original terrestrial writing system, and
the earthly system departed into cuneiform. This departure marked the
death of clay pictographs that were but remembered in the celestial pictures of astronomy... this departure was utilized to mark the death of Real
Adam by a Narrative Adam who is remembered in the virtual heaven of the
constellation pictures.   Adam's terrestrial death was translated into the
heavenly book (so to speak). Genesis can be seen here to merge (1) the
beginning of humanity with (2) the beginning of writing and (3) the beginning of the constellation pictures in its narrative as though they all happen
concurrently *because all of them are origins of recording-systems based
on writing*. The narrative time-frame of Genesis is chronological and thematic, **but the chronologies have multiple beginnings in real time that
are written as though they have a single beginning in narrative time.** The
description of the creation of the first man in terms of the first pictographic
books, combined with the fact that those books passed out of terrestrial
usage and were remembered as the constellation pictures, is the model
that became utilized to describe the remembrance of an earthly man in a
heavenly book. In other words, the literary description of the dead rising to
heaven seems to use the history of terrestrial pictographic writing's translation to astronomy while terrestrial writing morphed into cuneiform writing
and alphabetic writing. Consider:

> "...And at that time your people shall be DELIVERED, EVERYONE
> WHO IS FOUND WRITTEN IN THE BOOK. And many of those who
> sleep in the DUST OF THE EARTH shall awake, some to everlast-
> ing life, some to shame and everlasting contempt. Those who
> are wise shall SHINE LIKE THE BRIGHTNESS OF THE FIRMAMENT,
> and those who turn many to righteousness like THE STARS for-
> ever and ever" (Daniel 12: 1-3).

The idea of rising from the "dust of the earth" to shine like "the stars" appears to be a literary description of pictographic clay books (the dust of the
earth) being remembered celestially (the constellation pictures). Daniel's
references must be understood in light of the fact that Daniel wrote from
Babylon, the land that was formerly known as "Eden." In a manner of
speaking, the "breath of life" in clay (i.e. the first writing) ascended into
the winds or spirits or perception or vowels of the heavens (i.e. the stars):
"Then the dust will return to the earth as it was, and the spirit will return to
God who gave it" (Ecclesiastes 12:7). The resurrection, like the creation, is
described in literary and historic terms that anachronistically describe — in

a uniform program — a process otherwise inaccessible to us in the distant future relative to the composition of the Bible. Celestial luminaries were and are used to predict the future by understanding the cycles of the past, for it is in this way that we can predict eclipses exactly. Likewise, the Christ Child was found by reading Books and following stars, and it is this Christ Who describes Himself as the "Deliverance" or "Salvation" (which is what "Jesus" means) and Who has a Heavenly "Book" wherein the saved are remembered. Such terminology is comparative, not descriptive.

The link between "wind," "breath," "spirit," and "perception," is a matter of Hebrew etymology; however, connecting these four to "vowels" is specific to the consonantal (or incomplete) aspect of the Hebrew alphabet. To understand the constellation pictures as pictographs is to understand entire words represented by single pictures, and this system preceded the first alphabetic writing by nearly 800 years. Hebrew is alphabetic and consonantal. Hebrew does not write "wind," "breath," "spirit," "perception," i.e. vowels. To understand the constellation pictures as "vowels" can only be accomplished by grasping the consonantal nature of a vowel-less means of conveying a message older than alphabetic writing. Such an understanding elucidates that the written Hebrew message is a mnemonic of the message contained in the constellation pictures that, in turn, contain a message prior to the constellations having been imagined as such. The order of writing is (1) pictographs, (2) cuneiform, (3) incomplete alphabet, (4) and complete alphabet. This order is not an "evolution," for each system is complete by its own standards; each system is unique even though they all are writing or visible speech. Likewise, all of the zodiacal constellations exist along the same line, but each is unique and complete according to its own cluster. All history is subjective, but that does not mean that subjectivity is untruth. The human brain does not perceive every single aspect of sight, but it glues together a narrative that misses roughly two hours per day of waking time. This narrative is what is relevant with respect to a purpose. The purpose or reason of a history is determined prior to the composition of the record. Objectivity is a powerful tool for both deceit and truth, and subjectivity can be totally honest relative to a specific purpose. The perception of the Hebrew Text of Genesis can be understood in terms of the constellation pictographs as they were conceived when they first were marked out. In this sense, the starry heavens are as the vowels for the Hebrew Text. The wind, breath, spirit, perception, or vowels of the heavens, subjectively imagined as writing, objectively move in predictable, regular patterns that have been used for truthful and untruthful purposes throughout history. The synchronicity of the Hebrew Text, over centuries (or millennia), with the celestial bodies is evidence of a union that produced both the Man and the Book we read; for, in this sense, man is as writing (within a literate frame of reference) whereas man is as the celestial bodies (within a celestial frame of reference, like that of Daniel 12). Daniel 12 unifies man, writing, and the stars, as did Moses in Genesis, and as did Matthew and Luke. The frame of reference is the key to comprehending the mode of expression used to convey the message.

The written history of man, in terms of chronology established by Genesis' record of genealogy, only extends back to the history of the first writing and not to the first man. The Bible does not claim the material world to be six-millennia-old, but it tells the origins of the material world in parabolic terms that are chronologically tethered to the history of writing on literal earth or clay. As a result, the functionality of Genesis' organization and methodology is to tell a story of timelessness to those who live in time, i.e. to speak of eternity to those who will die. This approach reveals the intention of speaking across a vast interval of time into the future. The chronology accounted for, from Genesis to Revelation, is the chronology of Mesopotamian clay writing's existence (which has been "brought back to life" recently). The beginning of the world and the end of the world are put in terms of the beginning of the literate world of *clay* and the end of its *human* artificers; in this literary sense, the beginning and the end of the world unifies man with clay. Accordingly, it is foolish to think that people like Paul thought the material world was soon coming to an end, for that would mean that he wrote words to people who, like himself, would not be around to benefit from them. For whom then would Paul's letters be intended? It is not the end of the material world that Paul described, but the death of Mesopotamian clay writing that ceased to be a living system around the time of the destruction of the Second Temple. The end of a way of understanding was anticipated, and this understanding was used as a parallel for the end of the world in a chronologically undisclosed future.

The literate brain is structurally different from an illiterate or pre-literate brain. Likewise, the Torah's festivals are patterned after human gestation. The human brain was functionally altered by the invention of literacy since it requires the crossing of otherwise separate sensory perceptions in order to see spoken language. At the same time, the human brain's sensory and motor maps reveal the imprint of what appears to be the fetal positioning of a child in the womb. The ancient Mesopotamians who invented writing also used stars to count down to birth and to establish fixed agricultural cycles. The invention of writing facilitated this processes and helped future generations understand the celestial cycle called The Precession of The Equinoxes. The Bible maintains the imprint of a specific time within the roughly 26,000 years of Precession by describing the cherubs according to the pattern of the Autumnal Equinox that last occurred around 2,800 B.C. (when the constellation pictures were first devised), and the Bible does so by uniting this chronology with the time of Adam's death. This specific celestial pattern displays a battle between a man and a serpent; and, if one conceives of the constellation names in Hebrew, then the *scorpion* (Hebrew "infertility" combined with the letter "house/womb") the man treads would literally describe the destruction of infertility or the reestablishment of "Fertility," i.e. "Eden" at some point in the future. This reestablishment involves a resurrection, and the Bible describes resurrection in terms of clay pictographs being translated into constellation pictures. The Fall in "Eden" is the story of a gestation gone wrong, a gestation that resulted in death, and a death that was promised to be overturned through rebirth. In the Hebrew Bible, "womb" and "wisdom" are the same idea. "Eden" or "Fertility" is a story of "wisdom," and the brain is structured to resemble the gestation under discussion... a gestation that involves the stars, the breath of life, and the written word, through a literary method that engenders a timeless quality by merging different, but related, times in order to connect the reader to the timelessness that preceded him and to the eternity to which he is going.

The "Creationism vs. Evolution" debates have been but mental exercises wherein opposing sides conceded to the notion that the Bible dates the creation of the material world, when the Bible does not. The Hebrew Bible does provably describe man as the ancient Mesopotamians described clay writing thousands of years before Moses. Scripture, hybridizing man and writing in its explanation of origins, describes the emergence of a literate humanity that could be reintroduced to the long-forgotten truth as to *why* man suffers and dies.

The origin of human suffering has been the subject of this entire book, and it is bound up in the hideous death of the first human infant.

About the Author

Joshua Collins earned a Bachelor of Arts in English (Literature & Composition) from Northern Illinois University and a Master of Arts in English Education from The University of Kentucky. He is an independent researcher in the process of developing a field of knowledge for an academic discipline related to Investigative History.

Mr. Collins' research and communication skills have been utilized in teaching at the high school and college level, as well as in the publication of his previous works: *The Threshold of Paradise*, a historical novel, and *Did God Plant the Forbidden Tree?*, historical research.

This present volume, The Definitive Edition of *The Knowledge of Good & Evil* is an example of his detailed historical research. In addition to being a writer of Investigative History, Joshua is a devoted husband and father.